CW00403955

# German
# Aircraft

## of the Second World War

These three factory fresh Junkers Ju 88A-1s can be considered representative of German Second World War aircraft in their heyday. Built in larger numbers than any other German bomber, the earlier Ju 88s could easily be distinguished by their 'beetle eye' noses and annular engine cowlings. (*R. C. Seeley*)

# German Aircraft

## of the Second World War

J R Smith
Antony L Kay

PUTNAM

© J. R. Smith and A. L. Kay 1972
Drawings © E. J. Creek 1972
ISBN 85177 836 4
Printed in Great Britain for
Putnam, an imprint of
Conway Maritime Press Ltd
24 Bride Lane, Fleet Street
London EC4Y 8DR
Filmset in Photon Times 11 pt by
Richard Clay (The Chaucer Press) Ltd, Bungay
and printed in Great Britain by
Thomson Litho, East Kilbride
*First Published 1972*
*Sixth impression 1989*

# Contents

viii

ix

# Acknowledgements

The compilation of this work involved largescale research and would have been impossible without the co-operation of many individuals and organizations. For their generous assistance we wish to thank Horst Burgsmüller of Deutsche Lufthansa's public relations office, Peter M. Grosz, Hans Lächler, Alfred Price, Jaroslav Zazvonil, Ian Primmer, Hans Redemann, Karl Ries, Royal Canadian Air Force, Franz Selinger, Richard Seeley, Harold Thiele and the United States Air Force.

Correction of the manuscript, with particular attention to German terms, was undertaken by Hans Obert who also provided many photographs. Fritz Hahn contributed invaluable advice on the missile section, and Mrs Cecilie M. Buttery was responsible for typing the authors' drafts.

| A. L. Kay | J. R. Smith | E. J. Creek |
|-----------|-------------|-------------|
| Mitcham | Brimscombe | Clevedon |
| Surrey | Gloucestershire | Somerset |

# Authors' Note

This book describes alphabetically by design or manufacturing company all German aircraft built or used operationally during the Second World War, plus the main types of trainers in service with the Luftwaffe. It has proved impossible to describe every aircraft which served with the Luftwaffe's training elements because these were so many and varied. It is for this reason that pure trainers such as the Arado Ar 76 and Blohm und Voss Ha 135, which were only built in small numbers, and obsolete operational aircraft such as the He 51 and Do 23 have been excluded.

Luftwaffe Geschwader were always identified by an Arabic number (*e.g.*: JG 26) but Gruppen operating within a Geschwader were distinguished by a Roman figure (*e.g.*: III./JG 26). Individual Gruppen, that is those not operating as part of a Geschwader, utilized an Arabic number (*e.g.*: JGr 25) as did all Staffeln (*e.g.*: 3./JG 26). Therefore, II./KG 51 would be the second Gruppe of Kampfgeschwader 51, whereas 2./KG 51 would be the second Staffel of the same unit.

# Abbreviations

| | |
|---|---|
| Aufkl.Gr | Aufklärungsgruppe (Reconnaissance Group) |
| BFGr | Bordfliegergruppe (Shipboard Reconnaissance Group) |
| BK | Bordkanone (Cannon) |
| BMW | Bayerische Motorenwerke (Bavarian Engine Works) |
| Bramo | Brandenburgische Motorenwerke (Brandenburg Engine Works) |
| DFS | Deutsches Forschungsinstitut für Segelflug (German Gliding Research Institute) |
| DVL | Deutsche Versuchsanstalt für Luftfahrt (German Experimental Institute for Aviation) |
| DVS | Deutsche Verkehrsfliegerschule (German Commercial Pilot School) |
| EK | Erprobungskommando (Experimental Command) |
| Erg.Gr | Ergänzungsgruppe (Training and Replacement Group) |
| Erpr.Gr | Erprobungsgruppe (Experimental Group) |
| (F) | Fern (Long-range) |
| FAGr | Fernaufklärungsgruppe (Long-range Reconnaissance Group) |
| FFS | Flugzeugführerschule (Pilot School) |
| Flak | Fliegerabwehrkanone (Anti-aircraft gun) |
| FuG | Funkgeräte (Radio Equipment) |
| Fw | Feldwebel (Sergeant) |
| Gefr | Gefreiter (Corporal) |
| Gen Lt | Generalleutnant (Lieutenant General) |
| Gen Maj | Generalmajor (Major General) |
| Gr | Gruppe (Group) |
| (H) | Heeres (Army co-operation) |
| Hptm | Hauptmann (Captain) |
| Jabo | Jagdbomber (Fighter-bomber) |
| JG | Jagdgeschwader (Fighter Wing) |
| KG | Kampfgeschwader (Battle (Bomber) Wing) |
| KGr | Kampfgruppe (Battle (Bomber) Group) |
| Kü.Fl.Gr. | Küstenfliegergruppe (Coastal Reconnaissance Group) |
| LG | Lehrgeschwader (Instructional Wing) |
| LKS | Luftkriegsschule (Air Warfare School, for cadets) |
| LLG | Luftlandegeschwader (Air Landing Wing) |
| LT | Lufttorpedo (Air-launched torpedo) |
| Lt | Leutnant (Lieutenant) |
| MG | Maschinengewehr (Machine-gun) |
| MK | Maschinenkanone (Machine cannon) |
| NAGr | Nahaufklärungsgruppe (Short-range Reconnaissance Group) |

| | |
|---|---|
| NJG | Nachtjagdgeschwader (Night Fighter Wing) |
| NSGr | Nachtschlachtgruppe (Night Ground-attack Group) |
| Oblt | Oberleutnant (First Lieutenant) |
| Obstlt | Oberstleutnant (Lieutenant Colonel) |
| Ob.d.L. | Oberbefehlshaber der Luftwaffe (C-in-C of the Air Force) |
| Ofw | Oberfeldwebel (Flight Sergeant) |
| PC | Panzerbombe, zylindrische (Armour-piercing bomb) |
| (Pz) | Panzer (Armour, usually applied to a unit operating against armoured vehicles) |
| Rb | Reihenbildkamera (Photographic-reconnaissance camera) |
| RLM | Reichsluftfahrtministerium (German Aviation Ministry) |
| (S) | Schlacht (Ground-attack) |
| SG | Schweres Geschütz (Heavy gun or weapon) |
| SG | Schlachtgeschwader (Ground-attack Wing) |
| SKG | Schnellkampfgeschwader (Fast-bomber Wing) |
| St.G | Stukageschwader (Dive-bomber Wing) |
| TG | Transportgeschwader (Transport Wing) |
| Uffz | Unteroffizier (Warrant Officer) |
| Wekusta | Wettererkundungsstaffel (Meteorological Reconnaissance Squadron) |
| ZG | Zerstörergeschwader (Destroyer (Heavy-fighter) Wing) |
| zbV | zur besonderen Verwendung (On Special Operations) |

# FIXED-WING AIRCRAFT

INTRODUCTION

The Treaty of Versailles, which was finally signed by Germany on 28 June, 1919, contained clauses which called for a drastic reduction in size of both army and navy and the complete abolition of the old German Flying Corps. At least 15,000 aircraft and 27,000 aero-engines were included in the war material handed over to the Allies, and by 1920 military aviation in Germany was dead.

Although the Treaty of Versailles precluded Germany from any forays into military aviation, it only placed engine power restrictions on civil aircraft development. Even as early as December 1917 the first German airline, Deutsche Luft-Reederei (or DLR) had been formed, although the first scheduled flight was not made until February 1919. This company was followed shortly afterwards by several other small companies, all using converted military types such as the A.E.G. J II, the L.V.G. C VI and the Friedrichshafen G IIIa.

The first civil aircraft to be produced by Germany was the Junkers-F 13, an extremely advanced low-wing monoplane of all-metal construction with accommodation for two crew and four passengers. Although far in advance of most contemporary aircraft, the F 13 suffered initially from the glut of ex-military types and it was not until late 1919 that the first six

Perhaps more than any other aircraft, the Junkers-F 13 contributed to the revival of the German aircraft industry after the 1914–18 war. This machine (c/n 740) was operated by Luft Hansa. (*J. Zazvonil*)

1

Dr Ing Adolph Rohrbach should be remembered for his pioneering work on all-metal stressed-skin construction, seen here applied to one of his company's last designs, the three-engined Romar flying-boat. (*J. Zazvonil*)

machines were sold to the USA. This sale was soon frustrated by the efforts of the Inter-Allied Aeronautical Commission of Control which confiscated all machines under construction, explaining that the F 13 was equally suitable for military operations. Although this judgement was in many ways sound, the Commission relented in February 1920.

To help promote the F 13, Junkers established their own airline in 1921 known as Junkers-Luftverkehr. Eventually, on 6 January, 1926, Junkers-Luftverkehr and Deutscher Aero Lloyd (the successor of DLR) merged to form Deutsche Luft Hansa,* the company having $37\frac{1}{2}$ per cent of its shares owned by the government. The director of the new company was Erhard Milch, a shrewd businessman who rapidly built up the airline to become one of the largest and most efficient in the world.

* Written as Deutsche Lufthansa from 1 January, 1934.

The corrugated metal skinning developed by Junkers was in marked contrast to the smooth finish pioneered by Rohrbach. The G 24 D-1090 (c/n 915) was typical of Junkers aircraft of the late 1920s.

Although Germany's armed forces had been drastically reduced, a small Defence Ministry (Reichswehr-Ministerium) remained in Berlin. The chief of the army command was Gen Hans von Seeckt, a far-sighted officer who, as early as 1921, began to form a small aviation section within the ministry. In December 1923, the ministry signed an agreement with the Soviet government for the provision of training facilities at Lipezk, about 320 km (200 miles) east of Moscow. Training of the first recruits began in 1924, and for nine years the school was to provide Germany with several hundred pilots, mechanics, and observers.

Parallel with the training at Lipezk, initial flying instruction was given to potential pilots by the Deutscher Luftsportverband (DLV) with gliders,

Typical of Luft Hansa's fleet during the late 1920s is this Dornier Merkur D-1080 (c/n 128) and Junkers-F 13 D-410.

balloons and, later, powered aircraft. Organizer of these courses was Hptm Karl Student who later led VII. Fliegerdivision, the Luftwaffe's parachute corps. By 1929 the DLV had over 50,000 members and on 7 April, 1937, it was taken over by the Nazis and incorporated into the National-Sozialistisches Flieger-Korps (NSFK).

The NSFK, under Oberst Bruno Lörzer, was concerned with training young boys to fly gliders, the pick of the pilots being sent to the Deutsche Verkehrsfliegerschule (DVS). Based at List, Schleissheim, Brunswick and Warnemünde, this school continued the work of the Lipezk centre, training pilots to fly such aircraft as the Albatros L 68 and L 75, the Udet U 12, and the Arado SC 1.

On 30 January, 1933, Adolf Hitler was summoned to meet President

3

Hindenburg and within two hours had become Chancellor of the Third Reich. A few days later Hitler made Hermann Göring, a trusted friend and ex-fighter pilot, the Reichskommissar for Air, with Milch, who remained chairman of Luft Hansa, as his deputy. By March Göring had been appointed as Germany's first Air Minister with Milch as Secretary of State, and on 29 April, 1933, the Verkehrsministerium (Communications Ministry) was established.

## The Organization of the Air Ministry

In 1935 the Verkehrsministerium was renamed as the Reichs-luftfahrtministerium, the RLM or German Air Ministry. Gen Walther Wever was appointed as the first chief of staff, mainly at the instigation of

The Dornier company became famous for a long line of flying-boats. The Do 12 Libelle III was a two-seat sporting aircraft.

von Fritsch, commander of the army. Unfortunately for the Luftwaffe, Wever, a brilliant officer and proponent of the strategic bomber concept, was killed in a flying accident in 1936. He was succeeded in turn by Albert Kesselring, Hugo Stumpff in 1937 and Hans Jeschonnek in February 1939.

Another very important man in the early history of the RLM was Ernst Udet who, like Göring and Bruno Lörzer, was a fighter pilot of the First World War. Though not a Nazi, Udet was appointed by Göring in 1936 in an attempt to re-organize the Air Ministry's technical department.

As formed in 1935, the Technisches Amt, or technical office, was the main body of the RLM. Creation of the Generalluftzeugmeister (GL) or General of Air Production in 1938 brought into being seven staff divisions (Stabs-Abteilungen) numbered GL 1 to GL 7 which included subjects such as planning (Planung GL 1), research control (Fertigungs-Führung GL 3) and enemy armament (Auslandsrüstung GL 7). In addition there were three directorates:

GL/C  Technisches Amt (Technical Office)
GL/E  Nachschub-Amt (Supply Office)
GL/F  Wirtschafts-Amt (Contracts Office)

In 1939 the inspection department was transferred to the staff divisions and became GL 6. The service testing stations (Erprobungsstellen) came

One of the most important aircraft produced by the Dornier company before the Second World War was the Wal flying-boat. (*H. Thiele*)

directly under GL/C, development, supply and procurement being handled throughout divisions C2 to C8 of GL/C and GL/E.

The trend of the European war during the mid-war years led to the establishment of the Ministry for Armament and Munitions (Ministerium für Bewaffnung und Munition) under Albert Speer, which later became known as RüK. During this period the following changes took place:

(*a*) The union of the GL with the state secretariat, both controlled by Milch.

(*b*) The inclusion of the staff divisions under one directorate of projects—GL/A Planungsamt.

(*c*) Close association of the German anti-aircraft (flak) defence department with the GL, the former then being called GL/Flak-Rüstung in 1942.

(*d*) The placing of research control (Forschungsführung) on the same horizontal level as the GL/C directorate.

The creation of the Speer Ministry (RüK) introduced a new picture regarding the collaboration of the GL directorates with the industry, and its increasing influence, together with the friction and conflict that it

The Dornier Wal had considerable influence on the design of the Do 18 described later in this volume. D-ALOX (c/n 300) was one of six aircraft which operated Lufthansa's South Atlantic service. (*H. Thiele*)

brought with it on matters of production, necessitated a further change in the organization of the GL.

On 1 August, 1944, all departments and divisions of the GL organization connected with production were transferred to the Speer Ministry and the GL was renamed Chef der Technischen Luft-Rüstung (Chef TLR). The seven main departments of Chef TLR were:

Development (TLR/FL E Entwicklung)
Supply (TLR/FL Rüstungs- und Bestellwesen)
Research (Forschungsführung)
Testing (K.d.E. Erprobungsstelle)
Anti-aircraft (TLR/Flak)
Acceptance Inspection (BAL)
Field Liaison (BTT)

Scientific research on new weapons and production of armament was controlled not only by the established departments but also by the SS-Hauptamt—which worked concurrently with (and often in competition with) the Speer Ministry. After 20 July, 1944, the SS-Hauptamt unofficially took over the control of the RLM and Hitler ordered a certain proportion of all officers to join the Hauptamt. Obergruppenführer Dr Ing Kammler (one of the leading SS directors) and Speer became paramount authorities ranking with Heinrich Himmler after Hitler.

## The Experimental Stations

Initial testing and development of all new equipment for the Luftwaffe was undertaken by the various Service testing stations (Kommando der Erprobungsstellen—K.d.E.). These stations also undertook research up until 1941 when it was entrusted to the various research institutes such as the Deutsche Versuchsanstalt für Luftfahrt at Berlin-Adlershof and the Aerodynamische Versuchsanstalt Göttingen, or the manufacturing company itself.

Several Dornier F (or Do 11D) bomber/transports were delivered to Lufthansa, including D-3029 (c/n 262).

6

The death of Gen Walther Wever led to the abandonment of the Dornier Do 19 V1 four-engined bomber.

As the war progressed, co-operation between the manufacturing company and the K.d.E. gradually became more and more closely knit, and often the third element, the Erprobungskommando, made its operational tests at the same time. The object of this blurring of functions was to speed the development of the particular piece of equipment and introduce it into service as soon as possible.

At the end of the war, eight testing stations were operational under the control of Oberst Edgar Petersen. The oldest station was that at Rechlin near Neubrandenburg which eventually comprised seven different departments known as E2 to E8, all concerned with the development of aircraft and armament. Erprobungsstelle Travemünde on the Baltic coast near Lübeck was responsible for the testing of flying-boats and special weapons. The Tarnewitz station (north-west of Wismar) was developed from the E6 department at Rechlin and was responsible for the testing of aircraft guns and rockets.

Some of the most gruesome experiments were those carried out at Münster-Nord with chemical warfare methods. It was here that the various 'cross' groups of gases were developed but, fortunately for both sides, never used. Erprobungsstelle Tarnowitz (better known as Udetfeld to prevent confusion with Tarnewitz) was stationed in Upper Silesia and concerned mainly with bomb ballistic trials. The station at Gotenhafen was eventually transferred to Travemünde and dealt with the testing of torpedoes. The final station was that at Karlshagen (Peenemünde) which was responsible for the testing of aircraft-borne missiles. It had no connection whatsoever with the Flak-Versuchsstelle (anti-aircraft weapons) and the army establishment which developed the A4-type rockets.

7

Early Focke-Wulf aircraft were characterized by their Zanonia-form wing, here fitted to the prototype Fw 47 D-2295. (*F. Selinger*)

## The Aircraft Companies

*Arado Flugzeugwerke GmbH*   The Arado-Handelsgesellschaft was formed in 1925 as a successor to the Werft Warnemünde der Flugzeugbau Friedrichshafen GmbH. Capital for the new company was provided by Hugo Stinnes, a wealthy industrialist, and Ing Walter Rethel was appointed as chief designer. In 1925, Rethel produced the S I biplane trainer, followed a year later by the SC I and SC II advanced trainers. By 1928 the company had built the SD I single-seat fighter, the V 1 light airliner and the W 2 floatplane, and the following year saw the production of a large variety of aircraft types, but despite this, the Arado company failed to gain any large production contracts. Early in 1933, Hugo Stinnes died, Walter Blume was appointed as chief engineer and on 4 March, 1939, a new company was established as the Arado Flugzeugwerke GmbH.

*Blohm und Voss Schiffswerft, Abteilung Flugzeugbau*   On 4 July, 1933, the Blohm und Voss shipbuilding company at Hamburg formed an aircraft subsidiary known as the Hamburger Flugzeugbau GmbH directed by Walther Blohm. The company received few production orders during the Second World War, partly because production capacity was not available and possibly because a Nazi subsidy was resisted. Most production centred on the Bv 138 flying-boat until, from 1942, effort was increasingly absorbed on sub-contract work for Messerschmitt and Junkers. Although chiefly known for flying-boats and floatplanes, Blohm und Voss explored every facet of military and civil aviation, with the possible exception of rotary-wing aircraft, and even a few missiles were produced.

*Bücker Flugzeugbau GmbH*   Carl Clemens Bücker joined the German Naval Air Service in 1915 and became a seaplane pilot in the First World War. Thereafter he tested aircraft for the Swedish Navy and, in 1921, founded the Svenska-Aero AB (SAAB) at Stockholm. Heinkel-designed aircraft were included amongst SAAB's products, but in 1932, Bücker

8

sold his interests in the company and returned to Germany to found the Bücker Flugzeugbau at Johannisthal.

*Deutsches Forschungsinstitut für Segelflug*   Usually known by the abbreviation DFS, the German Gliding Research Institute was formed in 1925 from the Rhön-Rossitten-Gesellschaft, for research into unpowered flight. Under the leadership of Dr Walter Georgii, the company was established at the Wasserkuppe, but transferred to Darmstadt-Griesheim in 1933. As work increased, much of the institute's work was transferred to Ainring near Salzburg.

Typical of Gotha designs during the pre-war period, the Go 150 sporting aircraft was powered by two 50 hp Zündapp Z-092 engines. (*F. Selinger*)

*Dornier-Werke GmbH*   In 1910 Claudius Dornier joined the Zeppelin airship company and in 1914 was put in charge of the newly formed Zeppelin-Werke Lindau GmbH. Just after the war, the Dornier Gs I flying-boat was completed, but the Allies ordered its destruction, and it was sunk off Kiel on 25 April, 1920. In 1921 the first of the famous Komet and Merkur series of airliners was completed, and during 1922 the Zeppelin-Werke were renamed as the Dornier-Metallbauten GmbH. The Dornier Wal flying-boat brought the company much of its early fame, the prototype flying on 6 November, 1922, being followed in 1926 by the Super Wal. Three years later the Do X flying-boat was completed, then the largest aircraft in the world. In 1933 the company was renamed Dornier-Werke GmbH with factories at Friedrichshafen, Manzell, Löwenthal and Allmansweiler, plus a subsidiary at Wismar.

*Gerhard Fieseler Werke GmbH*   After distinguished service as a fighter pilot during the First World War, Gerhard Fieseler became one of the finest aerobatic pilots in the world. In 1928, the Raab-Katzenstein GmbH produced the F 1 Tigerschwalbe biplane to his design, and on 1 April, 1930, Fieseler purchased the Segelflugzeugbau Kassel. Renamed as the Fieseler Flugzeugbau in 1932, the company produced the F 2 Tiger, the unusual F 3 Wespe to the design of Dr Alexander Lippisch and the F 4 and F 5 sports monoplanes. During 1933 Erich Bachem and Rheinhold Mewes joined the company as technical director and chief designer and began work on the Fi 97 and Fi 98. On 1 April, 1939, the company became the Gerhard Fieseler Werke GmbH.

9

*Anton Flettner GmbH*   Flettner's work in the aeronautical field began as early as 1905 when he was employed by the Zeppelin company. In addition to his outstanding work on helicopters, he also developed the servo-tab aileron control which bears his name and also the Flettner rotor. These rotating cylinders were mounted vertically on the ships *Buchau* and *Baden-Baden* during the 1920s, producing a driving force by means of the Magnus effect.

*Focke Achgelis Flugzeugbau GmbH*   In 1931 Prof Heinrich Focke set up a research laboratory to pursue his very keen interest in rotary-wing flight, producing the Fa 61 helicopter and the Fw 186 gyroplane in 1936. During the following year, Focke left Focke-Wulf to establish his own company at Hoykenkamp near Delmenhorst, the Focke Achgelis Flugzeugbau GmbH.

*Focke-Wulf Flugzeugbau GmbH*   On 1 January, 1924, Prof Heinrich Focke, Georg Wulf and Dr Werner Neumann founded the Focke-Wulf Flugzeugbau AG at Bremen. Early Focke-Wulf designs were notable for their thick shoulder wings and included the A 16 light transport, the Möwe series of transports and the S 24 lightplane. In 1927, Georg Wulf was killed testing the unusual F 19 sportsplane, and from 1931 Focke turned to the design of rotary-wing aircraft. In September 1931, Focke-Wulf amalgamated with the Albatros works at Johannisthal and on 1 November, Dipl Ing Kurt Tank joined the company as chief designer. In June 1936 Focke-Wulf became a limited company under the new designation of Focke-Wulf Flugzeugbau GmbH.

*Gothaer Waggonfabrik AG*   The name of Gotha will always be associated with the large twin-engined bombers with which Germany attacked the British Isles during the First World War. The company was founded on 3 February, 1913, to build the famous Taube design and in July 1915 produced the Gotha G I, the first of many twin-engined bombers. The company was dissolved in 1919 but re-established in 1933 at Gotha with a subsidiary factory at Fürth.

*Ernst Heinkel AG*   After a short period as a designer with the L.V.G. and Albatros concerns, Ernst Heinkel joined the new Hansa und Brandenburgische GmbH as technical director. During the First World War he produced the famous W 12 and W 29 fighter floatplanes which proved extremely successful in operations around the Flanders coast. After the war, Heinkel joined the Caspar-Werke for a short period, but on 1 December, 1922, he formed his own company at Warnemünde. Ostensibly producing aircraft for the Swedish SAAB company, Heinkel continued the development of military aircraft for a large variety of customers. During 1932 a new factory was opened at Rostock, and on 4 May, 1937, the first aircraft was rolled out from Heinkel's ultra-modern factory at

One of the most important fighters of the early Luftwaffe was the Heinkel He 51. (*H. Thiele*)

Oranienburg near Berlin. After the invasion of Poland, Heinkel took over the P.Z.L. factory at Mielec and in 1942 his design staff were transferred to Vienna-Schwechat.

*Henschel Flugzeugwerke AG* Established in 1848, the locomotive manufacturing company of Henschel und Sohn later turned its attention to the construction of heavy lorries, machine tools, and on 30 March, 1933, to aircraft. The Henschel Flugzeugwerke were established at Schönefeld

Several Heinkel He 51B-1s were delivered to 1.J/88 of the Condor Legion at Leon in Spain. (*H. Obert*)

11

One of the fastest aircraft built by the German aircraft industry before the war was the He 119 V1.

The He 119 V3 reconnaissance floatplane.

with Walter Hormel as director and Friedrich Nicolaus as chief designer. Although Nicolaus produced a number of successful designs, the major part of the company's production facilities was devoted to the licence manufacture of such aircraft as the Do 17, Ju 88 and Me 410. The company, under the direction of Prof Herbert Wagner, later became the largest German producer of guided missiles.

*Junkers Flugzeug- und Motorenwerke AG*   In 1910 Prof Hugo Junkers patented a design for an all-metal aerofoil section for aircraft. This led to the design of the Junkers-J 1 all-metal cantilever monoplane of 1915 and the establishment, on 20 October, 1917, of the Junkers-Fokker-Werke AG. A number of successful all-metal aircraft were produced during the First World War including the J 4 ground-attack aircraft and the J 9 and J 10 fighters. After the war, the company was re-formed as the Junkers Flugzeugwerke AG, producing in June 1919 the J 13 (later F 13) – one of the world's most important transport aircraft. A number of successful aircraft followed and late in 1927 Dipl Ing Ernst Zindel took over as chief designer. By 1938 Junkers had factories at Dessau, Aschersleben, Bernburg, Halberstadt and Köthen and by the end of the war, a further nine major factories were in production.

12

The Junkers-R 42 was a military conversion of the G 24 airliner built in Sweden.

*Messerschmitt AG*   Before the First World War, Willy Messerschmitt had co-operated with Friedrich Harth in the construction of gliders. Messerschmitt's first powered aircraft was the S 15 which was followed in 1924 by the M 17 and in 1929 by the very successful M 23 lightplane. He also produced the M 18 and M 20 light transports but on 1 June, 1931, the Bayerische Flugzeugwerke with which he was closely associated had become bankrupt. After a considerable struggle, the bankruptcy was discharged in May 1933 and the Bayerische Flugzeugwerke AG re-established with 82 employees. On 11 July, 1938, it was renamed Messerschmitt AG with factories at Augsburg and Regensburg, and by the end of the Second World War, it was the largest German aircraft company.

*The German Aircraft Designation System*

From 1933 the technical department of the RLM (later known as the GL/C) standardized the designation system for all German aeronautical equipment. Each design was allocated a number, aircraft and missiles being

Both the Henschel and Junkers companies did considerable work on the problems of high-altitude flight before the war. The Junkers-EF 61 was designed to attain an altitude of 12,000 m (39,000 ft). (*H. Redemann*)

13

Two important early Messerschmitt aircraft were the tiny M 17 sportsplane and the M 20 airliner.

prefixed with the number 8, gliders with 108, piston engines with 9, and turbojet and rocket engines with 109. Therefore the 8-222 was the Blohm und Voss Bv 222 flying-boat and the 9-222 was the Junkers Jumo 222 piston engine.

These designations were also prefixed with the company's initial letters such as Ar for Arado, Go for Gotha and Ju for Junkers. The numbers themselves were normally allocated in batches, *e.g.* Messerschmitt Bf 108 to Bf 110, Heinkel He 111 to He 120 and Henschel Hs 121 to Hs 130. Another practice was the addition of 100 to the aircraft's designation when a radical modification of the basic design was made. An example of this practice was the Messerschmitt Bf 109 with subsequent Me 209, Me 309, Me 409, Me 509 and Me 609.

The aircraft designation was followed by a letter indicating a major modification and a number which signified a less radical alteration to the basic design, *e.g.* Bf 109A-1, B-1, B-2, etc. Pre-production aircraft were identified by a letter and the figure 0, *e.g.* Bf 109E-0. Experimental aircraft were identified by a small letter at first, the prototype being the Ar 66a, the second aircraft the Ar 66b and so on. By 1935 a new system had been

An early Luftwaffe unit, probably the Publicity Squadron Central Germany, on parade. The unit consists of a group of Heinkel He 51As and two rows of Arado Ar 65Es with Junkers-Ju 52/3m transports in the background.

14

adopted using the suffix letter V (for Versuchs) and a number. Thus the Fw 190 V1 was the first prototype of the Focke-Wulf fighter and the Ju 88 V30 was the thirtieth prototype of the Junkers bomber.

Minor modifications were identified by the addition of the letter U (for Umbau or rebuild) and a number, *e.g.* Bf 109G-6/U1. Conversion packs were identified in a similar manner, but by the letter R (for Rüstsatz or field conversion pack). Finally, aircraft with the suffix Trop after their designations carried tropical equipment.

Each piston-engine manufacturer was allocated a three-figure designation, those beginning with 100 being used by BMW, 200 by Junkers, 300 by Brandenburgische Motorenwerke, 400 by Argus, 500 by Hirth, 600 by Daimler-Benz, 700 by Deutz and 800 by BMW. Turbojet engine designations began with 109-001 and rocket engines with 109-500.

Küstenjagdgruppe 136 operated a number of He 51B-2 fighter floatplanes, the type being the Luftwaffe's first successful fighter.

## The Luftwaffe

Although German rearmament had been steadily growing for many years, it was not until 1 March, 1935, that the Luftwaffe was revealed to the world. As originally formed, the Luftwaffe comprised 20,000 men, many of whom had received flying training either acting as co-pilots on Lufthansa flights or by a course at the various DVS schools.

The basic Luftwaffe unit was the Staffel which, at that time, normally comprised between nine and twelve aircraft. Three Staffeln were combined together as the Gruppe, and three Gruppen could be combined as the Geschwader. With the exception of the reconnaissance units, virtually all Luftwaffe units were organized into Geschwader, with the Gruppe as an autonomous sub-division. Fighter units were known as Jagdgeschwader (JG), bomber units as Kampfgeschwader (KG) and dive-bomber units as Stukageschwader (St.G).

The reconnaissance units were organized into Gruppen with the Staffel as an autonomous sub-division. This was mainly because of the need for

15

each reconnaissance Staffel to co-operate closely with an army unit. Army co-operation Staffeln were distinguished by the abbreviation (H) for Heeres; long-range units being identified by the letter (F) for Fern or long-range. From the middle of 1942 the (H) Staffeln were organized into Nahaufklärungsgruppen or short-range reconnaissance squadrons.

In February 1939 the Luftkreis were reorganized into four Luftflotten or air fleets. Luftflotte 1 with its headquarters in Berlin controlled northeast Germany and East Prussia; Luftflotte 2 with headquarters in Brunswick controlled north-west Germany; Luftflotte 3 with headquarters in Munich controlled south-west Germany; and Luftflotte 4 with headquarters in Vienna controlled the Breslau area of Germany, most of Austria and the whole of western Czechoslovakia. Respective commanders were Generals Kesselring, Felmy, Sperrle, and Löhr.

Each air fleet contained one, two, or possibly three Flieger-Divisionen to which all operational commands were subordinated. When the Second World War began, the Luftwaffe had seven air divisions, but the total was soon increased and several were redesignated as Fliegerkorps. Towards the end of the war several specialized fighter commands were formed and known as Jagdkorps or Jagddivisionen. The administrative control of the Luftflotte was assigned to the Luftgau, which usually contained between six and twelve Flughafenbereichs-Kommandanturen or regional airfield commands.

The previously-described re-arrangement in the areas of command led to a complete redesignation of all Luftwaffe units, this being completed just before the war. As originally formed, the last digit in the three-figure Geschwader designation referred to the Luftkreis in which the unit was formed. For example, JG 132 was formed within Luftkreis II, KG 154 was formed within Luftkreis IV and St.G 168 within Luftkreis VIII.

The redesignation led to all Geschwader formed within Luftflotte 1 being designated from 1 to 25; those within Luftflotte 2 from 26 to 50; those within Luftflotte 3 from 51 to 75; and those within Luftflotte 4 from 76 to 99. At the same time, Gruppen ending in the number 0 or 1 were formed within Luftflotte 1; those ending in 2 within Luftflotte 2; those ending in 3 within Luftflotte 3, and those ending in 4 within Luftflotte 4. Naval units retained their three-figure designations ending in the number 6.

Three days after the invasion of Norway and Denmark on 9 April, 1940, a new Luftflotte was formed to control units based in the area. Designated Luftflotte 5, the air fleet was commanded by Gen Stumpff and had its headquarters in Oslo. In November 1942, Luftflotte 2 was withdrawn from the central Russian front to take over the units based on the Mediterranean front. The units that remained in Russia were placed under the control of Luftwaffen-Kommando Ost, this command eventually being redesignated in May 1943 as Luftflotte 6 with Gen Ritter von Greim at its head.

The final important command was Oberbefehlshaber Mitte formed in

March 1941 to control units operating in the defence of Germany. By February 1944 this had become one of the most important commands in the Luftwaffe, being redesignated as Luftflotte Reich and commanded by Gen Stumpff (Gen Josef Kammhuber taking over Luftflotte 5). The development of the Allied daylight bombing offensive from 1943 led to the rapid expansion of the Luftwaffe's fighter forces. Towards the end of 1944, two new conventional fighter Geschwaden were formed, JG 4 and JG 6, and most existing units were expanded to contain four groups of four squadrons each. At that time it was not unusual for a Geschwader to have 200 operational aircraft.

An Arado Ar 66C two-seat trainer of the Luftwaffe.

# Arado Ar 66

Before the Nazi Party came to power in 1933, the Arado company had produced a number of successful biplane fighters and trainers. Two years earlier design work began on a new two-seat trainer at Arado's Warnemünde factory.

Receiving the RLM type number Ar 66, the new trainer was designed by Ing Walter Rethel who had previously served with the Kondor and Fokker companies. The Ar 66 was a single-bay biplane of mixed wood and metal construction with fabric covering. It had tandem open cockpits, fixed undercarriage, and tailskid. The braced tailplane was mounted above a large rear fuselage fairing and there was no separate fin, the whole of the vertical surface being movable.

Following Rethel's transfer to the Messerschmitt company, Dipl Ing Walter Blume took over development of the Ar 66, which flew for the first time in 1932. The prototype was designated Ar 66a and powered by a single 240 hp Argus As 10C eight-cylinder liquid-cooled engine. The second landplane prototype was the Ar 66c which was essentially similar to the first aircraft. The major production model was designated Ar 66C. The second prototype was the Ar 66b, powered, like the other two

A large number of Ar 66Cs were delivered to the Luftwaffe. (*R. C. Seeley*)

prototypes, by an Argus As 10C engine, and fitted with two wooden floats supported by a large number of struts. The rudder was extended beneath the line of the rear fuselage, being faired into it by a large auxiliary fin. Ten Ar 66B production aircraft were completed during 1933, but the type failed to see operational service.

The Ar 66C began to reach the Luftwaffe in 1933, being delivered to several of the early operational units which were then in the process of being established. With the delivery of the more specialized military types, all Ar 66s were transferred to the many Luftwaffe training units, serving in this capacity until well into the Second World War. Pilot training schools operating the type during the war included FFS A/B 4 at Prague-Gbell, FFS A/B 11 at Schönewalde, FFS A/B 23 at Kaufbeuren and FFS A/B 116 at Göppingen.

On 7 October, 1943, an order was issued calling for the establishment of a number of night ground-attack groups within the Luftwaffe. Thus, the small number of Störkampfstaffeln (Harassing squadrons) already operational were put on a more organized footing. The main equipment of these units, which were engaged in night harassing attacks behind the Soviet lines, were the Ar 66 and Gotha Go 145 two-seat trainers equipped to carry 2 and 4 kg (4 and 9 lb) anti-personnel bombs. The main groups to operate the Ar 66 were NSGr 2, NSGr 3, NSGr 5 in Russia, NSGr 8 in Finland and NSGr 12 in Latvia.

*Wartime operational units:* 1., 2. and 4./NSGr 2, NSGr 3, 2./NSGr 4, NSGr 5, NSGr 8, 3./NSGr 11, NSGr 12 and the Flieger-Gruppe Ost.

Ar 66C: Span 10 m (32 ft 9¾ in); length 8·3 m (27 ft 2¾ in); height 2·93 m (9 ft 7⅓ in); wing area 29·63 sq m (318·93 sq ft).

Empty weight 905 kg (1,996 lb); loaded weight 1,330 kg (2,933 lb).

Maximum speed at sea level 210 km/h (130 mph); cruising speed 175 km/h (109 mph); landing speed 80 km/h (50 mph); climb to 1,000 m (3,280 ft) 4·1 min; service ceiling 4,500 m (14,764 ft); normal range 716 km (445 miles).

18

# Arado Ar 68 and Ar 197

The Arado Ar 68 was ordered as a replacement for the Luftwaffe's front-line biplane fighter, the Heinkel He 51, which had itself entered service in April 1935 as a replacement for the Arado Ar 65 biplane. Designed under the leadership of Ing Rethel, the Ar 68 fighter was also a biplane and, as such, was the last to enter front-line service with the Luftwaffe, being virtually phased-out of this rôle by the time the Second World War began.

The Ar 68 was a single-bay biplane with open cockpit and a fixed cantilever undercarriage—all wheels being enclosed in spats. The wings were of unequal span and chord, of wooden construction with plywood and fabric covering, braced by N-type interplane struts. The fuselage was a welded steel-tube structure covered on the top and forward sections with metal panels, the remainder being fabric-covered. The tailplane was strut-braced to the fin which, together with the rudder, formed a very distinctive shape seen on many later Arado designs. There was a large one-piece elevator, and the ailerons on the upper wings were also of notably generous area. All control surfaces were dynamically balanced.

Flying began in 1934 with the first prototype, the Ar 68a D-IKIN, which was powered by a 750 hp BMW VId twelve-cylinder vee liquid-cooled engine having a continuous rating of 550 hp. Although this aircraft handled well enough, its performance fell below expectations, and the second prototype, the Ar 68b D-IVUS was therefore fitted with one of the new supercharged 610 hp Junkers Jumo 210 twelve-cylinder inverted-vee liquid-cooled engines. This engine had advantages over the BMW engine because it maintained power up to a higher altitude and by improving the

The Arado Ar 68 was the last of the Luftwaffe's front-line biplane fighters. First put into small-scale production as the Ar 68F, shown here, and using the BMW VI engine, the fighter entered service in the late summer of 1936. (*K. Ries*)

19

pilot's view as a result of its inverted instead of upright vee form. A new problem arose, however, because performance was much reduced by the drag of a badly-designed chin-type radiator on the second prototype. The radiator was satisfactorily redesigned for the third prototype, the Ar 68c, or V3, D-IBAS, and this aircraft when it began flying in the summer of 1935 had a performance fully up to the original requirements.

The Ar 68 V3 was the first prototype to be armed, having two 7·9 mm MG 17 machine-guns in the upper engine cowling, and was to be the forerunner of the Ar 68C production aircraft, but insufficient supplies of the Jumo 210 engine caused a reversion to the BMW VI engine which was fitted in the Ar 68d, or V4, D-ITAR. The fifth prototype, Ar 68e D-ITEP, however, was powered by a Jumo 210 engine in anticipation of a later supply improvement when this machine was to act as the pattern for the Ar 68E production aircraft. In the interim, the Ar 68F powered by the BMW engine was put into small-scale production.

To those who were fully conversant with both aircraft, the Ar 68 was superior to the He 51 which it was to replace, but the General Staff of the Luftwaffe remained unconvinced of this and was reluctant to re-equip with another biplane. In January 1936, Ernst Udet was called in to take charge of technical matters for the Luftwaffe and, soon after, set about making a decision concerning the Ar 68. Udet was one of the RLM's few first-class men; he had been a First World War pilot, was regarded as the world's number one aerobatic pilot and was to do valuable work in the organiza- tion of the development of German air weapons. In his practical manner, Udet organized a mock combat between an He 51 and an Ar 68, the former being flown by a first-class pilot and the latter by himself. The result of this contest was that the Ar 68 out-performed the He 51 on every

When sufficient supplies of the Junkers Jumo 210 engine became available, the Ar 68F was supplanted in production by the Ar 68E, illustrated here. Most of the Luftwaffe's fighter units were equipped with the type during 1937 but the Messerschmitt Bf 109 soon outmoded the Ar 68 which was then relegated to the advanced trainer rôle. (*K. Ries*)

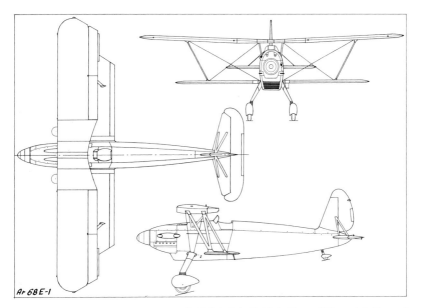

Ar 68 E-1

count and, by the late summer of 1936, I./JG 134 Horst Wessel followed by I./JG 131 became the first units to begin re-equipping with the Ar 68F-1.

By the spring of 1937, the Ar 68E was in production because 690 hp Junkers Jumo 210 Da engines were being made available for this aircraft. Armament was still only two MG 17 guns (500 rpg) and, at the cost of reduction in performance, a rack holding six 10 kg (22 lb) bombs could be fitted beneath the fuselage. At this time it was planned to have seven Jagdgruppen equipped with the Ar 68 and five with the He 51, but the phasing-out of the latter aircraft was accelerated after its poor combat performance in the Spanish Civil War. Prototypes of the later Messerschmitt Bf 109 were also tested in Spain and, by the time this fighter was being introduced into service in 1937, most of the Luftwaffe's Jagdgruppen were equipped with the Ar 68E.

In 1938, the Ar 68E had its own trials in Spain when two of these aircraft were despatched for night interceptions with Grupo 9, led by Capitan Javier Murcia from La Cenia airfield. Already, however, the Ar 68 was shown to be outmoded by the first Bf 109s and the last developments were begun in 1937 after production of the Ar 68E was under way.

The Ar 68G was intended to have an increased service ceiling but was not built because of lack of a suitable engine. The last prototype was therefore the Ar 68H D-ISIX which was powered by an 850 hp BMW 132 Da nine-cylinder radial air-cooled engine to increase considerably the maximum speed by 65 km/h (40 mph). Other new features included the fitting of two extra MG 17 guns (in the upper wing) and an enclosed cockpit with sliding canopy, so that the Ar 68H was reminiscent of one of

21

Evolved in parallel with the Ar 68H was the Ar 197 which was intended as a carrier-based interceptor and light bomber. The type was superseded by Messerschmitt designs but no German aircraft carriers were completed. Shown here is the Ar 197 V3 (production prototype) on which can be seen the arrester hook and an auxiliary fuel tank. (*F. Selinger*)

its more famous contemporaries, the Gloster Gladiator. No production of the Ar 68H was undertaken, but another, similar, aircraft, the Ar 197, was evolved in parallel with it.

The Ar 197 was intended for interception and light bombing duties and to operate from the German aircraft carriers *Graf Zeppelin* and *Peter Strasser* and ships converted for carrier operations. (Only the *Graf Zeppelin* was ever launched but was never completed and towards the end of the war was finally scuttled.) The Ar 197 V1 D-ITSE was generally similar to the Ar 68H with an enclosed cockpit but was fitted with a 900 hp Daimler-Benz DB 600A twelve-cylinder liquid-cooled engine driving a three-blade airscrew. Naval equipment, such as an arrester hook and catapult spools, was fitted to the Ar 197 V2 D-IVLE which was powered by an 815 hp BMW 132J nine-cylinder radial engine with a three-blade airscrew. These two prototypes flew in the spring of 1937 and were followed in the summer of that year by the Ar 197 V3 (which apparently had no registration). The V3 prototype had the more powerful 880 hp BMW 132 Dc radial engine and was armed with two 7·9 mm MG 17 guns (250 rpg) on top of the fuselage and two 20 mm MG FF guns (30 rpg) in the upper wing. Also, racks could be fitted below the lower wing for four 50 kg (110 lb) bombs, and either an auxiliary fuel tank or a smoke-laying unit could be fitted beneath the fuselage. This last prototype was delivered to E-Stelle -Travemünde for evaluation but no production was undertaken. The design was superseded in 1939 by the Bf 109T and in 1941 by the Me 155, but these aircraft never saw carrier service either.

By the time the Second World War began on 3 September, 1939, most of the Ar 68s had found their niche as advanced trainers with the

22

Jagdfliegerschulen but some were retained for a short time as night fighters with the units 10.(N)/JG 53, 10.(N)/JG 72 and 11.(N)/JG 72. The Arado Ar 80 low-wing monoplane fighter was intended as a replacement for the Ar 68 but was unsuccessful in the October 1935 trials which the Bf 109 and He 112 won.

Ar 68E: Span 11 m (36 ft $1\frac{1}{8}$ in); length 9·5 m (31 ft 2 in); height 3·3 m (10 ft 9 in); wing area 27·3 sq m (293·75 sq ft).

Empty weight 1,600 kg (3,528 lb); loaded weight 2,020 kg (4,454 lb).

Maximum speed at sea level 306 km/h (190 mph); maximum speed at 2,650 m (8,695 ft) 335 km/h (208 mph); landing speed 95 km/h (59 mph); initial rate of climb 755 m/min (2,476 ft/min); service ceiling 8,100 m (26,575 ft); range 415 km (258 miles).

Ar 197 V3: Span 11 m (36 ft $1\frac{1}{8}$ in); length 9·2 m (30 ft $2\frac{1}{4}$ in); height 3·6 m (11 ft $9\frac{3}{4}$ in); wing area 27·8 sq m (299·13 sq ft).

Empty weight 1,840 kg (4,057 lb); loaded weight 2,475 kg (5,457 lb).

Maximum speed at 2,500 m (8,200 ft) 400 km/h (248 mph); cruising speed 354 km/h (220 mph); landing speed 95 km/h (59 mph); climb to 4,000 m (13,120 ft) 5·3 min; service ceiling 8,600 m (26,213 ft); range 659 km (432 miles).

A development prototype of the Arado Ar 95, D-OHGV, patrol and light attack floatplane taxi-ing out to the take-off point. Tested in the Spanish Civil War, the Ar 95 was not ordered for German forces. (*R. C. Seeley*)

# Arado Ar 95 and Ar 195

Although not ordered by the German forces, the Ar 95 saw service with the Luftwaffe in small numbers by virtue of the war preventing the despatch of certain export orders. The aircraft was designed in 1935 by Dipl Ing W. Blume as a twin-float two-seat biplane for reconnaissance, patrol and light attack duties.

The first prototype, D-OLUO, was powered by an 880 hp BMW 132 Dc nine-cylinder radial engine and flew in 1936. The second prototype,

Another view of the Ar 95 D-OHGV, here beginning its take-off run. (*R. C. Seeley*)

D-OHEO, was powered by a 690 hp Junkers Jumo 210 twelve-cylinder inverted-vee liquid-cooled engine. These aircraft competed with the two prototypes of the Focke-Wulf Fw 62 which were of similar configuration but were both powered by BMW radial engines, the Fw 62 V2 having a central main float and two outrigger floats. The radial-engined Ar 95 V1 appears to have emerged from the trials as the most promising and six aircraft of this type were sent for trials with the Condor Legion in August 1938 in that universal testing ground, the Spanish Civil War. This trial batch of Ar 95s was probably made up of prototype and pre-production aircraft. The production prototype D-ODGX, had a long canopy over both

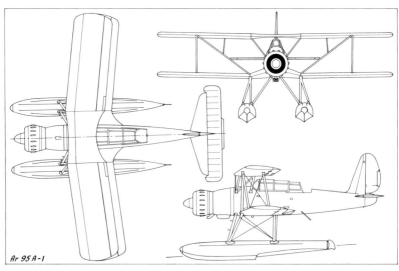

Ar 95 A-1

24

cockpits, with the aft end left open for the gunner. Armament comprised a 7·9 mm machine-gun fixed to fire forward and a similar weapon for the rear cockpit, and a 700 kg (1,544 lb) torpedo or various bomb loads could also be carried. All-metal construction was used and the single-step floats were braced to the lower wings and the fuselage. The parallel-chord wings had slightly positive stagger and a 6 deg sweepback, the lower wing having its inboard sections increased in chord and thickness, while for the upper wing, braced above the fuselage, the reverse was true.

When it became clear that the Ar 95 would not be ordered for the German forces, the type was offered for export in two forms, as the Ar 95W with floats or the Ar 95L with a non-retractable land undercarriage having trouser fairings around the main legs and a fairing over the tail-wheel. In 1938, Turkey ordered the Ar 95W and Chile ordered the Ar 95L, but only the Chilean aircraft were delivered before the outbreak of the Second World War. The floatplanes intended for Turkey were then completed and put into Luftwaffe service with the designation Ar 95A.

A production Ar 95A, D-ODGY, carrying a single torpedo. Only a few Ar 95s intended for export were put into Luftwaffe service during 1939.

In Luftwaffe service, the Ar 95A was used chiefly for training purposes in the Seeaufklärungsgruppen, the units concerned originally being 2./SAGr 125 and all three Staffeln of SAGr 126. By early 1943 the Ar 95s were transferred to SAGr 127, but from the end of that year until late 1944 only 1./SAGr 127 operated the type.

A design based on the Ar 95L landplane was the Ar 195 which was

25

The Ar 95 floatplane was produced in a landplane version as the Ar 95L for export. Shown here is a line-up of Ar 95Ls of the Chilean Air Force. No other Ar 95s were exported, due to the advent of war in 1939.

intended for operation from aircraft carriers planned for the German Navy. Three prototypes, the Ar 195 V1 D-OCLN, V2 D-OBBB, and V3 D-ODSG, were flown in 1937 and, in addition to the fitting of such items as arrester hook and catapult equipment, had a redesigned, heightened cockpit canopy. The leading edge of the top wing centre section was cut back to the canopy and the area slightly increased. The main undercarriage legs had slimmer fairings, and the wheels were enclosed in spats. A BMW 132 radial engine was fitted. The Ar 195 was not proceeded with because it was superseded by the Ar 197 development of which began in the same year.

*Wartime operational units:* 2./SAGr 125, SAGr 126, SAGr 127.

Ar 95A (or W): Span 12·5 m (41 ft 0⅛in); length 11·1 m (36 ft 5 in); height 5·2 m (17 ft 0¾ in); wing area 45·4 sq m (488·5 sq ft).

Empty weight 2,450 kg (5,402 lb); loaded weight 3,570 kg (7,872 lb).

Maximum speed at 3,000 m (9,840 ft) 309 km/h (192 mph); cruising speed at 1,200 m (3,936 ft) 253 km/h (157 mph); initial rate of climb 450 m/min (1,476 ft/min); service ceiling 7,300 m (23,944 ft); normal range 1,100 km (683 miles).

Ar 195 V1: Span 12·5 m (41 ft 0⅛ in); length 10·5 m (34 ft 5⅜ in); height 3·6 m (11 ft 9¼ in); wing area 46 sq m (495 sq ft).

Empty weight 2,380 kg (5,248 lb); loaded weight 3,745 kg (8,257 lb).

Maximum speed 282 km/h (175 mph); cruising speed 250 km/h (155 mph); time to 4,000 m (13,120 ft) 14 min; service ceiling 6,000 m (19,680 ft); normal range 650 km (404 miles).

# Arado Ar 96

Without doubt the most important advanced trainer produced for the Luftwaffe was the Arado Ar 96. Extremely advanced for its time, the Ar 96 was designed in 1938 by Dipl Ing Walter Blume, chief designer of Arado Flugzeugwerke GmbH. It was a neat cantilever low-wing monoplane built of light metal throughout with duralumin skin. The pupil and instructor were seated in tandem beneath an elongated and extensively glazed canopy. The fuselage was an oval-section monocoque structure built in two halves and the mainwheels retracted into the wing centre section. The tail assembly was of typical Arado design with a tall fin and rudder of narrow chord and the tailplane mounted at the extreme rear of the fuselage.

The Arado Ar 96 V1 which differed from subsequent aircraft in having an outwards retracting undercarriage.

The prototype, the Ar 96 V1 D-IRUU, powered by a 240 hp Argus As 10C eight-cylinder inverted-vee air-cooled engine, flew for the first time in 1938. As originally flown, the Ar 96 V1 had an outward-retracting undercarriage, but this was replaced by the inward-retracting type subsequently adopted for all production aircraft. The wide-track undercarriage was considered to be much more suitable for the rough landings associated with fledgling pilots.

The Ar 96 proved so successful that the RLM placed a large order for the machine in 1940. A small batch of Ar 96A-1 aircraft had been completed in 1939, these being powered, like the first prototype, by the 240 hp Argus As 10C engine. It was foreseen that the aircraft would provide the Luftwaffe's training schools with an excellent intermediate step between the standard initial trainers such as the Ar 66, Fw 44, Go 145 and He 72 biplanes and the advanced fighter monoplanes which were then in service.

27

The main production series was the Ar 96B which differed in being powered by a 465 hp Argus As 410A-1 twelve-cylinder inverted-vee air-cooled engine driving a two-blade metal airscrew with an Argus automatic pitch-change spinner. The Ar 96B also had a longer fuselage to accommodate more fuel. The first production model was the Ar 96B-1 unarmed pilot trainer. The Ar 96B-2 carried a 7·9 mm MG 17 machine-gun, for gunnery training, above the engine cowling and offset to starboard. A further five B-series aircraft have been reported including the Ar 96B-5 pilot gunnery trainer and the B-7 which could carry bombs for the training of ground-attack and dive-bomber pilots. Other aircraft were modified for night and blind flying, communications and navigational training, and at least one, D-IXWZ, carried a 7·9 mm MG 15 machine-gun in the rear of the cockpit for the training of air gunners.

At least one Ar 96B carried a flexibly-mounted MG 15 machine-gun in the rear cockpit.

Despite the success of the Ar 96, relatively few were built by the Arado company. Until mid-1941, the Ago Flugzeugwerke (a Junkers subsidiary) built most aircraft, but then, the Czechoslovak Avia company took over series production. The Letov company of Prague joined the Ar 96 programme in 1944 and by the end of the war no less than 11,546 aircraft had been completed.

The Ar 96C, of which only a pre-production batch was built, was powered by a 480 hp Argus As 410C engine and had a small window in the floor of the cockpit for bomb aiming practice. A development of the Ar 96B was the Ar 296 project to be powered by a 600 hp Argus As 411 twelve-cylinder inverted-vee air-cooled engine. This was abandoned in favour of the Ar 396 (*see page* 54) designed to use the minimum of strategically important materials. After the war the Ar 96B remained in production in Czechoslovakia until 1948 under the designation C.2B-1.

The Ar 96B formed the main equipment of the Jagdschulgeschwader (fighter-training wings) of which there were eventually thirteen, designated JG 101 to JG 110 and JG 114 to JG 116. The aircraft also served with the training and replacement fighter units (EJG), the pilot training schools (FFS A/B Schulen) and the officer cadet schools (LKS).

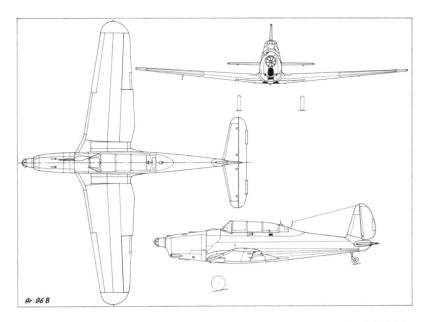

Ar 96 B

Ar 96B-2: Span 11 m (36 ft 1 in); length 9·13 m (29 ft 11¼ in); height 2·6 m (8 ft 6⅓ in); wing area 17.1 sq m (184·06 sq ft).
Empty weight 1,295 kg (2,854 lb); loaded weight 1,695 kg (3,747 lb).
Maximum speed at sea level 330 km/h (205 mph); cruising speed 295 km/h (183 mph); landing speed 100 km/h (62 mph); climb to 3,000 m (9,843 ft) 6·8 min; service ceiling 7,100 m (23,295 ft); normal range 990 km (615 miles).

# Arado Ar 196

With the object of replacing the Heinkel He 60 biplane in the shipboard reconnaissance rôle, the Arado Ar 196 two-seat low-wing floatplane was designed in 1937 for operation from German warships. In order to ascertain the best arrangement of floats, different prototypes were built in 1938. The first two prototypes, the Ar 196 V1 D-IEHK and V2 D-IHQI each had long twin floats, but the next three prototypes, the Ar 196 V3 D-ILRE, V4 D-OVMB and V5 D-IPOD, each had a single central main float and two small outrigger floats for lateral stability. Power was provided by a single 880 hp BMW 132Dc nine-cylinder radial engine driving a two-blade airscrew, but a three-blade variable-pitch airscrew was later fitted to the V1 and V5 prototypes.

After evaluation, including armament trials with the V4 prototype, a preference was established for the twin-float arrangement which was to appear on subsequent production aircraft. Thus, the Ar 196 was the

29

Designed as a shipboard reconnaissance floatplane, the Arado Ar 196 V1, D-IEHK, first flew in 1938.

nearest Germany came to using the single-float aircraft, a type which had a particular following in Japan and the USA. Later in 1938, production began of the Ar 196A-1 which differed from the first two prototypes chiefly in having a more powerful 960 hp BMW 132K radial engine. The fuselage was a basic structure of welded steel-tubes covered partly by fabric and partly by metal panels. The engine cowling had 18 streamlined bulges spaced around the outside to clear the engine valve gear. All-metal two-spar construction was used for the wings, which were strut-braced to the floats. These bracings were removed when the wings were folded, each wing hingeing at its trailing-edge root to lie back alongside the fuselage. For the tail assembly, a metal structure was used with metal-covered fixed surfaces and fabric-covered moving surfaces, the elevator being of the one-piece type. Catapult points were provided on the floats, which also had water rudders. Although the two seats were housed beneath the same

For comparative trials, three prototypes of the Ar 196 were built each with a single central main float but the twin float arrangement was chosen for production. Illustrated here is the Ar 196 V3, D-ILRE.

30

Following the equipment of the principal German warships with the Ar 196A-1, the Ar 196A-3 (illustrated here) went into production during 1940 to equip coastal patrol and reconnaissance units.

framed canopy, the rear-facing observer/gunner was only partially enclosed by a sliding portion of the canopy. Armament comprised one 7·9 mm MG 17 machine-gun in the forward fuselage and a similar weapon for the rear cockpit. Also, two 50 kg (110 lb) bombs could be carried beneath the wing.

The Ar 196A-1 entered service in the latter part of 1939 and the first unit to be thus equipped was the ship-based 5./BFGr 196 which later took part in the Norwegian campaign. By the end of 1939, the type was issued to the German warships *Gneisenau*, *Graf Spee*, *Lützow*, *Prinz Eugen*, *Scharnhorst*, and *Admiral Scheer*. The *Tirpitz* and *Bismarck* also received the floatplane.

With the principal warships equipped with the Ar 196A-1, a more aggressively-armed version was put into production for the prime purpose

An Ar 196A-3 or A-5 on coastal patrol.

31

of equipping land-based units employed on coastal and sea reconnaissance, patrol, and attack work. The new armament comprised two 20 mm MG FF cannon in the wings plus two paired 7·9 mm MG 17 machine-guns in the rear cockpit, and a small bomb load could still be carried. The Ar 196A-3 appeared as the major variant in 1940, which was the year in which Ar 196 production got into full swing. The first unit to receive the new version was probably the Kü.Fl.Gr.706. On 5 May, 1940, Lt Günther Mehrens, piloting an Ar 196A-3 from this unit, spotted the submarine HMS *Seal* (commanded by Lieut-Cdr R. Lonsdale). The submarine, which was unable to dive because of mine damage, was attempting to lay mines in the Kattegat when Mehrens attacked with his cannon and bombs, forcing the surrender of the submarine. Mehrens then alighted, picked up Lonsdale and flew him to Aalborg, the *Seal* later being towed into Frederikshavn.

An Ar 196A-3 (6H-LM) being handled at its coastal base. The A-3 was the principal production version.

By 1941, the Ar 196 was becoming increasingly active over the Mediterranean and Adriatic, and its patrols included attacking submarines and small vessels and protecting Axis ship convoys. Another activity was over the English Channel where the Ar 196s harassed RAF Coastal Command aircraft on their way to attack U-boats. Units which eventually operated the Ar 196 were 1./BFGr 196 (formed from 1./Kü.Fl.Gr. 906), 2., 3., 4., and 5./SAGr 126, Stab./SAGr 127, 1. and 2./SAGr 128, 1. and 2./SAGr 130, 2./SAGr 131, and 2./SAGr 132. There was also an Arado Kette operating the type.

In the spring of 1941, the *Bismarck* broke out into the Atlantic and used its Ar 196s to disperse the shadowing RAF Catalina flying-boats. The

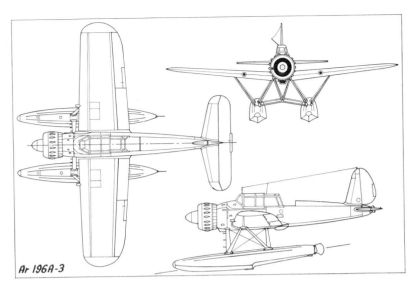

**Ar 196A-3**

following year, Ar 196 production reached its peak, thanks to a small contribution of 13 such aircraft being built by the French SNCA factory at St Nazaire. In 1943 SNCA built a further ten Ar 196s, and Fokker in the Netherlands joined in by beginning production of a new version, the Ar 196A-5, which was generally similar to the A-3. A total of 593 Ar 196s was produced (excluding prototypes) of which 401 were built by Arado.

*Wartime operational units:* 1./Kü.Fl.Gr. 706, SAGr 125, 126, 128 and 130, 2./SAGr 131, 2./SAGr 132, BFGr 196, 1. and 3./KG 200 (also used by III./KG 100—a temporary redesignation of SAGr 126).

Ar 196A-3: Span 12·4 m (40 ft 8¼ in); length 11 m (36 ft 1⅛ in); height 4.45 m (4 ft 7¼ in); wing area 28·4 sq m (305·58 sq ft).

Empty weight 2,990 kg (6,593 lb); loaded weight 3,730 kg (8,225 lb).

Maximum speed at 4,000 m (13,120 ft) 310 km/h (193 mph); cruising speed 253 km/h (157 mph); initial rate of climb 300 m/min (984 ft/min); service ceiling 7,000 m (22,960 ft); range 1,070 km (665 miles).

Ar 196As have been preserved in the Maritime Museum at Varna, Bulgaria; the Smithsonian Institution, Washington, DC; and at Willow Grove Naval Station, Pennsylvania.

Only two prototypes of this Arado Ar 199 light floatplane trainer were built, the V2
D-ISBC being shown here. The two floatplanes were, however, used by the Luftwaffe.

# Arado Ar 199

This light floatplane, though technically a success, became a victim of a
change in the official requirement for a floatplane trainer, with the result
that it did not go into production. The design of the Ar 199 was undertaken in 1938 as an all-metal low-wing monoplane stressed for catapult
launching and operation over water. Two strut frames attached the single-
step floats to the fuselage and bracing wires were fitted. The cockpit was
enclosed by a stepped canopy and provided side-by-side accommodation
for the pilot and his pupil, with a third, rear, seat for a trainee navigator or
radio operator.

Two prototypes, the Ar 199 V1 D-IRFB and the Ar 199 V2 D-ISBC,
were flown in 1939 using the 450 hp Argus As 410C twelve-cylinder
inverted-vee air-cooled engine driving a two-blade airscrew. At least one
aircraft had an Argus automatic pitch-change spinner fitted. With the
decision not to produce the Ar 199A, development of the type was stopped
but the prototypes went into Luftwaffe service as trainers.

Ar 199: Span 12.7 m (41 ft 8 in); length 10·57 m (34 ft 8$\frac{1}{8}$ in); height 4·36 m (14 ft
4$\frac{1}{4}$ in); wing area 30·4 sq m (327·1 sq ft).

Empty weight 1,675 kg (3,693 lb); fuel and oil 150 kg (331 lb); three crew 250 kg
(551 lb); loaded weight 2,075 kg (4,575 lb).

Maximum speed at 3,000 m (9,840 ft) 260 km/h (161 mph); cruising speed 212 km/h
(132 mph); alighting speed 80 km/h (50 mph); climb to 3,000 m (9,840 ft) 11 min; service
ceiling 6,500 m (21,320 ft); range 740 km (460 miles).

# Arado Ar 231

For some time before the Second World War consideration had been given to the design of a small aircraft which could operate from a U-boat. It was realized that such an aircraft could provide valuable reconnaissance reports of the position both of enemy convoys and warships. This speculation was to culminate in 1940 in the issuing of a specification to the Arado Flugzeugwerke GmbH for the construction of such a machine.

The Ar 231, as the aircraft was designated, was a small strut-braced parasol-wing monoplane designed to be stowed inside a 2 m (6·56 ft) diameter container. A canted centre section enabled the wings to be folded back on top of each other and the floats could be raised on either side of the fuselage. It was planned that during operations the Ar 231 would be lowered over the side of the submarine by means of a folding crane, the process of both launching and of retrieving the machine taking some six minutes.

The Arado Ar 231 V1 collapsible floatplane which could be stowed inside a 2-metre diameter container.

Six prototypes were completed during 1941, designated Ar 231 V1 to V6, all being powered by the 160 hp Hirth HM 501 six-cylinder inverted inline air-cooled engine. Trials showed that the machine was extremely difficult to handle both on the water and in the air. It was also feared that the parent U-boat would have to stay on the surface for some 10 minutes in order to recover the Ar 231, rendering the vessel extremely vulnerable to attack. Early in 1942 the whole Ar 231 programme was abandoned in favour of the more sophisticated Focke Achgelis Fa 330 which is described on page 606.

Ar 231 V1: Span 10·18 m (33 ft 4½ in); length 7·81 m (25 ft 7½ in); height 3·12 m (10 ft 2¾ in); wing area 15·2 sq m (163·61 sq ft).

Empty weight 833 kg (1,837 lb); loaded weight 1,050 kg (2,315 lb).

Maximum speed at sea level 170 km/h (106 mph); cruising speed at sea level 130 km/h (81 mph); service ceiling 3,000 m (9,843 ft); normal range 500 km (310 miles); endurance 4 hr.

The Arado Ar 232 V1 made its first flight in the summer of 1941.

# Arado Ar 232

From the time the Nazis came to power much emphasis had been placed on the mobility of the armed forces. It was realized that the most effective way of achieving this goal was to create a large and efficient air transport force. Thus, when Germany started the war in September 1939, it possessed the largest and most experienced air transport force in the world.

Until the capitulation in 1945, the backbone of this force was the elderly Ju 52/3m—'Tante Ju' as it was affectionately known throughout the Luftwaffe. Several replacements for the Junkers product had been ordered, including the Ju 252 and 352, the Messerschmitt Me 323 and Arado Ar 232, but none of these was produced in any numbers and the Ju 52/3m remained as the backbone of the Transportgeschwader until the end.

Of the four types designed to replace the Ju 52, perhaps the most radical was the Arado Ar 232, an ugly box-like design with several novel features. Early in 1940, the Arado design team at Warnemünde began detailed design work on the new transport, which was allocated the designation Ar 232. The machine featured a pod and boom type fuselage, angular wing

Another view of the Ar 232 V1, clearly showing the multi-wheel undercarriage employed during loading.

36

surfaces and twin tail fins. It was fitted with a specially-designed hydraulically-operated door in the rear of the fuselage pod which enabled large cargoes to be loaded. A maximum load of 4,500 kg (9,920 lb) could be carried, including such items as two Kübelwagen (four-seat scout cars) with their crews.

Perhaps the Ar 232's most unusual feature however was its multi-wheel static undercarriage on to which the aircraft was lowered during loading and unloading. The system originally comprised eleven separate idler wheels with low-pressure tyres on independently-sprung legs mounted in a row beneath the fuselage. The aircraft was provided with a conventional retractable nosewheel undercarriage which could be lowered by two hydraulic rams to clear the small wheels during take-off, and raised to enable the aircraft to rest on the idler wheels during loading.

The Ar 232 V1, which appeared early in 1941, and the generally-similar V2, were each powered by two 1,600 hp BMW 801MA radials as the forerunners of the proposed A-series. No less than 10 different subtypes of the basic Ar 232A were projected, although they differed only in internal equipment. Originally, two BMW 801 radials had been proposed as the powerplant for all Ar 232s, but following the largescale introduction of the similarly-powered Focke-Wulf Fw 190 fighter into service, these engines became scarce, and Arados were forced to consider a substitute.

Both twin-engined Ar 232 prototypes served with the Luftwaffe.

Eventually it was decided to replace the two BMW 801s with four 1,200 hp BMW-Bramo 323R-2 radials, but this decision came too late to influence the first two prototypes, the Ar 232 V3 being the first to have the BMW 323 engines. The third prototype, which received the alternative designation Ar 232B-01, had a 1·7 m (5 ft 7 in) increase in the span of the wing centre section to accommodate the extra pair of engines.

The Ar 232 V3, with ten instead of eleven idler wheels, was otherwise similar to the first two prototypes. Armament comprised a 13 mm MG 131 machine-gun in the nose, a similar weapon in the rear of the fuselage pod above the loading door and a 20 mm MG 151/20 cannon in a power-operated dorsal turret behind the cockpit transparency. These weapons could be supplemented by up to eight 7·9 mm MG 34 infantry machine-guns firing through the side windows.

37

The third prototype was the first of a batch of twenty Ar 232B-0s which received the alternative designations Ar 232 V3 to V22. Several of these aircraft were used for experimental purposes. One was fitted with a boundary layer control system, air being sucked from the leading edge of the wing and blown over the trailing edge. The pump for this system ran on hydrogen peroxide but was never tested because all such fuel was diverted to the Messerschmitt Me 163 programme. The Ar 232 V8 was fitted with four Gnome/Rhône 14M radial engines with fuel tankage increased by 2,295 litres (505 Imp gal)—almost double that of the standard Ar 232-0. The Ar 232 V11 (B-09) was fitted with a non-retractable undercarriage and with skis for operation in northern latitudes, and it eventually crashed in Norway.

Late in 1943, the Ar 232 V1 and V2, plus a batch of four Ar 232B-0s, were delivered to a Staffel commanded by Maj Pelz of the Ergänzungstransportgeschwader under Obstlt Fabiunke based on the Eastern Front. In March 1944, a second unit was equipped with the Ar 232, when a small number of aircraft were delivered to I./TG 5 based at Odessa under Maj Günther Mauss. I./TG 5, which had been formed in May 1943 from the Me 323 Gruppe, was equipped in the main with the huge Messerschmitt Gigant (Giant) and a few captured SIAI Marchetti S.M.82 transports.

In Luftwaffe service, the Ar 232s were appropriately nicknamed Tausendfüssler (Millipedes), but only a small proportion of the 22 aircraft constructed saw operational service. One was retained by Arado for transporting urgently-needed supplies in connection with the Ar 234 pro-

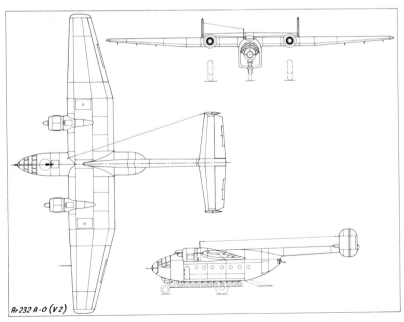

Ar-232 A-0 (V2)

One of a small batch of Ar 232B-0 transports produced by Arado.

gramme and was eventually flown to Britain after the war. In May 1943, the Ar 232 V8 (B-06) was used to carry meteorological equipment to Spitzbergen and subsequently saw operational service with Wekusta 5 at Banak in Norway.

Late in March 1944, an Ar 232B-0 was delivered to 1./KG 200, and the machine was used in very small numbers by both 1. and 3. Staffel of the unit. Towards the end of 1944, the Ar 232 equipped Ergänzungsstaffel was disbanded and its aircraft transferred to Transport-Staffel 5 based at Mühldorf under Hptm Wasserkampf. I./KG 200 and Transport-Staffel 5 often operated in close co-operation and during one notable mission on 5 September, 1944, an Ar 232B-0 carrying saboteurs for Operation Zeppelin (an attempt to destroy strategically important targets around Moscow) hit a tree and caught fire near the Soviet capital.

In March 1945, Transport-Staffel 5 was redesignated 14./TG 4 and possessed three Focke-Wulf Fw 200Cs, three Junkers Ju 90s, three Piaggio P.108Ts, four Ar 232B-0s and the Ar 232 V2; later in March, the unit was disbanded and its aircraft transferred to I./KG 200, all but one Ar 232 being destroyed on 8 May, 1945. The remaining aircraft was flown to the United Kingdom by Feldwebel Funk, and exhibited at the display of captured German aircraft held at Farnborough in October and November 1945.

Although only twenty-two Ar 232s were completed, it had been planned to switch production to the Ar 432. This was basically an Ar 232B-0 in which wood and steel were used in place of the strategically-important aluminium and duralumin alloys. Although several sub-assemblies were completed, the Ar 432 was abandoned before it could make its first flight.

*Wartime operational units:* I. and II./TG 5 and Transport-Staffel 5, 1./KG 200.

Ar 232B-0: Span 33·5 m (109 ft 10¾ in); length 23·5 m (77 ft 2 in); height 5·7 m (18 ft 8 in); wing area 143 sq m (1,535 sq ft).

Empty weight 10,280 kg (28,224 lb); normal loaded weight 21,160 kg (46,600 lb).

Maximum speed at 4,600 m (15,090 ft) 338 km/h (211 mph); maximum cruising speed at 2,000 m (6,560 ft) 288 km/h (180 mph); service ceiling 8,000 m (26,247 ft); normal range 1,050 km (658 miles).

The Arado Ar 234 V10 (c/n 130010) just after take-off.

# Arado Ar 234 Blitz (Lightning)

In addition to being the second jet-propelled aircraft to enter service with the Luftwaffe, the Arado Ar 234 was the world's first jet bomber. It was conceived late in 1940 in answer to a specification issued by the RLM for a high-speed reconnaissance aircraft to be powered by two of the new turbojets then under development at BMW and Junkers.

Early in 1941, the Arado design team, headed by Dipl Ing W. Blume and Ing Hans Rebeski, submitted the Ar E.370 project, later designated 8-234, a shapely shoulder-wing monoplane with underslung turbojets. The narrow fuselage of the design precluded the stowage of the undercarriage in the conventional position; therefore, two very novel layouts were proposed. One had nine very small wheels beneath the fuselage, with stabilizing skids below each turbojet. The other, and that finally chosen, proposed a special trolley which was to be jettisoned after take-off, the aircraft landing by means of three retractable skids.

Two prototypes, the Ar 234 V1 and V2, were completed during the winter of 1941–42, but it was not until February 1943 that the first pair of Junkers 004B-0 turbojets was delivered to Arado's Warnemünde plant. The first prototype began taxi-ing trials in March, but only in May was it transferred to Rheine airfield and fitted with two flight-cleared Junkers 004B-0 turbojets. The aircraft made its maiden flight on 15 June, 1943, piloted by Flugkapitän Selle. All went well with the aircraft, but the five braking parachutes failed to open and the trolley was destroyed. A similar fate was suffered by a second trolley, and finally it was decided to jettison the trolley on take-off rather than at 60 m (200 ft).

On 25 August, 1943, the Ar 234 V3 made its first flight. Intended to act as prototype for the Ar 234A, it had a pressurized cabin, an ejector seat and RATOG*, but was destroyed during an early flight. On 15 September,

* Rocket Assisted Take Off Gear.

40

the generally-similar V4 appeared, followed, on 20 December, by the V5 which was powered by two Junkers 004B-0 engines of 850 kg (1,848 lb) thrust.

The Ar 234 V6, which flew on 8 April, 1944, was powered by four 800 kg (1,760 lb) thrust BMW 003A-1 turbojets in four separate nacelles. The Ar 234 V8 which preceded the V6 and flew for the first time on 1 February, 1944, was also powered by four BMW 003A-1s, but in this case they were in paired nacelles.

The Ar 234 V7 was the last A-series prototype, being powered by two 900 kg (1,980 lb) thrust Junkers 004B-1 turbojets. During an early flight, the port engine caught fire and the control rods in that wing burnt through. In attempting to bring the aircraft in to land, Arado's chief test pilot, Flugkapitän Selle, was killed.

Although the launching trolley and landing skid arrangement had functioned well, it was realized that the aircraft's immobility on landing would be a severe disadvantage when it came to operational employment. After some consultation it was decided to fit the Ar 234 with a conventional wheeled undercarriage. The fuselage was marginally widened to accommodate two mainwheels midway along its length, a retractable nosewheel being mounted below the pilot's position. The narrow track of the installation caused some instability during taxi-ing but otherwise proved quite satisfactory.

With the retractable undercarriage installed, the aircraft was redesignated Ar 234B, and the first prototype of this version, the Ar 234 V9, flew

Close-up of the skid and three-wheeled take-off trolley employed by the early Ar 234 prototypes.

The Ar 234 V9 with two SC 250 bombs beneath the engine nacelles and RI 202b rocket assisted take-off pods under the wings.

The Ar 234B-1 jet-propelled reconnaissance aircraft, clearly showing the pilot entry hatch.

A mechanic at work on an Ar 234B.

on 10 March, 1944. The V10 followed on 2 April, differing in having neither pressurization nor ejector seat. It was fitted with two ETC 503 bomb racks beneath the turbojets and was used to test the BZA bomb-aiming computer.

The Ar 234 V11 was similar to the V9, making its first flight on 5 May, 1944, but the V15 and V17 were each fitted with two BMW 003A-1 turbojets for engine development purposes. Much trouble had been experienced with the thrust control of the BMW 003 turbojet, so it was hoped that flight trials using the two Ar 234s would considerably assist in the engine's development. The problem of thrust regulation was solved by the use of the Junkers 004 system, but the BMW engine always proved difficult to restart after suffering a flame-out during flight. The Ar 234 V12 and V14 were essentially similar to the V10, and the V13 was fitted with four BMW 003A-1 turbojets in a similar installation to the V8.

On 8 June, 1944, the first of 20 pre-production Ar 234B-0s left the assembly lines at Alt-Lönnewitz, on what is now the Czechoslovak-German border. Thirteen Ar 234B-0s, unpressurized and without ejector seats, were delivered to Rechlin for intensive development trials. They were followed by the Ar 234B-1 reconnaissance aircraft which could carry two Rb 75/30 cameras, two Rb 50/30 cameras or a combination of one of these and an Rb 20/30.

The Ar 234B-2 was a bomber which could carry a maximum bomb load of 2,000 kg (4,410 lb). Several sub-variants were produced including the B-2/b reconnaissance aircraft, the B-2/1 pathfinder and the B-2/r equipped with auxiliary fuel tanks. All aircraft were fitted with braking parachutes but these were rarely used operationally.

The bomber was equipped with a Patin PDS three-axes autopilot with LKS 7D-15 overriding control, enabling the pilot to swing the control column clear so that he could use the Lotfe 7K tachometric bomb sight. This manoeuvre called for some agility and not inconsiderable courage from the pilot, especially if enemy fighters were in the area. For shallow dive-bombing a BZA bombing computer was used in conjunction with an RF2C periscopic sight; steep dives were strictly forbidden because of jet surge and sensitivity of the lateral trim. The final proposed version of the B-series was the Ar 234B-3 bomber, but this was abandoned in favour of the Ar 234C.

Early in July 1944, the Ar 234 V5 and V7 were delivered to 1./Versuchsverband.Ob.d.L. based at Juvincourt near Rheims. The first operations were undertaken on 20 July, but due to constant Allied bombing of the airfield they proved extremely hazardous. A special grass landing strip was prepared because it was found that the skids were ripped off if any attempt was made to land on the torn-up concrete runway. The take-off trolley functioned well; only on one occasion did it fail to release. Both aircraft were fitted with Walter rocket-assisted take-off units. These RATO units proved very satisfactory apart from some tendency for the non-operation of their landing parachutes.

Considering the radical form of powerplant, operations proved very successful, the V5 and V7 respectively logging 22 and 24 flying hours. On 27 August, 1944, the unit transferred to Chièvres, three days later to Volkel and finally, on 5 September, to Rheine. Here 1./Versuchsverband Ob.d.L was joined by the third Staffel, the units taking on charge two Ar 234B-0s. Up to 1 November, 24 sorties were flown by the Ar 234s, engine failures being experienced during three of them. The mass-produced engines proved particularly vulnerable to cracks in the impeller, turbine wheels and vane rings, and eventually they were given a general overhaul before being installed in the aircraft. A subsequent overhaul was carried out after 10 hr, normal engine life being only 25 hr.

Photographic sorties were usually flown at a height of 9,000 m (29,530 ft), the aircraft obtaining a longitudinal overlap of 60 per cent, with an interval between exposures of 10 to 12 seconds. Each camera had a magazine containing 120 m (395 ft) of film. During operations, many of which were over the United Kingdom, the aircraft easily evaded Allied interception attempts, although the pilots were warned never to attempt to out-turn their adversaries as this would quickly reduce their speed.

In September 1944, a special test unit, designated Sonderkommando Götz, was formed at Rheine from a part of 1./Versuchsverband Ob.d.L. and equipped with four Ar 234B-1s. During the same period 1./Versuchsverb.Ob.d.L. test-flew the Ar 234 V6 and V8 four-engined aircraft, and in November two further experimental reconnaissance units were formed, designated Sonderkommando Hecht and Sperling.

By the end of January 1945, all three Sonderkommando had been

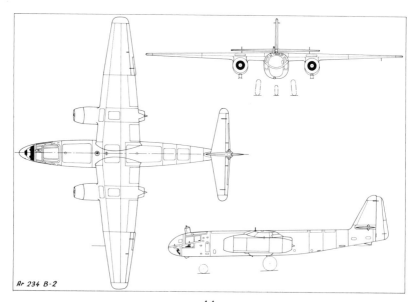

Ar 234 B-2

The first Ar 234 to fall into Allied hands was this B-2 coded F1-MT (c/n 140173) of 9./KG 76 which belly landed near Segelsdorf.

disbanded, but were replaced by 1.(F)/100 and 1.(F)/123 based at Rheine and 1.(F)/33 in Denmark. The Staffeln continued aerial reconnaissance sorties over the British Isles, the last recorded being that by an aircraft of 1.(F)/33 then based at Sola Airport, Stavanger, in Norway. 1.(F)/33 and 1.(F)/100 remained operational until the end of the war, the former at Stavanger, the latter at Saalbach.

The last Ar 234 reconnaissance unit to be formed was Sonderkommando Sommer based at Udine near Trieste. The unit was established with three Ar 234B-1s as a result of complaints received from German forces in northern Italy of inadequate surveillance of Allied troop movements. The unit radically altered the situation, making uninterrupted reconnaissance sorties over the Ancona and Leghorn sectors at altitudes of up to 12,000 m (39,372 ft).

In October 1944, IV.(Erg)/KG 76 was transferred to Alt-Lönnewitz with the task of introducing the Ar 234 bomber into service. Eventually, on 27 January, 1945, IV.(Erg)/KG 76 was redesignated III./EKG 1, the Gruppe employing two Messerschmitt Me 262B-1a two-seaters for conversion training. The first part of KG 76 to become operational with the Ar 234B-2 was the Stabsstaffel commanded by Oberstlt Robert Kowalewski, followed by 6.Staffel. 6./KG 76 undertook its first operations during the Ardennes offensive and I. and III. Gruppe joined the training programme during January 1945. Under Maj Hans-Georg Bätcher, III./KG 76 became operational in February, but sorties were severely limited owing to lack of fuel.

During the second week of February, the Stabsstaffel, 6.Staffel and III./KG 76 based at Achmer and Rheine, were heavily engaged in an attempt to relieve the Allied pressure on Kleve. On 24 February, 1945, following an attack by jet bombers from KG 51 and KG 76, an aircraft from III./KG 76 was brought down by USAAF P-47 Thunderbolts near Segelsdorf, providing the Allies with their first Ar 234.

From early March, operations by KG 76 steadily increased. Perhaps the most vital mission was the attempted destruction of the American-held

Ludendorff bridge over the Rhine at Remagen. Between 7 and 17 March, 1945, when the bridge finally collapsed, KG 76 made continuous and often almost suicidal attacks with SC 1000 bombs, supported by Me 262A-2 jet bombers from I. and II./KG 51.

By the end of March 1945, Ar 234 bomber sorties had virtually ceased. Stab/KG 76 was based at Karstädt with two aircraft, I./KG 76 at Leck, 6./KG 76 at Scheppern with five aircraft, and III./KG 76 at Marx/Oldenburg also with five aircraft. On 10 April, KG 76 was transferred to the control of Luftflotte Reich, and two days later, III./KG 76 received five new aircraft. Conditions were now chaotic, and few operations were undertaken before the end of the war in Europe.

Perhaps the least-known facet of Ar 234 operations was the sorties undertaken by the experimental night fighter unit, Kommando Bonow. The unit was formed late in March 1945 and equipped with two converted Ar 234s. Commanded by Maj Kurt Bonow, the unit operated under Luftflotte Reich until the end of the war.

Following trials with the four-engined Ar 234 V6, V8, and V13, it was decided to build a production variant to be designated Ar 234C. The first real prototype was the Ar 234 V19 which flew on 30 September, 1944. It was basically an Ar 234B-1 powered by four BMW 003A-1 turbojets and with such refinements as a larger nosewheel and experimental air-brakes. The Ar 234 V20 was similar, but was fitted with full cabin pressurization. The proposed initial production models, the Ar 234C-1 and C-2, were respectively similar to the B-1 and B-2, but embodied the refinements introduced on the V20. In addition, the C-1 could carry a pair of rearward-firing MG 151/20 cannon.

A partially completed Ar 234C-3 (c/n 250001). (*J. Zazvonil*)

Only a small number of Ar 234C-0 and C-1 aircraft was produced before the design was abandoned in favour of the C-3 multi-purpose version. Five prototypes were built, designated Ar 234 V21 to V25, all having a redesigned cabin, the roof of which was heightened to improve visibility. In addition to the rearward-firing MG 151/20 cannon, two similar weapons were to be installed beneath the nose. The aircraft could carry a variety of bomb loads on three ETC 504 racks.

The Ar 234C-3/N was a two-seat night fighter project, with provision for two forward-firing MG 151/20 and two MK 108 cannon. It was designed to use FuG 218 Neptun V radar and the FuG 350Zc Naxos homing device. The Ar 234C-4 was a specialized reconnaissance aircraft with provision for two cameras and four MG 151/20 cannon. The Ar 234 V28 was the prototype for the proposed C-5 two-seat multi-purpose aircraft in which the pilot and navigator/bomb-aimer sat side by side. The Ar 234 V29 was the forerunner of the proposed C-6 two-seat reconnaissance aircraft.

The Ar 234C-7 was a night fighter similar to the C-3/N, but with the crew of two seated side by side. It was designed to have FuG 245 Bremen O centimetric radar with a scanner installed in the nose. The early aircraft were to be powered by four BMW 003A-1 turbojets, although two 1,000 kg (2,205 lb) thrust Jumo 004C or two 1,300 kg (2,865 lb) thrust Heinkel-Hirth HeS 011A engines were projected. The final version of the C-series was the Ar 234C-8 single-seat bomber to be powered by two 1,050 kg (2,315 lb) thrust Jumo 004D turbojets.

Although of extremely poor quality, this photo shows the Ar 234 jet bomber towing an auxiliary winged fuel tank in the so-called Deichselschlepp (air trailer) arrangement.

The Ar 234 V31 to V40 which were under construction at the end of the war were prototypes for the proposed Ar 234D-1 reconnaissance aircraft and D-2 bomber. These variants were to be powered by two 1,300 kg (2,865 lb) thrust Heinkel-Hirth HeS 011A turbojets which were then under development. The Ar 234E destroyer was similar to the Ar 234D, and the Ar 234F was a scaled-up variant to be powered by four HeS 011 or two Junkers 012 turbojets.

Development of the Ar 234C-7 night fighter led to the specialized P-series. The Ar 234P-1 was to have been powered by four BMW 003A-1 turbojets and carry a crew of two in a pressurized cabin. FuG 245 radar was installed, with a scanner mounted in the nose, and the machine was provided with an armament of two MG 151/20 and two MK 108 cannon. The P-2 was similar, but with a heavily-armoured and redesigned cockpit constructed of 13 mm plate. The P-3 and P-4 were both similar to the P-2, but were powered respectively by two HeS 011A and two Junkers 004D engines. The Ar 234P-5 was a three-seat night fighter powered by two HeS 011 turbojets, with provision for one MG 151/20 and four MK 108 cannon.

The final proposed variant was the Ar 234R reconnaissance aircraft which was to be powered by a single 2,000 kg (4,410 lb) thrust Walter rocket engine. It would have been towed up to about 8,000 m (26,248 ft) by a Heinkel He 177A and then climbed to operational altitude under its own power. Other projected powerplants for the Ar 234 included the DB 007 bypass jet and the HeS 021 propeller-turbine.

Work did not centre on powerplants, however. In August 1944, Arado proposed four experimental wing designs for the Ar 234, designated Versuchsflügel I to IV. The first two, which were to be tested by the Ar 234 V16 and V18, were respectively wooden and metal wings of crescent planform. The Versuchsflügel III, which was to be tested by the Ar 234 V26, was an all-metal wing with laminar profile, and the Versuchsflügel IV, which was to be tested by the Ar 234 V30, was a swept wing with laminar profile. The Ar 234 V16 was to have been powered by two BMW 003R composite rocket and turbojet engines, but like the V18, V26 and V30, was destroyed to prevent it falling into Allied hands.

*Wartime operational units:* 1.(F)/33, 1.(F)/100 and 1.(F)/123, I., II. and III./KG 76, 1. and 3./Versuchsverband Ob.d.L., Kommando Bonow, Götz, Hecht and Sperling, III./ EKG 1.

Ar 234B-2: Span 14·44 m (46 ft 3$\frac{1}{2}$ in); length 12·64 m (41 ft 5$\frac{1}{2}$ in); height 4·29 m (14 ft 1$\frac{1}{2}$ in); wing area 27·3 sq m (284·167 sq ft).

Empty weight 5,200 kg (11,464 lb); normal loaded weight 8,400 kg (18,541 lb); maximum loaded weight 9,800 kg (21,715 lb).

Maximum speed at 6,000 m (19,685 ft) 742 km/h (461 mph), at 10,000 m (32,810 ft) 700 km/h (435 mph); climb to 6,000 m (19,685 ft) 12·8 min; service ceiling 10,000 m (32,810 ft); maximum range 1,630 km (1,013 miles).

Ar 234C-3: Dimensions as Ar 234B-2. Empty weight 6,500 kg (14,400 lb); loaded weight 11,000 kg (24,250 lb).

Maximum speed at sea level 800 km/h (496 mph), at 6,000 m (19,685 ft) 852 km/h (530 mph); climb to 10,000 m (32,810 ft) 16·7 min; service ceiling 11,000 m (36,091 ft); maximum range 1,215 km (765 miles).

An Ar 234B is preserved at the Smithsonian Institution, Washington, DC.

The Arado Ar 240 V3 bore little relation to the first aircraft.

# Arado Ar 240

It is an indisputable fact that the Luftwaffe never produced a really effective heavy bomber force, emphasis being placed on the fast medium bomber which could escape interception by virtue of its speed alone. Thus, it is not surprising that the German aviation industry failed to develop power-operated gun turrets to anything like the perfection achieved by the Western Allies. However, one very interesting foray was made into the field as early as 1938 when Arado, in co-operation with DVL and the Rheinmetall-Borsig concern, produced the FA-13 system of remotely-controlled armament.

Following a series of development trials with the barbettes, which were flight tested on the Messerschmitt Bf 110C-2/U1, the RLM issued a specification calling for a fast twin-engined multi-purpose aircraft to employ two of these advanced weapons. Two projects were submitted to the RLM; the little-known Ago Ao 225 and the Arado E 240, while Messerschmitt also proposed the installation of the FA-13 system in their Me 210 design. The Ago project was quickly abandoned mainly because of its radical remote drive concept, but construction of the Arado design, then redesignated Ar 240, was fully endorsed.

Development of the Arado design was entrusted to Ing Hans Rebeski, and the first prototype, the Ar 240 V1, made its initial flight on 10 May, 1940. It was a mid-wing monoplane powered by two 1,075 hp Daimler-

49

Benz DB 601A engines with annular radiators, and carried a crew of two seated in a pressurized cabin. Trouble was being experienced with the development of the FA-13 barbettes and consequently this feature was omitted from both the Ar 240 V1 and V2.

The second prototype, which appeared in July 1940, carried a fixed forward-firing armament of two 20 mm MG 151/20 cannon in the nose and two 7·9 mm MG 17 machine-guns in the wing roots. The development difficulties being experienced with the FA-13 barbettes were nothing to those suffered by the first two prototypes themselves. Both proved totally unstable, and the third aircraft, the Ar 240 V3, had to be completely redesigned.

Close-up of the double-slotted flaps fitted to the Ar 240 V1. The photograph shows the tail-mounted air-brake carried by the aircraft.

The third prototype was given a 1·25 m (4 ft 1½ in) increase in fuselage length, the tail-mounted dive-brake was replaced by a new short cone fitted with auxiliary fins, and the pressurized cabin was moved to the extreme nose of the aircraft. The first flight of the Ar 240 V3 was made during the spring of 1941 but, although improved, the handling characteristics of the machine still left much to be desired. The Ar 240 V3 was also the first machine to be fitted with the FA-13 barbettes, each of which were mounted either side of the fuselage aft of the cockpit and carried a 7·9 mm MG 81 machine-gun.

During flight trials, further attempts were made to improve the third prototype's characteristics and, amongst other modifications, new ailerons were fitted. During the late summer of 1941 the aircraft was delivered to 3./Aufklärungsgruppe Ob.d.L., based in northern France, for operational

Another view of the Ar 240 V3 which first flew during the spring of 1941.

trials. The FA-13 system was temporarily removed and the machine fitted with two Rb 50/30 cameras. Several flights were made over Britain by Oberst Knemeyer (who succeeded Oberst Rowehl as commander of the Aufkl.Gr.Ob.d.L.), the high performance of the Ar 240 enabling it to escape interception.

The Arado 240 V4, which was completed during the middle of 1941, had a tail-mounted dive-brake, and was powered by two 1,750 hp Daimler-Benz DB 603A engines. The Ar 240A-01 and A-02 (V5 and V6), the first two pre-production aircraft, made their appearance in October 1942. Intended for the reconnaissance rôle, both carried two 7·9 mm MG 17 machine-guns in the wing roots and two 7·9 mm MG 81 guns in each of two FA-13 barbettes.

The Ar 240A-03 was, like its predecessors, fitted initially with 1,175 hp DB 601E engines, but these were later replaced by two 1,880 hp BMW 801TJ radials. The Ar 240A-04 and A-05 (A-0/U1 and A-0/U2) were flown late in 1942, both powered by 1,750 hp Daimler-Benz DB 603A engines, but lacked armament. Tooling up began at Ago's Oschersleben plant for 40 production aircraft, but these were destined never to appear as

Three Ar 240A-0s on a test airfield with the V5 in the centre. Several of these aircraft subsequently saw service with the Luftwaffe.

the whole Ar 240 programme was cancelled by Erhard Milch in December 1942.

The Ar 240A-01 and A-02 were delivered to 13.(Zerstörer)/JG 5 dispersed around Petsamo, then in northern Finland. The aircraft were used to make reconnaissance flights over the all-important Murmansk railway. Shortly afterwards the Ar 240A-03 and A-05 were delivered to operational units on the Eastern Front, one to 3.(F)/10 in the north and one to 3.(F)/100 in central Russia.

The Ar 240A-02 in service with 13.(Z)/JG 5 in Finland during the winter of 1942/43.

In July 1943, the Ar 240A-02 was transferred to 2.(F)/122 at Frosinone, south of Rome, but it was written off when it crashed on landing while returning from its first operational mission. Shortly afterwards the Ar 240A-04 was transferred to the same unit, then based at Perugia, some miles north-east of Rome. The aircraft suffered constant engine troubles and was eventually flown back to Germany; there it was overhauled and sent, together with the V7 and V8, to join the other pre-production aircraft on the Eastern Front.

The Ar 240 V7 and V8, alternatively designated Ar 240B-01 and B-02, were forerunners of the proposed Ar 240B series. They were similar to the A-0 but were powered by two 1,475 hp Daimler-Benz DB 605A engines, and flew respectively in October and December 1942. The Ar 240 V7 was fitted with two fixed MG 17 machine-guns and four MG 81 weapons, two in each of two FA-13 barbettes. The V8 was similar, both machines being provided with MW-50 water-methanol injection, but carried a rearward-firing 20 mm MG 151/20 cannon.

The Ar 240 V9 (C-01) had a new wing of increased span and improved profile and was powered by two 1,900 hp Daimler-Benz DB 603G engines. The Ar 240 V10 (C-02) was intended for the night fighter rôle, an additional pair of MG 151/20s being installed below the fuselage. The Ar 240 V11 (C-03) was similar to the V9 and the V12 (C-04) was a destroyer sub-type.

Proposed production variants included the Ar 240C-1 destroyer, the C-2 night fighter, the C-3 light bomber and the C-4 fast reconnaissance aircraft. The proposed Ar 240D series were similar, but were to have been powered by 2,000 hp Daimler-Benz DB 614 engines. The projected Ar 240E bomber never passed beyond the drawing board stage, but four prototypes of Ar 440 multi-purpose aircraft powered by two 1,900 hp DB 603G or two 2,000 hp DB 627 engines were completed in 1942.

Between March and May 1944, a final attempt was made to utilize the high performance of the Ar 240 in the reconnaissance rôle over the British Isles. One aircraft was delivered to the Sonderaufklärungsstaffel of the Oberbefehlshaber der Luftwaffe based in France, while another was operated by 1./Versuchsverband Ob.d.L. Again the aircraft suffered interminable troubles from its poor flight characteristics, and, following the invasion of France, the type disappeared from front-line service.

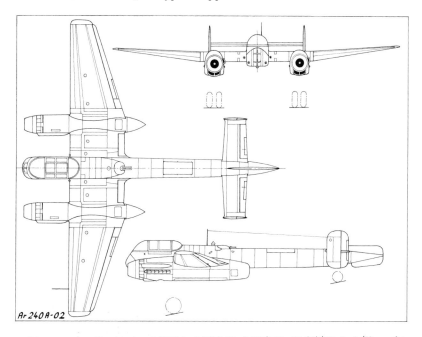

*Wartime operational units:* 3.(F)/10, 3.(F)/100, 3.(F)/122, 13.(Z)/JG 5, 1./Versuchsverband Ob.d.L., 3./Aufkl.Gr.Ob.d.L. and Sonder-Aufkl.Staffel/Ob.d.L.

Ar 240A-0: Span 13·33 m (43 ft 9 in); length 12·8 m (42 ft 0⅓ in); height 3·95 m (12 ft 11½ in); wing area 31·3 sq m (336·91 sq ft).
Empty weight 6,200 kg (13,669 lb); loaded weight 9,450 kg (20,834 lb).
Maximum speed at 6,000 m (19,685 ft) 618 km/h (384 mph); cruising speed at 6,000 m (19,685 ft) 555 km/h (345 mph); climb to 6,000 m (19,685 ft) 11 min; service ceiling 10,500 m (34,450 ft); maximum range 2,000 km (1,242 miles).

Ar 240B-0: Dimensions as Ar 240A-0. Empty weight 6,950 kg (15,323 lb); loaded weight 8,900 kg (19,624 lb).
Maximum speed at 6,000 m (19,685 ft) 630 km/h (392 mph); cruising speed at 6,000 m (19,685 ft) 580 km/h (360 mph); climb to 6,000 m (19,685 ft) 10·6 min; service ceiling 10,500 m (34,450 ft); maximum range 1,800 km (1,186 miles).

53

Designed as a two-seat trainer, the Arado Ar 396 was developed at the SIPA works near Paris but was too late for German service. Post-war production was for the French military services. (*J. Zazvonil*)

# Arado Ar 396

While superficially similar to the Ar 96B, the Ar 396 was a new design for a two-seat low-wing training monoplane. The aircraft was planned, late in 1944, to use a minimum of metal in its construction and to be powered by the new 580 hp Argus As 411 MA twelve-cylinder inverted-vee air-cooled engine driving a two-blade airscrew with automatic pitch control. Hand-operated flaps, and simple semi-retractable undercarriage were provided. The basic version had two seats in tandem with dual controls. Equipment changes were responsible for the designations Ar 396A-1 and Ar 396A-2. The A-1, to be used as a single-seater, was for fighter training and was equipped with a single 7·9 mm MG 17 machine-gun, UMG camera, Revi 16D gunsight and racks for two 50 kg (110 lb) bombs, while the A-2 was for blind-flying training and had no armament.

Designs and orders for the Ar 396 were given to the SIPA works near Paris where development was conducted on three prototypes, the first of which flew on 29 December, 1944, after the Allied liberation of France. The French then redesignated the type S.10 and after the war built over 200 examples, mostly of a modified design, for their military services. Construction of the Ar 396 was also undertaken by the Letov factory in Czechoslovakia but none of these were ready in time for Luftwaffe service.

Ar 396A-2: Span 11 m (36 ft 1⅛ in); length 9·29 m (30 ft 5¾ in); height 2·45 m (8 ft 0½ in); wing area 18·3 sq m (196·9 sq ft).

Empty weight 1,643 kg (3,623 lb); loaded weight 2,060 kg (4,542 lb).

Maximum speed at 2,400 m (7,872 ft) 354 km/h (220 mph); cruising speed at sea level 274 km/h (170 mph); landing speed 114 km/h (71 mph); climb to 4,000 m (13,120 ft) 10·3 min; service ceiling 7,000 m (22,960 ft); range 600 km (372 miles); duration at cruising speed 2·17 hr.

# Bachem Ba 349 Natter (Viper)

By 1944, it had become apparent even to the most ill-informed in Germany that the destruction being wrought by the Allied bomber streams was a prime factor in their country's declining fortunes and every effort was therefore put into investigating and producing the weapons to intercept and destroy the bombers. Principal concentration was upon fighters and missiles, but advanced designs of fighters were not being produced in the required quantity, while the more efficacious missiles were still under development, the chief obstruction being in the perfecting of guidance systems. The RLM, at the suggestion of its technical department, therefore directed four firms to submit designs of a weapon intended to combine the capabilities of interceptor aircraft and missile; such a weapon had to be rapidly and economically produced and swift and accurate in use, the pilot obviating the need for remote guidance control. The projects submitted in response to this requirement were the Heinkel P.1077 Julia, Junkers EF 127 Walli, Messerschmitt P.1104, and Bachem BP 20 Natter (Viper), from which the latter was chosen for development and given the official designation of Ba 349 on 1 August, 1944.

The design team at Bachem-Werke GmbH for the Ba 349 was led by Dipl Ing Erich Bachem, formerly technical director at Fieseler-Werke, and H. Bethbeder, formerly of Dornier-Werke. The resulting design was a semi-expendable single-seat rocket-powered interceptor which was to be launched vertically to the vicinity of the bombers, then steered by the pilot

To help combat the Allied bomber threat to Germany, the Bachem Ba 349 was conceived in 1944 as a semi-expendable, vertically-launched, piloted missile. This captured Ba 349 was being prepared for its vertical launcher in mountainous country. On the foremost trolley is a booster rocket and, in front of this, the nose section of another Ba 349. (*USAF*)

who fired the rocket armament and baled out. The aerodynamic shape was as simple as possible to ease production and consisted of a fuselage with stepped cockpit, and rectangular planform stubby wings without dihedral or sweepback and with a symmetrical section and constant profile. Vertical tail surfaces extended above and below the rear fuselage, the upper fin carrying a tailplane of similar design to the wing. Rudders and elevators were provided, but there were no ailerons, their effect being catered for by differential operation of the elevators. In September 1944 this design was wind-tunnel tested at the DVL in model form up to 500 km/h (310 mph) and pronounced satisfactory, and construction began at Bachem's Waldsee factory.

Construction entailed the minimum of elaborate jigs and tools and was made possible by the use of bonded and screwed wood for the airframe, with heavy, simple fittings. In addition, weight and refinement of finish were sacrificed so that most of the work could be done in small workshops dispersed throughout Germany. Superficially, the design was crude, but every element had been carefully planned and embodied many ingenious features to enable an operational machine to be turned out in about 1,000 man-hours, allowing for small-batch production and inexperienced labour.

The sustainer rocket motor housed in the rear fuselage was a Walter 109-509A-2 of the type used for the Messerschmitt Me 163, but modified, because of the vertical launch, to operate in any position. The propellants were T-Stoff (hydrogen peroxide plus 20 per cent water) and C-Stoff (hydrazine hydrate, methyl alcohol and water) contained in tanks above and below the wing main spar where it passed through the fuselage. The motor gave a maximum thrust of 1,700 kg (3,750 lb) for 70 seconds but thrust regulation down to 150 kg (330 lb) was possible for increased duration. For launching, four Schmidding 109-533 solid diglycol fuelled rocket units were fitted, two on each side of the rear fuselage, each giving a thrust of 1,200 kg (2,640 lb) for 10 seconds before jettisoning.

By October 1944, the first of 15 machines was available for the test programme which began with an unpowered example ballasted to operational weight less boost rocket weight. With Zübert, a test pilot, at the controls, the machine was towed by a Heinkel He 111 to an altitude of 5,500 m (18,040 ft) and released. The flight was conducted at speeds between 200 and 700 km/h (125 and 435 mph), when stability was excellent and controls were light and well co-ordinated. The rate of roll was about 360 deg/min and, at 400 km/h (250 mph), a 360 deg turn could be made in 20 seconds. The pilot, in summing up, pronounced the flying qualities superior to any standard German single-seat fighter. The only modification resulting from this and further piloted glide tests was that the explosive bolts, which released the nose section prior to baling out, were replaced by a mechanical release because of some bolt failures.

Starting on 22 December, 1944, eleven unmanned vertical launchings

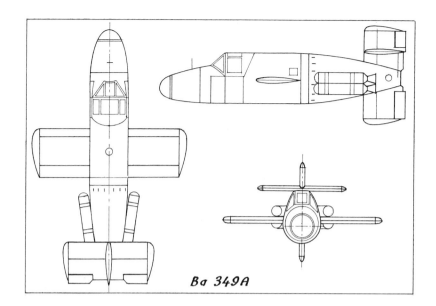

*Ba 349A*

were made using the booster rockets but without sustainer rocket. This stage of the programme was the most worrying since the speed of the Ba 349 was only about 60 km/h (37 mph) as it left the guidance of the launching rails and was therefore too low for aerodynamic control. Furthermore, there was considerable movement in the centre of gravity position once the booster rockets were dropped. With these problems in mind, some of the tests were made with 1 m (3·28 ft) square auxiliary stabilizing surfaces attached to the tailplane and fin tips, to be explosively jettisoned when the boosters fell away. In some of the tests, the boost rockets exploded and were generally erratic, with much variation in thrust and burning times but, when they operated satisfactorily, the launch was quite stable with or without the auxiliary surfaces. In most of the tests, wing tabs were fitted so that the machine rolled slowly, and the maximum height reached was 3,000 m (9,840 ft). One flight was very erratic due to the fitting of an under-developed autopilot device.

On 23 February, 1945, the first pilotless vertical launching was made with the Walter motor installed and fired at the same time as the booster rockets. For later tests, it was planned to use control vanes in the Walter motor exhaust instead of the auxiliary surfaces for control during launch. These vanes, designed by Bethbeder, were cooled by water which boiled away in 30 seconds after which the vanes melted.

The first piloted vertical launching took place before the end of February when, with Lothar Siebert at the controls, a Ba 349A thundered off the launching rails in a normal start but, at a height of about 150 m (492 ft), the cockpit cover and headrest combination flew off, probably injuring the pilot. The machine then turned onto its back, made a shallow

57

climb to 1,500 m (4,920 ft) and then dived inverted into the ground, killing Siebert. Further manned tests were planned, but it is uncertain if these were made.

The initial production orders for the Ba 349A were 50 for the Luftwaffe and 150 for the SS but only about 20 of these were completed. (By early 1945, the entire V-weapon offensive, together with many secret weapon programmes, was under the control of SS General Kammler.) The amount of dispersed manufacture begun is unknown but some manufacture was undertaken at the Wolf Hirth-Flugzeugbau in addition to the Bachem factory. No time was wasted, however, in setting up the first 10 available Ba 349As at Kirchheim (near the Wolf Hirth factory) ready for operations but, before any bombers could be intercepted, the machines had to be destroyed because of approaching United States troops.

A typical operational flight would have been as follows: As the bomber stream approached, the Natter would have been launched, producing sufficient g forces on the pilot to render him no more than a dummy at this stage. A standard Flak gun predictor sight was used to set the autopilot device which, at a height of 150 m (492 ft), commanded the controls for the interception course. Once the Natter was positioned slightly above the bombers, the pilot took over the controls and, in a shallow dive and with the Walter motor still burning, with the simplest of sights, he aligned his machine, ejected the nose fairing and fired the 24 Föhn 73 mm unguided rockets, each of which contained 0·4 kg (0·88 lb) of explosive. During the run-in, the pilot was protected by armoured steel and glass and, after diving clear of the bomber stream, speed was reduced to about 250 km/h (155 mph) and the pilot began the ejection drill. He uncoupled the control column and swung it forward to release the safety catch on the nose release attachments, having already undone his harness. Next, the pilot released the mechanical catches holding the nose section which was then immediately whisked away by the air flow, carrying with it the instrument panel, hood, armoured bulkhead and rudder pedals, leaving him completely exposed in front. A parachute then streamed from the rear fuselage causing deceleration and ejecting the pilot, who descended using his own parachute. The rear fuselage containing the Walter motor also descended by its parachute for recovery and re-use. For the entire sortie, a pilot could have been in his Natter for as little as two minutes!

In March 1945, tests in the Brunswick wind tunnel to just below Mach 1 indicated that improved performance could be obtained with more power and an increase in tail unit areas. Accordingly, a prototype of a version designated Ba 349B was built to have a 10 per cent increase in maximum speed and a greater rate of climb. The sustainer rocket motor for this version was the experimental Walter 109-509C which used T-Stoff and C-Stoff propellants to give a maximum thrust of 2,000 kg (4,410 lb) and could be throttled down to 200 kg (441 lb) with greater efficiency than the 109-509A-2 motor.

The plans for the Ba 349 were sold to the Japanese for whom it was of particular interest but they only managed to partially build a few before the end of hostilities. Only a small number of Ba 349s in completed condition was available for removal and examination by the Allies and, of these, only one is preserved today, at the Smithsonian Institution in Washington, and this bears the US evaluation number T2-1011.

Ba 349A: Span 3·6 m (11 ft 9¾ in); length 6·1 m (20 ft); wing area 2.75 sq m (29·6 sq ft).

Loaded weight including boost rockets 2,200 kg (4,850 lb); weight of four Schmidding 109-533 boost rockets 260 kg (572 lb); fuel weight 650 kg (1,430 lb).

Maximum speed near sea level 800 km/h (497 mph); initial rate of climb 185 m/sec (36,417 ft/min); service ceiling 14,000 m (45,920 ft); radius of action at 12,000 m (39,360 ft) 40 km (24·84 miles).

# Blohm und Voss Bv 138

The first aircraft to appear from the Blohm und Voss aircraft subsidiary, the Hamburger Flugzeugbau GmbH, was the Ha 135 two-seat biplane which was the responsibility of Reinhold Mewes. Dr Ing Richard Vogt soon replaced Mewes as chief engineer and the next designs were the Ha 136 single-seat monoplane and the Ha 137 dive-bomber, the latter competing unsuccessfully in 1936 against the Junkers Ju 87. (Use of the Ha designation ceased in 1937 when the parent company's title was used and aircraft designations then began with Bv.)

It was a logical step for the Hamburger Flugzeugbau to take up flying-boat work early in its career, considering the parent company's ship-building activities, and the works were ideally sited on the Elbe. After many flying-boat configurations had been studied, one, designated P.12, was selected for development as a long-range reconnaissance aircraft having a short hull and a high-mounted wing carrying floats and twin engines, the latter being faired back into twin tail booms. In the spring of 1935, a mock-up of the design was begun and this brought an order for three prototypes under the designation Ha 138. Each prototype was to use a different make of 1,000 hp category engine, for comparison, but difficulties in the development of the engines brought about a redesign of the Ha 138 to enable it to take three 650 hp Junkers Jumo 205C Diesel engines. The third engine was positioned above the centre of the wing and was thus mounted higher than the other two.

After a lengthy development and construction period, the Ha 138 V1 D-ARAK made its maiden flight as the first prototype on 15 July, 1937. The Ha 138 V2 D-AMOR, which differed mainly in the hull design, was completed in August, and by November testing was being undertaken at E-Stelle Travemünde, on the Baltic coast. This testing soon revealed numerous faults, the most serious being hydrodynamic and aerodynamic instability. To try to improve the latter, redesigned vertical tail surfaces with ventral extensions were tested on the V2 aircraft, but the situation warranted a general redesign. This work was therefore begun in 1938 and the partially-built Ha 138 V3 was abandoned.

Despite modifications made in this, the second prototype of the Blohm und Voss Ha 138, D-AMOR, long-range reconnaissance flying-boat, instability in the air and on the water persisted and a complete redesign resulted in the Bv 138A-0.

The new design, while retaining the same configuration as the previous aircraft, was unmistakably more refined. The most noticeable change was in the larger, longer and better-shaped hull, while the enlarged tail surfaces were carried by stronger booms of increased section. The prototype of the new design was designated Bv 138A-01, D-ADJE, following the change in the company's title, and it, together with five others (Bv 138A-02 to 06), were planned as pre-production aircraft. The Bv 138A-0 had a bow turret which could mount a 20 mm cannon and there were two 7·9 mm MG 15 machine-guns, one in an open position behind the centre engine and one in an open position in the rear of the hull.

Pre-production aircraft were followed by the Bv 138A-1 production type for the reconnaissance rôle. The first of these flew in April 1940 and, together with the second example, was used during the invasion of Norway. During October and November 1940, the Bv 138A-1 became operational in the long-range reconnaissance rôle. The first unit to be so

The first prototype of the new design, the Bv 138A-01, D-ADJE, with enlarged hull, fins and tail booms, and the addition of a bow turret. Resemblance to the previous Ha 138 prototypes lay in configuration only. (*F. Selinger*)

equipped was based in western France and was possibly 1./SAGr 130 which had been formed from 2./Kü.Fl.Gr. 706. Other units which eventually operated the Bv 138 type included 2. and 3./Kü.Fl.Gr. 406, 1./Kü.Fl.Gr. 706, 1., 2. and 3./Kü.Fl.Gr. 906, 1. and 3./SAGr 125, 3./SAGr 126, 1./SAGr 129, 1., 2. and 3./SAGr 130, 1. and 2./SAGr 131, 2./SAGr 132 and 1./BFGr 196. With regard to training and replacement, the operational units were served by Kü.Fl.Erg.Staffel 138.

Only a small number of Bv 138A-1s were produced, since early operations indicated that the structure still needed strengthening. This work was performed on the Bv 138A-04 which then became the first Bv 138B-0 and was followed by the production Bv 138B-1 at the end of 1940. Other important changes introduced with the Bv 138B-1, which supplanted the A-1, included increased power obtained from three 880 hp Junkers Jumo 205D Diesel engines and revised armament comprising one 20 mm MG 151 cannon in a power-operated bow turret and a similar cannon in the rear hull position. A 150 kg (330 lb) bomb load could be carried beneath the root of the starboard wing and, though rarely done, up to four times this load could be carried as an overload in the same position. Some of the pre-production Bv 138B-0s were later converted for use by the Minensuchgruppen in the mine-sweeping rôle. For this rôle, the converted

The Bv 138C-1 became the major production version and was the first in which the previous faults had been eliminated.

61

A Bv 138C-1 of 2./Kü.Fl.Gr.406 goes into action off Norway in February 1942. (*R. C. Seeley*)

aircraft were redesignated Bv 138MS, were each fitted with a dural hoop and field-generating equipment and had their armament removed. The diameter of the hoop was approximately the same as the length of the hull.

As with the Bv 138A-1, the B-1 version did not fare well in service, due in part to the need for more strengthening. Thus, in March 1941, another

A Bv 138C-1 (K6-KL) of 3./Kü.Fl.Gr.406 being hoisted on to a catapult. Note the four-blade centre airscrew. (*F. Selinger*)

62

version appeared. This was the successful Bv 138C-1 in which the previous troubles were finally eliminated and which became the major production type. The 880 hp Junkers Jumo 205D engines were again used but the centre engine drove a four-blade airscrew and the outers each drove a three-blade airscrew with broader blades, the different airscrews being used to modulate previous troublesome vibrations. Other new features included a modified centre-engine radiator and the addition of a 13 mm MG 131 machine-gun in the centre engine-nacelle position. Some aircraft were fitted with FuG 200 Hohentwiel search radar for anti-shipping duties. The crew comprised six members and, if necessary, up to 10 passengers could be carried.

A total of 279 Bv 138s were built between 1938 and 1943, this number including 227 Bv 138C-1s. A number of Bv 138s were fitted for catapult launching and all types could take-off with rocket assistance. The first type of rocket assistance used consisted of a pair of Walter 109-500 cold-type units each giving 500 kg (1,100 lb) thrust for 30 seconds but, when Walter hot-type units became available, either a pair of 109-501 units giving 1,000 kg (2,200 lb) thrust each for 42·5 seconds or a pair of 109-502 units giving 1,500 kg (3,300 lb) thrust each for 30 seconds could be fitted. All rocket units were jettisoned after use and recovered by parachute.

*Wartime operational units:* Kü.Fl.Gr. 406, 706 and 906, SAGr 125, 3./SAGr 126, 1./SAGr 129, SAGr 130, 131, 132 and BFGr 196.

Bv 138C-1: Span 27 m (88 ft 7 in); length 19·9 m (65 ft 3½ in); height 6·6 m (21 ft 7⅞ in); wing area 112 sq m (1,205·12 sq ft).

Empty weight 8,100 kg (17,860 lb); normal loaded weight 14,700 kg (32,413 lb).

Maximum speed at sea level 275 km/h (171 mph); cruising speed 235 km/h (146 mph); service ceiling 5,000 m (16,400 ft); maximum range 5,000 km (3,105 miles).

# Blohm und Voss Ha 139

Following the design of the military Bv 138 flying-boat was the design in 1935 of a four-engined float seaplane designated Ha 139. This seaplane was planned for operation by Deutsche Lufthansa whose requirements included the carrying of a 500 kg (1,102 lb) payload over stages of 5,000 km (3,106 miles) at a cruising speed of 250 km/h (155·3 mph). Also, a rugged but efficient structure was needed, with good handling characteristics, to enable take-offs and alightings on rough waters and to allow for catapult launching.

Accordingly, a low-wing monoplane layout was evolved around four 605 hp Junkers Jumo 205C Diesel engines. The parallel-chord inverted gull wing used a large-diameter steel tube for a main spar and had metal covering over the centre section and fabric covering over the outer panels, and was fitted with four hydraulically-operated landing flaps. Advantageously, the tubular spar also acted as the fuel tank. The fuselage was of circular cross-section and metal monocoque construction, while the stepped cockpit housed a crew of four including two pilots for long flights. The strut-braced tailplane carried twin fins and rudders and was mounted above a short stub-fin. The all-metal, single-step floats were attached by means of a steel stub, this being surrounded by a metal fairing providing both streamlining and a housing for a radiator.

The Blohm und Voss Ha 139 V3 taxi-ing. Also known as the Ha 139B, this aircraft was longer than previous prototypes and the engines were mounted lower on the wings. (*F. Selinger*)

DLH received their first Ha 139 in March 1937 and began trials over the North Atlantic with it and with the second aircraft. These two aircraft, which became known as Ha 139As, were the Ha 139 V1 (c/n 182) D-AJEY *Nordwind* (*North Wind*) and the Ha 139 V2 D-AMIE *Nordmeer* (*North Sea*). Using the seaplane depot ships *Schwabenland* and *Friesenland*, the North Atlantic trials, between the Azores and New York, began on 15 August, 1937. Although the average flight speeds achieved by the two prototypes were close to the specified cruising speed, various faults were revealed, and trials stopped at the end of November 1937 for modifications to be made. These included replacing the circular fins and rudders with redesigned larger surfaces to counteract directional instability, while to overcome cooling problems the inner-engine radiators were removed from the frontal mountings and underwing radiators were provided for all four engines.

Further trials were then made between 21 July and 19 October, 1938, by which time the Ha 139 V3 (c/n 217) D-ASTA *Nordstern* (*North Star*) was also being tested. The Ha 139 V3, known as the Ha 139B, differed from the earlier aircraft in having increased dimensions and weight, reduced chord float fairings, and the engines mounted lower on the wings. With the completion of trials, all three aircraft were put into regular service over the South Atlantic.

Soon after the outbreak of war, the Luftwaffe took over the three Ha

64

Another view of the Ha 139 V3, D-ASTA, later named *Nordstern* and used in Deutsche Lufthansa trials.

139s together with their crews. The Ha 139B was then considerably altered in appearance when modified for reconnaissance and mine-sweeping and was accordingly redesignated the Ha 139 V3/U1. To accommodate an observer, the V3/U1 had a lengthened extensively glazed nose which was compensated for by enlarged fins and rudders of a new shape. For mine-sweeping, a degaussing loop surrounded the aircraft and was connected to the noses of the fuselage and floats, the wings and the tail. Field generating equipment for the loop was carried in the fuselage.

Testing from E-Stelle Travemünde in January 1940 showed that the speed of the Ha 139 V3/U1 was slightly reduced by the degaussing equipment, but it was ready for use in the Norwegian campaign together with the Ha 139 V1 and V2, the latter two aircraft transporting troops and

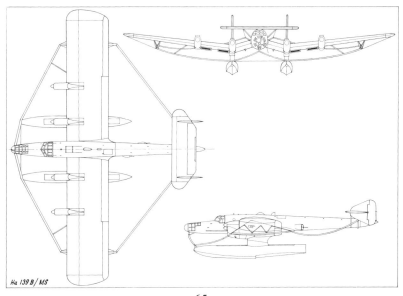

Ha 139 B/MS

65

The Ha 139 V3, after considerable modification for Luftwaffe service on mine-sweeping and reconnaissance duties, was redesignated Ha 139 V3/U1. It is seen here in modified form with new nose and fins, and degaussing loop. (*F. Selinger*)

freight. Coded P5-EH, the Ha 139 V3/U1 was operated by the Transozean-Staffel, and one of the three Ha 139s was later delivered to Stab/Kü.Fl.Gr. 406 in May 1940 at the end of the Norwegian campaign. Due to a lack of spares, the Ha 139s had only a short operational life, and an early proposal (under project number P.20) for a reconnaissance/-bomber version was never pursued. An offshoot of the Ha 139, the Ha 142 landplane, is described on page 71.

Ha 139A (V1 and V2): Span 27 m (88 ft 7 in); length 19·5 m (63 ft 11¾ in); height 4·8 m (15 ft 9 in); wing area 117 sq m (1,259·37 sq ft).
Empty weight 10,360 kg (22,839 lb); fuel 5,350 kg (11,794 lb); useful load 480 kg (1,058 lb); loaded weight, for catapult launch, 17,500 kg (38,581 lb).
Maximum speed 315 km/h (196 mph); normal cruising speed 260 km/h (161·5 mph); economic cruising speed 225 km/h (140 mph); climb to 1,000 m (3,280 ft) 6 min; service ceiling 3,500 m (11,482 ft); maximum range 5,300 km (3,293 miles).

# Blohm und Voss Bv 141

Early in 1937, tests were proceeding with prototypes of the Henschel Hs 126 two-seat single-engined aircraft with a view to making it the Luftwaffe's new short-range reconnaissance and army co-operation machine. At the same time, the RLM issued a specification calling for an Hs 126 successor which was again to be single-engined but carry a crew of three, and emphasis was placed on an all-round visibility superior to that of a parasol-wing aircraft such as the Hs 126. Designs built for the new requirement were the Arado Ar 198, Focke-Wulf Fw 189, and Blohm und Voss Bv 141.

The only noteworthy feature of the Ar 198 single-engined shoulder-wing monoplane was the enlarged and glazed ventral fuselage portion and,

The Blohm und Voss Bv 141 V3, handled well despite its asymmetric layout and was put forward as a production prototype. However, it was later superseded.

although this design was originally favoured, poor results with the Ar 198 V1, D-ODLG, led to the abandonment of the type. Focke-Wulf ignored the single-engine requirement (called for to reduce maintenance on temporary landing fields) but events were to prove their twin-engined Fw 189 a great success.

At the Hamburger Flugzeugbau, Dr Ing Richard Vogt elected to provide an aircraft with a single engine and also with excellent all-round view for the crew by using an asymmetrical layout where the engine was at the forward end of the tail boom and a crew nacelle was mounted separately on the wing to starboard of the engine. Suitable arrangement of the wing panel areas at each side catered for the displaced centre of gravity which fell outside the engine nacelle, and this in turn beneficially counteracted the airscrew torque during take-off. Power was to be provided by an 865 hp BMW 132N nine-cylinder radial air-cooled engine.

The RLM refused to finance development of Dr Vogt's unorthodox design although the capable Ernst Udet, who headed the technical

The Arado Ar 198 V1, D-ODLG, designed as a short-range reconnaissance aircraft, was unsuccessful compared with the Focke-Wulf Fw 189 and Blohm und Voss Bv 141. Note the glazed ventral fuselage portion of the Ar 198.

This Bv 141 V10, or B-02 (NC-RA), was delivered in the autumn of 1941 for Service trials with Aufklärungsschule 1.

department from January 1936, showed interest in it. The Hamburger Flugzeugbau, therefore, built at their own expense a prototype which first flew on 25 February, 1938, as the Ha 141-0 D-ORJE. This prototype showed few faults and, after being flown by Udet, was officially but reluctantly accepted as one of three development prototypes and redesignated Bv 141 V2 (c/n 172). The other two prototypes were the Bv 141 V1 D-OTTO (c/n 171) which first flew in September 1938 and the Bv 141 V3 D-OLGA (c/n 359) which flew soon after.

The Bv 141 V1 was of greater dimensions than the first machine and was the first prototype to have the crew nacelle with numerous flat glazed panels and without the cockpit step of the first (V2) prototype. On 5 October, 1938, the V1 suffered damage during a forced landing due to hydraulic failure and the test programme had to continue for a while with only the V3. The Bv 141 V3 was hopefully put forward as a prototype for production aircraft and increases in dimensions were again made,

The Bv 141 V12, or B-04 (NC-RF), seen here taking-off, was the last but one Bv 141 built.

68

together with a widening of the undercarriage track. Armament consisted of two fixed forward-firing 7·9 mm MG 17 machine-guns and two aft-firing movable 7·9 mm MG 15 machine-guns. One of the MG 15s was mounted in the rear glazed cone of the nacelle and this cone could be rotated through 360 deg. Other equipment included an automatic camera and racks for four 50 kg (110 lb) bombs or S125 gas or smoke-spraying equipment.

The Bv 141 V3 handled well and possessed in full measure all the characteristics desirable for its rôle, so that the RLM grudgingly ordered a further five aircraft as pre-production machines, these being designated Bv 141A-01 to A-05 inclusive (c/ns 360 to 364 respectively). In numerical

A Bv 141B-0. Endless troubles plagued the B-0 series and production plans for the asymmetric reconnaissance aircraft were finally cancelled in the spring of 1942.

order, the same aircraft received Versuchs numbers, these being V4 to V8. The first of the pre-production aircraft, the Bv 141 A-01 D-OLLE, began flying early in 1939. This machine had an increase in wing span and area over the previous V3 prototype and was to have been used for evaluation at E-Stelle Rechlin, but, because of an early hydraulic failure, it damaged its undercarriage during a landing. Its place at Rechlin was therefore taken by the Bv 141A-02 which finished its evaluation tests by January 1940 with a favourable report. Despite this, official conservatism prevailed in favour of the Fw 189 and production plans for the Bv 141A were cancelled in April on the grounds that it was underpowered.

Already, however, an intensive redesign had been made and a more powerful 1,560 hp BMW 801A fourteen-cylinder radial air-cooled engine allowed for. The redesign included attention to the structure, general enlargement, provision of equi-taper outer wing panels and, most noticeable, the fitting of an asymmetric tailplane which improved the rear field of fire. Five examples of the new design were ordered as Bv 141B-0s and were designated V9 to V13. The Bv 141 V9 (NC-OZ) first flew on 9 January, 1941, but it was evident that the new design suffered from various aerodynamic shortcomings and other defects, and modifications were necessary in addition to some structural strengthening. Endless teething troubles plagued the Bv 141B-0s, making progress slow, and the fifth and last example, the Bv 141 V13, was not delivered for official evaluation until

15 May, 1943, but well before then the Fw 189 was ably fulfilling the re
quisite rôles.

The last hopeful event for the Bv 141 occurred in the autumn of 1941
when the Bv 141 V10 (NC-RA) was delivered for Service trials to the
Aufklärungsschule 1 at Grossenhain in Saxony. Soon after, a number of
Bv 141Bs were required to equip a Sonderstaffel Bv 141 on the Eastern
Front, but these plans were cancelled in the spring of 1942 and the Bv 141
V13 was the last of the type to be built.

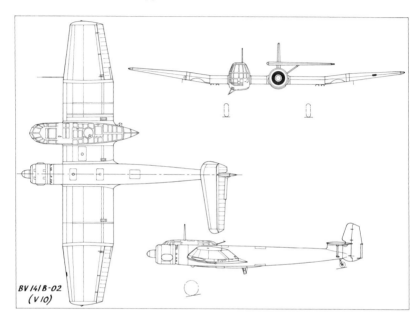

BV 141B-02
(V10)

Despite the discouraging progress of the Bv 141, Dr Vogt put forward
several other asymmetric designs, the most promising being the P.177 and
P.194. The P.177 was projected in 1942 as a single-seat dive-bomber,
substantially of wooden construction, of similar layout to the Bv 141 and
with a BMW 801 engine. Although an order was placed for the P.177
under the designation Bv 237, this was later cancelled because of an engine
supply problem which also affected the Bv 141. A similar asymmetric
layout was persisted with in the P.194 of early 1944, but this projected
dive-bomber was planned to have welded steel skin construction and extensive armouring. Also, the P.194 was to use a 900 kg (1,980 lb) static
thrust turbojet beneath the pilot's nacelle to supplement the BMW 801
radial engine when greater speed was required. Of more incidental interest
are the P.163 project studies for bombers which, while being of symmetrical layout, were asymmetric from the point of view of the crew, who
were accommodated in nacelles at the wingtips, leaving the central fuselage
to accommodate the fuel, bombs, and a coupled engine unit driving a single

70

airscrew. The unorthodox wingtip crew nacelle of the P.163 is said to have been tested on a modified Bv 141 to gain some idea of the piloting problems.

Bv 141B-02: Span 17·46 m (57 ft 3⅜ in); length 13·95 m (45 ft 9¼ in); height 3·6 m (11 ft 9¾ in); wing area 53 sq m (570 sq ft).
Empty weight 4,700 kg (10,363 lb); normal loaded weight 5,700 kg (12,568 lb).
Maximum speed at sea level 370 km/h (230 mph); service ceiling 10,000 m (32,800 ft); normal range 1,200 km (745 miles).

Bv 237: Span 14·46 m (47 ft 5¼ in); length 10·75 m (35 ft 3¼ in); loaded weight 6,685 kg (14,740 lb); maximum speed 575 km/h (357 mph); range 2,000 km (1,642 miles).

# Blohm und Voss Bv 142

Following the early trials with the Ha 139 float seaplane in 1937, work started on a landplane adaptation of this aircraft designated Ha 142. It is uncertain whether the Hamburger Flugzeugbau or Deutsche Lufthansa prompted this development, but the Ha 142 was intended for transatlantic mail-carrying and was to incorporate a maximum of Ha 139 components.

The landplane design was based most closely on the Ha 139 V3 (or Ha 139B) with its stepped cockpit but, apart from the obvious change to land undercarriage instead of floats, power was provided by four 880 hp BMW 132H nine-cylinder radial engines. Each main undercarriage member had twin wheels which retracted backwards into the longer inboard engine nacelles, and the twin tailwheel member also retracted. The maiden flight of the Ha 142 V1 D-AHFB (c/n 218) was made on 11 October, 1938, and was followed soon after by the first flight of the second prototype, the Bv 142 V2 D-ABUV *Kastor* (c/n 219), which received the Bv designation since it was begun after the change in the company's name.

Seen coming in to land is the Blohm und Voss Ha 142 V1, D-AHFB. This and three other examples were tested by Deutsche Lufthansa in 1939 but were subsequently converted for Luftwaffe duties.

By the summer of 1939, four prototypes were flying, and the type was tested by DLH but failed to make much impression, with the result that no plans materialized for regular service. In any event, the war began and, with the Ha 142s back at the works, Blohm und Voss set about adapting

The civil Bv 142 V2 was converted into the Bv 142 V2/U1, seen here, for military service. Illustrated with the military code PC-BC, the aircraft was later re-coded T5-CB for reconnaissance duties with 2./Aufkl.Gr.Ob.d.L. (*F. Selinger*)

the first two prototypes for military service. The military rôle was to be that of long-range maritime patrol and reconnaissance and, where suitable, modifications were made in line with those made for the redesignated Ha 139 V3/U1, such as the fitting of a lengthened extensively glazed nose section. Armament comprised an MG 15 7·9 mm machine-gun in the nose, one each side of the fuselage, in a ventral cupola and in an electrically-operated dorsal turret. In addition to these five guns, a small bomb load of 400 kg (880 lb) could be carried, and the crew, with extra equipment and armament to operate, was increased to six members.

The first converted aircraft, redesignated Bv 142 V2/U1 (PC-BC), was ready by the spring of 1940 and was delivered to the Luftwaffe that autumn. By January 1941, this aircraft was coded T5-CB and being employed by 2./Aufkl.Gr.Ob.d.L. attached to the headquarters of Luftflotte 3 in France. Similar employment was probably given to the Bv 142 V1/U1 conversion, while the unconverted Bv 142 V3 and V4 prototypes were pressed into transport service during the Norwegian campaign. Although, with its increased weight, the Bv 142 had unspectacular performance and was withdrawn from service by 1942, there was a plan to use the aircraft for launching the Henschel GT 1200C air-to-underwater missile described on page 685. Apart from its availability, the Bv 142 was probably chosen to test this missile because its inverted gull wing provided good fuselage ground clearance to carry the GT 1200C.

*Wartime operational units:* 2./Aufkl.Gr.Ob.d.L. and KGrzbV 105.

Bv 142 V2/U1: Span 29·53 m (96 ft 10¾ in); length 20·45 m (67 ft 1⅛in); height 4·44 m (14 ft 6¾ in); wing area 130 sq m (1,398·8 sq ft).
Empty weight 11,000 kg (24,255 lb); loaded weight 16,500 kg (36,383 lb).
Maximum speed at sea level 375 km/h (233 mph); cruising speed 325 km/h (202 mph); landing speed 100 km/h (62 mph); initial rate of climb 400 m/min (1,312 ft/min); service ceiling 9,000 m (29,520 ft); maximum range 3,900 km (2,422 miles).

# Blohm und Voss Bv 144

At the request of Deutsche Lufthansa, Blohm und Voss designed in 1940 a new short- and medium-haul airliner which received the designation Bv 144. In view of the favourable course the war was taking for Germany at that time, it was quite realistic for DLH to plan its post-war commercial services, when it was hoped that an advanced airliner, such as the Bv 144 with spacious accommodation for 18 passengers, would supplement and eventually replace the Ju 52/3m.

The Bv 144 was an all-metal high-wing monoplane designed to use two 1,600 hp BMW 801MA radial engines. The generally advanced nature of the aircraft centred largely around the wing which was designed to have variable incidence, electro-mechanical equipment rotating the wing by its tubular main spar by up to 9 deg. Thus, the angle of attack of the wings could be altered at low speeds and during landing without altering the level attitude of the fuselage. This ensured full maintenance of the airflow over the twin fin tail unit and avoided any blanketing of the control surfaces. It also maintained good pilot visibility during landings. Further landing aid was provided by long slotted flaps which were supplemented by the ailerons drooping when required. Another novel feature was the de-icing system for the leading edges of the wing and tail unit using air heated by an oil burner. The aircraft sat very low on its retractable nosewheel undercarriage, the main units of which retracted inwards into the wing.

The pilot and co-pilot were accommodated in a stepped cabin, with a radio-operator's compartment behind. Aft of this section was the forward freight hold, the passenger section, toilet and aft freight hold. A less spacious seating arrangement could increase the passenger accommodation from 18 to 23.

Since the Bv 144 design offered excellent performance with ample attention to safety, DLH ordered two prototypes. With the fall of France and the availability of that country's industry to the Germans, it was

Designed as an advanced, medium-range airliner for Deutsche Lufthansa, the Blohm und Voss Bv 144 was to be developed by the Breguet factory near Bayonne but only the prototype had flown by the time of the German withdrawal from France. Illustrated is the Bv 144 in French markings.

73

decided to put the development and prototype construction into the hands of the Breguet factory near Bayonne. Here, the first prototype, the Bv 144 V1, was completed and made its maiden flight by August 1944. By then, however, the Germans were in the process of retreating from France in the face of the advancing Allies and Bv 144 development was abandoned to the French. Although the French apparently carried on development for a while, they too abandoned it in due course.

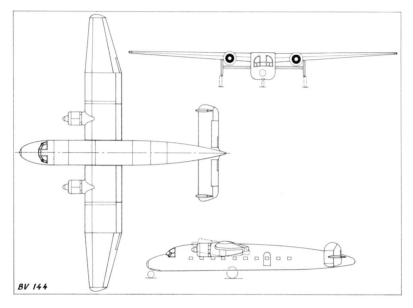

BV 144

Bv 144: Span 27 m (88 ft 7 in); length 21·8 m (71 ft 6¼ in); wing area 88 sq m (946·88 sq ft).

Loaded weight 13,000 kg (28,665 lb).

Maximum speed 470 km/h (292 mph); service ceiling 9,100 m (29,848 ft); range 1,550 km (931 miles).

A fine flying view of a Blohm und Voss Bv 222 Wiking. (*R. C. Seeley*)

# Blohm und Voss Bv 222 Wiking (Viking)

The Bv 222 flying-boat is noteworthy as being the largest flying-boat to attain operational status in the Second World War although the small number built fell very far short of its nearest operational rivals, the Short Sunderland and the Kawanishi H8K. Both these latter aircraft were considerably smaller than the Bv 222 although the Japanese H8K had a superior performance, and both were designed from the start as military aircraft. By contrast, the design of the Bv 222 was undertaken to satisfy a Deutsche Lufthansa requirement for a long-range flying-boat for the Atlantic routes, the requisite accommodation being for a maximum of 24 passengers.

The team which undertook the design work was headed by Dr Ing Richard Vogt (chief designer) and R. Schubert (chief of aerodynamics and hydrodynamics) and, following an order from Lufthansa in September 1939 for three aircraft, the first machine, the Bv 222 V1, was begun in January 1938 followed by work on the other two prototypes the same year.

The large hull of the Bv 222 was particularly spacious because, from the floor up, there were no bulkheads. Close-pitched bulkheads were fitted between the keel and the floor, which was riveted in position and provided with manholes for bilge access. The main step of the planing bottom was transverse and unfaired and varied in depth from 89 mm ($3\frac{1}{2}$ in) at the keel to 0·3 m (1 ft) at the chine, and the beam of the hull was about 3·05 m (10 ft). A large-diameter welded tubular steel wing spar not only contained the fuel and oil in separate compartments but also acted as the main member for carrying the six 1,000 hp BMW-Bramo Fafnir 323R radial engines. This tubular spar was of constant section as far as the outer engines but then tapered towards the wingtips. The float beneath each wingtip was split so that the two halves never quite met when extended and, for retraction, the two halves swung away from each other into the wing recesses. The metal skinning in general was of thick gauge offering good riveting conditions.

With the civil registration D-ANTE, the Bv 222 V1 (c/n 365) first flew on 7 September, 1940, piloted by Flugkapitän Helmut Rodig. Since wartime conditions now prevailed and Lufthansa had no prospect of using the Bv 222 in a civil rôle, the test programme which followed under K. Scherer (chief flight test engineer) also investigated military possibilities. To this end, larger loading doors were fitted, and Bv 222 V1 undertook its first freight mission for the Luftwaffe on 10 July, 1941, when it was flown from the Finkenwerder factory, near Hamburg, to Kirkenes, in the extreme north of Norway. During these initial trials, the chief criticism was that its controls were stiff and that its hydrodynamic qualities could be improved but, after a normal overhaul, the aircraft began flying supplies across the Mediterranean to the Afrika Korps. On these missions, the V1 had no defence apart from its Luftwaffe escort and was still flown by its civil crew.

At about this time, the generally similar Bv 222 V2 and V3 made their maiden flights, the former on 7 August, 1941, and the latter (c/n 0439) on 28 November, 1941, both being armed. Armament for the V2 comprised an MG 81 7·9 mm machine-gun in a bow position, two upper turrets, each with an MG 81, a single MG 81 in each of four hull waist positions and two MG 131 13 mm machine-guns in each of two gondolas under the wing centre section. The V3, on the other hand, started life with the sole armament of a single MG 81 in the bow position. During a refit in the winter of 1941/42, the V1 was also armed by installing an MG 81 in the bow position, two upper turrets each with an MG 131 and four hull waist positions each with an MG 81. Thus equipped, the Bv 222 V1 (with the military code X4-AH) was, on 10 May, 1942, the first such aircraft to be delivered to the specially-formed Luft-Transportstaffel (See) 222.

The Blohm und Voss Bv 222 Wiking was the largest flying-boat operational during the Second World War. This Bv 222 V2 was delivered to Luft-Transportstaffel (See) 222 in August 1942. (*H. Thiele*)

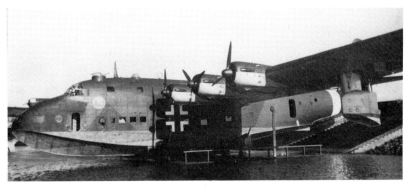

The Bv 222 V8, shown here with LTSta(See) 222, was lost in action on 10 December, 1942. (*F. Selinger*)

In the meantime, the Bv 222 V2 was undergoing trials at Erprobungsstelle Travemünde where the Service testing and development of flying-boats was undertaken. Here, it was confirmed that no heavy structure was needed to carry stresses from the hull bottom to the high wing spar but some strengthening of the rear hull and also the outer wing panels was undertaken. In an effort to improve the hydrodynamic qualities, five small steps about 25 mm (1 in) deep at 0·75 m (2 ft 5½ in) spacing were introduced into the planing bottom behind the main step, the rear keel had a deeper knife-edge fitted and flutes were added to the sides of the wing floats to throw off water. Finally, because of their bad aerodynamic effect, the two underwing gondolas carrying armament were removed. Thus modified, the V2 was delivered to LT Sta (See) 222 on 10 August, 1942, three months after the V1.

By the end of 1942, LT Sta (See) had received five more Bv 222s, these being the already-mentioned V3 plus the V4, V5, V6 and V8. Exact dates are unknown except for the V3 which was delivered on 9 December, 1942, after previously having been on supply duties between Italy and Tripoli. The previous month, on 24 November, the V6 (X4-FH) was the first to be destroyed when it was making an unescorted flight to Tripoli. Furthermore, the day after the V3 was delivered, LT Sta (See) 222 lost the V8, this being shot down by RAF Beaufighters when flying in company with the V1 and V4 flying-boats.

At about this time, attention began to turn towards using the Bv 222 as a maritime reconnaissance aircraft instead of a transport and, accordingly, LT Sta (See) 222 was redesignated Aufklärungsstaffel (See) 222 but retained its code of X4. There seems to be a strong possibility that the same unit was again redesignated during the spring of 1943 as 1.(Fern)/See-Aufklärungs-Gruppe 129 which alluded to long-range maritime reconnaissance. Beginning with Bv 222 V3 in February 1943 and following on with the V2, V4 and V5 the following month, the refitting of the flying-boats began. Previously, some aircraft, such as the V3, had

77

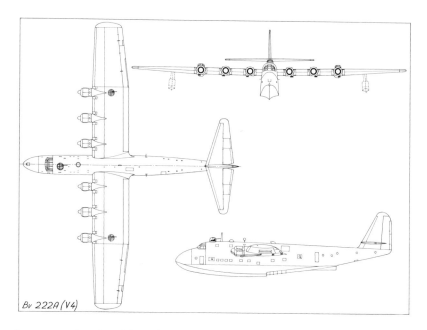

Bv 222A (V4)

been armed only with a single MG 81 in the nose; such armament was completely inadequate for defence and the reasoning here is obscure. During the refitting of aircraft, therefore, power-operated gun turrets were positioned: three along the top of the hull and two above the wings at the quarter-span positions. Other important equipment fitted included FuG 200 Hohentwiel search radar and FuG 216R Neptun rear warning equipment.

During this period, more flying-boats were lost. Bv 222 V1 was severely damaged and became partially submerged in Athens harbour where it hit a buoy during an alighting in February 1943. On the night of 21–22 June, 1943, the V3 and V5 were both strafed by RAF Mosquitos and sunk at their moorings at Biscarosse, this, apparently, being the base of 1.(F)/129. As already mentioned, both these aircraft had recently been refitted.

An important prototype, the V7, made its maiden flight on 1 April, 1943. This aircraft differed from previous examples primarily in having six 980 hp Junkers Jumo 207C Diesels in place of the BMW engines. In addition to armament in the turret positions, machine-guns were positioned in the nose and hull sides while the radar equipment for maritime reconnaissance was retained. Also, Walter assisted take-off units could be fitted to enable the aircraft to take-off in an overload condition. This aircraft was the prototype for the Bv 222C production series, previous prototypes in Luftwaffe service having been designated Bv 222A (although they were not production aircraft) while the Bv 222B was a proposal only for a Junkers Jumo 208 engined version.

With the building of Bv 222 V9 (Bv 222C-09), the first true production aircraft was begun. Detail manufacture and sub-assembly was mainly at the Blohm und Voss Steinwerder works, near Hamburg, and assembly of two Bv 222Cs at a time could be carried out at the ideally-sited Finkenwerder river island works. Here, the time to construct a hull in the gantry was reduced to six weeks, working day and night, and the production time for a complete airframe, less equipment and engines, averaged 350,000 man-hours. Although extensive corrosion troubles had been experienced with the first aircraft, these were now overcome simply by the application of a specially-developed paint, and a high-quality surface finish (usually associated with flying-boats) was not required.

Loading a Bv 222A in Norway. (*F. Selinger*)

By the time the Bv 222C appeared, the already-mentioned problem of stiff controls had been overcome, the chief culprit having been friction. It should be noted that, in large airframes of the Bv 222 type, many problems arise with the long control connection runs due to the magnification of structural deflections and temperature effects. For this reason, push-pull rods were discarded in favour of torsion tubes connected by gears and quadrants for the operation of all control surfaces. It is important to note that power-operated controls were not employed except for part of the elevator control, and the pilot applied the necessary control forces with consequent natural control feel. Each aileron was divided into two sections, the inboard section being fitted with a servo tab. Both aileron sections moved together in response to the controls under normal conditions but, when the servo tabs of the inner sections became ineffective, *e.g.* at low speeds or when taxi-ing downwind, the inner sections were picked up by stops on the outer sections. In the event of control tubes being severed, both sections of the ailerons were designed to float neutral. The elevator was divided into three sections on each side, the outer section being used only for trimming, the inner section being pilot-operated through a servo tab, and the centre section being operated by an autopilot. Such an auto-

A Bv 222C, showing the mooring hatch and radar antennae. (*F. Selinger*)

pilot was very useful for reducing fatigue on long flights but, since such equipment was not fully reliable at the time, it could always be over-ridden by the pilot and was switched off during take-off and alighting. The rudder was in a single section and operated through a servo tab. For trimming, an interesting tab box was designed instead of the usual three trimming wheels. This tab box had a miniature control column which was clicked back and forth in the requisite direction for longitudinal and lateral trim, while twisting the stick gave the requisite directional trim. This neat trimming arrangement was so well thought of that it was to have become standard equipment in German aircraft had time allowed.

Bv 222C-09 was delivered to 1.(F)/129 on 23 July, 1943, and was followed by Bv 222 V7 delivered to the same unit on 16 August, 1943. Only four other flying-boats were completed, these being Bv 222C-010 to Bv 222C-013 inclusive, and were delivered for operations by the end of 1943, although there are some doubts concerning the operational use of Bv 222C-013. This latter aircraft had been scheduled to be fitted with Junkers Jumo 205D Diesel engines to become the prototype for the projected Bv 222D but, in the event, Junkers Jumo 205C engines were fitted.

During October 1943, either Bv 222 V2 or V4 shot down an Avro Lancaster over the Atlantic but, a few months later, Bv 222C-010 was shot down by RAF night fighters. There had also been the loss of Bv 222C-09 which was strafed by Mustangs at Travemünde. As late as June 1944, 1.(F)/129 based at Biscarosse is recorded as having four Bv 222s on strength but, following the D-Day landings in that month, the unit appears to have been disbanded and its aircraft transferred to Stab and 1.(F)/130 and 2.(F)/131 which were operating Bv 138s in Norway. These units remained operational until at least January 1945 and probably until the end of the war when, to prevent their capture, they sank Bv 222 V4 at Kiel-Holtenau and Bv 222 V7 at Travemünde.

Only two Bv 222C Wikings survived the war. These were Bv 222C-011 and C-013 which were tested in the USA, C-013 subsequently being tested in the United Kingdom. Although some work was done on Bv 222C-014, C-015, C-016, and C-017 during 1944, these were abandoned because of German concentration on fighter production. Nothing is known concerning the 18th and 19th designations which are only mentioned because it is known that the Bv 222 V20 was projected to have the BMW Fafnir 323R engines used in the first six aircraft, to become the prototype for the Bv 222E.

*Wartime operational units:* Aufklärungsstaffel (See) 222, 1./SAGr 129, 1./SAGr 130, 2./SAGr 131, 3./Kü.Fl.Gr. 406, Luft-Transportstaffel (See) 222.

Bv 222C Wiking: Span 46 m (150 ft 11 in); length 36·575 m (120 ft); height 10·9 m (35 ft 9⅛ in); wing area 255 sq m (2,744 sq ft); hull beam 3·05 m (10 ft).

Empty weight 30,640 kg (67,565 lb); normal loaded weight 45,580 kg (100,500 lb); maximum loaded weight 48,980 kg (108,000 lb).

Maximum speed at 5,000 m (16,400 ft) 390 km/h (242 mph); cruising speed at 5,550 m (18,205 ft) 345 km/h (214 mph); alighting speed 130 km/h (81 mph); initial rate of climb 144 m/min (473 ft/min); service ceiling 7,300 m (23,945 ft); maximum range 6,100 km (3,788 miles).

# Blohm und Voss Bv 238

After completion of the basic design for the Bv 222 Wiking, during 1940 the team under Dr Ing Richard Vogt worked on a very large long-range flying-boat project for Deutsche Lufthansa, clearly showing that peacetime operations were still much in mind. This project, the P.200, was for an eight-engined aircraft with a span of 85 m (279 ft), a loaded weight of 200,000 kg (441,000 lb), a passenger capacity of 120, and a range of 8,600 km (5,340 miles), and the only flying-boat ever to exceed it in size was the post-war Hughes H-4. However, in January 1941, the P.200 was shelved in order to attend to an RLM request for a design of a long-range multi-purpose flying-boat. The new design, designated Bv 238, was to use four 2,500 hp Junkers Jumo 223 Diesel engines, but because the development of such engines required many years owing to Germany's lapse in this field, the original Bv 238 design was abandoned.

In July 1941, a completely fresh design was therefore started which, although considerably larger than the Bv 222, drew on that design for many of its features and general layout. This design was accepted and a

81

development order placed for four prototypes, the first three each to have six Daimler-Benz DB 603 liquid-cooled engines as prototypes for the Bv 238A and the fourth to have six BMW 801 air-cooled radial engines as the prototype of the Bv 238B. The aircraft which eventually emerged as the Bv 238 V1 was only exceeded in terms of wing span by one German-built aircraft, which was the Junkers Ju 322 Mammut (Mammoth) cargo glider.

Although the design could draw to a large extent on the Bv 222 for data, it was considered desirable to obtain extra information from a flying model in order to reduce the risk of failure in such a large undertaking. Accordingly, the Flugtechnische Fertigungsgemeinschaft, near Prague, were commissioned to build a flying-boat similar to, but about a quarter the size of, the Bv 238 design. This aircraft was designated FGP 227, built of wood and powered by six 21 hp engines but, although it was begun in 1942, it was not completed until early in 1944. Its use was then further delayed because of sabotage en route to Erprobungsstelle Travemünde, repairs not being completed until September 1944. The final scene in this unfortunate farce came when the FGP 227 (BQ-UZ) made its maiden flight only to be damaged in a forced alighting following a fuel blockage.

Far from obtaining any assistance from the FGP 227 programme, therefore, it would appear that it merely introduced delays and these were increased by various redesigns to provide for alterations in the extensive armament installations and so forth. Nevertheless, work had begun at the Steinwerder works on various Bv 238 components and jigs during 1942, and construction of the actual Bv 238 V1 hull began at the Finkenwerder works during January 1944. It is somewhat surprising that at this stage of the war, when Germany was on the defensive, the contract for such large

To obtain data for the huge Blohm und Voss Bv 238, this scaled-down flying-boat was built near Prague. Known as the FGP 227 (BQ-UZ), the small flying-boat was attended by misfortune and finally proved valueless.

82

aircraft was allowed to continue, but it must be remembered that, apart from the use of materials, the work at Blohm und Voss did not affect any plans for fighter production. As for the aircraft's operational feasibility, although it was to be capable of bombing, its prime rôle was to be that of long-range transport and reconnaissance and it was to be heavily armed and fly over sea areas where few Allied fighters were likely to be encountered.

The Blohm und Voss Bv 238 V1 was the sole prototype completed of this, the largest flying-boat built during the war. It was destroyed by strafing after only two months of test flying.

By about March 1945, the Bv 238 V1 was completed, although the fitting of armament was planned as a later stage. Apart from its greater size and some hydrodynamic refinements, the chief features in which it differed from the Bv 222 were that the elevator was in two sections only on each side (the outer, trimming, section being discarded) and the wing floats were not split but each retracted, as a whole, inwards. The system of using the tubular wing spar for carrying the engines, fuel and oil, was again employed, but the parallel centre-section tube was increased in diameter to about 1 m (3 ft $3\frac{3}{8}$ in) and its thickness was sufficient to withstand machine-gun bullets. In general, design features were simple to facilitate production and no magnesium was used at all.

Before the end of March 1945 the Bv 238 V1 was pronounced fit for service after only four test flights and its test programme was continued. Although this aircraft was flying for about two months, however, its armament had still not been installed when it was destroyed on Lake Schaal by Mustangs only four days before the war ended.

Although the Bv 238 V1 had taken some 14 months to complete, some 600,000 man-hours had been included for the manufacture of jigs and tools since Blohm und Voss hoped to produce the aircraft in some numbers. In production, it was planned to build a Bv 238 hull, for example, in eight weeks. At the end of the war, construction of the Bv 238 V2 and V3 was under way, V3 being at Finkenwerder with the hull 60 per cent completed but the wings barely started and V2 was 80 per cent complete at the Weser-Flugzeugbau Bremen, where detail components were sent from the Steinwerder works.

Although the Bv 238 was designed to a military specification, the design team had found time to make a preliminary layout for a civil version, but their attention was turned early in 1942 to the design of the Bv 250, a land-based derivative of the Bv 238 intended to undertake similar duties. The new aircraft was to use the same powerplants as the Bv 238 V1 and what was virtually a levelled-off hull and a multi-wheel undercarriage. Four prototypes of the Bv 250 were actually on order but by the end of the war only some component manufacture of the first prototype had been undertaken.

Bv 238 V1 (without armament): Span 60·17 m (197 ft $4\frac{3}{4}$ in); length 43·5 m (142 ft $8\frac{1}{2}$ in); height 13·4 m (43 ft $11\frac{1}{2}$ in); wing area 365·3 sq m (3,930 sq ft); hull beam 13·4 m (11 ft 8 in).

Empty weight 50,800 kg (111,985 lb); normal loaded weight 70,000 kg (154,325 lb); maximum loaded weight 80,000 kg (176,400 lb).

Maximum speed at 6,000 m (19,685 ft) 425 km/h (264 mph); alighting speed 125 km/h (78 mph); maximum range in reconnaissance rôle 6,100 km (3,788 miles).

Bv 250: Span 57·6 m (189 ft); length 46 m (149 ft 11 in); wing area 347 sq m (3,634 sq ft).

Empty weight 74,960 kg (165,285 lb); normal loaded weight 95,255 kg (210,035 lb).

Maximum speed 420 km/h (261 mph); maximum range in reconnaissance rôle 14,000 km (8,700 miles); range with normal payload 7,000 km (4,350 miles).

# Blohm und Voss Bv 40

The year 1943 was one which saw some of the greatest aerial dramas of the war over Germany. In that year the policy of round-the-clock bombing, with the USAAF operating by day and the RAF by night, was being put into effect on a scale whereby whole cities were being devastated by fire storms. At this time, however, the air war was still one of attrition and, whereas the summer of 1943 saw a large reduction in Allied bombing in order to regroup after severe losses, it also saw the Germans trying to offset their critical shortage of strategic materials by painstakingly salvaging all Allied aircraft wrecks. The Luftwaffe was also encountering the problem of keeping up the supply of well-trained aircrew.

Against this background, Dr Richard Vogt of Blohm und Voss proposed to the RLM the idea of an Ersatzjäger (substitute fighter) which would, in fact, be an engineless glider. The glider was to be towed into combat behind a standard fighter and then make a head-on gliding attack on its adversary. Although the airspeed of the glider-fighter would be low, it was anticipated that its chances of survival would be good because of the

Designed as an armed glider, the Blohm und Voss Bv 40 was to be rapidly and economically produced. This, the Bv 40 V1, PN-UA, made its first towed flight at the end of May 1944. Cannon were not, at that stage, fitted in the fairings beneath the wing roots.
(*H. Redemann*)

high closing speed of a frontal attack, the use of substantial cockpit armour, and the small frontal area made possible by its lack of an engine. The towing fighter could, of course, cover the glider-fighter attack and then follow it through. The prime attraction of the glider-fighter was not, however, its anticipated combat success but rather that good results could be obtained using very little strategic material and skilled man-hours, and pilots with only glider training could be used.

At the behest of the RLM, therefore, several firms prepared and submitted projects in the autumn of 1943. It is believed that at least one design incorporated a battery of small rockets in the rear fuselage sides to enable the aircraft to regain height after the first attack. The unpowered Blohm und Voss design was selected for development and received the designation Bv 40. Nineteen development prototypes were ordered for completion by March 1945 and, following satisfactory results from these, there was to be an initial production batch of 200.

The Bv 40 was a somewhat sinister-looking aircraft with straightforward, angular but quite clean lines. Throughout the design everything was kept as simple as possible and, apart from the cannon armament and instruments, all systems were manually operated. To keep the frontal area to the minimum, the pilot was in a prone position on a padded couch with

The Bv 40 V1, showing the jettisonable take-off wheels attached with adjustable cables. The lead hanging from the nose is the intercommunication connection with the towing aircraft.

85

padded chin and brow rests. His very restricted view was through small front and side panels, the windscreen being 120 mm ($4\frac{3}{4}$ in) armoured glass. The cockpit enclosure was of welded sheet metal construction with substantial armouring including armour steel panels which could be slid over the side windows during combat. By weight, the armour protection comprised about 26 per cent of the complete airframe. Access to the cockpit was given by the removal in one section of the top and port side. Riveted sheet metal construction was used for the fuselage centre section which was bolted to the rear wooden fuselage supporting the tail unit, also built from wood. The wing was attached to the fuselage by four bolts and consisted of a main plywood box-spar with two auxiliary spars and a skin of 4 mm plywood. Although the wing was of parallel chord, the thickness ratio of the outer wing sections was reduced by about a half near the quarter-chord positions. From these positions out to the wingtips ran the ailerons while the remainder of the wing trailing edge was occupied by slotted flaps. For normal landings, these flaps were lowered 50 deg but, in cases of emergency, a full 80 deg could be used to achieve a pin-point landing. Landings were made on a semi-extendable skid, the small wheels having been jettisoned at take-off.

Another view of the Bv 40 V1. Note the pitot head above the fuselage, the bracing for the tailplane, and the compass housing bulge on the nose.

The armament comprised two 30 mm MK 108 cannon, these being fitted inside bulged fairings at the fuselage sides beneath the wing roots. Each cannon was supplied with 35 rounds of ammunition from a feed channel inside the thick inboard section of each wing. At one stage, it was proposed that if it still had sufficient altitude the Bv 40 should make a second attack with a Gerät-Schlinge, a device consisting of a small bomb suspended by a cable beneath the aircraft; but the space required for it would have necessitated the removal of one cannon and it was felt that two cannon were essential for an effective discharge in the short attack time available. It was therefore settled that the Bv 40 would be cable-towed behind a Messerschmitt Bf 109G to an altitude of between 250 m (820 ft) and 750 m (2,460 ft) above the bomber pack, released, make a 20 deg angle diving attack and then glide back to base. It was also considered feasible for a single Bf 109G to tow two Bv 40s into combat.

By January 1944 the first prototype was being assembled, and this, the Bv 40 V1 (PN-UA), made its first towed flight behind a Messerschmitt Bf 110 at the end of May. After modifications, including improving the take-off trolley, a second flight was made on 2 June, 1944, with test pilot Rautenhaus at the controls. This flight was made from Wenzendorf airfield, and the Bv 40 V1 was cast-off for the first time; after performing well, the aircraft rapidly lost altitude when speed was reduced to 140 km/h (87 mph) and was badly damaged in the subsequent crash.

In the meantime, the Bv 40 V2 was being prepared and this made two short flights (because of poor visibility) on 5 June, 1944.

The Bv 40 V3 was a static test airframe, and the V4 was badly damaged in a crash late in June. Soon after this, the Bv 40 V5 began flight tests at Wenzendorf.

The first long flight of a Bv 40 was made by the Bv 40 V6 (PN-UF) which was towed behind a Bf 110 from Stade to Wenzendorf on 27 July, 1944, a flight which highlighted the strain imposed on the pilot flying from the prone position. The glider pilot on this occasion was Rautenburg who complained of the effort involved, but it should be remembered that the Bv 40 was subject to constant buffeting in the slipstream of the towing aircraft. The last prototype, the Bv 40 V7, was finished in August 1944 and by this time flight testing of the Bv 40 was complete.

The technical department of the RLM then proposed sub-variants of the

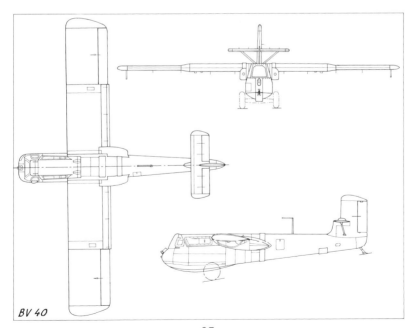

BV 40

basic design including some with the addition of pulsejets or rockets to give the glider climbing ability, various automatic control devices and even the conversion into a fuel tanker to increase the range of the towing fighter. Another proposal was for two Bv 40s to carry underwing bombs, the pair of Bv 40s being carried to the combat zone under the wings of a Heinkel He 177A-5 or B-5 bomber.

None of these proposals came to anything however because, by the autumn of 1944, the whole Bv 40 programme had been abandoned in favour of jet- and rocket-powered aircraft and missiles.

Bv 40: Span 7·9 m (25 ft 11 in); length 5·7 m (18 ft 8½ in); height 1·63 m (5 ft 4⅛ in); wing area 8·7 sq m (93·61 sq ft).

Empty weight 835 kg (1,842 lb); approx loaded weight 950 kg (2,095 lb).

Maximum speed of Bf 109G at 6,000 m (19,680 ft) towing one Bv 40—554 km/h (344 mph), or towing two Bv 40s—507 km/h (315 mph); towing time to 7,000 m (22,960 ft) 12 min with one Bv 40 or 16·8 min with two Bv 40s; maximum speed of Bv 40 in 20 deg dive at 2,000 m (6,560 ft) 470 km/h (292 mph); estimated maximum diving speed of Bv 40 900 km/h (559 mph) but aileron flutter set in before that speed was achieved.

# Blohm und Voss Bv 155

The chequered life of the Blohm und Voss Bv 155 started at Messerschmitt AG at the beginning of 1942 when that concern began the design of a shipboard fighter designated Me 155. Already, during 1940–41, sixty Messerschmitt Bf 109Es had been converted into Bf 109Ts for operation from German aircraft carriers, the first of which, the *Graf Zeppelin*, had been launched on 18 December, 1938. As with the Bf 109Ts, the Me 155 was also to employ a maximum of standard Bf 109 parts in order to facilitate development and was to use a Bf 109G fuselage with a new wing and undercarriage and the requisite naval equipment. This aircraft was not, however, proceeded with since German carrier and ship conversion work was abandoned by the end of 1942 with nothing to show for the effort.

A modified design was, however, begun in November 1942 as the Me 155A. This was to be a single-seat Schnellbomber (high-speed bomber) designed to carry a single 1,000 kg (2,205 lb) bomb for precision attacks on special targets. Since no official backing for this design was forthcoming, it was again re-worked, this time as the Me 155B-1 high-altitude fighter. This was to be powered by a Daimler-Benz DB 605 engine to operate at altitudes up to 11,000 m (36,080 ft) using a two-stage mechanical

The Blohm und Voss Bv 155 V3 high-altitude fighter prototype was put aside when partially completed and superseded by a fresh design. Note the exhaust duct leading back from the engine to a supercharger installed in the rear of the fuselage. Generous wing area and large radiators were also features.

supercharger and eight separate underwing radiators. A prototype of the Me 155B-1 was begun and consisted basically of a Bf 109G airframe with a new wing centre section to increase the span to 21 m (68 ft 10¾ in) and a new fin similar to one designed for the Me 209 V5. There was also some lengthening of the fuselage to accommodate the supercharger equipment and maintain balance. Before this machine was completed, however, the RLM ordered the transference of the development to Blohm und Voss in August 1943. Commensurate with this change of hands, the Me 155B-1 was redesignated Bv 155A-1 for which the first prototype was designated Bv 155 V1.

Although the aircraft begun by Messerschmitt retained many Bf 109 parts (and also main undercarriage members from a Junkers Ju 87D-6), extensive redesigning was carried out under Dr Richard Vogt's leadership, the most apparent change being the provision of a new wing with two large radiators mounted above it at about the quarter-span positions. Although the undercarriage had an exceptionally wide track, the main legs retracted outwards so that the mainwheels could be housed in the area of increased depth at the radiator sections. The Bv 155 V1 was built at the Finkenwerder works, Hamburg, and made its maiden flight on 8 February, 1945, powered by a 1,610 hp Daimler-Benz DB 603A engine. On this flight, the aircraft ran into trouble with overheating, and as a result the Bv 155 V2, which began flying on 15 February, had its wing radiators beneath instead of above the wing. Although the radiators had large air intake sections, their developed profiles followed a similar line and thickness/chord ratio to the wing and, accordingly, the radiator extended forward and aft of the wing chord. Other changes made in the V2 prototype included increasing the wing chord and the fitting of a new, bulged, cockpit canopy. This aircraft was similarly powered to the V1, and both prototypes tested the Hirth TKL 15 supercharger which was installed in the fuselage behind the cockpit, was exhaust-driven, and provided with a large ventral air intake.

Results provided by these aircraft and project studies brought about

89

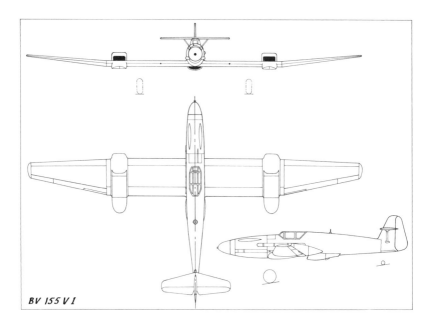

BV 155 V 1

some re-thinking of the design so that the Bv 155 V3 was put aside when partially completed, the proposed Bv 155B series was abandoned and the decision was made to proceed towards the Bv 155C series for which the Bv 155 V4 was to act as the prototype. The V4 prototype was powered by an 1,810 hp DB 603U engine with the Hirth TKL 15 supercharger and had both the wing span and undercarriage track reduced. Thirty Bv 155C-0 pre-production fighters were ordered, of which the Bv 155 V4 was the first, but this prototype had just been completed and was not flown by the time the war ended. The uncompleted Bv 155 V3 is believed to be held by the Smithsonian Institution in Washington, DC.

Bv 155 V2: Span 20·5 m (67 ft 3 in); length 12 m (39 ft 4½ in); wing area 39 sq m (419·8 sq ft).

Empty weight 4,860 kg (10,716 lb); loaded weight 5,625 kg (12,403 lb).

Maximum speed at 16,000 m (52,480 ft) 690 km/h (429 mph); climb to 16,000 m (52,480 ft) 29 min; service ceiling 16,950 m (55,610 ft); range about 1,500 km (932 miles).

# Bücker Bü 131 Jungmann

Following the establishment of the Bücker Flugzeugbau at Johannisthal in 1932, the company was fortunate in that its first aircraft, the Bü 131 Jungmann, was a success. This was largely due to the Swedish designer Anders J. Andersson under whose leadership all Bücker aircraft were designed before 1939.

The Bü 131 was a biplane for sports, aerobatic and training use and had two open cockpits in tandem. All wings had ailerons and dihedral, 11 deg sweepback and positive stagger, upper and lower wings being interchangeable. Construction consisted of a welded chrome-molybdenum steel-tube fuselage with forward metal and rear fabric covering, a tubular-steel tail unit with fabric covering and a wooden wing structure with I-section wooden spars and fabric covering. Fuel and oil tanks were carried in the fuselage. The landing gear consisted of two main legs hinged to the fuselage sides with springs and oil damping, the axles being hinged to a pyramidal structure beneath the fuselage. The mainwheels had balloon tyres and brakes while a sprung tailwheel was used.

The Bücker Bü 131 Jungmann went into service in 1935. As a primary trainer, it had to withstand mismanagement – as in this landing mishap! (*J. Zazvonil*)

The first prototype of the Bü 131, D-3150, first flew on 27 April, 1934, piloted by Joachim von Köppen, and powered by an 80 hp Hirth HM 60R four-cylinder inline engine. In the same year, production of the Bü 131A began with main deliveries to the Deutscher Luftsportverband. First examples were delivered to the Luftwaffe in 1935 for use as primary trainers, an example of a unit using the Jungmann being Flugzeugführerschule A/B 72 at Detmold. During 1936, production began of the Bü 131B, which differed mainly in having the more powerful 105 hp Hirth HM 504A-2 engine. An experimental type which was not put into production was the

91

Bü 131C which was powered by a 90 hp Cirrus Minor four-cylinder inline engine.

Although the Bü 131 continued in the training rôle throughout the war, quite a number were supplanted by the later Bü 181 Bestmann. Consequently, Bü 131s were available for use, together with other ex-trainer aircraft, by night ground-attack units which began forming at the end of 1942 with NSGr 2. In Esthonia and Latvia, NSGr 11 and 12 were formed and these units included the Bü 131 among their aircraft.

The considerable success of the Bü 131 as a primary trainer encouraged the Japanese to adopt the type. For the Imperial Japanese Army Air Force, 1,037 examples were built, using the 110 hp Hatsukaze engine, and designated Kokusai Type 4 (Ki 86). For the Imperial Japanese Navy, 217 examples were built and designated Watanabe-Kyushu Type 2 Momiji K9W1. Finland, Hungary, Spain, Sweden and Switzerland also used the Bü 131 and in Czechoslovakia it was built as the C-104.

Bü 131B: Span 7·4 m (24 ft 3¾ in); length 6·62 m (21 ft 8⅝ in); height 2·25 m (7 ft 4⅝ in); total wing area 13·5 sq m (145·3 sq ft).

Empty weight 390 kg (860 lb); loaded weight 680 kg (1,500 lb).

Maximum speed at sea level 183 km/h (114 mph); cruising speed 170 km/h (106 mph); landing speed 82 km/h (51 mph); climb to 1,000 m (3,280 ft) 6·3 min; service ceiling 3,000 m (9,840 ft); range 650 km (404 miles).

# Bücker Bü 133 Jungmeister (Young Champion)

With the Bücker company's move from Johannisthal to Rangsdorf completed and the Bü 131 production in full swing, the Bü 133 Jungmeister (Young Champion) was produced. Using many of the previous type's components, the Bü 133 looked very similar but was a single-seater, had a more powerful engine, and was smaller. The result was a highly aerobatic aircraft with good characteristics commending it to the advanced flying and training rôle. With the successful flight of the prototype D-EVEO powered by a 135 hp Hirth HM 6 inverted inline air-cooled engine, the Jungmeister was ordered by the Luftwaffe for training, including fighter pilot training. Examples of units using the type were FFS A/B 11 at Schönewalde and Jagdfliegerschule 2.

The standard production version was the Bü 133C, which was powered by a 160 hp Siemens Sh 14A-4 seven-cylinder radial engine. This version was produced in Germany and, from 1936, by Dornier-Werke at Altenrhein in Switzerland where 47 were built for the Swiss Air Force. The other production model was the Bü 133B which was powered by a

Prototype of the Jungmeister, the Bücker Bü 133 V1 with inline engine. (*J. Zazvonil*)

160 hp Hirth HM 506 engine but was not built in Germany. Production of the Bü 133B was undertaken in small numbers from 1941 by the Spanish CASA concern which built 50 Jungmeisters, most of which were of the C version.

Bü 133C: Span 6·6 m (21 ft 7$\frac{7}{8}$ in); length 6.02 m (19 ft 9 in); height 2·2 m (7 ft 2$\frac{5}{8}$ in); total wing area 12 sq m (129·12 sq ft).
Empty weight 425 kg (937 lb); loaded weight 585 kg (1,290 lb).
Maximum speed at sea level 220 km/h (137 mph); landing speed 90 km/h (56 mph); climb to 1,000 m (3,280 ft) 2·8 min; service ceiling 4,500 m (14,760 ft); range 500 km (310 miles).

The standard production version of the Jungmeister trainer was the Bü 133C with radial engine. Here, one is landing on skis. (*H. Obert*)

93

Originally designed as a sports aircraft, the Bücker Bü 181 Bestmann largely supplanted previous Bücker trainers in the Luftwaffe. (*R. C. Seeley*)

# Bücker Bü 181 Bestmann

After the Bü 133 came the Bü 134 two-seat cabin monoplane which had a 105 hp Hirth HM 504 engine and high-mounted wings which could be folded back. This aircraft was, in fact, unsuccessful and the sole prototype (D-EQPA) flew in 1936. Next came the Bü 180 Student, the company's first low-wing monoplane. First prototype of the Bü 180 (D-ELIO) flew in the autumn of 1937 and although only a small number was built (it was a two-seat touring aircraft for civil use only) the type was the first Bücker aircraft to use the new constructional methods described for the Bü 181.

The Bü 181 Bestmann was a cabin monoplane with two side-by-side seats and, although originally designed for sports and touring use, it supplanted to a large extent previous Bücker aircraft in service with the Luftwaffe training elements. The low-mounted wings of the Bü 181 tapered sharply in chord and thickness and consisted of an all-wood structure with plywood covering over the leading edge back to the rear spar and then fabric covering to the trailing edge. There were narrow-chord ailerons over half the wing trailing edge and split flaps between ailerons and fuselage. For the fuselage, which was principally of oval section, the forward section consisted of a chrome-molybdenum steel-tube structure with metal panels while the rear section was a wooden monocoque. A wooden framework was used for the tail unit with plywood covering for the fixed surfaces and fabric covering for the rudder and elevators. Trim tabs on the elevators were adjustable in the air but those on the rudder were adjustable only on the ground. A fixed, cantilever-type undercarriage was fitted, the single legs having steel springs and oil dampers. There were fairings on the main legs and on the inner sides and behind the wheels while the tailwheel could castor. In the cabin there were dual controls, adjustable seats arranged for seat-type parachutes and a large baggage compartment at the rear. Fuel and oil tanks were also in the fuselage.

In February 1939, the first prototype (D-ERBV) of the Bü 181 made its

94

maiden flight. After being selected as a standard basic trainer for the Luftwaffe, deliveries were begun by the end of 1940 of the Bü 181A which was powered by a 105 hp Hirth HM 504 four-cylinder inline air-cooled engine. Several thousand Bestmann aircraft were built during the war at the Rangsdorf factory and examples of training schools which employed the type include FFS A/B 23 at Kaufbeuren and FFS A/B 112 at Langenleborn. Soon, the Bü 181 was available for other rôles such as communication, glider-towing and even transporting Panzerfaust weapons. (The Panzerfaust was an infantry weapon which simply consisted of a light launching tube and a rocket projectile with a hollow-charge warhead. It effectively knocked out tanks.)

A Bü 181 at Zell-am-See, Austria, in May 1945. A German pilot is demonstrating the aircraft to US Army personnel. (*USAF*)

Production of both the Bü 181A and the slightly modified Bü 181D was begun by Fokker in Amsterdam in 1942 and its total wartime production was 708 aircraft. Between 1944 and 1946, AB Hagglund och Söner in Sweden built 125 Bü 181s as the Sk 25 for the Swedish Air Force. Just prior to the German withdrawal from Czechoslovakia, production of the Bü 181D was initiated in the Zlin plant at Otrokovice, and production continued after the war, when the type was designated C.6 and C.106 for the Czechoslovak Air Force and Zlin Z.281 and Z.381 in various versions for civil club use.

A final tribute to the soundness of Bücker design came during the 1950s when the Egyptian Heliopolis Aircraft Works acquired a Czechoslovak licence to produce the Bestmann in a version similar to the Zlin Z.381 with 105 hp Walter-Minor engine. Produced for the Egyptian Air Force, the type was named Gomhouria (Republic) and subsequent versions were supplied to other Arab air forces.

One other aircraft type was produced by Bücker, the Bü 182 Kornett (Cornet) which first flew late in 1938 and therefore before the Bü 181. It was, like the Bü 181, developed from the Bü 180 in using a similar type of construction. The Kornett was an enclosed single-seat advanced training monoplane having a single 80 hp Bücker Bü M700 four-cylinder inverted inline engine. Although its performance and flying qualities were good, it was not ordered by the Luftwaffe and only a few examples were built.

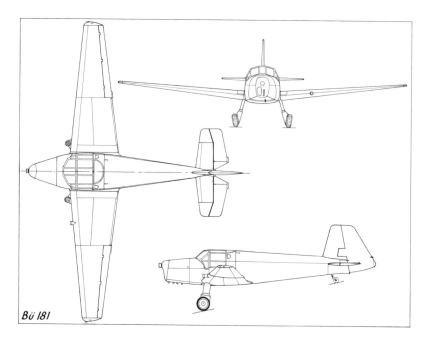

Bü 181

Bü 181A: Span 10·6 m (34 ft 9 in); length 7·85 m (25 ft 9 in); height 2·06 m (6 ft 9⅛ in); wing area 13·5 sq m (145·3 sq ft).
Empty weight 480 kg (1,056 lb); loaded weight 750 kg (1,650 lb).
Maximum speed at sea level 215 km/h (133 mph); cruising speed 195 km/h (121 mph); landing speed 80 km/h (50 mph); climb to 1,000 m (3,280 ft) 5·3 min; service ceiling 5,000 m (16,400 ft); range 800 km (497 miles).

# DFS 54

The original work of the Deutsches Forschungsinstitut für Segelflug (German Gliding Research Institute), or DFS, dealt with the construction and employment of gliders. Interest in this work was maintained by the DFS throughout most of the war years despite an ever-increasing variety of aeronautical research programmes undertaken. In the last few years before 1939, heights reached by ordinary sailplanes were considerably increased but an altitude of 11,600 m (38,050 ft) was the limit set when the pilot simply wore an oxygen mask. It was, of course, realized that thermals carrying the sailplane aloft extended considerably higher than this limit.

In the autumn of 1940, therefore, the DFS studied the problems

96

involved in building a high-altitude sailplane with pressurized cabin, and the main problem was found to be that of reconciling high aerodynamic efficiency, low weight and wing loading with a sturdy pressure cabin. Thus, the need for a light-weight pressure cabin was fundamental and, when tests showed that such a cabin could be made from wood, design work went ahead on the high-altitude sailplane designated DFS 54. Although development work was complete and construction of a mockup was about 80 per cent complete, due to the war situation the project was abandoned for other work. Most parts were to hand for the building of a prototype, but certain design features of the DFS 54 would soon have been obsolete in the light of the DFS 228. The RLM '8' number 54 was re-issued in 1941 for Nagler-Rolz helicopters.

# DFS 228

In 1940, the DFS planned an ambitious research programme concerned with investigating supersonic flight which it was realized could be most easily achieved at high altitude, given the power of German rocket motors then in existence. In order methodically to achieve a solution to all the problems involved it was decided to divide the programme into three parts. The first was concerned with development and testing of the pressure cabin, the emergency pilot-rescue equipment and the performance of the rocket unit at high altitudes, for which purpose the subsonic DFS 228 was designed; the second part was to investigate the performance and characteristics of sweptback wings with various versions of the projected aircraft, the P.1068; and the third part of the programme was to build an actual supersonic aircraft, the DFS 346. The P.1068 and DFS 346 projects are described on page 636.

Approaching for a skid landing, this rocket-powered DFS 228 V1 was built for high-altitude research and (ultimately) reconnaissance. Remarkable in many ways, it foreshadowed the turbojet-powered American Lockheed U-2 which achieved unwelcome fame in the 1950s.

Working on the basis of DFS information, the technical department of the RLM requested in 1941 that the DFS 228 be planned for high-altitude reconnaissance in addition to its research purpose, but the required range and fuel load made the design work particularly difficult. The operational plan was that the DFS 228 should be towed or carried to an altitude of about 10,000 m (32,800 ft), released near the reconnaissance zone, where the rocket would be ignited until the aircraft reached 23,000 m (75,440 ft). By alternately gliding and then climbing again under rocket power, it was estimated that this altitude could be maintained for about 45 minutes until the rocket propellants were exhausted, when the aircraft, after the reconnaissance photographs had been taken, would make a long glide back to base. Depending on thermal current conditions, it was estimated that the DFS 228 would travel a total distance of about 1,050 km (652 miles) when released from its parent aircraft.

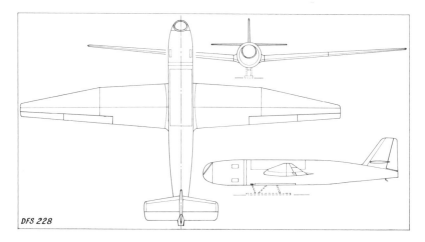

DFS 228

Due to the difficulties of design and the general pressure of other work, the first prototype of the DFS 228, the V1 D-IBFQ, was not completed until 1943. Its airframe and pressure cabin, and that of the subsequent V2 aircraft, were built by the DFS, but the landing skid and control sections were produced by Schmetz of Herzogenrath. The design was a very clean mid-wing monoplane with a single vertical fin and rudder and the horizontal tail surfaces were attached near the base of the fin. The wing, which had an aspect ratio of 9·5 and considerable dihedral, was fitted with wide-span divided ailerons, the inner sections of which acted as flaps during landings, and there were also lift spoilers on the upper and beneath the lower surfaces. Wood construction was used wherever possible in the airframe, the wing having a single, laminated wooden spar with wooden ribs and plywood skinning.

Despite the previous belief that a pressure cabin could be constructed from wood, a metal pressure cabin was built for the DFS 228. This cabin

98

comprised the nose section only and was of double-walled construction with aluminium foil insulation between the inner and outer walls. Inside the cabin a pressure equivalent of 8,000 m (26,240 ft) was intended to be maintained up to about 25,000 m (82,000 ft) and an air-conditioning unit controlled temperature and humidity. In the DFS 228 V1 the pilot sat on a conventional seat behind a small hemispherical Plexiglas (safety glass) nose panel and small side panels, these panels being double-walled and provided with hot-air circulation to prevent frosting. For emergency escapes, the entire self-contained nose section was detached from the aircraft by firing four explosive bolts connected to the cabin rear bulkhead, and a parachute deployed to stabilize and decelerate the nose section. At a predetermined altitude, the pilot's seat was ejected by compressed air, and he then made a normal parachute descent.

The rocket motor intended for the DFS 228 was the Walter 109-509A-1 fuelled by C-Stoff and T-Stoff to give a step-controlled thrust from 300 to 1,500 kg (660 to 3,300 lb). This rocket worked on the so-called hot system, used regenerative cooling for the combustion chamber and was the type first used in the Messerschmitt Me 163B-0. The main section of the rocket unit, comprising the framework with steam generator, turbine, pumps, control valves and electrics, was attached to a bulkhead in the fuselage centre section immediately aft of the propellant tanks, and the thrust tube and propellant piping led aft to the combustion chamber in the tail.

Trials with the DFS 228 V1 were made by the DFS at Hörsching and by Erprobungsstelle Rechlin. In these tests, the DFS 228 V1 was carried above the Dornier Do 217K V3 but, although some 40 flights were made, no testing of the rocket unit was done. However, these flights brought to light the inadequacies of the pilot's cabin, in that the safety installations were insufficient and it proved extremely difficult to seal the cabin sufficiently because of the large area involved. The decision was therefore made to position the pilot on a horizontal couch. This new arrangement offered two main advantages. First, the prone position allowed for a smaller, more-easily sealed pressure cabin inside the nose and, second, much of the stress was removed from the cabin walls by attaching the rear of the pilot's couch only to the main bulkhead aft. The new cabin design was incorporated into the DFS 228 V2 which was tested without rocket power but was eventually destroyed at Hörsching in May 1945 leaving only parts of the cabin worthy of salvage.

Plans were made to construct further aircraft, including two by the Wrede company at Freilassing. For these two, which were not even started, the DFS designed another new metal pressure cabin which was developed by Henschel. At the end of the war, only the DFS 228 V1 survived, at Ainring, and this aircraft was removed by the Americans for examination.

Apart from the early troubles with the pressure cabin, the chief faults found with the DFS 228 in its gliding trials were that aileron effectiveness was poor at high altitude while the elevators were abnormally sensitive, but the general handling was satisfactory and good control harmony was not essential to the aircraft's rôle. On the question of powered flight, however, there appear to be grounds to believe that the proposed Walter rocket unit would have been unsuitable for the intended high altitude operation, even given that the 109-509A-2 rocket was an improvement on the A-1 model. Although this type of rocket unit was fitted, for example, to the Messerschmitt Me 163B-1a Komet interceptor and operated at altitudes where the temperature was about $-56°$ C, they were rarely operated intermittently and were never airborne for more than 15 minutes. For the DFS 228, the rocket unit had to work in similar temperatures but was also required for intermittent operation for much longer periods and greater altitudes in the reconnaissance rôle. Thus, apart from on short research flights, rigorous demands would have been made on the motor's valves and pumps and, for long operations, it seems likely that either special heating arrangements or a new type of rocket unit would have been necessary. Suitable new rockets were possible, developed along the lines of, for example, the later Schmidding system using M-Stoff (methanol) fuel and gaseous A-Stoff (oxygen) which needed no propellant pumps and could easily operate at temperatures down to $-70°$ C.

It is not known how effective the emergency pilot-rescue arrangements were. The following data include estimated performance figures.

DFS 228 V1: Span 17·56 m (57 ft 7¼ in); length 10·58 m (34 ft 8½ in); wing area 30 sq m (323 sq ft).

Empty weight 1,650 kg (3,638 lb); loaded weight 4,200 kg (9,261 lb).

Maximum speed at 10,000 m (32,800 ft) 900 km/h (559 mph); release altitude from parent aircraft 10,000 m (32,800 ft); service ceiling 23,000 m (75,440 ft); absolute ceiling 25,000 m (82,000 ft); maximum range about 1,050 km (652 miles).

# DFS 230

In 1932 the Rhön-Rossitten-Gesellschaft built an experimental glider with high aspect ratio wings for meteorological research. Development of the glider passed to the DFS when that institute took over the company's work in 1933. Udet became very interested in the aircraft after seeing it flying at Darmstadt and, following a conversation with Ritter von Greim (*see below*), a contract was placed for the development of a military version, the DFS 230.

The DFS 230 was designed by Hans Jacobs and was test flown by Flugkapitän Hanna Reitsch, Germany's famous woman pilot, with a Ju 52/3m as the towing aircraft. The DFS 230 had a square box-like fuselage

100

An early prototype DFS 230 after landing in the snow. This aircraft is almost certainly the first prototype. (*H. Redemann*)

structure, shoulder wing and a jettisonable wheeled undercarriage. The glider was first tested without load and then gradually more and more weight was added until it was proved that the craft could carry a full military load, of eight heavily-armed troops.

In 1937 the DFS 230 was demonstrated before a gathering of senior officers including Gen Robert Ritter von Greim who later commanded Luftflotte 2, Kesselring, Model, Udet, and Milch. Hanna Reitsch cast off from the Ju 52/3m at about 1,000 m (3,280 ft), dived the DFS 230 and landed virtually at the feet of the officers. Within seconds eight soldiers had disembarked and taken up their positions. These trials were followed by a series of towing demonstrations and were so successful that a contract was placed for a batch of DFS 230A production aircraft to be built by the Gothaer Waggonfabrik.

During the autumn of 1938 a small glider assault command was formed under Leutnant Weiss, and it was found that the use of glider-borne troops had many advantages over those dropped by parachute. Their approach was silent, they were not dispersed and they did not have to spend precious time extricating themselves from cumbersome parachutes.

The world's first operational use of glider-borne troops came on 10 May, 1940, with the capture of the Belgian fort of Eben-Emael which occupied a strategic position on the Albert Canal. By 04.35 hr that morning, forty-one Ju 52/3ms took-off from Cologne-Ostheim and Cologne-Butzweilerhof airfields, each towing a DFS 230 glider. The force, from

A DFS 230A-1 glider transport in flight. A dual-control version, the DFS 230A-2, was also built in small numbers.

101

Sturm-Abteilung Koch, was in four groups, each of which was given a specific task. The most important mission was that allocated to 'Granite' section under Oblt Witzig, entrusted with the demolition of the outer fortifications. The other groups were each entrusted with the capture of a bridge over the canal.

Only nine of the 11 gliders from the 'Granite' section actually reached the target, but these landed among the bewildered Belgian troops and held the position until the arrival of German ground forces at 07.00 hr on 11 May. Total losses of the 'Granite' section were six killed and 20 wounded.

The next major operation in which the DFS 230 took part was the invasion of Crete in May 1941. The attack was led by fifty-three DFS 230 gliders from I.Bataillon/Luftlande-Sturmregiment commanded by Maj Walter Koch. The Staff of I.Bataillon landed near Maleme airfield, but the gliders were scattered owing to the rocky terrain. Then, during an attempt to capture Hill 107 which dominated the airfield, Maj Koch was seriously wounded and several of his men killed.

The DFS 230B-1 under tow just before jettisoning its wheeled take-off dolly. (*F. Selinger*)

Another group of gliders led by Gen Lt Wilhelm Süssmann, commander of 7. Fliegerdivision, was given the task of capturing the town of Canea. Soon after take-off a Heinkel He 111 bomber passed so close to Gen Süssmann's DFS 230 that the towing cable snapped and the glider was forced into a wild manoeuvre. Within seconds the wings had disintegrated and Süssmann plunged to his death. When the other gliders landed at Canea their troops suffered heavily and it was only desperate hand-to-hand fighting that finally captured the island from the Allies. Despite heavy losses the Crete operation was successful although such an operation was never again attempted.

Perhaps the most notable operation in which the DFS 230 took part was the rescue of Benito Mussolini from his mountain prison in the Abruzzi. During the afternoon of 12 September, 1943, twelve DFS 230C-1s led by Otto Skorzeny crash-landed on a tiny strip of land just in front of the Rifugio Hotel in which Mussolini was imprisoned. The Italian guards, taken by surprise, capitulated without resistance and Mussolini was flown out in a Fieseler Storch.

Several variants of the DFS 230 were produced. The DFS 230B-1 was fitted with a braking parachute; the DFS 230C-1 had three braking rockets fitted in the nose; and the final variant, the DFS 230F-1, for which the

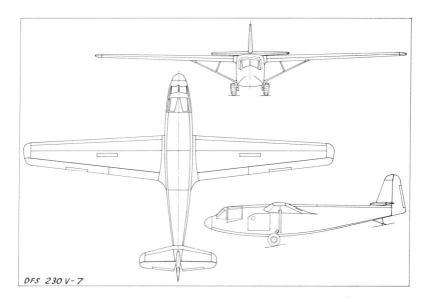

DFS 230 V-7

DFS 230 V7 was prototype, had an enlarged and more streamlined fuselage with provision for 15 troops, but no production was undertaken.

Three ATO rockets were also developed for use with the DFS 230, the Schmidding 109-593 which delivered 750 kg (1,654 lb) of thrust for four seconds, and the Rheinmetall-Borsig 109-505 and 109-515 which produced respectively 500 kg (1,102 lb) and 1,000 kg (2,205 lb) thrust, both for a period of six seconds. Production of the DFS 230 between 1938 and 1941 was 1,022 aircraft.

*Wartime operational units:* Schleppgruppe 1, 2 and 3, LLG 1 and LLG 2.

DFS 230A-1: Span 20·87 m (68 ft 5½ in); length 11·24 m (36 ft 10½ in); height 2·74 m (9 ft); wing area 41·3 sq m (444·55 sq ft).

Empty weight 860 kg (1,896 lb); loaded weight 2,100 kg (4,630 lb).

Maximum diving speed 290 km/h (180 mph); maximum towing speed 210 km/h (130 mph).

# DFS 331

The design of the DFS 331 cargo glider is believed to have been undertaken during 1940 when the DFS was forced to revert for a time from advanced research to conventional glider work. Also co-operating in the work was the Gothaer Waggonfabrik but only the DFS 331 V1 prototype was built and no production undertaken. The main features of the DFS

This DFS 331 V1 was the sole example of this cargo glider. Note the aerofoil profile of the square-sectioned fuselage.

331 V1 were a square-section fuselage with an aerofoil profile to generate some of the lift, a fully-glazed nose, and a pair of sprung landing skids which were attached by their front ends very near the front of the fuselage. Far forward on the port side was a loading door of the largest possible size and this made it necessary to position the pilot on a raised platform offset to port and covered by a bubble-type canopy. The shoulder-mounted strut-braced wings were of equi-taper planform, had considerable dihedral and the usual lift-spoilers. The braced tailplane was raised above the fuselage and carried twin fins and rudders.

DFS 331 V1: Span 23 m (75 ft 5½ in); length 15·81 m (51 ft 10⅜ in); height 3·55 m (11 ft 7¾ in); wing area 60 sq m (645·6 sq ft).
Empty weight 2,270 kg (5,005 lb); loaded weight 4,770 kg (10,518 lb).
Speed at 1:18 gliding angle 270 km/h (168 mph).

# DFS 332

The DFS 332 was designed to be used as a research aircraft to investigate various wing profiles in free flight. The need arose because of the limiting factors of working with small-scale model sections in wind tunnels and also because of a growing need to work with Reynolds numbers without applying estimated correction factors to allow for wind tunnel effects. Objectives of the design were that measurements of aerodynamic loads, pressure distribution, effects of CG movement, and drag, could be measured on a given wing test section flying at a constant speed and at varying angles of attack. An important point governing the aircraft layout was that the wing test section should be in the plane of symmetry of the aircraft in order to avoid disturbing influences such as cross-flow on the wing, and this requirement led to a tailless aircraft with two fuselages having fixed outer wing panels and the test wing between the two fuselages.

The centre test wing was built around a dural box spar which carried all the loads between the two fuselages and could be rotated by an electric motor to alter the angle of incidence of the test wing by up to 20 deg in relation to the outer wings. Three different box spars were designed to carry test wings of 9, 12, and 15 per cent thickness/chord ratio, and wooden ribs were screwed to the spar and then covered with plywood. The dimensions of the test wing were standardized in planform at 4·5 m (14 ft 9$\frac{1}{8}$ in) span by 3·6 m (11 ft 9$\frac{3}{4}$ in) chord. To take pressure measurements there were some 80 to 90 holes in each wing test section and connections made to manometer valves in the port fuselage where a camera continuously recorded the readings. To determine the loss of impulse, and hence the test wing profile drag, a test rake was situated behind the wing (following typical German wind tunnel practice) and this was also photographed. The pilot of the DFS 332 sat in the starboard fuselage and an observer sat in the port.

A typical test flight with the DFS 332 was that it should be towed to a height of 6,000 m (19,680 ft), released and then put into a gliding dive until the desired speed was reached. The aircraft was then to be levelled off and the test speed maintained constant by the use of two controllable-thrust Walter RII-203 rocket motors using T-Stoff propellant decomposed by Z-Stoff (calcium or sodium permanganate) catalyst on the so-called cold principle. These motors were to be calibrated to give a maximum thrust of 650 kg (1,430 lb) each and the normal level flight speed was to be 500 km/h (310 mph). The original choice of the RII-203 rocket motor (which was tested in the Messerschmitt Me 163 V1) dates the conception of the DFS 332 to the latter half of 1941, but it is fairly certain that improved Walter rocket motors were selected later in place of the early, unreliable RII-203 type.

The DFS 332, however, was destined never to fly. Wrede at Freilassing made the control surfaces and fuselage covering, while Caudron in Paris made the steel tubing parts and the dural spar for the 15 per cent thick test wing. Due to spasmodic deliveries, the first DFS 332 was not fully completed at Prien and the rocket motors were not fitted. In the autumn of 1944 the DFS made a new request to the RLM for a requisition permit to cover the construction of a second DFS 332 and also for dural spars for the 9 and 12 per cent thick test wings. The parts for this second aircraft were finished, but transport difficulties prevented deliveries from the various sub-contractors, although the rocket motors did arrive.

DFS 332: Span 14·98 m (49 ft 1¼ in); length 12·24 m (40 ft 1⅞ in); wing area 33·5 sq m (360·4 sq ft). Typical towed release height 6,000 m (19,680 ft); typical level speed 500 km/h (310 mph).

# Dornier Do 17

Until the appearance of the Do 17, the name of Dornier had always been associated with the Komet and Merkur transports and the development of superb flying-boats. It was in fact an accident that produced what was to become one of the most famous bombers of the Second World War, and certainly one of the most attractive.

In 1933 Lufthansa issued a requirement for a high-speed mailplane capable of carrying six passengers. In answer, towards the end of 1934, Dornier produced the beautiful Do 17 V1. The aircraft had an exceptionally slim fuselage with a shoulder-mounted wing and a single fin and rudder, and was of all-metal construction with metal skinning to the fuselage, and mixed metal and fabric covering to the wing.

Three prototypes of the aircraft were completed during 1934, all being powered by 660 hp BMW VI engines. These were passed to Lufthansa for evaluation in 1935, but, despite their exceptional performance, were rejected because it was found that passengers would find it very difficult to enter the two very small cabins. The three aircraft were therefore returned to Dornier and were stored in a hangar at Löwenthal.

Here, in all probability, they would have remained had it not been for the resourcefulness of Flugkapitän Robert Untucht who acted as liaison officer between Lufthansa and the RLM. Discovering the prototypes in their hangar, Untucht asked to fly one of them and was so impressed that he suggested that the Do 17 should be used as a bomber. Untucht had previously gained eight international records during the spring of 1933 while flying the Heinkel He 70 V2 D-2537, and was killed

The Dornier Do 17 V1 was designed as a high-speed passenger-carrying mailplane for Lufthansa. (*F. Selinger*)

when the Junkers Ju 90 V2, D-AIVI, crashed at Bathurst in November 1938.

During the late summer of 1935, the Do 17 V4 made its first flight. This aircraft differed from the first three prototypes in being shorter and in having twin fins and rudders and a radio operator's cabin aft of the cockpit. The Do 17 V6 was similar to the V4, but the V5 was powered by two 860 hp Hispano Suiza 12Ybrs twelve-cylinder liquid-cooled engines. The Do 17 V7 was fitted with a single 7·9 mm aft-firing MG 15 machine-gun in a blister above and behind the cockpit. The V8, described below, was retained by Dornier.

The first production model was the Do 17E-1 for which the V9 D-AHAK acted as prototype. This aircraft had a shortened and extensively glazed fuselage nose, enlarged vertical tail surfaces and an aerodynamically refined dorsal gun blister. The Do 17 V10 D-AKUZ was used to test the 750 hp BMW VI 7·3 engines, but was otherwise similar to the V6.

The Do 17E-1 bomber and F-1 reconnaissance aircraft were both similar to the V9, the former carrying a 500 kg (1,102 lb) bomb load, the latter fitted with two cameras and increased fuel tankage.

In the spring of 1937 fifteen Do 17F-1s were transferred from Aufkl.Gr 122 to 1.A/88 of the Condor Legion in Spain. They, and the Do 17E-1 bombers delivered to 1 and 2.K/88, proved able to evade with ease the obsolescent aircraft employed by the Republican air force.

The first public appearance of the new Dornier bomber came in July

The Do 17 V9 fitted with 1,000 hp Daimler-Benz DB 600 engines.

107

An early production Do 17E-1 carrying both civil and military markings.

1937 at the International Military Aircraft Competition held at Dübendorf near Zürich. The eighth prototype, the Do 17 V8, as the forerunner of the proposed Do 17M, had been fitted with two DB 600A engines which produced 1,000 hp for take-off. Alternatively designated Do 17M V1, and nicknamed the 'Flying Pencil', the aircraft successfully outperformed the fighters of all other nations participating in the contest.

Because of the shortage of DB 600 engines, Dornier were forced to consider an alternative powerplant for the Do 17M bomber and its contemporary Do 17P reconnaissance aircraft. Eventually the 900 hp Bramo 323A-1 radial was chosen for the Do 17M, and two prototypes powered by these engines, the Do 17 V13 and V14, were built. The Do 17 V15, first prototype for the P-series, was powered by two 865 hp BMW 132N radials and could carry two Rb 50/30 or two Rb 75/30 cameras.

The standard production Do 17M-1 was armed with three 7·9 mm MG 15 machine-guns, one protruding through the starboard windscreen, one in the rear of the dorsal position and one below the fuselage firing aft. Standard bomb load was 1,000 kg (2,205 lb). The Do 17M-1/U1 carried an inflatable dinghy in a housing forward of the dorsal gun position and the Do 17M-1/Trop and Do 17P-1/Trop were both tropical variants fitted with sand filters and desert survival equipment.

Following the successful demonstration of the Do 17M V1 at Zürich, the Yugoslav government placed an order for a similar aircraft to be powered by two licence-built 980 hp Gnome/Rhône 14N1/2 engines.

A Do 17E-1 bomber of the Luftdienst after the port undercarriage leg collapsed.
(*J. Zazvonil*)

A Do 17E-1 of 2./KG 255 which took part in the 1938 war games as part of the 'enemy' force.

The Do 17 V13 D-AYZE, the second prototype for the M-series bomber. (*F. Selinger*)

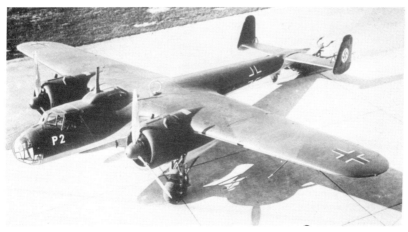

A Do 17P reconnaissance aircraft.

Essentially similar to the Do 17M V1 with an elongated glazed nose, three variants were proposed, the Do 17Kb-1 bomber and the Ka-2 and Ka-3 reconnaissance aircraft. The export versions were delivered from October 1937, and licence production was undertaken by the Drzavna Fabrika Aviona at Kraljevo early in 1940.

Work also proceeded on several experimental variants for the Luftwaffe. The Do 17 V11 and V12 (also designated L V1 and L V2) were the forerunners of the proposed Do 17L-1 pathfinder. Powered by two 900 hp Bramo 323A-1 engines, this aircraft would have carried a fourth crew member, but no production was undertaken. The Do 17R was an engine test bed, the two examples built being delivered to the Luftwaffe for Service evaluation. The Do 17R V1 D-AEEE was powered initially by two BMW VI engines but these were later replaced by two 950 hp Daimler-Benz DB 600G units. The Do 17R V2 D-ATJU was similar but was fitted with two 1,000 hp Daimler-Benz DB 601Aa units.

Experience in Spain with the Do 17 had shown that an increase in defensive armament, particularly for the underside, was desirable. Accordingly the forward fuselage was bulged to accommodate a prone gunner with a hand-held MG 15 gun firing aft. The nose was fully glazed with a series of 'beetle eye' transparent panels, and the pilot was provided with an improved all-round view. Designated Do 17S-01 and registered D-AFFY, the first variant to be fitted with this nose was essentially similar to the M-1, but was powered by two DB 600G engines. Three pre-production aircraft were built, being delivered to the Luftwaffe for Service trials.

An early production Do 17P-1 being refuelled by a mobile tanker. (*R. C. Seeley*)

The next variant was the Do 17U pathfinder which, similarly to the Do 17S, carried a second radio operator and extensive radio equipment. Three Do 17U-0 and twelve Do 17U-1 aircraft were completed, two being delivered to 7.Kompanie/Luftnachrichten-Abteilung 100 late in 1938. Ln.Abt.100 had been formed to experiment with new radio and navigational equipment, and was based at Köthen. Its two Kompanien (7. and 8.)

A number of Do 17P-1s were delivered to Aufklärungsstaffel 88 of the Condor Legion.

were redesignated as 1. and 2./KGr 100 on 18 November, 1939, the Do 17Us being transferred to the group's staff flight. The final, and most important production model, was the Do 17Z which appeared late in 1938. The Do 17Z-0 was a four-seat bomber with a similar nose section to that introduced in the Do 17S, but powered by two 900 hp Bramo 323A-1 radials. The Do 17Z-0 carried three MG 15 machine-guns, but the Z-1 production aircraft was fitted with a fourth weapon firing through the nose. Although retaining the delightful handling characteristics of the previous variants, the Do 17Z-1 was underpowered, and the bomb load had to be reduced to a mere 500 kg (1,102 lb).

The Do 17Z-2 was powered by two 1,000 hp Bramo 323P engines and again carried the 1,000 kg (2,205 lb) bomb load, could carry a fifth crew member, and defensive armament was often increased to as many as eight MG 15 machine-guns. The Do 17Z-3 was a photographic reconnaissance variant with two Rb 20/30 cameras installed in the entry hatch and had provision for a 500 kg bomb load. The Do 17Z-4 was a dual control trainer variant, and the Do 17Z-5 was similar to the Z-1 but was fitted with special inflatable flotation bags and other survival equipment in the event of an enforced alighting on the sea. Total production of the Do 17 was in the region of 1,700.

Following night-bombing attacks by the RAF, consideration was given in Germany to the conversion of several bomber aircraft to the night fighting rôle. A standard Do 17Z-3 was taken from the production line and had its nose replaced by one from a Junkers Ju 88C-2 fighter. Redesignated Do 17Z-6 Kauz I (Screech-owl I), the marriage of the two airframes was not successful and the variant was abandoned in favour of the Do 17Z-10 Kauz II. This was fitted with a specially redesigned nose which carried four 7·9 mm MG 17 machine-guns, and two 20 mm MG FF cannon, the breeches of which were accessible from the cockpit for reloading. The infra-red detection device (Spanner-Anlage) was fitted, this being used in conjunction with a Q-Rohr sighting screen. Only nine Do 17Z-10s were completed, these serving for a short period late in 1940 with I./NJG 2 under Hptm Heyse.

The invasion of Poland began with an attack on the Dirschau railway bridge by a squadron of Do 17Z-2s from III./KG 3 on 1 September, 1939. Poor weather hampered early operations, but on that day, KG 77

111

The Do 17Z-1 could easily be distinguished from early versions of the bomber by its extensively glazed cockpit. (*H. Obert*)

succeeded in bombing Cracow, Krosno and Moderowka; KG 76 struck at Kielce, Lodz, Radom, Skierniewice, Tomaszow and Tschenstochau, and KG 2 attacked Biala-Podlaska, Lida and Plozk. Subsequent operations were directed against airfields, troop concentrations and ammunition dumps, but KG 77 did take part in the bombing of Warsaw on 25 September.

On 2 December, 1939, the Luftwaffe was recorded as having 493 Do 17s operational, a total which comprised 12 Do 17Fs, 41 Do 17Ms, 83 Do 17Ps, the two Do 17Rs, the three Do 17S-0s and 352 Do 17Zs. The only Do 17 unit to take part in the Norwegian campaign was 1.(F)/120 based at Lübeck-Blankensee and later Stavanger-Sola.

On 10 May, 1940, Germany invaded France and the Low Countries. The Do 17Zs which equipped KG 2, KG 3, KG 76, KG 77 and KGr 606, struck at Allied communications and airfields, destroying many aircraft before they could leave the ground. The invasion proceeded swiftly, Wehrmacht forces reaching the Somme by 18 May. Nine days later, British forces who were awaiting evacuation from Dunkirk were heavily bombed by the Do 17Zs of KG 2 and KG 3.

Following the successful conclusion of the French campaign, the Luftwaffe turned its attentions to the British Isles. Do 17Z bombers now equipped only nine Kampfgruppen: I., II. and III./KG 2, I., II. and III./KG 3, I. and III./KG 76 and KGr 606. Both II./KG 76 and KG 77 had converted to the Junkers Ju 88A-1, and the Do 17 was also rapidly disappearing from the ranks of the Aufklärungsgruppen.

The first phase of the attack on the British Isles began with an attempt to block the English Channel to Allied shipping. A force of bombers from

KG 2 and two Stuka-Gruppen were placed under the command of the Geschwader-Kommodore of KG 2, Oberst Johannes Fink, who was appointed Kanalkampfführer. The first attack came on 10 July when twenty Do 17Z-2s from KG 2 bombed a convoy off Dover. On 15 July a force of fifteen Do 17s attempted to bomb another convoy in the Channel but were driven off by Hurricanes from Nos. 56 and 151 Squadrons. Attacks on shipping continued until 12 August, 1940, when KG 2 attacked Manston, dropping 150 bombs and putting the airfield out of action for a day. Next day, two formations totalling seventy-four Do 17s from KG 2 set out to attack Eastchurch and Sheerness. The first group led by Fink severely damaged Eastchurch, but lost four Do 17s. The rear formation was intercepted before reaching Sheerness and was repulsed.

On 15 August, KG 3 under Oberst Wolfgang Chamier-Glisczinski took-off to attack Eastchurch and Rochester, and next day West Malling was bombed by Do 17s from KG 76. On 18 August, KG 76 bombed

Close-up of the 'beetle eye' glazed nose fitted to the Do 17Z-series.

Kenley and Biggin Hill, only two aircraft from 9.Staffel returning unscathed. Eight days later, a combined force from KG 2 and KG 3 set out to bomb North Weald and Hornchurch. Apart from one Staffel which damaged Debden, the aircraft were turned back by Allied fighters. The same two units, in concert with Heinkel He 111s from KG 26 and KG 53, set oil tanks on fire at Thameshaven on 5 September, and two days later London was bombed by 625 aircraft.

By January 1941, only I., II. and III./KG 2, III./KG 3 and KGr 606 were still equipped with the Do 17. On 6 April, 1941, the first four

113

Two Do 17Z-2 bombers parked on a Luftwaffe airfield during the Polish campaign. (*R. C. Seeley*)

Gruppen mentioned took part in the invasion of Greece and Yugoslavia, and some two and a half months later the same units joined Operation Barbarossa, the attack on the Soviet Union. During August, both II. and III./KG 2 began to re-equip with the new Do 217E, and by the end of the year the whole Geschwader had converted to the new type.

In October 1941, III./KG 3 was joined by 10.(Croat)/KG 3, a unit made up of Croatian volunteers. When III./KG 3 re-equipped with the Ju 88, its aircraft were transferred to the Croatian Staffel, but the latter was withdrawn after a short time. It returned in July 1942 as 15.(Croat)/KG 53, remaining operational until November 1942 on the Eastern Front. The final units to use the Do 17 operationally were the four Nachtaufklärungs-staffeln which re-equipped with Do 217s in 1942.

*Wartime operational units:* 3.(F)/10, 2., 3. and 4.(F)/11, 1.(H)/13, 4.(F)/14, 2. and 3.(F)/22, 3.(F)/31, 1. (F)/120, 1., 2., 3. and 4.(F)/121, 1., 2., 3. and 5.(F)/122, 1., 2. and 3.(F)/123, 1.(F)/124, 1., 2., 3. and 4./Nachtaufklärungsstaffeln, 7. and 8.(F)/LG 2., 3. and 4./NJG 1, KG 2, 3, 15.(Croat)/KG 53, KG 76, KG 77, KGr 100 and KGr 606. Also used in small numbers by the staff flights of St.G 1, 2, 3, 51, 76 and 77.

Do 17M-1: Span 18 m (59 ft 0$\frac{2}{3}$ in); length 16·1 m (52 ft 9$\frac{1}{4}$ in); height 4·55 m (14 ft 11$\frac{1}{4}$ in); wing area 55 sq m (592·014 sq ft).
Empty weight 5,160 kg (11,377 lb); loaded weight 8,000 kg (17,640 lb).
Maximum speed at sea level 345 km/h (214 mph), at 4,000 m (13,124 ft) 410 km/h (255 mph); cruising speed at 3,000 m (9,843 ft) 350 km/h (218 mph); service ceiling 7,000 m (22,967 ft); normal tactical range 500 km (311 miles); maximum range 1,360 km (845 miles).

Do 17Z-2: Span 18 m (59 ft 0$\frac{2}{3}$ in); length 15·79 m (51 ft 9$\frac{2}{3}$ in); height 4·55 m (14 ft 11$\frac{1}{4}$ in); wing area 55 sq m (592·014 sq ft).
Empty weight 5,210 kg (11,488 lb); maximum loaded weight 8,590 kg (18,940 lb).
Maximum speed at sea level 345 km/h (214 mph), at 4,000 ft (13,124 ft) 410 km/h (255 mph); cruising speed at 4,000 m (13,124 ft) 300 km/h (186 mph); service ceiling 8,200 m (26,904 ft); normal tactical range 330 km (205 miles); maximum range 1,160 km (721 miles).

# Dornier Do 18

The Do 18 flying-boat, ordered in 1934 by Deutsche Lufthansa to replace the Dornier Wal, was of similar layout but aerodynamically improved. Possessing clean aerodynamic and hydrodynamic lines, the Do 18 had an all-metal structure with metal skin except for fabric covering over the wings. The low aspect ratio wing was high-mounted on a pylon and braced to the so-called Stummel sponsons which projected from the hull sides to give lateral stability on the water in place of wing-floats. Also mounted on the wing pylon was a single streamlined nacelle which housed two engines in tandem driving a tractor and a pusher airscrew. Since the aircraft was required for long transoceanic flights, particularly to carry mail across the Atlantic, the crew comprised two pilots in addition to a radio-operator and an engineer. The crew was accommodated forward, and the mail compartment and four fuel tanks with a total of 3,920 litres (862·4 gallons) capacity were amidship.

On 15 March, 1935, the Do 18 V1 D-AHIS *Monsun*, powered by two 540 hp Junkers Jumo 5 Diesel engines, made its maiden flight. Beginning in 1936, DLH received four more aircraft, D-AANE *Zyklon* (Do 18 V2 c/n 677), D-ABYM *Aeolus* (Do 18 V3 c/n 661), D-AROZ *Pampero* (c/n 255) and D-ARUN *Zephir* (c/n 663). They were fitted with 600 hp Junkers Jumo 205C Diesel engines and received the designation Do 18E. The sixth and last machine delivered to DLH was a special equipment-testing aircraft, D-ANHR, designated Do 18F, which first flew on 11 June, 1937. This aircraft was heavier and had a greater wing area than the previous versions, and it established a new straight-line nonstop distance record for seaplanes of 8,392 km (5,214 miles) in 43 hours on 27–29

Six Dornier Do 18s were delivered to Deutsche Lufthansa by 1937, chiefly to carry transatlantic mail. The last delivered was the Do 18F D-ANHR, illustrated, which established a new distance record for seaplanes in March 1938. (*Lufthansa*)

115

Principal user of the Do 18 was the Luftwaffe. The prototype of the first military variant, D-AJII, the Do 18D, is seen here. (*R. C. Seeley*)

An operational Do 18D being launched.

A Do 18D of 2./Kü.Fl.Gr.406 under tow. (*F. Selinger*)

March, 1938. The same aircraft was later redesignated Do 18L when fitted with two 880 hp BMW 132N radial engines with which it first flew on 21 November, 1939. Both versions could be catapult-launched.

Although DLH was the first to use the Do 18, the type's principal rôle was with the Luftwaffe which also acquired it to replace the Dornier Wal 32 and 33 flying-boats. The first military variant, the Do 18D, was operational by September 1938. This type, which was in production as the Do 18D-1 and D-2, was powered by two Jumo 205C engines and carried a crew of four. Armament consisted of a single 7·9 mm MG machine-gun in an open bow position and a similar gun behind the wing in an open hull position. During 1939, the D version was supplanted in production by the Do 18G-1 which had more powerful 880 hp Jumo 205D engines and heavier armament comprising a single 13 mm MG 131 machine-gun in the bow position and a single 20 mm MG 151 cannon in a new, power-operated, hull turret.

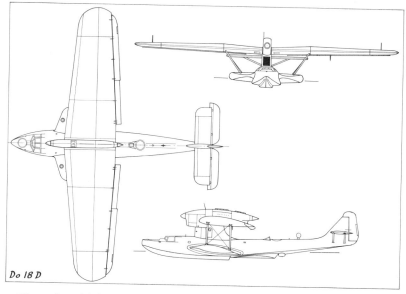

Do 18 D

The units which operated the Do 18 were normally, but not always, the second Staffel of the Küstenfliegergruppen, which undertook coastal reconnaissance work. The first Luftwaffe aircraft to become a victim of any of the British services was, in fact, a Do 18 (of 2./Kü.Fl.Gr. 106) which was destroyed by a Blackburn Skua of No. 803 Squadron from HMS *Ark Royal*. This occurred on 26 September, 1939, when three Do 18s were shadowing *Ark Royal* steaming in company with the battleships HMS *Rodney* and *Nelson*. Nine Skuas attacked the Dorniers but, although hits were scored, two of the flying-boats made their escape. The third flying-boat was forced down by Lieut B. S. McEwen and was eventually sunk by HMS *Somali* after the four crew members had been taken on board.

Two Do 18Ds of 2./Kü.Fl.Gr.306 (later, 3./406) at Wilhelmshaven in October 1939. (*F. Selinger*)

For the Battle of France, units operational with the Do 18 were 2./Kü.Fl.Gr. 106, 1., 2. and 3./Kü.Fl.Gr. 406, and 2./Kü.Fl.Gr. 906, but, during the Battle of Britain, only 2./Kü.Fl.Gr. 106 was operational. Before the middle of 1942, by which time the Do 18 was replaced by the Blohm und Voss Bv 138, the third Staffel of Kü.Fl.Gr. 906 was also operating the Do 18. For training, a few Do 18Hs were produced which were little different from the operational aircraft apart from having dual controls and lacking armament.

By about September 1939, production of the Do 18 had ceased after just over 100 had been built, including about 70 of the Do 18G type. However, a new version was created during 1941–42 by modifying some of the Do 18Gs as they were replaced in the Küstenfliegergruppen. These modified flying-boats, which were designated Do 18N-1, carried no armament and were fitted with air-sea rescue equipment to work with the Seenotstaffeln (air-sea rescue squadrons). They carried Red Cross markings, in accordance with the Geneva Convention, in order to operate unscathed, but it was alleged that they were sometimes used for clandestine military duties.

*Wartime operational units:* 2./Kü.Fl.Gr 106, 1., 2. and 3./Kü.Fl.Gr 406, 2. and 3./Kü.Fl.Gr 906.

Do 18G-1: Span 23·7 m (77 ft 9 in); length 19·25 m (63 ft 2 in); wing area 97·5 sq m (1,049·1 sq ft).

Empty weight 5,850 kg (12,900 lb); loaded weight 10,000 kg (22,050 lb).

Maximum speed at sea level 260 km/h (162 mph); cruising speed 220 km/h (137 mph); alighting speed 90 km/h (56 mph); climb to 1,000 m (3,280 ft) 7·9 min; service ceiling 4,200 m (13,776 ft); maximum range 3,500 km (2,174 miles).

# Dornier Do 22

The Dornier Do 22 was designed in 1934 under the initial designation Do C3 as a three-seat utility floatplane for reconnaissance and light attack duties. Development was undertaken at Altenrhein in Switzerland by Dornier-Werke AG, which built two prototypes but subsequently left production to Dornier's Friedrichshafen plant in Germany. Although the official designation of Do 22 was issued, the type was not ordered for the Luftwaffe and permission was eventually granted to solicit orders for it elsewhere. Buyers were therefore found in Greece, Latvia, and Yugoslavia, for a small number of Do 22s, and the first production aircraft flew on 15 July, 1938.

The Do 22 was powered by a single 860 hp Hispano-Suiza 12Ybrs twelve-cylinder vee liquid-cooled engine driving a three-blade airscrew although at least one of the two prototypes had a four-blade airscrew. The parallel-chord wing had $7\frac{1}{2}$ deg sweepback and was attached slightly above the fuselage by short struts, and the single-step twin floats were braced to both the fuselage and the wing. The rudder was dynamically balanced in the normal way but the elevators were linked to and moved small control surfaces mounted above the fixed tailplane. Metal construction with fabric covering was used throughout, except for the forward part of the fuselage which was metal covered. The pilot and gunner were accommodated in open cockpits, but the radio/camera operator, seated in the forward half of the gunner's cockpit, was partially enclosed by a bubble windscreen. A single torpedo or small bomb load could be carried beneath the fuselage, and typical armament comprised four 7·9 mm machine-guns, these being disposed two for the rear cockpit, one above the engine and one protruding from the rear of the shallow ventral fuselage step.

The various floatplanes were designated Do 22Kg for Greece, Do 22Kj

The Dornier Do 22 utility floatplane was not ordered for the Luftwaffe but exported. Here, a Do 22Kj for Jugoslavia is seen. (*H. Thiele*)

119

A later version of the Do 22 floatplane, the Do 22L, was flown with a land undercarriage.
(*F. Selinger*)

for Yugoslavia, and Do 22Kl for Latvia. On 10 March, 1939, a landplane version, designated Do 22L, was flown. This had a non-retractable tail-wheel undercarriage with the spatted mainwheels braced in a similar manner to the floats of the seaplane, but production of the landplane seems not to have been undertaken.

When Yugoslavia was overrun, four of the 12 Do 22Kj floatplanes supplied to its naval air service were flown to Egypt in April 1941 and subsequently operated by their crews with the Allies in the Mediterranean. Four other Do 22 floatplanes were captured by the Germans in either Yugoslavia or Greece, and, from 1942, these were operated on both floats and skis by the Finnish Air Force. Only about thirty Do 22s were built.

Do 22 (float version): Span 16·2 m (53 ft 1¾ in); length 13·12 m (43 ft 0½ in); wing area 45 sq m (484·2 sq ft).

Empty weight 2,600 kg (5,734 lb); fuel and oil 800 kg (1,764 lb); crew 300 kg (661 lb); ammunition and torpedo or bombs 300 kg (661 lb); loaded weight 4,000 kg (8,820 lb).

Maximum speed at 3,000 m (9,840 ft) 350 km/h (217 mph); cruising speed at 3,000 m (9,840 ft) 310 km/h (193 mph); alighting speed 85 km/h (53 mph); climb to 5,000 m (16,400 ft) 13 min; service ceiling 9,000 m (29,520 ft); maximum range 2,300 km (1,428 miles).

# Dornier Do 24

Once flight tests of the Do 18 were under way, design work began on a similar, but larger, three-engined flying-boat to fulfil a requirement of the Royal Netherlands Naval Air Service. The Do 24 design was begun in 1935 as an all-metal flying-boat with a two-step hull and typical Dornier sponsons extending from the hull sides for lateral stability on the water. All three engines, with tractor airscrews, were carried on the tapered wing which was mounted above the hull on a system of struts. Twin fins and rudders were carried by a tailplane which was supported at about wing height by the upward-curving hull. Although the Do 24 saw its share of front-line hazards, it was chiefly employed during the war on air-sea rescue duties.

Initially, three prototypes were begun and the first flight was made on 3 July, 1937, by the Do 24 V3 D-ADLR. This aircraft was powered by three 890 hp Wright R-1820-F52 Cyclone radial engines and, as the prototype for the Do 24K, was delivered to the Netherlands late in 1937 for evaluation. After acceptance of the type, the Netherlands Navy received eleven Do 24Ks built by Weser-Flugzeugbau near Bremen and another twenty-five Do 24Ks built under licence in the Netherlands.

At the beginning of the war, only the Do 24 V1 and V2 prototypes were available in Germany. Of these the V1 was first to fly, on 10 January, 1938, and the two machines differed from the V3 primarily by having 600 hp Junkers Jumo 205 Diesel engines in nacelles with ventral radiators. The Do 24 V1 and V2 were later fitted with armament and, with the invasion of Norway in April 1940, were pressed into transport service in that campaign.

Following the defeat and occupation of Holland on 15 May, 1940, all semi-completed Do 24Ks were shipped to Germany and were equipped for

This, the Dornier Do 24 V3, was delivered for evaluation late in 1937 as the prototype of the Do 24K for the Netherlands Navy. (*H. Thiele*)

This Do 24N-1 was one of the Netherlands-built Do 24Ks modified for Luftwaffe service.
(*F. Selinger*)

air-sea rescue duties under the designation Do 24N-1. Production also continued in the Netherlands at the Aviolanda and De Schelde factories under the supervision of the Weser-Flugzeugbau, and about 170 Do 24Ts were produced before the liberation. Both T-1s and T-2s were produced, with differences in internal equipment, and both versions used the 1,000 hp BMW-Bramo 323R-2 Fafnir radial engine (later redesignated BMW 301R). The Do 24 went into Luftwaffe service with the three Seenot-staffeln (known also as 1., 2. and 3./Seenotgruppe) based at Berre (near Marseilles) and Biscarosse, and these units also operated captured examples of the antiquated Breguet 521 Bizerte three-engined biplane flying-boat on their air-sea rescue missions. 3./Seenotgruppe also used the Heinkel He 59. Other units employing the Do 24 were 2. and 3./KG 200 and probably the small air-sea rescue flights known as Seenotdienstführer units. The wartime activities of the Do 24 were quite unaggressive and never included such missions as reconnaissance and bombing, although the standard armament comprised a 20 mm MG 151 cannon in a power-operated dorsal turret and a single 7·9 mm MG 15 machine-gun in each of the bow and tail positions. There was also capacity enough to carry twelve 50 kg (110 lb) bombs or extra fuel.

Netherlands Do 24Ks were still operational in 1941 in the East Indies, but, by the end of that year, the Japanese had destroyed nine. The rest were eventually flown to Australia where another four were strafed and sunk at Broome in March 1942. Six surviving Do 24Ks were used by the RAAF (as the A-49), one of these having previously been used by the Netherlands Forces Intelligence Service until October 1943.

As more flying-boats were required by the Luftwaffe, the Chantiers Aéro-Maritimes de la Seine (CAMS) plant at Sartrouville, France, began production of the Do 24T, and, from 1942 until the liberation, this plant produced about 50 complete and semi-complete aircraft. All Do 24Ts were eventually completed, and those that did not go to the Luftwaffe during the occupation were subsequently used by the French Navy until 1953.

In the spring of 1944, Germany persuaded neutral Spain to buy twelve Do 24T-3s to augment the air-sea rescue service in the Mediterranean. The first Do 24T-3s were collected from Germany in June 1944 and were flown to the base of operations at Pollensa. The Spanish air-sea rescue group was organized by Colonel Pombo, with the first headquarters at Berre flying-boat base, and initial training was given on Arado Ar 196 floatplanes, probably with German instructors. The Spanish Do 24s (later known as HR.5s) rescued pilots of any nationality and, although none was shot down, there was always a risk that Allied aircraft would mistake their identity. At the present time, the Spanish HR.5s are still in service, albeit modernized, and will apparently continue thus until lack of spares forces their withdrawal.

In Luftwaffe service, the Do 24 was employed for air-sea rescue duties. (*R. C. Seeley*)

During the war, two German Do 24s were flown to neutral Sweden. The first (c/n 3343) was coded CM-RY and was flown to Hällevik on 31 October, 1944, by a German pilot and his Estonian girl friend! This aircraft was bought for the Swedish Air Force which designated it Tp 24. The second Do 24 (c/n 42) was coded 5W-BU and flown to Trelleborg on 9 May, 1945, with the astonishing cargo of 37 refugees. One of these flying-boats was possibly flown by a Soviet crew to the USSR in August 1945, but the other was finally scrapped by the Swedish Air Force in 1952.

Throughout the life of the Do 24, little part was played by Dornier after the initial development. There was, indeed, little development carried out, but an interesting improved version of the Do 24T-2 was built by Weser-Flugzeugbau under the designation Do 318. The new feature of this version was a wing with boundary layer suction to reduce drag and increase the range, but only one prototype was completed.

Do 24T: Span 27 m (88 ft 7 in); length 22 m (72 ft 2⅓ in); height 5·75 m (18 ft 10⅜ in); wing area 108 sq m (1,162·1 sq ft).

Empty weight 9,200 kg (20,286 lb); fuel and oil 4,200 kg (9,261 lb); loaded weight armed but without bombs 17,800 kg (39,249 lb).

Maximum speed at 3,000 m (9,840 ft) 340 km/h (211 mph); cruising speed 295 km/h (183 mph); alighting speed 122 km/h (76 mph); climb to 1,000 m (3,280 ft) 7·5 min; service ceiling 5,900 m (19,352 ft); normal range 2,900 km (1,801 miles).

The Dornier Do 26 V1, D-AGNT *Seeadler*, was the first of two such flying-boats delivered to Deutsche Lufthansa by 1939 for nonstop Atlantic mail flights. (*F. Selinger*)

# Dornier Do 26

The last of a long line of Dornier flying-boat designs to be built, the Do 26, embodied the company's extensive experience, but in layout a break was made from typical Dornier practice. The most obvious changes, made in the interests of aerodynamic refinement, were the cantilever shoulder-mounted wing and retractable stabilizing floats instead of the high-mounted braced wings and Stummel sponsons used on previous designs. Deutsche Lufthansa ordered three Do 26s in 1937 to carry mail nonstop across the North Atlantic from Lisbon to New York. For this duty, the aircraft was designed to carry a crew of four, 500 kg (1,100 lb) of mail, and 7,300 litres (1,606 gallons) of fuel to give adequate range. Passenger versions were also ordered later, but only six Do 26s were built.

On 21 May, 1938, the prototype, Do 26 V1 D-AGNT *Seeadler* (*Sea Eagle*), made its maiden flight, powered by four 600 hp Junkers Jumo 205 Diesel engines driving three-blade airscrews. The engines were mounted in tandem pairs at the ends of the dihedralled centre section of the wing, this section being built integral with the hull. The two rear pusher propellers were shaft-driven and could be tilted upwards by 10 deg to be clear of spray during take-off. The all-metal structure was stressed for catapult launching and the extremely clean lines were enhanced by the stabilizing floats being completely enclosed when retracted into the wings.

Early in 1939, the second prototype, Do 26 V2 D-AWDS *Seefalke* (*Sea Falcon*) (c/n 792) was flying, and the two prototypes were delivered to DLH as Do 26As; but they were not used over the North Atlantic and only made 18 mail crossings over the South Atlantic before the war began. The war also prevented the planned completion of the Do 26 V3, D-ASRA

This Do 26 V6 (P5-DH) was one of the Do 26Ds used by the Transozean-Staffel in Norway. (*H. Thiele*)

*Seemöwe* (*Seagull*), as the Do 26B, which differed from the first two prototypes in having accommodation for four passengers, and the Do 26 V4, V5 and V6 as Do 26Cs with 700 hp Junkers Jumo 205 engines. These last four aircraft were therefore modified before completion as Do 26Ds for service with the Luftwaffe in the transport and reconnaissance rôle.

Beginning with the Do 26 V3, each Do 26D had one 20 mm MG 151 cannon in an electrically-operated bow turret and three 7·9 mm MG 15 machine-guns disposed in two waist positions and one watertight ventral position in the hull. Up to 12 equipped troops could be carried. The first Do 26D entered service early in 1940 and by April all six Do 26s were performing transport work in the Norwegian campaign. The Do 26 V4, V5 and V6 (coded P5-DF, P5-DG, and P5-DH respectively) are known to have been used by the Transozean-Staffel in Norway and were later transferred to 1./Kü.Fl.Gr 406. Two Do 26s were shot down by Hurricane fighters on 28 May, 1940, when ferrying troops to Rombaksfjord, and one crash-landed at Narvik where the pilot, Graf Schack, and 10 troops were captured.

Do 26A: Span 30 m (98 ft 5¼ in); length 24·6 m (80 ft 8½ in); height 6·85 m (22 ft 5¾ in); wing area 120 sq m (1,291·67 sq ft).

Empty weight 10,700 kg (23,594 lb); fuel and oil 6,750 kg (14,884 lb); loaded weight 20,000 kg (44,100 lb).

Maximum speed 335 km/h (208 mph); maximum cruising speed 310 km/h (193 mph); long-range cruising speed 265 km/h (164·6 mph); alighting speed 125 km/h (77·6 mph); service ceiling 4,800 m (15,748 ft); maximum range 9,000 km (5,592 miles).

Another view of the Do 26 V6, showing the rear airscrews tilted upwards to clear spray during take-off. (*F. Selinger*)

125

A standard production Dornier Do 215B-1 reconnaissance aircraft.

# Dornier Do 215

The Zürich international flying meeting in July 1937 stimulated considerable foreign interest in the Do 17 bomber, particularly in Yugoslavia. Consequently a Do 17Z-0, D-AIIB, was redesignated Do 215 V1 and used as a demonstration aircraft for foreign air forces. The Do 215 V1 was essentially similar to the Do 17Z-0, but the Do 215 V2 was fitted with a pair of Gnome/Rhône 14N 1/2 radial engines. These power units did not offer sufficient increase in performance over the Yugoslav Do 17K, so a third aircraft, the Do 215 V3, was re-engined with Daimler-Benz DB 601As each rated at 1,075 hp for take-off.

These engines offered a substantial increase in performance and a production variant was proposed under the designation Do 215A-1. During the autumn of 1939, the Swedish government placed an order for 18 machines, but before they could be delivered, the Luftwaffe placed an export embargo on the bomber. The aircraft under construction were converted for Luftwaffe use as the Do 215B-0 and B-1, carrying a 1,000 kg (2,205 lb) bomb load, photographic reconnaissance cameras and a crew of four.

The Do 215B-2 was a pure bomber variant which was abandoned at an early stage, and the Do 215B-3, two examples of which were completed, was delivered to the USSR early in 1940. The Do 215B-4 was a reconnaissance aircraft similar to the B-1, but carried an Rb 50/30 camera in the lower gun position and an Rb 20/30 in the crew entry door.

The first Luftwaffe unit to operate the Do 215B was 3.Aufkl.St./Ob.d.L. which received the type early in 1940. By May 1940, all three Staffeln of Aufkl.Gr./Ob.d.L. had received the type as well as 1.(F)/124, the Richthofen-Aufklärungsstaffel. The aircraft also saw service with 1.(F)/100 and the Nachtaufklärungsstaffeln in Russia, but never with a pure bomber group.

In 1940 a night-fighter/intruder conversion of the aircraft was completed under the designation Do 215B-5. This was fitted with a new unglazed nose similar to that of the Do 17Z-10 which permitted the installation of two 20 mm MG FF cannon and four 7·9 mm MG machineguns. The first Do 215B-5s were delivered to 4./NJG 2 in the spring of 1941, the Staffel operating intruder sorties over the British Isles. Use of the aircraft in small numbers was also made by I., III. and IV./NJG 1 and I. and II./NJG 2. By 1942 the Do 215 had disappeared from operational Luftwaffe service, being replaced by the Junkers Ju 88 and Do 217.

*Wartime operational units:* 1.(F)/100, 1.(F)/124, 1./Nachtaufklärungsstaffel, 1., 2. and 3./Aufkl.Gr.Ob.d.L., I., III. and IV./NJG 1, I. and II./NJG 2.

Do 215B-1: Span 18 m (59 ft 0⅔ in); length 15·79 m (51 ft 9⅔ in); height 4·56 m (14 ft 11½ in); wing area 55 sq m (592·014 sq ft).
Empty weight 5,780 kg (12,727 lb); loaded weight 8,800 kg (19,404 lb).
Maximum speed at sea level 385 km/h (239 mph), at 4,000 m (13,124 ft) 470 km/h (292 mph); service ceiling 9,000 m (29,529 ft); normal range 2,450 km (1,522 miles).

The Dornier Do 217E-2 with its electrically-operated dorsal turret. (*R. C. Seeley*)

# Dornier Do 217

In 1937, Dornier proposed a larger development of their Do 17 bomber which was just entering service with the Luftwaffe. The Do 217, apart from being slightly larger, closely followed the outlines of its predecessor, the Do 215. One novel feature was the provision of an 'umbrella'-type dive-brake which, comprising a long extension to the rear of the fuselage when folded, opened out at right angles into four separate ribs to slow the aircraft in a dive.

The Do 217 V1, powered by two 1,075 hp Daimler-Benz DB 601A engines, made its first flight in August 1938. It proved to have much less forgiving flight characteristics than the Do 215, particular trouble being experienced with directional instability. About a month after its first flight the aircraft crashed during a low-level pass, killing both pilot and observer.

127

The first prototype was followed by two generally-similar aircraft, the Do 217 V2 and V3, these differing only by being powered by 950 hp Junkers Jumo 211A engines.

The fourth aircraft, D-AMSD, was similar to the two previous prototypes, but was fitted with defensive armament, modified dive-brakes, and enlarged rear surfaces, the latter designed to cure stability problems. The machine was delivered to Rechlin, but reports from test pilots were not favourable, complaints being made about inadequate performance, instability, and failure to carry heavy offensive weapons and full fuel.

Meanwhile, construction of three further aircraft proceeded at Dornier's Löwenthal factory, the machines being designated Do 217 V1E (E indicating Ersatz or replacement), V5 and V6. All three were powered by Jumo 211A engines, the V1E having fixed slots in the leading edges of the tail fins which substantially improved stability. The prototypes underwent extensive trials during the summer of 1939, but it soon became obvious that the type would never attain a useful performance with the power provided. The Do 217 V7 D-ACBF and V8 D-AHJE were therefore each fitted with two of the new 1,550 hp BMW 139 radial engines which were then under development. The increased power of the engines enabled Dornier to redesign the aircraft to carry much heavier loads, but in the autumn of 1939 the BMW 139 was abandoned in favour of the improved BMW 801.

The initial production variants were the Do 217A-0 reconnaissance aircraft, of which eight were completed, and the Do 217C-0 bomber of which five were built including the prototype. Carrying an armament of three MG 15 machine-guns and two cameras, the Do 217A-0s entered service early in 1940 with the Aufklärungsgruppe/Ob.d.L. operating clandestine surveillance missions over Soviet and other neutral territory.

First variant to be powered by two 1,550 hp BMW 801MA radial engines was the Do 217 V9, forerunner of the proposed Do 217E. In addition to the new engines, the prototype featured a substantially deepened fuselage which enabled it to carry much heavier bombs or even a torpedo internally. The first pre-production Do 217E-0s appeared late in 1940, followed early in 1941 by a batch of E-1 production aircraft.

This Do 217E-4 (c/n 4340) awaits delivery to a Luftwaffe unit. (*H. Redemann*)

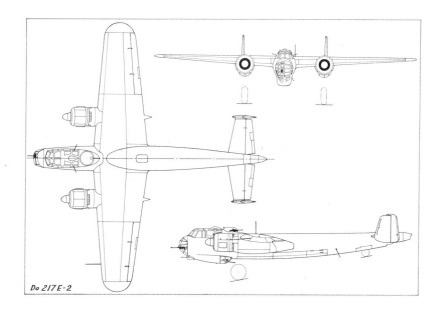

Do 217E-2

The variant could carry a 2,000 kg (4,410 lb) bomb load and had a defensive armament of five MG 15 machine-guns and a 15 mm MG 151 cannon.

The first operational use of the Do 217E was made by the long-range reconnaissance unit, 3.(F)/11, late in 1940 when it undertook the mapping of areas of the Soviet Union from Rumania. The first bomber unit to receive the machine was II./KG 40 which was formed in March 1941 for anti-shipping duties in the Atlantic. In August 1941 a number of Do 217E-1s were delivered to II./KG 2 in the west, and III. Gruppe, based in Russia, also began to retrain on the type. By the end of the year the whole of KG 2 under Oberstlt Paul Weitkus had re-equipped with the Do 217E and was operating from Eindhoven and Gilze-Rijen in the Netherlands.

The Do 217E-3 preceded the E-2 into production, the variant featuring increased armour protection and an armament of seven MG 15 machine-guns and a 20 mm MG FF cannon. No less than 25 Rüstsätze (standard field conversion packs) were produced for the Do 217E series, the majority enabling various armament installations to be mounted. Perhaps most interesting were the R 10 and R 15 conversion packs which enabled two Henschel Hs 293A missiles to be carried. The Do 217E-2 was basically similar to the E-1 but introduced an electrically-operated dorsal turret mounting a 13 mm MG 131 gun, a further MG 131 in the ventral position, an MG 151 cannon in the nose and three MG 15s in the forward fuselage. The Do 217E-4 was a modified version of the E-2 with BMW 801C engines and balloon-cable cutters on the wings. The final E-series aircraft was the Do 217E-5 which was designed specifically to carry two Hs 293A missiles on ETC 500/XII racks.

129

A Do 217E-4 (c/n 4381) prepares for take-off. (*H. Redemann*)

Following an RAF raid by 234 bombers on the old Hanseatic city of Lübeck, Hitler issued an order calling for a series of Terrorangriffe (terror attacks) on the British Isles. To become notorious as the Baedeker raids, the attacks were mainly directed against towns of historic or aesthetic importance but little strategic value.

The first raid was made on 23 April, 1942, against Exeter by 45 aircraft, the majority drawn from KG 2. The attack on Exeter, which proved abortive, was followed by another, and, on 25 and 26 April, by two raids on Bath which suffered heavily from the low-flying raiders on the second night. Three further raids were carried out on successive days against Norwich, York (severe damage by incendiary bombs), and Norwich again. The most successful attack was that of 3 May, when 131 tons of bombs were dropped on Exeter, severely damaging the city centre. Cowes was bombed on 4 May, followed by raids on Norwich and historically less important towns such as Hull, Poole, and Grimsby, none of which were particularly successful. The final raid of the month, on Canterbury, did cause some damage.

The preceding 14 attacks resulted in the loss of 40 Luftwaffe aircraft, a large proportion of them Do 217Es. Losses were particularly high among the training unit IV.(Erg)/KG 2 which joined the assault in April. From the end of May 1942 raids began to tail off, with emphasis shifting to more important strategic targets such as Birmingham, Southampton, and Middlesbrough. The last four raids were made on 27, 29, 30, and 31 July, but resulted in the loss of 27 aircraft. During the period from April to September 1942, KG 2 lost 65 out of the 88 crews with which it began the offensive.

The Do 217F and G were not built, and the Do 217H was an experimental high-altitude version of the E-series powered by two Daimler-Benz DB 601 engines with turbo-superchargers. The Do 217J was an interim night fighter with a redesigned nose housing two MG FF cannon and four MG 17 machine-guns. Two variants were completed, the Do 217J-1 intruder and the J-2 night fighter which had its bomb bays faired over and carried FuG 202 Lichtenstein BC radar as standard. The Do 217J entered service during the early summer of 1942, being used in small numbers by II., III. and IV./NJG 1, II. and III./NJG 2, the whole of NJG 3 and III./NJG 4.

During the autumn of 1942 the Do 217K entered service with KG 2. Based on the E-series, the Do 217K had an entirely new nose in which the cockpit step was eliminated. The aircraft carried a defensive armament of two MG 131 and four to six MG 81 machine-guns. The Do 217K V1 was powered by two 1,700 hp BMW 801D engines and was flown initially with a single fin and rudder. The Do 217K V2 and V3 were followed by the Do 217K-1 which could carry the same Rüstsätze (conversion packs) as the Do

The Do 217J-2 night fighter with Lichtenstein C-1 radar equipment.

217E. The Do 217K-2 was specially designed to carry two Fritz X rocket-propelled missiles with FuG 203a and FuG 230a radio guidance equipment being installed. The Do 217K-3 was similar, but with FuG 203c or 203d equipment, and could carry either two Fritz X or Hs 293A weapons.

The Do 217L V1 and V2 were prototypes of a proposed series in which the cockpit and armament installation was re-arranged. The Do 217M-1 was similar to the K-1 but was powered by two 1,750 hp Daimler-Benz DB 603A engines. Produced almost simultaneously with the Do 217K, only two variants of the M-series saw operational service—the Do 217 M-1 and the M-11 which was a missile carrier similar to the K-3. Also built

The first K-series pre-production aircraft was the Do 217K-01 which began flight trials during the spring of 1942. (*H. Redemann*)

The Do 217K-1 was basically an E-series airframe with a completely redesigned forward fuselage. (*USAF*)

A Do 217K-1 bomber of KG 2. The unit received its first Do 217Ks during the autumn of 1942. (*H. Redemann*)

A Do 217K, with two winged torpedoes underwing, taxies towards its take-off point. (*H. Redemann*)

132

were the Do 217M-5 which carried a single Hs 293A below the fuselage and the Do 217 V13 and V14 which were used to test turbo-super-chargers.

In April 1943, II./KG 100 with Heinkel He 111s was withdrawn from the Eastern Front to Graz for re-equipment with the Do 217E-5. Also based at Graz during this period was the experimental test unit Lehr- und Erprobungskommando 21 which was redesignated as the second III./KG 100, an offshoot forming 13./KG 100. In August 1943, II./KG 100 became operational with the Do 217E-5/Hs 293A combination at Cognac, with III./KG 100 operating the Do 217K-2/Fritz X and being based at Marseilles-Istres.

The first operational sortie was on 25 August when aircraft from II./KG 100 under Hptm Molinus attacked a British submarine in the Bay of Biscay. This attack proved unsuccessful, but a second, on 27 August, damaged the destroyer HMCS *Athabaskan* and the corvette *Egret*. The first operation by III.Gruppe was undertaken on 29 August in the Mediterranean area.

At the end of August 1943, Germany made preparations to attack the Italian fleet if it attempted to move out of La Spezia harbour. At that time Italy was still technically part of the Axis, but on 9 September news reached III./KG 100 that the Italian fleet was sailing south to join the Allies. At 14.00 hr six Do 217K-2s took-off from Marseilles and about an hour later a hit was scored by a Fritz X on the battleship *Roma*. Following a second hit by a missile, the vessel sank at 05.10 hr carrying 1,255 men with her. The battleship *Italia* was also hit but managed to reach Malta under her own steam.

III./KG 100's next operations were against Allied shipping off the Salerno beachhead when Maj Bernhard Jope's missile hit the battleship *Warspite*. Although severely damaged, the *Warspite* was towed back to Malta but took no further part in the war. Also damaged by missile-carrying Do 217s were the cruisers *Uganda* and *Savannah*. On 22 January, 1944, the unit operated against the Anzio landings, but heavy anti-aircraft defences proved difficult to penetrate and the only Allied losses were the cruiser *Spartan*, which was sunk on 29 January, and the destroyer *Janus*.

Paradoxically, the final variant of the Dornier bomber to see operational service was a night fighter, the Do 217N. The Do 217N was based on the M-series airframe with a similar nose to that of the Do 217J-2. The initial variant, of which few were produced, was the Do 217N-1 with four MG 151/20 cannon and four MG 17 machine-guns in the nose and an MG 131 weapon in the dorsal turret. The Do 217N-1/U3 could carry two or four MG 151/20 cannon in a Schräge Musik upward-firing gun installation, and the N-2 was the main production variant with the dorsal turret deleted.

The Do 217N was used operationally by II./NJG 1, II./NJG 2 in the Mediterranean area, and by parts of NJG 5 and NJG 6, but the two major units to operate the type were NJG 3 under Oberstlt Helmut Lent and NJG 4 under Oberst Stoltenhoff. By October 1943 the Do 217 night fighter had virtually disappeared from service, being replaced by the Messerschmitt Bf 110 and Junkers Ju 88.

Perhaps the most interesting experimental variant was the Do 217P high-altitude reconnaissance and bomber aircraft. Based on a Do 217E-2 airframe, the Do 217P V1 was fitted with the HZ-Anlage, a supercharger system similar to that used by the Henschel Hs 130E. The aircraft was powered by two 1,750 hp Daimler-Benz DB 603B engines with a 1,475 hp DB 605T mounted inside the fuselage driving a large two-stage supercharger. The Do 217P V1 made its first flight in June 1942 and during trials reached an altitude of 13,400 m (43,965 ft). The crew were in a pressurized cabin and defensive armament was limited to four MG 81 machine-guns. Two Rb 75/30 and an Rb 20/30 camera was carried, and it was proposed that two 500 kg (1,102 lb) bombs should be carried underwing. The Do 217P V2 and V3 differed in having extended outer wing panels and were followed by a batch of three Do 217P-0 pre-production aircraft. Although capable of reaching an altitude in excess of 16,000 m (52,497 ft), no Do 217P production was undertaken.

The final variant was the Do 217R missile carriers which were in fact converted from five of the six Do 317A-0 aircraft. Fitted with underwing racks for two Hs 293 missiles, the Do 217Rs were powered by two 1,750 hp Daimler-Benz DB 603 engines and carried an armament of two MG 81 and two MG 131 machine-guns and a 15 mm MG 151 cannon. The aircraft were delivered to III./KG 100 at Orléans-Bricy during the sum-

Close-up of the smoothly glazed nose of the Do 217K/M-series. (*H. Redemann*)

The Do 217N-2 night fighter differed from the N-1 in having the dorsal gun turret removed. (*F. Selinger*)

mer of 1944, but it is doubtful whether they were used operationally. A total of 1,730 Do 217s were built.

During Operation Steinbock, Hitler's last major bombing attack on London, the Do 217 made its last major appearance over the British Isles. Early in 1944 I. and III./KG 2 and I./KG 66 began a series of attacks against British cities but losses to Allied fighters proved severe. By June 1944 only parts of I./KG 2 based at Gilze-Rijen and the missile-carrying III./KG 100 were still operational with the Dornier bomber.

The operations by III./KG 100, then based at Toulouse-Francazal or Orléans-Bricy under Hptm Heinrich Schmetz, were limited to nocturnal strikes against the invasion ports and other military targets. One of the last important missions by the unit was on 7 August, 1944, against the American-held bridge over the Sélune at Pontaubault. Six Do 217s took-off, each with an Hs 293A missile on board. In the event they achieved little success, and one aircraft, (6N-GR) of 7./KG 100, was shot down by a Mosquito of No. 604 Squadron.

About a week later, III./KG 100 withdrew from Orléans, taking its Hs 293 missiles with it by train. By late September 1944 both KG 2 and KG 100 had been disbanded, their personnel going to various other Luftwaffe and army units. The final operation by missile-carrying Do 217s was made on 12 April, 1945, when twelve aircraft from the Versuchskommando/KG 200 launched their Hs 293As against the Oder bridges. Although several hits were claimed, little success was achieved.

*Wartime operational units:* 2.(F)/11, 6.(F)/123, 4./FAGr 5, 1., 2., 3. an
4./Nachtaufklärungsstaffeln, II./NJG 1, II./NJG 2, I., II., III. and IV./NJG 4, II., III. an
IV./NJG 5, I./NJG 6, I./NJG 100, I., II. and III./KG 2, 15./KG 6, II./KG 40, I./KG 66
II., III. and 13./KG 100, 1., 2. and Versuchskommando/KG 200, Lehr- un
Erprobungskommando 21.

Do 217E-2: Span 19 m (62 ft 4 in); length 18·2 m (59 ft 8½ in); height 5·03m (16 f
6 in); wing area 57 sq m (613·542 sq ft).
Empty weight 8,950 kg (19,522 lb); normal loaded weight 15,000 kg (33,075 lb)
maximum loaded weight 16,640 kg (36,294 lb).
Maximum speed at 5,500 m (17,045 ft) 516 km/h (320 mph), at sea level 440 km/h
(273 mph); maximum cruising speed 416 km/h (258 mph); initial rate of climb 215 m/min
(705 ft/min); service ceiling 9,000 m (29,529 ft); maximum range on internal fuel 2,300
km (1,429 miles), maximum range with drop tanks 2,800 km (1,740 miles).

Do 217M-1: Span 19 m (62 ft 4 in); length (without dive-brake) 16·98 m (55 ft 7⅓ in),
length (with dive-brake) 17·79 m (58 ft 4½ in); height 5·03 m (16 ft 6 in); wing area
57 sq m (613·542 sq ft).
Empty weight 9,000 kg (19,845 kg); maximum loaded weight 16,700 kg (36,823 lb).
Maximum speed at 5,700 m (18,700 ft) 560 km/h (348 mph), at sea level 473 km/h
(294 mph); cruising speed 400 km/h (248 mph); initial rate of climb 210 m/min
(688 ft/min); service ceiling 9,500 m (31,170 ft); maximum range on internal fuel
2,150 km (1,335 miles), maximum range with drop tanks 2,500 km (1,550 miles).


# Dornier Do 317

Towards the end of 1939 the RLM issued its notorious 'Bomber B'
specification for an advanced medium bomber to be powered by two
twenty-four cylinder piston engines, then under development, to replace
the Heinkel He 111 and Junkers Ju 88. The new type had to have the
range to operate to any part of the British Isles from French bases, have a
maximum speed comparable with that of the best contemporary fighters,
and carry a bomb load of 4,000 kg (8,820 lb). The aircraft was to
have a pressurized crew compartment and be powered by two of the
new twenty-four cylinder Junkers Jumo 222 or Daimler-Benz DB 604
engines.

Four companies produced designs and of these the Focke-Wulf Fw 191
and Junkers Ju 288 were awarded full development contracts, the Arado
Ar 340 was abandoned, and the Dornier Do 317 was retained as an
insurance against the failure of the two more favoured projects, but was
allocated low development priority. The projected Do 317 was basically
similar to the Do 217 but was to be powered by two 2,660 hp Daimler-
Benz DB 604 engines and be pressurized.

Only a mockup of the bomber was constructed before emphasis shifted
to the Do 217P high-altitude reconnaissance aircraft in 1940. The project

Only one prototype of the Dornier Do 317 was completed. This type could easily be distinguished from the Do 217 by its triangular-shaped vertical tail surfaces.

was revived in 1941 and this time two variants were proposed: the Do 317A with two 1,750 hp Daimler-Benz DB 603 engines and the Do 317B with two 2,870 hp Daimler-Benz DB 610s. The Do 317 V1, which first flew in 1943, was similar to the Do 217M apart from a new tail unit with triangular twin fins and rudders. Five further prototypes, designated Do 317 V2 to V6, were eventually completed without pressurization as the Do 217R missile carrier. The aircraft, which carried a Henschel Hs 293 missile below their fuselages, were used operationally by III./KG 100 during the autumn of 1944.

The projected Do 317B was to have had the same fuselage as the Do 317A but longer-span wings, remotely controlled defensive armament and two DB 610 engines, but the design was finally abandoned in 1943.

Do 317A-1: Span 20·65 m (67 ft 8¼ in); length 16·8 in (55 ft 1½ in); height 5·45 m (17 ft 10½ in); no further information available.

# Dornier Do 335 Pfeil (Arrow)

In addition to having a unique engine layout, the Dornier Do 335 was potentially the fastest piston-engined fighter ever built. It would have provided the Luftwaffe with an extremely effective night and heavy day fighter, but vacillation on the part of the RLM was to delay its introduction into service until just before the end of the war. The Do 335 was powered by a conventionally mounted Daimler-Benz DB 603 engine in the nose, with a second engine buried in the rear fuselage driving an airscrew behind the tail via an extension shaft.

This unconventional layout was patented by Dr Ing Claudius Dornier in 1937, and, to test its feasibility, the Göppingen Gö 9 was built by Schemp-Hirth at Wüsterberg. The Gö 9, D-EBYW, was a small experimental machine with a single 80 hp Hirth HM 60R engine mounted in the fuselage aft of the cockpit and driving a four-blade airscrew by means of an extension shaft. The Gö 9 was successfully tested in 1940 and spurred the Dornier design team to produce a fighter employing the tandem engine layout.

Although the RLM showed interest in the idea, they were adamant that Dornier should concentrate on the production of bomber aircraft. Therefore they placed a development contract for a tandem-engined intruder, designated Do P.231, which would carry a 1,000 kg (2,205 lb) bomb load. By 1942 design work was almost complete, but changes in the war situation led the RLM to cancel the project and to resurrect the idea of a tandem-engined fighter.

The new aircraft was designated 8-335, and the first prototype, the Do 335 V1, made its maiden flight in September 1943 from Dornier's Oberpfaffenhofen airfield. For a single-seat fighter the machine possessed quite massive dimensions, the top of the fin being some 5 m (16 ft 4$\frac{3}{4}$ in) above ground level. The first prototype was powered by two 1,800 hp Daimler-Benz DB 603 twelve-cylinder inverted-vee liquid-cooled engines.

The Do 335 was a low-wing monoplane with a cruciform tail and a nosewheel undercarriage. The fuselage was an all-metal monocoque structure with the cockpit positioned just behind the forward engine. The wings and tail were also built entirely of metal with stressed skin covering. The propeller of the rear engine was mounted just behind the tail, and explosive bolts allowed the airscrew and top fin and rudder to be jettisoned to prevent the pilot being injured when baling out.

The second prototype, the Do 335 V2, differed in having modified undercarriage doors and the oil cooler transferred from the original position beneath the nose to above the engine. The machine was destroyed when the rear engine caught fire during a test flight, and this resulted in a

The second pre-production aircraft, the Dornier Do 335A-02, was captured by American forces and is now in storage for the Smithsonian Institution.

After the war a number of Do 335s were captured by American forces. This aircraft, the Do 335A-05, stands derelict with an Arado Ar 234B jet bomber in the background. (*USAF*)

small modification to the fuel system of subsequent prototypes. For a twin-engined machine, the Do 335 possessed exceptional performance: it could fly easily on the power of one engine with none of the asymmetrical troubles associated with a conventional twin-engined layout, and during tests it was found that it could even take-off with one engine inoperative—an exceptional feat.

The Do 335 V3 was similar to the V2, both flying late in 1943, apart from the modification to the rear engine, but the V4 was the prototype for the proposed Do 435, a side-by-side two-seat night fighter to be powered by two 2,500 hp Junkers Jumo 222 engines. It was a simplified version of the Do 335, with almost straight upper fuselage decking apart from the bulged cockpit cover. The Do 335 V5 was the first of the type to carry armament, two 15 mm MG 151 cannon being mounted above the forward engine, with a single 30 mm MK 103 gun firing through the spinner. It was later delivered to Erprobungsstelle Tarnewitz for armament trials.

The Do 335 V6 and V7 were similar to the V5 and were both used by Dornier for extensive development tests. The Do 335 V7 was later delivered to Junkers for trials with the Jumo 213E engine, and the V8 went to Daimler-Benz for DB 603 development.

The Do 335 V9 was delivered to Rechlin during the summer of 1944 and was the forerunner of the Do 335A-0 pre-production model. Ten Do 335A-0s were built at Oberpfaffenhofen between July and October 1944, all being powered by a 1,750 hp Daimler-Benz DB 603A-2 engine in the nose and with a DB 603A-2 of similar power installed in the rear position. One of the first Do 335A-0s was delivered to 1./Versuchsverband Ob.d.L. late in July 1944 for preliminary operational trials.

Early in 1945, the first Do 335A-1 production aircraft left the final assembly line at Oberpfaffenhofen. These were similar to the A-0, with a single 30 mm MK 103 cannon firing through the spinner and two 15 mm MG 151/15 cannon mounted above the front engine. One 1,102 lb SC

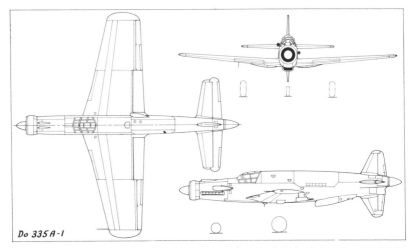

Do 335 A-1

500J, SD 500C or AB 500-1 bomb or two SC 250 bombs could be carried in an internal bay below and just behind the cockpit.

A special procedure was adopted for abandoning the aircraft in emergency. The rear propeller and upper tail fin were jettisoned, followed by the cockpit cover, and the pilot then left the cockpit by conventional means; but at least one aircraft was fitted with an ejector seat.

One Do 335A-0 was taken from the production line and equipped with two Rb 50/30 cameras as the forerunner of the proposed Do 335A-4 reconnaissance aircraft. The Do 335 V10 was the prototype of the Do 335A-6 two-seat night fighter, being fitted with FuG 220 Lichtenstein SN-2 radar with aerials mounted on the leading edges of the wings. A second crew member was seated beneath a small transparent blister to operate both the FuG 220 and FuG 350 Naxos radar equipment.

The Do 335 V11 and V12 were also two-seaters, but the second crew member was seated above and behind the pilot, occupying a similarly shaped cockpit transparency. These variants were intended to act as prototypes for the proposed Do 335A-10 tandem two-seat training aircraft.

The Do 335 V11, prototype for the A-10 two-seat conversion trainer.

140

The Do 335A-12 was similar but was powered by DB 603A-2 engines in place of the DB 603E and QE of the A-6 and A-10.

As the war drew to a close, design work was switched to the Do 335B heavy fighter. The Do 335B-1, similar to the A-1 but carrying an armament of two 20 mm MG 151/20 cannon in place of the previous 15 mm weapons, was quickly abandoned in favour of the Do 335B-2 which had an additional pair of 30 mm MK 103 cannon in the wings and installed in a special mounting which pivoted downwards for ease of loading and maintenance. Two prototypes were completed before the end of the war, the Do 335 V13 and V14, the former being captured by French forces and test flown south of Paris.

The Dornier factory at Oberpfaffenhofen as captured by American troops. The machine in the foreground (c/n 121) is a Do 335A-12 two-seat conversion trainer. (*USAF*)

The Do 335B-3 was similar to the B-1, but was powered by the more powerful 2,100 hp Daimler-Benz DB 603LA engine, and the B-4 was to have had a higher aspect ratio wing spanning 18·4 m (60 ft 4½ in.). The Do 335B-5, B-6, B-7, and B-8 were two-seat night fighter versions of the B-1, B-2, B-3, and B-4. Six further prototypes were under construction at the end of the war, designated Do 335 V15 to V20, and production of the Do 335A was 37 aircraft, including prototypes.

Many other projected variants of the basic design were also under consideration at the end of the war. These included the Do/He 535, in which the rear DB 603Q engine was to be replaced by an HeS 011A turbojet; and the coupled Do 635 project which comprised two Do 335 airframes joined together by a new wing centre section. Intended for the long-range reconnaissance rôle, the Do 635 design work was transferred first to Heinkel under the designation He P.1075 and finally to Junkers as the Ju 635 which it was anticipated would have a maximum range of 6,520 km (4,060 miles) at 640 km/h (398 mph).

During the spring of 1945, a special operational test unit was established to evaluate the Do 335, designated Erprobungskommando 335. Production deliveries of the machine were increasing rapidly when the war drew to a close, but it is doubtful that any were delivered to an operational Geschwader.

Do 335A-1: Span 13·8 m (45 ft 3⅓ in); length 13·85 m (45 ft 5¼ in); height 5 m (16 ft 4¾ in); wing area 38·5 sq m (414·14 sq ft).
Empty weight 7,400 kg (16,314 lb); normal loaded weight 9,610 kg (21,186 lb).
Maximum speed at 6,400 m (21,000 ft) 763 km/h (474 mph); maximum cruising speed at 7,100 m (23,300 ft) 685 km/h (426 mph); landing speed 180 km/h (112 mph); service ceiling 11,400 m (37,400 ft); normal range 1,380 km (858 miles).

A Do 335A-0 is preserved by the Smithsonian Institution.

The Fieseler Fi 156 V1 made its first flight during the late spring of 1936.

# Fieseler Fi 156 Storch (Stork) and Fi 256

One of the most remarkable aircraft produced by the German aviation industry was the Fieseler Fi 156 Storch. In these days of short and vertical take-off aircraft, it is interesting to note that over 35 years ago an aeroplane was designed which could take-off in 65 m (213 ft) and land in 20 m (61 ft) and virtually hover against a 40 km/h (25 mph) wind.

In 1935, the RLM issued a requirement for an aircraft which could be used for army co-operation, casualty evacuation and liaison duties. Three companies produced designs: Fieseler, the Fi 156; Messerschmitt, the Bf 163 (not to be confused with the Me 163 Komet); and Siebel, the Si 201.

The Fieseler design was a high-wing cabin monoplane with long-stroke undercarriage legs, powered by a 240 hp Argus As 10C inverted-vee air-cooled engine. The wing and tail were braced and the extensively glazed

142

The Focke-Wulf Fw 186 V1 autogyro which was designed as a private venture to the same general requirement as the Fieseler Fi 156 Storch.

cabin afforded the crew of three an excellent view. The fuselage of the Fi 156 was built of welded steel-tube with fabric covering. The wings and tail were both built of wood, respectively with fabric and plywood covering.

The Messerschmitt Bf 163, of which only one prototype was completed, was similar to the Fi 156, but the Siebel Si 201 was a strange design with a box-like forward fuselage, a shoulder wing, above and behind which was mounted a pusher engine, and a slim boom to carry the conventional tail surfaces. Two Si 201 prototypes were built, but of the three designs, the Fi 156 was preferred because of its cheapness and quickness of construction.

The Fi 156 V1, D-IKVN, first flew during the spring of 1936, being followed by the V2, D-IDVS, with a wooden instead of a metal airscrew, and the V3, D-IGLI, production prototype with military equipment. The Fi 156 V4, D-IFRM, was fitted with skis and a drop tank beneath the fuselage, and the V5, D-IYZQ, was similar to the third aircraft. Two production versions were proposed, the Fi 156A with fixed leading-edge slots and the Fi 156B with movable slots.

The Fi 156A-0 and A-1 production variants, which were delivered from the spring of 1937, were similar to the V3, possessing remark-

One of the ten pre-production Fi 156A-0s completed during the spring and summer of 1937.

The wings of the Fi 156 could be folded back for ease of storage.

A number of Fi 156Cs were fitted with ski undercarriages for operations from snow and ice. (*R. C. Seeley*)

An Fi 156D-1 ambulance aircraft operating from Ain El Gazala in North Africa during May 1942.

able slow-flying characteristics. The secret of the aircraft's performance lay in the combination of leading-edge slots and full-span flaps, the latter being extended chordwise at the tips to further increase area. The Fi 156B-1, which was intended mainly for civilian use, was never built.

The major production variant was the C-series, the Fi 156C-0 leaving the assembly lines in 1939. This model differed in having the rear of the extensively glazed cabin raised to allow a single 7·9 mm MG 151 machine-gun to be carried. The Fi 156C-1 was used as a staff aircraft by the Luftwaffe, the C-2 being equipped for aerial reconnaissance. The Fi 156C-3 was a multi-purpose design, most aircraft being powered by the improved Argus As 10P engine. The Fi 156C-4 was not built, and the C-5 was fitted with a drop tank which increased range from 385 km (239 miles) to 1,015 km (631 miles). Tropical variants were also produced under the designations Fi 156C-3/Trop and C-5/Trop.

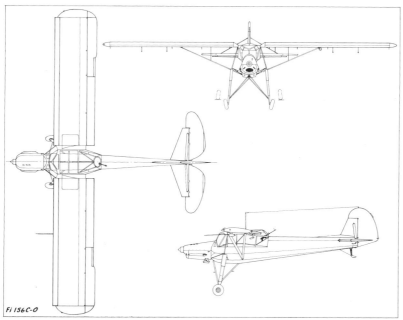

Fi 156C-0

The Fi 156D-0, which appeared in 1941, was the forerunner of a specialized casualty evacuation variant. Powered by an Argus As 10C engine, this version could carry a single stretcher case and had larger doors to facilitate loading; the Fi 156D-1 was similar, but had the more powerful As 10P engine. The final variant was the Fi 156E-0 which was experimentally fitted with a caterpillar-type undercarriage for operation from rough terrain.

The Storch became one of the most common of all Luftwaffe aircraft, operating in the Arctic, the Western Desert, all areas of the Russian

The Fi 156D-1 desert rescue aircraft over North Africa. (*R. C. Seeley*)

front, and in the West. Many of the more important members of the General Staff had their own Fi 156, and those used by Rommel and Kesselring were perhaps the most famous. In addition, nearly every operational Geschwader had at least one Storch on hand, the aircraft usually bearing similar markings to those of the unit's major equipment. Several reconnaissance units also operated the Fi 156 including Aufklärungsgruppe 14 and 21.

The main units to operate the Fi 156D-1 were the two Wüstennotstaffeln (desert rescue squadrons) which rescued pilots stranded in North Africa. A total of 2,549 aircraft was built during the war, production also being undertaken by the Morane Saulnier factory in France and the Mraz company in Czechoslovakia. Three variants were produced by the French factory, the M.S. 500, M.S. 501 and M.S. 502, and the Czech aircraft was known as the Mraz K-65 Cap. An improved variant was also built by the French factory, the Fi 256 which was powered by an As 10P engine, but

A Flettner Fl 282 helicopter hovers above one of the two Fieseler Fi 256s completed at the French Puteaux factory during 1943/44.

146

was a five- instead of a three-seater. Only two aircraft, the Fi 256 V 1 and V2 were built.

One of the last, and most memorable, wartime flights by the Storch was on 26 April, 1945, when Hitler ordered General Ritter von Greim and Hanna Reitsch to fly from Berlin-Gatow into Berlin. The journey, which is vividly described in Hanna Reitsch's book *The Sky my Kingdom*, was made to enable Hitler to promote von Greim to command the Luftwaffe in place of Göring who had fallen from favour.

*Wartime operational units:* 1.(H)/14, 4.(H)/21, NAGr 14, the desert rescue squadrons. (The Fi 156 was also used by many communications and training units).

Fi 156C-1: Span 14·25 m (46 ft 9 in); length 9·9 m (32 ft 5¾ in); height 3 m (9 ft 10 in); wing area 26 sq m (279·86 sq ft).

Empty weight 930 kg (2,051 lb); loaded weight 1,320 kg (2,911 lb).

Maximum speed at sea level 175 km/h (109 mph); cruising speed 145 km/h (90 mph); minimum speed 51 km/h (32 mph); climb to 1,000 m (3,280 ft) 4 min; service ceiling 4,600 m (15,092 ft); normal range 385 km (239 miles).

Numbers of Fi 156s still exist, examples being known in Germany, South Africa, Switzerland and the United States.

# Fieseler Fi 167

With the beginning of construction, late in 1936, of Germany's first air-craft carrier, later named *Graf Zeppelin*, the RLM issued specifications for various types of aircraft for carrier operation. To fulfil the rôle of a carrier-borne multi-purpose attack aircraft, the Arado Ar 195 and Fieseler Fi 167 were designed in competition, but only one prototype of the Ar 195 was built since it was little more than a redesigned Ar 95L and failed to meet the requirements.

The Fi 167 V 1, on the other hand, completed in the summer of 1938, soon showed that it more than met the official specification, only one other development prototype was deemed necessary, and this early success brought an order for twelve pre-production Fi 167A-0s. Of distinctive appearance, the Fi 167 was designed by Reinhold Mewes as a two-seat biplane powered by a 1,100 hp Daimler-Benz DB 601B twelve-cylinder liquid-cooled engine driving a three-blade airscrew. The undercarriage was designed to withstand heavy deck-landings and its main members could be jettisoned in an emergency, the aircraft being designed to stay afloat. There was a tailwheel and deck arrester hook. Full-span automatic slots on the leading edges of both wings, large flaps on the lower wings, and tail surfaces of generous area endowed the Fi 167 with very exceptional low-speed characteristics so that near-vertical descents were possible. Arma-ment consisted of a forward-firing 7·9 mm MG 17 machine-gun and an

One of twelve pre-production Fieseler Fi 167A-0s, this aircraft ably fulfilled a carrier-based, multi-purpose, attack aircraft specification. However, a German aircraft carrier was not completed and most of these aircraft were sold to Rumania in 1943.

observer's 7·9 mm MG 15 machine-gun, and an offensive load of up to 1,000 kg (2,205 lb) of bombs or one torpedo could be carried. The torpedo could be the Blohm und Voss L 10 Friedensengel, which consisted of a normal LT 950 torpedo fitted with wings and tail unit to allow drops to be made at greater altitude and range than normal. For reconnaissance, the range could be increased by carrying a 300 litre (66 gal) drop tank.

By the summer of 1940, the twelve Fi 167A-0s were ready for Service evaluation, and the Erprobungsstaffel 167 was formed for this duty although, earlier that year, all aircraft carrier work had been stopped. Later, Erprobungsstaffel 167 transferred to the Netherlands for coastal trials with nine of the Fi 167A-0s. Although work on carriers was resumed by May 1942, the design of the Fi 167 was by then considered less desirable than proposed naval versions of existing aircraft such as the Junkers Ju 87. Consequently, all Fi 167s were withdrawn from Service testing by 1943 and, after overhaul, all but three were sold to Rumania. The remaining three were then used by the DVL at Budweis for under-carriage landing-shock tests in which the high range of sinking speeds obtainable with the Fi 167 was highly useful and was further increased in some of the tests by reducing the span of the lower wings.

Fi 167A-0: Span 13·5 m (44 ft 3½ in); length 11·4 m (37 ft 4⅞ in); wing area 45·5 sq m (489·6 sq ft).

Empty weight 2,800 kg (6,174 lb); maximum loaded weight 4,850 kg (10,695 lb).

Maximum speed at sea level 320 km/h (199 mph); cruising speed 250 km/h (155 mph); climb to 1,000 m (3,280 ft) 2·7 min; service ceiling 7,500 m (24,600 ft); maximum range 1,300 km (807 miles).

# Fieseler Fi 103R

In Germany, towards the end of 1943, consideration was given to the possibility of using piloted missiles for precision attacks against well-defended targets of high strategic value, such as warships, even though such attacks would involve the death of the missiles' pilots. This form of weapon was only considered because of the seriously reduced capability of the Luftwaffe and the threat of Allied landings in Continental Europe. However, sanctioning of suicide operations would have been an admission of desperation and the idea was initially rejected.

Nevertheless, premature or not, a conference of various interested experts, scientists and Luftwaffe personnel took place at the DFS to discuss

The Fieseler Fi 103R-IV, operational version of the piloted bomb. Based on the Fi 103 (V1) flying bomb, it used the same Argus pulse-jet power unit.

ways and means. At first, a conversion of the Fieseler Fi 103 (V1) flying-bomb was considered but then rejected in favour of a glider-bomb version of the Messerschmitt Me 328. By March 1944, the war situation was such that Hitler sanctioned the necessary research and development work for suicide attacks. While work was going ahead on the special Me 328, from May 1944 experiments were conducted by the 5th Staffel of II./KG 200 with Focke-Wulf Fw 190s at Dedelstorf. This special unit was known as Kommando Lange (after its Staffelkapitän) or, alternatively, as the Leonidas-Staffel. The experiments consisted of very steep dives and excessive manoeuvres with each Fw 190 fitted with a maximum calibre bomb, the intention being for the pilot to aim the aircraft at a target and then bale out. Although some consideration was given to using the Fw 190 itself for operations, it was decided that its chances of penetrating Allied defences were minimal with its maximum payload. Furthermore, the special Me 328s which had been ordered showed no signs whatever of materializing by the time D-Day arrived.

A new impetus was now initiated by Otto Skorzeny who urged the adaptation of the Fi 103. Four design conversions were worked out by the DFS, which had become responsible for development. Later, when the piloted Fi 103 programme had been given the operational code name Reichenberg, the four design conversions were designated Fi 103R-I, R-II, R-III and R-IV, the R-II and R-III types being for training purposes and the R-IV for operations. An example of each type was converted from standard flying-bombs by Henschel in only fourteen days and were laid out as follows: the R-I was a single-seater with ballast (in place of the warhead), skids and landing flaps but no pulse-jet unit, and was for the test programme; the similar R-II had a second cockpit in the nose-section for use in the training programme; advanced training was to be undertaken on the R-III, which had a single cockpit, landing skid and flaps and was powered by the 350 kg (770 lb) thrust Argus 109-014 pulse-jet, but had no warhead; finally, the operational R-IV was similar to the R-III but had no landing aids and was fitted with a warhead.

Testing began in the summer of 1944 by releasing piloted Fi 103Rs from a Heinkel He 111 parent-aircraft. This work was done at Lärz by pilots from Rechlin but, after two had crashed, testing was continued by Hanna Reitsch and Heinz Kensche who were both working for DFS. Flights with the unpowered R-I and R-II were successful enough, though not without various nerve-racking incidents, and these machines handled easily enough in the air but required great skill upon landing because of the high speed during that phase.

In the meantime, production of the Fi 103R-IV was begun at an assembly plant in a densely-wooded area near Dannenberg and also in a second factory known as the Pulverhof V1 assembly plant.

Before looking at the piloted Fi 103R-IV in more detail, the standard self-guided Fi 103 flying bomb should first be mentioned. Its cigar-shaped fuselage, which contained the warhead, fuses, fuel, guidance and control equipment, consisted largely of pressed steel sheet with an aluminium alloy nose fairing. The rectangular fin and tailplane were of pressed sheet metal and had control surfaces, but the simple, rectangular wing had none. This wing was of plywood construction with a single steel-tube spar which passed through the centreline of the fuselage. Finally, the simple Argus pulse-jet power unit was mounted above the fuselage with its bulged intake cowling starting some distance aft of the wing trailing edge and its tubular tail-pipe passing along the top of, and beyond, the bomb's fin and rudder.

The Fi 103R-IV, of which about 175 were produced in the above-mentioned factories, differed from the standard Fi 103 flying bomb in the following respects. Ailerons, each measuring 2·377 m by 248 mm (7 ft 8 in by $9\frac{3}{4}$ in) were added to the trailing edges of the standard parallel-chord wings, and conventional stick and rudder controls operated these and the elevator and rudder surfaces. Since one of the two standard compressed air containers was not now required for control power operation, its space was occupied by the cockpit just behind the wing trailing edge. The remaining air container, used for fuel tank pressurization, was repositioned in the aft compartment formerly occupied by the automatic pilot. The simple cockpit equipment consisted of a panel with, from left to right, a warhead arming switch, a clock, an airspeed indicator, an altimeter, and a combined inclinometer and turn indicator. Below this panel, between the pilot's knees, was positioned an assembly of a gyro compass, battery and 3-phase inverter. Although there was no radio, headphones and microphone were provided for wire contact between the Fi 103R-IV and its Heinkel He 111H parent aircraft. The standard faired warhead of the V1 was replaced by one of a truncated cone shape, and this was enclosed by a new aerodynamic plywood nose fairing.

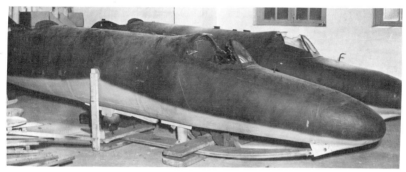

Two fuselages of the two-seat Fieseler Fi 103R-II trainer for the piloted bomb. They were superficially damaged before abandoning to US troops at the Pulverhof V1 assembly plant. (*USAF*)

After aiming his R-IV at, and diving it close to, the target, the pilot was to release the cockpit canopy (which had to hinge 45 deg to starboard before it would fall away) and then bale out using his back-parachute. It was generally agreed, however, that the pilot had practically no chance at all of surviving; since the rear edge of the canopy interfered with the pulse-jet cowling, and the canopy's mechanism was in any case inefficient, it would have been almost impossible to release it at high diving speeds but, if it were released, the pilot's chances of escaping injury from the pulse-jet cowling would have been slim. There must have been a strong case here for considering the more extensive modification involved in providing downward seat ejection through a hatch; it must be remembered, however, that the guidance by the pilot was required until almost the last second if accuracy was to be achieved, and the very act of ejection could upset the bomb's trajectory. Interestingly enough, Japanese pilots were sealed into their Ohka bombs (mentioned later) once their mission was started. These problems were never put to a practical test, however, because, although some 70 pilots were selected as the first training batch from thousands of volunteers, they never saw service. This was due to several factors including difficulties experienced in tests with the powered Fi 103R-III and inertia produced by clashes of personality and the unwillingness of high officials to treat the Reichenberg plan seriously. From the time Werner Baumbach took over as the new Geschwader-Kommodore of KG 200 in October

These close-ups of the Fi 103R-IV show the cockpit canopy and pulse-jet intake cowling to advantage. Although the pilot was hopefully intended to bale out after diving his flying bomb close to the target, his chances were slim since the cockpit canopy would jam against the pulse-jet cowling.

1944, the plan was allowed to drop. There were, in any case, promising schemes for employment of the Mistel combinations (described on page 570) being fostered within KG 200.

Although the men who were to fly the Fi 103R-IV would have had little chance of survival once their carrier, or parent, aircraft had taken off, there

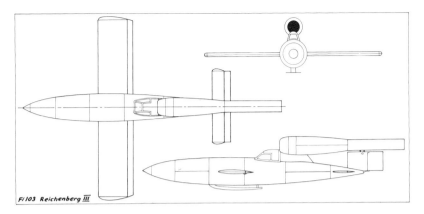

F/103 Reichenberg III

is a subtle difference to be noted between the term suicide pilot and the one applied to them of Selbstopfermänner (self-sacrifice men). This is the same difference as between a selfish suicide and a sacrifice of one to save many and was the same distinction insisted upon by the Japanese Kamikaze (Divine Wind) pilots. Although the German plans came into being without knowledge of the Kamikaze, a vague idea of the results the Germans could have expected from the Fi 103R-IV can be gleaned by a brief glance at the results obtained with the Japanese rocket-propelled piloted Ohka bomb which was also carried to the battle zone by another aircraft.

Japanese Kamikaze operations began with conventional aircraft on 13 October, 1944, but the Ohka bomb was not used until 21 March, 1945, and figures for the Ohka alone are not available. However, from 21 February until 15 August, 1945, when most attacks were with the Ohka bomb, some 17 ships were sunk and 198 were damaged in the Okinawa area; this score entailed the expenditure of 930 Kamikaze and escort aircraft out of a total of 1,809 used for the Okinawa operations. Space does not permit a detailed analysis of the respective German and Japanese battle environments, but brief details of the Ohka bomb are given for comparative purposes.

Fi 103R-IV: Span 5·715 m (18 ft 9 in); length 8 m (26 ft 3 in); fuselage diameter 0·838 m (2 ft 9 in).

Launching speed as parent aircraft speed; maximum horizontal speed approx 650 km/h (405 mph).

Static thrust of Argus 109-014 pulse-jet at sea level 350 kg (770 lb); approximate efficient life of 109-014 inlet valves 20 min; pulse frequency 47 cycles per second constant. Other details similar to Fi 103.

Yokosuka Ohka (Model 11): Span 5·12 m (16 ft 9½ in); length 6·066 m (19 ft 10¾ in); height 1·16 m (3 ft 9⅝ in); wing area 6 sq m (64·583 sq ft).

Loaded weight 2,140 kg (4,718 lb).

Launching speed as carrier aircraft speed, *i.e.* approximately 290 km/h (180 mph); maximum horizontal speed 649 km/h (403 mph); diving speed 927 km/h (576 mph); typical range after launch 37 km (23 miles).

153

# Fieseler Fi 333

A very interesting general-purpose transport aircraft, the Fieseler Fi 333, was evolved during 1942. This aircraft was designed to have a detachable freight or passenger pod which could be rapidly replaced by another pod with a new load for a quick turn-round. When complete, the Fi 333 was of a pod and single-boom layout with a very tall braced non-retractable undercarriage with tandem wheels, the undercarriage giving ground clearance for pod removal. The main undercarriage legs extended from the nacelles of the two 1,000 hp BMW-Bramo 323D radial air-cooled engines which were mounted on the rectangular centre section of the wing. The outer panels of the wing had considerable dihedral and roughly equi-taper planform. The conventional tail unit had a strut-braced tailplane, single fin and rudder. There was accommodation for a crew of two.

Three prototypes of the Fi 333 were built, but the designed tandem-wheeled undercarriage was not fitted to any of them; scaled-down versions of the undercarriage were, however, tested on Fieseler Fi 156 Storch and Messerschmitt Bf 108 Taifun aircraft. In addition to carrying freight and passengers, the Fi 333 could have been used without its pod to transport either complete wings or fuselages of fighter aircraft or similar loads, but no production was undertaken.

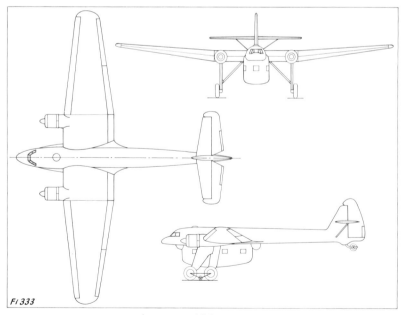

Fi 333

Fi 333: Span 30 m (98 ft 5$\frac{1}{8}$ in); length 22 m (72 ft 2$\frac{1}{8}$ in); height 5·8 m (19 ft).
Empty weight, including pod, 6,100 kg (13,450 lb); fuel 1,400 kg (3,087 lb); crew 200 kg (440 lb); normal loaded weight 9,200 kg (20,285 lb); maximum overload weight 11,500 kg (25,358 lb).
Maximum speed at 4,500 m (14,760 ft) 300 km/h (186 mph); minimum speed 65 km/h (40 mph); range 1,500 km (930 miles).

An example of the Focke-Wulf Fw 44C, principal production version of the Stieglitz training and sports aircraft. (*J. Zazvonil*)

# Focke-Wulf Fw 44 Stieglitz (Goldfinch)

Early Focke-Wulf aircraft were characterized by their thick, high-mounted wings and bulky fuselages and began in 1924 with the A 16 light transport which saw service with several airlines. Subsequent aircraft included the Möwe series of transports, the S 24 Peewit light aeroplane, the A 39, A 40 and the Fw 43 Falke high-wing monoplanes. No great successes were recorded with the early aircraft but 1931 saw an amalgamation with the old Albatros-Flugzeugwerke and the arrival at Focke-Wulf's Bremen plant of Kurt Tank who was to become one of the world's leading aeronautical engineers. Tank took up leadership of the design department and also flight testing and, under his guidance, work began on the Focke-Wulf Fw 44 Stieglitz in 1931. The Fw 44 was designed as a two-seat biplane for sporting and primary training use and the aircraft was instrumental in establishing the Focke-Wulf Flugzeugbau since it was the first for which the company received substantial orders.

155

The prototype of the Fw 44A first flew in the late summer of 1932 with a 150 hp Siemens Sh 14a seven-cylinder radial air-cooled engine but displayed innumerable faults. Exhaustive test flying by Tank led to considerable detail redesign until the Fw 44 emerged as an aircraft with excellent flight characteristics and capable of taking considerable stresses. The reputation of the Fw 44 was enhanced by its use in aerobatic displays by such pilots as Gerd Achgelis, Ernst Udet, and Emil Kopf whose aircraft was easily recognized because it bore the registration D-EMIL. Orders for the aircraft from flying schools and clubs grew to such an extent that a new factory had to be established for production. Not only did orders come from within Germany, but also from Argentina, Bolivia, Brazil, Bulgaria, Chile, China, Czechoslovakia, Finland, Rumania, Sweden and Turkey, and it became necessary to grant licensed production abroad to satisfy the demand. The first type which went into small-scale production was the Fw 44B powered by a 120 hp Argus As 8 four-cylinder inverted inline air-cooled engine (giving the aircraft a more slender nose), but the principal production version was the Fw 44C which reverted to the Siemens radial engine.

A line-up of Fw 44Cs at a training school. (*J. Zazvonil*)

The Fw 44C was a single-bay strut- and wire-braced biplane, the wings having equal span and slight sweepback, stagger and dihedral. The lower wings were attached directly to the bottom of the fuselage, the upper wings were attached to the top of the fuselage by struts, and a single set of N struts interconnected the wings on each side. Pinewood spars and plywood ribs with a mixture of fabric and plywood covering were used for the wings, and ailerons were fitted to upper and lower wings. The fuselage was a welded steel-tube structure, covered with metal panels back as far as the rear cockpit and the remainder with fabric. The tail unit was of mixed construction with plywood and fabric covering, and the tailplane incidence was adjustable in flight. A duralumin bulkhead with fire-proof glands for control leads was provided behind the tubular engine mount. Total capa-

156

Wheels could be replaced with skis as shown by this Fw 44C of a Luftwaffe training school.

city of the two fuselage fuel tanks was 135 litres (29·7 gal), the lower, smaller tank being used for inverted flying, while a third tank contained 15 litres (3·3 gal) of oil, all tanks being forward of the fireproof bulkhead. Seat-type parachutes could be used in the open cockpits, and the rear cockpit seat could be folded down for access to the luggage locker.

In the training rôle, the Fw 44 saw service with the Luftwaffe throughout the war. Training units which used the type were Flugzeugführerschulen (pilot schools) FFS A/B 4 (Prague-Gbell), A/B 14 (Klagenfurt), A/B 23 (Kaufbeuren), A/B 43 (Crailsheim), A/B 51 (Elbing), A/B 72 (Detmold), A/B 112 (Langenleborn), A/B 113 (Brünn), A/B 125 (Neukuhren) and C 22 (Oels). Luftkriegsschule (officer candidate school) LKS 4 at Fürstenfeldbruck also used the Fw 44.

Fw 44C: Span 9 m (29 ft 6¼ in); length 7·3 m (23 ft 11⅜ in); height 2·7 m (8 ft 10¼ in); wing area 20 sq m (215·2 sq ft).
Empty weight 525 kg (1,158 lb); loaded weight for aerobatics 770 kg (1,698 lb); loaded weight for training 870 kg (1,919 lb); loaded weight for touring 900 kg (1,985 lb).
Maximum speed at sea level 185 km/h (115 mph); cruising speed 172 km/h (107 mph); landing speed 72 km/h (45 mph); climb to 1,000 m (3,280 ft) 5·5 min; climb to 3,000 m (9,840 ft) 23·6 min; service ceiling 3,900 m (12,792 ft); maximum range 675 km (420 miles).

A Focke-Wulf Fw 56 Stösser of the Hungarian Air Force. (*F. Selinger*)

# Focke-Wulf Fw 56 Stösser (Falcon)

The Focke-Wulf Fw 56 Stösser was a single-seat high-wing monoplane advanced trainer first built in 1933. It was the first Focke-Wulf aircraft with which Kurt Tank was fully involved from the start and the first for which he chose the name, the tradition for bird names having been started by Heinrich Focke. Early in its career, the Fw 56 showed good flying qualities. In particular, its exceptionally clean lines gave it a high diving speed and its sound construction enabled it to withstand considerable pull-out forces. These characteristics came to the attention of Ernst Udet who, after having been impressed by a demonstration in the USA of a Curtiss Helldiver dive-bomber, arranged in 1935 to test the dive-bombing technique for himself using an Fw 56. Makeshift racks were fitted for small concrete bombs, and results superior to normal bombing techniques were obtained when aiming at a target on Bremen airfield. It was not, however, until Udet headed the RLM's technical department in 1936 and arranged a similar official demonstration that the Stuka (dive-bombing) technique was officially adopted with, later, well-known results.

The Fw 56 was powered by a 240 hp Argus As 10C eight-cylinder inverted-vee air-cooled engine. The high, braced wing had elliptical tips and slight sweepback and consisted of two spruce and plywood spars, spruce ribs, and plywood covering back to the rear spar, with fabric covering for the remainder. An alternative design allowed for a metal wing structure. The fuselage was a welded steel-tube structure with metal panels covering the forward section and fabric the rear. The tail unit was a mixture of wood, metal and fabric, the triangular tailplane being mounted on top of the truncated fin and forward of the rudder. A fuel tank of 100 litres (22 gal) capacity and a tank containing 12 litres (2·64 gal) of oil was contained in the fuselage behind the fireproof engine bulkhead. Wide-chord light metal fairings covered the cantilever main undercarriage legs, and the wheels were fitted with hydraulic brakes.

The prototype, the Fw 56a (later designated Fw 56 V1) D-JSOT, was flown for the first time in November 1933. It was followed by the generally similar V2 D-IIKA and the V3 D-ILAR which had a modified undercarriage with unspatted wheels. A batch of three Fw 56A-0 pre-production aircraft was completed in 1934, each bearing consecutive Versuchs numbers. The Fw 56A-01 D-ITAU was also known as the V4, the A-02 D-IGEU as the V5 and the A-03 D-IXYO as the V6. The first two pre-production aircraft were each fitted with two 7·9 mm MG 17 machine-guns and a rack for three 10 kg (22 lb) bombs. The Fw 56 V6 carried only one MG 17 gun.

A line-up of Fw 56s, the type adopted by the early Luftwaffe as a single-seat, advanced trainer.

During the summer of 1935, the Fw 56 competed with the Heinkel He 74 and Arado Ar 76 for an RLM contract which called for a home defence fighter and advanced trainer. The Stösser proved superior to the other machines and a batch of Fw 56A-1 production aircraft was ordered for the Luftwaffe. Substantial orders were obtained for the Fw 56, total production being in the region of 1,000 aircraft. It was also adopted by the Austrian and Hungarian air forces, and many civil flying clubs.

Fw 56: Span 10·5 m (34 ft 5½ in); length 7·6 m (25 ft 3¼ in); height 2·55 m (11 ft 7¾ in); wing area 14 sq m (150·64 sq ft).

Empty weight 695 kg (1,532 lb); loaded weight 996 kg (2,196 lb).

Maximum speed at sea level 278 km/h (173 mph); maximum speed at 4,000 m (13,120 ft) 258 km/h (160 mph); landing speed 90 km/h (56 mph); climb to 1,000 m (3,280 ft) 2·2 min; climb to 5,000 m (16,400 ft) 17·9 min; service ceiling 6,200 m (20,336 ft); maximum range 400 km (250 miles).

# Focke-Wulf Fw 58 Weihe (Kite)

Following on from the Fw 56, the next important Focke-Wulf aircraft designed under Kurt Tank's leadership were: the Fw 159, virtually an enlarged version of the Fw 56 but the first Focke-Wulf aircraft with retractable undercarriage; the Fw 57, the first Focke-Wulf aircraft with all-metal monocoque construction; and the Fw 58 Weihe. Of these three, only the relatively innocuous-looking Fw 58 achieved the success of production status, and it was, in fact, an excellent aircraft. The Fw 58 was designed to the same specification as the Arado Ar 77, each being powered by two 240 hp Argus As 10C eight-cylinder inverted-vee air-cooled engines. The Fw 58 had a welded steel-tube fuselage with mixed covering and a metal wing with fabric covering aft of the spar. The wing of semi-cantilever type, was set low, the centre section being braced from the tops of the engine mountings to the fuselage. Conversely, the tailplane, which was mounted forward of the fin, was strut-braced from below. The engine nacelles housed the main undercarriage units when retracted.

The prototype, Fw 58 V1, D-ABEM, made its first flight in 1935 as a six-seat light transport. The second aircraft was the Fw 58 V2, prototype for the A-series. It was a military variant and was fitted with single 7·9 mm MG machine-guns in open nose and dorsal positions. Very few aircraft were completed before production was switched to the Fw 58B, the

Three Focke-Wulf Fw 58s ready for export, the far aircraft for Hungary and the other two for Czechoslovakia. (*J. Zazvonil*)

The Fw 58B could be fitted with floats as the Fw 58BW. (*F. Selinger*)

forerunner of this variant being the Fw 58 V4 fitted with a glazed nose carrying an MG 15 machine-gun, with a similar weapon in an open dorsal position. The Fw 58B was also capable of carrying bombs, and some were fitted with floats and designated Fw 58BW.

The major production model was the Fw 58C, the first prototype for which was the Fw 58 V11. This was a light transport with a faired-in nose and accommodation for six passengers. One of the first examples, D-ALEX, was used by Kurt Tank as his personal aircraft.

Eight Weihes were delivered to Lufthansa during 1938 and 1939, these being D-ONBR (c/n 2697), D-OAFD (c/n 2698), D-OORK (c/n 2699), D-OBJH (c/n 2700), D-OKDN (c/n 3103), D-OTRE (the Fw 58 V13 c/n 3100), D-OHLM (the Fw 58 V14 c/n 3101) and D-OVXF (c/n 3104). The last three mentioned aircraft were each powered by two 260 hp Hirth HM 508D engines. Another Fw 58, registered D-OXLR, was fitted with a nosewheel undercarriage for flight refuelling trials with a Junkers Ju 90.

A large number of Fw 58Bs and Cs were delivered to the Luftwaffe, being used in small numbers by many operational units for communications and light transport duties. The type also saw service as an ambulance, being dubbed the Leukoplast-Bomber (adhesive-tape bomber) by Luftwaffe personnel. Perhaps the Fw 58's most unusual task was that of pest control, this work being performed by the unit known as the Flieger-forstschutzverband (later EKdo 40) under Oberst von Borstell. One successful undertaking, in the middle Danube district, for many years was the protection of seed potatoes against spring frosts by smoke spraying. Later, the work included spraying of areas on the Eastern Front which were actual or potential sources of disease for German troops. Various aircraft were used including about thirty Fw 58s. These were fitted with a tank, behind the pilot's seat, containing the solid substances which were electrically stirred for spraying in dust form, the pilot's cockpit being sealed against the ingress of the dust. The development work for the aircraft

161

An Fw 58C which suffered a damaged airscrew. The Fw 58 Weihe was used in considerable numbers by the Luftwaffe for communications and light transport duties.

modifications was done by Flugzeug-Werke Vegesack (near Bremen). Ekdo 40 was originally based at Göttingen and then later at Coburg until lack of fuel forced its final disbandment.

Fw 58C: Span 21 m (68 ft $10\frac{3}{4}$ in); length 14 m (45 ft $11\frac{1}{4}$ in); wing area 47 sq m (505·9 sq ft).

Empty weight 2,400 kg (5,291 lb); loaded weight 3,600 kg (7,936 lb).

Cruising speed 242 km/h (150 mph); landing speed 85 km/h (53 mph); service ceiling 5,600 m (18,372 ft); normal range 800 km (497 miles).

# Focke-Wulf Fw 187 Falke (Falcon)

Before the start of the Second World War, several excellent fighting aircraft were designed by the German aircraft industry, only to be virtually ignored by the RLM. Included among these were the Heinkel He 100 single-engined fighter, the He 119 high-speed reconnaissance aircraft, and the Focke-Wulf Fw 187 Falke (Falcon).

Projected early in 1936 by Dipl Ing Kurt Tank, the Fw 187 was a neat low-wing monoplane with a retractable tailwheel undercarriage and an

The Focke-Wulf Fw 187 V1 single-seat fighter prototype was initially fitted with Junkers-built Hamilton airscrews. (*H. Redemann*)

162

extremely slim fuselage. The cockpit was so small that it had to be made to fit the pilot, and some of the instruments were placed on the inboard sides of the engine cowlings. The Fw 187 was built of metal with stressed metal skin covering. The aircraft was designed around a pair of 960 hp Daimler-Benz DB 600 engines, but the first prototype, the Fw 187 V1, D-AANA, which appeared during the summer of 1937, was powered by two 680 hp Junkers Jumo 210Da engines.

The Fw 187 V1, although considerably underpowered, attained a maximum speed of 525 km/h (326 mph). In addition, its handling characteristics proved to be superb, the machine possessing a turning circle

The third two-seat Fw 187 prototype was the V5, D-OTGN, which was completed during the autumn of 1938.

superior to that of many contemporary single-engined fighters, plus exceptional climb and dive performance. Two 7·9 mm MG 17 machine-guns were proposed as armament for the aircraft.

The Fw 187 V2 was similar but was powered by two 670 hp Jumo 210G engines, but the V3, D-ORHP, was a two-seater with armament increased to four MG 17 machine-guns. The Fw 187 V4, D-OSNP, and V5, D-OTGN, were both similar to the V3, all three having abbreviated engine nacelles to allow for the provision of full-span flaps. Extensive trials were undertaken with the prototypes, the Fw 187 V1 being destroyed on 14 May, 1938, when it failed to recover from a dive.

The only variant to be fitted with the Daimler-Benz DB 600 engines was the Fw 187 V6 which appeared late in 1938. This aircraft was powered by two 1,000 hp DB 600A units, a surface evaporation cooling system being developed to take the place of conventional radiators. The Fw 187 V6 attained a maximum speed of 630 km/h (390 mph), an exceptional performance when one considers that the contemporary Messerschmitt Bf 109E was only capable of 570 km/h (354 mph). The surface evaporation cooling system was not very successful however, but even with conventional radiators it was anticipated that the Fw 187 would have a maximum speed of 560 km/h (348 mph) with DB 600 engines.

Though the Fw 187 had demonstrated its excellent performance, the RLM refused to proceed with series production, limiting their orders to three Fw 187A-0 pre-production aircraft. These aircraft were generally similar to the fourth and fifth prototypes, although a flat bullet-proof

Only three Fw 187A-0 pre-production aircraft were completed although these did manage to see service with the Luftwaffe. (*R. C. Seeley*)

windscreen replaced the free-blown type of the earlier examples. Each aircraft was powered by two 700 hp Jumo 210G engines and carried an armament of two 20 mm MG FF cannon and four MG 17 machine-guns.

By the time the three Fw 187A-0s had been completed early in 1940, the RLM had lost interest in the type, and the three aircraft were used during the summer to defend the Focke-Wulf factory at Bremen. During

During 1940, several propaganda photographs of the Fw 187A-0 were issued in an attempt to deceive Allied Intelligence into thinking that the aircraft was in largescale Luftwaffe service.

164

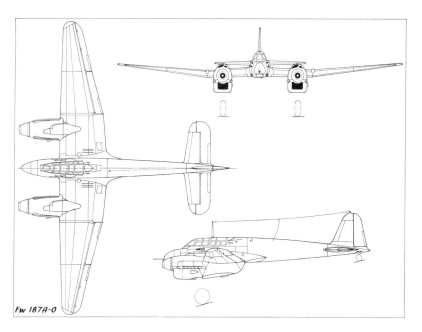

Fw 187A-0

the winter of 1940–41, the three Fw 187s were unofficially delivered to 13 (Zerstörer) Staffel of JG 77 based in Norway. The Service pilots much preferred the Falke to their Messerschmitt Bf 110s, but as soon as the RLM learned of their existence they were returned to Bremen. After overhaul the Fw 187s served as development aircraft for the Ta 154 programme.

Fw 187A-0: Span 15·3 m (50 ft 2½ in); length 11·01 m (36 ft 5 in); height 3·85 m (12 ft 7 in); wing area 30·4 sq m (327·22 sq ft).

Empty weight 3,600 kg (8,160 lb); loaded weight 5,000 kg (11,025 lb).

Maximum speed at 4,000 m (13,124 ft) 525 km/h (326 mph); service ceiling 10,000 m (32,811 ft).

The Fw 189 V2 D-OVHD which made its first flight in August 1938. (*F. Selinger*)

# Focke-Wulf Fw 189 Uhu (Owl)

The Luftwaffe was basically a tactical force supporting the Wehrmacht and it is therefore somewhat surprising that only two German short-range reconnaissance aircraft were to achieve prominence during the Second World War, the Henschel Hs 126 and the Focke-Wulf Fw 189 Uhu.

The Fw 189, popularly known as Das Fliegende Auge (the Flying Eye), was conceived in February 1937 in answer to an RLM specification calling for an advanced successor to the Hs 126 which was then undergoing trials. Three projects were produced in answer to the specification, all revealing in their layout the designer's individual approach to creating an aircraft with an excellent all-round view.

Least unconventional of the three was the Arado Ar 198, a shoulder-wing monoplane with a radial engine and an extensively glazed fuselage. The Blohm und Voss design, the Bv 141, employed an asymmetric layout, and was one of the strangest-looking aircraft ever built. The Fw 189 was certainly more conventional, employing a twin-boom layout with two small engines and an extensively glazed central fuselage nacelle. The RLM viewed the Bv 141 and Fw 189 with some suspicion but awarded contracts to both Arado and Focke-Wulf to each produce three prototypes.

Construction of the Fw 189 V1, D-OPVN, began in April 1937 under the supervision of Dipl Ing E. Kosel, the aircraft flying for the first time in July 1938 with Kurt Tank at the controls. It was powered by two 430 hp Argus As 410 twelve-cylinder inverted-vee air-cooled engines and proved to have delightful flying characteristics. The Fw 189 V2, D-OVHD, which joined the test programme in August 1938 was similar to the V1, but was armed, a 7·9 mm MG 17 machine-gun being carried in each wing root and an MG 15 of similar calibre in the nose, dorsal and tail positions. In addition the aircraft could carry four 50 kg (110 lb) SC 50 bombs on ETC 50 racks beneath the wings.

The unarmed Fw 189 V3, D-ORMH, made its first flight in September 1938. It was fitted with special Argus-designed propellers, the pitch of which was controlled automatically by special vanes on the nose of the spinners. Following the successful testing of the first three Fw 189s and the unsatisfactory performance exhibited by the cumbersome Ar 198 V1, D-ODLG, the RLM awarded a development contract for the construction of four further Uhu prototypes.

The Fw 189 V4, D-OCHO, was completed late in 1938 and was intended as the prototype for the proposed A-series production model. It was powered by two 465 hp Argus As 410A-1 engines, and defensive armament was reduced to two MG 15 machine-guns. The aircraft was later used for trials with various offensive weapons including spray containers for the Yellow Cross group of mustard gases.

The Fw 189 V5 was the prototype for the proposed B-series, a dual-control trainer. The glazed fuselage nacelle of the Fw 189A was replaced by an elegant structure of more refined aerodynamic shape and a conventional stepped cockpit. The RLM ordered the construction of three Fw 189B-0s and ten B-1s during the summer of 1939, and before the end of the year all of the former and three of the latter had been delivered. Each could carry a crew of five, but all defensive armament was deleted. The remaining seven Fw 189B-1s were completed during the first two months of 1940 and delivered to the Luftwaffe for familiarization pending the introduction of the operational Fw 189A.

An Fw 189A of an unidentified army co-operation squadron of the Luftwaffe. (*H. Redemann*)

167

Close-up of the fuselage nacelle of the Fw 189A-1 photographic-reconnaissance aircraft. (*H. Redemann*)

Late in 1939, the Fw 189 V1 was withdrawn from the test programme and returned to Focke-Wulf for modification as the V1b close-support aircraft. The original fuselage nacelle was replaced by a small structure composed mainly of armour plate with small armoured glass screens for the pilot and gunner. Seated with his back to the pilot, the gunner was provided with a single 7·9 mm MG 15 machine-gun. Initial flight trials with the modified aircraft were very disappointing. The abbreviated nacelle

The rear of the glazed crew nacelle of the Fw 189A-1. (*J. Zazvonil*)

168

severely reduced the aircraft's performance, and the small glass screens markedly restricted the pilot's and the gunner's view. Consequently the aircraft was returned to the experimental shop where the pilot's screen was enlarged and the gunner's visor replaced by an armoured position with a considerably improved view.

With these modifications the Fw 189 V1b competed with the Hs 129 V2 and V3. Neither aircraft was received with any enthusiasm, both possessing poor handling characteristics and limited cockpit visibility. The Hs 129 was however smaller and therefore cheaper, and also offered a much smaller target to enemy anti-aircraft gunners. Eventually the Fw 189 V1b was destroyed during a demonstration when the pilot crash-landed the aircraft to avoid hitting a hangar. The Fw 189 V6 was similar to the modified V1b, but carried an armament of two 20 mm MG 151/20 cannon and four 7·9 mm MG 17 machine-guns, the rear gunner being provided with a twin MG 81Z installation. The Fw 189 V6 first flew early in 1940,

Fourteen Fw 189A-1s were delivered to the Slovakian Air Force during 1942. (*F. Selinger*)

but by that time the Hs 129A-0 was undergoing Service trials and the proposed Fw 189C-0 was abandoned.

Early in 1940 the first of ten Fw 189A-0 pre-production aircraft left the assembly line at Bremen, followed by an initial batch of twenty Fw 189A-1 production machines. These were essentially similar to the Fw 189 V4, but had two fixed MG 17 machine-guns in the wing roots, a movable MG 15 in the dorsal and tail positions, and four ETC 50 bomb racks which could carry four SC 50 bombs or two S 125 smoke-laying containers. In addition, a fixed Rb 20/30 or 50/30 camera was carried in the fuselage and could be supplemented by a hand-held HK 12·5/7 or HK 19.

During the spring of 1940, five Fw 189B-1 five-seat trainers were delivered to 9.(H)/LG 2, and in the autumn of that year, the unit received its first Fw 189A-0s for operational trials. Although very successful, the RLM saw no reason to replace the proven Henschel Hs 126 with the new Fw 189. Therefore it was not until the early summer of 1942 that the Fw 189A-1 and A-2 began to appear in any numbers. The first unit to re-equip with the aircraft was 2.(F)/11 based in Russia, and, by May 1942, Aufklärungsgruppe 10 Tannenberg had begun to receive the type.

Several developments of the basic Fw 189A-1 airframe were produced during the summer of 1941. These included the Fw 189A-1/Trop with desert survival equipment and the A-1/U2 (c/n 0159) and A-1/U3 (c/n

169

Ten Fw 189B-1 two-seat trainers were completed early in 1940. The photograph shows the third production aircraft. (*H. Redemann*)

0178), which were personal transports for Generalfeldmarschall Kesselring and General Jeschonnek respectively. The Fw 189 V7 was the prototype for the proposed Fw 189D-1 floatplane; essentially a B-series airframe fitted with twin floats, it was converted to B-0 standard before it could be completed.

The Fw 189 V9 (c/n 0030) had the two movable MG 15 guns replaced by twin 7·9 mm MG 81Z installations, providing the aircraft with a defensive armament of no less than six machine-guns. The Fw 189 V9 led to the construction of the Fw 189A-2 production model which began to appear on the production lines in the middle of 1941. The Fw 189A-3 was a two-seat dual-control trainer, and the A-4, which appeared late in 1942, was intended to double as a light ground-attack aircraft. It carried two 20 mm MG 151/20 cannon and two MG 17 machine-guns in the wing roots and armour plate to protect the engines, fuel tanks, and lower part of the fuselage.

Late in 1940, a second production line was laid down at the Aero factory in Czechoslovakia, and, during the middle of 1941, a complete set of jigs and tools was delivered to factories in the Bordeaux area. By the middle of 1942 production of the Fw 189 had virtually ceased at Bremen, the factory concentrating on the production of the superlative Fw 190 interceptor.

Of the 317 short-range reconnaissance aircraft listed as operational on

An Fw 189A-2 of 1. (H)/31 operating on the Eastern Front during the summer of 1942. (*H. Redemann*)

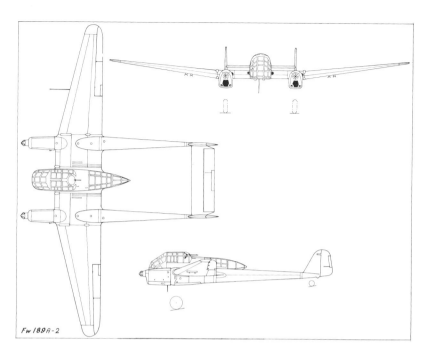

Fw 189A-2

the Eastern Front in September 1942, 174 were Fw 189A-1s and A-2s, 103 were Hs 126s and the remainder were made up of Messerschmitt Bf 109s and Bf 110s. The Fw 189 was eventually to form the equipment of Aufklärungsgruppen 10, 11, 12, 13, 14, 21, 31, 32, and 41, and when these were eventually formed into the Nahaufklärungsgruppen, only NAGr 7 did not operate the machine.

The only reconnaissance Staffel to operate the Fw 189 in the Middle East was 4.(H)/12 which operated under Fliegerführer Afrika. Besides operating reconnaissance missions with its Bf 109s and Fw 189s, 4.(H)/12 also provided Kesselring with his personal transport, the Fw 189A-1/U2 (c/n 0159) coded H1-IN. Reconnaissance and communications were not the only tasks performed by the Fw 189 however. Several aircraft were used by I./NJG 100, the Eisenbahn-Nachtjagd, or railway night fighter unit, as it was known. This unit operated against the small Po-2 biplanes of the Soviet Air Force which carried out nuisance raids against German rail targets at night.

Development of the aircraft continued at Focke-Wulf's Bremen factory, a further six prototypes being constructed. The first two of these, the Fw 189 V10 (c/n 0047) and V11 (c/n 0048), were fitted with electrically-operated undercarriages, the latter as a development aircraft for the Fw 189E-0. The Fw 189 V12 was a development aircraft for the proposed Fw 189F-2, also being fitted with an electrically-operated undercarriage, the armament of the A-2, increased armour protection and enlarged fuel tanks.

171

The Fw 189 V13 was a development machine for the Fw 189F-1 and was basically an A-2 airframe but with an electrically-operated under-carriage.

One Fw 189A-1 airframe was taken from the assembly line at Bordeaux and modified with the aid of drawings supplied by SNCASO at Chatillon-sur-Seine, to use two 700 hp Gnome/Rhône 14M 4/5 fourteen-cylinder radial engines. The aircraft, designated Fw 189 V14 (c/n 0090), was the prototype for the proposed E-0 production model, but was destroyed when it crashed near Nancy during a ferry flight to Germany for evaluation.

The final production model was the Fw 189F-series which was powered by two 580 hp Argus 411MA-1 engines. The first aircraft to be powered by these engines was a converted A-1 airframe and designated Fw 189 V15. The Fw 189F-1 was basically an A-2 airframe powered by the new engines, but the F-2 had such refinements as increased armour protection, increased fuel capacity and an electrically-operated undercarriage. Only seventeen Fw 189F-1s were completed at Bordeaux before production ceased early in 1944.

One further project was proposed by the Focke-Wulf design team, the Fw 189G powered by two 950 hp Argus As 402 engines and having a number of structural alterations. It was anticipated that this version would achieve a maximum speed of 435 km/h (270 mph) at 4,500 m (14,765 ft), but in the event the As 402 engine never reached the production stage and the Fw 189G was abandoned.

Production of the Fw 189 finally ceased at Bremen in February 1943, eleven aircraft being produced by Focke-Wulf in that year. Production also ceased at the Aero factory in Prague, but 206 aircraft were built by the French SNCASO factory at Bordeaux-Mérignac until it too ceased production early in 1944. A total of six aircraft were built in 1939, 38 in 1940, 250 in 1941, 327 in 1942, 226 in 1943 and 17 in 1944, making a total of 864 including prototypes.

*Wartime operational units:* The army co-operation squadrons of Aufkl.Gr. 10, 11, 12, 13, 14, 21, 31, 32, 41, 9.(H)/LG 2, NAGr 1, 2, 3, 4, 5, 6, 8, 9, 10, 11, 12, 13, 14, 15 and 16.

Fw 189A-1: Span 18·4 m (60 ft 4½ in); length 11·9 m (39 ft 5½ in); height 3·1 m (10 ft 2 in); wing area 38 sq m (409·029 sq ft).

Empty weight 2,805 kg (6,185 lb); loaded weight 3,950 kg (8,708 lb); maximum loaded weight 4,175 kg (9,193 lb).

Maximum speed at 1,700 m (5,578 ft) at 3,950 kg (8,708 lb) 334 km/h (208 mph), and at 6,000 m (19,686 ft) 308 km/h (191 mph); cruising speed at 1,700 m (5,578 ft) 318 km/h (197 mph); landing speed 120 km/h (75 mph); service ceiling 7,000 m (22,967 ft); maximum range 830 km (506 miles) at 5,000 m (16,405 ft).

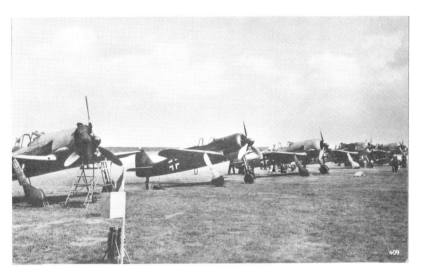

A line-up of Fw 190 prototypes. Second from the left is the V1 followed by the V5k and two A-0s. (*H. Thiele*)

# Focke-Wulf Fw 190

When the Focke-Wulf Fw 190 first appeared in action over the coast of France during the autumn of 1941 it was certainly the most advanced fighter in the world. For the first time the Luftwaffe fighter pilots were to have an ascendancy over the contemporary Spitfire, an ascendancy which they enjoyed at least until the introduction of the Spitfire IX during the autumn of 1942. The Fw 190, unofficially named Würger (Butcher Bird), was perhaps the most perfect radial-engined fighter built, influencing the design of such aircraft as the Hawker Fury fighter monoplane of the early 1950s.

During the autumn of 1937, the RLM placed a development contract with the Focke-Wulf Flugzeugbau GmbH for a single-seat interceptor fighter to supplement the Messerschmitt Bf 109. Work on the project began late in 1937 under the direction of Dipl Ing Kurt Tank, the design team being headed by Ober-Ingenieur R. Blaser. Two alternative power-plants were specified, the Daimler-Benz DB 601 twelve-cylinder vee liquid-cooled engine and the BMW 139 eighteen-cylinder two-row radial. Rather to the surprise of everyone concerned, the radial-engined design was chosen, and detailed work on the aircraft began in the summer of 1938.

Following a period of very intensive work, the first prototype, the

173

Fw 190 V1, D-OPZE, took-off from Bremen airfield on 1 June, 1939. It was powered by a fan-cooled 1,550 hp BMW 139 radial which was fitted with a special ducted spinner to reduce drag. Flugkapitän Hans Sander, Focke-Wulf's chief test pilot, was extremely impressed with the aircraft but complained that the engine overheated rapidly.

Close-up of the ducted spinner fitted to the Focke-Wulf Fw 190 V1.

After five test flights, the aircraft was transferred to Rechlin where a speed of 595 km/h (370 mph) was achieved. During October 1939 a second prototype, the Fw 190 V2, was completed. This aircraft had two 13 mm MG 131 machine-guns and two 7·9 mm MG 17 weapons and was also fitted with a ducted spinner. Sander still complained that the engine overheated, and eventually the ducted spinner of the V1 was removed and replaced by a new tightly-fitting NACA cowling.

The Fw 190 V1 first flew with this feature on 1 December, 1939, and later made comparative trials with the V2. It was found that no loss was suffered in performance, and consequently the ducted spinner of the V2 was also removed. During June 1939 the BMW 139 engine was abandoned, work being concentrated on the potentially more powerful fourteen-cylinder BMW 801. Because the new engine was considerably heavier, the Fw 190 V3, which was all but complete, and the generally similar V4 were abandoned.

An Fw 190A-0 pre-production aircraft shows off its attractive lines.

The first examples to be powered by the new 1,660 hp BMW 801C-0 engine were the Fw 190 V5k and V5g. To compensate for the greater engine weight the cockpit was moved further aft. The V5k (k indicating klein or small) had a wing area of 15 sq m (161·46 sq ft) and the V5g (g indicating gross or large) a wing area of 18·3 sq m (196·98 sq ft). The Fw 190 V5g, although 10 km/h (6 mph) slower than the V5k, was considerably more manoeuvrable and had a superior climb.

The Fw 190 was a small low-wing monoplane with a fully retractable undercarriage. The bulky radial engine was neatly faired into the slim fuselage and an extensively glazed cockpit canopy afforded an excellent all-round view. The aircraft was built of metal with stressed duralumin skin. The tall undercarriage legs retracted inwards, their wide track providing a considerable improvement in ground handling over that of the narrowly spaced mainwheels of the standard Bf 109 fighter.

The success of the BMW 801-engined Fw 190 led to the construction of 30 pre-production aircraft designated Fw 190A-0. Nine of these (c/ns 0006 to 0014) were fitted with the small wing, the remainder having the larger surfaces. One hundred production Fw 190A-1s were ordered, the first five of which bore the alternative designations V7 to V11. The Fw 190A-1 was essentially similar to the V5g, being powered by a 1,660 hp BMW 801C-1 radial and having four 7·9 mm MG 17 machine-guns and FuG 7a radio equipment.

An early production Fw 190A-1 (c/n 067) under test. This variant was merely an interim model pending the introduction of the improved A-2.

175

Early trials with the Fw 190 were undertaken at Erprobungsstelle Rechlin, and in March 1941 a team from Jagdgeschwader 26 began the task of introducing the new fighter into Luftwaffe service. The team was headed by Oblt Karl Borris, Staffelkapitän of 6./JG 26 with Oblt Otto Behrens as technical officer. In August 1941 the first Fw 190A-1s were delivered to 6./JG 26 based at Le Bourget, and on 27 September Spitfires and Fw 190s clashed for the first time.

It quickly became apparent that the Fw 190A was more manoeuvrable in every respect than the Spitfire V, apart from the latter's superb turning circle. The German fighter also had a higher maximum speed and was able to break off combat at will.

In November 1941 the first Fw 190A-1s were delivered to the Geschwader-Stab of JG 26 under Obstlt Adolf Galland. By January 1942 both II./JG 26 under Hptm Joachim Müncheberg and III./JG 26 under Hptm Josef Priller were operational with the Fw 190A-2, I. Gruppe receiving their first aircraft in March.

A Focke-Wulf Fw 190A-3 (c/n 2387) of 8.Staffel/JG 2 with the unit's eagle emblem on the fuselage sides. (*R. C. Seeley*)

The first major operation in which the Fw 190 was involved was the protection of the battle cruisers *Scharnhorst* and *Gneisenau* and the heavy cruiser *Prinz Eugen* as they attempted to flee from Brest to the safety of North German ports. From 11.00 hr on 12 February, 1942, when the warships were first spotted by RAF reconnaissance aircraft, the Bf 109s from JG 1 and 2 and the Fw 190s from JG 26 were heavily engaged in preventing attempts by British aircraft to bomb them. One of the most notable actions was the destruction of six Swordfish torpedo-bombers from No. 825 Squadron by Fw 190s from III./JG 26. The Swordfish attack was led by Lieut-Cdr E. Esmonde who was posthumously awarded the Victoria Cross.

Following operational experience, the RLM placed an order for the improved Fw 190A-2. The first prototype was the Fw 190 V14 which had two 7·9 mm MG 17 machine-guns above the engine cowling and two 20 mm MG FF cannon in the wing roots. The production Fw 190A-2 was powered by the improved BMW 801C-2 engine and often carried an extra pair of MG 17 guns in the outboard wing panels.

The first major production variant was the Fw 190A-3 which was powered by the 1,700 hp BMW 801D-2 engine and had the MG FF

A pair of Fw 190A-3s (c/n 278 in the foreground) of 9./JG 2 in France, 1942.
(*R. C. Seeley*)

cannon moved outboard and replaced by two of the much faster firing 20 mm MG 151/20 weapons. The cockpit canopy could be jettisoned with the aid of explosive bolts and the pilot was protected by 8 and 14 mm armour plate. Several minor modifications of the basic design were produced including the A-3/U1 and U7 fighter-bombers, the A-3/U4 reconnaissance aircraft and the A-3/U3 ground attack machine.

From early 1942 production of the Fw 190 rapidly increased. In addition to the Focke-Wulf factories at Tutow/Mecklenburg, Marienburg, Cottbus, Sorau/Silesia, Neubrandenburg and Schwerin, the fighter was

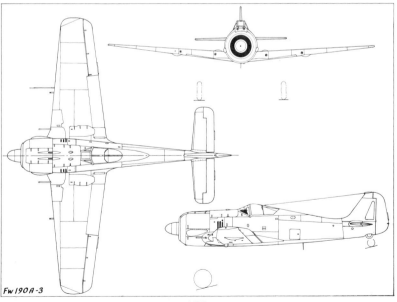

Fw 190A-3

177

also built by the Ago factory at Oschersleben, the Arado factories at Brandenburg and Warnemünde and by Fieseler at Kassel. By early 1942 over 250 Fw 190s were being produced monthly.

In March 1942, II./JG 26 was re-equipped with the Fw 190A-3, and during the same month 9.(H)/LG 2 became operational on the Eastern Front with a specially modified Fw 190A reconnaissance aircraft. In April 1942, the whole of Jagdgeschwader 2 under Oberst Walter Oesau was equipped with the Fw 190A-3. The machines flown by III./JG 2 under Maj 'Assi' Hahn were distinguished by a large black eagle's head painted on the fuselage sides.

During the late summer of 1942, the Fw 190A-4 entered service. This version was powered by the BMW 801D-2 engine which, with the addition

An Fw 190A-4 (c/n 6735) of 8./JG 2 based in France during the summer of 1942. *(R. C. Seeley)*

of MW-50 water-methanol injection could provide 2,100 hp for short periods. The Fw 190A-4 was fitted with FuG 16Z radio equipment which necessitated the introduction of a short radio mast on top of the fin. Several sub-variants were produced including the A-4/Trop, the A-4/U1 and U8 fighter-bombers, and the A-4/R6 which could carry two underwing WGr 21 rocket tubes.

In June 1942 the Fw 190 was delivered to Jagdgeschwader 1 which was engaged in the daylight defence of Germany and to IV./JG 5 based at Banak and Bodø in Norway. Also in June, 10.(Jabo)/JG 26 was re-equipped with the Fw 190A-3/U1 fighter-bomber. This machine had the outboard MG FF cannon removed and beneath the fuselage was an ETC 501 bomb rack which could carry a 500 kg (1,100 lb) bomb. By September, both this Staffel and 10.(Jabo)/JG 2 had been re-equipped with the Fw 190A-3/U1. One notable attack by the fighter-bomber force was on 31 October, 1942, when 30 aircraft bombed Canterbury.

Some Fw 190A-4s probably of IV./SKG 10, parked in front of a pair of camouflaged hangars at Cognac in 1943. (*H. Thiele*)

During dog-fights between Fw 190s and RAF fighters it was not uncommon for the Luftwaffe aircraft to flick on their backs from a very tight turn and crash at full throttle. The cause of this disastrous behaviour was the pilot making excessive use of the electric tail-trimmer, an ingenious invention of Focke-Wulf, in an attempt to tighten an already very high 'g' turn, the aircraft eventually entering a high-speed stall from which there was no recovery.

On 23 June, 1943, the first Fw 190A-3 (c/n 313) fell into British hands. The machine was piloted by Oblt Armin Faber of III./JG 2 who landed by mistake at Pembrey, South Wales, providing the Allies with valuable information on the fighter.

One of the fiercest air battles of the war took place on 19 August, 1942, when British and Canadian troops were landing at Dieppe. The Luftwaffe's reaction to the raid was slow at first, but by mid-morning dog-fights

An operational Fw 190A-4 fitted with tropical filters. (*R. C. Seeley*)

179

between RAF fighters and Fw 190s of JG 26 were taking place in the vicinity of the beaches. The fighter-bombers of 10.(Jabo)/JG 2 and JG 26 flew numerous sorties against the landing craft, and by nightfall operations had ceased. During the Dieppe raid, the RAF lost 106 aircraft of which JG 2 claimed 59 and JG 26 claimed 38.

By the end of 1942, several other Luftwaffe units had received the Fw 190. Late in August, I./JG 51 under Hptm Heinrich Krafft was withdrawn to Jesau and re-equipped with the Fw 190A-4, becoming the first fighter unit to operate the aircraft on the Eastern Front. II./JG 51 was re-equipped with the aircraft in October, III./JG 51 in December and IV./JG 51 in January 1943. In November 1942 the newly-formed NAGr 13 became operational in France with the Fw 190A-3/U4 reconnaissance aircraft, and several other units received this version. The first ground attack unit to receive the Fw 190 was I./Sch.G 2 formed in November 1942 and based at Zarzun in North Africa.

Meanwhile, fighter-bomber attacks on the British Isles had been continuing, severe damage being caused during a daylight raid on London on 20 January, 1943. Just before this, III./ZG 2 had been redesignated as III./SKG 10 in North Africa and in February a Geschwader-Stab, I. and II./SKG 10 had been formed; all equipped with the Fw 190A-4/U8. This aircraft had an internal armament of two MG 151/20 cannon and two MG 17 machine-guns, and could carry an SC 500 bomb under the fuselage on an ETC 501 rack and two 300 litre (66 Imp gal) drop tanks beneath the wings.

In March 1943, SKG 10 attacked Eastbourne, Hastings and Ashford, and made another raid on London. Early in April, Eastbourne was again attacked, and on the 14th a ball-bearing factory at Chelmsford was destroyed. On 16 April, 10.(Jabo)/JG 26 (which had temporarily been re-designated 10./JG 54) and 10./JG 2 were renamed as 14. and 15./SKG 10, the two units forming IV./SKG 10.

One Fw 190A-5 airframe was modified to carry 550 lb SC 250 bombs underwing with a 1,100 lb SC 500 weapon beneath the fuselage.

The Fw 190A-5 carrying a 1,100 lb SC 500 bomb and two 300 litre (66 Imp gal) drop tanks. (*R. C. Seeley*)

Early in 1943, the Fw 190A-5 appeared on the production line. This was essentially similar to the A-4 but had a revised engine mounting which enabled the BMW 801D-2 to be carried 15 cm (5·9 in) further forward. This was done to cure a tendency for the engine to overheat in early aircraft. Many sub-variants of the Fw 190A-5 were produced including the A-5/U2 night ground attack aircraft which carried two MG 151/20 cannon, an ETC 501 bomb rack, two 300 litre drop tanks and flame-damping equipment.

The Fw 190A-5/U3 had similar internal armament but could carry an SC 500 bomb under the fuselage and two SC 250 bombs under the wings. The A-5/U4 was a reconnaissance aircraft with two Rb 12·5/7 cameras, the U6 and U8 were fighter-bombers, and the U11 could carry two 30 mm MK 103 cannon under the wings. The Fw 190A-5/U12 had six MG 151/20 cannon, four of these mounted in two WB 151A weapon containers, and two MG 17 machine-guns. The A-5/U13 was a fighter-bomber similar to the U2, and the U 14 and U15 were torpedo fighters carrying respectively an LT F5b and an LT 950 weapon. The A-5/U16 could carry a 30 mm MK 108 cannon in the outboard wing position, and the U17 was the prototype for the Fw 190F-3 ground attack machine.

By May 1943, at least half the Jagdgeschwader were re-equipped with the Fw 190A. JG 11 which had been formed on 1 April, 1943, was equipped with the aircraft, I. and II./JG 54 used them on the Eastern Front in May, and ground attack variants were in service with both Schlachtgeschwader 1 and 2.

On the Western Front conditions were beginning to improve for the Allies. In July 1942 the first Spitfire IXs had entered service with the RAF and were able to meet the Fw 190 on almost equal terms. It proved almost impossible for the Luftwaffe pilots to distinguish the Spitfire IX from the V at combat range, and this resulted in all Spitfires being treated with a healthy respect.

181

Until 18 June, 1943, when II. and IV./SKG 10 were transferred to Sicily, Schnellkampfgeschwader 10 was extremely active in its fighter-bomber raids against the British Isles. I./SKG 10 remained operational on the Western Front until June 1944 when it was redesignated III./KG 51 and then NSGr 20. The Fw 190 proved an extremely tough opponent for the Mosquito night fighters of the Air Defence of Great Britain, although many aircraft were shot down by the defenders.

When II. and IV./SKG 10 were transferred to Sicily to join III.Gruppe, only one other Fw 190 equipped unit was operational in the Middle East, II./Sch.G 2 based at Gerbini. It was joined by I.Gruppe in July, all five units being heavily engaged during the Allied invasion of Sicily. Due to the overwhelming Allied superiority in the Mediterranean, both SKG 10 and Sch.G 2 suffered heavily and were withdrawn to Italy and Sardinia. Early in October 1943, Sch.G 2 under Maj Wolfgang Schenk and II., III. and IV./SKG 10 under Maj Heinz Schumann formed the basis of two new Schlachtgeschwader, SG 4 and SG 10.

From the beginning of 1943 the four-engined bombers of the USAAF began to challenge the Luftwaffe in daylight over Europe. By July 1943 the American raids had begun to reach serious proportions and the Luftwaffe was forced to denude other fronts of urgently needed fighter units. In addition to the newly-formed JG 11, JG 3 was transferred from Russia, II./JG 27 from southern Italy, II./JG 51 from Sardinia, and III./JG 54 from northern Russia to take part in the defence of Germany.

By late August 1943, six Jagdgruppen were recorded as operational under Befehlshaber Mitte equipped with the Fw 190A-4 and A-5. These were I. and II./JG 1, I./JG 11, I. and II./JG 26 and II./JG 300. In addition, both I. and II./NJG 1 were experimenting with the use of the Fw 190 as a night fighter. I. and III./JG 2 were still operational on the Channel coast with the Fw 190A-5 and fighter units equipped with the aircraft on the Eastern Front included IV. and 14./JG 5, I., III. and 15./JG 51 and I., II. and IV./JG 54. 15./JG 51 was a Spanish unit, a component of the Blue Division under the command of Maj Mariano Cuadra.

On 17 August, 1943, the US Eighth Air Force attempted to bomb Regensburg and Schweinfurt. The aircraft were intercepted by over 300 fighters drawn from JG 1, JG 2, JG 3, JG 11, JGr 25, JG 26, II./JG 27, II./JG 51, III./JG 54, JG 300 and ZG 26, with the result that 60 bombers were shot down and a further 100 damaged. On 14 October, 1943, the USAAF again attempted to bomb the ball-bearing factories at Schweinfurt and 79 bombers were destroyed and a further 121 damaged, out of a total of 228 dispatched. Prominent amongst the defending fighters were the Fw 190A-5/R6 equipped Staffeln from JG 1 and 26. These aircraft carried two underwing 210 mm WGr 21 rocket tubes, the rockets being used to blast the neat bomber formations apart and render them easy prey to the more conventionally-armed fighters.

Late in June 1943, at the instigation of a famous bomber pilot, Maj Hajo Herrmann, a special 'Wilde Sau' (Wild Boar) night fighter unit was formed. Designated Jagdgeschwader 300, the unit was placed under the command of Herrmann and was based variously at Bonn/Hangelar, Rheine and Oldenburg. I. and III./JG 300 were equipped with the Bf 109G, the Geschwader-Stab and II./JG 300 operating the Fw 190A-5/U2. The Geschwader, unlike the conventional radar-equipped night fighters, would attack the enemy bombers over the target itself, making use of the light from fires, searchlights or flares.

The first major operation by JG 300 was on the night of 17–18 August when the RAF attacked Peenemünde. In a masterly piece of bluff, the RAF successfully gave the impression that it was attacking Berlin and JG 300 was ordered to intercept. Units of the Flakartillerie were ordered to restrict their fire to 7,000 m (22,967 ft) so that the fighters could operate in comparative safety. When Herrmann reached Berlin, he realized that the German defences had been tricked, but with only 15 minutes' fuel in the tanks of his Fw 190, he was forced to lead his Geschwader back to base.

In September 1943, Herrmann was acclaimed as a national hero, promoted to the rank of Oberstleutnant, and appointed to command a group of three Geschwader, designated Jagddivision 30. The three Geschwader were JG 300 commanded by Obstlt Kurt Kettner, JG 301 formed in October and November 1943 under Maj Helmut Weinrich based at Neubiberg and JG 302 formed in December under Maj Ewald Janssen based at Döberitz near Berlin.

Operating during the bright summer nights of 1943, the Geschwader proved extremely successful, but with the onset of winter, losses began to rise alarmingly. Although some machines were fitted with blind approach aids, many of them crashed on landing, or even failed to find the airfield at all. At the end of December 1943, II./JG 300 had four serviceable Fw 190s, III./JG 300 had one Bf 109G, II./JG 301 had three and II./JG 302 had two Fw 190s.

On the Eastern Front, the Fw 190 was becoming very popular with the Luftwaffe pilots. I./JG 51 under Maj Erich Leie was often given the unenviable task of escorting III./St.G 2 under Hptm Walter Krauss, but acquitted itself well against the opposing Soviet fighters. In February 1943, the first Lavochkin La-5 fighters were encountered, the Soviet fighter providing the Luftwaffe with an unpleasant surprise. It was very similar in appearance to the Fw 190, and had similar performance.

The next major variant of the Focke-Wulf to enter service was the Fw 190A-6. The aircraft was developed from Fw 190A-5/U10 (c/n 861) and had a redesigned wing which was lighter and could take four 20 mm MG 151/20 cannon. The aircraft retained the two MG 17 machine-guns mounted above the engine and could carry FuG 16ZE and FuG 25 radio equipment. Following successful trials with the Fw 190A-5/U12 (c/n 813), the A-6/R1 was developed. This had six 20 mm MG 151/20 cannon and was used operationally by JG 11. The Fw 190 V51 (c/n 530765) was the forerunner of the A-6/R2 which could carry a 30 mm MK 108 in the outboard wing position.

The Fw 190A-6/R3 could carry two 30 mm MK 103 cannon in underwing gondolas, and the A-6/R4 was to be fitted with a BMW 801TS engine with a turbo-supercharger. The only prototype, the Fw 190 V45 (c/n 7347), was initially fitted with a BMW 801D-2 engine with GM-1 power-boosting, being re-engined with the BMW 801TS in July 1944 and tested at Langenhagen. The Fw 190A-6/R6 was the final variant, and carried a 210 mm WGr 21 rocket tube beneath each wing.

Several fighter-bomber variants of the Fw 190 were produced, each carrying an ETC 501 bomb rack under the fuselage. They could carry a 300 litre (66 Imp gal) drop tank, a 250 kg (550 lb) SC 250 bomb, a 500 kg (1,100 lb) SC 500 bomb, 1,000 kg (2,205 lb) SB 1000 bomb (with cropped lower fin) or a supplementary ER-4 rack with four 50 kg (110 lb) SC 50 bombs.

In December 1943, the Fw 190A-7 was introduced on the production line. The first prototype was the Fw 190A-5/U9 (c/n 812) which had two MG 151/20 cannon in the wings and two 13 mm MG 131 machine-guns above the engine cowling. The second prototype, the Fw 190 V35 (c/n 816), was similar but had four MG 151/20s in the wings and a strengthened undercarriage. It was later re-engined with a 2,000 hp BMW 801F engine, which was also tested in the V36. The Rüstsatz (conversion packs) produced for the A-7 were similar to those for the A-6, much emphasis being placed on the A-7/R6 with WGr 21 rocket tubes.

Final production version of the A-series was the Fw 190A-8. The aircraft could have GM-1 power boosting equipment with an extra 115 litre (25 Imp gal) internal fuel tank, and had FuG 16ZY radio equipment, with the ETC 501 bomb rack shackles moved 20 cm (7·9 in) forward. Some aircraft were fitted with skis for operation from frozen airfields in Russia, this installation being tested as early as October 1941.

The Fw 190A-8/R1 to R6 were again similar to the A-6/R1 to R6, but

One of the three prototype Fw 190A-8/U1s (c/n 410011) converted early in 1944 from A-5 airframes.

184

The Fw 190A-8/U1 two-seat trainer. The instructor sat behind the pupil and was provided with rudimentary dual controls.

the A-8/R7 for use by the newly established Sturm-Gruppen had a specially armoured cockpit. The A-8/R8 was similar, but had the same armament as the A-8/R2, and the A-8/R11 was an all-weather fighter with PKS 12 radio navigation equipment, heated cockpit windows and FuG 125 Hermine radio equipment. The Fw 190A-8/R12 was similar, but had MK 108 cannon in the outboard wing positions.

The Fw 190A-8/U1 was a two-seat conversion trainer, intended to precede the proposed Fw 190S-8 production aircraft. In the event, all two-seat Focke-Wulfs were conversions of the standard A-series, no Fw 190S being built. The Fw 190A-8/U3 was the upper component of the Fw 190/Ta 154 Mistel (Mistletoe), and the A-8/U11 was a fighter-bomber, which, in addition to the standard bomb loads described earlier, could carry a 700 kg (1,540 lb) BT 700 torpedo bomb.

Late in 1943 a unit known as Sturmstaffel 1 was created under the direct control of Göring and equipped with specially armoured Fw 190A-6s. Its pilots were either volunteers, or those who had committed some misdemeanour and had been asked to join the unit as a way to atone for their wrong-doings. Each pilot had to sign a declaration that he would bring down at least one enemy bomber during each mission, if necessary by ramming. Failure to do this would be treated as 'cowardliness in the face of the enemy'.

In April 1944, the unit formed the basis of IV.(Sturm)/JG 3 under Hptm (later Maj) Wilhelm Moritz. The unit was very successful, and

185

during one notable mission on 7 July, 1944, brought down 32 USAAF bombers for the loss of two Fw 190A-8/R7 fighters. Finally, in November 1944, Moritz was forced to give up command of the unit because of complete exhaustion.

A second Sturm unit was formed in March 1944 at Quedlinburg under the command of Maj Hans Günther von Kornatski. Initially called the Ramm-Staffel, the unit was later redesignated II.(Sturm)/JG 4 and equipped with the Fw 190A-8/R7 and R8. Following the Allied landings in Normandy in June 1944, IV.(Sturm)/JG 3 was placed under the control of JG 300, and in July a II.(Sturm)/JG 300 was created under Maj Kurt Peters. When IV.(Sturm)/JG 3 rejoined its parent Geschwader in October 1944, a new Gruppe was formed, designated IV.(Sturm)/JG.300, equipped with the Fw 190A-8 and commanded by Hptm Ofterdingen.

Luftwaffe mechanics at work on an Fw 190A. (*R. C. Seeley*)

On D-Day, 6 June, 1944, only two fighters opposed the huge Allied air armada. These were the Fw 190A-8s flown by Oberst Josef Priller, Geschwader-Kommodore of JG 26, and his wingman Fw Wodarczky, but the front was rapidly reinforced and, by 20 June, the following Fw 190 equipped fighter units were operational: I. and II./JG 1, 1. and III./JG 2, IV.(Stürm)/JG 3, IV./JG 5, I./JG 11, I., II. and III./JG 26, I., II. and III./JG 54, JGr 200 and II./JG 300.

Many units were reduced to ground attack sorties against Allied ground forces. Typical of these was II./JG 1 which was temporarily placed under the command of Oblt Kirchmayer after Hptm Karl-Heinz Weber had been shot down by Allied fighters on 7 June. The unit operated with 250 kg (550 lb) SC 250 bombs but achieved little success because of the overwhelming Allied air superiority. On 31 July, Maj Staiger took over the command of II./JG 1, and in August the Gruppe was withdrawn to Reinsehlen in Germany.

Two interesting fighter units equipped with the Fw 190 at this time were JGr 10 and JGr 200. The former was a special Fw 190 armament test unit formed in July 1944 from Erprobungskommando 25. It was commanded by Maj Georg Christl and comprised no less than nine Staffeln. It was this unit that was responsible for the testing of the 'Doppelreiter' streamlined auxiliary fuel tank which was mounted above the wing. Two aircraft were fitted with the device, Fw 190A-8 (c/n 380394) and Fw 190F-3 (c/n 67007). Tests ended on 5 January, 1945, with the result that the project was abandoned, mainly because the tanks caused severe instability in flight.

Jagdgruppe 200 was formed late in June 1944 under the command of Maj Herbert Kroack for the defence of southern France. Two Staffeln were equipped with the Bf 109G and based at Aix, the other equipped with the Fw 190A and based at Avignon. During the invasion of southern France during the night of 14–15 August, the unit had only 15 serviceable aircraft and, on the 28th, was transferred to Wiesbaden where it was disbanded.

One of the last production versions of the A-series was the Fw 190A-9. It was similar to the A-8 but was to be powered by a 2,000 hp BMW 801F engine which was tested in the Fw 190 V34 (c/n 410230) and the V36. In addition, the machine was to have had armoured wing leading edges, designed mainly for use with ramming tactics. The Fw 190 A-9/R11 was fitted with a BMW 801TS engine with turbo-supercharger, and the R12 was similar but had two 30 mm MK 108 cannon in the outer wing positions.

The last projected variant of the A-series was the Fw 190A-10. This was to have been powered by a BMW 801TS/TH engine, have two MG 131 machine-guns, four MG 151/20 cannon, an ETC 503 bomb rack, and a 1,750 kg (3,860 lb) bomb load or three 300 litre (66 Imp gal) drop tanks. Continued development of the aircraft led to the construction of many prototypes, the last recorded being the Fw 190 V80 (c/n 586600).

One of the most interesting A-series prototypes was the Fw 190 V74 (c/n 733713) fitted with the SG 117 Rohrblock weapon. This comprised no less than seven 30 mm MK 108 cannon barrels combined, each loaded with a single shell for rapid salvo firing. The weapon was aimed with the aid of a Revi 242 gunsight, and it was planned to mount two for operations.

The Fw 190 V75 (c/n 582071) was used to test the SG 113A Förstersonde anti-tank weapon which grouped six 77 mm barrels in a vertical mounting. Each contained a 45 mm armour-piercing sabot type shell which was fired from a height of 5 to 10 m (16 to 32 ft). Experiments were made with several triggering devices including radar, electrical and magnetic induction. Yet another interesting weapon tested on the Fw 190 was the SG 116 Zellendusche, which comprised three, four or six vertical-firing 30 mm MK 103 barrels. Using the SG 116, the fighter was to fly on an opposite course to the bomber, some 100 to 200 m (328 to 656 ft) below it, the weapon being triggered by the shadow of the bomber falling on to a photo-electric cell.

Although the Fw 190A had proved an extremely effective fighter, operational experience had shown that the power of its BMW 801 engine tended to drop off at altitudes of 7,000 m (22,967 ft) and above. Therefore in 1942 an attempt was made to improve the high altitude performance of the aircraft, with the Fw 190B and C versions.

The first three Fw 190A-1s (c/ns 0046 to 0048) were taken from the production line and modified under the designation Fw 190B-0. The first aircraft (c/n 0046) was fitted with a larger wing which had an area of 20·3 sq m (218·5 sq ft), a BMW 801D-2 engine, a pressurized cabin with double glazing, and GM-1 power boosting. It was completed early in 1943 and was transferred to Rechlin on 9 January. The Fw 190B-02 (c/n 0047) was similar but had the standard wing and two MG 17 machine-guns and two MG 151/20 cannon. It was delivered to Rechlin on 4 May, 1943, and was followed by the generally similar B-03 (c/n 0048) on 10 August.

One further Fw 190A-1 (c/n 0055) was converted as the prototype for the B-0, the machine being extensively tested at Langenhagen. The Fw 190 V12 was intended to be the prototype for the proposed Fw 190B-1 production series, but was never completed. One Fw 190A (c/n 811) was converted to B-1 standard, being similar to the B-0s, but had the two MG FF cannon in the outboard wing panels. The aircraft proved none too successful, many difficulties being experienced with the pressurized cabin, and eventually the design was abandoned in favour of the Fw 190C.

The Fw 190 V13 (c/n 0036) after being re-engined with a Daimler-Benz DB 603 engine.

The first prototype for the C-series was the Fw 190 V13 (c/n 0036) which was converted from an A-0. This was powered by a 1,750 hp Daimler-Benz DB 603A twelve-cylinder liquid-cooled engine with annular radiator but was otherwise similar to the A-series. The second prototype, the Fw 190 V18 (c/n 0040), was considerably different, having a pressurized cabin and being powered by a DB 603G engine with Hirth 9-2281 turbo-supercharger which drove a four-blade airscrew. The new engine had a large air intake below the fuselage, and necessitated the fitting of enlarged wooden vertical tail surfaces. The machine was later fitted with the DB 603A-1 engine under the designation Fw 190 V18/U1.

The second prototype, the Fw 190 V29 (c/n 0054), was similar, and the third aircraft was the Fw 190 V30 (c/n 0055) which had previously been used for trials with the proposed B-series. The Fw 190 V31 (c/n 0056) and V32 (c/n 0057) were again similar, the former being totally destroyed in a crash at Rechlin on 29 April, 1943. The final prototype for the C-series was the Fw 190 V33 (c/n 0058), which had two MG 131 machine-guns and two MG 151/20 cannon. Although the aircraft was an extremely effective high-altitude fighter, the Hirth 2281 turbo-supercharger proved too unreliable for Service use, and it was abandoned.

During the spring of 1944, Fw 190A-0 V17 (c/n 0039) was re-engined with a 1,776 hp Junkers Jumo 213A-1 twelve-cylinder liquid-cooled unit as prototype for the proposed D-series. To compensate for the increased fuselage length, the machine, redesignated Fw 190 V17/U1, was fitted with enlarged vertical tail surfaces. It first flew in May 1944 from Langenhagen and proved an immediate success.

The Fw 190 V53 (c/n 170003), prototype for the D-series, was powered by a Jumo 213A engine.

The second prototype, the Fw 190 V53 (c/n 170003), was similar but had increased armament—four MG 151/20 cannon in the wings and two engine-mounted MG 131 machine-guns. The Fw 190 V54 (c/n 174024) was similar; but the fourth aircraft, the Fw 190 V21 (c/n 0043), was fitted with a new wing, the area of which was increased to 19·6 sq m (211 sq ft). In August 1944 a small pre-production batch of ten Fw 190D-0s (c/ns 210001 to 210010) were converted from A-7 airframes, the ninth aircraft being delivered to Junkers for engine tests.

The first production model was designated Fw 190D-9 as it was intended that it would replace the A-8 on the assembly lines. The aircraft had two MG 151/20 cannon in the wings and two MG 131 machine-guns mounted above the engine. Early aircraft were fitted with a conventional cockpit cover, but most machines had the bulged hood of the F-series. Provision was made for MW-50 water-methanol injection which could boost the power of the Jumo 213A engine to 2,240 hp for short periods. These aircraft were equipped with the ETC 504 bomb rack which could carry either a 300 litre (66 Imp gal) drop tank or an

A standard production Fw 190D-9 (c/n 601444) photographed during the early months of 1945. (*R. C. Seeley*)

SC 250 bomb. The Fw 190D-9/R11 was an all-weather fighter with FuG 125 Hermine D/F.

The Fw 190D-9, or 'Dora 9' as it was nicknamed by the Jagdflieger, entered service with III./JG 54 commanded by Maj Robert 'Bazi' Weiss in the autumn of 1944. After re-equipment, the unit transferred to Hesepe and Achmer to protect the activities of the experimental jet fighter unit, Kommando Nowotny. The next Gruppe to be equipped with the aircraft was I./JG 26 under Maj Karl Borris, the pilot who had first introduced the Fw 190A into Luftwaffe service in August 1941. The unit was based at Handrup, northwest of Osnabrück, and became operational early in October 1944.

At first, pilots of these two units treated the aircraft with some distrust, but operations soon proved that the 'Dora-9' had a much superior performance to the Fw 190A-8. In fact many fighter pilots considered that the Fw 190D-9 was the finest piston-engined fighter to enter Luftwaffe service.

On 25 December, 1944, III./JG 54 was transferred to Varrelbusch between Achmer and Oldenburg and placed under the control of Oberst Josef Priller's Jagdgeschwader 26. Four days later the Kommandeur, Hptm Weiss, and five other pilots were in combat with a large Spitfire formation over Lingen/Ems and were killed. Both III./JG 54 and I./JG 26

The Fw 190D-9 could carry a 300 litre (66 Imp gal) drop tank under the fuselage.

190

took part in the famous attack on Allied airfields on 1 January, 1945, and, shortly afterwards, II./JG 26 under Maj Anton Hackl was equipped with the D-9. During the first months of 1945, the Fw 190D-9 was also delivered to JG 2 under Obstlt Kurt Bühligen and JG 301 under Obstlt Aufhammer.

In April 1945, Jagdgeschwader 6 under Maj Gerhard Barkhorn based at Sorau/Silesia was equipped with no less than 150 brand-new Fw 190D-9 fighters from the nearby Focke-Wulf factory. Only Barkhorn and his wing-man retained their Messerschmitt Bf 109G-14s, but lack of fuel resulted in the Geschwader having to restrict patrols to four aircraft at a time.

The first two Fw 190D-0s (c/ns 210001 and 210002) were modified during the late summer of 1944 as prototypes for the proposed Fw 190D-10 production series. The aircraft differed from the D-9 in having the two MG 131 machine-guns replaced by a single 30 mm MK 108 cannon firing through the spinner. The next proposed model was the Fw 190D-11 for which seven prototypes were constructed.

The Fw 190 V55 (c/n 170923) and V56 (c/n 170924) were each powered by a Jumo 213F engine with MW-50 water-methanol injection, the latter aircraft flying for the first time on 31 August, 1944. The V57, V58 and V59 (c/ns 170926, 170933 and 350156) were all rebuilt from Fw 190A-8s, c/n 350156 crashing on 9 October, 1944. The Fw 190 V60 (c/n 350157) was similar but unarmed, and the V61 (c/n 350158) was delivered to Junkers as an engine test bed. The Fw 190D-11 had two MG

An Fw 190D-9, probably of I./JG 26, after capture by American troops during the spring of 1945. (*R. C. Seeley*)

151/20 and two MK 108 cannon but never went into production. Two sub-variants of the aircraft were proposed: the D-11/R20 with PKS 12 directional control and the D-11/R21 with FuG 125 Hermine D/F.

The Fw 190D-12 was designed as a ground attack fighter, with two MG 151/20 cannon in the wing roots and a single MK 108 cannon firing through the spinner. It was powered by a 2,060 hp Jumo 213F engine, the installation being surrounded by armour plate. The first prototype was the Fw 190 V65 (c/n 350167) which was intended to precede the D-12/R5 production model. It was fitted with four extra fuel tanks containing a further 310 litres (69 Imp gal), and was re-engined with a Jumo 213EB.

The Fw 190 V63 and V64 (c/ns 350165 and 350166) were converted from Fw 190A-8 airframes and completed in November and December 1944 respectively. Intended to precede the Fw 190D-12/R11 all-weather fighter, these aircraft were fitted with PKS 12 directional control and FuG 125 radio equipment. The Fw 190D-12/R21 was fitted with MW-50 water-methanol injection and could attain a maximum speed of 730 km/h (453 mph) at 11,000 m (36,091 ft). The Fw 190D-12/R25 was similar to the D-12/R5 but was powered by a Jumo 213EB. Production of the Fw 190D-12 began at the Arado and Fieseler factories in March 1945, but it is doubtful whether the type saw operational service.

The Fw 190D-13 was powered by a Jumo 213EB and had three MG 151/20 cannon. Two prototypes were built, the Fw 190 V62 (c/n 732053) and the V71 (c/n 732054), both converted from standard production A-8s. The Fw 190D-13/R5, R11, R21, and R25 were all similar to the D-12 series apart from their armament. The Fw 190D-14 was similar to the previous D-series aircraft, but was powered by a 1,800 hp Daimler-Benz DB 603A. Two prototypes were built, the Fw 190 V76 (c/n 210040) converted from a D-9 and the Fw 190 V77 (c/n 200043) converted from a D-12. Final proposed production version was the Fw 190D-15 which was to have been powered by the DB 603EB and was to be built from Fw 190A-8 and F-8 airframes.

The Fw 190E-1 reconnaissance fighter was not built, this being a conversion of the A-4 with provision for two Rb 12.5/7 cameras. The Fw 190F and G were both specialized ground attack versions of the Fw 190A and appeared in service some time before the Fw 190D-9. The first of these to see service was the Fw 190G, a modification of the A-4/U8 and A-5/U8.

The Fw 190G-0 was fitted with an ETC 501 bomb rack under the fuselage and could carry a maximum of 1,000 kg (2,205 lb) of bombs.

Luftwaffe mechanics prepare an Fw 190G-3 fighter-bomber, probably from II./SG 10.
(*R. C. Seeley*)

192

Close-up of the ER-4 supplementary bomb rack which enabled the Fw 190 to carry four SC 50 bombs beneath the fuselage.

Internal armament was reduced to two 20 mm MG 151/20 cannon, and the machine could carry two 300 litre (66 Imp gal) drop tanks. The Fw 190G-1 was similar but was fitted with a strengthened undercarriage which enabled it to carry a 1,800 kg (3,970 lb) SC 1800 bomb under the fuselage. It was fitted with wing-mounted drop-tank racks similar to those devised for the Junkers Ju 87R, the Fw 190G-2 having Messerschmitt-designed carriers. The undercarriage of one Fw 190G-2 was extensively tested at Berlin-Adlershof.

The Fw 190G-3 was similar to the G-0 and G-1, but was fitted with Focke-Wulf designed wing racks and had PKS 11 directional control. The G-3/R5 could carry four 50 kg (110 lb) SC 50 bombs under the wings and the G-4 was fitted with three ETC 503 bomb racks. The Fw 190G-5 and G-6 were not built, but the G-7 tested a 900 litre (198 Imp gal) torpedo-shaped drop tank, the tailwheel unit being lengthened so that the tank cleared the ground during taxi-ing.

Final production version of the G-series was the Fw 190G-8 which was similar to the G-3, but with all the modifications introduced on the A-8 as standard. It was powered by a 1,700 hp BMW 801D-2 engine and could be fitted with a 115 litre (25 Imp gal) auxiliary tank. The G-8/R4 had GM-1 power-boosting equipment, and the G-8/R5 was similar to the G-3/R5. The proposed Fw 190G-9 and G-10, fighter-bomber conversions of the A-9 and A-10, were not built.

The Fw 190F series were also fighter-bombers but could be distinguished by the clear-blown bulged cockpit hood. This hood was fitted with suspended armour for the pilot's head, and the lower part of the engine cowling and wheel covers were constructed of 6 mm plate. Total weight of armour was some 360 kg (794 lb). The aircraft carried an internal arma-

An Fw 190F-8 fighter-bomber prepares to take-off from a snow-covered Luftwaffe airfield.
(*H. Obert*)

ment of two MG 151/20 cannon in the wing roots and two MG 17 machine-guns above the engine.

The first production model was the Fw 190F-1 which had an ETC 501 bomb rack under the fuselage and two ETC 50 racks under each wing. The Fw 190F-2 was similar, but a supplementary ER-4 rack could be carried beneath the ETC 501 to enable the aircraft to carry eight 50 kg (110 lb) SC 50 bombs. The F-3 was fitted with the wing of the A-6 and could carry a 300 litre (66 Imp gal) drop tank beneath each wing. The F-3/R1 was fitted with simplified bomb release gear, and the F-3/R3 could carry two 30 mm MK 103 cannon under the wings.

The Fw 190F-4, F-5, and F-6 were renamed the F-8, F-9, and F-10; the F-7 was never built. The Fw 190F-8 was the most important production model, carrying a variety of weapons including 24 R4M unguided rockets, 14 RBS B/F21 rocket bombs, two clusters of three WGr 28 rocket tubes, or various anti-personnel bombs. The Fw 190F-8/U1 was a proposed trainer version, and the F-8/U2 and U3 were to carry the BT 400, BT 700 and BT 1400 torpedo bombs. The Fw 190F-8/U14 was to carry a torpedo and the F-8/R1 could carry two ETC 71 racks in place of the ETC 50s.

Several other conversion packs were produced for the Fw 190F-8 including the F-8/R2, R3, R5, R8, R11, R14, R15, and R16—all of which introduced changes in armament. The Fw 190F-9 was produced in parallel with the A-9, being powered by the BMW 801TS engine. It could employ the same conversion packs as the F-8, but few aircraft were built. The Fw 190F-10 to F-14 were projects only, but the F-15 was to be powered by the BMW 801TS/TH engine and have the wing of the A-8. Only one prototype, the Fw 190 V66 (c/n 584002), was completed. The Fw 190 V67 (c/n 930516), which was due to fly in May 1945, was the prototype for the proposed Fw 190F-16. This was to have had larger wheels, increased armour and a BMW 801TS/TH engine.

The first unit to be equipped with the Fw 190G-1 ground attack aircraft was II./Sch.G 2 based at Zarzun in North Africa. In February 1943, Schlachtgeschwader 1 under Obstlt Hubertus Hitschold was re-equipped with the aircraft. When the Luftwaffe launched its last great offensive of the war on 5 July, 1943, against the Kursk salient, virtually all its ground attack forces were marshalled for the assault. The Fw 190G-1s from I./Sch.G 1, under Maj Georg Dörffel, and II./Sch.G 1, under Maj Alfred Druschel, were both heavily engaged. On 8 July Henschel Hs 129s succeeded in repulsing a surprise attack by a Soviet tank brigade, II./Sch.G 1 assisting by scattering the escorting infantry with their fragmentation bombs.

Early in October a complete redesignation of the Luftwaffe's ground-attack formations took place. Sch.G 1 was incorporated into the new Schlachtgeschwader and I. and II./Sch.G 2 became III. and I./SG 4 respectively. II./SG 4 was formed from II./SKG 10, and III. and IV./SKG 10 became I. and II./SG 10. In January 1944 the following units were equipped with the Fw 190G series: I. and II./SG 4 in Italy, 4./SG 5 in Finland, I. and II./SG 10 in southern Russia and, in addition, II./SG 2 had begun converting to the aircraft.

In March 1944, II./SG 77 received the Fw 190, but it was not until August of that year that the whole of the Schlachtgeschwader were re-equipped. The one remaining Junkers Ju 87G equipped Gruppe was III./SG 2 under Maj Hans-Ulrich Rudel, which often co-operated with the Fw 190s from Maj Kurt Kennel's II./SG 2—the latter unit providing fighter cover for Rudel's attacks against tanks. The only Fw 190F-9 equipped Panzer-Gruppe was I.(Pz)/SG 9, formed on 10 January, 1945, from 12./SG 9, 10./SG 1 and 10./SG 3. The unit's aircraft were fitted with twelve underwing R4M rockets, but it is somewhat doubtful whether these were used operationally.

Perhaps the most interesting of the Fw 190 ground attack units were NSGr 20 and III./KG 200. NSGr 20 had been formed in November 1944 from III./KG 51 and was put under the command of Maj Kurt Dahlmann. The unit was based at Twente and was equipped with Fw 190G-1s each carrying a single SC 1800 bomb. During the winter and early spring of 1944–45 the unit made many near suicidal attacks on bridges.

III./KG 200 (comprising 9., 10., and 11. Staffeln) was formed at Staaken from I./SG 5 late in 1944. It was equipped with the Fw 190F-8 carrying two AB 250 or one AB 500 weapon container, or a single SC 1000 bomb. The unit was later joined by an experimental anti-shipping formation known as Sonderverband Einhorn which eventually became 13./KG 200. III./KG 200 was commanded by Maj Helmut Viedebantt who is reputed to have flown the Fw 190A-5/U14 torpedo fighter opera-tionally. He was killed on 1 May, 1945, near Wusterhausen when attempt-ing to drop a supply container.

Several Fw 190F-8 airframes were used for armament trials. The Fw 190 V69 (c/n 582072) was fitted with two ETC 715 racks to carry two Ruhrstahl X-4 wire-guided air-to-air missiles. The V70 (c/n 580029) was similar but crashed on 25 August, 1944. Three further Fw 190F-8s (c/ns

583431, 583438 and 584221) were converted to carry the X-4, but the weapon was not ready for operational use when the war ended. Three other aircraft, the Fw 190 V78, V79, and V80 (c/ns 551103, 581304, and 586600), were fitted with AG 140 rocket racks. Other weapons tested on the Fw 190 included the previously mentioned SG 113A, SG 116, and SG 117, and the Blohm und Voss Bv 246 missile.

Final proposed production variant was the Fw 190H-1 high-altitude fighter to be powered by a DB 603G engine, but it was abandoned in favour of the Focke-Wulf Ta 152H. In addition to the numerous weapons tested by the Fw 190, several advanced powerplants were proposed for the aircraft. Included among these were the 2,400 hp BMW 802 eighteen-cylinder radial, the 3,900 hp BMW 803 twenty-eight-cylinder radial, the 2,660 hp Daimler-Benz DB 609 sixteen-cylinder inverted vee, the twelve-cylinder 2,400 hp Daimler-Benz DB 623 and the 2,500 hp Junkers Jumo 222 twenty-eight-cylinder four-row radial.

*War-time operational units:* 1. (F)/121, 3.(F)/122, 1., 4. and 5.(F)/123, NAGr 13, I., II., III. and IV./JG 1, I., II., III. and IV./JG 2, IV.(Sturm)/JG 3, II.(Sturm) and III./JG 4, I., II., III., IV. and 14./JG 5, I., II. and III./JG 6, JGr 10, I., III. and 10./JG 11, I., II., III. and IV./JG 26, I., II., III., IV. and 15.(Spanish)/JG 51, I., II., III. and IV./JG 54, JGr 200, I., II. and IV./JG 300, I., II. and III./JG 301, I., II. and III./JG 302, I. and II./Sch.G 1, I. and II./Sch.G 2, I., II., III. and IV./SKG 10, I., II., III. and 10.(Pz)/SG 1, I. and II./SG 2, I., II., III. and 10.(Pz)/SG 3, I., II. and III./SG 4, I./SG 5, I.(Pz)/SG 9, I., II. and III./SG 10, I., II. and III./SG 77, NSGr 9 and 20, III./KG 51, III./KG 200. Also used in small numbers by several night fighter Geschwader.

Fw 190A-8: Span 10·5 m (34 ft 5½ in); length 8·84 m (29 ft); height 3·96 m (13 ft); wing area 18·3 sq m (196·98 sq ft).
Empty weight 3,170 kg (7,000 lb); loaded weight 4,430 kg (9,750 lb); maximum loaded weight 4,900 kg (10,805 lb).
Maximum speed at 6,000 m (19,686 ft) 654 km/h (408 mph), at sea level 571 km/h (355 mph); cruising speed 480 km/h (298 mph); initial rate of climb 720 m/min (2,363 ft/min); service ceiling 11,400 m (37,403 ft); normal range 805 km (500 miles).

Fw 190C-0: Span 10·5 m (34 ft 5½ in); length 9·75 m (32 ft); height 3·96 m (13 ft); wing area 18·3 sq m (196·98 sq ft).
Maximum speed at 11,000 m (36,091 ft) 668 km/h (415 mph), at sea level 566 km/h (352 mph); service ceiling 12,000 m (39,372 ft).

Fw 190D-9: Span 10·5 m (34 ft 5½ in); length 10·24 m (33 ft 5¼ in); height 3·35 m (11 ft 0¼ in); wing area 18·3 sq m (196·98 sq ft).
Empty weight 3,590 kg (7,694 lb); loaded weight 4,300 kg (9,480 lb); maximum loaded weight 4,850 kg (10,670 lb).
Maximum speed at 6,500 m (21,326 ft) 685 km/h (426 mph), at sea level 574 km/h (357 mph); climb to 4,000 m (13,124 ft) 2·1 min, to 10,000 m (32,810 ft) 16·8 min; service ceiling 12,000 m (39,372 ft); normal range 837 km (520 miles).

At least eleven Fw 190s are believed to exist. An A-3 is in the South African National War Museum; there are A-8s in Britain, the United States and the Paris Musée de l'Air; and four D-series—one in the Air Force Museum at Wright-Patterson Air Force Base, one in the Smithsonian Institution and two others in the USA. The Smithsonian also has the fuselage of a G-3 model.

196

The Focke-Wulf Fw 191 V 1 showing the four sections of landing flaps/dive-brakes.

# Focke-Wulf Fw 191

During the winter of 1939–40, four companies received from the RLM the outline specification for a new medium bomber. This was known as the B medium bomber type which was to have a maximum speed of 600 km/h (373 mph) and carry a 4,000 kg (8,820 lb) bomb load to any part of the British Isles from French or Norwegian bases. In addition, a pressurized crew compartment, remote-controlled armament, and dive-bombing ability were required. For power, either two Junkers Jumo 222 or two Daimler-Benz DB 604 twenty-four-cylinder liquid-cooled engines, which were under development for the 2,500 hp class, were to be used.

By July 1940, the four firms submitted their design proposals, the Arado Ar 340, Dornier Do 317, Focke-Wulf Fw 191, and the Junkers Ju 288, with the result that the Fw 191 and Ju 288 were selected for full development, the Ar 340 was eliminated, and the Do 317 was put on a low priority development contract. A condition of the Focke-Wulf contract was that the Fw 191 should be designed with electrical systems throughout; this ill-founded and illogical directive precluded any hydraulic or similar systems, however appropriate they might be, and later earned the aircraft the appellation of Fliegendes Kraftwerk (flying power-station).

Under the leadership of Dipl Ing E. Kösel, the Fw 191 was designed as an all-metal, twin-engined aircraft possessing clean lines. The shoulder-mounted wing, which was to carry two Jumo 222 engines, had a parallel-chord centre section and an approximately equi-taper planform outboard of the engines. In addition to ailerons divided chordwise into two sections near each wingtip, there were special combination landing flaps/-

197

dive-brakes (designed by Hans Multhopp) divided chordwise into four sections along each wing trailing edge. From the engine nacelles (which projected slightly beyond the wing trailing edge) extended the main undercarriage members which swung rearwards and turned through 90 deg for retraction into the bottom of the nacelles. The tailwheel retracted forwards and was covered by two small doors. Twin fins and rudders, of an almost square shape, were carried at the tips of the tailplane which had moderate dihedral. In the fuselage, behind the crew's pressurized nose compartment, was situated the bomb bay with long, folding bomb doors, while above this bomb bay were the main fuel tanks. These were supplemented by tanks in the inboard wing sections. The hemispherical fuselage nose consisted of a framework with glazing to provide a view for the pilot and bomb-aimer/navigator, the latter lying prone for bomb-aiming and firing the chin-mounted turret guns. Above and just behind the glazed nose section was a clear Plexiglas canopy which provided a sighting-station for navigation and also gave the radio operator a rear view when firing the three upper gun barbettes (two at the rear of the engine nacelles and one on top of the rear fuselage). Beneath the nose was a gondola with a glazed rear step which provided a view for the flight engineer when he lay prone to fire the rear ventral gun barbette. All armament was to be remotely-controlled.

By the time construction started on the Fw 191 V1 and V2 prototypes late in 1940 it was obvious that the proposed Jumo 222 engines were far from ready and so the two prototypes were fitted with less-powerful 1,600 hp BMW 801A air-cooled radial engines to begin flight testing. Furthermore, these prototypes had no cabin pressurization, and only dummy armament installations. With Dipl Ing Mehlhorn at the controls, the Fw 191 V1 first flew early in 1942 and, after ten flights, was joined by the similar Fw 191 V2.

The flight tests with the Fw 191 V1 and V2 machines proved very disappointing but this did not reflect any incompetence on Focke-Wulf engineers. Much of the trouble stemmed from the enforced underpowering, while the aircraft had suffered a weight penalty due to the profusion of electrical equipment which was also a source of constant breakdown (which said nothing for its chances under combat conditions). More surprising, Multhopp's special flaps were susceptible to serious flutter. No-one at Focke-Wulf had any illusions about the design and, late in 1942, after repeated requests, permission was given to abandon work on the Fw 191 V3, V4, and V5 prototypes and to modify and complete the V6 machine. The most important modifications were that all the main systems were made hydraulic and two specially-prepared Jumo 222 engines were fitted although these were still only producing less than 90 per cent of their design power. Thus modified, the Fw 191 V6 made its maiden flight in the spring of 1943 with Flugkapitän Hans Sander at the controls and, shortly after, made its last flight, from Delmenhorst to Wenzendorf. Already, in 1942, the Daimler-Benz DB 604 engine development had been abandoned and development prospects for the Jumo 222 engine appeared bleak

Only three prototypes of the Focke-Wulf Fw 191 bomber were completed.

because of the shortage of special metals. With no other 2,500 hp class engine available, therefore, the whole B medium bomber programme was officially shut down.

The Fw 191 V6 would have been a prototype for the Fw 191A production bomber. In addition to the pressurized nose compartment, the Fw 191A was to have had a complex arrangement of remote-controlled armament. For forward defence, there would have been a chin turret with two 7·9 mm MG 81 guns and, for rear defence, a small barbette in the rear of each engine nacelle (each with an MG 81) and a dorsal and ventral rear-fuselage barbette each with twin MG 81s or a single 20 mm MG 151 cannon. The internal bomb load of 4,000 kg (8,820 lb) was designed to be supplemented with up to 2,000 kg (4,410 lb) of external bombs or torpedoes. To guard against engine supply difficulties, at the end of 1941 Focke-Wulf had proposed the Fw 191B which was to be powered either by two Daimler-Benz DB 606 or two DB 610 engines which provided take-off power of 2,700 hp and 2,870 hp respectively by coupling pairs of DB 601 or DB 605 twelve-cylinder engines in each case. The development of these coupled engines was proceeding but their lower power-to-weight ratios would have reduced the Fw 191's armament and payload. The Fw 191C was also put forward as a solution, when the Fw 191A was cancelled, and was to have had four standard engines of the Jumo 211, DB 601E, DB 605 or similar type. The Fw 191C was to have been generally simplified with unpressurized cabin and manually-operated guns only. In the event, the Fw 191 V6 was the last Fw 191 ordered or built.

Fw 191B with DB 601 engines (estimated data): Span 26 m (85 ft $3\frac{5}{8}$ in); length 19·63 m (64 ft $4\frac{3}{4}$ in); height 5·6 m (18 ft $4\frac{1}{2}$ in); wing area 70·5 sq m (758·58 sq ft).

Empty weight 16,300 kg (35,942 lb); normal loaded weight 23,600 kg (52,038 lb); maximum loaded weight 25,600 kg (56,448 lb).

Maximum speed at 5,000 m (16,400 ft) 600 km/h (373 mph); initial rate of climb with normal load 450 m/min (1,476 ft/min); service ceiling 8,500 m (27,880 ft); maximum range 3,850 km (2,390 miles).

The prototype Condor, the Focke-Wulf Fw 200 V1, after being re-registered D-ACON and named *Brandenburg*.

# Focke-Wulf Fw 200 Condor

The British have always been famous for their ability to improvise, but in the matter of a long-range anti-shipping aircraft it was Germany that was forced to a makeshift. The famous Focke-Wulf Condor airliner which had established several records before the war, was adapted at the instigation of Oberstlt Edgar Petersen as a long-range reconnaissance and anti-shipping aircraft. The improvisation was never a particularly successful one, the many broken Condors that lay on Luftwaffe airfields proving that the machine was not designed for military work. Nevertheless, the aircraft was to become notorious in Britain as one of Germany's most potent anti-shipping weapons.

The Fw 200 was designed during 1936 by Dipl Ing Kurt Tank as an airliner for use by Lufthansa. It was a neat low-wing monoplane of all-metal construction with the exception of the control surfaces which were fabric covered. Accommodation for 26 passengers was provided in two cabins and the machine featured a fully-retractable undercarriage. The mainwheel legs, which retracted forward into the inboard engine nacelles, were of rather unusual design, this resulting from an attempt to produce an undercarriage, which, in the event of an emergency, would extend with the aid of the slipstream. Previous undercarriage design had been such that the airflow tended to prevent the legs from extending following a loss of hydraulic pressure.

The first prototype, the Fw 200 V1 D-AERE, later named *Saarland*, made its first flight on 27 July, 1937, one year and 11 days after the placing of the initial contract. The machine was powered by four 875 hp Pratt & Whitney Hornet radials, and was quickly followed by two further aircraft, the Fw 200 V2 D-AETA *Westfalen* and the V3 D-2600 *Immelmann III*. The latter was nominated as Hitler's personal aircraft to replace his Junkers-Ju 52/3m D-2600 *Immelmann II*. The second and

200

third machines differed from the prototype only in that they were powered by four 720 hp BMW 132G-1 radials. The Fw 200A-01 or V4 D-ADHR was named *Saarland* after the V1 had been renamed *Brandenburg*.

The A-02 OY-DAM *Dania* and A-05 OY-DEM *Jutlandia* were delivered to DDL Danish Air Lines. Of the remaining six aircraft, four went to Lufthansa: these were the A-03 or V5, D-AMHC *Nordmark*; the A-04 or V6, D-ACVH *Grenzmark*; the A-06 or V7, D-ARHW *Friesland*; and the A-09 or V9, D-AXFO *Pommern*. The other two machines, the A-07 or V8, PP-CBJ *Arumani* and A-08 PP-CBI *Abaitara* were delivered to Syndicato Condor of Brazil.

Late in 1938 the Fw 200 V1 (re-registered D-ACON *Brandenburg*) and bearing the special designation Fw 200S-1, was flown from Berlin to Tokyo. The arrival of the aircraft created much interest in Japan and resulted in an order for five Fw 200B transports and a single aircraft for use by the JNAF on reconnaissance duties. The Fw 200B-1 powered by four 850 hp BMW 132Dc engines and the B-2 with four 830 hp BMW 132H engines were intended as the main production variants, several being delivered to Lufthansa.

In the event, no Condors reached Japan, but the order for the military variant did result in the construction of the Fw 200 V10. This was a long-range reconnaissance variant with a dorsal turret containing a 7·9 mm MG 15 machine-gun. Two further MG 15s were fitted to fire fore and aft from a special gondola carried beneath the forward fuselage and offset to starboard.

Just before Germany went to war, the Luftwaffe Chief of Air Staff, Gen Hans Jeschonnek, ordered Oberstlt Edgar Petersen, an experienced reconnaissance pilot, to establish a long-range anti-shipping squadron. The only aircraft immediately available possessing the requirements for such a task was the Condor, but it was by no means the ideal. Its structure was much too weak for a military aircraft, but nevertheless construction of an armed production variant began.

Designated Fw 200C-0, a batch of ten pre-production aircraft were delivered in September 1939. The Fw 200C was structurally strengthened

An Fw 200C retracts its undercarriage after take-off. (*A. Price*)

and the first four C-0s were completed as unarmed transports and served, together with four Fw 200Bs, with KGrzbV 105 during the invasion of Norway in April 1940. The six armed aircraft were delivered to Petersen's Fernaufklärungsstaffel which was formed in November 1939. The unit's first operational sortie was on 8 April, 1940, when, in company with Heinkel He 115s of Kü.Fl.Gr 506, it reconnoitred the North Sea for signs of activity by the Royal Navy. The unit later saw action against British shipping, being redesignated 1./KG 40 towards the end of the month.

The first military production variant was the 830 hp BMW 132H powered Fw 200C-1. It carried an armament of one 20 mm MG FF cannon in the nose and an MG 15 machine-gun in the rear of the considerably lengthened ventral gondola, plus a further MG 15 in a simplified forward dorsal position. A third MG 15 gun was carried in a rear glazed dorsal position and provision was made for four 250 kg (550 lb) bombs, two beneath the extended inboard engine nacelles and two immediately beyond the outboard engines on special racks. A 250 kg (550 lb) concrete bomb for aiming purposes could be carried beneath the ventral gondola. The Fw 200C-1 carried a crew of five including pilot, co-pilot, navigator/radio operator/gunner, flight engineer/gunner and rear dorsal gunner.

In June 1940, 1.Staffel/KG 40 was redesignated I.Gruppe and soon afterwards was re-equipped with the Fw 200C-1. After being transferred to Bordeaux-Mérignac, the unit went into action against the British Isles. During experimental mine-laying operations, each Condor carried two 1,000 kg (2,200 lb) mines, the aircraft dropping the weapon at the entrance to British east coast ports. The weapon was so unwieldy that little success

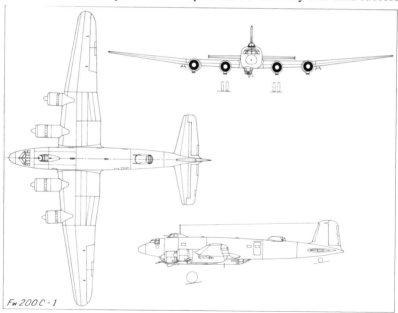

Fw 200C-1

202

was achieved. Another experimental use of the Fw 200 was the bombing of the Liverpool/Birkenhead area during the last four nights of August 1940.

During August and September 1940, I./KG 40 sank no less than 90,000 tons of shipping, and on 26 October Oblt Bernhard Jope bombed the 42,000 ton liner *Empress of Britain*, the vessel later being sunk by a U-boat. In January 1941, Hitler placed I./KG 40 under direct control of the German Navy, and between 1 August, 1940, and 9 February, 1941, the unit claimed no less than 363,000 tons of Allied shipping. Previously, on 16 January, Hptm Verlohr sank two ships totalling 10,857 tons and early in February Hptm Fritz Fliegel, Staffelkapitän of 2./KG 40, led an attack on Iceland.

The Bramo 323 powered Fw 200C-3 was delivered from mid-1941. (*R. C. Seeley*)

The next production model was the Fw 200C-2 which was also powered by BMW 132H engines but featured new 'cutaway' outboard engine nacelles which allowed a 250 kg (550 lb) bomb or 300 litre (66 Imp gal) drop tank to be carried, with much reduced drag. The first really major modification to the aircraft was in the Fw 200C-3 which appeared during the summer of 1941. This was structurally strengthened and powered by four 1,000 hp Bramo 323R-2 radials and normally carried a load of four 250 kg (550 lb) bombs. The Fw 200C-3/U1 had its defensive armament boosted by the addition of a 15 mm MG 151 cannon in a hydraulically-operated dorsal turret and the replacement of the 20 mm MG FF cannon by an MG 151/20 of similar calibre. The Fw 200C-3/U2 was fitted with the original type of dorsal gun position and had the MG 151/20 cannon replaced by a 13 mm MG 131 gun, which allowed a Lotfe 7D bombsight to be carried. The C-3/U3 had two additional MG 131 weapons, and the C-3/U4 mounted MG 131 guns in place of the MG 15s and carried an additional gunner.

The Condor continued to experience trouble with its weak structure, the usual cause being the failure of the rear spar resulting in the aircraft breaking its back on landing.

The machine was never produced in large numbers, 26 Condors being delivered in 1940, 58 in 1941, 84 in 1942, 76 in 1943 and eight in 1944.

An Fw 200C-3 of I./KG 40 with the unit's famous 'world in a ring' insignia on the nose. (*H. Redemann*)

It became usual for a crew from KG 40 to be sent to the Cottbus factory to collect each aircraft as it came off the assembly line. Production was also slowed by the bombing of the factory, final assembly work then being transferred to Blohm und Voss.

With the increase in anti-aircraft defences and the Allied use of catapult aircraft on merchant ships, offensive operations by the Condors were severely curtailed, activities being confined to shadowing their quarry and reporting its position to Fliegerführer Atlantik. The catapult merchant ship carried a Hurricane fighter which was launched when an enemy aircraft came within sight. The first success by such a ship came on 3 August, 1941, when Lieut Everett of No. 804 Squadron shot down a Condor from I./KG 40. Only five aircraft were lost to the catapult-equipped merchantmen, but their presence did have an important effect on the morale of both sides.

Early in 1942 the Fw 200C-4 appeared on the production lines. Essentially similar to the C-3, the new variant was fitted with FuG Rostock search radar; later machines being equipped with FuG 200 Hohentwiel radar which allowed blind bombing attacks to be carried out. An MG 151/20 cannon or MG 131 machine-gun could be installed in the nose of the gondola depending on whether a Lotfe 7D bombsight was carried. The Fw 200C-4/U1 and U2 were both high-speed transport aircraft, but only one variant of each (respectively c/n 0137 and 0138) was completed.

Late in 1941 several Condors were lost to Grumman Wildcats from HMS *Audacity*, one of the first escort carriers to see operational service. During the early part of 1942, I./KG 40 was transferred to Trondheim-

Photographed in April 1943, this Fw 200C-3/U1 was fitted with an HDL 151 dorsal turret. (*H. Redemann*)

204

A Condor of I./KG 40 on patrol over the Atlantic. (*A. Price*)

Vaernes in Norway and played an important rôle in the operations against the PQ series of Arctic convoys. In May 1942 Oberst Pasewaldt took over from Petersen as commander of KG 40, but the unit was split up towards the end of the year.

On 9 January, 1943, 1. and 3./KG 40 with eighteen Fw 200s flew to Stalino in southern Russia. Here they were redesignated KGrzbV 200 and placed under the command of Maj Hans-Jürgen Williers to operate in support of the beleaguered German garrison at Stalingrad. Initially the Condors landed near Stalingrad, but the airfield was soon overrun by Soviet troops, and it became necessary to drop their supply containers by parachute. After about a month of operations KGrzbV 200 was withdrawn to Berlin-Staaken and redesignated 8./KG 40.

The re-united II./KG 40 was then based at Bordeaux and Cognac, with 2.Staffel remaining at Trondheim. III.Gruppe concentrated solely on anti-shipping attack, acting on sighting reports provided by the Ju 290s from

Close-up of the Fw 200C's ventral gondola with a flexibly-mounted 20 mm MG FF cannon in the nose. (*H. Redemann*)

205

An Fw 200C-6 fitted with FuG 200 Hohentwiel radar equipment with a nose-mounted antenna. (*H. Redemann*)

FAGr 5. Reports would be received from Algeciras in Spain when Allied convoys left Gibraltar and aircraft from FAGr 5 would then report their exact position. A minimum of four Fw 200s from KG 40 would then attack, making full use of FuG 200 search radar. The Condor was then forbidden to attack at altitudes of below 3,000 m (9,843 ft) because of danger from anti-aircraft fire.

In an attempt to improve the Condor's offensive capabilities, several

Luftwaffe mechanics of KG 40 loading bombs aboard an Fw 200C at Bordeaux. (*K. Ries*)

aircraft were modified to carry two Henschel Hs 293 missiles, under the designation Fw 200C-6. A definitive version was also built, the Fw 200C-8, both variants being equipped with FuG 203b Kehl III missile control equipment. The first operational use of the Fw 200/Hs 293 combination was made on 28 December, 1943, but the aircraft encountered a patrolling RAF Sunderland flying-boat and was forced down. In the event, no successes were recorded with the combination, and by early 1944 the Condor had virtually disappeared from operations.

Condors remained in service with the Luftwaffe until the end of the war, but in the rôle for which they were originally designed. The Fw 200 V3 and V6 were used by the special unit commanded by Flugkapitän Hans Baur which carried the Nazi leaders around Germany. Based at Berlin-Tempelhof, the unit later acquired a number of Fw 200Cs. Perhaps the most interesting of these was the specially equipped C-4/U1 used by Heinrich Himmler as his personal transport. The machine was captured after the war and exhibited at RAE Farnborough in 1945.

The last scheduled flight by a Lufthansa aircraft was made on 14 April, 1945, when the Fw 200B-2 D-ASHH flew from Barcelona to Berlin. The machine was lost a week later while attempting the return flight. Several Condors were also used by the clandestine I./KG 200 for spy-dropping activities.

*Wartime operational units:* 1.(F)/120, 1.(F)/122, I., III. and IV./KG 40, II./KG 100, I./KG 200, KGrzbV 200, Führerkurierstaffel, Transportfliegerstaffel Condor, Transportstaffel 200.

Fw 200C-3/U4: Span 32·84 m (107 ft 9½ in); length 23·85 m (76 ft 11½ in); height 6·3 m (20 ft 8 in); wing area 118 sq m (1,290 sq ft).

Empty weight 17,000 kg (37,485 lb); loaded weight 22,700 kg (50,053 lb).

Maximum speed at 4,700 m (15,410 ft) 360 km/h (224 mph); cruising speed at 4,000 m (13,124 ft) 335 km/h (208 mph); service ceiling 6,000 m (19,685 ft); normal range 3,560 km (2,211 miles); endurance at economic cruising speed 14 hr.

# Focke-Wulf Ta 152 and Ta 153

The Focke-Wulf Fw 190, designed by Dipl Ing Kurt Tank, had proved so successful that the RLM allowed him to use the first letters of his surname to prefix all subsequent Focke-Wulf designs. Only six designs were ever to carry this designation, these being the Focke-Wulf Ta 152, Ta 153, Ta 154, Ta 183, Ta 283 and Ta 400. The Ta 154, Ta 183 and Ta 283 are described elsewhere in this volume, the Ta 400 was a six-engined bomber project, and the Ta 152 and Ta 153 were high-speed fighter developments of the Fw 190D.

During the autumn of 1944 the Fw 190 V18 (c/n 0040) was fitted with a 1,750 hp Junkers Jumo 213E engine and long-span wings of high aspect ratio. Having the designation V18/U2, the aircraft was the first prototype for the Ta 152H series which in fact followed on from the Fw 190G. The V18/U2 crashed on 8 October, 1944, but was replaced by the Fw 190 V20 (c/n 0042) which, although retaining the standard Fw 190 wing, was powered by a Jumo 213E engine.

The first Ta 152H prototype with full equipment was the Fw 190 V29/U1 (c/n 0054) which had a pressurized cabin and a wing span of 14·5 m (47 ft 6¾ in). The aircraft had two 20 mm MG 151/20 cannon in the wings plus an engine-mounted 30 mm MK 108 cannon, and was powered by a Jumo 213E engine. The Fw 190 V30/U1 (c/n 0055) was similar to the previous aircraft but without armament. The V32/U1 (c/n 0057) was the final Ta 152H-0 prototype, and it was later fitted with an experimental 20 mm MG 213 cannon which had a rate of fire of no less than 1,300 rounds per minute, the machine being redesignated Fw 190 V32/U2.

Twenty Focke-Wulf Ta 152H-0 pre-production aircraft (c/ns 150001 to 150020) were built at the Cottbus factory from October 1944.

The Ta 152H-0 pre-production model was similar to the V29/U1, being powered by a 1,880 hp Jumo 213E/B engine, the power of which could be boosted to 2,250 hp by the addition of MW-50 water-methanol injection. The Ta 152H-0/R11 was an all-weather fighter fitted with LGW K 23 navigational control and FuG 125 radio equipment. The H-0/R21 had the GM-1 nitrous-oxide boosting removed, and the H-0/R31 featured increased GM-1 capacity.

The first production model was the Ta 152H-1 for which the Ta 152 V26 (c/n 110026) was the prototype. Apart from increased fuel capacity, the H-1 was similar to the H-0, and the H-2 project was to have had improved radio equipment. Final projected variant was the Ta 152H-10 fighter-reconnaissance aircraft with an Rb 20/30, Rb 50/30 or Rb 75/30 camera.

The Ta 152A-1 and A-2 projects were similar to the Fw 190D-9 but were to have carried four 20 mm MG 151/20 cannon and FuG 24 radio in place of FuG 16. The Ta 152B series were similar, but were equipped with an engine-mounted MK 108 cannon and GM-1 boosting. The Ta 152B-1 and B-2 were projects only, the B-3 a ground attack variant with extensive

A rare photograph of a number of Ta 152H-1 fighters in service with JG 301 during April 1945. (*Dölling via R. C. Seeley*)

armour and the B-4 a heavy fighter. Two variants were proposed, the B-4/R1 with standard armament and the B-4/R2 with three MK 108s and two MG 151/20s. The Ta 152B-5, for which the modified Fw 190 V53 or V68 (c/n 170003) was prototype, had three MK 103 cannon. An all-weather variant was designated Ta 152B-5/R11 and three prototypes were built, the Ta 152 V19, V20, and V21.

The second major production variant (the first being the Ta 152H) was the Ta 152C. First prototype was the Fw 190 V21/U1 (c/n 0043) which was fitted with a Daimler-Benz DB 603L engine and made its first flight on 19 November, 1944. This was followed on 28 February, 1945, by the generally similar Ta 152 V6 (c/n 110006) and V7 (c/n 110007), the latter with all-weather equipment. The Ta 152 V8 was fitted with a Revi EZ 42 gunsight, but the V13 and V15 were never completed.

The Ta 152C-0 and C-1 were essentially alike, both being powered by the 2,100 hp DB 603L engine and armed with one MK 108 and four MG 151/20 cannon. A similar series of conversion packs were produced for the Ta 152C as for the H, the Ta 152C-1/R14 being a fighter-bomber with ETC 504 racks. The Ta 152C-2 was similar to the C-1, apart from improved radio equipment, and the C-3 had an engine-mounted MK 103 cannon in place of the MK 108. Prototypes included the Ta 152 V16 (c/n 110016), V17 (c/n 110017), V 27 (c/n 110030) and V28 (c/n 110031). The Ta 152C-4 project was to have carried WGr 21 rocket tubes, three prototypes (Ta 152 V22, V23, and V24) being ordered.

The Ta 152E-1, for which the V9 (c/n 110009) and V14 (c/n 110014) were prototypes, was a photographic-reconnaissance aircraft with a camera installation similar to that of the H-10. The Ta 152E-1/U1 had an obliquely-mounted camera and the E-2 was a high-altitude variant with the wing of the H-series. Only one prototype was completed, the Ta 152 V26. Final proposed models were the Ta 152S-1 tandem two-seat trainer and variants powered by the 3,000 hp Junkers Jumo 222E/F engine.

Early in 1945 a number of Ta 152Hs were delivered to the newly-formed Erprobungskommando 152 at Rechlin under Hptm Bruno Stolle. The first operational unit to be equipped with the aircraft was the Geschwader-Stab of JG 301 under Obstlt Aufhammer, the unit being charged with the protection of Messerschmitt Me 262 fighter bases.

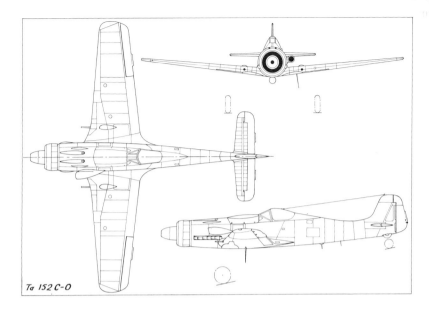

Ta 152 C-0

Parallel with the Ta 152, a more radical variant was proposed, designated Ta 153. This was similar in layout to the Ta 152C series but was to have had an entirely new wing of high aspect ratio and increased span. Only one prototype was completed, the Fw 190 V32/U1 (c/n 0057), but the design was abandoned as it was thought that it would have seriously disrupted production lines at a critical stage in the war.

Ta 152H-1: Span 14·5 m (47 ft 6¾ in); length 10·8 m (35 ft 5½ in); height 4 m (13 ft 1½ in); wing area 23·5 sq m (252·95 sq ft).

Normal loaded weight 4,750 kg (10,472 lb); maximum loaded weight 5,220 kg (11,508 lb).

Maximum speed at 10,500 m (34,451 ft) 695 km/h (431 mph), at 9,000 m (29,529 ft) 750 km/h (466 mph) with MW-50, and at 12,500 m (41,012 ft) with MW-50 and GM-1 760 km/h (472 mph); service ceiling 14,800 m (48,560 ft); normal range 1,200 km (745 miles).

The Smithsonian Institution has the Ta 152H-0 (c/n 110003).

# Focke-Wulf Ta 154

During 1942, the Luftwaffe was increasingly in need of a new type of night fighter to replace the adapted versions of the Messerschmitt Bf 110 and Junkers Ju 88 it was using, but the RLM's plans for such a replacement were set back mainly because Allied bombing delayed development of the Heinkel He 219. In September 1942 therefore, two months before the He 219 V1 flew, the RLM issued a new requirement for a specialized night fighter which, unlike the He 219, was to be largely of wooden construction. The reason was not simply to economise in metal but was also to make the best use of skilled wood-workers since it had proved difficult to retrain them to work with metal.

The Focke-Wulf Ta 154 V1 (TE-FE), prototype of a fighter planned to use a maximum of wood in its construction. (*F. Selinger*)

Focke-Wulf at Bremen undertook to meet the new requirement with a twin-engined two-seat shoulder-wing aircraft and had basic calculations completed by 14 October, 1942, and layout drawings ready about five days later. Several variants were proposed including two- and single-seat day fighters, but the basic design required materials in the approximate proportions of 57 per cent wood, 30 per cent steel and very little duralumin in the remaining 13 per cent. Satisfied with this, the RLM issued a general development contract together with the designation Ta 154. Unofficially the Ta 154 was known as the Moskito.

The Ta 154 was a neatly laid-out aircraft designed to be powered by two 1,340 hp Junkers Jumo 211F twelve-cylinder inverted-vee liquid-cooled engines driving three-blade airscrews. Since steel tubes were becoming scarce, the main and auxiliary wing-spars were of wooden box construction while extensive use was to be made of bonding in the assembly of the wooden airframe in general. A nosewheel undercarriage was used, with wheels of generous diameter to facilitate take-offs from grass surfaces; the main undercarriage members retracted backward into engine nacelle recesses and the nose member pivoted back into the fuselage with the wheel swivelling through 90 deg to lie flat under the pilot's seat. The windscreen of the stepped cockpit canopy was of armoured glass and some 150 kg (330 lb) of armour plating was distributed around the cockpit. The radio/radar operator sat behind the pilot and faced forward, with his screen and equipment filling most of the space in front of him. In the fuselage sides, and flanking the radio/radar operator, were two 30 mm MK 108 cannon (with 110 rounds) and two 20 mm MG 151 cannon (with 150 rounds), while a single MK 108 cannon (with 150 rounds) was mounted at a forward angle of 45 deg to fire from the top of the rear fuselage (Schräger Waffeneinbau or oblique weapon installation). Fuel was equally disposed in two 750 litre (165 gal) fuselage tanks situated one behind the wing main spar and one behind the auxiliary spar where these passed through the fuselage.

By the summer of 1943, the Ta 154 V1 was complete and made its maiden flight on 1 July, 1943, flown by Kurt Tank, and was subsequently flown on 7 July with the test pilot Flugkapitän Hans Sander at the controls. Flying at this time was from Hanover-Langenhagen, Lower Saxony, where Focke-Wulf's testing had to be done because of Allied air attacks. Both the V1 and V2 aircraft were powered by 1,500 hp Jumo 211N engines, improved versions of the 211F engines originally envisaged, but no radar equipment was fitted at this early stage. The success of flight trials with these aircraft led the RLM to order the Ta 154A night-fighter version and, accordingly, Ta 154 V3 was fitted with FuG 202 Lichtenstein BC-1 radar equipment to become the prototype of the Ta 154A-0/U1 pre-production aircraft. Making its first flight on 25 November, 1943, the V3 was powered by two 1,500 hp Jumo 211R engines (forerunner of the 213 series) and achieved a speed of 620 km/h (385 mph) with the short radar antennae installed. Various other types of radar and electronic equipment were also tested in four other prototypes built before the end of 1944.

The Ta 154 V3 (TE-FG) was the first Moskito to be fitted with radar equipment as the prototype for the Ta 154A-0/U1 pre-production night fighter. (*H. Redemann*)

212

The Ta 154 V7 (TE-FK). (*F. Selinger*)

In March 1944, the Jägerstab laid down the following short-term delivery schedules for the Ta 154, although they could not be met; the Focke-Wulf concern was to deliver 37 aircraft by May 1944, the Reparatur-Werk (Erfurt) and Famo (Breslau) were to deliver 21 and five aircraft respectively by the same month, and combined production was to rise to 250 aircraft a month by November that year. It was not, however, until August that the Ta 154 V8 to V15 were built at the Reparatur-Werk as the first eight pre-production Ta 154A-0s and, after a brief trial period with a Service test unit, they were then put back into the development programme. Also built at the Reparatur-Werk were the first two Ta 154A-1 production aircraft, subsequent aircraft apparently being built elsewhere. Production was slowed up by transport difficulties which affected delivery of the various components from the sub-contractors, and the somewhat high production figure of 12,000 man-hours per airframe was arrived at.

The delayed and slow production was a bad start for the Ta 154, but its official cancellation came about before the end of 1944 as a result of troubles with the special Tego-Film used to bond the wooden parts. When the factory producing the so-called Goldschmitt Tego-Film was bombed, various new bonding agents had to be tried and these proved unsatisfactory. In the first two Ta 154A-1 aircraft the new bonding agent weakened the wood by containing too much acid (insufficiently neutralized), and both these aircraft disintegrated during high-speed flights. The problem of supplying adequate bonding agents was not, in fact, solved until the intensified programme for Heinkel's He 162 (Germany's second aircraft to use wood substantially) got under way and then not only were adequate new bonding agents brought out, but a special bureau to study the problems of wooden construction was set up.

Only seven of the other Ta 154A-1 night fighters under construction were completed and these were used operationally for a short period by I./NJG 3 at Stade, and NJGr 10. Other aircraft were modified for special rôles; six of the Ta 154A-0 pre-production machines were adapted as Mistel bombers (redesignated Ta 154A-2/U3) with the cockpit space occupied by a warhead and attachments fitted for an Fw 190 director fighter, while six other aircraft also had warheads fitted and a rear cockpit with downward-firing ejector seat to enable a pilot to aim his aircraft at a

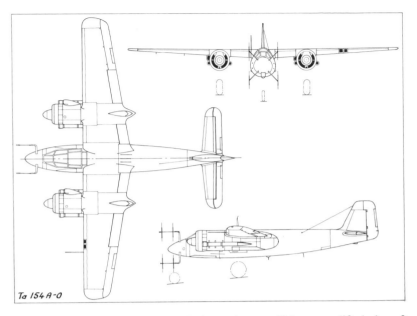

Ta 154 A-0

bomber pack and then bale out. It is not known if these modified aircraft were ever used.

Other developments proposed were the Ta 154C-1 night fighter with armament increased to six MK 108 cannon and a fuselage lengthened by 1·1 m (3 ft 7¼ in) to accommodate more fuel, and the similar Ta 154C-2 day fighter which dispensed with radar equipment. The projected Ta 254 night fighter was a redesign of the Ta 154C with the same lengthened fuselage and the same 1,750 hp Jumo 213A engines but with the wing area increased by 30 per cent to allow the weight of the very formidable armament of eight MK 108 cannon to be carried.

Ta 154A-1: Span 16 m (52 ft 6 in); length (excluding antennae) 12·1 m (39 ft 8⅜ in); height 3·5 m (11 ft 5¾ in); wing area 32·4 sq m (348·6 sq ft).

Empty weight 6,405 kg (14,123 lb); crew 200 kg (440 lb); ammunition 320 kg (704 lb); fuel and oil 1,325 kg (2,922 lb); loaded weight 8,250 kg (18,191 lb).

Maximum speed at 6,100 m (20,008 ft) 635 km/h (395 mph); maximum speed at sea level 540 km/h (335 mph); climb to 6,000 m (19,680 ft) 10 min, to 8,000 m (26,240 ft) 14·5 min; landing speed (empty) 163 km/h (101 mph); take-off distance on grass 600 m (1,968 ft); service ceiling 10,500 m (34,440 ft); single-engine ceiling 5,500 m (18,040 ft); endurance at 510 km/h (317 mph) at 6,000 m (19,680 ft) 2·75 hr.

Four Gotha Go 145As of a Luftwaffe pilot training school. (*R. C. Seeley*)

# Gotha Go 145

When the Gotha company was re-established on 2 October, 1933, its first aircraft was the Go 145 biplane trainer designed by Dipl Ing Albert Kalkert. It was a conventional single-bay two-seat biplane with a fixed undercarriage. The machine was built of wood with fabric covering and was powered by a 240 hp Argus As 10C eight-cylinder inverted-vee air-cooled engine driving a two-blade fixed-pitch wooden propeller.

The prototype first flew in February 1934 and was followed by the Go 145A production aircraft which entered service in 1935 with the Luftwaffe's training elements. The design proved so successful that production was later undertaken by the Ago, Focke-Wulf and BFW companies. Licence production of the Go 145 was also undertaken in Turkey and Spain, and eventually almost 10,000 were built. The Spanish variant was built by Construcciones Aeronauticas SA as the CASA 1145-L, remaining in service with the Spanish Air Force until long after the war.

Development of the aircraft continued in Germany, the experimental Go 145B with an enclosed cockpit and spatted undercarriage appearing in 1935. The Go 145C was used for gunnery training and carried a single 7·9 mm MG 15 machine-gun in the rear cockpit. Luftwaffe training units that operated the Go 145 included FFS A/B 4 at Prague-Gbell, FFS A/B 23 at Kaufbeuren, FFS A/B 41 at Frankfurt-an der -Oder, FFS A/B 72 at Detmold and FFS A/B 116 at Göppingen.

During 1942, the Russians began to use the Polikarpov Po-2 biplane on night harassing missions behind the German lines, and these operations were so successful that the Luftwaffe, in addition to setting up counter-measures, established its own harassing squadrons. The first of 13 Störkampfstaffeln were established in December 1942, being mainly equipped with Gotha Go 145 and Arado Ar 66 two-seat trainers. They also proved successful, so that in October 1943 they were redesignated

The Go 145C was fitted with a 7·9 mm MG 15 machine-gun in the rear cockpit for gunnery training. (*R. C. Seeley*)

NSGr 1, 2, 3, 4, 5, and 6. Part of 1. and 2./NSGr 1, NSGr 2, 1./NSGr 3 and NSGr 6, the last mentioned commanded by Maj Rupert Frost, a holder of the Ritterkreuz, all originally operated the Go 145.

In February 1944, the Go 145 was delivered to NSGr 5 under Maj Böllner based in southern Russia. On Christmas Day 1944 the unit was at Somlovvasarholy, moving to Batolnapuszta for operations with the Go 145 in the Budapest area. When the war drew to a close in May 1945, the Go 145 and Ar 66 still formed the major equipment of the Nachtschlachtgruppen.

*Wartime operational units:* Störkampfstaffeln, 1., 2. and 3./NSGr 1, NSGr 2, NSGr 3, NSGr 4, NSGr 5, NSGr 6 and the Ost-Flieger-Gruppe.

Go 145A: Span 9 m (29 ft 6¼ in); length 8·7 m (28 ft 6½ in); height 2·9 m (9 ft 6 in); wing area 21·75 sq m (234·10 sq ft).
Empty weight 800 kg (1,940 lb); loaded weight 1,380 kg (3,043 lb).
Maximum speed at sea level 212 km/h (132 mph); cruising speed 180 km/h (112 mph); landing speed 90 km/h (56 mph); climb to 1,000 m (3,280 ft) 5·5 min; service ceiling 3,700 m (12,139 ft); normal range 630 km (391 miles).

# Gotha Go 242

The only Gotha aircraft type to see anything like large-scale operational service during the Second World War was the Go 242 transport glider. Designed by Dipl Ing Albert Kalkert, the Go 242 was an unusual twin-boom design with shoulder-mounted wings. The fuselage pod was capable of carrying 21 fully-equipped troops and was hinged at the rear for ease of access. Apart from troops, the aircraft could also carry a Kübelwagen military vehicle and other heavy loads.

The Go 242 was allocated high priority by the RLM after they recognized that the design would provide the Luftwaffe with a useful troop-

A Gotha Go 242A-1 glider transport of the Luftwaffe's Schleppstaffeln. (*H. Lächler*)

carrying glider with roughly three times the capacity of the DFS 230. Two prototypes were constructed, the Go 242 V1 and V2, both of which flew early in 1941. The wings and tail surfaces were built of wood with part fabric and part plywood covering. The fuselage pod was built of welded steel tube and had fabric covering, and the twin-wheel undercarriage was jettisoned after take-off, the glider landing with the aid of two retractable skids.

The pre-production Go 242A-0 was similar to the V1 and V2, but the Go 242A-1 introduced deeper tailbooms and could carry an armament of up to four 7·9 mm MG 15 machine-guns. The first production variant was intended to carry freight, but the Go 242A-2 was an assault glider with provision for 21 troops.

The Go 242A entered service in 1942 with six special glider squadrons. The most usual towing aircraft was the Heinkel He 111H, and in some instances the He 111Z five-engined tug was used. A variety of rocket-assisted take-off units could also be used to help the Go 242 into the air, including four 1,102 lb thrust Rheinmetall-Borsig RI 502 solid fuel rockets. The first operational use of the Go 242 was in the Middle East, some being based at Athens-Tatoi, various airfields in Sicily and in the Western Desert. The aircraft later took part in operations on the Eastern Front.

In 1942 the Go 242B series appeared which was fitted with a fixed nosewheel undercarriage. The Go 242B-1 had a simple twin-wheel arrangement with a cross axle, but the B-2 introduced a more refined undercarriage

The Go 242A-1 which underwent assisted take-off trials with four RI 502 solid-fuel rockets mounted behind the fuselage. (*H. Redemann*)

The Go 242A-2 which served as a development aircraft for the Kalkert Ka 430 glider
(*R. C. Seeley*)

with spring oleo legs attached to the fuselage sides. The Go 242B-3 and
B-4 were paratroop versions of the B-1 and B-2 respectively, with a
double rear loading door. The Go 242B-5 was a dual control variant for
training.

The last production version was the Go 242C-1, a special conversion of
the A-1 capable of alighting on water. It had a planing hull, and twin
stabilizing floats mounted beneath the wings. This variant could carry a
small catamaran assault boat with a 1,200 kg (2,646 lb) charge of explosive suspended between its hulls. The boat would have been placed
alongside an enemy ship, the one-man crew escaping to be picked up later
by a submarine or seaplane. A number of Go 242C-1s were delivered to
6./KG 200 under Oblt Kempke during the autumn of 1944. The glider
was to have been towed to the vicinity of its target by an He 111Z of the
same unit, and it was planned to make an assault with the weapon on the
British fleet at Scapa Flow, but Germany's shortage of fuel prevented the
operation from being undertaken.

Perhaps the most interesting development of the Go 242 was the
Kalkert Ka 430, a smaller, and more refined version of the basic design.
The Ka 430 had a single fin and rudder mounted atop a slim tail boom. It
carried a 13 mm MG 131 machine-gun in a manually-operated cupola
above and behind the cockpit. Full dual controls were fitted. A Go 242A-2
was fitted with the single fin and rudder assembly in 1944 and at least one
Ka 430A-0 was built and flown.

Total production of the Go 242 was 1,528 of which 133 were converted
to Go 244 standard.

*Wartime operational units:* 1. to 6./Go 242 Staffeln, 6./KG 200. Also used in small
numbers by the Schleppgruppen (towing groups) and LLG 1 and 2.

Go 242A-2: Span 24·5 m (80 ft 4½ in); length 15·8 m (51 ft 10 in); height 4·4 m (14 ft
4¼ in); wing area 64·4 sq m (693·20 sq ft).
Empty weight 3,200 kg (7,056 lb); loaded weight 7,100 kg (15,656 lb).
Maximum towing speed 240 km/h (149 mph).

# Gotha Go 244

With a large number of captured French Gnome/Rhône 14M fourteen-cylinder two-row radial engines available to the Germans, the decision was made to produce a twin-engined version of the Go 242 transport glider. Designated Go 244, the aircraft was basically a Go 242B airframe with the forward portion of the twin booms extended to accommodate two 700 hp Gnome/Rhône 14M 4/5 engines. Five variants were built, designated Go 244B-1 to B-5, respectively conversions of the Go 242B-1 to B-5.

A small number of Go 244s were delivered in March 1942 to KGrzbV 104 in Greece and KGrzbV 106 in Crete. The aircraft were used for a short period in the Western Desert but proved extremely vulnerable to Allied air and anti-aircraft action and were soon withdrawn. KGrzbV 106 was re-equipped with the Junkers-Ju 52/3m during the summer of 1942 and KGrzbV 104 with the Messerschmitt Me 323 in November. The only other unit to operate the Go 244 was 7./TG 4 based in southern Russia.

The Gotha Go 244B-1 was a development of the Go 242 glider powered by two Gnome/Rhône 14M radial engines. (*H. Redemann*)

Some Gotha Go 244s were fitted with captured Russian Shvetsov M-25A radials which produced 750 hp for take-off and the native BMW 132Z, but the French engine was by far the most successful. The Go 244 was also projected with an Argus As 10C or Junkers Jumo 211 engine mounted in the nose, but no such aircraft was completed.

Perhaps the most interesting Gotha glider project, however, was the Go 345 which was proposed in 1944. An attractive shoulder-wing monoplane, the Go 345 was projected in two major versions: the Go 345A with a pointed nose and large upward hingeing doors in the fuselage sides, and the Go 345B with an abbreviated nose which could be folded aside to facilitate loading. Both machines were projected with a 300 kg (660 lb) thrust Argus As 014 pulse-jet under each wing. The Go 345 was to be capable of carrying a crew of two and ten troops or the equivalent weight of freight. A prototype of the Go 345B was completed in 1944, but no production of the aircraft was undertaken. The Go 345A is illustrated on page 613.

Go 242B-2: Span 24·5 m (80 ft 4⅓ in); length 15·8 m (51 ft 10 in); height 4·7 m (15 ft 5 in); wing area 64·4 sq m (693·2 sq ft).

Empty weight 5,100 kg (11,245 lb); loaded weight 7,800 kg (17,199 lb).

Maximum speed at 3,000 m (9,843 ft) 290 km/h (180 mph); service ceiling 7,500 m (24,607 ft); normal range 600 km (373 miles); maximum range 740 km (460 miles).

# Heinkel He 45

In 1930 Ernst Heinkel AG began work on two combat aircraft at the behest of the Reichswehr Ministry. These were the He 45 light bomber and the He 46 tactical reconnaissance aircraft. The He 45 was a sturdy single-bay biplane of conventional layout and three prototypes were built early in 1932. The He 45a, D-2477, was an unarmed two-seater powered by a 750 hp BMW VI 7·3Z twelve-cylinder vee liquid-cooled engine. The second prototype was the He 45b with a four-blade airscrew, and the He 45c was the first model to carry armament, one fixed forward-firing MG 17 and one movable MG 15 machine-gun being installed.

The major production variant was the He 45C which was essentially similar to the He 45c. Because of limited production capacity at Heinkel's Warnemünde factory, the He 45 was built under licence by Focke-Wulf, BFW and Gotha. By the time the He 45C entered service it had been rejected as a bomber and was delivered to the Aufklärungsverbände, each Staffel receiving three.

A number of He 45Cs equipped a Kette of A/88 serving in the Spanish Civil War, but at the start of the 1939–45 war only 21 aircraft of this type

A Heinkel He 45C of Aufklärungsgruppe 122.

220

were recorded as operational with the Luftwaffe. These were serving with 4.(H)/12, 5.(H)/13, 4.(H)/21, 4.(H)/23 and 4.(H)/31, but were so out-dated that they were virtually incapable of performing useful service and were soon relegated to training units. Several experimental conversions of the basic design were completed, including one powered by the 880 hp Daimler-Benz DB 600 engine and another with the experimental BMW 116 unit.

He 45C: Span 11·5 m (37 ft 8¼ in); length 10 m (32 ft 9¾ in); height 3·6 m (11 ft 9¾ in); wing area 34·59 sq m (372·32 sq ft).
    Empty weight 2,105 kg (4,642 lb); loaded weight 2,745 kg (6,053 lb).
    Maximum speed at sea level 290 km/h (180 mph); cruising speed 220 km/h (137 mph); landing speed 105 km/h (65 mph); climb to 1,000 m (3,280 ft) 2·4 min; service ceiling 5,500 m (18,046 ft); normal range 1,200 km (746 miles).

The Heinkel He 46 short-range reconnaissance and Army co-operation aircraft first flew late in 1931. An early sub-variant, the He 46f, D-ILHE, is seen here.

# Heinkel He 46

When the build-up of German military aircraft began to speed up in the early 1930s, Ernst Heinkel moved into a favourable position due to his willingness to design and build every type of aircraft called for. The Reichswehr-Ministerium wanted rapidly-built aircraft so that large num-bers would be available in various tactical categories to train personnel for a future Luftwaffe. Heinkel aircraft formed much of this early equipment and, to cover the category of a short-range reconnaissance and army co-operation aircraft, the He 46 was designed in 1931.

The He 46 was a two-seat sesquiplane of mixed wood and metal con-struction with fabric covering. The upper mainplane had 10 deg sweepback, the tailplane was high-mounted and strut-braced, and there was a fixed undercarriage with a tailskid. Powered by a 450 hp Siemens-built Bristol Jupiter nine-cylinder radial air-cooled engine, the He 46a flew as the first prototype late in 1931 and was followed by the He 46b early the next year. Flying characteristics were satisfactory but a major modification was decided on. This was the removal of the small lower wing from the first prototype in order to improve downward view. The mainplane was strut-braced to the base of the fuselage and its area was increased by 22 per cent. Thus, without detracting from its flying qualities, the He 46 was transformed into a parasol-wing monoplane. The He 46a was then improved by fitting a more powerful engine, the 660 hp Siemens SAM 22B (later known as the Bramo 322B) nine-cylinder radial. During 1932, a third prototype, the He 46c, was built incorporating all previous improvements together with operational equipment and a single 7·9 mm MG 15 machine-gun in the rear, observer's, cockpit.

After official acceptance, production began at Heinkel's Warnemünde factory in 1933 with the He 46C-1, which could carry either a camera or up to 200 kg (440 lb) of small bombs beneath the rear cockpit. Although Warnemünde was responsible for the bulk of production, it was necessary to bring in companies such as MIAG (Leipzig), Gotha and Fieseler as subcontractors to produce the required number of aircraft within a reasonable time. The Siemens SAM 22B engines were not, however, mass-produced so easily and quality was initially sacrificed, with the result that some He 46s vibrated alarmingly. Nevertheless, by the end of 1934 about five hundred He 46s had been produced.

Minor changes in the He 46C-1 produced the He 46D, and when this

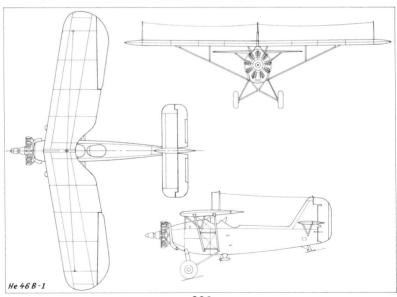

He 46 B-1

222

An He 46E-2 (BB-CK) taking-off. Engine cowlings were usually left off in Luftwaffe service to facilitate maintenance of troublesome engines. On the ground, a Ju 52/3m.

type was fitted with a NACA engine cowling it was designated He 46E. Although this cowling improved the maximum speed by about 25 km/h (16 mph), it was rarely used in Luftwaffe service because of the engines needing constant attention. A more reliable engine, the 560 hp Armstrong Siddeley Panther, with a cowling, was fitted to the He 46F of which a small number was built for training purposes.

By 1936 the Luftwaffe's Aufklärungsstaffeln (H) were fully equipped with the He 46 and, before production ceased, the type was offered for export. Bulgaria acquired eighteen He 46C-2s, which differed from the C-1 mainly in having NACA cowlings, and Hungary acquired some He 46E-2s. In September 1938, twenty He 46C-1s were despatched for use by the Spanish Nationalists.

From the spring of 1938, the Luftwaffe began the gradual replacement of the He 46 with the Henschel Hs 126A-1, and this process was complete by the time Germany invaded France. Only a small percentage of the He 46s were used in their original rôle by the Luftwaffe in the Second World War, chiefly with Aufklärungsstaffeln 2.(H)/31 and 4.(H)/31 during the invasion of Poland.

In July 1941, an air contingent accompanied the Hungarian Army's Fast Corps advancing into the USSR with the Germans, and included a strange collection of aircraft such as the Fiat C.R. 42, Reggiane Re 2000, Junkers Ju 86, Caproni Ca 135, WM 21 Sólyom and He 46E-2, the last named being with the 1st Short-Range Reconnaissance Squadron. Because

223

of the rapid advance and constant changes of airfield, Hungarian aerial sorties were few, and the units withdrew in December 1941 when many of the aircraft suffered from winter conditions. After the Hungarian Air Force had reorganized in mid-1942, it despatched about 100 aircraft to Russia, including twelve He 46E-2s with the 3/2 Short-Range Reconnaissance Squadron. Following a short period of reconnaissance work, the He 46s were used for bombing sorties and, while only one was lost, they managed to destroy three Soviet fighters. By the spring of 1943, the Hungarian He 46s appear to have been replaced by Focke-Wulf Fw 189s of the 3/1 Short-Range Reconnaissance Squadron. The Luftwaffe wrote the final operational chapter for the He 46 when some of these aircraft were taken from training schools along with various other ageing trainers and pressed into service with the Nachtschlachtgruppen (NSGr). During 1943 these aircraft harassed the Russians at night with small bombs.

*Wartime operational units:* 1. (H)/11, 3. and 4.(H)/12, 4.(H)/13, 1. and 3.(H)/14, 2. and 4.(H)/23, 2. and 4.(H)/31, 3.(H)/41, NSGr 1.

He 46C: Span 14 m (45 ft 11¼ in); length 9·5 m (31 ft 2 in); wing area 32·2 sq m (346·5 sq ft).

Empty weight 1,765 kg (3,892 lb); loaded weight 2,300 kg (5,071 lb).

Maximum speed at sea level 250 km/h (155 mph); cruising speed at sea level 210 km/h (130 mph); landing speed 95 km/h (59 mph); climb to 1,000 m (3,280 ft) 2·6 min; service ceiling 6,000 m (19,680 ft); range 1,000 km (621 miles).

# Heinkel He 50

Early in 1931, the Japanese Navy placed a specification with the Heinkel company for the construction of a two-seat dive-bomber. It was to be capable of carrying a 250 kg (550 lb) bomb load and to operate with either wheel or float undercarriages.

The prototype, the Heinkel He 50aW, was completed during the summer of 1931. It was a sturdy two-bay biplane of mixed wood and welded steel tube construction with fabric covering. The aircraft had twin floats and was powered by a 390 hp Junkers-L 5 liquid-cooled engine. This engine was found to provide insufficient power, and the second aircraft, the He 50aL, D-2471, was powered by a 490 hp Siemens Jupiter VI radial driving a four-blade wooden propeller, and had a landplane undercarriage. A second Jupiter-powered landplane was completed under the designation He 50b and production of a small batch of similar aircraft was completed for the Japanese Navy under the designation He 66.

The He 50aL (later redesignated He 50 V1) was demonstrated before

A Heinkel He 50A, D-IMAA, prior to being delivered to I./St.G 162 in 1935. (*F. Selinger*)

the Reichswehr-Ministerium (Defence Ministry) in 1932 and resulted in an order for three development aircraft. These were completed in the summer of 1932 and were powered by uncowled 600 hp Siemens SAM 22B radial engines driving three-blade metal airscrews. A production batch of 60 of the generally-similar He 50A was produced for the Luftwaffe during 1933. An order for 12 aircraft from China resulted in the He 66b, a similar machine to the He 50A but with a NACA cowling around the SAM 22 engine. These aircraft were commandeered by the Luftwaffe in 1933 and designated He 50B.

The He 50 was delivered to Fliegergruppe Schwerin in 1935, the Luftwaffe's first dive-bomber unit, and served with that arm for a short period. With the introduction of the Henschel Hs 123 and Junkers Ju 87, the He 50s were transferred to the FFS A/B training schools.

Another view of the He 50A D-IMAA. (*H. Redemann*)

225

The Heinkel He 66 was an export version of the He 50 developed for use by the Chinese Nationalist Air Force. (*H. Redemann*)

During the winter of 1943–44 a new night harassing group was established in Estonia, designated NSGr 11. This unit was mainly equipped with a number of He 50s which had been brought out of retirement, although a squadron is known to have operated the Fokker C.V. The aircraft often operated from snow-covered airfields and were painted in a distinctive finish of white upper surfaces and black undersides. The unit was disbanded in September 1944.

He 50: Span 11·5 m (37 ft 8¾ in); length 9·6 m (31 ft 6 in); height 4·5 m (14 ft 9¼ in); wing area 34·8 sq m (374·59 sq ft).

Empty weight 1,600 kg (3,528 lb); loaded weight 2,620 kg (5,778 lb).

Maximum speed at sea level 235 km/h (146 mph); landing speed 95 km/h (59 mph); climb to 1,000 m (3,280 ft) 3 min; service ceiling 6,400 m (20,998 ft).

# Heinkel He 59

The Heinkel He 59 was designed in 1930 as a large twin-engined attack and reconnaissance biplane which could be operated either on wheels or floats, and two prototypes were constructed to test both versions. In September 1931, the second prototype became the first He 59 to fly. This was the He 59b D-2215, which was fitted with wheels and large trouser-type fairings around the main undercarriage members. The first prototype, the He 59a D-2214, first flown in January 1932, was fitted with a pair of long single-step floats. In the spring of 1932, a small production batch of He 59As was begun, these were generally similar to the He 59a floatplane prototype and were ordered for evaluation.

226

Following these successful trials, a pre-production batch of sixteen He 59B-1s was produced. These aircraft were later redesignated He 59B-0 and differed from the He 59A in minor equipment changes and in having a single 7·9 mm MG 15 machine-gun in an open nose position. The first major production model was the He 59B-2 which was produced by both Heinkel and Arado. Like its predecessors, this version was powered by two 660 hp BMW VI 6,0 ZU twelve-cylinder vee liquid-cooled engines and was of mixed construction but had a new all-metal nose with bomb-aiming panels while glazed panels were also fitted for a ventral position gunner. Armament consisted of an MG 15 gun in this ventral position and a similar gun in the nose and dorsal positions. The He 59B-2 floatplane was the first version to see operational service when in 1936 some were sent to Spain where the Condor Legion used them for night bombing, and for anti-shipping patrols when a 20 mm MG FF cannon comprised the nose

The Heinkel He 59 was designed in 1930 as an attack and reconnaissance aircraft to be built with either floats or wheels. Seen here is the second prototype, the He 59b, D-2215, which was fitted with wheels and was the first to fly. Subsequent He 59s were built with floats.

armament. In 1937, an Arado-built B-2 was fitted with a complete He 115 V1 nose section to conduct tests for that floatplane.

With the establishment of He 59B-2 production, more specialized operational versions were produced. The first was the He 59B-3 which was similar to the B-2 but was for reconnaissance work only and had its armament reduced to two MG 15 guns and the normal fuel supply in the floats supplemented by tanks in the fuselage. The He 59C-2 was without glazed nose panels, bomb-aiming equipment and armament, but could carry six dinghies and equipment for air-sea rescue duties.

By the time war began, the He 59 was in service with Staffel Schwilben and the Seenotdienststaffel for air-sea rescue work and with the third Staffel of each of four Küstenfliegergruppen for coastal reconnaissance and anti-shipping duties, these Staffeln being 3./Kü.Fl.Gr.106, 3./Kü.Fl.Gr. 406, 3./Kü.Fl.Gr.506 and 3./Kü.Fl.Gr.706. For training, special versions of the He 59 were gradually introduced. The He 59C-1 was stripped for long-range reconnaissance but could also be used for training, while the He 59D-1 was similar to the C-2 but was used for training pilots, radio operators and navigators. More advanced navigation training was given with the He 59N with its special radio equipment, while training in torpedo

In addition to reconnaissance, anti-shipping and training duties, the He 59 was used for air-sea rescue as illustrated by this floatplane, D-ARYX.

dropping could be given with the He 59E-1 which was similar to the D-1. Six examples of the He 59E-2 floatplane were built for long-range reconnaissance, and each had three cameras installed.

With the outbreak of war, He 59s were busy patrolling the shipping lanes of the Baltic and North Sea but were soon more actively engaged in

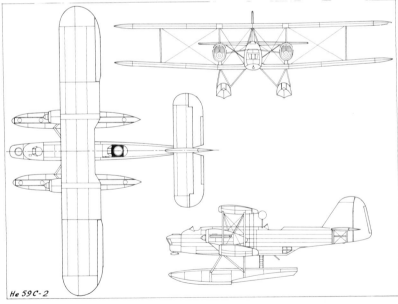

He 59C-2

dropping mines in the Thames Estuary at night. By the summer of 1940, Staffel Schwilben and the Seenotdienststaffel were rescuing pilots from the English Channel and became increasingly busy as the Battle of Britain increased in tempo. For this rescue work, the He 59s were painted white and carried red crosses, but some were shot down after incidents where the crews had been radioing information to German bombers. One He 59, D-ASUO, was beached at Walmer Harbour, Kent, on 11 July, 1940. Before the He 59 was supplanted by other seaplanes, it took an active part in the Norwegian campaign. An especially noteworthy operation was when twelve He 59s from Staffel Schwilben landed troops on the Maas to capture the main bridge at Rotterdam. One hundred and twenty troops were disembarked and four of the floatplanes were lost. No production was undertaken of the He 59 landplane.

*Wartime operational units:* 3./Kü.Fl.Gr. 106, 3./Kü.Fl.Gr. 406, 3./Kü.Fl.Gr.506, 3./Kü.Fl.Gr.706, KGrzbV 108, 1., 2. and 3./KG 200 and the air-sea rescue squadrons.

He 59B-2: Span 23·7 m (77 ft 9 in); length 17·4 m (57 ft 1 in); height 7·1 m (23 ft 3½ in); total wing area 153·3 sq m (1,649 sq ft).

Empty weight 6,215 kg (13,704 lb); fuel 2,000 kg (4,410 lb); loaded weight 9,000 kg (19,845 lb).

Maximum speed at sea level 220 km/h (137 mph); cruising speed 215 km/h (133 mph); alighting speed 87 km/h (54 mph); initial rate of climb 225 m/min (738 ft/min); service ceiling 3,500 m (11,480 ft); maximum range 1,750 km (1,087 miles).

# Heinkel He 60

Although designed in 1932 for reconnaissance operations from German warships, the Heinkel He 60 saw most of its service with the coastal and sea reconnaissance units and remained in service until late in the Second World War. The He 60 was a single-engined twin-float single-bay biplane of sturdy construction to withstand punishment from rough seas and catapult-launches. Mixed construction was used, with fabric and metal covering. The angular parallel-chord wings had considerable positive stagger, ailerons being fitted to upper and lower wings, and there were N interplane struts. The single-step floats were braced to the fuselage and the lower wing.

The first prototype, the He 60 V1, D-2325, flew early in 1933 powered by a 660 hp BMW VI 6,0 ZU twelve-cylinder vee liquid-cooled engine driving a two-blade airscrew. This power was somewhat insufficient and so a 750 hp BMW VI engine was tested in the He 60 V2, but, because the uprated engine proved troublesome, subsequent aircraft had to be powered by the 660 hp engine. The He 60 V3, D-IROL, was the first example to be equipped for catapult launching and was delivered to the Kriegsmarine for

The Heinkel He 60 V4, D-IHOH, which was the first of fourteen pre-production examples of this shipboard reconnaissance floatplane. (*F. Selinger*)

trials, although the decision had already been made to put the He 60A into production. By the summer of 1933, fourteen pre-production He 60As had been delivered to Navy training schools; these fourteen floatplanes began with the He 60 V4, D-IHOH, and were possibly designated He 60A-01 to A-014. The operational production version, the He 60B, was then begun with minor improvements and provision for a 7·9 mm MG 15 machine-gun in the observer's cockpit, but by 1934 this version was supplanted by the generally redesigned, but similar, He 60C. Prototypes for the He 60C

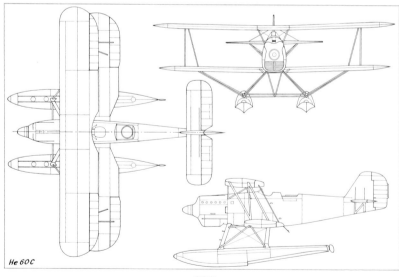

He 60C

were registered D-ILRO and D-IXES. One other attempt was made to provide the floatplane with more power when one He 60C was tested with a 1,000 hp Daimler-Benz DB 600 liquid-cooled inverted-vee engine, but delivery problems resulted in all He 60Cs being built with the 660 hp BMW VI engine.

Although the He 60 had only a small payload capacity, spraying equipment could be fitted in the floats. This equipment was designated SN 40 and, using compressed air, could be used for making smoke screens or spraying non-volatile war gas such as mustard gas (Lost/Senfgas).

The He 60C served on all the major German warships, until replaced by the Heinkel He 114 and Arado Ar 196, and, before the war, went into service with the first Staffel of each of four coastal reconnaissance units, namely Kü.Fl.Gr. 106, 206, 306, and 406. (1./Kü.Fl.Gr. 306 was later redesignated 3./Kü.Fl.Gr. 806). Operational testing of the He 60C was done during the Spanish Civil War in which six of the floatplanes were used on coastal reconnaissance missions.

An He 60C transferred from an operational to a training rôle and probably redesignated He 60D.

On 22 September, 1939, an He 60 (K6-QH) from 1./Kü.Fl.Gr. 406 had engine trouble and made a forced alighting at Ystad in Sweden, and the crew were later exchanged for a Swedish Air Force Ju 86K and its crew which had force-landed in Germany. As the war progressed, the He 60 was relegated more to training and communications duties but was still active in reconnaissance work in the Mediterranean theatre until the end of 1942 with the Seeaufklärungsgruppen. From Crete and Greece, SAGr 126 operated the He 60 until it was gradually supplanted by the Ar 196. From the end of 1942, SAGr 127 used the He 60, the Arado Ar 95 and the Henschel Hs 126, while 15./SAGr 127 used the He 60 together with various captured aircraft. When transferred from an operational to a training rôle, it seems likely that the He 60C was redesignated He 60D.

231

*Wartime operational units:* 1./Kü.Fl.Gr. 106, 206, 306, 406 and 506, SAGr 125, 126 and 127.

He 60: Span 13·5 m (44 ft 3½ in); length 11·5 m (37 ft 8¾ in); height 5·3 m (17 ft 4⅝ in); total wing area 56·2 sq m (604·7 sq ft).

Empty weight 2,725 kg (6,009 lb); fuel and oil 500 kg (1,102 lb); crew 200 kg (441 lb); loaded weight without armament 3,425 kg (7,552 lb).

Maximum speed at sea level 240 km/h (149 mph); cruising speed at sea level 215 km/h (134 mph); alighting speed 90 km/h (56 mph); climb to 1,000 m (3,280 ft) 3·2 min; service ceiling 5,000 m (16,400 ft); maximum range 950 km (590 miles).

The Heinkel He 70 Blitz was used on express domestic services by Deutsche Lufthansa, the He 70G illustrated being the definitive civil version of the Blitz. However, the subsequent military career of the He 70 proved disappointing.

# Heinkel He 70, He 170 and He 270

The Nazis claimed, soon after they came to power in 1933, to have rebuilt German aviation from nothing but this was a distortion for by that time the major German companies were already sufficiently well-established to tackle work on modern military aircraft and the Nazis simply brought about a quantitative expansion of the industry.

The Heinkel He 70 proved to be the forerunner of the company's modern military aircraft, although it was as much a military failure as it was a civil success. The He 70 did not, in fact, lend itself readily to adaptation for new rôles since it was designed as a specialized four-passenger high-speed transport.

The fast Lockheed Orion had appeared in the autumn of 1931 and, in February 1932, Deutsche Lufthansa had commissioned Ernst Heinkel A.G. to design an aircraft with which the airline could maintain its prestige against the Orion. Accordingly, work began on the He 65 mono-plane which, with a non-retractable undercarriage, was designed to have a maximum speed of 285 km/h (177 mph). By May 1932, however, this design was abandoned because a speed of 300 km/h (186·4 mph) was being called for, with Swissair's introduction of the Orion on the Zürich–Munich–Vienna route.

A new low-wing monoplane design, the He 70, was then begun by the brothers Siegfried and Walter Günter, and every aerodynamic refinement was resorted to in order to obtain the maximum speed from the single 630 hp BMW VI 6,0 Z twelve-cylinder vee liquid-cooled engine. This engine was cooled by ethylene-glycol instead of water, and the higher evaporation rate permitted the use of a smaller radiator which was made retractable to reduce resistance still further at high speeds. The engine, driving a two-blade airscrew, was enclosed by a closely fitting cowling which blended into the oval-section fuselage, this being of duralumin monocoque construction with all rivets countersunk, giving a very smooth finish. Slightly offset to port was the pilot and radio operator's cockpit which had a low windscreen, sliding canopy and a long fairing running back from the seat headrest, and the cabin had seats for four passengers in facing pairs. The wing and tail surfaces were elliptical, and the wing was a two-spar structure with trailing-edge flaps and highly-polished plywood covering. The main undercarriage units retracted outwards into wing wells, this being a new feature in Germany, but the tailwheel was not retractable.

By June 1932, the preliminary design work was complete and, soon after, work began not only on a prototype but also on an initial production series. The prototype, the He 70 V1, made its first flight with Flugkapitän Werner Junck at the controls when it was flown from the Warnemünde

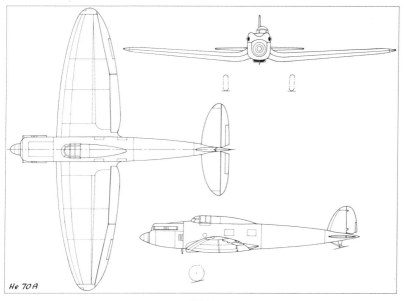

He 70 A

233

works to Travemünde airfield on 1 December, 1932. This aircraft had its undercarriage fixed down with the wheel wells faired over. The second aircraft (c/n 403), first of the He 70As, was later registered D-2537, and the name *Blitz* (*Lightning*) on its nose became general for the He 70. The name was certainly apt, since the aircraft could outstrip almost every contemporary fighter and the He 70 V1 was attaining a level speed of 377 km/h (234 mph) early in 1933. In March and April of that year, Flugkapitän R. Untucht, the well known Lufthansa pilot, established eight new speed records in various categories with the He 70 V2. These events culminated in the display of the He 70 at the Paris Salon in November and the type gained new prestige for the German aviation industry.

After proving flights, the He 70A entered DLH domestic passenger service on 15 June, 1934. Also introduced were a few examples of the He 70B, C, and D, the only significant modification being in the D version which was re-engined with the more powerful 750 hp BMW VI 7,3. The same type of engine was fitted to the definitive civil model, the He 70G which had the cockpit on the fuselage centreline and did not carry a second crew member. Other modifications included an increase in length and loaded weight. The He 70G-1 D-UBOF (c/n 1692) was modified in 1935 to take an 810 hp Rolls-Royce Kestrel engine and was used up to 1944 by Rolls-Royce at Hucknall as a flying test-bed. In this form the aircraft was re-registered G-ADZF and attained a maximum speed of 410 km/h (255 mph).

In 1934, the Luftwaffe was using commercial models of the He 70 for high-speed communication work and, by the time the Luftwaffe was officially announced in March 1935, military He 70s were in service. These were the He 70F-1 long-range reconnaissance type and the He 70E-1 high-speed light bomber, both types having a crew of two. The He 70E was similar to the D version but could carry a 300 kg (660 lb) bomb load and had a 7·9 mm MG 17 machine-gun in the rear cockpit for defence.

An event of some significance for the Luftwaffe occurred on 3 June, 1936, when the first Chief of Staff, General Wever, was killed when taking-off in his He 70. Since Wever was one of the few men in authority who favoured the build-up of a strategic bomber force, his death played a major part in such a force being denied to Germany, the implications of this being manifest.

As with many of the Luftwaffe's prewar aircraft, the He 70 made its first sorties in the Spanish Civil War. Eighteen He 70F-2s were sent, in the autumn of 1936, to Spain where they were used by A/88, the Condor Legion's reconnaissance component, and some remained in Spanish service until scrapped in the early 1950s. By 1938, all He 70s had been withdrawn from DLH service and were also being replaced in Luftwaffe front-line service. Units which principally operated the type were the Aufklärungsgruppen (F)/121, 123, 124, 125, and 127, and their He 70F-1s were gradually replaced by Dornier Do 17F-1s.

Early in 1937, a new design of the He 70 was produced as the He 170 for export to Hungary. The He 170A-01, D-OHEW, is seen here. The Hungarians first operated the He 170 in March 1939. (*H. Redemann*)

Early in 1937, a new design was brought out as the He 170 for export to Hungary, the principal change being the fitting of a 910 hp Gnome/Rhône 14K Mistral-Major fourteen-cylinder radial air-cooled engine enclosed in a new circular cowling. Following the prototype D-OASA, about twenty He 170s were delivered to the I Independent Long-Range Reconnaissance Group which first operated the Heinkels in Carpatho-Ruthenia in March 1939. On 26 June, 1941, the He 170s were first flown against the Russians but, with a defensive armament of only a pair of machine-guns, the aircraft were seen to be very vulnerable and the type was withdrawn from front-line service by July 1941. Maximum speed of the He 170 was 435 km/h (270 mph) at an altitude of 3,400 m (11,155 ft).

The final development of the He 70 was the one-off He 270 D-OEHF which flew in 1938. This was the most powerful version, being powered by a 1,175 hp Daimler-Benz DB 601A engine driving a three-blade airscrew. It was intended for a dual light bombing and reconnaissance rôle and had a maximum speed of 460 km/h (286 mph) at 4,000 m (13,120 ft). Armament was still very light and comprised one forward-firing plus two rear-firing MG 15 machine-guns whilst the 300 kg (660 lb) bomb load was no improvement over that for the He 70E.

The poor military qualities of the He 70 did nothing to endear it to its Service crews, and Spanish crews appear to have been the only ones which had any liking for the type as an operational aircraft. Also,

Final development of the He 70 was this sole prototype of the He 270, flown in 1938 as D-OEHF. This was the most powerful version, being intended for military use.

the aircraft proved troublesome in low temperatures. Nevertheless, the He 70 was a prestige-builder in its proper civil transport rôle and was a milestone in Heinkel aircraft development. Altogether, 324 examples of the He 70 and its derivatives were built, including 28 commercial examples.

He 70F: Span 14·8 m (48 ft 6½ in); length 11·7 m (38 ft 4⅝ in); height 3·1 m (10 ft 2 in); wing area 36·5 sq m (392·88 sq ft).

Empty weight 2,300 kg (5,072 lb); loaded weight 3,420 kg (7,541 lb).

Maximum speed at sea level 360 km/h (224 mph); cruising speed at sea level 335 km/h (208 mph); landing speed 105 km/h (65·2 mph); initial rate of climb 452 m/min (1,483 ft/min); service ceiling 5,250 m (17,220 ft); range at cruising speed 1,000 km (621 miles).

Line-up of Heinkel He 72A production aircraft. (*H. Redemann*)

# Heinkel He 72 Kadett (Cadet)

One of the most important primary trainers of the Luftwaffe was the Heinkel He 72 Kadett. This was a conventional tandem two-seat, single-bay biplane of fabric-covered metal construction. It was designed in 1933, the prototype being powered by a 140 hp Argus As 8B four-cylinder inverted-inline engine. It was followed by a small batch of the generally-similar He 72A production aircraft. The main production model, however, was the He 72B which was powered by a 160 hp Siemens Sh 14A seven-cylinder radial.

In addition to the standard He 72B-1 landplane, a twin-float variant was built, designated He 72BW although it remained in the prototype stage.

236

The He 172 was a development of the He 72 Kadett trainer.

The He 72B-3 Edelkadett (Leading Cadet) was an improved variant for civil use and had its mainwheels enclosed in spats. Only thirty of this variant were built.

The He 72A and B equipped several NSFK (National Socialist Flying Corps) units and was later to see service with many Luftwaffe training schools. Examples of units that operated the type included FFS B 7 at Kolberg, FFS A/B 11 at Schönwalde, FFS A/B 72 at Detmold, and Luftkriegsschule 3 at Oschatz. In addition to serving widely as a trainer, the He 72 was also notable in being the first aircraft to fly with a liquid-fuelled rocket engine when, during the autumn of 1936, trials were undertaken with a 135 kg (300 lb) thrust Walter engine carried under the fuselage of an He 72B.

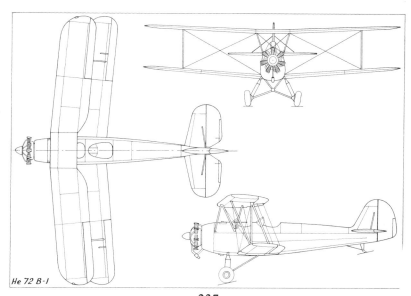

He 72 B-1

237

In 1934, Heinkel proposed an improved version of the He 72, designated He 172. Only one prototype was completed, the He 172 V1 D-EEHU, the aircraft differing mainly from the earlier He 72B in having a NACA cowling closely enclosing its Siemens Sh 14A engine.

He 72B-1: Span 9 m (29 ft 6⅓ in); length 7·5 m (24 ft 7¼ in); height 2·7 m (8 ft 10¼ in); wing area 20·7 sq m (221·81 sq ft).
Empty weight 540 kg (1,191 lb); loaded weight 865 kg (1,907 lb).
Maximum speed at sea level 185 km/h (115 mph); cruising speed at sea level 170 km/h (106 mph); landing speed 80 km/h (50 mph); climb to 1,000 m (3,280 ft) 6 min; service ceiling 3,500 m (11,484 ft); normal range 475 km (295 miles).

First flown in January 1938, the Heinkel He 100 V1 was sent to E-Stelle Rechlin in March. Note absence of a conventional, main radiator due to the use of an enclosed cooling system.

# Heinkel He 100

By 1936 it was clear that the production contract for the Luftwaffe's new single-seat fighter had been won by Messerschmitt's Bf 109 and lost by Heinkel's He 112 (*see* page 261), although many thought the latter aircraft superior. Undaunted by this failure, Heinkel proposed to Ernst Udet a new, superior fighter with the then-incredible speed of 700 km/h (435 mph). The proposed speed was so high that it was decided the aircraft could also be used to establish world speed records. Under Heinrich Hertel (Heinkel's technical director) and Siegfried Günter (chief project designer) drawings for the new aircraft were ready by 25 May, 1937, and prototypes

The He 100 V2 D-IUOS, broke the 100 km closed-circuit, landplane speed record on 6 June, 1938. From this time, the He 100 was used in various prestige and propaganda schemes. (*F. Selinger*)

were sanctioned under the designation He 113, but this was changed at some time to He 100.

At the beginning of the project it was clear that a new fighter would need more than high speed to stand any chance of going into production alongside the Bf 109, which was firmly entrenched in official favour, and the experience gained from the failure of the He 112 was also taken into account. Thus, to facilitate production, the He 100, as compared with the He 112, needed only one third the number of individual parts and 40 per cent of the number of rivets, while standardized components had been increased by 70 per cent. Curved profiles, such as those for elliptical wings, were eliminated or reduced to a minimum. The 1,000 hp Daimler-Benz DB 601 twelve-cylinder inverted-vee liquid-cooled engine was chosen, which it was hoped could be boosted to about 1,700 hp for record flights. For both military and record aircraft, it was decided to develop a special cooling system to dispense with drag-producing radiators, but an evaporative cooling system where water was constantly lost was not acceptable for military aircraft though it had served previous record aircraft well enough. Thus, a cooling system was chosen whereby pressurized hot water surrounding the engine was piped out to form depressurized water and steam. The steam was condensed back into water through piping in the wings, and all water was recirculated by pumping it back to the engine. A similar enclosed system could not be developed for cooling the engine oil (for which a normal radiator was employed) since insufficient area was available.

On 22 January, 1938, the He 100 V1 made its first flight, with the test pilot Gerhard Nitschke at the controls, and in March was sent for tests at E-Stelle Rechlin. The V1 prototype had a rounded fin, but the He 100 V2, D-IUOS, had a square-tipped fin as did subsequent versions. It was soon apparent that these prototypes were greatly superior to the earlier He 112, and so the He 100 V2 was prepared for a speed-record attempt using a

On 30 March, 1939, this He 100 V8, D-IDGH, established a new absolute world speed record of 746·606 km/h (463·92 mph). (*F. Selinger*)

normal DB 601M engine. A few days before the attempt was planned, Ernst Udet took-off in the He 100 V2 at 16·21 hr on 6 June, 1938, from Marienehe for a test flight, and succeeded in taking the 100 km closed-circuit landplane record from the Italians, since a speed of 634·73 km/h (394·6 mph) was officially recorded between Wustrow and Müritz. The new record was much publicized but was deceptively attributed to a non-existent He 112U to gain prestige for the He 112 then being exported.

The He 100 V3, D-ISVR, was then made ready for an attempt on the world absolute speed record, being given a wing with a reduced span of 7·60 m (24 ft 11¼ in), and other refinements such as a new canopy, and a special Daimler-Benz DB 601 engine, which could be boosted to give 1,800 hp, was received in August. However, the V3 crashed in September while being tested at Warnemünde, the pilot, Nitschke, being forced to bale out when a jammed undercarriage leg prevented a landing. In the meantime, the He 100 V4 and V5 had been built and sent for evaluation at Rechlin as prototypes for the proposed He 100B, the previous aircraft having been known as He 100As.

The crashed V3 was replaced by the similar He 100 V8, D-IDGH, which established a new absolute world speed record of 746·606 km/h (463·92 mph) on 30 March, 1939, when Hans Dierterle took-off at 05·23 hr, and flew four times over a course at Oranienburg to obtain the record for Germany for the first time. In Britain, news of this event led to the abandonment of planned record attempts using the special Speed Spitfire, N.17, which was expected to achieve 675 km/h (419 mph). Nevertheless, victory for Heinkel was short-lived because only 27 days later the Messerschmitt Me 209 V1 just succeeded in setting a new absolute world speed record.

An improved fighter version was by now planned as the He 100C, and the first prototype for this, the He 100 V6, was delivered to Rechlin as an engine test bed on 25 April, 1939. This was followed by the He 100 V7, which first flew on 24 May, 1939. The third and last He 100C prototype, the V9, was the first He 100 to have armament, comprising two 20 mm MG FF cannon and four 7·9 mm MG 17 machine-guns, but this aircraft was later tested to destruction to obtain structural data. The final prototype, the He 100 V10, was a static-test airframe only.

For speed there was nothing to touch the He 100 in the fighter category, but the pilots at Rechlin reported unfavourably that the type was difficult to handle and had a high landing speed. In order to improve control, therefore, the He 100D was designed with new enlarged tail surfaces, and three pre-production He 100D-0s plus twelve production He 100D-1s

Fifteen He 100D fighters were produced but did not go into Luftwaffe service, partly because of engine supply difficulties. Some were used in propaganda photographs such as this. Note the semi-retractable, ventral radiator which supplanted the enclosed cooling system of previous prototypes. (*H. Redemann*)

were constructed. The He 100D fighter dispensed with the enclosed cooling system which was still not satisfactorily developed and used instead a semi-retractable ventral radiator. Some of the previous He 100 prototypes had also tested small radiators, while the Me 209 V4 later had to be fitted with radiators instead of an enclosed evaporative cooling system when an attempt was made to produce a fighter from this record-breaking design. Armament for the He 100D comprised one nose-mounted 20 mm MG FF cannon and two wing-mounted 7·9 mm MG 17 machine-guns.

The He 100D, though superior at least in speed to the Messerschmitt Bf 109E, did not go into Luftwaffe service. Production orders might have been given had the He 100 been suitable for another engine, but it was tailored very closely to the DB 601 and production of that engine was

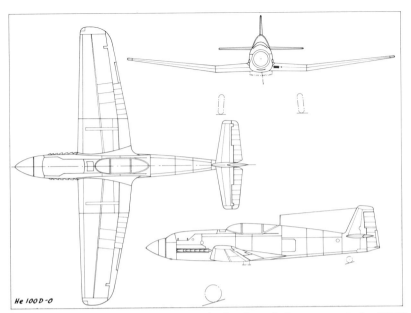

He 100 D-0

almost entirely taken up by Messerschmitt aircraft. In any event, the RLM
was satisfied with the existing fighter production plans and instructed
Heinkel to concentrate on bombers. Permission was therefore given to
export the existing He 100s and to sell manufacturing licences to friendly
countries, and both Soviet and Japanese commissions visited the Heinkel
works to examine the aircraft in October 1939. Six of the He 100 prototypes
(V1, 2, 4, 5, 6, and 7) were sold to the USSR; while the three He
100D-0s were sold to Japan where they arrived in May 1940, going
to the JNAF as the AXHei, but the Japanese plans to manufacture this
type were frustrated because certain Heinkel jigs were not forthcoming.

The twelve He 100D-1s were eventually used for a while to equip a
Heinkel-staffed unit formed to help defend the Rostock-Marienehe factory.
These aircraft appeared in many successful propaganda photographs and,
by carrying a variety of markings and spurious unit emblems, gave the
impression of a number of units equipped with a remarkable new fighter.
The record-breaking He 100 V8, retained by Heinkel, also featured in such
photographs and was painted grey with the false coding 42C-11 added.
Thus, the He 100, which had begun its career with such promise came to a
relatively ignominious end, never having fired its guns in action.

He 100 V1: Span 9·4 m (30 ft 10 in); length 8·18 m (26 ft 10 in); wing area 14·5 sq m
(156·02 sq ft).
Empty weight 2,070 kg (4,564 lb); loaded weight 2,500 kg (5,512 lb).
Maximum speed at 4,000 m (13,120 ft) 670 km/h (416 mph); cruising speed 555 km/h
(345 mph); landing speed 150 km/h (93 mph); initial rate of climb 1,000 m/min (3,280
ft/min); service ceiling 10,500 m (34,440 ft); range 900 km (559 miles).

An early production Heinkel He 111B-2 bomber banks steeply over a Heinkel He 112.
(*H. Thiele*)

# Heinkel He 111

There will be few people who lived in the British Isles during those fateful winter nights of 1940–41 who will forget the dull throbbing note of the unsynchronized engines of the Heinkel He 111, a twin-engined bomber with a peculiar asymmetric glazed nose, which although in service in large numbers with the Luftwaffe, was rapidly becoming obsolete.

The He 111 was designed by Siegfried and Walter Günter for dual rôles, as a high-speed transport and as a bomber for the still-secret Luftwaffe. Design work began early in 1934, the machine owing much to the earlier single-engined He 70 which had captured several international records. The new machine was considerably larger than the He 70, but retained much of that aircraft's beauty of line. The first prototype, the He 111a, was powered by two 660 hp BMW VI 6,OZ engines and made its first flight on 24 February, 1935, with Flugkapitän Gerhard Nitschke at the controls. Performance was comparable with that of contemporary fighters, and its handling characteristics were much superior to those of the He 70.

The He 111a (which was redesignated V1) was followed by the V2 which made its first flight on 12 March, 1935. This aircraft, D-ALIX (c/n 715), was a transport version with reduced span and a straight trailing

243

edge. The machine was delivered first to Lufthansa and named *Rostock* and was later passed to Kommando Rowehl for clandestine reconnaissance missions. The He 111 V3, D-ALES, was a bomber with further reduced wing span but otherwise similar to the V1, and was the forerunner of the He 111A production model.

The He 111 was an orthodox cantilever low-wing monoplane with a fully retractable undercarriage. The line of its beautifully streamlined fuselage was broken only by the step formed by the pilot's cockpit. The wing and tail surfaces were elliptical in planform and hydraulically-operated trailing edge flaps were fitted. The aircraft was built of metal throughout with duralumin stressed skinning.

Following the success of the He 111 V3, Heinkel were ordered to go ahead with the construction of a pre-production batch of ten He 111A-0s. Two aircraft, the He 111A-02 and A-03, were delivered to Rechlin for official trials but proved totally unsuitable for operational conditions. The weight of full military equipment severely interfered with its handling characteristics and considerably reduced its top speed. Following rejection by the Luftwaffe, all ten He 111A-0s were exported to China for use against the Japanese.

The He 111C-04 (c/n 1831) delivered to Lufthansa late in 1936. (*Lufthansa*)

Meanwhile, development of the civil transport series continued with the He 111 V4 D-AHAO, c/n 1968. This was similar to the V2, but could seat 10 passengers in two cabins and was the forerunner of the proposed He 111C production model. The machine was delivered to Lufthansa and revealed to the press at Berlin-Tempelhof on 10 January, 1936, with the name *Dresden*. The first of six He 111C-0s left the assembly lines at Rostock-Marienehe in the summer of 1936. These were the He 111C-01 D-AMES *Nürnberg*, c/n 1828; the C-02 D-AQYF *Leipzig*, c/n 1928; the C-03 D-AXAV *Köln*, c/n 1830; the C-04 D-ABYE *Königsberg*, c/n 1831; the C-05 D-AQUA *Breslau*, c/n 1832; and the C-06 D-ATYL *Karlsruhe*, c/n 1833.

Even before the He 111A-0 was rejected by the Luftwaffe, the Heinkel design team were completing a replacement, the He 111B, the prototype for which was the V5 D-APYS. This aircraft was basically an He 111A airframe fitted with two of the new Daimler-Benz DB 600A engines which each developed 1,000 hp for take-off. Although substantially heavier than the A-0, the He 111 V5 had a maximum speed of 360 km/h (224 mph) and was ordered into production for the Luftwaffe as the He 111B-1.

Early in 1936, the RLM proposed the building of a very large new factory specifically for He 111 construction. The new factory was at Oranienburg, north of Berlin, and it was completed on 4 May, 1937. The new complex was built on the factory estate principle and became a showpiece for foreigners visiting the German aviation industry.

The pre-production He 111B-0s were similar to the A-0 apart from the engines. The He 111B-1 production aircraft began to leave the Marienehe assembly lines during the autumn of 1936 and were augmented by deliveries from the Oranienburg factory from May 1937. Powered by two 880 hp Daimler-Benz DB 600C engines, the B-1 carried an armament of three 7·9 mm MG 15 machine-guns in the nose, and ventral 'dustbin' positions. The He 111B-1 was superseded on the production lines by the B-2 which was powered by two 950 hp DB 600CG engines with supplementary radiators on either side of the nacelles beneath the wings.

The first He 111B-1s were delivered to 1./KG 154 Boelcke at Hannover-Langenhagen late in 1936. By the autumn of 1937 the Geschwader comprised three Gruppen, the second at Wunstorf and the third at Delmenhorst, all equipped with the He 111B. In October, with the establishment of Luftkreiskommando VII, KG 154 was redesignated KG 157, and He 111B-1s were delivered to I. and II./KG 152 Hindenburg, I., and II./KG 155, I., II. and III./KG 253 Wever, I., II. and III./KG 257 and I., II. and III./KG 355.

Anxious to test the aircraft under operational conditions, the Luftwaffe sent a batch of thirty He 111B-1s to Kampfgruppe 88 in Spain in February 1937. Forming the bomber component of the Condor Legion, K/88 undertook its first operational sortie on 9 March when it bombed the

An He 111F-4 with the type of nose used on all early bomber variants. (*H. Redemann*)

Republican airfields at Alcala and Madrid-Barajas. The bomber proved eminently successful in Spain, being able to evade fighter interception by virtue of its speed alone.

The next proposed production model was the He 111D in which the DB 600CG engines were replaced by two 950 hp DB 600Ga units. The forerunner of this series was the He 111 V9, D-AQOX, which retained the drag-producing external radiators and began flight trials during the summer of 1937. A batch of He 111D-0s was produced late in 1937, but only a few D-1s were completed before production switched to the He 111E series following a shortage of DB 600 engines.

The He 111 V6, D-AXOH, was a B-0 airframe experimentally fitted with two 700 hp Junkers Jumo 210Ga engines. These lacked sufficient power to take full advantage of the airframe, and were soon replaced by two Jumo 211A-1 units which produced 1,000 hp for take-off. Development of the V6 led to the V10, D-ALEQ, which was similarly powered and was the immediate predecessor of the E-series. A small batch of He 111E-0s was followed in February 1938 by the first E-1 production model which carried a 2,000 kg (4,410 lb) bomb load. Relatively few E-1s were completed before production was switched to the heavier E-3. The He 111E-4 carried half its 2,000 kg bomb load externally, and the E-5 had several auxiliary fuel tanks inside the fuselage.

About 200 He 111Es were built before production changed to the F-series. The He 111 V7, a standard B-0 airframe, had been fitted with a new wing during the summer of 1936. This wing was of simpler construction and had straight instead of curved taper. The new wing was accepted for the He 111G transport, but it was some time before the RLM became convinced of its merits. Eventually the V7 was developed by way of the V11 into the He 111F which was virtually an E-5 fitted with the new wing and powered by two 1,100 hp Jumo 211A-3 engines. A small batch of He 111F-1 and F-4 bombers were produced, the former being delivered to Turkey, the latter to the Luftwaffe.

Nine G-series aircraft were produced, five of these receiving alternative experimental designations. The He 111 V12, D-AEQA *Halle* (c/n 2534), and V13, D-AYKI *Magdeburg* (c/n 2535), were both similar to the C-0 but were fitted with the wing of the V7. The He 111 V14, D-ACBS *Augsburg* (c/n 1884), was fitted with two 880 hp BMW 132Dc radial engines and was known alternatively as the He 111G-3 or He 111L. These designations were also applied to the He 111 V15, D-ADCF *Dresden* (c/n 1885), which was powered by two 870 hp BMW 132H-1 engines. The He 111 V16 D-ASAR, which was also known as the He 111G-4, was fitted with two 900 hp DB 600G engines. A production batch of four DB 600Ga engined aircraft was produced under the designation He 111G-5 and delivered to Turkey.

The He 111J was produced in parallel with the F-series and was basically an F-4 powered by two 950 hp DB 600CG engines. The He 111J-0 was designed as a torpedo-bomber, but the 90 or so completed J-1 produc-

The He 111 V8 D-AQUO was the first aircraft to be fitted with the offset glazed nose later carried by the P- and H-series.

tion models reverted to the original bomber layout. Although eighty-eight He 111J-1s were delivered to the Luftwaffe, only one unit is recorded as having been equipped with the machine when Germany started the war in 1939: this was the naval unit, KGr 806.

The first really radical modification to the appearance of the Heinkel bomber came with the eighth prototype. This machine, D-AQUO, was fitted with a new asymmetric glazed nose and first flew during January 1938. Although effective from an aerodynamic point of view, this feature certainly added nothing to the appearance of the bomber. The He 111 V7 which had previously tested the straight-tapered wing was now fitted with a new glazed nose as prototype for the He 111P.

The He 111P-0 was powered by two 1,150 hp Daimler-Benz DB 601Aa engines and had a new ventral gondola in which the gunner lay prone. First deliveries of the He 111P-1 were made to KG 157 Boelcke during the spring of 1939, these machines having three 7·9 mm MG 15 machine-guns. The He 111P-2 had FuG 10 radio in place of FuG III, and the P-3 was a dual-control trainer. The He 111P-4 had increased armour protection, three extra MG 15 machine-guns and provision for two externally-mounted PVC 1006 bomb racks. Final production model was the He 111P-6, which was powered by two 1,175 hp DB 601N engines.

Relatively few He 111Ps were completed before production switched to the He 111H powered by two Junkers Jumo 211 engines. The He 111 V19, D-AUKY, was basically a P-2 airframe powered by two 1,010 hp Jumo 211A engines, and was followed by a batch of generally similar H-0

At least one He 111P was fitted with rocket-assisted take-off units beneath the wings.
(*F. Selinger*)

The He 111H was similar to the P-series, but was powered by Jumo 211 engines. (*H. Thiele*)

and H-1 production aircraft. The He 111H-3 was powered by two 1,100 hp Jumo 211A-3 engines and had the same armament as the P-4. The first He 111H-4s were fitted with 1,100 hp Jumo 211D engines, but later production aircraft had the Jumo 211F-1 which developed 1,400 hp for take-off. The aircraft had two external PVC 1006 racks which could carry two 1,000 kg (2,205 lb) SC 1000 or one 1,800 kg (3,968 lb) SC 1800 bomb. The H-5 was similar but had increased fuel capacity and carried its bomb load entirely externally.

An He 111H-2 of the reconnaissance group of the Luftwaffe's High Command during the winter of 1939/40. (*H. Thiele*)

248

Bad weather hampered early operations against Poland, but during the morning of 1 September, I. and III./KG 4 took-off from Langenau to bomb an airfield at Cracow. Escorted by the Messerschmitt Bf 110s of I./ZG 76, the Gruppen of KG 4 caused heavy damage. II./KG 4 under Obstlt Erdmann attacked the airfield at Lemberg and unloaded 22 tons of bombs on the runway. I./KG 1 directed its first attack against the Polish naval base of Putzig-Rahmel, and I./KG 152 struck the airfield at Thorn.

II./KG 26 directed its assault against railway installations at Posen, I./KG 53 attacked the air base at Gnesen, and II./LG 1 took-off from Powunden to bomb Warsaw-Okecie Airport. Besides damage to the runways, a number of bombs hit the PZL aircraft factory. A major attack on

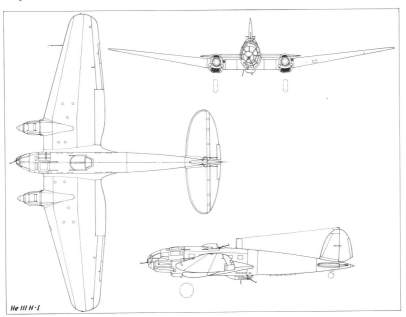

*He III H-1*

Warsaw followed when nearly ninety He 111Ps from KG 27 bombed the city. They were met by some very courageous Polish fighter pilots who braved their own flak and the Messerschmitt Bf 110 escort to intercept the German bombers. Despite the attentions of the Polish fighters, very few He 111s were lost.

Subsequent operations by KG 1 under Oberst Ulrich Kessler, KG 4 under Oberst Martin Fiebig and KG 26 under Oberst Siburg, were directed mainly against railway and industrial targets east of the Vistula. The final operation was the bombing of Warsaw which took place on 25 September. This was preceded by five leaflet raids on the city, the first of which, by I./KG 4, took place on 16 September.

During the winter of 1939–40, KG 26 undertook some sorties against British shipping, but the next major operation was against Norway and

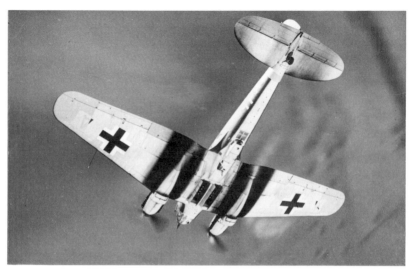

An exhaust-blackened He 111H with its bomb-bay doors open. (*J. Zazvonil*)

Denmark on 9 April, 1940. Three Heinkel units were deployed, KG 4 with the He 111P, KG 26 with the He 111H-3 and H-4 and KGr 100 with the He 111H-3. Early operations were limited to 'demonstration flights' and leaflet raids, although some bombing of Oslo-Kjeller airfield and flak positions in the area was undertaken by the units. On 10 April, 41 bombers from KG 26 Löwen in company with Junkers Ju 88s from KG 30 attacked Royal Naval units off Norway, damaging the cruisers HMS *Devonshire, Glasgow* and *Southampton* and sinking the destroyer HMS *Gurkha.*

As the campaign progressed, KG 26 transferred first to Oslo and Stavanger and then to Trondheim. At one stage the aircraft of III./KG 26 under Maj Viktor von Lossberg operated from a frozen lake, but after a short time a sudden thaw set in and one aircraft sank through the ice. Von Lossberg quickly ordered the rest of his unit to jettison their bombs and take-off immediately, and his prompt action saved the remaining aircraft from destruction.

On 10 May, 1940, German forces invaded France and the Low Countries. Operations against the Netherlands began with an attack by He 111s from KG 4 on Amsterdam and Rotterdam Airports and Ypenburg airfield. Following the Dutch refusal to surrender Rotterdam on 14 May, one hundred He 111Ps from KG 54, under Oberst Lackner, took-off from Delmenhorst, Hoya-Wester and Quakenbrück to bomb the city. German sources have subsequently stated that an attempt was made to recall the aircraft, but 97 tons of bombs were in fact dropped on Rotterdam. The fire that followed completed the destruction, and in the centre of the city only two buildings, the town hall and the post office, were left standing.

The widespread introduction of the Junkers Ju 88 into Luftwaffe service was accompanied by a reduction in units equipped with the He 111. For the Battle of Britain, the following bomber units were equipped with the He 111P and H: I. and II./KG 1, I and II./KG 4, I. and III./KG 26 (in Norway), KG 27, KG 53, KG 55, KGr 100 and KGr 126. In addition, the aircraft was used in small numbers by Staffeln of Aufklärungsgruppe 120, 121, and 122.

The main phase of the battle was preceded by German strikes across the Straits of Dover, but it was obvious from the start that the Luftwaffe was not going to have it all its own way. On 14 August, the Geschwader Kommodore of KG 55, Oberst Alois Stöckl, was killed when his He 111 (G1-HA) was shot down near Eastdene while attempting to bomb the airfield at Upavon. Next day the first major attack on Britain by an He 111 unit was mounted when 63 aircraft from I. and III./KG 26 left Stavanger to bomb airfields at Dishforth and Linton-upon-Ouse in Yorkshire. The unit was escorted by Messerschmitt Bf 110s from I./ZG 76 but was intercepted by Spitfires from Nos. 72, 41, and 607 Squadrons and lost eight bombers, five of them from a Staffel of III./KG 26.

One disastrous mission was undertaken early in September following German insistence that RAF Fighter Command had been destroyed. III./KG 27 took-off from Bordeaux without fighter escort to bomb east-coast towns, but only 14 badly-damaged Heinkels returned. III./KG 27 was subsequently recorded as having four serviceable aircraft. On 5

The forward gunner of the He 111H was provided with a 7·9 mm MG 15 machine-gun on an Ikaria flexible mounting. (*H. Redemann*)

251

After the Battle of Britain, the defensive armament of the He 111H-series was considerably increased. (*H. Redemann*)

September, 1940, sixty-eight bombers from KG 2, KG 3, KG 26 and KG 53 bombed the London docks and this was followed by a raid on Croydon by seventy He 111s from KG 55. No less than fourteen RAF squadrons were scrambled to intercept and the German unit returned badly mauled. Two days later the Luftwaffe made its first major attack on the City of London, and on 15 September, 56 aircraft were lost including ten He 111s.

It was now becoming obvious that the He 111 and Dornier Do 17 in particular could no longer survive in daylight against the RAF fighters. To continue the offensive against the British Isles, the Luftwaffe gradually shifted its emphasis to night operations. For some time Germany had been developing several radio navigational beams for use at night. The first of these was Knickebein, a simple system of cross beams, but this was soon jammed by the RAF; the second, and much more complex, system was X-Gerät carried by the He 111s of KGr 100 under Hptm Friedrich Aschenbrenner based at Vannes in Brittany.

The first operation by the unit using this device was on 13 August, 1940, when 11 bombs hit the Spitfire factory at Castle Bromwich, Birmingham. The best known operation by KGr 100 was on 14 November, 1940, when it led a raid by 449 bombers on Coventry. As a result of the raid, some 400 people were killed, a further 800 injured, and production in the city came to a standstill. The next raid, on Birmingham five days later, was successfully countered by the Bromide jamming device, but unfortunately this system was not in position to counter the Luftwaffe raid on London on 29 December, 1940, in which much of the City was destroyed.

The second Luftwaffe unit to be equipped with a specialized pathfinding device was III./KG 26 under Maj von Lossberg based at Poix. This unit was equipped with the more sophisticated Y-Geräte which proved more difficult to jam. However, with the use of decoy sites and the Benjamin and Domino jamming devices, the RAF succeeded in preventing another raid of the magnitude of that on Coventry. Eventually III./KG 26 was redesignated III./KG 100.

Until May 1941, most He 111 units took part in night raids against the British Isles but, in January 1941, II./KG 26 under Maj Bertram von Comiso was transferred from Norway to Sicily, and one Staffel went to Benghazi. In April 1941, II./KG 4 was transferred to Rumania and took part in mine-laying operations in the Suez Canal, a section from the unit later being assigned to Iraqi insurgent forces attempting to take over the RAF base at Habbaniyah.

The reconnaissance group of the Luftwaffe's High Command flew clandestine surveillance missions over the Soviet Union prior to the German invasion. The photograph shows one of the unit's He 111H-2s. (*H. Redemann*)

During May and early June 1941, a large proportion of Luftwaffe units were transferred to the Eastern Front. Included among these were three Geschwader equipped with the He 111: KG 27 Boelcke, KG 53 Legion Condor, and KG 55 Grief, and these units were joined a month later by KG 4 General Wever and KGr 100 from France. The only He 111 units retained on the Western Front were I. and III./KG 26 in Norway and III./KG 40 in France, all operating anti-shipping sorties.

From early in 1941 the Luftwaffe had begun to build up its anti-shipping offensive against Britain, but these attacks increasingly proved that the bomb was not an effective weapon against heavily-armed ships. Consequently the Luftwaffe gave much thought to the re-introduction of the torpedo, sponsoring extensive trials at the bombing school at Grossenbrode on the Baltic. These trials and further tests at the Italian school (known as KSG 2) at Grosseto proved that the He 111 was an extremely effective torpedo-bomber.

The first variant of the He 111 to be developed to carry torpedoes was the H-6 which was introduced late in 1941. It was powered by two Jumo 211F-1 engines, had six MG 15 machine-guns and a 20 mm MG FF

An He 111H-6 bomber of the Luftwaffe. (*H. Redemann*)

cannon, and could carry two 765 kg (1,686 lb) LT F5b torpedoes externally. The first unit to re-equip with the He 111H-6 was I./KG 26 which underwent the three weeks conversion course at Grosseto early in 1942. By June the complete Gruppe, based at Bardufoss and Banak in northern Norway, were ready for operation against the Arctic convoys.

The first notable mission undertaken by the torpedo-bombers of I./KG 26 under Hptm Gernot Eicke was on 5 July, 1942, when it struck the ill-fated PQ 17 convoy. The Heinkels flew in low from several directions and sank two ships for the loss of two aircraft. Eicke himself sank the United States freighter *William Hopper*, and subsequent operations by I./KG 26 and KG 30 virtually destroyed the complete convoy.

It was not until 13 September, 1942, that the next convoy, PQ 18, came within range of the Luftwaffe aircraft, now joined by III./KG 26 with Junkers Ju 88 torpedo-bombers. The fighter escort from the carrier HMS *Avenger* intercepted the initial assault by Ju 88s from KG 30, but this

Two LT F5b practice torpedoes carried beneath the fuselage of an He 111H-6 on PVC weapon racks. (*R. C. Seeley*)

254

allowed KG 26 under Maj Werner Klümper to attack without hindrance, sinking a total of eight vessels. Next day the unit attempted to repeat its success, directing its attacks on the *Avenger* herself. This time the Hurricanes were waiting and six He 111s were shot down and nine more written-off on landing in Norway. Bad weather prevented further operations by KG 26 and KG 30, and in November 1942 they were transferred to the Mediterranean front.

Development of the Heinkel bomber continued with the He 111H-8, a modification of an H-3 or H-5 airframe with a large and cumbersome balloon-cable-fending device. This weighed no less than 250 kg (550 lb) and, after a brief period of operations by KG 54, the 30 or so aircraft converted had the fender removed and were modified as glider tugs under the designation He 111H-8/R2. The He 111H-10 was similar to the H-6, but carried the MG FF cannon in the ventral gondola and was fitted with Kuto-Nase balloon-cable-cutters in the wing leading edge.

Although tested over the British Isles by KG 54, the He 111H-8 with the balloon-cable-fending device proved too cumbersome for successful operation. (*H. Obert*)

255

The He 111H-11 had a fully-enclosed dorsal gun position and increased defensive armament. The H-11/R1 had a pair of beam-mounted MG 81Z twin-gun installations, and the H-11/R2 was a glider tug. The He 111H-12 was fitted with an FuG 203b Kehl III transmitter for use with two under-wing Henschel Hs 293A missiles. The He 111H-12 was never used operationally, but a few aircraft were used in connection with the Hs 293D and G programmes described on pages 679 and 681.

One of the most interesting of the early H-series to see operational service was the He 111H-14 which was a pathfinder with a crew of six and FuG Samos with Peil-GV and APZ 5 and FuG 351 Korfu radio equipment. The variant was used operationally by Sonderkommando Rastedter of KG 40 during 1944. The He 111H-15 was a torpedo-bomber, and the next major production series was the H-16. Powered by two 1,350 hp Jumo 211F-2 engines, this version carried extensive defensive armament including the MG 81Z twin-gun installation, the 13 mm MG 131 weapon and the MG FF cannon. The He 111H-16/R1 had an MG 131 gun in a power-operated dorsal turret, the H-16/R2 was a glider tug and the R3 was a pathfinder.

The He 111H-20 for which three prototypes, the V46, V47 and V48, were completed late in 1942. (*H. Thiele*)

The He 111H-18 was a specialized pathfinder variant based on the H-16/R3. Intended specifically for night operations, it had the same radio equipment as the H-14 and flame-damping equipment over the exhausts. The next important model was the H-20 which was produced in four different versions. The H-20/R1 had accommodation for 16 paratroops, the H-20/R2 was a freighter and glider tug, the H-20/R3 was a night bomber with racks for a 2,000 kg (4,410 lb) bomb load, and the H-20/R4 carried a load of twenty 50 kg (110 lb) SC 50 bombs. As part of their heavy defensive armament, several H-20 variants were fitted with an electrically-operated dorsal turret housing an MG 131 machine-gun.

With the abandonment of the Junkers Ju 288 (*see* page 437) and the continued trouble being experienced with the He 177, Heinkel proposed a new variant of the He 111 to be powered by Jumo 213 engines. This model was designated He 111H-21 and was basically an H-20/R3 powered by two 1,750 hp Jumo 213E-1 engines with two-stage superchargers. It had a maximum speed of 480 km/h (298 mph) without bomb load.

The most fascinating of all He 111H operations were those undertaken

Close-up of a late production He 111H showing the nose-mounted 20 mm MG FF cannon and the aerial array for the FuG 200 anti-shipping radar. (*H. Redemann*)

by KG 53 with the He 111H-22. Following experiments at Peenemünde in 1943, several He 111H-6s, H-16s and H-21s with the designation He 111H-22, were modified to carry a Fieseler Fi 103 missile (the V1) under either wing. After a short period of training, the newly re-formed III./KG 3 became operational with the type at Venlo and Gilze Rijen in the Netherlands. By August the unit had launched three hundred V1 flying bombs against London, 90 against Southampton and 20 against Gloucester. The flying bomb made the Heinkel bomber extremely unwieldy in the air, and the attackers were forced to adopt a special procedure to evade interception by Allied fighters. Taking-off at night, the aircraft would fly low over the sea to evade the Allied radar cover, climb to about 450 m (1,475 ft) to release their missiles, and then make good their escape, again at low level.

In September 1944, with the Allied advance into German-held territory, III./KG 3 was forced to withdraw to bases at Aalhorn, Handorf bei Münster, Varelbusch, and Zwischenahn. During October the unit was redesignated I./KG 53 and, within a month, two further Gruppen had been added to the unit. II./KG 53 was formed in November 1944, and the aircraft from KG 27, which had been disbanded as a bomber unit in September, were hurriedly re-equipped as Fi 103 carriers and delivered to III./KG 53, which had become operational in December.

Now operating with a strength of some one hundred He 111H-22s, KG 53 launched its missiles mainly against London, but made some attacks on other cities towards the end of the year. Perhaps the most notable was the launching of some fifty Fi 103s against Manchester on 24 December,

1944; of the 50 launched, 30 crossed the British coastline but only one actually hit the city. During the period from late July 1944 to 14 January, 1945, when operations by KG 53 finally ceased, the unit lost seventy-seven He 111s, 16 of these to Mosquito night fighters. Of the 1,200 or so missiles launched, only a small proportion actually reached their targets.

The final production version of the H-series was the He 111H-23, which was a paratroop-carrier somewhat similar to the H-20/R1 but powered by two 1,776 hp Junkers Jumo 213A-1 engines. The aircraft was often con-verted for use as a bomber. The final bomber project was the He 111R series, which was intended for high-altitude operations. The proposed He 111R-1 was a bomber to be powered by two turbo-supercharged 1,350 hp Jumo 211F-2 engines in annular cowlings. This was abandoned in favour of the R-2, which was to have been powered by two 1,810 hp Daimler-Benz DB 603U engines with either Hirth 2281 or TKL 15 turbo-superchargers, but only one prototype was produced—the He 111 V32 which was fitted with two DB 603U engines and TK 9AC superchargers.

Basically two He 111H-6 airframes coupled together, the five-engined He 111Z-1 saw limited Luftwaffe service. (*R. C. Seeley*)

Without doubt the strangest variant was the He 111Z (the Z indicating Zwilling or twin). The machine comprised two He 111 airframes coupled by a new centre section fitted with a *fifth* engine. The He 111Z-1 was designed to tow the very large Messerschmitt Me 321 or up to three Gotha Go 242 transport gliders, and carried a crew of seven, four of these (including the pilot) sitting in the port fuselage, and the remainder in the starboard fuselage.

The He 111Z-1 had a span of 35·2 m (115 ft 6 in), an all-up weight of some 28,500 kg (62,850 lb), and could tow an Me 321 up to 4,000 m (13,124 ft) at 225 km/h (140 mph). The He 111Z-2 was a long-range bomber project similar to the Z-1 but capable of carrying up to four Henschel Hs 293A missiles. The He 111Z-3 was a proposed reconnais-sance variant carrying four 300 litre (66 Imp gal) drop tanks.

Towards the end of 1942, the He 111 was being used in some numbers for transport duties. One of the first major operations in which the He 111 transport was involved was an attempt to deliver supplies to the German army at Stalingrad. On 24 November, 1942, the Luftwaffe's Commander-

258

The peculiar five-engined He 111Z-1 takes off with two Go 242 gliders in tow. (*H. Lächler*)

in-Chief ordered that 300 tons of supplies should be flown daily into Stalingrad. With the Junkers-Ju 53/3ms alone this was clearly impossible, so it was decided to make use of several He 111 equipped bomber units.

Following this decision, Gen Richthofen appointed Oberst Dr Ernst Kühl, commander of KG 55 at Morosovskaya, as Lufttransportführer 1 in charge of all He 111 transport units. Kühl had at his disposal, in addition to his own I. and II./KG 55, the whole of KG 27 under Obstlt Hans-Henning von Beust at Millerovo, I./KG 100, and KGrzbV 5 and KGrzbV 20 at Morosovskaya. The last of these was equipped with such obsolete variants as the He 111D and F, but the others were equipped with either P- or H-series machines.

The first operation took place on 30 November when the Heinkels flew to Pitomnik, but bad weather and Soviet fighters took a heavy toll of the German aircraft. Finally, on 23 December, 1942, Soviet tanks were advancing on Morosovskaya airfield so Kühl ordered his aircraft to fly to Novocherkassk. The bad weather cleared for a few days, and the aircraft of KG 27, KG 55, I./KG 100, Sch.G 1 and St.G 2, were able to strike at the Soviet tanks, temporarily making Morosovskaya airfield safe again. Bad weather soon returned, and on Boxing Day the units were forced to return to Novocherkassk.

By the time the Stalingrad campaign ended on 2 February, 1943, the units of Lufttransportführer 1 (joined on 1 January by III./KG 55) had lost no less than one hundred and sixty-five He 111s, more than half the aircraft committed. The Kampfgeschwader were never to recover from this blow.

As the war progressed, the He 111 was gradually relegated more and more to duties such as glider towing with Luftlandegeschwader 1 and

An He 111Z-1 five-engined transport. (*H. Thiele*)

259

Schleppgruppe 1. Apart from operations by KG 53 with the He 111H-22 mentioned earlier, one of the last major missions undertaken by the Heinkel bomber was that of the night of 21/22 June, 1944. Earlier in the day 114 United States Boeing B-17 Fortresses together with their Mustang fighter escort had landed at Poltava airfield in the USSR after a flight from Britain during which they had bombed Berlin. They were followed to the airfield by a Heinkel He 177 and, during the night, bombers of KG 4, KG 27, KG 53, and KG 55 attacked, following the dropping of flares by I./KG 4, with the result that 43 Fortresses and 15 Mustangs were destroyed.

One of the last units to be equipped with the He 111 was TGr 30 based at Gross-Ostheim and later Zellhausen. The unit dropped paratroops behind the Allied lines during the battle of the Ardennes in 1944, and was later engaged in transporting supplies to the German garrisons at Dunkirk, St Nazaire, Lorient and La Rochelle. Although based at Zellhausen, the unit usually operated from Stuttgart-Echterdingen, and one notable mission was on 10 February, 1945, when two aircraft from 2./TGr 30 carried mail and food supplies to Guernsey and St Nazaire.

When the war ended in May 1945, only four Gruppen were still operational with the He 111: I. and III./KG 4 based at Königgrätz, II./KG 4 at Greifswald, and TGr 30 based at Neubiberg and Rerik. These units, joined by a part of Schleppgruppe 1, equipped with the He 111 at Königgrätz, operated purely as transports. The wheel had turned full circle.

Total He 111 production was about 7,000.

*Wartime operational units:* I.(F)/120, 1. and 3.(F)/121, 2., 3. and 5.(F)/122, 3.(F)/123, 1.(F)/124, the Nachtaufklärungsstaffeln, 1., 3. and 4./Aufkl.Gr.Ob.d.L., the meteorological reconnaissance squadrons, I., II. and III./KG 1, III./KG 3, I., II. and III./KG 4, 15./KG 6, I., II. and III./KG 26, I., II., III. and 14.(Eis)/KG 27, I., II. and III./KG 28, I. and III./KG 40, I., II. and III./KG 51, I., II. and III./KG 53, I., II. and III./KG 54, I., II., III. and 14.(Eis)/KG 55, I., II., III. and 13./KG 100, KGr 100, 126 and 806. KGrzbV 20, 23 and 25, III./TG 3, TGr 30, TGr 111, I., II. and III./LG 1, I. and Versuchskommando/KG 200, Erprobungskommando 17, Lehr- und Erprobungskommando 36 and 100, Kommando Koch.

He 111E-3: Span 22·6 m (74 ft 1¾ in); length 17·5 m (57 ft 5 in); height 4·4 m (14 ft 5¼ in); wing area 87·6 sq m (942·917 sq ft).
Loaded weight 9,600 kg (21,168 lb).
Maximum speed at 4,000 m (13,124 ft) 420 km/h (261 mph), at sea level 350 km/h (218 mph); cruising speed at 4,000 m (13,124 ft) 381 km/h (237 mph), at sea level 325 km/h (202 mph); service ceiling 7,500 m (23,620 ft); maximum range 1,500 km (932 miles).

He 111H-16: Span 22·6 m (74 ft 1¼ in); length 16·4 m (53 ft 9½ in); height 4 m (13 ft 1¼ in); wing area 86·5 sq m (931·07 sq ft).
Empty weight 8,680 kg (19,136 lb); loaded weight 14,000 kg (30,865 lb).
Maximum speed at sea level 364 km/h (227 mph), at 2,000 m (6,562 ft) 400 km/h (248 mph), and at 6,000 m (19,686 ft) 435 km/h (270 mph); climb to 2,000 m (6,562 ft) 8·5 min, to 6,000 m (19,686 ft) 42 min; service ceiling 6,700 m (21,982 ft); absolute ceiling 8,500 m (27,888 ft); normal range 1,950 km (1,212 miles).

The Royal Air Force has an He 111H and parts of others still exist.

The Heinkel He 112 V2 (c/n 1291) which made its first flight in November 1935.
(*R. C. Seeley*)

# Heinkel He 112

Late in 1933 the RLM issued a specification calling for a monoplane fighter design to replace the Heinkel He 51 and Arado Ar 68 biplanes then under development for the still-secret Luftwaffe. Four designs were produced: the Arado Ar 80, the Focke-Wulf Fw 159, the Heinkel He 112, and the Messerschmitt Bf 109. The He 112, which was designed by Dipl Ing Heinrich Hertel, competed with the other three at a competition held at Travemünde in October 1935. The trials left little doubt that the Bf 109 and He 112 were far superior to the other designs, but there remained the question of which would receive the development contract. Eventually, and rather to the surprise of informed observers, who considered the He 112 superior, a contract was awarded for ten aircraft from both companies.

The Heinkel He 112 was a sturdy low-wing monoplane with an inverted gull wing of semi-elliptical planform and exceptionally broad chord. The deep-section fuselage with its large open cockpit afforded the pilot a good view when taxi-ing, and the wide-track retractable undercarriage eased ground handling problems. The oval-section monocoque fuselage and two-spar wing were both built of metal and covered in flush-riveted stressed metal skin.

The He 112 V1, D-IADO, was powered by a 695 hp Rolls-Royce Kestrel V engine with which it achieved a maximum speed of 466 km/h (289 mph). The V2, D-IHGE, and generally similar V3, D-IDMO, differed from the first prototype in having 600 hp Junkers Jumo 210C engines and reduced span. Two 7·9 mm MG 17 machine-guns were installed in the V3, which was later fitted with a new wing of full elliptical planform, and a sliding cockpit canopy. The He 112 V4, D-IZMY, was powered by a 680 hp Jumo 210Da engine, had the modified wing from the outset, and was intended to act as prototype of the proposed He 112A production model.

The He 112A series did not meet with RLM approval and Heinkel was allowed to offer the fighter for export. The He 112 V4, which was followed by the generally similar V5, was demonstrated at the International Flying Meeting at Zürich in July 1937. During the summer of 1936, the He 112 V4 had been evaluated under operational conditions by the Condor Legion in Spain.

The He 112 V6, D-ISJY, had some modification to the radiator bath and less rounded vertical tail surfaces, and it was later fitted with a new clear vision cockpit cover which considerably improved the rear view. The final He 112A series prototype was the V8, D-IRXO, which was virtually a test bed for the Daimler-Benz DB 600 engine.

After trials with the He 72, an early production He 112 was used as a static test airframe for the rocket engine designed by Wernher von Braun. The engine was installed in the rear fuselage of the He 112 with fuel tanks fore and aft of the cockpit. Successful experiments with the rocket were made at Kummersdorf although both the original, and a second He 112 airframe, exploded during these. Eventually a third airframe was donated for flight tests, the aircraft using the power from its piston engine for normal flight, the rocket being fired in a 30 second burst. Successful development of the rocket-propelled He 112 led to the design of the He 176 described on page 276.

The He 112 V4 just after completion. The aircraft was later registered D-IZMY and demonstrated at the Zürich International Flying Meeting in 1937.

With the failure of the He 112A series, Hertel undertook a complete structural redesign of the aircraft under the designation He 112B. The fuselage was given improved aerodynamic contours and was considerably lightened, and there were new wing and tail surfaces. The first B-series prototype was the He 112 V7, D-IKIK, which was powered by a 1,000 hp Daimler-Benz DB 600Aa engine. The first real production prototype was the He 112 V9, D-IGSI, which first flew in July 1937. Although powered by a 680 hp Junkers Jumo 210Ea engine, it proved to be some 40 km/h (25 mph) faster than the Messerschmitt Bf 109B-1 which had just entered service with the Luftwaffe.

The first B-series aircraft was the He 112 V7, seen here in its later form with revised air intakes.

The performance of the He 112 V9 was such that the Japanese government placed an order for thirty generally similar He 112B-0 pre-production aircraft during the autumn of 1937. The He 112B-0 had two 20 mm MG FF cannon in the wings and two 7·9 mm MG 17 machine-guns mounted above the engine cowling. The first twelve aircraft were delivered to Japan during the spring of 1938, but a second batch of twelve, due to be delivered in the summer, were hurriedly impressed into the Luftwaffe because of the Sudeten crisis. The machines were delivered to III./JG 132 (later II./JG 141) at Fürstenwalde and enthusiastically received by the Luftwaffe pilots who considered them much superior to the Bf 109C-1s with which the other two Gruppen were equipped. But, following the signing of the Munich Agreement, the fighters were returned to Heinkel for export, and replaced by the new Messerschmitt Bf 110.

Mainly because of what they considered poor manoeuvrability, the Japanese Navy cancelled their contract for the remaining eighteen He 112B-0s, and Heinkel immediately offered them to Spain. The last of the initial batch of He 112B-0s was retained by Heinkel for development work, but the other seventeen were delivered to Grupo 5-G-5 under Maj Muños of the Spanish Nationalist Air Force in November 1938.

The unit comprised two squadrons, one equipped with the Bf 109E-1, the other with the He 112B, and operated as top cover for Fiat C.R. 32 fighters. When the Spanish Civil War ended, the fifteen He 112B-0s that remained were transferred to Grupo 27 based in Spanish Morocco. As late as 1943 one of these aircraft destroyed an American Lockheed P-38 Lightning fighter which strayed into Spanish air space.

The previously mentioned He 112B-0 retained by Heinkel was redesignated He 112 V11, D-IYWE, and fitted with the 700 hp Jumo 210G engine with direct fuel injection. The He 112 V10, D-IQMA, was fitted with a 1,175 hp Daimler-Benz DB 601Aa engine as a prototype for the proposed He 112E (E for export) model. The He 112 V10 attained a maximum speed of 570 km/h (354 mph) and had a range of 1,150 km

Powered by a 1,175 hp Daimler-Benz DB 601 engine, the He 112 V10 D-IQMA was the prototype for a proposed export model. (*H. Redemann*)

(715 miles)—the latter considerably better than that of the comparable Bf 109E-1. The final prototype was the He 112 V12, D-IRXS, which was powered by a 1,100 hp DB 600Aa engine, and was eventually sold to Japan for research purposes.

The only air arm to use the He 112 operationally during the Second World War was the Royal Rumanian Air Force. Early in 1939, the Rumanian government, anxious to replace its rather ancient PZL P.11 and P.24 fighters, signed a contract with Heinkel for the delivery of twenty-four He 112B fighters. The first thirteen of these were of the He 112B-0

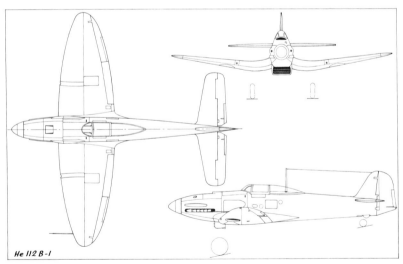

He 112 B-1

264

sub-type similar to the previous batch of thirty produced initially for the Japanese Navy, the remainder being of the improved B-1 series.

The He 112B-1 was powered by a 700 hp Junkers Jumo 210G engine with direct fuel injection and had individual exhaust stubs which provided a slight increase in performance. By September 1939, when production of the He 112 finally terminated, the Rumanian Air Force had received its total complement of twenty-four aircraft.

Twelve aircraft were delivered to each of two units, the 20th Squadron, engaged in the fighter defence of Bucharest, and the 51st Squadron, which supported the Rumanian 3rd and 4th Armies' drive across Bessarabia from June 1941. The latter unit's aircraft were engaged mainly in strafing the retreating Soviet troops, and lost several of their aircraft to ground fire. By the middle of 1942, the remaining Rumanian He 112Bs had been relegated to training units.

The last air arm to receive the Heinkel fighter was the Royal Hungarian Air Force which purchased three He 112B-1s and three Bf 109E-1s during the spring of 1939. In addition, the He 112 V9 was delivered to the Manfred Weiss factory and influenced the design of the indigenous WM-23 fighter. The Hungarian Service pilots preferred the He 112 to the Bf 109, but yet again the latter fighter was chosen by the Hungarian government.

He 112B-0: Span 9·1 m (29 ft 10¼ ins); length 9·3 m (30 ft 6 ins); height 3·85 m (12 ft 7½ ins); wing area 17 sq m (182·99 sq ft.).

Empty weight 1,620 kg (3,571 lb); loaded weight 2,250 kg (4,960 lb).

Maximum speed at sea level 484 km/h (301 mph), at 4,000 m (13,120 ft) 510 km/h (317 mph); landing speed 135 km/h (84 mph); climb to 6,000 m (19,685 ft) 10 min; service ceiling 8,500 m (27,890 ft); normal range 1,100 km (683 miles).

# Heinkel He 114

This two-seat twin-float sesquiplane was designed in 1935 to succeed the He 60 in the rôle of shipboard reconnaissance. Although the He 114 was no spectacular performer and was somewhat outdated by the time the Second World War began, it nevertheless saw service for more than half the duration of the war, but its numbers were supplemented by the more modern Arado Ar 196 float monoplane which was designed about two years later and was also to replace the He 60.

The He 114 had an all-metal fuselage and single-step twin floats and the wings were metal structures with fabric covering. The upper wing was mounted above the fuselage on splayed struts and V-struts connected the two wings. The floats were attached to the fuselage by a pair of struts on each side and wire-braced to each other and the lower wing. Water rudders were fitted to the tails of the floats. The tailplane was low set and the rudder

This view of the Heinkel He 114 V2, D-UGAT, float sesquiplane clearly illustrates the difference in span between the two wings.

dynamically balanced. The two cockpits were in tandem and partially enclosed.

Although the BMW 132 nine-cylinder radial air-cooled engine was eventually chosen to power the He 114, various engines were tried out in the prototype floatplanes. Twelve-cylinder inverted-vee liquid-cooled engines were tested in the first two prototypes, which flew during the spring of 1936, the He 114 V1 having a 960 hp Daimler-Benz DB 600 driving a two-blade airscrew and the He 114 V2, D-UGAT, having a 640 hp Junkers Jumo 210 driving a three-blade airscrew. These engines were closely cowled and had chin radiators. The next two prototypes were each flown with nine-cylinder radial air-cooled engines, the He 114 V3, D-IOGD, having an 880 hp BMW 132Dc driving a two-blade airscrew and

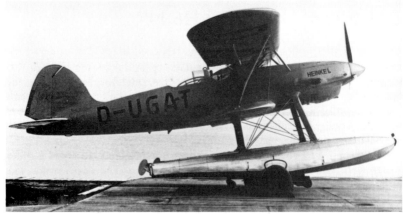

The He 114 V2. The type was designed to succeed the Heinkel He 60 in the shipboard reconnaissance rôle.

266

the He 114 V4, D-IDWS, having a 960 hp BMW 132K driving a three-blade airscrew. One or other of these BMW radial engines powered all subsequent machines apart from a few for export.

The He 114 V5 with a BMW 132Dc engine was the prototype for the pre-production He 114A-0 of which ten were built and of which four were also designated He 114 V6 to V9 as development aircraft. The He 114 V8, or A-03, D-IDEG, was the prototype for the first production model, the He 114A-1, of which 33 with BMW 132Dc engines were built for training purposes. The He 114 V9, or A-04, D-IHDG, was the prototype for the first operational production model, the He 114A-2.

Put into production in 1938, the He 114A-2 was powered by the BMW 132K engine and had one fixed forward-firing 7·9 mm MG 17 machine-gun and a similar weapon in the observer's cockpit. Also, either two 50 kg (110 lb) bombs or SN 50 spraying apparatus could be carried. The spraying equipment was installed in the floats in a similar manner to that for the

The He 114 V3, D-IOGD, was the first prototype to be tested with a radial engine. This engine, the BMW 132, was the type eventually chosen for production aircraft.

He 60 and could be used for smoke screening or the spraying of non-volatile war gases such as mustard gas. The few He 114s operated from Kriegsmarine warships were flown by 5./BFGr 196 but, contrary to the original aim, the principal bases of operation for the He 114 were coastal, and one of the first coastal units to receive the type was 1./Kü.Fl.Gr.506. Also, in 1939, four unarmed examples of the He 114A-2 were built, and these were designated He 114C-2s for operation from German commerce-raiding ships plying the South Atlantic and Pacific oceans.

Before the war began, fourteen He 114A-2s were exported to Sweden as He 114B-1s. Six He 114B-2s exported to Rumania were reminiscent of the first two prototypes, since three had Daimler-Benz DB 600 engines and three had Junkers Jumo 210 engines. A further 12 aircraft exported to Rumania were designated He 114B-3s, but these were virtually standard He 114A-2s. Before production ceased in 1939, fourteen He 114C-1s

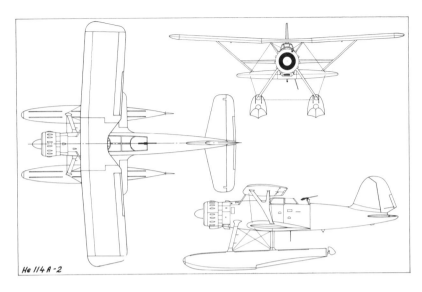

He 114 A-2

were produced for the Luftwaffe. These were similar to the A-2 version but had an extra forward-firing MG 17 machine-gun.

During the war, the He 114 was operated both by Germans and Rumanians over the Black Sea, but its chief bases were in Greece and Crete when flown on Mediterranean reconnaissance missions during 1942. The units concerned in these latter operations were SAGr 125 and SAGr 126, but their He 114s were gradually phased out by increasing numbers of the Arado Ar 196 which were further supplemented with the Blohm und Voss Bv 138.

*Wartime operational units:* SAGr 125 and SAGr 126, BFGr 196 and 1./Kü.Fl.Gr 506.

He 114 A-2: Span 13·6 m (44 ft 7$\frac{1}{2}$ in); length 11·09 m (36 ft 4$\frac{1}{2}$ in); height 5·15 m (16 ft 10$\frac{1}{4}$ in); wing area 42·3 sq m (455·15 sq ft).

Empty weight 2,315 kg (5,105 lb); fuel and oil 600 kg (1,323 lb); loaded weight including ammunition 3,400 kg (7,497 lb).

Maximum speed at 3,500 m (11,480 ft) 335 km/h (208 mph); maximum cruising speed 290 km/h (180 mph); alighting speed 95 km/h (59 mph); initial rate of climb 330 m/min (1,082 ft/min); service ceiling 4,800 m (15,744 ft); normal range 1,050 km (652 miles).

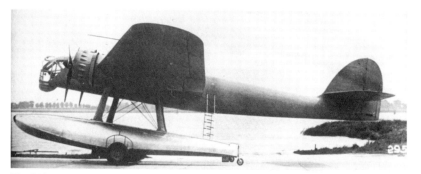

The Heinkel He 115 V1 before being registered as D-AEHF in 1936. This floatplane was later modified, mainly by streamlining the nose and fuselage, and gained eight new speed records in its class on 20 March, 1938.

# Heinkel He 115

Although the Heinkel He 115 twin-engined twin-float seaplane was developed well before the Second World War, it continued without much modification in front-line service almost to the end. The chief reason for this was that its main duty was the dropping of mines over the sea at night, and in this rôle it was relatively unmolested and harassed Allied shipping considerably although other rôles included bombing, torpedo launching and reconnaissance. The aircraft's general handling qualities were very good, and its usefulness was such, in fact, that it was put back into production late in 1943 at a time when most German production was turning to defensive fighters.

The He 115 was an all-metal mid-wing monoplane having twin floats attached by struts beneath the engine nacelles. The wing was built in three sections around two spars and the monocoque fuselage had a stepped

Designed to the same requirement as the Heinkel He 115, the Blohm und Voss Ha 140 was abandoned at an early stage. (*R. C. Seeley*)

269

cockpit which faired back to a stepped, rearward-facing, observer's compartment. A crew of three was carried.

The first prototype, the He 115 V1, D-AEHF, flew in 1936 and was powered by two 960 hp BMW 132K nine-cylinder radial air-cooled engines and had a single 7·9 mm MG 15 machine-gun in the glazed nose and a similar weapon in the rear observer's position. This aircraft was later modified for record-breaking purposes, and aerodynamic cleaning included replacing the angular glazed nose with a wooden fairing and removing the rear compartment step by further fairing. On 20 March, 1938, the He 115 V1 gained eight new speed records for its class by flying at an average speed of 325 km/h (202 mph) with varying payloads over various distances. Generally similar to the prototype in its original form, the He 115 V2, D-APDS, flew soon after. On the He 115 V3, D-ABZV, there was a continuous glazed canopy extending from the windshield to the rear position, and this feature appeared on subsequent aircraft.

Refuelling an He 115 (M2-MH) of 1./Kü.Fl.Gr.106. (*H. Thiele*)

The first production prototype was the He 115 V4, D-AHME, and this introduced angled bracing struts between the vertical struts of the floats and dispensed with the previous complex of bracing wires. During 1937, ten pre-production He 115A-0s were built, each having only a single MG 15 gun at the observer's position. The following year saw deliveries of the He 115A-1 production aircraft which differed chiefly in reverting to a twin MG 15 armament, and a small number of this type was later sold to Norway and Sweden as the He 115A-2. The first version received by the Luftwaffe in large numbers was the Hē 115A-3 which had a revised bomb bay and radio equipment.

During 1939, the He 115B-1 was introduced, which had the important modification of increased fuel capacity to extend the range to 3,350 km (2,080 miles) from the 2,000 km (1,242 miles) of the A-series. Some of these B-1s could carry, at the expense of their increased range, a 1,000 kg (2,200 lb) magnetic parachute mine together with a 500 kg (1,100 lb) bomb load. There was also the He 115B-2 which had reinforced floats to permit operation from snow and ice.

270

An He 115B-1 (of 1./Kü.Fl.Gr.506) used to ferry spare He 115 floats. (*H. Thiele*)

The units which operated the He 115 were the Küstenfliegergruppen which undertook mining, bombing, reconnaissance, and other coastal duties. Staffeln of the various Gruppen which operated this floatplane were 1. and 3./Kü.Fl.Gr. 106, 1./Kü.Fl.Gr. 406, 1. and 3./Kü.Fl.Gr. 706 and all three Staffeln of both Kü.Fl.Gr. 506 and Kü.Fl.Gr. 906. In November 1939, German seaplanes began supplementing the efforts of the Kriegsmarine vessels by dropping magnetic parachute mines in critical sections of the Allied shipping lanes. 3./Kü.Fl.Gr. 906 inaugurated such missions on the night of 20/21 November after bad weather had prevented a mission two nights previously. The unit dropped its mines without loss off Harwich and at the mouth of the Thames, and performed similar work

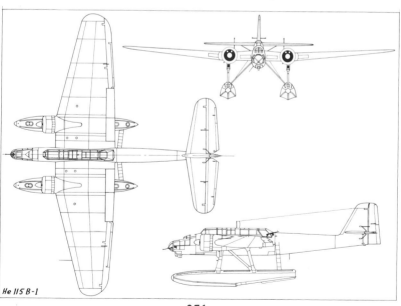

He 115 B-1

271

the following night. On these occasions, the mines were probably dropped without their parachutes from altitudes of less than 1,000 m (3,280 ft), and a magnetic or acoustic fuse was armed, with or without a time delay, by water pressure.

On the night of 22/23 November, 1939, 3./Kü.Fl.Gr. 906 was again in action but was joined this time by the He 115s of 3./Kü.Fl.Gr. 106, one of which dropped a mine off Southend. This particular mine proved fortuitous for the Allies since, when the tide receded that night, it was de-fused by a team led by Lieut-Cdr J. G. D. Ouvry of HMS *Vernon* and then removed for dissection. The secrets thus revealed aided subsequent de-fusing and provided information for exploding the submerged German mines, such work being done by low-flying Wellingtons fitted with de-gaussing rings. Another Allied counter-measure to the new menace was the bombing of the He 115 bases on the island of Sylt.

From May to early June 1940, some of the Germans occupying Norway found themselves at the receiving end of He 115A-2s of the Norwegian Naval Air Service which, together with two captured He 115B-1s, attacked the Germans, principally in the Narvik area. Subsequently, two of these aircraft were flown to Helensburgh on the Clyde and were modified by the British for clandestine operations such as transporting agents.

During the Battle of Britain, both Kü.Fl.Gr. 106 and 506 were active with the He 115. In the same year, the He 115C-0 appeared, and a

Hoisting a torpedo into an He 115C from the special servicing platform beneath the weapons bay. The He 115 was the Luftwaffe's most-used attack and reconnaissance float seaplane.

272

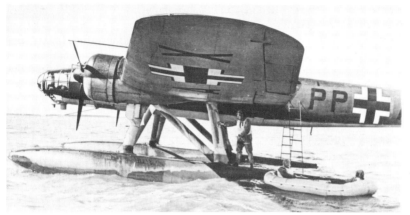

An He 115 (PP-AX), probably during air-sea rescue practice. (*H. Redemann*)

production version, the He 115C-1, entered service in 1941. This version had the previous armament augmented by a single 20 mm MG 151 cannon in a bulged housing beneath the nose, and some aircraft also had a further MG 17 machine-gun fixed in each wing root. Another modification gave the option of fitting auxiliary fuel tanks in the bomb bay, but at the expense of bomb capacity. The He 115C-2 version, like the B-2, differed in having reinforced float bottoms to permit operations from snow and ice, while the C-3 was specifically for mine-laying and the C-4 for torpedo dropping and had armament reduced to one aft-firing MG 15 machine-gun. Also used on operations in 1941 was the one and only He 115D-0 which was the sole version to have more powerful engines, namely two 1,600 hp BMW 801C radials, and for this prototype, an He 115A-1 had been converted; but the D-series was not proceeded with due, apparently, to the discontinued development of the BMW 800 radial engines for which it was designed.

Before 1941, production of complete He 115s had ceased in order to concentrate on other types of aircraft, and Kü.Fl.Gr. 106 and 506 were re-formed into K.Gr. 106 and 506 with the Junkers Ju 88 in May 1941. The other He 115 Gruppen, however, continued operations as the following example shows. On 2 July, 1942, the Allied convoy PQ 17 was attacked by eight He 115s of 1./Kü.Fl.Gr. 406 flying from Sörreisa, near Tromsö in Arctic Norway, and led by Hptm Herbert Vater. The ships' flak was severe and Vater's aircraft was forced down, but he was rescued by the aircraft of Oblt Burmester before his own aircraft sank. An He 115 from the same unit and piloted by the Staffel-Kapitän, Hptm Eberhard Peukert, then spotted the convoy at 05.00 hr on 4 July and the unit made a torpedo attack in which the US freighter *Christopher Newport* was severely damaged.

In view of the good results obtained with the He 115, particularly in the mine-laying rôle over the Atlantic, Baltic, and North Sea, it was decided that it was worthwhile keeping the type in service by restarting production

273

late in 1943. Already, late in 1942, the duties of Kü.Fl.Gr. 906 had been taken over by the Blohm und Voss Bv 138 flying-boats. Production began again with the He 115E-1, which was generally similar to the C-series but had two nose-mounted 7·9 mm MG 81 machine-guns and two similar guns in the aft position, while some machines also had a single forward-firing 20 mm MG 151 cannon. The He 115, of which about 500 were built, can be summed up as the Luftwaffe's most-used and most successful attack and reconnaissance float seaplane.

*Wartime operational units:* 1. and 3./Kü.Fl.Gr. 106, 1./Kü.Fl.Gr 406, 1., 2. and 3./Kü.Fl.Gr 506, 1./Kü.Fl.Gr 706, 1. and 2./Kü.Fl.Gr 906, 1., 2. and 3./KG 200.

He 115B-1: Span 22·2 m (72 ft 2$\frac{1}{8}$ in); length 17·3 m (56 ft 9$\frac{1}{8}$ in); height 6·6 m (21 ft 7$\frac{7}{8}$in); wing area 87·5 sq m (934·5 sq ft).

Empty weight 5,300 kg (11,687 lb); maximum mixed attack payload 1,500 kg (3,300 lb); normal loaded weight 9,100 kg (20,065 lb); maximum loaded weight 10,400 kg (22,932 lb).

Maximum speed at 3,400 m (11,152 ft) 355 km/h (220 mph); cruising speed at 3,400 m (11,152 ft) 295 km/h (183 mph); alighting speed 115 km/h (72 mph); initial rate of climb 235 m/min (770 ft/min); service ceiling 5,500 m (18,040 ft); normal range 2,000 km (1,242 miles); maximum range 3,350 km (2,080 miles).

# Heinkel He 116

The Heinkel He 116A was produced for Deutsche Lufthansa to serve as a long-distance mail carrier, primarily on the South Atlantic route and to the Far East. The design borrowed much from the clean aerodynamic shapes of the He 70 and He 111, particularly the elliptical planform wing and tail surfaces, but was a four-engined machine. The engines were of the 240 hp Hirth HM 508 eight-cylinder inverted-vee air-cooled type, driving two-blade airscrews, and 2,650 litres (583 gal) of fuel could be carried. The wing was a two-spar wooden structure with plywood covering, the fuselage was a metal monocoque structure with watertight bulkheads, and all undercarriage members retracted. The crew of four included two pilots.

Eight aircraft, all bearing V numbers, were put in hand and the first appeared in the summer of 1937 as the He 116 V1 *Lübeck*, but this did not see regular service and apparently received no civil registration. The He 116 V2 (c/n 545) was D-AJIE *Schlesien* and the He 116 V4, also known as the He 116A-02, was D-ATIO *Hamburg*. Two of the eight He 116As were bought by the Japanese for Manchurian Air Transport's mail service on the Tokyo-Hsinking route. These two aircraft were the He 116 V5, J-BAKD *Nogi*, and the He 116 V6, J-EAKF *Togo*, and they arrived in Tokyo on 29 April, 1938.

Eight Heinkel He 116A civil mail-carriers were built. One of them, the He 116 V2, is shown here. (*J. Zazvonil*)

Six examples of the He 116B were built for testing in the long-range reconnaissance and bomber rôles. An He 116B under evaluation is shown here. Note the new, fully-glazed nose compared with the civil type. (*R. C. Seeley*)

Another He 116B, still with its civil registration D-ADEG. (*R. C. Seeley*)

275

The He 116 V7 and V8 were unregistered but the He 116 V3, also known as the He 116A-03, was D-ARFD *Rostock*. This aircraft was modified for record-breaking when it had the pseudo-designation He 116R; its engines were 240 hp Hirth HM 508Hs, and a wing of greater span and area was fitted. On 30 July, 1938, the He 116R established a new international record by flying a distance of 10,000 km (6,213 miles) in 48 hr 18 min.

The performance of the He 116A suggested to the RLM that the aircraft might be useful as a long-range reconnaissance aircraft and, accordingly, a ninth aircraft was built as the prototype for an He 116B. Unlike the civil version which had conventional crew cabin and metal nose, the military version had a fully-glazed rounded nose reminiscent of the He 111H. The possibility of using the type as a bomber was also considered, but, although five more examples of the He 111B version were built, no production or Service use resulted. Thus, only 14 examples of the He 116 type were constructed.

He 116A: Span 22 m (72 ft 2 in); length 13·7 m (44 ft 11$\frac{1}{2}$ in); height 3·3 m (10 ft 10 in); wing area 62·87 sq m (676·72 sq ft).

Empty weight 4,050 kg (8,929 lb); loaded weight 7,130 kg (15,719 lb).

Maximum speed at sea level 325 km/h (202 mph), at 5,000 m (16,400 ft) 355 km/h (220 mph); cruising speed at 5,000 m (16,400 ft) 300 km/h (186 mph); landing speed 110 km/h (68·3 mph); service ceiling 6,600 m (21,653 ft); range 4,100 km (2,548 miles).

# Heinkel He 176

Although the Heinkel He 176 was not the first aircraft to use rocket power, it was the first to fly solely with a liquid-fuelled rocket motor fitted and it represents the culmination of early Heinkel experiments in this field. Some time before the He 176, interest in applying rocket power to aircraft had begun in Germany and the first such flight, with a man on board, occurred on 11 June, 1928, when Fritz Stamer flew a rocket-driven glider. In September the following year, von Opel also flew a glider powered by a battery of solid-fuelled rockets, but this glider caught fire soon after take-off and crashed. There followed similar experiments, notably by Stamer and Espenlaub. Later, significant trials were conducted by Prof Hugo Junkers at Dessau when an overloaded Junkers-W 33 floatplane took-off with the assistance of under-wing powder rockets. By 1936, attention was turning to liquid-fuelled rockets when a 300 kg (660 lb) thrust motor was fitted to a Junkers-A 50 Junior which was used in centrifugal but not flight trials. The first flights with a liquid-fuelled rocket were made in the autumn of 1936 when a Heinkel He 72 was used to test a simple Walter motor using hydrogen peroxide and paste catalyst to give a thrust of about 135 kg (300 lb) for 45 seconds.

The Heinkel company then began to take serious interest and donated two He 112 airframes for a series of dangerous ground tests with a von Braun liquid oxygen/alcohol rocket which eventually gave about 1,000 kg (2,200 lb) thrust for 30 seconds. Late in April 1937, an He 112 fitted with this motor flew at Kummersdorf with Flugkapitän Erich Warsitz at the controls but crash-landed after a rocket malfunction. After repairs, the programme continued and Warsitz eventually made an all-rocket-powered flight with this aircraft in the summer of 1937. By this time, the H. Walter KG at Kiel had improved the hydrogen peroxide system used on the He 72 by using liquid instead of paste catalyst, and a new motor produced 300 kg

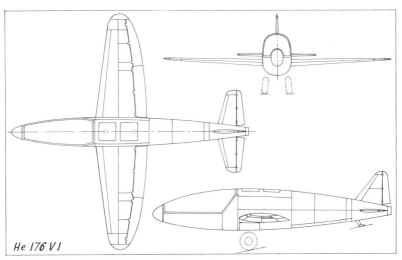

He 176 V1

(660 lb) thrust for 30 seconds; motors of this type were used in assisted take-off trials with an overloaded Heinkel He 111 at Neubrandenburg in the summer of 1937. Although liquid oxygen motors were also tested in He 111s, the Walter motors proved more reliable and suitable and, beginning with the RI-201 model, were eventually adopted for ATO work. Finally, Walter KG developed the liquid catalyst motor into the first variable-thrust motor in which a turbine-driven pump could alter the flow of hydrogen peroxide and hence vary thrust. The motor gave a maximum thrust of 950 kg (2,000 lb) for 30 seconds and was fitted to the previously-mentioned He 112 and flown from Peenemünde in the autumn of 1938.

After the 1937 trials with the He 112, it was clear that dramatic results could be obtained from rocket-propelled aircraft, and Heinkel decided to build an aircraft to be entirely powered by a rocket motor for the purpose of high-speed research and the prestige of possibly exceeding the, then magic, 1,000 km/h (621 mph) mark which far exceeded the contemporary world speed record. Thus, late in 1937, the design of the He 176 was begun by Hans Regner, and the construction of a prototype began in a secluded hangar at Marienehe. The aircraft was of the minimum size possible, the fuselage having a maximum diameter of 0·8 m (2 ft 7½ in), and was in fact made-to-measure for the pilot Warsitz, who was provided with a slightly reclining seat. The fuselage, into which the mainwheels retracted, contained two tanks for the hydrogen peroxide and methanol propellants and a Walter RI rocket motor. This motor was a further development of the type used in the He 112, and control of the hydrogen peroxide flow allowed a thrust variation between 45 kg (100 lb) and 500 kg (1,100 lb), maximum thrust being possible for 60 seconds.

The low-set elliptical planform wings had a symmetrical profile section, and were fitted with wingtip skids as a precaution because of the narrow track of the undercarriage. Control surfaces were generally conventional, the principal indication of high-speed flight being the generally clean lines exemplified by the Plexiglas cockpit cover being flush with the fuselage profile. A particularly novel feature of the He 176 was the system specially designed for emergency escape because of the anticipated high speeds. The arrangement was for the whole cockpit section to be ejected by compressed air and, when slowed down sufficiently, to deploy a parachute for further deceleration. When the speed of the cockpit section had dropped sufficiently, the pilot would release the cover and bale-out with his own parachute in the conventional manner. The only drawback was that, according to tests conducted by dropping cockpits and dummies from an He 111, the minimum altitude for ejecting the cockpit section was about 6,000 m (19,680 ft).

In the summer of 1938, the completed He 176 was taken to Usedom island where attempts were made to conduct taxi-ing trials by towing the aircraft behind a large Mercedes car, but without much success. Therefore, using the Walter motor in short bursts, powered taxi-ing was carried out and then progressively longer hops off the ground. Finally, on 30 June, 1939, the He 176, with Warsitz at the controls, made its first full rocket flight which lasted 50 seconds, and ended in a smooth landing, and on the following day, a second flight was made before Milch, Udet and other RLM personnel. Several other flights were made during the month. On 3 July, 1939, a demonstration of new aircraft types was staged at Rechlin, and, at the nearby Roggentheim airfield, the He 176 was flown before Hitler, Goering, von Keitel and others.

Despite its accident-free, albeit short, history, the performance of the He 176 was not impressive, and it appears to have been flown only at low altitude in more or less straight and level flight and never exceeded 700 km/h (434 mph), which was below the world speed record at that time. The aircraft was heavy for its size, resulting in a very high wing loading and underpowering. At an early stage, the RLM had requested that provision for armament be made, and, although the He 176 was a purely private venture for research, a gesture was made by fitting small blisters which did not enclose armament but contained instruments.

Although it was planned to build a second, improved, model, the He 176 programme was abandoned once war started, and the only prototype was sent to the Berlin Air Museum where it was destroyed in a bombing raid during 1943. Ernst Heinkel has maintained that the first signs of political machinations against him appeared with lack of official interest in the He 176, but this was not the only reason for the programme being abandoned. The RLM saw more promise in the rocket aircraft programme it had instituted, (after the proposal of Hans M. Antz of the Technisches Amt) with the designer Dr Alexander Lippisch and which did, after all, result in the Me 163B Komet interceptor. In any event, Heinkel's attention was being increasingly concentrated on the possibilities of the turbojet-powered He 178 even before the He 176 was abandoned.

He 176: Span 4 m (13 ft 1½ in); length 5 m (16 ft 4⅞ in); wing area 5 sq m (53·8 sq ft). Empty weight 1,570 kg (3,455 lb); loaded weight 2,000 kg (4,400 lb). Maximum speed at sea level 700 km/h (435 mph).

The Heinkel He 177 V1 (c/n 00 001) which made its first flight on 19 November, 1939, at Rostock.

# Heinkel He 177 Greif (Griffon)

Gen Walther Wever, the Luftwaffe's first Chief of Staff had proposed, as early as 1934, the construction of a four-engined long-range bomber. Two aircraft were built to his specification, the Dornier Do 19 and the Junkers Ju 89. The former was a low-wing monoplane with a box-like fuselage, twin fins and rudders, powered by four Bramo 322 radials. The underpowered aircraft was comparatively slow and only one prototype was completed. The Junkers Ju 89 was more promising. It was similar in basic layout to the Do 19, but much more streamlined, and was powered by four Daimler-Benz DB 600 engines. Two prototypes of the Ju 89 were built, but following the death of Wever in an air accident on 3 June, 1936, the

279

The He 177 V7 (c/n 00 007) prior to delivery to IV.(Erg)/KG 40 at Bordeaux on 2 August, 1942. (*R. C. Seeley*)

design was abandoned. Only one subsequent attempt was made by the Luftwaffe to produce a strategic bomber: the He 177.

Even had this aircraft proved an unqualified success, there is reason to believe that the Luftwaffe could never have mounted a large strategic air offensive. The reasons are threefold. First, it is doubtful whether Germany could have produced sufficient crews to replace those lost to the RAF and ground defences of the British Isles, defences which were often superior to those of Germany. Second there was the problem of provision of effective radio aids which were not subject to Allied jamming; although Germany pioneered the use of such bombing aids, these were quickly jammed by British technicians, and the Luftwaffe soon fell behind the Allies in this field.

Finally, and possibly most serious of all for Germany, there was the problem of fuel supplies. Even though she had pioneered the development of synthetic fuels, from the middle of 1942 Germany was faced with a steadily worsening fuel situation. Assuming that each bomber would have needed an average of six tons of fuel for an operation, a mission by 500 aircraft would have called for 3,000 tons of fuel. Allowing for six missions per month, and adding one third on top for training, the average monthly fuel consumption for the force would have totalled some 24,000 tons, or roughly one sixth of Germany's monthly fuel production in 1943. And this before the decision by the Allies for a major offensive against Germany's oil production centres.

Early in 1938, the RLM's technical department issued a requirement for a heavy bomber design capable of carrying a 2,000 kg (4,410 lb) bomb load over a radius of 1,600 km (1,000 miles) at a speed of 500 km/h (310 mph). The specification was issued to only one company, Ernst Heinkel AG, which submitted its He P.1041 project during the late spring of 1938. The project, which received the RLM designation He 177, was designed by Siegfried Günter, and proposed many radical features to attain the performance called for by the specification.

Günter would have preferred to have used two 2,000 hp engines to power the bomber, but no such engine was available at the time. In fact the German aviation industry never managed to produce in quantity an engine of this power before the end of the war. One of the major reasons for this was lack of sufficiently high-octane fuel, and here again the question of fuel comes into the story of the He 177. Realizing that no engine of 2,000 hp would be available to power his design, Günter resorted to the idea of coupling two 1,000 hp Daimler-Benz DB 601 units together. The resultant engine, the DB 606, produced 2,600 hp for take-off but was never particularly reliable.

The He 177 was an attractive mid-wing monoplane with a semi-circular-section fuselage and square tail surfaces. The high aspect ratio wing was built in three sections, the centre portion having parallel chord. The coupled engines were mounted in the outboard parts of the centre section, the huge twin mainwheel units being hinged in the cowlings to retract, one inwards and one outwards, into the wing. Large Fowler-type flaps occupied the complete trailing edge of the wing, the outboard portions forming the lower part of the ailerons. The aircraft was built of metal throughout with conventional stressed duralumin skin.

A revolutionary feature was the system of evaporation cooling, similar to that used on the He 100 and He 119, which dispensed with the need for radiators and thus helped to decrease drag. Although the feature had worked well in previous Heinkel aircraft, Günter was finally forced to admit, in the spring of 1939, that it was not suitable for large operational aircraft. The decision resulted in the provision of external radiators which increased drag and shortened the aircraft's range. To compensate for this, more fuel had to be carried which, in turn, meant that the aircraft had to be structurally strengthened. A further twist was given to the spiral when the RLM specified that the aircraft be capable of releasing its bombs in a dive, a somewhat ludicrous requirement for such a large machine.

On 19 November, 1939, Dipl Ing Francke, head of Rechlin's Erprobungsstelle E-2 flight-test section, took the He 177 V1 (c/n 00 001) on its initial test flight from Rostock-Marienehe airfield. The flight lasted only 12 minutes because the engines began to overheat. Francke was generally complimentary about the aircraft, but complained of some tail flutter, vibration of the airscrew shafts and inadequate tail surfaces.

The He 177 V1 was followed by the generally similar V2, (c/n 00 002), neither prototype being fitted with armament. Francke also took the V2 on its maiden flight, the machine then being handed over to another Rechlin pilot, Rickert. He carried out the first diving trials with the machine, and it was during these that severe flutter developed and the machine disintegrated. The loss of the aircraft led to the modification of the V1, the area of tail surfaces being increased by some 20 per cent. The V3, V4, and V5 which were nearing completion at Rostock were all similarly modified.

The He 177 V3, D-AGIG, was flown to Rechlin for engine trials, but the V4 was retained by Heinkel for diving tests. It was during one of these that the machine failed to recover and crashed into the Baltic, killing its pilot, Flugkapitän Ursinus. The He 177 V5 was the first of the type to carry armament, triple bomb bays being installed and a hand-operated MG 15 machine-gun in the nose, dorsal, ventral and tail positions. Early in 1941 the engines of the V5 caught fire, and the machine hit the ground and exploded.

The He 177 V6 and V7 both had modified nose sections, the latter carrying an armament of two MG FF cannon and an MG 131 machine-gun. Both machines were delivered to IV.(Erg)/KG 40 on 2 August, 1941, for operational trials, but they proved extremely unpopular with all who flew them. The He 177 V8 (c/n 00 008) was the last machine to be built as a prototype, the 16 additional machines (V9 to V24) being conversions of pre-production and production aircraft.

Thirty-five He 177A-0s were built at the Heinkel and Arado factories. The photograph shows the third aircraft (c/n 00 021) taxi-ing to its take-off point.

Fifteen He 177A-0 aircraft were laid down at Rostock, the first, the He 177A-01 (c/n 00 016), being flown in November 1941. Simultaneously the Heinkel plant at Oranienburg produced fifteen He 177A-0s (c/ns 32 001 to 015) and the Arado factory at Warnemünde a further five (c/n 05 001 to 005). The thirty-five He 177A-0s built were employed for a wide variety of trials, much emphasis being placed on engine development. The A-02 blew up in May 1942, and the A-05, A-06, and A-07 were redesignated V9, V10, and V11.

Between March 1942 and June 1943, about 130 production He 177A-1s were completed, some of the first being delivered to I./KG 40 at Bordeaux-Mérignac in July 1942 for operational trials. It was during one of these, on 28 August, that one of them dropped a single 250 kg (550 lb) bomb on the Broad Wier district of Bristol, killing 45 people and injuring a further 66— the worst single bomb incident suffered by the city during the war.

The tail of the He 177A-0 pre-production aircraft.

Four sub-variants of the He 177A-1 were produced, designated A-1/R1 to R4, but these differed only in armament. The He 177 V11 was fitted with a pair of DB 610 engines and served as a test bed for the Junkers Ju 288 programme at Dessau. The V15 and V16 were prototypes for the He 177A-3 production aircraft. They were powered by two DB 610 engines, these being moved 20 cm (8 in) further forward in an attempt to ease the problems associated with the extremely cramped engine installation of the

The He 177A-04 (c/n 00 022) which was completed during the spring of 1942.

An He 177A-3/R1 of 1./KG 40 which arrived at Châteaudun late in 1943 for operations over the British Isles. (*R. C. Seeley*)

early machines. The first production variant, the He 177 A-3/R1, retained the DB 606 engines but was given an additional fuselage bay. The A-3/R2 had an improved armament installation and electrical equipment, and the A-3/R3 could carry three Henschel Hs 293 missiles. The He 177A-3/R4 had a gondola to house the FuG 203 control unit for the Hs 293. The He 177A-3/R5 had a 75 mm cannon in a ventral gondola and was powered by DB 610 engines, and the A-3/R7 could carry two L5 or LT 50 torpedoes. Only three A-3/R7s were completed, these being tested by KG 26.

The first He 177A-3s were delivered to the training unit I./KG 50 at Brandenburg-Briest. The unit, which was undergoing winter trials at Zaporozh'ye, was hurriedly transferred to the Stalingrad front to operate supply missions for the beleaguered VI. Army. Redesignated FKGr 2, it undertook its first operation in January 1943, and during twelve subsequent operations seven He 177s were lost due to engine fires.

The He 177A-4 was a high-altitude project developed into the He 274, the A-5 being the next major He 177 production variant. This differed in having shorter undercarriage legs, a strengthened wing to allow it to carry heavier external loads, and the Fowler flaps removed. The He 177A-5/R1 to R4 differed only in armament installations, the A-5/R5 being fitted with a remote-controlled ventral barbette aft of the bomb bay. The A-5/R6 was similar, but the two forward bomb bays were deleted, and the R7 had a pressurized cabin. The final variant, the A-5/R8, was fitted with two remote-controlled barbettes in the chin and tail positions.

Following trials with the He 177A-012, five He 177A-5s were converted in 1944 for use as interceptor fighters. The bomb bays were replaced by 33 rocket tubes mounted so as to fire forwards and upwards at an angle of 60 deg. The aircraft were delivered to the Kampfstaffel of EKdo 25, under Lt Frodl, based at Tarnewitz, in June 1944. The Staffel moved to Parchim in July and was redesignated VJGr 10, but no operational use of the He 177 Zerstörer (destroyer) is recorded.

The first determined operational use of the He 177A-5 came on 21 November, 1943, when II./KG 40 (which had been formed from I./KG 50) attacked a convoy with Hs 293 missiles. The unit was commanded by

284

Maj Mons, and its operations are described more fully in the missile section of this book.

Early in 1943, I./KG 40 began converting from the Focke-Wulf Fw 200 to the He 177 at Fassberg, but it was not until 19 December that the Gruppe's first Staffel arrived at Châteaudun for operations against the British Isles. On 1 October, 1943, I./KG 4, which had also been trained on the He 177, was redesignated I./KG 100, its third Staffel preceding 1./KG 40 to Châteaudun by one day. The two Staffeln operated as a single unit, being placed under the control of Gen Maj Peltz's Angriffsführer England (Attack-leader England).

The first attack was made by 447 bombers, only a small proportion of which were He 177s, on 21 January, 1944, but the RAF was ready and the raiders suffered heavily. The first He 177 to be shot down over the British Isles was lost on that day when Flg Off Kemp flying a Mosquito destroyed it near Haslemere in Surrey. Operation Steinbock, as the offensive was code-named, continued until May 1944, the focus of the attack shifting from London to the southern ports in April.

Typical of the operations was an attack made by 125 bombers on the City of London on 18 April, 1944. The raiders included five He 177A-5s from I./KG 100 under Hptm von Kalkreuth, based at Rheine near Münster. After taking-off, the crews climbed as high as possible while still over German-held territory. The actual penetration of the defences was made in a shallow dive at high speed, tactics which made it difficult for even the superlative Mosquito to combat. After making their attack, the He 177s returned at low level.

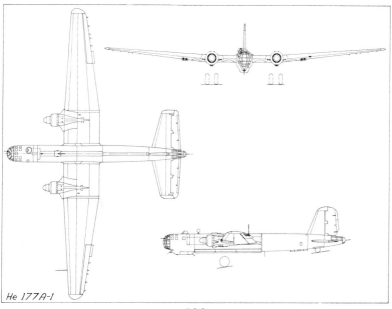

He 177A-1

285

In January 1944, II./KG 40 was temporarily transferred to the command of Luftflotte 2 to combat the Allied landings at Anzio. Several missions were undertaken with the He 177/Hs 293 combination, but they proved abortive, and serviceable strength sank from 18 to six aircraft. In February, the unit returned to Luftflotte 3 control and during the same month 3./KG 40 was transferred to Trondheim-Vaernes in Norway.

On 6 June, 1944, the Allies landed in France. Anti-shipping forces from IX. Fliegerkorps attacked, but were largely ineffective against the impenetrable barrier provided by the Allied fighter escort. During the first ten days of the invasion, only five vessels were lost to Luftwaffe air action. During the next six weeks the Luftwaffe resorted to mining operations, but, although these caused great inconvenience, they did not severely hamper the movement of Allied shipping. By mid-July 1944, all Luftwaffe anti-shipping units had been withdrawn to Norway and Germany. Only one He 177 unit was retained in France, Wekusta 2, a meteorological unit based at Mont de Marsan.

Although the He 177A-5 was the last variant in service, several other variants were projected. The He 177A-6 was based on the A-5 but had heavily-armoured fuel tanks, more protection for the crew, and increased defensive armament. Only six He 177A-6/R 1s were completed, and these by the use of a large number of standard A-5/R6 components. The He 177 V22 was the prototype for the proposed He 177A-6/R2 which differed in having an entirely new forward fuselage with a defensive armament of two MG 151/20 cannon, three MG 131 machine-guns and a dorsal turret with four MG 81 weapons. The He 177A-6 was abandoned in favour of the He 277.

The final projected variant was the He 177A-7, a specialized high-altitude bomber, to be powered by two Daimler-Benz DB 613 engines which comprised two DB 603G units coupled together to provide 3,600 hp for take-off, and was fitted with an extended wing spanning 36 m (118 ft $1\frac{1}{2}$ in); only six were completed and these were converted from standard A-5 airframes, retaining the DB 610 engines.

Perhaps the most interesting He 177, however, was the He 177 V38

The He 177 V38 which was modified at the Letov factory near Prague. (*J. Zazvonil*)

Close-up of the enlarged bomb bay of the He 177 V38 designed to carry the German atom bomb. (*J. Zazvonil*)

which was flown to the Letov factory near Prague in 1942. Its wings were removed and modifications made to its bomb bay to enable it to carry the German atomic bomb, when and if that terrifying weapon was ever completed. As one German engineer remarked, 'if we succeed in this, we shall rule the world'. In August 1944 work stopped on the He 177 V38 and other aircraft to be similarly modified, all being badly damaged in an American air raid on 25 March, 1945.

The Japanese Navy, which never possessed an efficient heavy bomber, showed considerable interest in the He 177 and especially the A-7 variant, and this resulted in the Japanese Hitachi company proposing to build the machine under licence. To this end, Heinkel sent sample tools to Japan by U-boat and readied the third He 177A-7 (completed in May 1944) to make a nonstop flight from Germany to Japan. Much of the aircraft's armour protection was replaced by additional fuel tanks and the flight was planned to cross Soviet territory at extreme altitude. The Japanese were not at all happy about the crossing of Russia, and eventually the plan was abandoned and the aircraft remained in Germany.

The end of He 177 operations in the West was by no means the end of the He 177 in Luftwaffe service. During the late spring of 1944, Kampfgeschwader 1 under Obstlt Horst von Riesen began converting to the aircraft, the first Gruppe moving to its operational airfields in East Prussia in May. Before the end of the month, I./KG 1 was joined by II and III. Gruppe, and the Geschwader now comprised some ninety He 177As, undoubtedly the most powerful striking force on the Eastern Front.

Operations began almost at once, the bombers striking at troop concentrations and Soviet supply centres in support of the German army. No attempt was made to strike at strategic targets although many were within

287

An He 177 fitted with a mockup of a special tail turret housing two 20 mm MG 151/20 cannon. (*H. Thiele*)

range. The bombers attacked in daylight at about 6,000 m (20,000 ft) and losses were very low. The few Soviet fighters that managed to reach the bombers' attacking altitude rarely pressed home their attacks because of the formidable defensive armament of the He 177. Also, very few He 177s were lost because of engine fires; constant modifications had ensured that troubles suffered by the coupled engine installation were reduced to a minimum. The machines that did crash due to this cause were mainly those flown by inexperienced pilots who mishandled the throttles, causing the engines to overheat.

At one time, KG 1 made several pattern bombing attacks, the only time such tactics were employed by the Luftwaffe. During one such operation, von Riesen led 87 bombers in a mass attack on the railway centre of Velikye Luki. Flying in three waves, each comprising a Gruppe of some 30 aircraft, the He 177s must have been a most impressive sight.

On 23 June, 1944, Soviet forces launched their major offensive on the Central Front and the German lines collapsed. Desperate attempts were made by the Luftwaffe to stem the tide, the final ignominy for the German long-range bomber coming when Göring ordered von Riesen's unit to attack the Soviet tanks. For such a huge aircraft to attack a very small, moving target such as a tank was similar to using the proverbial sledgehammer to crack a nut. In an attempt to make the best of a bad job, von Riesen sent out his aircraft in pairs at low level, but nearly a quarter of the bombers assigned to the operation failed to return and the tactics were never repeated.

One of the last operations undertaken by KG 1 was on 20 July, 1944. The first of 80 or so He 177s took-off and orbited the Masury lakes where it was gradually joined by the rest of the Geschwader. Two aircraft suffered engine fires and were ordered to jettison their bombs, following which the unit set off to bomb its target. When von Riesen returned he was told that he would be court martialled for allowing bombs to be dropped on Hitler's nearby headquarters at Rastenburg! After some very anxious hours, von Riesen was informed that the explosion at Rastenburg was in fact a deliberate attempt on Hitler's life—the famous July bomb plot—and he was cleared of any charges.

Shortly after this, operations by KG 1 ceased, mainly because of lack of fuel. For an 80-aircraft attack, KG 1 needed 480 tons of fuel, which equalled a day's output from the entire German oil industry in August 1944. Therefore, the He 177s were flown back to Germany and the unit disbanded, its personnel being incorporated into newly-established fighter units. A few He 177s were operated by II./KG 100 in January 1945, but by then it was far too late to make any effective use of an aircraft which must be regarded as having had one of the saddest careers in German aviation history.

*Wartime operational units:* JGr 10, I., II. and III./KG 1, I./KG 4, I. and II./KG 40, I., II., III. and 13./KG 100, Versuchskommando/KG 200, Lehr- und Erprobungskommando 36.

He 177A-5/R2: Span 31·44 m (103 ft $1\frac{3}{4}$ in); length 19·4 m (66 ft $11\frac{1}{4}$ in); height 6·4 m (20 ft $11\frac{3}{4}$ in); wing area 102 sq m (1,097·9 sq ft).

Empty weight 16,900 kg (37,038 lb); normal loaded weight 27,200 kg (59,866 lb); maximum loaded weight 31,000 kg (68,343 lb).

Maximum speed at 6,000 m (19,686 ft) 488 km/h (303 mph), at sea level 400 km/h (249 mph); cruising speed at 6,000 m (19,686 ft) 415 km/h (258 mph); initial rate of climb 190 m/min (623 ft/min); service ceiling 8,000 m (26,248 ft); range with two Hs 293 missiles 5,500 km (3,417 miles), with two FX 1400 missiles 5,000 km (3,107 miles).

The world's first aircraft to fly purely on turbojet power, the Heinkel He 178. Its first true flight was on 27 August, 1939.

# Heinkel He 178

The events which led to the world's first flight by an aircraft powered solely by a turbojet began when Ernst Heinkel employed Dr Hans Joachim Pabst von Ohain and his assistant Max Hahn in March 1936. Von Ohain had been conducting pioneering experiments on jet propulsion at Göttingen University and continued to do so in a secret shed at Heinkel's Marienehe airfield. By September 1937, the first demonstration turbojet, the HeS 1, was bench-running (albeit somewhat uncontrollably and only on hydrogen) to give a thrust of about 250 kg (550 lb) and it resembled in principle Frank Whittle's early patents although it was in no way influenced by them. It is unlikely that an HeS 2 design was built, but, by March 1938, the HeW 3 design was bench-running at a thrust of about 500 kg (1,100 lb) and had made the further advances of being controllable and of running on petrol. The HeS 3 engine used an axial-flow impeller and a centrifugal compressor. Some of the air from this compressor passed forward into a reverse-flow annular combustion chamber while some went rearwards to mix with the combustion gases before entering the turbine. The radial inflow turbine was of similar configuration to the compressor and the whole engine had a somewhat large diameter for its size, due to the compressor and combustion chamber arrangement. Maximum rotor speed was 13,000 rpm and the weight was 360 kg (795 lb).

Flight tests began with this engine suspended beneath a Heinkel He 118, and, at the same time, the design began of the He 178 to be powered by the HeS 3 for more extensive experiments. The HeS 3 made many flights beneath the He 118 until the turbine burned out but, by that time, much had been learned and an improved engine (though of similar performance) was ready. The decision was made to install the new engine, the HeS 3b, in the He 178 airframe which was nearing completion in the same secret hangar as the He 176.

The He 178 was a shoulder-wing monoplane with the pilot's cockpit well forward of the wing leading edge. The wings were largely of wooden construction, had moderate dihedral, an equi-taper planform, and large inboard trailing-edge flaps. The HeS 3b engine was installed in the duralumin monocoque fuselage with its forward end roughly on a level with the wing trailing edge, and air was drawn from a nose intake through a duct which curved beneath the pilot's seat and then up to the engine; the tailpipe was of considerable length, being about one third of the aircraft's total length. The single petrol tank was immediately behind the cockpit, and the tailwheel-type undercarriage retracted into the fuselage.

The date when taxi-ing trials with the He 178 began is uncertain, but, with Flugkapitän Erich Warsitz at the controls, the aircraft made a short hop along the runway on 24 August, 1939. The first true flight followed three days later when Warsitz circled Marienehe airfield, but this flight was marred because the undercarriage could not be induced to retract and the engine cut out soon after take-off when a bird was sucked into the intake. However, a safe power-off landing was made and the flight occurred exactly one year before the first flight of the Italian Caproni-Campini C.C.2, which used a much cruder ducted-fan jet system but was, nevertheless, the world's second jet aircraft to fly. Not until more than 20 months after the He 178 flight, did the first serious competitor appear when, on 15 May, 1941, the Gloster E.28/39 first flew with a turbojet born out of Whittle's work.

Up until the completion of the He 178's first flight, this jet project had been kept strictly as a private venture, but from that time every effort was made to interest the RLM. It was not, however, until 1 November, 1939, that Udet, Milch, Lucht and others were induced to witness a flight of the He 178 at Marienehe. One reason for this long delay in making only the

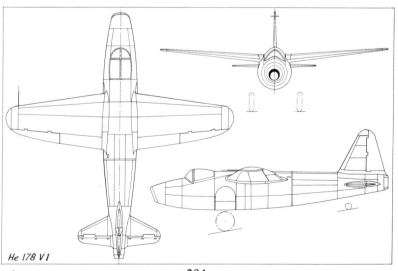

He 178 V1

second flight was that once war had started the order had been given to concentrate on normal aircraft production and experimental work was slowed down. Nevertheless, time had been found to make modifications to the HeS 3b engine which resulted in the HeS 6, giving a thrust of 590 kg (1,300 lb) at 13,300 rpm but with a weight of 420 kg (925 lb). This was the engine used on the second flight, but the performance was rather poor because of the lower power-to-weight and power-to-diameter ratios of the engine and defects in the airframe, the most noteworthy of which was the directional instability above a certain speed and the fact that the under-carriage still refused to retract. The He 178 only flew at about 600 km/h (373 mph) maximum but Dr von Ohain believed that his HeS 6 engine could have pushed it up to about 700 km/h (534 mph) if the airframe defects alone had been remedied.

Although the demonstration in November had received a cool reception, the period of official disinterest in Heinkel's turbojet development was coming to an end by the late autumn of 1939. Up until that time, the turbojet programme instituted by the technical department of the RLM saw no place for engine development in an airframe company. This policy was largely that of Hans A. Mauch (who headed the jet engine development section of the Technisches Amt) but, when he left the RLM at the end of 1939, Helmut Schelp moved into a more influential position and he approved the backing of Heinkel's turbojet programme.

By this time, the work at Heinkel was expanding to explore various types of turbojet engine, but no attempt was made to continue development of the He 178 because the problems encountered with a fuselage-mounted engine were considered too great at that stage. Instead, attention turned to the development of a fighter with wing-mounted turbojet engines, the He 280. The He 178 was finally despatched to the Berlin Air Museum where it was destroyed, along with the He 176, in a 1943 bombing raid.

He 178: Span 7·2 m (23 ft 3½ in); length 7·48 m (24 ft 6½ in); height 2·1 m (6 ft 10⅝ in); wing area 9·1 sq m (97·9 sq ft).

Empty weight 1,620 kg (3,565 lb); loaded weight 1,998 kg (4,396 lb).

Cruising speed at sea level 580 km/h (360 mph); estimated maximum speed at sea level 700 km/h (435 mph); landing speed 165 km/h (103 mph).

# Heinkel He 280

When, on 2 April, 1941, the Heinkel He 280 made its first powered flight, it was the first flight ever to be made by a turbojet-powered aircraft which had been designed as a potential fighter. As already related, the end of the He 178 programme saw attention turning towards the design of the He 280 and the expansion of Heinkel turbojet development. The He 280 was designed as an all-metal mid-wing monoplane powered by two turbojets attached to the undersides of the wing. The wing had a straight leading edge, a curved trailing edge and slight dihedral outboard of the engines, while the tail unit consisted of a high-mounted tailplane carrying a fin and rudder at each tip. Controls comprised ailerons, landing flaps, twin rudders and a one-piece elevator. A slender fuselage, which carried the fuel and nose-mounted armament, had a stepped cockpit with rearwards-sliding canopy. For the tricycle undercarriage, the main members were attached to the wing just inboard of the engines and retracted inwards (partly into the wing and partly into the fuselage) while the nose member retracted rearwards into the fuselage.

The Heinkel He 280 V1 taking-off on the first flight by a turbojet-powered aircraft designed as a potential fighter. The two HeS 8 turbojets were left uncovered and the undercarriage was not retracted on the first flight.

The expansion of the Heinkel turbojet development programme began when Max A. Mueller arrived at Rostock-Marienehe and brought with him a design for an axial-flow engine he had been working on at Junkers' Magdeburg factory. This engine was to be known as the HeS 30 or 109-006 and, while its development was proceeding, the original group at Rostock under Dr Hans Joachim Pabst von Ohain worked on a new centrifugal-flow engine based on the HeS 3/6 series which was designated HeS 8, or 109-001. Both these new engines were scheduled for testing with the He 280 aircraft, the HeS 30 being designed initially for a static thrust of 800 kg (1,760 lb) and the HeS 8 for a static thrust of 700 kg (1,540 lb). Also proceeding, but at a lower priority, was work towards other forms of jet such as the ducted fan engines which Mueller had also brought with him; these were the HeS 50 and HeS 60 designed to use 1,000 bhp and 2,000 bhp reciprocating engines respectively.

These events were taking place at the end of 1939 when the jet development programme of the RLM was finalized and, despite the scepticism of Wolfram Eisenlohr (in charge of powerplant development) concerning the new power form, certain firms were officially engaged on turbojet development. Junkers were working on the conservative 109-004 which was speedily to attain production status, while BMW (Bramo) were doing longer-term work on the 109-003 engine scheduled as a more advanced replacement. There was also work proceeding very slowly at Daimler-Benz on the 109-007, an advanced engine with a counter-rotating axial compressor. It should be noted that, with the exception of von Ohain's engines, all the designs mentioned employed axial type compressors. In the HeS 8 design, von Ohain had succeeded, despite the centrifugal compressor, in obtaining an overall diameter only fractionally greater than that of the Junkers 109-004 and at less than half the weight, and the design looked very promising on paper, as also did that for Mueller's axial HeS 30.

By September 1940, however, none of the new Heinkel turbojets were ready for use although the airframe of the first He 280 prototype, the V1, was completed and work had begun on four other prototypes. Unpowered flight tests with the He 280 V1 were therefore begun in which the aircraft was towed to altitude by a Heinkel He 111B and cast off for gliding flight, the first of these being made on 22 September, 1940. In these tests, little fault could be found with the handling of the He 280 V1 despite the fact that the design was intended to be as generally advanced as considered prudent, one radical feature which was not immediately obvious being the compressed-air ejection seat. By March 1941, the He 280 V1 had made some 40 gliding flights, and the work of fitting two HeS 8 engines beneath the wings began, although the development of this engine had been lagging and it was only producing about 500 kg (1,102 lb) static thrust. Nevertheless, the He 280 V1 took-off on its first powered flight on 2 April, 1941, with the works' test pilot Fritz Schäfer at the controls. On this flight no engine cowlings were fitted (because the engines tended to leak fuel) and the undercarriage was not retracted, but the aircraft made a circuit of Marienehe airfield at a height of about 300 m (985 ft) and landed.

A demonstration before Luftwaffe and RLM officials was then arranged and, on 5 April, 1941, the He 280 V1, with engine cowlings fitted, was flown at Marienehe before Udet, Lucht, Eisenlohr, Reitenbach and Schelp. This flight did much to secure official backing for Heinkel's jet development programme, since it convinced Eisenlohr of the soundness of the new developments with the result that he was to do all he could to facilitate jet development in the future. At the same time Schelp, of the RLM's technical department, became more enthusiastic about Heinkel's work and he proposed that they should begin work on a new second-generation turbojet of 1,300 kg (2,866 lb) static thrust, the 109-011, which was intended to supersede the first-generation 109-003 and 109-004. Official arrangements were made on 9 April, 1941, for Ernst Heinkel AG to control Hirth Motoren GmbH (a firm experienced in the production of aircraft reciprocating engines, auxiliaries and turbo-superchargers) at Stuttgart-Zuffenhausen and Berlin. This move was essentially made to ease the problem of the acute shortage of specialized skilled labour.

Mueller's work, in particular the HeS 30, was moved to Stuttgart, leaving the entire facilities at Rostock at von Ohain's disposal to continue development of the HeS 8 and begin design of the 109-011 (HeS 11). However, development of the HeS 8 did not go at all well and was, by the end of 1941, overtaken by the Junkers Jumo 109-004. The chief problems with the HeS 8 arose as a result of striving for small diameter, and it was not until early in 1943 that the He 280 V2 (GJ-CA) and He 280 V3 (GJ-CB) were flown with HeS 8 engines, but each engine was still delivering little more than 600 kg (1,323 lb) static thrust and the He 280 itself was showing signs of tail flutter. Already, however, von Ohain had completed the layout of the 109-011 and development had begun, and, because Mueller's HeS 30 was also showing much greater promise, the HeS 8 development was abandoned. The engine was still used, however, in the development programme of the 109-011, and the He 280 V3 flew HeS 8 engines for this purpose, crash-landing on one occasion because of turbine failure.

The He 280 V3 (GJ-CB), which first flew in July 1941, is seen here after skidding. A more serious crash-landing was made on another occasion.

By this time Mueller had left Heinkel and his ducted fan engines were simultaneously abandoned, but the HeS 30 had made remarkable progress and was delivering 900 kg (1,985 lb) static thrust so that it was proposed continuing with this engine alongside development of the 109-011, also moved to Stuttgart in the autumn of 1942. However, in what must be considered a major blunder of the war, Schelp decreed that work on the 109-006 engine should be discontinued in order to concentrate on the 109-011. Thus, the He 280 was left without the prospect of a Heinkel engine and the company had to consider other engines.

The first move in this direction came in April 1943, when the He 280 V2 was re-engined with Junkers Jumo 109-004s, but this aircraft was destroyed soon after when the undercarriage failed during landing. The He 280 V4 was built from the start to use two BMW 109-003 engines and flew, thus equipped, on 15 August, 1943. This flight was preceded by the flight of the He 280 V5 which initially had HeS 8 engines but was converted two months later to 109-003 engines. The He 280 V6 (NU-EA), which flew in the same month as the V5, had 109-003 engines from the outset.

During this period, although the He 280 was being used to study many problems, it was in direct competition with Messerschmitt's Me 262 jet fighter for an official production order. The He 280 V5 and V6 had been used in armament trials (with such installations as three MG 151 20 mm cannon in the nose) and mock combat between the He 280 and Fw 190 had indicated the superiority of the former over the best German fighter in service at that time. Furthermore, the He 280, when using the same power as the Me 262, had superior maximum speed, rate of climb and service ceiling, but its development as a fighter was abandoned in 1943 in favour of the Me 262 chiefly for technical reasons. Some of these reasons may have been politically contrived, but the most reasonable criticisms of the He 280 were that it had only about two-thirds of the range of the larger Me 262, was under-gunned, and had shown some weakness in its tail, all these shortcomings apparently having been carried into the projected He 280A fighter design. Over-optimistic estimates of the fuel consumption of Heinkel turbojets had led to fuel tanks of inadequate capacity being designed into the He 280. The He 280B-1 was then proposed which was to have a fuselage lengthened by 0·8 m (2 ft 7 in) to accommodate more fuel, an increased nose armament of six MG 151/20 cannon, a bomb rack beneath the fuselage and an improved tail unit. With the loaded weight thus increased, the He 280B-1 was to have more wing area but a reduction in certain performance aspects was inevitable and no production order was forthcoming.

With the prospect of military service gone, the He 280 was not abandoned but was continued for use in various research and test programmes, for which, aerodynamically and structurally, it was suitable in many ways. The He 280 V1, for example, had its turbojets replaced by four Argus 109-014 pulse-jets for trials at Erprobungsstelle Rechlin. The pulse-jets, of course, did not develop sufficient static thrust for an unassisted take-off and the He 280 V1 had to be towed behind two Messerschmitt Bf 110s. Its flight, with Argus pilot Schenk at the controls, was short-lived because icing-up of the aircraft forced the pilot to use the ejector seat, the first use of this equipment making aviation history. Similar trials were again made at Rechlin in August 1943, when the He 280 V4 was powered by six Argus 109-014s, somewhat more successfully.

After the He 280 V7 (NU-EB) had flown in April 1943 on the power of two Junkers 109-004 engines, it was transferred to the DFS at Ainring with its engines removed for an extensive aerodynamic research programme in the hands of the test pilot Dipl Ing Wilhelm Mohr. This pro-

After powered flights in April 1943, the He 280 V7 (NU-EB) had its engines removed and was used by the DFS in an extensive aerodynamic research programme.

gramme was a continuation of that started several years previously with the DFS 230 glider to determine ways of raising the Reynolds and Mach numbers of wings, and many other aerodynamic problems were also investigated. The He 280 V7 was equipped with instruments to record aircraft attitude and to film light threads attached to the wings, and a long pitot tube extended from above the nose. The actual flights (about 115 altogether) were made from Hörsching, near Linz, and the aircraft was towed to altitude by an He 111H-6. The maximum altitude reached was 7,000 m (22,960 ft), and during one dive the He 280 V7 attained 930 km/h (578 mph). This speed was probably the highest attained by any He 280 and no bad effects were encountered. Most flights, however, were made with the wing near the stall, and in 50 trials with the aircraft in a spin behaviour was never critical.

While these trials were proceeding, the He 280 V8 (NU-EC) was flown with two Junkers 109-004 engines on 30 June, 1943. Later, on 29

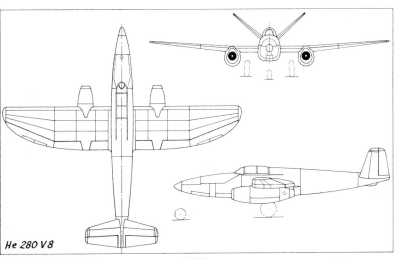

He 280 V8

September, 1944, this aircraft was flown with new V-type tail surfaces, in place of the previous twin fin and rudder assembly, the 109-004 engines being retained. These comparative trials yielded data which was used in the design of the He 162 tail assembly. The final aircraft in the He 280 series, the V9, was designed as a BMW turbojet test bed and flew on 31 August, 1943, with 109-003 engines.

Despite its pioneering work on jet aircraft and engines, success in the shape of production orders for jet aircraft was to elude the Heinkel concern until near the end of the war when the He 162 appeared. After the He 280, design work turned to projects such as the He 343 bomber, and the P.1078 and P.1079 fighters, which were all based on the use of the 109-011 turbojet. In many ways, therefore, much reliance was placed on this new engine to which the whole of the Heinkel-Hirth engine development had been turned. Although very promising, however, the difficulty of manufacturing the 109-011 (particularly in regard to the complex diagonal-flow compressor) resulted in no production engines being produced and, by the war's end, only bench-running and a few flights beneath a Junkers Ju 88 had been made. The following data relate to the He 280 V5, but performance was enhanced, of course, with more powerful engines such as the 109-003 or 109-004.

He 280 V5 with two HeS 8A (109-001A) engines rated at 750 kg (1,650 lb) static thrust each and with three MG 151 20 mm cannon: Span 12·2 m (40 ft); length 10·4 m (34 ft 1½ in); height 3·06 m (10 ft 0½ in); wing area 21·5 sq. m (231·5 sq ft).

Empty weight 3,215 kg (7,073 lb); fuel 810 kg (1,782 lb); pilot 100 kg (220 lb); ammunition 185 kg (407 lb); loaded weight 4,310 kg (9,482 lb).

Maximum speeds at 6,000 m (19,680 ft)—900 km/h (559 mph) burst for 30 seconds or 820 km/h (510 mph) maintained; landing speed 140 km/h (87 mph); initial rate of climb 1,145 m/min (3,755 ft/min); theoretical service ceiling 11,500 m (37,720 ft); maximum range at 6,000 m (19,680 ft) 650 km (404 miles).

# Heinkel He 219 Uhu (Owl)

On the night of 11/12 June, 1943, Maj Werner Streib of I./NJG 1 took-off from Venlo airfield in the Netherlands in a pre-production Heinkel He 219A-0. He soon succeeded in guiding his fighter among a stream of RAF Avro Lancaster bombers heading for Berlin and within 30 minutes had succeeded in destroying no less than five of them with bursts from the He 219's powerful armament of six cannon. The only sour note for Streib was sounded when the flaps of the He 219 refused to function on landing and the oil-bespattered fighter crashed and broke into three pieces, Streib and his observer escaping without injury.

Thus ended the first mission by what was certainly the best night fighter

Two prototypes of the Heinkel He 219 (the V4 and V6) were used to test the Heinkel-designed compressed-air ejector seat.

possessed by the Luftwaffe. Fast, manoeuvrable and with devastating fire-power, the He 219 was the only piston-engined night fighter capable of meeting the Mosquito on equal terms. But it, like the Messerschmitt Me 262, was never made available in sufficient numbers to have a significant effect on the course of the air war over Germany.

The He 219 Uhu was conceived in the summer of 1940 as a private venture by Ernst Heinkel AG. It was originally intended as a multi-purpose aircraft with such advanced features as remote-controlled arma-ment, a pressurized cabin and a steerable nosewheel, but little interest was shown in the design by the RLM. However, by late 1941, night raids by the RAF were beginning to reach serious proportions, and the RLM requested a redesign of the He 219 as a night fighter.

The Uhu was a shoulder-wing cantilever monoplane with underslung engines and a retractable nosewheel undercarriage. The tailplane had con-siderable dihedral and terminated in twin fins and rudders. The extensively glazed cockpit canopy was faired neatly into the nose of the aircraft, affording the crew of two (seated back to back) an exceptional view. The single-spar wing, rectangular-section fuselage, and tail surfaces were of metal construction with stressed-skin covering.

The majority of the drawings for the He 219 had been completed by March 1943 when an RAF raid on the Rostock works destroyed over three-quarters of the drawings. This resulted in transfer of the design office to Vienna-Schwechat where it was intended to set up the main He 219 assembly line. The He 219 V1 made its first flight on 15 November, 1942,

The He 219 V11 (c/n 310189) which was evaluated in Britain during 1945.

powered by two 1,700 hp Daimler-Benz DB 603A engines. In February 1943, the aircraft was fitted with four 30 mm MK 108 cannon in a ventral tray, but this demonstrated a tendency to part company with the fuselage when the cannon were fired, and subsequent prototypes were fitted with six MG 151/20 cannon.

On 8 January, 1943, the He 219 V2 was flown in competition with the Junkers Ju 188, but these trials proved somewhat inconclusive and were followed, on 25 March, by more extensive tests. The He 219 V2 piloted by Maj Streib was pitted against a Ju 188S, piloted by Oberst Viktor von Lossberg, and a Do 217. The Dornier retired early, but the other two machines continued an exhaustive series of trials. Eventually the He 219 Uhu emerged as clear victor and an order for 300 was placed by the RLM.

The He 219 V3 had a lengthened fuselage, the V4 was fitted with FuG 220 Lichtenstein SN-2 radar, and the V5 introduced a dorsal fairing which eliminated the rear fuselage 'step'. A number of He 219A-0 pre-production aircraft followed, many bearing alternative Versuchs numbers. Many different armament combinations were tested on these machines and resulted in a most complicated series of designations, an example of this being the He 219A-0/R1-U3 which was fitted with four MK 103 cannon and modified radar equipment.

In April 1943 the first of a small batch of He 219A-0s were delivered to I./NJG 1 based at Venlo. The first operational sortie by Maj Streib, which has already been recounted, was followed by 10 days of operations during which no less than 20 RAF bombers were shot down, including six Mosquitos.

The He 219A-1 reconnaissance bomber project was abandoned, the first production model being the He 219A-2/R1 night fighter. This version was powered by two 1,750 hp Daimler-Benz DB 603A engines and had two MG 151/20 cannon in the wing roots and two MK 108s in the ventral tray. It was also proposed that two MK 108 cannon should be installed behind the cockpit in a Schräge Musik obliquely upward-firing gun installation. This device was tested on the He 219 V19 in August 1943, but was not fitted to the A-2/R1 until much later.

The He 219A-3 was a three-seat high-speed bomber project, and the A-4 was a proposed high-altitude reconnaissance aircraft with long-span wooden wings and two 2,500 hp Jumo 222A/B engines, somewhat similar in concept to the Hütter Hü 211 project of which two prototypes were under construction when destroyed in December 1944.

The first variant to leave the assembly line in numbers was the He 219A-5 in which the rear of the cockpit was neatly faired into the fuselage and the MG 131 machine-gun removed. The He 219A-5/R1 had the same armament as the later A-2/R1s, the A-5/R2 was powered by two 1,800 hp Daimler-Benz DB 603E engines which had been tested previously in the V16 and V20, and the A-5/R3 had two DB 603Aa units of similar power. The He 219A-5/R4 was a three-seater powered by two DB 603E engines and having a single MG 131 gun for rearward defence.

The He 219A-053, prototype for the A-5/R1 which carried an armament of two 20 mm and two 30 mm cannon. (*H. Redemann*)

In December 1943, Milch suggested that the whole He 219 programme be discontinued in favour of the Ju 88G. Milch's main objection to the He 219 was that it would have disrupted production lines at a vital time and that in any case the performance of the Junkers aircraft was sufficient to take on such bombers as the Lancaster and Halifax. The major flaw in this argument was that the RAF began to use Mosquitos to escort their night bombers, and the Ju 88G proved incapable of combatting this superb British fighter.

Milch put forward three proposals: (1) that Heinkel should abandon the He 219 altogether in favour of the Junkers Ju 88G and Dornier Do 335; (2) that the production of the He 219 be reduced in favour of the Ju 88G; and (3) that the production of the He 219 should continue as planned. For a time the third proposition was chosen, but on 25 May, 1944, Milch

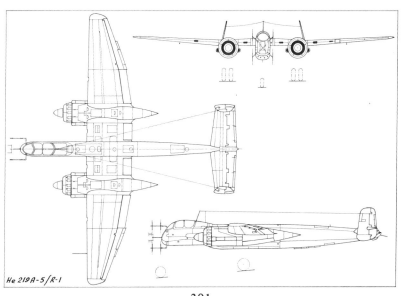

He 219A-5/R-1

301

finally got his way. He persuaded the RLM to abandon the He 219 in favour of two new night fighters, the Ju 388J and the Focke-Wulf Ta 154. The Ju 388J never in fact went into operational service, and the all-wood Ta 154, although an excellent design, regularly disintegrated because of faults in its adhesives. Although the He 219 was officially abandoned, Heinkel continued to produce the aircraft in small numbers, although both Allied bombing and official interference resulted in very few machines being delivered for operational service.

Universally popular with air and ground crews alike, the He 219 introduced several new features. It was the first German operational aircraft with a nosewheel undercarriage, a feature which was looked upon with complete distrust by the RLM; it was the world's first operational aircraft fitted with an ejector seat, a device which was subsequently to save the lives of several aircrew; the concentration of the aircraft's armament behind the pilot prevented him from being temporarily blinded when the weapons were fired; and it provided excellent maintenance accessibility.

The advent of the Mosquito fighter escort to RAF bombers resulted in the introduction of the He 219A-6 variant based on the A-2/R2. This was a specially stripped variant powered by two 1,980 hp Daimler-Benz DB 603L engines and with armament reduced to four MG 151/20 cannon, and it had a maximum speed of 650 km/h (404 mph) and an initial rate of climb of 550 m/min (1,805 ft/min).

The major production version of the Uhu was the He 219A-7 which was essentially similar to the A-5 apart from enlarged supercharger intakes. Three prototypes were produced, the He 219 V25, V26, and V27, the latter fitted with warning radar in the tail. The He 219A-7/R1 had an armament of no less than eight cannon, two MK 108s in the wing roots, two MK 103s and two MG 151/20s in the ventral tray and two MK 108s in a Schräge Musik installation aft of the cockpit.

The He 219A-7/R2 had MK 108 guns in place of the MK 103s, the A-7/R3 had the wing-mounted MK 108s replaced by MG 151/20s, and the A-7/R4's armament was reduced to four MG 151/20s. The He 219A-7/R5 had similar armament to the A-7/R3 but was intended for anti-Mosquito duties, being powered by two 1,900 hp Junkers Jumo 213E

An He 219A production aircraft with FuG 220 Lichtenstein SN-2 radar.

302

engines with MW-50 water-methanol injection. Fastest of all A-series aircraft was the He 219A-7/R6 which was experimentally fitted with two 2,500 hp Jumo 222A/B engines and achieved a maximum speed of 700 km/h (435 mph).

Up until May 1944 it was only possible to re-equip I./NJG 1 with the He 219, the unit gradually exchanging its Messerschmitt Bf 110Gs for the Uhu. After Streib was promoted to Geschwader-Kommodore of NJG 1 on 1 July, 1943, Hptm Hans-Dieter Frank took over command of the Gruppe. He was killed on 27 September when his aircraft collided with another night fighter and was succeeded by Hptm Manfred Meurer. Meurer, who claimed 65 victories, was killed on 21 January, 1944, near Magdeburg when his He 219 collided with a four-engined bomber.

The second unit to re-equip with the He 219 was the experimental anti-Mosquito Gruppe, NJGr 10, based at Werneuchen near Berlin. Shortly afterwards a number of Uhus were delivered to II./NJG 1 at Arnhem-Deelen under Hptm Eckhart-Wilhelm von Bonin, and late in June 1944 IV./NJG 1 at St Trond under Hptm Schnaufer was equipped with a few He 219s. Although a small number of He 219s were delivered to the units mentioned, it was only I./NJG 1 and NJGr 10 that retained the machine in any quantity. By October, I./NJG 1 under Hptm Werner Baake had moved to Handorf, the only other unit to re-equip with the He 219 before the collapse being III./NJG 5 under Hptm Piuk.

The He 219B-1 was a high-altitude version of the Uhu originally projected with 2,000 hp DB 614 engines but replaced by the two 2,500 hp Jumo 222A/B units. The He 219B-1 had a lengthened fuselage and increased span, but only one example was completed, powered by DB 603Aa engines, because of the problems associated with the Jumo 222 programme. The He 219B-2 was an anti-Mosquito variant similar to the A-6 powered by DB 603L engines, and the B-3 was a two-seater with an armament of four MG 151/20s and two MK 108s. Originally to be powered by DB 603L engines, the RLM ordered that Jumo 222 units should be substituted, and consequently the B-3 never flew.

The He 219C-1 had the wing and tail surfaces of the B-series but a new fuselage of improved aerodynamic shape. Both the He 219C-1 and C-2 were three-seaters to be powered by Jumo 222 engines, the former having four MK 108 and two MG 151/20 cannon, the latter two MK 103 weapons. Both machines were fitted with a Rheinmetall-Borsig pressurized tail turret carrying four MG 131 guns, the C-2 also having provision for three 500 kg (1,100 lb) SC 500 bombs beneath the fuselage.

The He 319 was a night fighter projected in parallel with the He 219, differing mainly in having a single fin and rudder. The design was abandoned in November 1942 in favour of the He 419. The He 419A-0 was basically an He 219A-5 fitted with a new enlarged wing and DB 603G engines. This machine was followed by six He 419B-1/R1s which had exhaust-driven turbo-superchargers and a wing area of no less than 59 sq m (635 sq ft). Standard armament was four MK 108 and two MG 151/20 cannon, the B-1/R2 being projected with four MG 212 weapons and the B-1/R3 with four MK 103s. One other interesting variant was the He 219 V14 which had a BMW 109-003 turbojet carried below the fuselage in connection with the He 162 programme. He 219 production was 268.

*Wartime operational units:* I./NJG 1, III./NJG 5, NJGr 10, Nachtjagdstaffel Norwegen (also used in small numbers by II. and IV./NJG 1).

He 219A-7/R1: Span 18·5 m (60 ft 8½ in); length 15·33 m (50 ft 11¼ in); height 4·1 m (13 ft 5½ in); wing area 44·5 sq m (478·994 sq ft).
Empty weight 11,200 kg (24,692 lb); loaded weight 15,300 kg (33,730 lb).
Maximum speed at 7,000 m (22,967 ft) 670 km/h (416 mph); cruising speed 540 km/h (355 mph); absolute ceiling 12,700 m (41,668 ft); normal range 1,545 km (960 miles); maximum range 2,000 km (1,243 miles).

# Heinkel He 274

Early in 1941 Heinkel proposed a high-altitude development of their Greif bomber, the He 177A-4. The machine was to be powered by two coupled Daimler-Benz DB 610 engines, and have a pressurized cabin and remote-controlled defensive armament. The design was gradually improved, a high aspect ratio wing and Hirth 2291 turbo-superchargers being added, the type eventually being redesignated He 274.

Because of Heinkel's preoccupation with the He 177, detailed design work for the He 274 was transferred to the Société Anonyme des Usines Farman at Suresnes near Paris. The He 274 was a mid-wing monoplane powered by four separate 1,750 hp Daimler-Benz DB 603A-2 engines in annular cowlings. The wing was of high aspect ratio and the twin main-

Only one Heinkel He 274 prototype was completed, this being built in France as the AAS 01A.

wheels retracted backwards into the engine cowlings. The fuselage was similar to that of the He 177A-3 apart from the pressure cabin, but during the early production stage was lengthened to 23·8 m (78 ft $1\frac{1}{4}$ in). A new tail assembly was developed for the design, with twin fins and rudders. All-metal stressed-skin construction was used throughout. In May 1943, an order was placed for two prototypes and four pre-production aircraft, the latter to be powered by four 1,900 hp DB 603G engines.

Construction of the He 274 V1 and V2 began during the late summer of 1943, but later in the year the four He 274A-0s were abandoned. The He 274 V1 was nearing completion in July 1944 when the Allied advance forced the Germans to withdraw from Paris. An attempt was made to destroy the airframe but with little success, and the He 274 V1 was eventually flown in December 1945, under the designation AAS 01A, from Orléans-Bricy. The AAS 01A was subsequently used to test-fly scale models of the French SO 4000 and NC 270, but was scrapped at Marseilles in 1953.

He 274 V1: Span 44·2 m (145 ft $0\frac{1}{4}$ in); length 23·8 m (78 ft $1\frac{1}{4}$ in); height 5·5 m (18 ft $0\frac{1}{2}$ in); wing area 170 sq m (1,829·86 sq ft).
Empty weight 21,300 kg (46,966 lb); loaded weight 36,000 kg (79,380 lb).
Maximum speed at sea level 430 km/h (267 mph), at 11,000 m (36,091 ft) 580 km/h (360 mph); cruising speed at sea level 400 km/h (248 mph); climb to 6,000 m (19,686 ft) 32·5 min, to 13,000 m (42,653 ft) 90 min; absolute ceiling 14,300 m (46,918 ft); normal range 2,850 km (1,770 miles).

# Heinkel He 277

In 1940, when much trouble was being experienced with the coupled-engine installation of the He 177, Heinkel proposed a new version powered by four separate Daimler-Benz DB 603 units. The machine failed to find favour with the RLM as it was held that too many delays would result in replacing the original He 177 on the production lines. Eventually, in the autumn of 1941, because of continued demands from Ernst Heinkel that production should be switched to the He 277, Göring formally forbade any further *mention* of the new bomber.

This did not prevent work continuing under the cover designation He 177B and finally, during a conference of aircraft manufacturers held at Obersalzberg on 23 May, 1943, Hitler demanded immediate production of a heavy bomber which could make round-the-clock attacks on London and destroy Allied shipping far out in the Atlantic. Heinkel at once suggested the He 177B and was awarded a development contract for the machine.

The He 277 V1 (or He 177B-0) was converted from an He 177A-3/R2 airframe and fitted with four separate DB 603A engines. The first flight

The only known photograph of the Heinkel He 277 V1, which differed from the He 177 in being powered by four separate engines.

was made at Vienna-Schwechat late in 1943, and the He 277 V2 (He 177B-5/R1), which followed on 28 February, 1944, was a conversion of the A-5/R1. Both machines suffered from some directional instability which was not effectively cured until the modified V3 appeared with twin fins and rudders similar to those used on the He 274. The first production model was the He 277B-5/R2 which was powered by four 1,750 hp DB 603A engines, but only eight machines were completed before all heavy-bomber development was cancelled in favour of the emergency fighter programme on 3 July, 1944.

Several other variants of the He 277 were projected. The He 277B-6/R1 had increased span, four 2,060 hp Junkers Jumo 213F engines, enlarged tail surfaces, the nose of the He 177A-6/R2, and an HL/131V tail turret containing four MG 131 machine-guns. The He 277B-6/R2 had a longer fuselage and a more streamlined nose, and the B-6/R3 had a deeper fuselage, more extensive glazing and manually-operated gun positions. The He 277B-7 was a long-range reconnaissance variant based on the He 177A-7 but was powered by four Jumo 213 or Jumo 222 engines.

He 277B-5/R2: Span 31·44 m (103 ft 1¾ in); length 22·15 m (72 ft 8 in); height 6·66 m (21 ft 10½ in); wing area 100 sq m (1,076 sq ft).

Empty weight 21,800 kg (48,069 lb); maximum loaded weight 44,490 kg (98,105 lb).

Maximum speed at 5,700 m (18,701 ft) 570 km/h (354 mph), and at sea level 486 km/h (302 mph); cruising speed at 5,400 m (17,717 ft) 460 km/h (286 mph); absolute ceiling 15,000 m (49,215 ft); maximum range 6,000 km (3,728 miles).

# Heinkel He 162

When, in the latter half of 1944, the Messerschmitt Me 262 turbojet fighter and the Me 163B rocket interceptor were put into Luftwaffe service, great hopes were justifiably held that they would effectively combat the crippling Allied air offensive against Germany. However, the Me 163B could not be effectively employed for a number of reasons while, for both aircraft, mass production required considerable amounts of scarce material and skilled labour and was never fully achieved.

During this period, the RLM underwent its final major reorganization, with staunch Nazis directly assuming further positions of influence. On 1 August, 1944, all departments connected with aircraft production were transferred to Albert Speer's Ministry for Armament and Ammunition (R.f.Ruk.), which had already absorbed the departments connected with supply (Nachschub-Amt). The technical department, with Karl Otto Saur as its chief, now came directly under the control of the Speer Ministry, and the RLM with its remaining departments (including the Chief of Technical Air Armament or Chef TLR) was subordinated to the new structure. There then arose, largely under Saur, the concept of the Volksjäger (People's Fighter) lightweight fighter which would use the minimum of strategic materials, be suitable for rapid mass-production and still have a performance superior to contemporary piston-engined fighters, and this concept was discussed at a conference of industrial leaders and Speer Ministry officials in the late summer of 1944. The outcome was a basic project requirement issued on 8 September to Arado, Blohm und Voss, Focke-Wulf, Junkers, Heinkel and Messerschmitt, out of which only the last mentioned declined to consider the project.

In addition to the qualities already mentioned, the new fighter had to weigh no more than 2,000 kg (4,410 lb), have a minimum endurance

A rare flying view of the Heinkel He 162 V1 Spatz (c/n 200 001). (*F. Selinger*)

307

of 30 minutes, take-off within 500 m (1,640 ft) and be armed with two 30 mm cannon. For power, a single BMW 109-003 turbojet of 800 kg (1,760 lb) static thrust was to be used. This engine was originally planned for the Me 262 (under which heading its early development is discussed) but was, by this time, reserved chiefly for the proposed Volksjäger. The great pressure behind the programme is indicated by the fact that material had to be submitted for consideration by 14 September and the aircraft itself had to be ready in less than four months, by 1 January, 1945.

Conferences were held on 15 and 19 September, 1944, to consider the various proposals, and the P.211 design submitted by Blohm und Voss was judged the best, with Heinkel's P.1073 design as possible second best. On 23 September, a mockup of the Heinkel proposal was inspected at the Vienna-Schwechat plant by Gen Lucht of the technical department, together with other officials, and Heinkel was awarded the contract on 30 September despite the general opinion that the Blohm und Voss design was superior. In the meantime, at a conference held on 23 September an enthusiastic Göring finalized the details of the whole programme at his Rastenburg headquarters. The tricky problems of supplying thousands of new pilots and maintaining thousands of the new aircraft were soon solved. Pilots were to come from the Hitler Youth, and those who could not fly (and many could) were to receive speedy training which would be completed by actually flying the jet fighters on operations. As for the maintenance of the aircraft, it was felt that this would hardly be necessary since damaged aircraft could easily be replaced by the vast numbers which would be produced. Such extravagant claims were typical of certain elements during that desperate period and were strongly opposed by more realistic men such as Adolf Galland.

By 29 October, 1944, detail drawings of the Heinkel design were ready after day and night work under the chief project designer Siegfried Günter and the chief designer Karl Schwärzler. Within the firm the design was known as the Spatz (Sparrow) and it received the official designation He 162 (which number had previously been used for Messerschmitt's Bf 162 Jaguar) although Ernst Heinkel had tried to obtain the designation He 500 for prestige purposes. Later, the unofficial name Salamander was given to the aircraft, after the creature which has the mythical ability of being able to live through fire.

The most noteworthy features of the He 162 were its low span/length ratio, the mounting of the turbojet above the fuselage, the nosewheel undercarriage retracting into the fuselage and the pronounced dihedral of the tailplane. The mounting of the engine outside the fuselage was in line with Heinkel policy to avoid problems with jet intake and tailpipe ducting, such a policy having begun with the He 280. The He 162 had a semi-monocoque fuselage of duralumin construction, but with the nosewheel doors and radio compartment of plywood. The cockpit had various standard fittings, a minimum of instruments and a simple cartridge-operated ejector seat. Cockpit visibility was allegedly good though the mounting of the engine must have caused a blind spot at the rear. The shoulder-mounted wings were of wooden construction throughout except for aluminium alloy tips, these being removable to allow internal servicing with the aid of special tools and a mirror since the wing skin was permanently bonded in position with no access panels. The complete wing was attached to the fuselage by four vertical bolts, and there were three other connections for the turbojet, the standard 109-003A-1 engine being modified for this type of mounting and redesignated 109-003E-1. The wing auxiliary spar

A line-up of He 162A Salamander jet fighters of JG 1 at Leck. This airfield was captured by the British in May 1945 before the new fighters became fully operational. (*F. Selinger*)

carried the ailerons and flaps, the latter being hydraulically operated as was the undercarriage during retraction, the hydraulic pump being driven from the engine. For longitudinal trimming, the incidence of the entire tailplane could be altered about a hinge at its forward end while, for directional trimming, the twin rudders could be offset. These trim changes could be effected in flight but the trim tabs on the ailerons could only be adjusted on the ground. The normal fuel capacity of 695 litres (153 Imp gal) was contained behind the cockpit in a fuselage tank and could be increased to a maximum of 765 litres (168 Imp gal) and further augmented by carrying another 180 litres (39·6 Imp gal) in the space between the main and auxiliary wing spars, the wood being suitably sealed. Throughout the design, every effort was made to simplify and use materials easily available. As an example, the airframe was planned for plain or bushed bearings throughout, although, in the event, ball bearings were used since sufficient supplies were available.

Indicative of the urgency of the He 162 programme is the fact that development, pre-production and mass-production were all proceeded with more or less simultaneously, such a step having no precedent. The Vienna-Schwechat plant of Heinkel was ordered to produce ten development prototypes (V1 to V10), which would also serve as He 162A-0 pre-production aircraft, and then begin mass-production, using the underground salt mine at nearby Hinterbrühl as a factory.

On 24 September, 1944, six days before the written contract was received, work began on the first prototype and on 6 December, 1944, this aircraft made its maiden flight from Vienna–Schwechat with Flugkapitän Peter at the controls. This was the He 162 V1 (c/n 200 001) which behaved reasonably well on this first flight although a defectively-bonded undercarriage door was torn away when the aircraft was flown at maximum speed. This incident made both Peter and Heinkel engineers anxious to examine fully the general bonding of the aircraft. Similar bonding troubles had afflicted Focke-Wulf's Ta 154 following the bombing of the Goldschmitt Tego-Film factory and the introduction of new bonding agents but, whereas these troubles ended production of the Ta 154, not even a delay was to be allowed with the He 162, especially as a second, demonstration, flight had been arranged before many officials on 10 December. Consequently, when Peter was making a low-level high-speed pass on this day, he was killed when the aircraft crashed following disintegration of the starboard wing. Subsequent investigation showed that the insufficiently neutralized acid in the bonding agent had eaten into the wood, and further development was obviously required. This incident, however, in no way held up the programme and the He 162 V2 (c/n 200 002) made its first flight 12 days later, and, at the insistence of the RLM, was later used for firing trials with two MK 108 30 mm cannon, although designed for two smaller MG 151/20 20 mm cannon.

When more flying had been done by the Heinkel test team, the first aerodynamic deficiencies in the He 162 design came to light. These were lateral instability and snaking at high speed and a tendency for severe instability during left hand turns of more than 4 g. Accordingly, the He 162 V3 (c/n 200 003) and V4 (c/n 200 004) aircraft, which both flew on 16 January, 1945, had been modified to have enlarged vertical tail surfaces, extended wingtips with 55 deg anhedral, and the centre of gravity slightly adjusted by fitting a weight over the nosewheel. These modifications alleviated the problems, particularly during turns.

After further testing of MK 108 cannon in the He 162 V6, which first flew on 23 January, it was finally conceded that this armament was too heavy for the lightweight airframe. With the He 162 V8 (c/n 200 008) therefore, the originally proposed pair of MK 151 20-mm cannon was finally fitted, and the generally similar V9 and V10 machines completed the batch of 10 prototype-cum-pre-production aircraft from the Vienna–Schwechat factory though, as related later, this by no means saw the end of the prolific development work. The He 162 V7 (c/n 200 007) was the unarmed forerunner of the He 162A-1 production series.

For the mass-production of the He 162, Lt-Gen Kessler (who after the Schweinfurt bombing had successfully re-established anti-friction bearing production within three months) laid down schedules known as K-programmes or Kurzfristige Lieferpläne (short-term delivery schedules) which also covered the production of V-weapons and turbojets. The He 162 production programme was managed by Baugruppe Schlempp headed by Heinrich Lübke, such a co-ordination group being necessary because of

An He 162A-1 (c/n 120 077) with the American evaluation serial T-2-489 on the fins. This aircraft was evaluated at Edwards Air Force Base in 1946. (*USAF*)

the large network of subcontractors and enforced dispersal of production centres.

Most of the existing, albeit diminished, factories of Heinkel and Junkers were drawn into making fuselages and components for the He 162, and these concerns also operated newly-established works located underground in potassium and salt mines. In many cases, completed fuselages had to be lined up in the open or in farm buildings to await the fitting of wings and engines. Wooden parts, such as for wings, were made by many small wood-working firms in the Erfurt and Stuttgart areas. At Wendlingen/Neckar, a technical bureau for wooden aircraft construction was set up under the title of Firma Erwin Behr. Here techniques for wood and metal bonding were developed using a new agent of phenol base, known as FZ Tego-Film, in place of the normal Goldschmitt Tego-Film; these new techniques were also applied to the Me 262 and Me 163 aircraft. Overall wing production was controlled by the Hermann Wachter technical bureau, and final assembly of all the wing parts was done in a most modern factory, the Möbelfabrik May in Zeulenroda. There was also a new department of the Gothaer Waggonfabrik set up to investigate new constructional methods for aircraft in general; here, Dipl Ing Fritz Stensel developed a new He 162 wing which used a wooden double-skin structure consisting of skins, tapered pressure plates, lattice work or grill, and all bonded with Kaurit WHK agent, but this did not go into production. Helped by top priority ratings, all the sub-manufactured sections reached the final assembly factories surprisingly well under the chaotic conditions prevailing. The final assembly plants and their scheduled outputs of aircraft per month were Heinkel at Rostock-Marienehe (1,000), Junkers at Bernburg (1,000) and the vast manufacturing centre of Mittelwerke GmbH (2,000) beneath the Harz mountains near Nordhausen. This total target of 4,000 aircraft per month was to be worked up to from 1,000 per month by April 1945 and 2,000 per month by May 1945.

As for the 109-003 turbojets, although the decision had been made in March 1944 to move production underground, most of the 500 or so A-1

311

and E-1 models actually finished came from the BMW Zühlsdorf plant. The production schedules called for a total underground production of 109-003 engines of 6,000 per month (plus spare parts), 2,000 per month of which were to come from the Mittelwerke GmbH. However, as with the K-programmes for the airframes, these figures were gradually considerably written down as difficulties increased. The planned spare-part production for the engines gives an insight into the use-and-discard nature bestowed on the He 162. For the Arado Ar 234 jet bomber (which also used the 109-003 engine) 40 to 50 per cent engine spares were planned but, for the He 162, planned spares amounted to only about 20 per cent.

An He 162A-2 (c/n 120 222), formerly of JG 1, seen here in France. This fighter was later tested in the USA as T-2-504. The tail in the left background belongs to the damaged. He 162 c/n 120 233. (*USAF*)

As production of the He 162 went ahead, so too did its development. Most of this work was done at the Heinkel Hinterbrühl plant where production aircraft were taken off the lines and modified for experimental work. (The first production aircraft were of the A-1 series, but these were soon replaced by the slightly modified A-2 series. All the Hinterbrühl aircraft had construction numbers beginning 220.) With the He 162 V11 (c/n 220 017) and V12 (c/n 220 018), the BMW engine was replaced by a Junkers Jumo 109-004B-1 turbojet of 900 kg (1,980 lb) static thrust, although no switch-over to this engine was planned, while the He 162 V16 (c/n 220 019) and V17 (c/n 220 020) were prototypes for the He 162S two-seat training glider with lengthened fuselage. There was also a single-seat version of the He 162S, but it is not known if such gliders were actually used in training.

Following closely on the flight testing by the Heinkel team, pilots at Erprobungsstelle Rechlin began evaluating the He 162 from the Service point of view, though there can be little doubt that, whatever the verdict, the aircraft would have been put into service. The chief faults found with the machine were that it had a tendency to early tip stall, there was little harmony between its controls and it still snaked at high speed. The following aircraft were therefore used to try out cures for these troubles: with

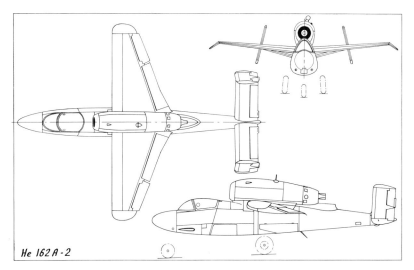

He 162 A-2

the He 162 V25 (c/n 220 008), which was first flown on 17 February, 1945, and the similar V26 and V27 machines, an increase in the fuselage length was made; this had the same effect as the increase in tail-surface area, made previously, of increasing stability and bringing yaw and pitch control more in line with the high rate of roll control. With the He 162 V22 (c/n 220 005) and V23, which were first flown on 25 and 27 February, 1945, respectively, the wing root incidence was increased to cause it to stall before the tip and also spoilers were fitted to the leading edge of the wing root. These important modifications, scarcely noticeable at a glance, were introduced on the He 162A-2 production aircraft.

Nevertheless, the production aircraft were still very hot to handle and certainly not recommended for novice pilots. Even experienced pilots were at a disadvantage because they had to learn to use the He 162's controls in smooth, flowing movements, whereas they had been able to handle the controls more roughly when manoeuvring their piston-engined fighters.

An incorrectly repainted He 162A-2 in the United States.

313

The He 162 was to remain aerodynamically unstable, despite the afore-mentioned modifications, and its critical Mach number was rather low at 0·75. These deficiencies arose chiefly from interference between the engine fairing and fuselage and between the wing and fuselage, at which points considerable displacement of the airflow was caused (at high speeds) by high local air velocities. (In the later, similarly-arranged, Henschel Hs 132, some of these troubles were to be avoided by mounting the wing at right angles to the fuselage skin; whereas the wing of the He 162 had a cavity beneath it where the fuselage skin began to curve inwards.) Against this the He 162 was quite a tough aircraft, being designed for a load factor of 7·5 (similar to dive-bombers) and a safety factor of 1·8.

If any plan existed for the operational employment of the He 162, and there was certainly no chance to test such plans, it was that hordes of He 162s would swarm over the Allied bombers' fighter escorts, leaving the unprotected bombers to the attentions of Me 262s. This was an interesting reversal of a former plan where the Me 262s would have engaged Allied fighters, leaving the bombers to the piston-engined Messerschmitt Bf 109s and Focke-Wulf Fw 190s.

The first unit to receive the He 162 was Erprobungskommando 162 (or Einsatzkommando Bär) based at E-Stelle Rechlin under the command of Obstlt Heinz Bär. From this base and, later, from Munich-Riem, the unit worked from January 1945 on the operational proving of the He 162. Simultaneously, ground crew were trained in its maintenance, and, in this work, the 109-003 engine proved amenable since, for example, the turbine could be replaced in two hours, certainly not a feature of the Junkers 109-004.

On 6 February, 1945, I./JG 1 under Oberst Herbert Ihlefeldt trans-ferred from the Eastern Front for He 162 training at Parchim where the unit was later joined by Stab/JG 1. On 8 April, the unit, reduced from four to three Staffeln, moved to nearby Ludwigslust, whilst II./JG 1 had trans-ferred the previous month from Insterburg, in East Prussia, to Warne-münde for its own training on He 162s. The planned conversion to He 162s of the third Gruppe of JG 1 could not be put into effect.

I./JG 1 moved again on 14 April to Leck in Schleswig-Holstein where the unit began its final working up under the temporary command of Oblt Demuth. By the end of April, the training programme of II./JG 1 had to be abandoned because the Red Army was approaching Warnemünde; Hptm Dahne, the Kommandeur of II./JG 1, was killed during a training flight on 24 April and was replaced by Maj Zober. By 3 May, 1945, the remnants of II./JG 1 had joined the Geschwader Stab and I. Gruppe at Leck and, on the following day, all units were regrouped into one Gruppe designated I. (Einsatz) Gruppe/JG 1 which was commanded by Zober and had three Staffeln with a total nominal strength of about fifty He 162s.

By this time, also, the Einsatzkommando Bär with its He 162s had moved to Salzburg-Maxglam to join up with JV 44, Galland's élite Me 262 unit formed as a last-ditch effort by the Luftwaffe. Since the He 162 units were not considered ready for action, combat was forbidden and only scant Allied reports are available of contacts with it. One typical report was given, together with photographs, of a brief encounter between an He 162 and a North American P-51 Mustang in April 1945. This encounter took place at between about 150 and 300 m (500 and 1,000 ft), and the He 162 was stated to be quite manoeuvrable and be able to turn and climb on a par with the P-51 but had a higher level speed and acceleration.

On 3 May, the units at Salzburg-Maxglam surrendered, while, at Leck, the I. (Einsatz) Gruppe/JG 1 surrendered on 8 May, 1945, only four days after its formation. Thus, despite prodigious efforts and an organizational network which ran uncommonly smoothly, the Volksjäger programme came to nothing.

An He 162A-1 (c/n 120 076) excellently refurbished in July 1966 and preserved at the Canadian War Museum. This aircraft was captured at Leck and evaluated in flight by the British as AM 59 (RAF serial VH523). (*National Aeronautical Collection – Ottawa*)

Such great hopes were placed on the He 162 that considerable development and experiment with the basic aircraft was undertaken and projected, some of the former work having already been mentioned. Much work centred around improving performance by increasing engine thrust. In the BMW 109-003C turbojet, an increased static thrust of 900 kg (1,980 lb) was obtained by fitting a more efficient compressor of Brown-Boveri design, and one test engine was built. In April 1945, therefore, the 003D turbojet was ordered which was to have an increased static thrust of 1,100 kg (2,425 lb) and be interchangeable with the standard 003E engine, but only calculations were made. There were also the possibilities of employing the BMW 109-003R combination turbojet/rocket engine (described on page 544) for improving the rate of climb, or of fitting the Heinkel-Hirth 109-011A turbojet of 1,300 kg (2,866 lb) static thrust. Although the 109-011A engine was not in production and was still proving difficult to manufacture by the war's end, much reliance had been placed on it. At the same time as it was applied to the He 162, it was hoped to raise the low critical Mach number of the aircraft by fitting new swept-forward wings (He 162C) or sweptback wings (He 162D), both versions being planned with new butterfly tails. Both types of wing were to be

315

tested, using interchangeable fittings, with the He 162A-14, but the first prototype was only partially built when the war ended. Finally, mention must be made of the proposed He 162B-1 and B-2 which were to be powered by two Argus 109-014 pulse-jets and one Argus 109-044 pulse-jet respectively. These proposals came about as a result of a request for an even more simplified fighter and, although performance would have been poor, a greater fuel load could have been carried. The projected use of the He 162 in the Mistel composite aircraft rôle is described on page 577.

Today, some seven He 162s are known to be preserved in various establishments, out of some 275 completed and about 800 nearly completed.

*Wartime operational units:* Erprobungskommando 162, I. and II./JG 1.

He 162A-2 with one BMW 109-003E-1 or E-2 turbojet of 800 kg (1,760 lb) static thrust: Span 7·2 m (23 ft 7¾ in); length 9 m (29 ft 8½ in); height 2·55 m (8 ft 4⅜ in); wing area 11·15 sq m (120 sq ft).

Empty weight 1,750 kg (3,859 lb); pilot 100 kg (220 lb); ammunition 50 kg (110 lb); normal fuel 590 kg (1,301 lb); normal loaded weight 2,490 kg (5,490 lb); maximum loaded weight with extra fuel 2,700 kg (5,953 lb).

Maximum level speed at 6,000 m (19,680 ft) 835 km/h (522 mph); limiting Mach number 0·75; landing speed 165 km/h (103 mph); initial rate of climb 1,290 m/min (4,231 ft/min); approximate service ceiling 11,000 m (36,080 ft); endurance 20 min at sea level or 57 min at service ceiling; maximum range with maximum fuel at service ceiling 1,000 km (620 miles).

He 162D project with Heinkel-Hirth 109-011A turbojet of 1,300 kg (2,866 lb) static thrust and sweptback wings: Span 8 m (26 ft 3 in); length 9 m (29 ft 8½ in); height 2·65 m (8 ft 8¼ in); wing area 13·6 sq m (146·3 sq ft).

Empty weight 2,050 kg (4,520 lb); pilot 100 kg (220 lb); normal fuel 900 kg (1,985 lb); normal loaded weight 3,050 kg (6,725 lb).

Maximum level speed at 7,000 m (22,960 ft) 920 km/h (571 mph) or Mach 0·82. Other estimated performance data not known.

The Henschel Hs 123 V1 which made its public debut on 8 May, 1935, at Berlin-Johannisthal. (*R. C. Seeley*)

# Henschel Hs 123

Apart from a few training aircraft which served with the Nachtschlachtstaffeln towards the end of the war, the Luftwaffe's last operational biplane was the Henschel Hs 123. The aircraft originated from a specification for a dive-bomber, placed in 1933 under the aegis of Ernst Udet. Two companies competed for the contract, Fieseler with the Fi 98 and Henschel with the Hs 123.

Both powerful-looking biplanes, the Fieseler design suffered from a preponderance of interplane, centre-section and undercarriage struts. In contrast the Henschel aircraft, a neat sesquiplane, had single streamlined interplane struts and a large spatted undercarriage. The Hs 123 was built of metal, the fuselage and fixed tail surfaces having light alloy covering. All control surfaces and the rear portion of both wings were fabric covered. The wings, forward of the main spars, were metal skinned.

The prototypes of both designs, the Hs 123 V1 and Fi 98a, appeared during the spring of 1935, the former making its public debut on 8 May. It was immediately apparent that the Henschel machine was superior and a contract was awarded, the Fi 98 being abandoned.

Both the Hs 123 V2, D-ILUA, and V3, D-IKOU, like the first prototype, were powered by a single 650 hp BMW 132A-3 nine-cylinder radial air-cooled engine but had smaller-diameter cowlings, in which the valve gear was enclosed by 18 streamlined blisters. The Hs 123 V3 was the first of these aircraft to carry armament, a pair of forward-firing 7·9 mm MG 17 machine-guns in the upper decking of the fuselage. During August 1935

317

The Hs 123 V2 which was fitted with a modified cowling carried by all subsequent production aircraft. (*F. Selinger*)

the three prototypes were extensively tested at Rechlin, two of them shedding their wings during dives. Investigations revealed that the wing had ripped away from the centre-section struts, and therefore the fourth aircraft, the Hs 123 V4, D-IZXY, had considerable structural strengthening.

These structural alterations proved effective, and, during the summer of 1936, the first Hs 123A-1 production aircraft left the assembly lines at Schönefeld and Johannisthal. The Hs 123A-1 was powered by an 880 hp BMW 132Dc and had two MG 17 machine-guns in the fuselage top decking. A 250 kg (550 lb) bomb or an auxiliary fuel tank could be carried beneath the fuselage, and there was provision for four 50 kg (110 lb) bombs under the lower wing.

On 1 October, 1935, the Luftwaffe set up an experimental dive-bomber unit at Schwerin, the formation eventually becoming I./St.G 162, the first Gruppe of the subsequently famous Immelmann-Geschwader. At first, the Gruppe, together with II./St.G 162 and I./St.G 165 formed at Kitzingen, were equipped with such aircraft as the Heinkel He 50, He 51 and Arado Ar 65, but during the autumn of 1936 it received its first Hs 123A-1s. In December 1936, five Hs 123As were delivered to the Condor Legion in Spain, the aircraft making its operational debut early in 1937. Although designed as a dive-bomber, the Hs 123 was used mainly as a Schlachtflugzeug, that is, a close-support aircraft rather than a Sturzkampfflugzeug which made pinpoint attacks on the more strategic targets.

During the early spring of 1937, the first Junkers Ju 87A-1s had begun to enter service with I./St.G 162, and by the middle of the year Ju 87s were also equipping II./St.G 162, III./St.G 165 and I./St.G 262. Now only I. and II./St.G 165 were equipped with the Hs 123A-1, and by 1 August, 1938, with the establishment of the Schlachtfliegergruppen, these two units were also converted to the Ju 87A. Only two of the five Schlachtfliegergruppen, SFG 10 and SFG 50, were equipped with the Hs 123A,

318

but on 1 November, 1938, these too were disbanded, their aircraft passing to the newly established II. (Schlacht)/LG 2.

Just before production of the Hs 123A was phased out during the autumn of 1938, two further prototypes were produced. The Hs 123 V5, D-INRA, fitted with a 960 hp BMW 132K engine in a longer, streamlined cowling and intended as prototype for the proposed Hs 123B series, although no development of the aircraft was undertaken. The final prototype was the Hs 123 V6, D-IHDI, forerunner of the proposed C-series. Similar to the V5, the sixth prototype had an enclosed cockpit and two additional MG 17 machine-guns.

When the Luftwaffe struck against Poland on 1 September, 1939, only II.(S)/LG 2, under Maj Werner Spielvogel based at Alt-Rosenberg, was

Luftwaffe mechanics at work on an Hs 123A-1 ground attack aircraft. (*R. C. Seeley*)

equipped with the Hs 123A. The Gruppe concentrated on the support of the German XIVth Army as it advanced towards Warsaw, striking against pockets of Polish resistance. Although carrying only light armament, the Hs 123 terrorized troops and horses alike with the roar from its BMW 132 radial, its success being out of all proportion to the actual damage it caused.

On 10 May, 1940, II.(S)/LG 2, commanded by Hptm Otto Weiss, attacked Belgian troops attempting to hold bridges over the Albert Canal, and then joined in smashing two French divisions on 13 May. Although effective against ground forces, the elderly biplane was very vulnerable to enemy fighters, so much so that a Jagdgruppe, I./JG 21, under Hptm Werner Ultsch, was assigned for II.(S)/LG 2's protection. During one notable operation on 22 May, 1940, the two Gruppen held off an attack by some 40 tanks against their own advanced base at Cambrai.

319

An Hs 123A-1 ground attack aircraft of Schlachtgeschwader 2 on the Eastern Front, 1943/44. (*R. C. Seeley*)

After the successful completion of the French campaign, II.(S)/LG 2 was withdrawn to Brunswick for re-equipment with the Messerschmitt Bf 109E fighter-bomber, but when the unit participated in the attack on the Balkans in April 1941, it still had some Hs 123s. During the winter of 1941–42, II.(S)/LG 2 was withdrawn from operations to form the basis of a new unit, designated Schlachtgeschwader 1. Eventually comprising two Gruppen of four Staffeln each, Sch.G 1 was equipped with a mixture of Bf 109Es, Hs 123A and Hs 129B aircraft.

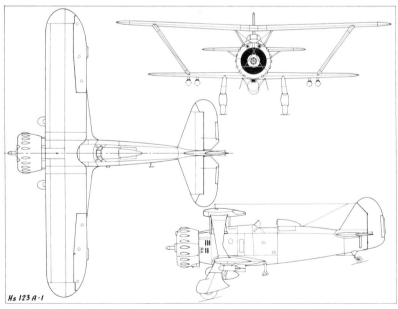

Hs 123 A-1

320

Although obsolescent, the Hs 123 still proved to be a valuable part of the Luftwaffe ground attack forces, being capable of operating from the roughest of temporary airfields. Some machines had two 20 mm MG FF cannon and others carried ninety-two 2 kg (4·4 lb) SD 2 anti-personnel bombs. The aircraft was so successful that on 16 January, 1943, Gen von Richthofen demanded that the aircraft be put back into production, but the proposal was impracticable as all tools and jigs had been scrapped in 1940. In October 1943, II./Sch.G 1 was redesignated II./SG 2, and the Hs 123A remained with that unit until mid-1944 when normal attrition caused it to disappear from the ranks of the Luftwaffe.

*Wartime operational units:* II.(S)/LG 2, I. and II./Sch.G 1, I. and II./Sch.G 2, II./SG 2.

Hs 123A-1: Span (upper wing) 10·5 m (34 ft 5½ in), span (lower wing) 8 m (26 ft 3 in); length 8·33 m (27 ft 4 in); height 3·21 m (10 ft 6⅓ in); wing area 24·8 sq m (267·4 sq ft). Empty weight 1,500 kg (3,307 lb); loaded weight 2,215 kg (4,884 lb).

Maximum speed at 1,200 m (3,937 ft) 341 km/h (212 mph), at sea level 333 km/h (207 mph); cruising speed at 2,000 m (6,562 ft) 317 km/h (197 mph); initial rate of climb 900 m/min (2,952 ft/min); service ceiling 9,000 m (29,529 ft); maximum range 860 km (534 miles).

# Henschel Hs 126

At the beginning of 1939, the Luftwaffe's short-range reconnaissance units were still mainly equipped with the Heinkel He 45 and He 46. Both these types were slow, possessed limited altitude performance, and were extremely vulnerable to ground fire. In addition, their mixed steel-tube and wood construction and fabric covering made them so sensitive to bad weather that they had to be housed in protective tents.

The appearance of the Henschel Hs 126, with its all-metal stressed-skin construction, in the middle of 1939 provided the Luftwaffe with its first really effective short-range reconnaissance aircraft. The Hs 126 was in fact based on an earlier design, the Hs 122, which appeared during the summer of 1935. Three prototypes had been completed, the Hs 122 V1, D-UBYN, powered by a Rolls-Royce Kestrel liquid-cooled engine, and the Hs 122 V2, D-UDIZ, and V3, D-UBAV, both powered by 660 hp Siemens SAM 22B air-cooled radials. These machines were followed by a small batch of Hs 122A-0 pre-production aircraft, but the type failed to provide any marked improvement in performance over the He 46.

Early in 1936, Dipl Ing Friedrich Nicolaus, chief designer of the Henschel company, began work on a more sophisticated variant of the Hs 122 which later received the designation Hs 126. The new type retained the basic parasol-wing layout of the Hs 122, but had a redesigned wing, a cantilever undercarriage and a semi-enclosed cockpit. The Hs 126 V1,

The Henschel Hs 122 V3 was developed into the Hs 126, one of the Luftwaffe's most important reconnaissance aircraft.

which made its first flight during the autumn of 1936, was converted from the Hs 122A-04, was powered by a 610 hp Junkers Jumo 210 liquid-cooled engine and was flown initially without the cockpit cover.

The Hs 126 V2, D-UJER, and V3, D-OECY, were each powered by an 830 hp Bramo-Fafnir 323A-1 nine-cylinder radial, but the former was fitted with an exhaust-driven supercharger and had an enlarged rudder and twin tailplane bracing struts. The third prototype was fitted with vertical tail surfaces of similar shape to those of the first aircraft, but the under-carriage legs were set at right angles to the fuselage datum rather than having a rearward slope.

By the end of 1937, Henschel had completed a pre-production batch of

One of the batch of ten Henschel Hs 126A-0s completed before the end of 1937 at Schönefeld.

322

ten Hs 126A-0s, these being essentially similar to the Hs 126 V3. During the spring of 1938 several Hs 126A-0s were delivered to the reconnaissance Lehrgruppe for Service evaluation and were well received by the Luftwaffe. The machine proved to have excellent handling characteristics and an extremely good short-field performance.

The first Hs 126A-1s began to leave the Henschel assembly lines at Schönefeld and Johannisthal early in 1938, and the type entered service with the Luftwaffe later that year. The Hs 126A-1 differed from the pre-production model in being powered by the BMW 132Dc which produced 880 hp for take-off. The type was provided with a single Zeiss camera mounted in the rear fuselage bay, concealed when not in use by a movable panel controlled by the observer. In addition to this fixed camera, a hand-held Rb 12.5/9x7 camera was attached to the port side of the cockpit.

An Hs 126A-1 of 7.(F)/LG 2 with the observer leaning over the side holding a hand camera.

Armament was standardized as a fixed forward-firing 7·9 mm MG 17 machine-gun and a movable MG 15 of similar calibre in the rear cockpit. The machine could also carry five 10 kg (22 lb) SD 10 bombs or a single 50 kg (110 lb) SC 50 bomb on a special rack under the fuselage, behind the port undercarriage leg.

The Hs 126A-1 entered service with Aufklärungsgruppe 35, and in the autumn of 1938 six aircraft were delivered to a Kette of Aufklärungsstaffel 88 in Spain which had previously been equipped with the Heinkel He 45 biplane. Operating during the closing stages of the Spanish Civil War, the aircraft proved extremely successful and were later transferred to the Spanish Air Force. Sixteen aircraft were also delivered to the Greek Air Force's 3rd army co-operation squadron.

During the summer of 1939 the Hs 126B-1 appeared on the assembly lines. This was basically an A-1 powered by an 850 hp Bramo 323A-1 or Q-1 engine or a 900 hp Bramo 323A-2 or Q-2. The new variant proved to have a much-enhanced performance at altitude and an even shorter take-off run. The machine also had FuG 17 VHF radio equipment; but no navigational aids for inclement conditions, a grave limitation since many missions had to be performed in bad weather by the long-range reconnaissance units.

When the Second World War began, the Hs 126 was in service with the majority of the army co-operation reconnaissance units, including 9.(H)/LG 2, Aufkl.Gr 10, 11, 12, 13, 14, 21, 23, 31, 32 and 41. At this time a total of 257 of the Hs 126s were in service with the Luftwaffe as compared with sixty-four Heinkel He 46s and twenty-one Heinkel He 45s. By May 1940, when Germany launched its assault on France and the Low Countries, the He 45 and He 46 had virtually disappeared from the ranks of the Aufklärungsstaffeln. Between 1 September, 1939, and January 1941 a total of 505 Hs 126s were built. Pre-war production was in the region of 100 aircraft.

A flight of three Hs 126A-1s from 7.(F)/LG 2 photographed before the war.

During the Polish and French campaigns, it was normally possible to assign an Aufklärungsstaffel to each army corps, thus providing each ground unit with an up-to-date view of the tactical situation. Daylight reconnaissance flights over the battle area were normally made at altitudes of below 2,000 m (6,562 ft), but night missions usually had to be flown at almost tree-top level.

The normal method of operation was for the army command to issue its instructions to the Staffelkapitän who then passed them on to the individual crews, ensuring the most efficient use of the men and aircraft at his command. It was very rarely that a request for a sortie was issued direct

An Hs 126A-1, probably of Aufklärungsgruppe 21, in France, May 1940.

from the army command to individual aircraft pilots. The information gathered on each sortie was normally reported orally after landing, but in exceptional cases a direct radio report was made.

In addition to co-operating with the conventional ground troops, a squadron of Hs 126s was allocated to each of the Panzer-Korps. These Staffeln were identified by the abbreviation (Pz) after their designation, and eventually included 1. and 5.(H)/11, 1.(H)/13, 1. and 5.(H)/14, 3.(H)/21, 1., 2. and 3.(H)/23, 2.(H)/31, 2. and 6.(H)/32 and 3.(H)/41. Two Staffeln were reserved to co-operate with the artillery batteries and were identified by the abbreviation (Art). These were 3.(H)/10 and 3.(F)/11.

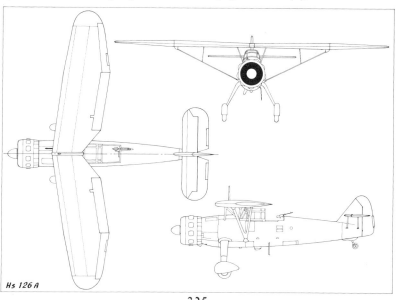

Hs 126 A

An Hs 126B-1 of an unidentified Luftwaffe unit with a number of Ju 52/3ms in the background. (*R. C. Seeley*)

At the beginning of the Russian campaign in June 1941, no less than 48 army co-operation squadrons were operational with the Luftwaffe, all equipped with the Hs 126, making a total of well over 400 aircraft. Although the number of Staffeln had been increased, the establishment of the units was reduced from nine to seven, and to six in the case of the formations assigned to the Panzer-Korps. Although the Hs 126 suffered only light losses in the French campaign, in Russia it began to suffer quite heavily and units often had to be given fighter protection.

The only unit to operate the Hs 126 in the Middle East was 4.(H)/12 based in North Africa, but gradually re-equipped with Messerschmitt Bf 109 and Bf 110 fighter-reconnaissance machines and disappeared from the area in August 1942.

From the spring of 1942 a gradual switch was made to the Focke-Wulf Fw 189 and by the end of the year the Hs 126 had been virtually withdrawn from front-line units. Several Hs 126s were used for towing DFS 230 gliders with II. and III./LLG 1. The final use of the aircraft was as a night harassing bomber with NSGr 7 in the Balkans, 3./NSGr 11 in Estonia and 2./NSGr 12 in Latvia. The units were composed of instructors from the pilot training schools and operations included anti-partisan missions.

*Wartime operational units:* Used by the army co-operation squadrons of Aufkl.Gr 10, 11, 12, 13, 14, 21, 23, 31, 32 and 41, NAGr 1, 2, 3, 4, 5, 6, 7, 8, 10, 11, 12. 9.(H)/LG 2, NSGr 7, 3./NSGr 11, 1./NSGr 12, 1. and 3./SAGr 127, IV./KG 200.

Hs 126B-1: Span 14·5 m (47 ft 6¼ in); length 10·85 m (35 ft 7 in); height 3·75 m (12 ft 3½ in); wing area 31·6 sq m (340·14 sq ft).
  Empty weight 2,030 kg (4,476 lb); loaded weight 3,090 kg (6,813 lb).
  Maximum speed at sea level 310 km/h (193 mph), at 3,000 m (9,843 ft) 356 km/h (221 mph), at 6,000 m (19,686 ft) 335 km/h (208 mph); climb to 4,000 m (13,124 ft) 7·2 min, to 6,000 m (19,686 ft) 12·7 min; service ceiling 8,300 m (27,232 ft); normal range 580 km (360 miles); maximum range 720 km (447 miles).

# Henschel Hs 128 and Hs 130

For some time before the start of the Second World War, the Deutsche Versuchsanstalt für Luftfahrt had been working on the problems associated with high-altitude flight. The Henschel company, under the direction of their chief designer, Dipl Ing Friedrich Nicolaus, had simultaneously been working on the design of a pressurized cabin and during 1938 the two organizations decided to pool their research to produce the Hs 128 high-altitude research aircraft.

The pressurized cockpit shell of the Henschel Hs 128 V1 under test by the DVL at Berlin-Adlershof.

The pressurized cabin for the aircraft was patented on 16 December, 1939, and seated two. It was only joined to the actual airframe of the aircraft by a ring mounted midway along its length, air being circulated between it and the fuselage walls to provide insulation.

The Hs 128 V1, which first flew from Berlin-Adlershof in 1939, was a cantilever low-wing monoplane with a high aspect ratio wing and fixed spatted undercarriage. The aircraft was built entirely of metal with a stressed light alloy skin. The first prototype was powered by two 1,000 hp Daimler-Benz DB 601 engines, it being proposed that these should be fitted with TK 9 exhaust-driven superchargers. These were not ready in time for the aircraft's first flight and were installed later.

Later in 1939, the Hs 128 V2 (D-ARHD) joined the test programme, this being powered by two Junkers Jumo 210 engines with TK 16

The Henschel Hs 130E-0 extreme-altitude reconnaissance aircraft fitted with the HZ-Anlage supercharger system.

mechanically-driven superchargers. During the research programme, the Hs 128 V2 attained an altitude of 12,000 m (39,372 ft). Both aircraft were later used to test superchargers developed by the DVL and the Hirth company.

Following a suggestion by Oberst Theodor Rowehl, commander of the reconnaissance group of the Luftwaffe's High Command, the RLM asked Henschel to produce a high-altitude reconnaissance version of the Hs 128. Designated Hs 130A, the aircraft differed in having a retractable undercarriage and was originally projected with DB 601D engines with TK 16 superchargers. The first prototype, the Hs 130 V1, was powered by 1,100 hp DB 601R engines driving three-blade VDM airscrews. With the addition of GM-1 nitrous oxide power-boosting equipment, the aircraft could reach an altitude of 13,200 m (43,309 ft)—an exceptional performance for 1940.

The Hs 130 V2 and V3 were essentially similar to the V1 apart from the re-introduction of four-blade airscrews; all three aircraft had the wing span reduced to 22·1 m (72 ft 6 in) when compared with the Hs 128 which had a span of 26 m (85 ft 2¾ in). Two Rb 75/30 cameras were mounted in the rear fuselage, these being operated by remote control from the cabin. Early in 1941, the first Hs 130A-0 pre-production aircraft were delivered to Stuttgart-Echterdingen for flight testing. Essentially similar to the prototypes, they had new outer wings, the span being increased to 25·5 m (83 ft 8 in) in an attempt to further increase performance in the rarefied air at high altitudes.

The Hs 130A-06 and A-07 (or A-0/U6 and U7), which appeared in November 1943, had the span further increased to 29 m (95 ft 1¾ in) to improve altitude performance. Both aircraft were powered by two 1,475 hp Daimler-Benz DB 605B engines with Hirth 9-2281 turbo-superchargers plus GM-1 power-boosting equipment. In this system, nitrous oxide was injected into the superchargers to increase the power of the engines above their rated altitude. With a crew of two and carrying two 300 litre (66 Imp gal) drop tanks, they had an absolute ceiling of no less than 15,500 m (50,750 ft)—an altitude which was only exceeded by one other German piston-engined aircraft, the Blohm und Voss Bv 155. A

328

further modification of the basic design was projected with two 1,500 hp Junkers Jumo 208 Diesel engines.

The Hs 130B-0 was a proposed bomber conversion of the A-0 with provision for a 1,000 kg (2,205 lb) bomb load, but only a mockup was completed.

The Hs 130C-0 was a complete departure from the previous aircraft. Produced late in 1942, it was in fact Henschel's contender for the ill-fated B Bomber specification which was responsible for the production of such aircraft as the Junkers Ju 288, Focke-Wulf Fw 191 and Dornier Do 317. The first two prototypes, the Hs 130C V1 and C V2, were each powered by two 1,600 hp BMW 801A radial engines and had entirely new and fully-glazed pressurized cabins capable of accommodating a crew of four. Early in 1943, the Hs 130C V2 was re-engined with two 1,810 hp BMW 801TJ radials with turbo-superchargers. The production prototype, the Hs 130C V3, was powered by two 1,750 hp Daimler-Benz DB 603A engines. It had two 13 mm MG 131 machine-guns in each of two remote-controlled barbettes mounted above and below the cabin and a remote-controlled 7·9 mm MG 15 machine-gun in the extreme tail. The aircraft could carry a 2,000 kg (4,410 lb) bomb load which could include a single SC 1800 bomb or two LT F5b torpedoes.

During the summer of 1943, the RLM discussed with Henschel the possibility of producing one hundred Hs 130C-1 production aircraft, but, following the abandonment of the entire B Bomber programme late in 1943, the scheme was cancelled. The Hs 130D-0 was a projected high-altitude aircraft powered by DB 605 engines with an extremely complicated two-stage supercharging system developed jointly by DVL and Argus. The system was so complex that it was quickly abandoned, work being switched to the Hs 130E.

The Hs 130E-0 had the Höhen-Zentrale Anlage supercharging system comprising two conventionally-mounted 1,750 hp DB 603B engines which were supercharged by a 1,475 hp DB 605T engine within the fuselage driving a large turbo-blower. The initial project was designated Hs P.80 and was similar in size to the Hs 130A-06, but early design work led to the lengthening of the fuselage and the provision of a high aspect ratio wing.

The Hs 130E V1 first flew in September 1942, the V2 following two months later. For the initial flights neither prototype was fitted with the HZ-Anlage system, but during subsequent tests altitudes of up to 15,000 m (49,200 ft) were achieved. The Hs 130E V2 was lost during its seventh flight, because of an engine fire, but was quickly replaced by the Hs 130E V3.

Results were so encouraging that the RLM placed an order for one hundred Hs 130E-1 production aircraft during the spring of 1943. The first of seven Hs 130E-0s flew in May 1943, but shortly afterwards the RLM reduced the production order to 30 and then, mainly because of unreliability of the HZ-Anlage system, abandoned the design altogether.

The final projected design was the Hs 130F-0 to be powered by four 1,800 hp BMW 801TJ radials or four 1,750 hp Daimler-Benz DB 603s with either Hirth 9-2279 or 9-2281 turbo-superchargers.

Hs 130E-01: Span 33 m (108 ft 3¼ in); length 22 m (72 ft 2 in); height 5·6 m (18 ft 4½ in); wing area 85 sq m (914 sq ft).
Empty weight 12,200 kg (26,901 lb); loaded weight 16,700 kg (36,823 lb).
Maximum speed at 14,000 m (45,935 ft) 610 km/h (379 mph); cruising speed at 12,000 m (39,372 ft) 515 km/h (320 mph); landing speed 130 km/h (81 mph); service ceiling 15,100 m (49,545 ft); maximum range 3,000 km (1,864 miles).

Luftwaffe mechanics prepare a Henschel Hs 129B (c/n 0350) for an operational sortie.
*(R. C. Seeley)*

# Henschel Hs 129

In April 1937, the technical department of the RLM issued a specification for a small twin-engined ground-attack aircraft to the Hamburger Flugzeugbau, Focke-Wulf, Gotha, and Henschel companies. The aircraft was to be heavily armoured and have at least two 20 mm MG FF cannon. After examining the four designs, on 1 October, 1937, the RLM issued a development contract for the Focke-Wulf and Henschel projects, respectively designated Fw 189C and Hs 129.

The Henschel aircraft was designed by Dipl Ing Friedrich Nicolaus, detailed work being completed on the aircraft by the middle of 1938. The first prototype, the Hs 129 V1, flew in the spring of 1939. It was a small low-wing monoplane with a triangular-section fuselage and two 465 hp Argus As 410 twelve-cylinder inverted-vee air-cooled engines. The airframe was built of light alloy with stressed skin and 5 mm armoured plate protecting the engines. The nose, in which the pilot sat, comprised a 'box' of 6 to 12 mm armour plates spot-welded together with the windscreen of 75 mm armoured glass. The cockpit was so small that several of the

Schlachtgeschwader 1 operated a number of Hs 129B-2s on the Eastern Front. Here an aircraft of 4.Staffel prepares for take-off. (*R. C. Seeley*)

instruments had to be mounted on the inboard sides of the engine cowlings. Standard armament was two 20 mm MG FF cannon and two 7·9 mm MG 17 machine-guns.

Two further prototypes were completed, the Hs 129 V2 and V3, these competing in trials with the Focke-Wulf Fw 189 V1b, forerunner of the proposed Fw 189C. Test pilots were far from enthusiastic about the Henschel design, which was obviously underpowered and extremely difficult to control. The cramped cockpit limited movement of the control column which was excessively short, and the smallness of the armoured glass windscreen severely restricted the pilot's view.

The Fw 189 was even less popular than the Hs 129 and the RLM awarded a development contract for eight Hs 129A-0 pre-production aircraft. Some of these were delivered to 5.(Schlacht)/LG 2 in the late autumn of 1940, but the Luftwaffe pilots were even less enthusiastic about the aircraft.

It was underpowered, extremely sluggish, and difficult to control in the air, and the pilot's view from the tiny armoured cockpit was little short of complete blindness.

The results of these tests brought a tacit refusal from the Luftwaffe to accept the proposed Hs 129A-1 production model, and Nicolaus began work on a larger and entirely new design, the Henschel P.76. However,

Several Hs 129Bs were delivered to the Rumanian Air Force and saw service in the Zaporozh'ye area during the summer of 1943. (*R. C. Seeley*)

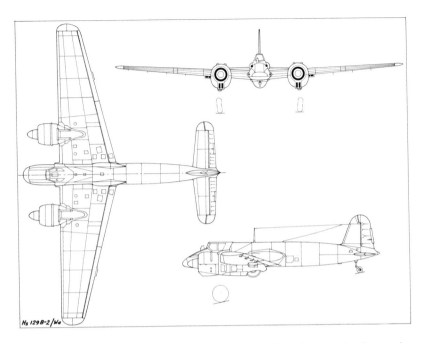

Hs 129 B-2/Wa

because of the urgent need for a ground-attack aircraft to equip the newly-established Schlachtgeschwader, the RLM refused to countenance the delay that would result in the Hs P.76 being tooled-up for production. Therefore the Henschel company was ordered to produce a modified version of the Hs 129A-0 powered by captured Gnome/Rhône 14M 4/5 radial engines, the Hs 129B.

Early in 1941, two Hs 129A-0s were returned to Schönefeld to be fitted with Gnome/Rhône radials, the remaining six aircraft being transferred to 4./SG 101 at Paris-Orly. The modified Hs.129A-0s proved to have a much improved performance over their Argus-engined predecessors, although Luftwaffe test pilots continued to complain about high stick forces and severely restricted forward vision. Therefore, on the Hs 129B-0 new electrically-operated trim tabs and a new canopy with more extensive glazing were fitted. The canopy was first tested on the Hs 129 V3, and considerably increased available space inside the cockpit. A special external Revi C12/C sight was mounted just forward of the windscreen, the pilot aligning the angled fins with the horizon during a diving attack to assist him to correctly aim his bomb.

The first of a batch of ten Hs 129B-0s (c/ns 0151 to 0160) was delivered in December 1941, the Hs 129B-1 being placed on the production lines in March 1942. During 1942, 219 aircraft were built, followed by 414 in 1943 and 225 up to September 1944, when production ceased. Both versions were powered by two 700 hp Gnome/Rhône 14M 4/5 engines and had two 20 mm MG 151/20 cannon and two 7·9 mm MG 17 machine-guns. but the B-1 differed in having exposed blast troughs for the guns and the radio equipment repositioned.

During 1942 a number of Schönefeld-built Henschel Hs 129B-1s were modified to carry a large variety of weapons. The Hs 129B-1/R1, in addition to the standard built-in armament, carried two 50 kg (110 lb) SC 50 bombs or two packs each containing forty-eight SD-2 anti-personnel bombs. The most widely used variant was the Hs 129B-1/R2 which carried below the fuselage a 30 mm MK 101 cannon with 30 rounds. The Hs 129B-1/R3 had four additional MG 17 machine-guns with 1,000 rounds, the R4 could carry four SC 50, one SC 250 or ninety-six SD 2 bombs, and the Hs 129B-1/R5 was a reconnaissance variant with an Rb 50/30 camera and reduced ammunition capacity.

The first Hs 129B-1s were delivered to the newly-formed 4./Sch.G 1 at Lippstadt in northwest Germany. The unit received 16 aircraft by the middle of April 1942 and, after a period of intensive working-up, was transferred to the Eastern Front in May. Even at this early stage in the career of the Hs 129, the engine trouble that was to persist throughout the aircraft's life began to manifest itself. The Gnome/Rhône engines were found to seize at the slightest provocation and were extremely vulnerable to even the slightest battle damage.

Therefore it was not until September 1942 that a second Hs 129 equipped unit was formed. Designated 4./Sch.G 2, the Staffel was established at Deblin-Irena in Poland on 30 September, 1942, with a strength of twelve Hs 129B-1s. On 10 November, the unit arrived in North Africa, but by then its strength had been reduced to eight aircraft, only half of which were serviceable. After relatively few appearances over the Allied lines, the Hs 129s were withdrawn to Tripoli, minus two of their number captured after making forced landings. At Tripoli, an attempt was made to produce a satisfactory sand filter for the Gnome/Rhônes but with little success. The remaining aircraft were eventually destroyed when the Allies entered Tripoli on 23 January, 1943, and 4./Sch.G 2, minus its aircraft, was transferred to Bari in southern Italy for refitting.

Undismayed by this debacle, 8.Staffel of II./Sch.G 2, which had recently been formed by amalgamating the Jabo-Staffeln of JG 27 and JG 53, was equipped with the Hs 129B-1. Based at Tunis-Aouina, the unit became operational in February 1943 and proved much more successful than its predecessor. Strength rose from 10 aircraft in February to 16 in April, but serviceability steadily declined. In May 1943, 8./Sch.G 2 was transferred to Decimomannu in Sardinia and in July 1943 to the Eastern Front.

The appearance of the Soviet T-34 and KV-1 tanks had caused much surprise and no little trepidation among the Germans as they proved superior to the Pz.Kw III and IV tanks then in service with the Panzer-Divisions. Fortunately for the Wehrmacht, the Soviet tanks did not appear in numbers until the end of 1942. Soviet tank battalions, comprising 65 vehicles, were formed and these created severe problems among the

German armoured divisions. The KV-1 had a 76 mm gun and 75 mm plate, and the T-34 had the same calibre gun but only 45 mm armour although better distributed. The frontal armour of both was able to withstand the Hs 129B-1/R2's 30 mm MK 101 cannon shells and in fact difficulty was experienced in penetrating the vehicles' frontal armour even with the 50 mm gun of the Pz.Kw III and 75 mm gun of the Pz.Kw IV.

Tests were made with new weapons for the Hs 129 during the autumn of 1942. The 30 mm MK 103 (an MK 101 with increased muzzle velocity), the 37 mm BK 3·7 and the 50 mm BK 5 weapons were all tested, eventually resulting in a new production series, the Hs 129B-2. Before the introduction of the new sub-type, the Hs 129B-1 was equipped with 4 kg (9 lb) SD 4 bombs which had hollow-charge warheads and were capable of penetrating the armour of the Russian tanks.

The Hs 129B-2 was purely a gun carrier, the bomb racks being removed and the MG 17 machine-guns replaced by 13 mm MG 131 weapons. The Hs 129B-2/R1 had the standard armament, the R2 a 30 mm MK 103 cannon in an underfuselage mounting, and the B-2/R3 was fitted with a 37 mm BK 3·7 weapon with the MG 131s removed.

In parallel with the development of the Hs 129B-2 weapon carrier, several specialized anti-tank units were established. These included the Versuchs-Staffeln für Panzerbekämpfung, equipped with the Junkers Ju 87G and Ju 88P; Staffel 92 also equipped with the Ju 88P-1; I./ZG 1, equipped with the Messerschmitt Bf 110; and the Panzerjäger-Staffel of JG 51 with the Hs 129B. The units carried out a long series of tactical trials at Rechlin using captured Soviet tanks, and were eventually transferred to the Eastern Front, being placed under the control of the Führer der Panzerjäger. By July 1943, five Hs 129 equipped units were operational on the Eastern Front: 4. and 8./Sch.G 1, 4. and 8./Sch.G 2 and the Pz.Jäg. Sta./JG 51.

On 5 July, 1943, the Germans launched Operation Citadel in an attempt to regain the initiative on the Eastern Front after the Stalingrad defeat. The German offensive plan was to use a great pincer movement to encircle Soviet troops at the Kursk salient and then strike eastwards as far as possible. In addition to 900,000 troops and 2,700 tanks and assault guns, no less than 2,000 aircraft were concentrated for the offensive.

Three days after the launching of the attack, German forces had failed to penetrate more than 40 km (25 miles) into Soviet-held territory. The eastern flank of the southern jaw of the pincer movement was dominated by a wooded belt around Belgorod, and the Luftwaffe was given the task of keeping the area under careful surveillance. Early on the morning of 8 July this task had fallen to a section of Hs 129s led by Hptm Bruno Meyer. Meyer, who was in overall command of 4. and 8./Sch.G 1 and 4. and 8./Sch.G 2, spotted a number of Soviet tanks moving in the woods and realized that a whole brigade was about to descend on the flank of the II.SS Panzer-Korps.

An Hs 129B-2/R2 of 8.(Pz)/Sch.G 2 at Apostolovo in southern Russia, September 1943. (*R. C. Seeley*)

An Hs 129B-2/R2 (c/n 141586), probably of 8./Sch.G 2, being refuelled by a Luftwaffe ground crew. (*R. C. Seeley*)

A snow-camouflaged Hs 129B-2/R2 in service with IV.(Pz)/SG 9 during the winter of 1943/44. (*R. C. Seeley*)

335

Meyer radioed his base at Mikoyanovka, and within 15 minutes the first of four Staffeln, each equipped with sixteen Hs 129B-2/R2s, was reaching the target area. 4./Sch.G 2 under Hptm Matuschek attacked first, followed by 8./Sch.G 2 under Oblt Oswald, 4./Sch.G 1 under Oblt Dornemann and 8./Sch.G 1 under Lt Orth. Thus, while one Staffel was actually attacking the tanks, two more spaced at intervals were approaching, and another was returning to refuel and re-arm. The attacks were directed mainly at the Soviet tanks' thinly-protected sides and rear, and within an hour they had either fled or were on fire. During Operation Citadel 37,421 sorties were flown and 20,000 tons of bombs were dropped, the Luftwaffe claiming the destruction of 1,100 tanks and 1,300 vehicles.

On 10 October, 1943, a complete redesignation of the Luftwaffe's ground attack formations took place, the Stukageschwader being renamed Schlachtgeschwader, and the old Sch.G 1 and 2 and SKG 10 being incorporated into the newly-formed SG 4, SG 9 and SG 10. The five Hs 129 Staffeln were reorganized into IV. (Pz)/SG 9; 4. and 8./Sch.G 1 becoming 10. and 11./SG 9; 4. and 8./Sch.G 2 becoming 12. and 13./SG 9; and Pz.Jäg.Sta./JG 51 under Hptm Russer becoming 14./SG 9.

The new Gruppe, which was placed under the command of Hptm (later Maj) Bruno Meyer operated on a roving commission over the whole of the central and southern sectors of the Russian front. Ten days after the formation of IV.(Pz)/SG 9, 11.Staffel was withdrawn from operations and transferred to Udetfeld, being redesignated Erprobungskommando 26 on 20 January, 1944.

A wooden mockup of the 75 mm PaK 40 cannon installation fitted to an Hs 129B-2 (c/n 141258) at Travemünde experimental station.

336

Even the MK 103 and BK 3·7 cannon were unable to penetrate the frontal armour of the Soviet tanks and therefore the Hs 129B-2/R4 was developed. This was fitted with a 75 mm Pak 40 gun which was designed for ground-based anti-tank use. The gun was carried below the fuselage in a large streamlined fitting, tested in wooden mockup form on a standard Hs 129B-2 (c/n 141258) in May 1944 at Travemünde. The aircraft was fitted with wool tufts around the rear fuselage and tail for airflow measurements and was extensively tested. The installation was much improved over that of the Ju 88P-1, a feature being the ejection of the gun gases to the rear, thus preventing interference with the airflow from the airscrews.

Following successful trials, the Hs 129B-2/R4 was developed into the Hs 129B-3 which appeared in June 1944. This differed in having a 75 mm BK 7·5 gun (originally designated Pak 40L) which was fired electro-pneumatically instead of mechanically. The gun was about 6 m (20 ft) long, could carry 12 rounds, each weighing some 12 kg (26·4 lb), the intervals between shots being $1\frac{1}{2}$ seconds. The recoil distance of the barrel was 91 cm (35·8 inches), and this, combined with the flash, had a rather unfortunate effect on the pilot when the gun was fired. The whole was jettisonable in an emergency, thus enabling the pilot to retain control of the aircraft with one engine out of action.

The first three Hs 129B-3s (c/ns 162033, 162034 and 162035) were delivered to EKdo 26 at Tarnewitz in early August 1944 for trials. These were completed by September and about twenty-five Hs 129B-3s were built at Henschel's Schönefeld plant. The aircraft were delivered to 10. and 14.(Pz)/SG 9 in the winter of 1944–45 and operated quite successfully, even against the giant Josef Stalin tanks.

A variety of other weapons were tested in the Hs 129 including the 210 mm WGr 21 and 280 mm WGr 28 rocket tubes, the 70 mm Panzer-blitz 1 and 55 mm Panzerblitz 2 rockets and the Gero flame thrower. One of the most interesting was the SG 113A Förstersonde rocket mortar with which three Hs 129s were fitted. This advanced weapon consisted of six single-barrelled mortars in a rhomboid-shaped mounting firing vertically downwards and triggered by a photo-electric cell. The shell comprised a 77 mm soft metal jacket, which, after leaving the barrel, was discarded, leaving a hard 45 mm core. The weapon was never developed to a reliable operational state.

By the early months of 1944 it was becoming increasingly obvious that the Allies would soon attempt to liberate Europe. Several Luftwaffe units were withdrawn from Russia and Italy to strengthen German forces in Western Europe, and some Ergänzungsgruppen were temporarily made operational. Among the latter was an Hs 129 unit, probably a Staffel of III./SG 151. This formation was based at Caen-Carpiquet and appeared over the Allied beachheads during the D-Day landings. One aircraft was captured in July 1944, but its subsequent fate is not recorded.

With the improvement in Russia's fighter and anti-aircraft defences, it

One of three Hs 129B-2s (c/n 0249) fitted with the downward-firing SG 113A rocket mortar device.

Close-up of the 77 mm SG 113A rocket-launching tubes tested on the Hs 129B-2 (c/n 0249).

was realized that the Hs 129's performance was far from adequate. Pilot losses of 20 per cent were being experienced and it was proving almost impossible to keep the Schlachtgeschwader fully manned. Several advanced studies were made for coupling the armoured cockpit of the Hs 129 to other airframes. One project was to have combined the Hs 129 cockpit with a Ju 188 airframe having Jumo 222 engines, while another was to have made use of a Go 229 airframe with a 1,750 hp Jumo 213 engine installed as a pusher.

Perhaps the most interesting study was for fitting the aircraft with two 840 hp Isotta-Fraschini RC 17/40 Delta engines, the project being designated Hs 129C. The proposed production model, the Hs 129C-1, was to have been fitted with two 30 mm MK 103 cannon installed side by side, each in a remote-controlled barbette under the fuselage, but only extensive wind-tunnel tests were undertaken.

*Wartime operational units:* 4. and 8./Sch.G 1, 4. and 8./Sch.G 2, Pz.Jäg./JG 51, 5.(S)/LG 2, IV.(Pz)/SG 9, Erprobungskommando 26.

Hs 129B-1/R2: Span 14·2 m (46 ft 7 in); length 9·75 m (31 ft 11¾ in); height 3·25 m (10 ft 8 in); wing area 29 sq m (312·153 sq ft).

Empty weight 3,984 kg (8,400 lb); loaded weight 5,109 kg (11,266 lb).

Maximum speed at 3,830 m (12,750 ft) 407 km/h (253 mph); climb to 3,000 m (9,843 ft) 7 min; service ceiling 9,000 m (29,529 ft); normal range 560 km (348 miles).

The maximum sea level speeds of the Hs 129A-0 and Hs 129B-3 were 355 km/h (220 mph) and 320 km/h (199 mph) respectively.

# Henschel Hs 132

Much of Germany's military success in the early stages of the war was due to the dive-bomber, but its principal type, the Junkers Ju 87, had proved to be a failure when its operations were opposed by high-performance Allied fighters. Furthermore, precision level bombing presented problems at the higher speeds of the jet aircraft towards the end of the war because of a lack of suitable bombsights. To overcome this problem, Henschel designed the Hs 132 turbojet dive-bomber and, because of Germany's desperate military situation, this design was well received by the RLM and prototypes were ordered.

For the Hs 132 to have any chance of success in operation, it had to be capable of using very high speed to elude the defences and this involved high pull-out forces—a load factor of 12 being considered necessary in contrast to the more usual factor of about eight for piston-engined dive-bombers.

To enable pilots to withstand such high g forces, it was considered

This Henschel Hs 132 V1, prototype of a turbojet dive-bomber, was scheduled to fly in June 1945 but was captured by Soviet forces. This is the only known photograph of the Hs 132.

essential that the pilot in the Hs 132 should occupy a prone position and, in fact, prone-position tests had already been undertaken with the special twin-engined Berlin B.9 low-wing monoplane at Rechlin.

Germany's shortage of materials and skilled labour made necessary the simplest design and one using the smallest quantity of strategic materials. As part of the plan to produce a simple structure and one that was easily maintained, the turbojet was mounted above the fuselage. This was not considered to be the ideal position for the engine because of possible decreased ram effect at the intake, increased drag at high speed resulting from interference at the fuselage/engine fairing junctions, and the risk of other aerodynamic problems, but a similar layout was used in the Heinkel He 162s which were already flying and it was decided to adopt the layout for the Hs 132.

In layout the Hs 132 was a mid-wing monoplane with twin fins and rudders and retractable nosewheel undercarriage. The wing, mostly of wooden construction, tapered sharply in chord and thickness, had trailing-edge flaps and housed the main undercarriage units which were attached far out towards the tips and retracted inwards.

The fuselage was a metal structure of circular section, the pilot's position being in the extreme nose (which was extensively glazed and completely faired into the fuselage profile) whilst the nosewheel retracted backwards to be housed in the lower fuselage. The turbojet was mounted on top of the fuselage immediately above the wing, with its intake immediately aft of the cockpit and its tailpipe ending in line with the wing trailing-edge roots. The tailplane had marked dihedral and supported inclined end-plate fins and rudders. All control surfaces, including the ailerons, were fitted with trim tabs but, because steep dives to the target were not envisaged, there were no dive-brakes.

Three Hs 132 prototypes were ordered, construction began in March 1945 at Henschel's Schönefeld factory, and at the end of the war the Hs

132 V1, prototype for the A-series, was nearing completion. It was scheduled to fly in June 1945, but together with the well-advanced V2 and V3, was captured by Soviet forces and it is not known whether the type ever flew.

Three versions of the Hs 132 had been proposed: the Hs 132A to be powered by an 800 kg (1,760 lb) static thrust BMW 109-003E-2 turbojet and capable of carrying a single 500 kg (1,100 lb) SD 500 bomb semi-recessed beneath the fuselage; the Hs 132B to be powered by a 900 kg (1,980 lb) static thrust modified Junkers Jumo 109-004B and capable of carrying a 500 kg bomb load and two nose-mounted MG 151 20 mm cannon for ground attack; and the Hs 132C which would have used the 1,300 kg (2,866 lb) static thrust Heinkel-Hirth 109-011A if this had become available. The greater power of the latter would have been used to enable the aircraft to carry the normal bomb load while armed with two MG 151 20 mm and two MK 103 30 mm cannon, or a bomb of up to 1,000 kg (2,205 lb) if only the 20 mm cannon were fitted. The 1,000 kg bomb load could have comprised an SC 1000 Hermann or a PC 1000 RS Pol rocket-assisted armour-piercing bomb.

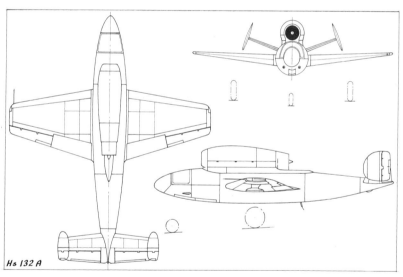

Hs 132A: Span 7·2 m (23 ft 7$\frac{1}{2}$ in); length 8·9 m (29 ft 2$\frac{1}{2}$ in); wing area 14·82 sq m (159·4 sq ft).

Loaded weight 3,400 kg (7,497 lb).

Maximum speed at 6,000 m (19,685 ft) 780 km/h (485 mph) without bomb load, 700 km/h (435 mph) with bomb load; landing speed 153 km/h (95 mph); service ceiling 10,250 m (33,625 ft); range at 4,000 m (13,125 ft) 680 km (422 miles), at 10,000 m (32,800 ft) 1,120 km (696 miles).

From left to right, the Horten Ho II, Ho III (8-250), Ho IV (8-251) and Ho V (8-252).

# Horten Tailless Aircraft

Most of the original ideas for Horten tailless aircraft stemmed from Reimar Horten, but his brother Walter also made valuable contributions because he later had good contacts within the RLM and was on good terms with Ernst Udet. In 1931, following many experiments with models, the Horten brothers started work on their first full-size aircraft at their home in Bonn. This was the Ho I sailplane, which consisted of a wing in which the pilot occupied a prone position in the centre section which had a small cockpit canopy. Wooden construction with chiefly fabric covering was used and there was a central, fixed landing skid. The wing had 24 deg leading edge sweepback, an almost straight trailing edge and slight dihedral confined mainly to the undersurfaces. The depth of the wing centre section was sufficient without a bulge or gondola to accommodate the pilot. As with all Horten aircraft, the Ho I had no vertical or tail surfaces. Elevons were used for pitch and roll control and yaw control was obtained from brake flaps above and below the leading edges near the wingtips. (These brake flaps have also been called drag rudders and, in action, were similar to air-brakes.) Although it logged about seven flying hours and won a prize at the 1934 Rhön sailplane competitions, the Ho I did not satisfy the Hortens, who burned it in 1934.

In the same year, the Hortens built another sailplane, the Ho II, which incorporated their previous experience. Using wood and fabric construction, the Ho II consisted of a wing with the pilot accommodated in a prone position in the centre section with a canopy above him. The principal new

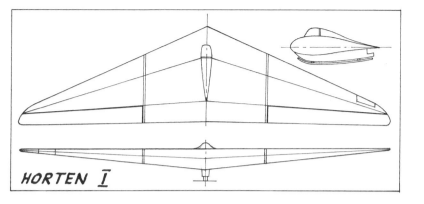

HORTEN I

features were the introduction of sweepback on the wing trailing edges (as well as the leading edges), two sets of elevon controls, and a tandem wheel undercarriage with retractable nosewheel and faired rear wheel. Wingtip brake flaps were again fitted for yaw control, and dihedral was mainly confined to the undersurfaces of the wing. Four examples of the Ho II were built, all as sailplanes but, in 1935, the first example was fitted with a Hirth 80 hp engine mounted in the wing to drive a pusher propeller via an extension shaft. This powered version was tested by Hanna Reitsch at Darmstadt airfield on 12 November, 1938, at the request of Ernst Udet. These tests indicated that, although the flying qualities were generally good, much further development was needed although some of the faults were caused by improvisations due to lack of funds. Turns were impossible with the elevons alone and use of the brake flaps for this purpose produced very sudden responses. Due to the large amount of wing wash-out, it was almost impossible to spin the aircraft and it could not be side-slipped.

Following a period of military training, the Hortens were able to start work on a more elaborate aircraft in 1938. Since some official backing was now available, they moved to better facilities at Tempelhof Airport, Berlin,

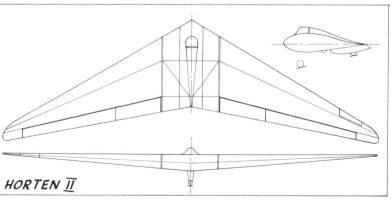

HORTEN II

343

A Horten Ho III (8-250) sailplane which was externally similar to the Ho II but had a greater span and a third pair of trailing-edge control surfaces. (*Smithsonian Institution*)

where they constructed the Ho III sailplane, designated 8-250 by the RLM. The Ho III was externally generally similar to the Ho II but had increased span and aspect ratio, and a third pair of control surfaces were added to the wing trailing edge at the innermost position to act as landing flaps. A departure from all-wood construction was made by building the

344

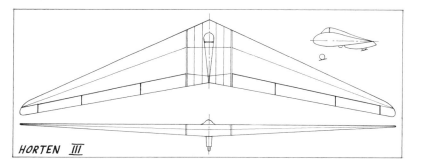

HORTEN III

wing centre-section from welded steel tubes and the tandem wheel under-carriage was made fully retractable. A second aircraft, the Ho III B, was built by the Peschke-Flugzeugbau in Berlin. Various modifications were made to these two experimental aircraft, including the fitting of dive-brakes above and below the centre section at the leading edges, automatic flaps to limit diving speed, and wingtips which rotated for lateral control. Two other examples, the Ho III C and D, were also built, though by whom is uncertain. The Ho III C was fitted with a small auxiliary wing forward of the main wing for low-speed control. Of the four examples, only the Ho III D was fitted with an engine (type unknown); during gliding flight the propeller blades folded to reduce drag.

Horten's next sailplane, the Ho IV (8-251), was designed principally to investigate the effects of high aspect ratio and although the span remained the same as that of the Ho III, the aspect ratio was, at 21·16 to 1, twice as great. Sweepback was again employed on both leading and trailing edges but pronounced dihedral was given to the wing, and its thin section neces-sitated a bulged cockpit section. In the cockpit, the pilot occupied a curious half-kneeling position. Construction was of wood and fabric except for the outer wing panels which were so thin that metal had to be used, and there was a retractable landing skid. The wing again had three sets of differential elevons and wingtip brake flaps but the dive-brakes were moved to a more central position along each wing. The first Ho IV was built at Königsberg-Neuhaus in 1941 and a development of it, the Ho IV B with a laminar-flow wing incorporating plastic leading edges, was built at Hersfeld near Kassel.

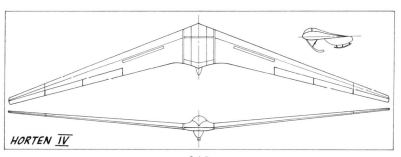

HORTEN IV

345

This closer view of the Horten Ho IV (8-251) effectively illustrates the extremely high aspect ratio that was being investigated. The three differential elevons on the port wing can be clearly seen. (*Smithsonian Institution*)

Unfortunately, the Ho IV B suffered from bad stalling characteristics and eventually crashed after going into a spin.

Although the next design, the Ho V (8-252), was, like the previous aircraft, a flying wing, it differed in being designed from the outset as a powered research machine. Its wing had marked sweepback on the outer panels but the centre section had greatly reduced sweep on the leading edge and a straight, unswept trailing edge. The centre section had a welded steel

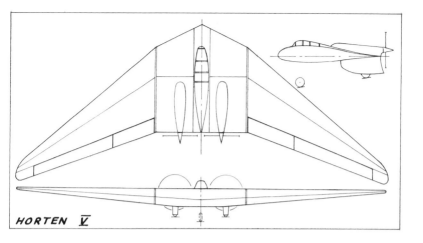

HORTEN V

tube structure and carried two 80 hp Hirth HM 60R four-cylinder inline
air-cooled engines which drove handed pusher propellers through extension shafts. A non-retractable tricycle undercarriage was fitted and there
were centre-section landing flaps. The Ho V had a completely new control
system to the previous Horten flying wings. In order to eliminate wing
twisting and consequent yaw, its control surfaces were in two sections on
each side. They acted differentially as elevons, the two outer sections
producing nose-up pitch and the inner sections nose-down pitch. Banking
was achieved by use of an outer section on one side and an inner section on
the opposite side.

As originally built, at Ostheim between 1936 and 1938, the Ho V
had two side-by-side seats but, in 1942, the aircraft was converted to a
single-seater by Peschke-Flugzeugbau at Minden. The Ho V was test-
flown at Göttingen in 1943. With the object of offering rapid, light construction, a second Ho V was built by an entirely new method in which
extensive use was made of bonded plastic materials. Plastic sheet was
used for wing covering and rib webs, plastic laminate for main spar
booms and stringers, and wood for rib booms. On its maiden flight, this
second Ho V was badly damaged in a rough landing caused by a high
wind.

In an endeavour to obtain further funds, the Horten brothers proposed a
development of the Ho V as a glider tug with the advantage that the towing
line would be close to the tug's centre of gravity, but the proposal was not
taken up.

As an experiment in flying-wing planforms, the single-seat glider known
as the Horten Parabola was built at Aegidienberg near Koblenz. The
planform of this glider was approximately quarter-moon shaped, the parabolic leading edges of the wing curving more acutely to join the parabolic
trailing edges at the tips. At the centre section the wing was relatively thick
and the outer panels tapered to the tips without dihedral. Two sets of

347

The only prototype of the Horten experimental parabolic glider was destroyed en route to the test field and never flew.

elevons were fitted for control. The tandem wheel undercarriage had a rearward-retracting nosewheel and a fixed rearwheel in a ventral fairing. Only one example of this glider was built but it was not flown because it was destroyed by fire while being transported to the test aerodrome. However, this digression in parabolic flying-wing planforms was not followed up by the Hortens.

Following up the high aspect ratio investigations begun with the Ho IV (8-251), the Ho VI (8-253) was built with similar features and the same control layout but with the span increased (to give a very high aspect ratio of 32·4 to 1) and with dihedral decreased. The resulting wing proved to be structurally poor and was too flexible for practical ground handling.

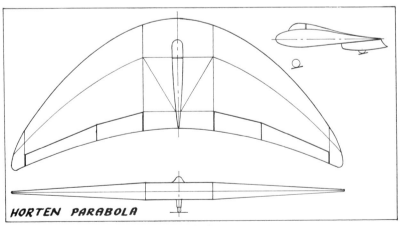

HORTEN PARABOLA

348

Nevertheless, the sole Ho VI, built at Aegidienberg, was flown before being scrapped but details of its flight history are lacking.

A flying wing generally similar to the Ho V (8-252) was the Ho VII (8-227). A more powerful aircraft, however, the Ho VII was fitted with two 240 hp Argus As 10C engines and had the prime purpose of familiarizing pilots with tailless aircraft characteristics. An innovation in the design was the drag bars which moved out, spanwise, from either wingtip for directional control but these proved very unsatisfactory in flight. Although twenty of these aircraft were to have been built by Peschke-Flugzeugbau, only one was completed and one other nearly completed. The sole Ho VII completed is believed to have been test-flown at Oranienburg where it is known to have been in March 1945. In order to jettison the propellers in an emergency, explosive hubs were being designed for the Ho VII.

The sole example of the Horten Ho VII (8-227), which flew in March 1945. Purpose of the type was to familiarize pilots with the characteristics of powered tailless aircraft. (*F. Selinger*)

By far the largest of the Horten flying-wing designs was the Ho VIII. This was designed as a commercial aircraft with accommodation for about 60 passengers but, subject to satisfactory test results, would doubtless have been used as a military transport. There was also a proposal to suspend a flying wind tunnel, 3 m (9·84 ft) long, beneath the wing centre section. The Ho VIII was under construction by the Luftwaffe Sonderkommando 9 at Göttingen, this unit having been set up early in the war by the Hortens specifically to develop tailless aircraft. Originally the span of the Ho VIII was to have been about 80 m (262·5 ft) but this had to be restricted to 48 m (157 ft $5\frac{3}{4}$ in) because that was the largest that could be accommodated at Göttingen. The centre section of the wing had a tubular-steel structure but the outer panels were of wooden construction built around main and auxiliary spars. Constant sweepback was employed on the wing leading edges but the sweepback on the trailing edges gave way to a straight centre trailing edge and there were large, semi-circular wing tips. Along the straight section of the wing trailing edge were six pusher propellers which were driven by extension shafts from six BMW 600 hp engines mounted inside the wing. Power operation was planned for the control surfaces which comprised two sets of elevons and wingtip drag bars. All payload was to be carried within the wing centre section, the forward part of which had glazed panels, but there was no cabin pressurization. A raised canopy was set as far forward as possible along the top of the wing to give the pilot an acceptable view. The undercarriage was of the tricycle type, the nosewheel being self-centring and the multiple mainwheels bogie-mounted.

It was anticipated that the Ho VIII would have had a range of about 6,000 km (3,725 miles) at a cruising speed of between 300 and 350 km/h (186 and 217 mph) at an altitude of between 1,000 and 2,000 m (3,280 and 6,560 ft). However, although the prototype was expected to fly in about November 1945, it was not completed by the end of the war. After the war, the concept of this aircraft was re-thought when Reimar Horten designed the I.A.38 tailless cargo aircraft for Argentina's Instituto Aerotecnico. The I.A.38 was only about two-thirds of the size of the Ho VIII and differed chiefly in having four 450 hp engines and a large cargo container suspended beneath the wing centre section. Although the prototype was built in 1958, its development was plagued by engine cooling troubles and prevented by political influences.

To return to Horten wartime work, we come next to the Ho IX (later 8-229) tailless fighter. In designing this, the first Horten aircraft intended specifically for combat, the design team of Sonderkommando 9 had a fund of tailless aircraft data to draw upon. Design work began in 1942 and, in particular, the Ho V superficially resembled the Ho IX although the latter, with its twin turbojets, was of very advanced concept.

As with previous types, Ho IX construction consisted of a welded steel tube centre section structure and a wooden structure for the outer panels, plywood covering being used extensively. The wing leading edges were sweptback some 32 deg and there were rounded tips. As the sweptback trailing edges approached the centre, they were curved aft to form a large, pointed fairing trailing from the centre section. The entire trailing edge was occupied by three control surfaces at each side. Outer and centre surfaces gave lateral and longitudinal control and the inner surfaces acted as landing flaps. For directional control, one large and one small brake flap was provided above and below each wingtip. A spring link system ensured that the larger brake flaps did not operate until the smaller flaps had fully extended, thus affording much smoother control than with the previous single brake flap systems. The pilot's cockpit was set as far forward as possible to provide an adequate view when landing and was equipped with a spring-operated ejection seat and a control column which could be raised vertically for increased leverage at high speeds. The undercarriage consisted of inwards-retracting mainwheels and a rearwards-retracting nose-wheel.

With all the principal items of equipment mounted in the wing centre section, a very compact design had to be made, with the result that, when the two BMW 109-003A-1 turbojets proved to have larger diameters than anticipated, they could not be installed through the spars of the Ho IX V1 which had almost been completed at Göttingen. This aircraft was there-fore completed as a glider with non-retractable nosewheel and test flown at Oranienburg in the summer of 1944. Because of their greater avail-ability, two Junkers 109-004B-1 turbojets (which had even larger diameters) were then fitted to the redesigned Ho IX V2, also constructed at Göttingen. These engines, each rated at 900 kg (1,980 lb) static thrust, were installed close to the sides of the cockpit and had very short air intakes. The hot gases from the engines were ejected above the upper sur-face of the wing which was protected by steel plates separated from the wing surface by a small air space. Five fuel tanks were distributed inside each outer wing panel, self-sealing tanks being planned for operational aircraft.

Thus equipped, the Ho IX V2 was flown successfully from Oranien-burg but was destroyed in an enforced single-engine landing after logging only a few hours. Nevertheless, it had flown at speeds up to 800 km/h (597 mph) and the general promise of the type was such that the RLM instructed Gothaer Waggonfabrik to investigate the design, with a view to adapting it for mass production and producing various Service test aircraft, and issued the designation Go 229. The third prototype was, therefore, designated Go 229 V3 and built at the Gotha facility at Fried-richsrode under somewhat cramped conditions. This aircraft was fitted with more-powerful Junkers 109-004C turbojets of 1,000 kg (2,205 lb) static thrust and had been completed by the time the workshops were captured by the VIII Corps of the US Third Army. Under construction at the same workshops were the two-seat Go 229 V4 and V5, each of which had an extended, pointed nose, and were intended as test aircraft for the night fighter rôle. Work was also just beginning on the Go 229 V6 and V7 which were intended as an armament trials aircraft and two-seat trainer respectively. No time was left to begin production of the twenty Go 229 A-0 fighter-bomber aircraft (on order for Luftwaffe evaluation), each of which was to be fitted with four MK 103 30 mm cannon and carry a 1,000 kg (2,205 lb) bomb load.

While the Ho IX (Go 229) was a twin-jet flying wing, the possibility of more powerful turbojets becoming available, such as the Heinkel-Hirth 109-011A, made possible the building of single-engined jet fighters with adequate performance. The Göttingen team therefore made the decision to design a Horten jet fighter powered by a single 109-011A turbojet of 1,300 kg (2,866 lb) static thrust and work started in the autumn of 1944. In order to make preliminary investigations, a tailless aircraft was designed with a configuration similar to the Ho III and with the wingtips

The Gotha Go 229 V3, developed from the Horten Ho IX, under construction at a Gotha factory at Friedrichsrode. This work was part of the programme to produce a tailless twin-jet fighter-bomber. Behind the V3 prototype can be seen the tubular centre section of another prototype under construction. The abandoned state of the workshop is as found by the VIII Corps of the US Third Army on 14 April, 1945. (*US Army*)

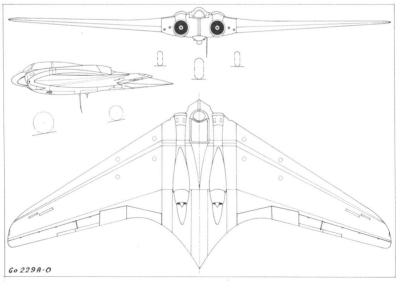

Go 229A-O

352

rotating on skew hinges for lateral control. Although this control method had never met with much success, the Hortens had faith and persisted with it. The prototype of this aircraft was under construction at Hersfeld and was to be used for low-speed flight trials powered by a single 240 hp Argus As 10C piston engine with a pusher propeller. Following this, the actual Ho X was to have a deep, smoothly-faired structure housing the pilot's cockpit and rear-mounted turbojet. Air intakes for the engine were on either side just aft of the cockpit and the planned armament was one 30 mm MK 108 plus two MG 151/20 cannon.

Before the war ended, a number of other Horten flying-wing aircraft were either projected or designed but only two, which were under construction, will be mentioned. First, there was the Ho XI which was being built at Hersfeld when the war ended. Little is known of this aircraft other than that it was a single-seat tailless glider of about 8 m (26 ft 3 in) span which was designed to be fully aerobatic. Second, there was the Ho XII under construction at Kirtof near Kassel. The Ho XII was intended as a private aircraft but, since it was designed at Göttingen, had two side-by-side seats, and RLM interest backing it, it would undoubtedly have been used for training pilots in tailless aircraft flying techniques. The layout was similar to the Ho III but a laminar-flow wing section was used and a 50 hp DKW piston engine drove a pusher propeller.

Horten Ho I: Span 23 m (40 ft 9⅝ in); wing area 21 sq m (226 sq ft); aspect ratio 7·27; empty weight 120 kg (264 lb); sinking speed 0·85 m/sec (2·8 ft/sec).

Horten Ho II (unpowered): Span 16·5 m (54 ft 1⅝ in); wing area 32 sq m (334·3 sq ft); aspect ratio 8·48; empty weight 275 kg (605 lb); loaded weight 375 kg (825 lb); sinking speed 0·80 m/sec (2·62 ft/sec).

Horten Ho III (8-250. Sailplane version): Span 20 m (65 ft 7⅜ in); wing area 37·5 sq m (403·5 sq ft); aspect ratio 10·66; empty weight 250 kg (550 lb); sinking speed 0·65 m/sec (2·13 ft/sec).

Horten Ho IV (8-251): Span 20 m (65 ft 7⅜ in); wing area 18·9 sq m (203·4 sq ft); aspect ratio 21·16; empty weight 200 kg (441 lb); sinking speed 0·54 m/sec (1·77 ft/sec).

Horten Ho V (8-252). Data for first example built: Span 16 m (52 ft 5⅞ in); wing area 42 sq m (452 sq ft); aspect ratio 6·1; empty weight 650 kg (1,433 lb); loaded weight 1,100 kg (2,426 lb); maximum speed 215 km/h (134 mph); landing speed 75 km/h (47 mph).

Horten Parabola: Span 12 m (39 ft 4½ in); wing area 33 sq m (355 sq ft); aspect ratio 4·37; empty weight 90 kg (198 lb); sinking speed 0·65 m/sec (2·13 ft/sec).

Horten Ho VI (8-253): Span 24 m (78 ft 8⅞ in); wing area 17·8 sq m (191·5 sq ft); aspect ratio 32·4; empty weight 250 kg (550 lb).

Horten Ho VII (8-227): Span 15·24 m (50 ft); wing area 43·95 sq m (473 sq ft); aspect ratio 5·3; loaded weight 3,200 kg (7,056 lb); maximum speed 340 km/h (211 mph) at sea level.

Gotha Go 229A-0 (from Ho IX): Span 16·78 m (55 ft 0$\frac{5}{8}$ in); length 7·47 m (24 ft 6$\frac{1}{8}$ in); wing area 51·5 sq m (554 sq ft); loaded weight 8,500 kg (18,743 lb); maximum speed 1,000 km/h (621 mph) at 6,100 m (20,000 ft); landing speed 130 km/h (81 mph).

Horten Ho X: Span 14 m (45 ft 11$\frac{1}{8}$ in); length 7·2 m (23 ft 7$\frac{1}{2}$ in); wing area 35 sq m (376·6 sq ft); loaded weight 6,000 kg (13,230 lb); maximum speed 1,100 km/h (683 mph) at 6,000 m (19,680 ft) or Mach 0·87; service ceiling 15,000 m (49,280 ft); range 1,500 km (932 miles).

In the preceding descriptions it will be noted that certain aircraft were issued with RLM '8' numbers. However, most of these RLM numbers were issued twice, in the following manner:

8-250—Ho III and Blohm und Voss Bv 250 project.
8-252—Ho V and Junkers Ju 252 transport aircraft.
8-253—Ho VI and Fieseler Fi 253 sports aircraft.
8-227—Ho VII and scale-model version of Blohm und Voss Bv 238.

As far as is known, 8-251 was only issued for the Ho IV and 8-229 for the Ho IX. Some of the early Horten aircraft described do not strictly come within the scope of this book but have been included since they were an essential part of a continued development theme.

# Junkers-W 33 and W 34

In 1926 Junkers produced developed versions of their F 13 single-engined four-passenger transport which had such an impact on German aviation and air transport in many parts of the world. The new aircraft, the W 33 and W 34, were primarily intended for cargo carrying, but had provision for six passengers in their airline versions. Both types were cantilever low-wing monoplanes with the familiar Junkers corrugated metal skin. The pilot was seated in an open cockpit behind the single engine, but the passenger or cargo compartment was fully enclosed. The two types differed solely in that the W 33 was normally powered by an inline liquid-cooled engine and the W 34 by an air-cooled radial.

The first prototype for the W 33, D-921 (c/n 794), was powered by a 280 hp Junkers-L 5 engine and could have either float or land under-carriage. This was followed in 1927 by the first production example, D-1048 (c/n 2500), and subsequent variants included the W 33b, W 33c, W 33d, W 33f, and W 33h, the majority being powered by the 280/310 hp Junkers-L 5 unit.

The first Junkers-W 34 was, like the prototype W 33, converted from an F 13, and was powered by a 420 hp Gnome/Rhône Jupiter VI radial. The

A Luftwaffe Junkers-W 34hi. (*J. Zazvonil*)

production series began with D-1119 (c/n 2600) and included variants such as the W 34b, W 34c, W 34d, W 34f, W 34g, and W 34h, powered by engines such as the Jupiter VI, Armstrong Siddeley Panther, Bristol Mercury, Siemens Sh 20 and Pratt & Whitney Hornet.

Both types of aircraft saw service with a large number of airlines and set up several world records. Production ceased in 1934, but both types, particularly the W 34, remained in largescale service with the Luftwaffe for both communications and training duties until the end of the Second World War. The main variants in Luftwaffe service were the W 34hau powered by a 650 hp Bramo 322 in a long-chord cowling driving a four-blade airscrew, and the W 34hi powered by a 660 hp BMW 132 driving a two-blade airscrew.

In addition to being used by KGrzbV 4 (later redesignated Verbindungsgruppe) the W 34 also saw service with several of the Fliegerführer-Transportstaffeln. But it was perhaps as a trainer that the

The W 34hi provides an interesting contrast with the later Ju 52/3m seen in the background right. (*H. Redemann*)

355

W 34 was most frequently seen on Luftwaffe airfields. Units known to have operated W 34s included FFS B 1 at Schweinfurt, FFS A/B 2 at Luxeuil, FFS C 3 at Alt-Lönnewitz, FFS A/B 5 at Quakenbrück, FFS A/B 11 at Schönewalde, FFS A/B 14 at Klagenfurt, FFS A 32 at Pardubitz and BFS 33 at Prague-Ruzyne.

W 34hi landplane: Span 17·75 m (58 ft 2¾ in); length 10·27 m (33 ft 8¼ in); height 3·53 m (11 ft 7 in); wing area 43 sq m (462·84 sq ft).
Empty weight 1,700 kg (3,748 lb); loaded weight 3,200 kg (7,056 lb).
Maximum speed 265 km/h (165 mph); cruising speed 233 km/h (145 mph); landing speed 116 km/h (72 mph); climb to 1,000 m (3,280 ft) 3·2 min; service ceiling 6,300 m (20,670 ft); normal range 900 km (559 miles).

The second Junkers-G 38, D-2500 (c/n 3302), during its service with Lufthansa. (*Lufthansa*)

# Junkers-G 38

One of the most striking designs produced by the pre-war German aircraft industry was the Junkers-G 38. Embodying many of the ideas for a flying wing originally proposed by Prof Junkers in 1909, the aircraft was powered by four engines, two 800 hp Junkers-L 88 twelve-cylinder and two 400 hp L 8a six-cylinder liquid-cooled units buried in the wings. The G 38 was a cantilever monoplane with a huge shoulder-mounted wing which was about 1·7 m (5 ft 7 in) thick. The biplane tail surfaces were mounted above the comparatively short fuselage, with three fins and rudders. Originally the huge tandem-wheel undercarriage was partly enclosed by spats, but these were removed at an early stage. Typical Junkers all-metal construction was used with corrugated duralumin skin.

The prototype G 38, D-2000 (c/n 3301), made its first flight on 6 November, 1929. A second aircraft was delivered to Lufthansa on 1 September, 1931, being designated G 38b and registered D-2500 (c/n 3302). The aircraft differed from the first G 38 in having a much deeper fuselage with a two-deck cabin. Accommodation was provided for 34 passengers in four compartments. The first aircraft was later modified to the same standard, but, after being re-registered D-AZUR, crashed at Dessau in 1936 and was written-off.

The second machine originally had a similar engine arrangement to that of the first, but was later fitted with four 650/800 hp Junkers-L 88a engines under the designation G 38ce. In 1935, the aircraft was re-engined with four 750 hp Junkers Jumo 204 Diesel engines, and then bore the registration D-APIS.

In September 1939 the aircraft was impressed by the Luftwaffe and operated by KGrzbV 172 as GF-GG during the invasion of Norway when it transported a military band to Oslo-Fornebu. Although carrying military markings, the machine still carried Lufthansa's name and its own name *Generalfeldmarschall von Hindenburg*. The aircraft was finally destroyed on 17 May, 1941, during an RAF bombing attack on Athens-Tatoi airfield.

G 38ce: (Jumo 204 engines): Span 44 m (144 ft 4¼ in); length 23·2 m (76 ft 1¼ in); wing area 300 sq m (3,229·17 sq ft).
Empty weight 14,880 kg (32,805 lb); loaded weight 24,000 kg (52,911 lb).
Cruising speed 208 km/h (127 mph); landing speed 78 km/h (48 mph); service ceiling 3,700 m (12,139 ft).

# Junkers-Ju 52/3m

The Junkers-Ju 52/3m is probably rivalled only by the Douglas DC-3 for the honour of being the most famous transport aircraft of all time. It was conceived in 1930 as the last of a long line of corrugated metal skinned aircraft which began with the construction of the Junkers-J 4 of 1917. Used by a large number of the world's airlines and air forces, the Ju 52 remained in service for nearly 40 years. Its best known exploits were those as a transport aircraft with the Luftwaffe, where it was known universally as 'Tante Ju' (Auntie Junkers). Names such as Norway, Crete, Demyansk, Stalingrad, the Kuban Peninsula—all figured prominently in

The Junkers-Ju 52/3m was delivered in large numbers to Lufthansa. This aircraft (c/n 6650) awaits passenger embarkation.

357

the history of this machine which formed the backbone of the German military air transport force.

The first Junkers all-metal aircraft was the J 1 which was completed in 1915 under the direction of Professor Hugo Junkers. This aircraft was developed via the Junkers D I monoplane fighter into the F 13 four-passenger transport which played a most important part in the development of the world's airlines, and had corrugated duralumin load-bearing skin which gave great strength for little weight penalty. The prototype Junkers-F 13, which flew on 25 June, 1919, was one of the most advanced aircraft of its time.

The basic design of the Junkers-F 13 was continuously developed between the two world wars, resulting in the G 23/24, the G 31, the W 33, the W 34, and, in 1930, in the Junkers-Ju 52.

The Ju 52 was a low-wing cantilever monoplane with a fixed undercarriage and tailskid, powered in its original form by a single engine in the nose. Construction of the aircraft followed standard Junkers practice, metal being used throughout with corrugated duralumin sheet covering. The Ju 52 was fitted with the Junkers double-wing, a full-span auxiliary flying surface hinged to the wing trailing edge, which provided the aircraft with both ailerons and flaps.

Designed primarily as a transport aircraft, the Ju 52 had a 16·7 cu m (590 cu ft) capacity cargo hold, plus small auxiliary compartments aft of the main cabin and below the floor. Access to the freight compartment was gained via a large horizontally divided door, the lower half acting as a platform when open. A number of smaller doors gave access to the main and underfloor compartments. When used as an airliner, the Ju 52 could carry 15–17 passengers.

The first Ju 52 flew on 13 October, 1930, powered by a single 800 hp Junkers L 88 twelve-cylinder liquid-cooled engine. A large variety of engines were fitted to Ju 52s including the 600/755 hp BMW VIIau, the 780 hp BMW IXu and the 825 hp Rolls-Royce Buzzard twelve-cylinder liquid-cooled units and the 700/750 hp Armstrong Siddeley Leopard air-cooled radial.

Five single-engined Ju 52s have been identified; D-1974 (c/n 4001), D-2133 (c/n 4002 or 4003), D-2317 (c/n 4004), D-2356 (c/n 4005) and CF-ARM (c/n 4006). The last of these was delivered to Canadian Airways in 1931, operating with land, float and ski undercarriages. D-2133 and D-2317 also flew with twin floats.

Development of the basic Ju 52 design led Dipl Ing Ernst Zindel to produce a three-engined version, the Ju 52/3m. Essentially similar to the single-engined variant, the Ju 52/3m had an enlarged vertical fin and two engines in the wings. The prototype, c/n 4007, flew in April 1932 powered by three licence-built 525 hp Pratt & Whitney Hornet nine-cylinder radials. The next two aircraft, c/ns 4008 and 4009, were delivered to Lloyd Aereo Boliviano and named *Juan del Valle* and *Huanuni* respectively. In all, seven aircraft were delivered to the Bolivian company, being

358

used as airliners and as military transports during the dispute with Paraguay over the Gran Chaco during 1932–35.

The first aircraft to be delivered to Deutsche Lufthansa were D-2201 (c/n 4013) and D-2202 (c/n 4015) which were named *Boelcke* and *Richthofen* after famous fighter pilots of the First World War. Eventually no less than 230 Ju 52/3ms were registered in the name of Lufthansa, the aircraft becoming one of the most reliable types in the world. DLH themselves stated that forced landings were reduced from 7 per million km (621,370 miles) to 1·5 after the introduction of the machine. The aircraft entered service on the Berlin–London and Berlin–Rome routes in 1932 and eventually formed 85 per cent of the airline's fleet.

One of the seven Ju 52/3ms delivered to the Swedish airline, AB Aerotransport.

By no means all passenger-carrying Ju 52/3ms were delivered to Lufthansa. A Hispano-Suiza powered Ju 52/3mbe, CV-FAI (c/n 4016), was delivered to Prince Bibesco of Rumania, and other early aircraft were operated by the airlines of Finland, Sweden, and Brazil. Most machines were powered by three 525 hp BMW 132A-3 engines, but many other powerplants were installed. The Ju 52/3mho was powered by three 700 hp Junkers Jumo 205 Diesel engines, and others had Pratt & Whitney Hornet and Wasp radials and at least one had Bristol Pegasus engines.

Eventually, the Ju 52/3m was used by the airlines of Argentina, Australia, Belgium, Bolivia, Brazil, China, Colombia, Czechoslovakia, Denmark, Equador, Estonia, Finland, France, Great Britain, Greece, Hungary, Italy, Lebanon, Mozambique, Norway, Peru, Poland, Portugal, Rumania, South Africa, Spain, Sweden, and Uruguay. Many aircraft were fitted with floats, the first Ju 52/3m floatplanes being Aero O/Y's OH-ALK *Sampo* (c/n 4014) and AB Aerotransport's SE-ADR *Södermanland* (c/n 4017). Perhaps the most interesting German civil aircraft was D-ALYL *XI. Olympiade* (c/n 5180) used to fly the Olympic Torch from Greece to Berlin for the 1936 Olympic Games.

The Ju 52/3m D-ALYL (c/n 5180) which carried the Olympic torch from Athens to Germany in 1936.

In 1934 a military version of the Ju 52/3m was produced for use by the still secret Luftwaffe. Designated Ju 52/3mg3e, the aircraft was designed as a heavy bomber with a crew of four and armed with two MG 15 machine-guns. One gun was mounted in the dorsal position, the other being carried in a retractable 'dustbin' suspended beneath the fuselage. Four hundred and fifty Ju 52/3ms were delivered to the Luftwaffe during 1934–35, the type entering service with KG 152 Hindenburg.

In October 1937, IV./KG 152 was redesignated KGrzbV 1, the group eventually being expanded to Geschwader strength. KGrzbV was an abbreviation of the term Kampfgruppe zur besonderen Verwendung (bomber group on special operations), a designation applied to all early German air transport units. The main reason for adopting this designation and not the term Transportgruppe was that it was intended that all such formations could double as bomber units should an emergency arise. It was not until May 1943 that the term was finally abandoned.

Little use of the aircraft as a bomber was made by the Luftwaffe, the Kampfgeschwader quickly switching to the Ju 86, Dornier Do 17 and Heinkel He 111. On 18 July, 1936, civil war began in Spain, and the

Troops loading military stores into a Ju 52/3mg3e transport during the Polish campaign.

360

warring factions received immediate help from various foreign countries. Germany, who supported the Nationalist movement, quickly dispatched twenty Ju 52/3ms and six Heinkel He 51 fighters to Spain, and in November 1936 the Condor Legion was formed under Gen Hugo Sperrle.

In Spanish service, the Ju 52/3m was first used to ferry 10,000 Moorish troops from Morocco to Spain, and the aircraft then formed the equipment of the three-squadron-strong Kampfgruppe 88. Initial operations by the group included the bombing of the Republican-held Mediterranean ports and the support of the land battle around Madrid in November 1936. By the summer of 1937, the Ju 52/3mg3e bomber had been replaced in Condor Legion by the new Do 17E-1 and He 111B-2 which proved more effective fighting machines.

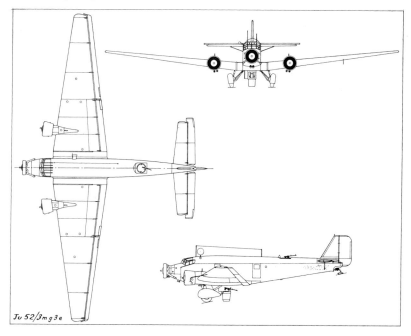

Ju 52/3mg3e

A number of Ju 52/3ms were delivered to the Spanish Nationalist Air Force, the first unit to receive the aircraft being Escuadra B. The Spanish pilots initially received their training from German aircrews at Seville, and the Ju 52/3m proved an immediate success. It was given the affectionate nickname Pava (turkey) and first went into action in September 1936. During the following months, wherever Nationalist troops were engaged, the Ju 52/3m acted in support, although by early 1937 Republican fighters were becoming a serious menace. One particular Ju 52 was attacked by 24 Soviet-built I-15 biplane fighters before being shot down.

The Ju 52/3m was delivered to many other Spanish units including Escuadra 4-E-22, Grupo 1-G-22 and Grupo 2-G-22 and, during the push to the Mediterranean, the bitter fighting around the Ebro (July to December 1938) and the victorious campaign in Catalonia, the Ju 52/3m was rarely molested by Republican fighters. The last operational sortie was made on 26 March, 1939, when Ju 52/3 ms bombed targets at Belmez.

The Nationalist Ju 52/3ms had operated throughout the Spanish Civil War and their activities can be considered to have played a major part in Franco's ultimate success. In 13,000 hours of operations, they had flown 5,400 missions and dropped over 6,000 tons of bombs. Eight aircraft were lost, five in the air and three on the ground. In April 1939 the remaining twenty-five Ju 52/3ms were mustered at Leon and subsequently used for many years as transports for the Spanish Air Force.

The port undercarriage leg of this Ju 52/3mg4e collapsed after a heavy landing at Prague, 1945. (*J. Zazvonil*)

Following the demise of the Ju 52/3m as a bomber, the Luftwaffe ordered the development of a specialist variant with provision for carrying heavier loads. Designated Ju 52/3mg4e, this version appeared in 1935 and differed from the g3e in having a tailwheel in place of a skid. The Ju 52/3mg5e was similar but had the more powerful BMW 132T-2 engines which developed 830 hp for take-off. It had provision for wheel, float and ski undercarriages to be readily interchanged, and had de-icing equipment.

During the Austrian Anschluss of March 1938, the Ju 52/3m played a prominent part in the Luftwaffe's show of strength, KGrzbV 1 being based at Fürstenwalde (later moving to Burg bei Magdeburg) and KGrzbV 2 at Brandenburg-Briest. Each group comprised a staff flight of five aircraft and four squadrons, each comprising an establishment of twelve Ju 52/3ms. The German air transport Gruppe differed from other formations of its size in that it always contained four Staffeln, this practice not being followed by other units until late in the war.

It is some indication of the numbers of Ju 52/3ms in Luftwaffe service

362

that, when Germany invaded Poland on 1 September, 1939, it possessed 552 freight-carrying aircraft of which no less than 547 were Ju 52/3ms.

The first major operation in which German air transport units were involved was Operation Weserübung—the invasion of Norway and Denmark. No less than 573 Junkers-Ju 52/3ms were gathered together from the transport Gruppen including I., II., III. and IV./KGrzbV 1, KGrzbV 101, 102, 103, 104, 105, 106 and 107. The meticulously planned operations were placed under the control of Oberstlt Carl-August Baron von Gablenz. Each Gruppe was given a specific task which it had to undertake with the utmost precision.

One of the most important tasks, the capture of Oslo's Fornebu Airport was allocated to the paratroops of 1./FJR 1 embarked in the Ju 52/3ms of 5. and 6./KGrzbV 1. After the paratroops had captured the airport, it was proposed that Ju 52/3ms from KGrzbV 103 would land and disembark the troops of II./IR 324 who would consolidate the German hold on the area. In the event, bad weather prevented the dropping of the paratroops, and KGrzbV 103 was forced to make a landing on Fornebu Airport, which was still in Norwegian hands. By late morning, the Germans had captured the airport, allowing further landings to be made by KGrzbV 102 and KGrzbV 107.

The troops embarked in 8./KGrzbV 1's Ju 52/3ms were given the task of capturing the Vordingborg bridge which they successfully accomplished within minutes of landing. Important landings were made at Aalborg by Ju 52/3ms and paratroops were dropped on Stavanger-Sola Airport by the aircraft. During the Norwegian campaign a total of 3,018 sorties were flown, 1,830 with troops and 1,188 with supplies of various kinds. A total of 29,289 men, 2,376 tons of supplies, and 1,178,000 litres (259,300 Imp gal) of aviation fuel were landed by the Ju 52/3ms taking part in the operation. Losses amounted to 150 aircraft.

A Ju 52/3mg5e of an unidentified Luftwaffe unit. (*H. Redemann*)

Several further developments of the Ju 52/3m were beginning to enter service at this time. The Ju 52/3mg6e was a specialized military transport similar to the g5e, but fitted with improved radio equipment. Several aircraft were fitted with a large-diameter duralumin hoop, which, when energized by a small additional motor, was used for exploding magnetic mines, and aircraft carrying this device were used by the Minensuchgruppe based variously at Cognac, La Leu and Biarritz.

The Ju 52/3mg7e was one of the major production variants, differing from the g6e in having an automatic pilot, wider cabin doors and accommodation for 18 fully-equipped troops or 12 stretcher cases. Defensive armament varied, a typical combination being a 7·9 mm MG machine-gun in the dorsal position and two guns of similar type firing through the side windows.

The Ju 52/3mg8e was similar to the Ju 52/3mg7e but had more cabin windows and unspatted wheels. Several earlier variants had the spats removed as it was discovered that they tended to be fouled by mud during operations from rain-soaked airfields. The Ju 52/3mg8e (c/n 7730) and subsequent aircraft were fitted with a single 13 mm MG 13 machine-gun in the dorsal position, and some aircraft were powered by 850 hp BMW 132Z engines.

The Ju 52/3mg9e which entered production in 1942 was similar to the BMW 132Z powered previous model, but was provided with a glider towing hook as standard, and the undercarriage was strengthened to permit a take-off weight of 11,500 kg (25,357 lb).

The Ju 52/3mg10e had provision for floats and naval equipment and the g12e was powered by 800 hp BMW 132L engines. A few of these machines were delivered to Deutsche Lufthansa under the designation Ju

A Ju 52/3mg6e of the Minensuchgruppe fitted with a large dural hoop which could be energized by an auxiliary motor to provide 300 amps D/C for exploding magnetic mines. (*H. Redemann*)

364

A Ju 52/3mg6e floatplane of Seetransportstaffel 1 off the coast of Crete, 1941.
(*R. C. Seeley*)

52/3m-12. The final production model was the Ju 52/3mg14e which, delivered in the late autumn of 1943, introduced armour protection for the pilot and had an MG 15 machine-gun mounted over the cockpit in a streamlined cupola.

The Ju 52/3mg4e, g5e, g8e, g10e, and g14e could all be fitted with floats, under the general designation Ju 52/3m Wasser. Total production of the Ju 52/3m is reported as 4,835, although the exact number completed before 1939 has yet to be confirmed. Production figures from that year were 145 in 1939, 388 in 1940, 502 in 1941, 503 in 1942, 887 in 1943 and 379 in 1944.

On 10 May, 1940, Germany launched Operation Yellow, the invasion of the Netherlands, Belgium and France. For the attack, 475 Ju 52/3m and forty-five DFS 230 gliders were amassed, the whole being placed under a special command staff under Gen Putzier.

The operations against Holland began with a paratroop drop on four major locations: north and south of the Moerdijk bridges; near Dordrecht; around Rotterdam's Waalhaven Airport; and near The Hague, the last with the intention of capturing the royal family. During the five days of the campaign against Holland no less than 167 Ju 52/3ms were lost, mostly falling victim to anti-aircraft fire.

After the initial assault, operations by the transport units began to tail off, the capture of Belgium and northern France being entrusted to ground-based army units. The Luftwaffe's air transport units were held in readiness for Operation Sea Lion, the proposed invasion of the British Isles, but in that fateful summer of 1940, the 'Few' successfully repulsed the might of the Luftwaffe and the invasion was postponed indefinitely.

The transport units were instrumental in the rapid build-up of German forces for the invasion of Greece and Yugoslavia which took place on 6 April, 1941. The assault opened with a dive-bomber attack on Belgrade and 11 days later Yugoslavia capitulated. By 24 April, British and Greek forces were beginning to retreat from Thermopylae and the Germans planned a large-scale parachute drop to capture intact the road bridge over the Corinth Canal, but were unsuccessful. The paratroop assault took place on 26 April, 1941. Despite this setback, the Germans successfully captured the Peloponnese and only Crete stood in the way of Axis domination of the Balkans.

On 20 April, 1941, Gen-Leut Kurt Student, leader of the new XI.Fliegerkorps which took in under its control all air transport units, suggested to Göring that an attempt be made to invade Crete from the air. The plan was put to Hitler on 21 April and four days later he issued Directive No. 28—Operation Mercury. Gen Maj Gerhard was made air commander of a force of transport aircraft which was to include 493 Ju 52/3ms and over eighty DFS 230 gliders.

Even before the huge aerial armada took-off, things had begun to go wrong. Enough fuel for the first attack wave arrived only a few hours before take-off, and the pilots had no idea whether they would have sufficient petrol for the two succeeding waves.

Only seven Ju 52/3ms were lost during the initial assault, but when they returned to their airfields many could not land because of the heavy dust. Those that did attempt a landing collided with others and the whole situation became chaotic. A second attack wave was planned to depart at 13.00 hr to drop paratroops against Retimo and Heraklion, but the confusion led to the spreading of the unit's take-off times, and the last Ju 52/3m unit arrived three and a half hours after the first, KGrzbV 105. Despite defiant resistance from the British Commonwealth and Greek troops, Crete finally fell to the Axis powers on 31 May, 1941. Germany lost over 7,000 men killed or wounded, including one out of every four paratroopers dropped. The Luftwaffe's air transport units lost over 170 Ju 52/3ms destroyed or very seriously damaged.

When Germany invaded the Soviet Union on 22 June, 1941, six transport Gruppen were operational on the Eastern Front. The Soviet scorched-earth policy meant that a large proportion of supplies had to be flown in by the Luftwaffe and this strained German resources to the utmost.

On 9 January, 1942, four Soviet armies penetrated the German front between Army Groups Centre and North, and by 8 February the whole of Gen Graf Brockdorff-Ahlefeldt's X.Armee-Korps was surrounded at Demyansk. Six divisions totalling some 100,000 men were surrounded and within a few days were separated from the yielding German front. On 18 February, a conference was called in which Gen Oberst Keller, commander of Luftflotte 1 asked Oberst Fritz Morzik if his air transport units could supply the Demyansk pocket.

At the time only two units were in the area, but on 19 February five more Gruppen were flown in to assist the operation. Airfields used by the units included Pskov (already crowded with Heinkel He 111s), Korovje-Selo, Ostrov and even Riga in the far west. On 20 February the first Ju 52/3ms landed at Demyansk and by the end of the month three more units had joined the operation.

In March 1942 a second airfield was established at Pyesky, some 13 km (8 miles) north of Demyansk. Initially the Ju 52/3ms flew in singly at low level, but increasing losses to Soviet air action forced the German pilots to adopt tight formations with fighter escort provided by Messerschmitt Bf 109Fs. In May 1942, a land corridor was opened up to Demyansk, and by 18 May only three groups remained to transport supplies by air.

Between 20 February and 18 May, 1942, an average daily figure of 273 tons of supplies was taken in by air transport units, making a total of 24,303 tons. In addition, 15,446 troops were flown into the pocket and 20,093 wounded flown out. Losses totalled 262 aircraft and 385 officers and men killed, including Maj Walter Hammer, commander of KGrzbV 172.

A Ju 52/3m which suffered slight damage to the port wing after a collision. (*J. Zazvonil*)

The success of the Demyansk operation was however to create a dangerous precedent. On 23 November, 1942, a Soviet pincer movement closed at Kalach and trapped the 250,000 men of Germany's Sixth Army under Gen Paulus in and around Stalingrad. Göring with his usual mixture of ineptitude and boastfulness, assured Hitler that the huge army could be supplied from the air, and from that moment Paulus' men were doomed.

In the middle of November 1942 only five Ju 52/3m transport units were in the area. During the first two days only 65 tons of supplies were landed, but the Luftwaffe high command had specified that 300 tons should be delivered daily. This was soon recognized to be impossible with the forces available, and by December a further 13 groups were operational including some 176 He 111s.

Weather conditions were little short of atrocious, and scarcely more than a third of the aircraft were serviceable at any one time. On 30 November 100 tons of supplies were delivered at Stalingrad for the first time, but this was far from enough to keep the German army supplied. Next day the airfields were covered by a heavy snow-fall, and this was followed by ice. Between 19 and 21 December the units succeeded in flying 450 sorties and landing over 700 tons of supplies at Pitomnik airfield near Stalingrad. On 22 December the area was covered in freezing fog, and two days later Russian shells began to fall on the Ju 52/3ms' airfield at Tazinskaya. With only minutes to spare, 108 Ju 52/3ms and Ju 86s took-off in thick fog, amidst a scene of utter chaos, and landed at Rostov and Novocherkassk. Among the machines which landed at the latter airfield was one piloted by Hptm Lorenz of Luftnachrichten-Regiment 38 who had never previously handled an aircraft.

A Ju 52/3mg6e of 6./TG 3 after crashing in the snow, early spring 1945. (*US Army*)

By Christmas 1942 the Ju 52/3m formations had withdrawn to Sal'sk. Operations continued amidst terrible weather, Russian fighters and other hazards, but on 16 January Pitomnik airfield was captured. The transports were now forced to land at Gumrak which was strewn with the wrecks of crashed aircraft. On the same day Ju 52/3ms were forced to withdraw from Sal'sk to Sverevo, and within 24 hours no less than 52 of them were destroyed in a Russian bombing attack.

The final landings at Gumrak were made during the night of 21/22 January, 1943, and after that the Luftwaffe had to resort to the parachuting of supplies. On 3 February, 1943, Lt Kuntz of I./KG 100 flew the last supply mission over Stalingrad, dropping his load among the frozen dead of a once-proud army.

As the Allied blockade of Axis shipping in the Mediterranean grew in intensity, the Luftwaffe was increasingly called upon to bring supplies to the hard-pressed Afrika Korps. During one notable action on 10/11 April, 1943, towards the end of the campaign, four Ju 52/3ms and fourteen Messerschmitt Bf 109 and Bf 110 escorts were shot down by Allied fighters. On 18 April fifty-two from a force of over one hundred Ju 52/3ms were shot down near Cap Bon, many of the petrol-laden aircraft blowing up in a most spectacular fashion. Between 5 and 22 April no less than 432 German transport aircraft were destroyed for the loss of 35 Allied fighters.

Operations by Ju 52/3ms continued until the end of the war in Europe, and, although an attempt was made to replace the machine with the Ju 352 Herkules, the latter aircraft never appeared in numbers.

The next notable action in which the transport units were engaged was the supply of German troops in and around Odessa in March and April 1944.

In May 1944 two emergency transport units were formed from the remnants of other defunct groups to operate in support of the German troops in trying to prevent the Allied invasion of France.

368

Final operations were centred around the supply of Breslau and Posen and by 25 April, 1945, only eight Ju 52/3m units remained operational.

In addition to performing a vast number of mundane transport tasks, the Ju 52/3m was also widely used as an engine test bed, the centre unit being replaced by the powerplant under test. In 1939, D-ATOF (c/n 5369) was used to test the 1,200 hp Daimler-Benz 601N engine, and in November of that year the DB 601 V21, prototype for the 1,300 hp DB 601E series, was tested in the same aircraft.

At least one Ju 52/3m was used by the E-2 department of Rechlin for their regular turbojet performance tests. The engine under test was mounted in a parallel-motion frame beneath the aircraft. The German method of taking measurements of thrust, consumption, etc, was to make all readings at a constant weight and therefore because of fuel consumption this meant that a separate flight had to be made for each reading. There must, therefore, have been a great many flights undertaken with the Ju 52/3m testbed at Rechlin. Most of these flights are likely to have been made during 1944 and probably started no earlier than mid-1943.

This winter-camouflaged Ju 52/3mg6e of 6./TG 3 is being examined by American troops after the clearance of snow. (*US Army*)

The end of the war was not the end of the Ju 52/3m. The type was built by Ateliers Aéronautiques de Colombes in France as the AAC.1 Toucan and used by the French Aéronavale, the Armée de l'Air, Air France and a number of other airlines. Aircraft based at Hanoi were used in some numbers against the Viet Minh in French Indochina during 1949 and 1950. One hundred and seventy aircraft were built in Spain by Construcciones Aeronauticas SA as the C-352-L powered by Elizalde-built BMW 132 radials, and were used widely by the Spanish Air Force for many years. Some were also delivered to the Swiss Air Force. The Ju 52/3m was even used by British European Airways; ten captured Ju 52/3mg8es were rebuilt by Short Brothers and Harland at Belfast and were put into service in November 1946 on the airline's domestic services, but all were withdrawn at the end of August 1947. Several Ju 52/3ms have been preserved.

*Wartime operational units:* KGzbV 1 and 2, KGrzbV 3, 5, 6, 7, 8, 9, 11, 12, 40, 50, 60, 101, 102, 103, 104, 105, 106, 107 and 108, KGzbV 172, KGrzbV 300, 400, 500, 600, 700, 800, 900 and 999, KGrzbV Brindisi, Frankfurt, Naples, Oels Posen, Reggio, and Wittstock. (Many of these groups were created for specific campaigns and only existed for short periods). TG 1, 2, 3, 4 and 5, TGr 20 and 30 plus a large number of Korps transport flights. The Minensuchgruppen. Seetransportstaffel 1 and 2. LVG Bronkow and Mobil.

Ju 52be: Span 29 m (95 ft $1\frac{3}{4}$ in); length 18·5 m (60 ft $8\frac{1}{4}$ in); wing area 116 sq m (1,248·6 sq ft).
Empty weight 3,890 kg (8,576 lb); payload 1,845 kg (4,067 lb); loaded weight 7,000 kg (15,432 lb).
Maximum speed 190 km/h (118 mph); cruising speed 160 km/h (99·4 mph); landing speed 77 km/h (47·8 mph); take-off run 315 m (1,033 ft); landing run 175 m (574 ft); service ceiling 2,800 m (9,186 ft); range 1,500 km (932 miles).

Ju 52/3mg4e: Span 29·25 m (95 ft $11\frac{1}{2}$ in); length 18·9 m (62 ft); height 4·5 m (14 ft 9 in); wing area 110·5 sq m (1,189·4 sq ft).
Empty weight 6,510 kg (14,354 lb); loaded weight 10,500 kg (23,157 lb).
Maximum speed 270 km/h (168 mph); cruising speed 200 km/h (124 mph); landing speed 100 km/h (62 mph); service ceiling 5,500 m (18,046 ft); normal range 915 km (568 miles); maximum range 1,280 km (795 miles).

# Junkers Ju 86

The Junkers Ju 86 is one of those less-familiar aircraft which had its origin in the mid-1930s, was supplied to the Luftwaffe in the days of its clandestine build-up, but which was considered obsolescent when war came and therefore saw little active service. Although the aircraft was not, in fact, very successful, it is of interest as an early example of a Diesel-engined aircraft and for its use in later high-altitude work.

Developed under the leadership of Dipl Ing Ernst Zindel, the Ju 86 was a contemporary of the more successful Heinkel He 111 and, like the latter aircraft but to a greater extent, was designed to fulfil both military bomber and commercial transport rôles. To formulate and, as far as possible, to integrate the specifications for these two rôles, the RLM (which was not fully organized until 1935) and Deutsche Lufthansa worked together. This was not to be a case of Lufthansa flying the aircraft until the Luftwaffe was ready to expand and take them over; distinct civil and military versions of the Ju 86 were to be built. Nevertheless, the requirements were not fully compatible, and the development of the high-speed medium-bomber version was to be emphasized to the detriment, if necessary, of a 10-passenger airliner for Lufthansa, which was wanted more for prestige than economic purposes.

The basic design was that of a twin-engined low-wing monoplane with

A landing mishap with a Junkers Ju 86E. This version of the bomber went into Luftwaffe service in the late summer of 1937 with a great improvement in serviceability due to the introduction of BMW 132 radial engines. (*J. Zazvonil*)

twin fins and rudders. Metal stressed-skin construction was used but was untypical of Junkers' practice in that the skin was smooth and not corrugated. The tapered wing had two main spars and one auxiliary spar and the usual Junkers auxiliary-wing type of flaps and ailerons. An unusual feature for this size of aircraft was that the main undercarriage members were attached at the wing roots and retracted outwards into the wings, this arrangement giving a very narrow track.

With the ordering of three military and two civil prototypes, Junkers at Dessau began building the first prototype, the Ju 86a or V1 (c/n 4901), which first flew on 4 November, 1934, as the forerunner of the bomber version. Because the two 600 hp Junkers Jumo 205 Diesel engines for which the aircraft was designed were not ready, it was fitted with two Siemens SAM 22 radial air-cooled engines driving two-blade airscrews. Flight trials with this aircraft were disappointing, stability and control being unsatisfactory. During subsequent modifications, the open dorsal and ventral gun positions were added.

In January 1935, the Ju 86 V3, D-ALAL (c/n 4903), became the second prototype to fly and, although originally fitted with Siemens 22 engines, was re-engined in March with the first available Jumo 205C Diesels driving three-blade airscrews. The V3 was similar to the V1 but had the lower part of the nose glazed for a bomb-aimer's position and a manual turret fitted to the top of the nose in front of the stepped cockpit. The Diesel engines resulted in slim nacelles but there was a large, sloping, radiator beneath each.

The first prototype of the civil version flew in April 1935. This was the Ju 86b or V2, D-ABUK (c/n 4902), which was fitted with Diesel engines from the outset, and it was joined the following month by the similar Ju 86 V4, D-AREV (c/n 4904). The V5, which first flew in August 1935 as D-AHOE (c/n 4905), and V4 aircraft were prototypes for the production Ju 86A bomber and Ju 86B commercial transport respectively. Flying characteristics were still poor and a new wing was therefore designed with

371

increased area, achieved by increasing the chord towards the tips, and both the V4 and V5 received the new wing. The V4, together with the V2, was tested by Lufthansa for a trial period ending in December 1935, by which time production had begun at Dessau of both the Ju 86A-0 and Ju 86B-0 pre-production aircraft, the first of which appeared in February 1936.

A Ju 86E with a modified nose. (*J. Zazvonil*)

By the spring of 1936, the Ju 86A-0 bomber had been evaluated, and the first production Ju 86A-1s were received by KG 152 Hindenburg. During this period, also, the first few Ju 86Bs began going into Lufthansa service, and one also went to Swissair. Sweden then acquired three examples of the Ju 86K-1 bomber in December 1936 for her air force which designated them B3. The K-1s were powered by two 875 hp Pratt & Whitney Hornet radial engines, and one aircraft was later fitted with skis and was designated K-2. Other versions of the Ju 86K were later sold for the air forces of Chile, Hungary and Portugal, and both Gnome/Rhône radial engines (Ju 86K-9) and Bristol Pegasus radial engines (Ju 86K-4 and K-5) were fitted. Following evaluation of its three Ju 86K-1s, the Swedish Air Force acquired sixteen Ju 86 bombers which were licence-built by SAAB and were fitted with licence-built Pegasus radial engines. These aircraft were designated Ju 86K-13 in Germany and B3 in Sweden, deliveries beginning late in 1939. For all the export and licence-built bombers, engines other than the Diesel type were fitted.

In February 1937 a second aircraft went to Swissair as a Ju 86Z-1, HB-IXE, with Jumo engines but was re-engined with BMW 132Dc radial engines in 1939. It was then redesignated Ju 86Z-2 and registered HB-IXA but crashed in July 1939 leaving only the Ju 86B, HB-IXI, in Swissair service. Exported civil Ju 86s were acquired by other airlines following Swissair's example. South African Airways ordered Ju 86 transports in 1936 with 745 hp Rolls-Royce Kestrel XVI twelve-cylinder liquid-cooled engines. The Ju 86 V7 flew in the autumn of 1936 as the prototype for the South African aircraft but only a few Kestrel-engined Ju 86s were actually built before being re-engined with Pratt & Whitney Hornet radial engines, these being more suitable for commercial use. With Hornet engines, the aircraft was designated Ju 86Z-7, SAA receiving seventeen of these (the first arriving in June 1937) together with a single Ju 86K-1 bomber. The bomber was presumably for South African Air Force evaluation which, in any case, took over all eighteen aircraft in 1939.

1937 saw Southern Airlines and Freighters in Australia briefly operating a Jumo-powered Ju 86Z-1 but this was returned to Junkers in August of that year. The Swedish airline, AB Aerotransport, received a Ju 86Z-7 with Hornet engines and used it on night mail service as SE-BAE *Svalan* (*The Swallow*) but the Swedish Air Force took it over in 1940 as the Tp 9 No.911. Similarly, two other Ju 86Z-7s were acquired by Lloyd Aereo Boliviano in 1937 only to have them taken over by the Bolivian Air Force in May 1941. Finally, 1938 saw three Jumo-powered Ju 86Z-1s sold to LAN-Chile and five BMW-powered Ju 86Z-2s sold to South Manchurian Railway, one of the latter being M-212.

Among the fifteen or so Ju 86s eventually delivered to Lufthansa were a few Ju 86Cs (received in 1937) which were similar to the B-series but with a modification intended to improve stability. This modification, tested on the Ju 86 V6, consisted of a new dorsal, spine-like, fin added to the tail-end of the fuselage.

The same modification for improved stability was also introduced on the Luftwaffe Ju 86 bombers with the appearance of the Ju 86D-1 in 1936.

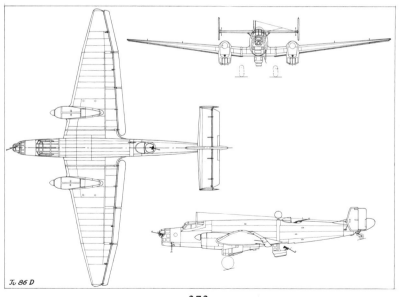

Ju 86 D

Jumo Diesel engines were still employed and the only other important difference from the few Ju 86A-1s built was that fuel capacity was increased by 50 per cent. The Ju 86D-1 bomber was the first version to see operational service when five were used by K/88 of the Condor Legion in Spain late in 1937. These aircraft carried a crew of four, were fitted with a single 7·9 mm MG 15 gun in each of the dorsal, ventral, and nose turret positions, and could carry up to 800 kg (1,764 lb) of bombs inside the fuselage. During the Spanish Civil War the Ju 86D-1 did not give a good account of itself since it was let down by its Jumo 205 Diesel engines which proved difficult to keep serviceable under combat conditions.

In the spring of 1937, therefore, the Ju 86 V9, D-ADAA, was successfully tested with 810 hp BMW 132F radial engines. This aircraft was converted from a production D-1 and was the prototype for the Ju 86E-1 which was put into service in the summer of that year and was followed by the Ju 86E-2 with improved 865 hp BMW 132N radials. An E-1 bomber was then modified as the Ju 86 V10 prototype which featured a shorter, fully-glazed, hemispherical nose to improve the pilot's take-off vision, and the new aircraft was introduced into service in the summer of 1938 as the Ju 86G-1.

The Ju 86G-1 went into Luftwaffe service in the summer of 1938 with the new feature of a fully-glazed nose.

From 1937, production of the Ju 86 bomber was increased in concert with the increasing Luftwaffe build-up and, accordingly, Henschel's Schönefeld factory also took part in Ju 86 production. Nevertheless, the Luftwaffe did not find the performance of the Ju 86 too spectacular, and, by September 1939, the type was almost completely phased out of front-line service in favour of such bombers as the superior Heinkel He 111. As the Kampfgruppen re-equipped, the Ju 86s were transferred to the Kampflehrgeschwader or bomber-training units.

This downgrading of the Ju 86 as a bomber by no means saw the end of the development of the type, since Junkers directed their attention to turning it into a high-altitude bomber and reconnaissance aircraft. Junkers had done more high-altitude work than most firms, having, for example, gained early experience with their Ju 49 of 1931 and their Ju (EF) 61 of 1936. Such aircraft had been useful primarily in the development of the necessary high-altitude pressure cabins, and by 1939 Junkers were working on a high-altitude engine based on their Jumo 205 Diesel. This was the 950 hp Jumo 207A fitted with two centrifugal superchargers driven in

The Junkers EF 61 high-altitude research aircraft which provided valuable data for the Ju 86P and R programmes. (*H. Redemann*)

series from an exhaust gas turbine fitted to the first supercharger. The proposal to fit such engines with new three-blade airscrews to modified Ju 86D airframes was accepted and the official designation of Ju 86P was issued for the new aircraft.

The prototype of the new version, the Ju 86P V1 D-AUHB, flew in February 1940. In addition to the new engines, modifications from the D version included an entirely new, shorter nose section (which almost amounted to a rounding off of the main fuselage cross-section) and the removal and fairing over of the dorsal and ventral gun positions. The new nose contained the pressure cabin for a crew of two, the pressurization being provided by bleeding air from one of the engine superchargers. In March 1940, the Ju 86P V1 was joined in the air by the similar V2 and these aircraft had little difficulty in exceeding altitudes of 10,000 m (32,800 ft). Such altitudes were modest enough and were soon improved upon by the Ju 86P V3, which had a span of 25·6 m (83 ft 11⅛ in) compared with the previous 22·5 m (73 ft 9¾ in). This enabled altitudes of up to 12,000 m (39,360 ft) to be attained. During the summer of 1940, one of these protoypes was delivered for evaluation to the Aufklärungs-gruppe of the OKL. This unit was led by Obstl Theodor Rowehl and conducted with the prototype at least one high-altitude reconnaissance mission over Britain without mishap.

Following these successes, the order was given for the conversion of forty Ju 86Ds into the Ju 86P-1 and P-2 types, the former being a high-altitude bomber with up to 1,000 kg (2,205 lb) bomb capacity and the latter a high-altitude photographic reconnaissance type with three automatic

375

cameras. There was also a projected Ju 86P-3 high-altitude bomber which was not, however, proceeded with, although the Ju 86 V37 (c/n 5161) was the prototype for it and was flown in November 1941. Ju 86P-1s and P-2s were received by the OKL's 2./Aufklärungsgruppe which flew them over Britain during 1940. On such missions, altitudes up to 12,500 m (41,000 ft) provided immunity and no defensive armament was carried. The same types were delivered in January 1941 to a new 4th Staffel of the Aufklärungsgruppe known as the Versuchsstelle für Höhenflüge (test centre for high-altitude flights), which also had the Ju 88B-0 and possibly the Henschel Hs 130A-0. The work of this unit included testing new aircraft on actual missions, including reconnaissance over the USSR prior to Operation Barbarossa, plus the normal flights over Britain.

On 22 June, 1941, the invasion of the Soviet Union began, and 1., 2. and 3.Staffel of the OKL's Aufklärungsgruppe moved to the Russian Front for more intensive reconnaissance. Some reorganization occurred in January 1942 when the Versuchsstelle für Höhenflüge was disbanded and its Ju 86Ps transferred to 1. Staffel of the Versuchsverband Ob.d.L. at Berlin-Rangsdorf.

Some Ju 86P-2s were transferred in May 1942 to 2.(F)/123 at Kastelli in Crete, this long-range reconnaissance Staffel already being equipped with the Ju 88D. Siegfried Kneymeyer (later to become Chief of Technical Air Armament) made the first reconnaissance mission in a Ju 86P-2 over North Africa, and the aircraft continued unchallenged over that theatre until 24 August, 1942. On that day a Ju 86P was shot down by a special Spitfire V at 12,800 m (42,000 ft), with the result that a token armament of one remote-controlled 7·9 mm MG 17 gun was fitted in the rear fuselage of the Ju 86P-2. This was of little use, however, and after two more aircraft had been shot down by Spitfires, the Ju 86Ps were withdrawn in May 1943. Prior to this, the Ju 86P-1 bomber was delivered to 14./KG 6 in August 1942 for operations on the Western Front; about 12 sorties were made, flying at between 9,000 m (29,520 ft) and 12,000 m (39,360 ft), but with very little success. Elsewhere, fighting with the Allies, the ageing Ju 86Zs taken over by the South African Air Force were finally phased out in September 1942 after undertaking bombing and coastal patrol duties.

Early in 1942, before any Ju 86Ps had been intercepted, plans were worked out at Junkers to increase the operational ceiling of the aircraft in order to ensure its continued immunity. These provided for Ju 86P-1s and P-2s to be converted into what were later designated Ju 86R-1s and R-2s, designed to operate at altitudes up to 14,400 m (47,230 ft). This $12\frac{1}{2}$ per cent increase in altitude was achieved by further increase of wing area by extending the span to 32 m (104 ft $11\frac{7}{8}$ in), while power was maintained by the 1,000 hp Jumo 207B-3 with GM-1 (nitrous oxide) boosting supplementing the superchargers, and new four-blade airscrews. Other equipment remained unchanged, but fuel capacity was increased. Only a small number of the new type were built, and the 1./Versuchsverband Ob.d.L. received a few Ju 86R-1s in 1943 but had relinquished them by July 1944.

A Ju 86P-1 (c/n 0439) high-altitude bomber. Ju 86P-1s and P-2s were first employed by 2./Aufklärungsgruppe of the OKL for missions over Britain during 1940.

The relatively small number of high-altitude Ju 86s were virtually the only aircraft of this type in front-line Luftwaffe service during the war although a considerable number were, as already related, with the bomber-training units. On 24 November, 1942, the Luftwaffe was given the desperate order to air-lift supplies to the doomed German Sixth Army cut off at Stalingrad. For such a task, every available transport aircraft was needed, and the training Ju 86s were therefore pressed into service with the transport units KGrzbV 21 and 22. Since the Red Air Force by then enjoyed air superiority over the Stalingrad area, old aircraft such as the Ju 86 did not prove very successful, and over 40 were lost by the time Stalingrad fell on 2 February. By March 1943, the few Ju 86s left were back with the training units but were again pressed into service, at the end of the year, in the Balkans. There were also some Ju 86s (exact designations unknown) delivered in September 1943 for a short operational period to 1.(F)/100 on the Eastern Front. In the meantime, the Hungarian Air Force was still using the Ju 86K-9 against the USSR on bombing and reconnaissance missions and continued to do so until the middle of 1944.

The Ju 86 was an aircraft which was obviously suitable for adaptation and considerable development, as indicated by the last projected variants. The Ju 86R-3 was proposed for operation at an altitude of 15,850 m (52,000 ft) and was to be powered by two 1,500 hp Jumo 208 Diesel engines fed at altitude by a large two-stage supercharger. This supercharger was mounted inside the fuselage and driven by a separate Daimler-Benz DB 605 inverted-vee engine which had its own supercharger and was of about 1,500 hp. Also projected were the Ju 186 high-altitude research

377

aircraft to be powered by either four Jumo 208s or two Jumo 218s (coupled pairs of Jumo 208s), and the Ju 286 high-altitude bomber to be powered by six Jumo 208 engines. These projects all remained on paper apparently because of Jumo 208 engine development being abandoned. Altogether, about 500 Ju 86s were built.

*Wartime operational units:* 1.(F)/100, 2.(F)/123, 14./KG 6, KGrzbV 21 and 22, 2. and 4./Aufkl.Gr.Ob.d.L., 1./Versuchsverbänd Ob.d.L.

Ju 86D-1: Span 22·5 m (73 ft 9¾ in); length 17·6 m (57 ft 8⅞ in); height 4·7 m (15 ft 5 in); wing area 82 sq m (882·3 sq ft).

Empty weight 5,355 kg (11,795 lb); normal loaded weight 8,050 kg (17,750 lb); maximum loaded weight 8,200 kg (18,080 lb).

Maximum speed at sea level 300 km/h (186 mph); cruising speed at 1,000 m (3,280 ft) 275 km/h (171 mph); service ceiling 5,900 m (19,360 ft); maximum range with auxiliary fuel tanks 1,500 km (932 miles).

Ju 86P-1: Span 25·6 m (83 ft 11⅞ in); length 16·46 m (54 ft); height 4·7 m (15 ft 5 in); wing area 92 sq m (990 sq ft).

Empty weight 6,660 kg (14,685 lb); loaded weight 10,400 kg (22,930 lb).

Maximum speed at 6,000 m (19,680 ft) 360 km/h (224 mph); cruising speed at 11,000 m (36,090 ft) 260 km/h (161 mph); service ceiling 12,000 m (39,360 ft); normal range 1,000 km (621 miles).

Ju 86K-4 c/n 0860412 is in the Swedish Air Force Museum at Malmslätt.

# Junkers Ju 87

The progenitor of the Stuka—an abbreviation of the German word Sturzkampfflugzeug, or dive-bomber—was the Swedish-built Junkers-K 47 which made its first flight in 1928. But it was not until 27 September, 1933, that Germany placed a contract for the design of such an aircraft, a decision engendered mainly by Ernst Udet who had earlier witnessed a demonstration by US Navy Curtiss Helldivers at Cleveland, Ohio.

Four companies submitted proposals, the Ju 87 designed by Dipl Ing Hans Pohlmann being the Junkers entry. The Ju 87 V1 was a two-seat all-metal monoplane with an unusual inverted gull wing and twin fins and rudders. For ease of construction, the fuselage was built in two halves which were joined along the centreline. Large trousers covered the fixed mainwheels and the Junkers double-wing principle (as described in the Ju 52/3m history) was used. The prototype first flew, from Dessau, in the late spring of 1935, being powered by a 640 hp Rolls-Royce Kestrel V liquid-cooled engine. After some overheating was experienced, it was fitted with a new radiator of substantially larger dimensions. The aircraft was destroyed during diving trials in the summer of 1935 when it developed tail flutter.

378

The Junkers Ju 87 V3 D-UKYQ made its first flight late in 1935.

As originally designed, the second prototype was similar to the first, but was powered by a Junkers Jumo 210Aa engine which provided 610 hp for take-off. Following the crash of the Ju 87 V1, the second aircraft was fitted with a single fin and rudder and joined the test programme in 1935. In March 1936 the four competitors were pitted against each other at Rechlin. Taking part were the Arado Ar 81 V2, D-UPAR; the Blohm und Voss Ha 137 V4, D-IFOE; the Heinkel He 118 V1, D-IKYM; and the unregistered Ju 87 V2. The Heinkel and Junkers designs immediately proved their superiority, although it came as some surprise when the slower and less manoeuvrable Ju 87 was finally chosen.

Before being delivered to Rechlin, the Ju 87 V2 had been fitted with special slats beneath the wing just outboard of the undercarriage fairings. These could be rotated through 90 deg, and acted as dive-brakes. The bomb itself was carried on a special underfuselage cradle hinged just aft of the radiator bath, this being swung forward during a dive to enable the weapon to clear the airscrew.

The Arado Ar 81 (here represented by the V3) was designed to the same specification as the Junkers Ju 87 dive-bomber.

379

Five Blohm und Voss Ha 137 dive-bombers were built to compete with the Arado Ar 81, Heinkel He 118 and Junkers Ju 87. (*F. Selinger*)

Of more advanced concept than the Junkers Ju 87, the Heinkel He 118 was finally abandoned when the V2 crashed with Ernst Udet at the controls.

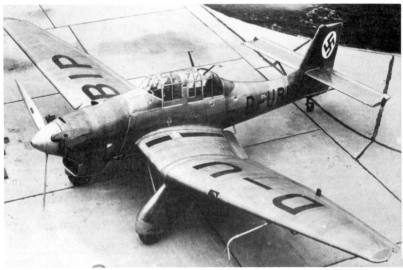

The Ju 87 V4 was the production prototype of the A-series dive-bomber.

The 12th production Ju 87A-1, D-IEAU, prior to delivery to St.G 162 in 1937.
(*H. Redemann*)

The Ju 87 V3, D-UKYQ, was similar to the modified V2, but had an improved forward view. The fourth aircraft, D-UBIP, was the production prototype, making its first flight during the autumn of 1936. It had larger vertical tail surfaces and carried a single 7·9 mm MG 17 machine-gun in the starboard wing. Ten Ju 87A-0 pre-production aircraft were laid down in the summer of 1936, differing from the V4 in having straight wing leading edges (in place of the double-tapered section of the earlier aircraft) to simplify production. The first production Ju 87A-1s left the assembly line early in 1937, being followed later that year by the improved A-2 powered by a 680 hp Jumo 210Da engine and with a broader-bladed airscrew.

During the early spring of 1937, the first Ju 87A-1s were delivered to I./St.G 162 Immelmann, the unit being entrusted with the task of evolving operational tactics. In December 1937 a flight known as the Jolanthe-Kette was sent to Spain as part of the Condor Legion. The unit had only three Ju 87A-1s, these being flown by pilots from St.G 162 who were

One of the three Ju 87A-1s flown by pilots of St.G 162 during the Spanish Civil War.
(*H. Obert*)

381

constantly changed to provide as many as possible with operational experience. Operating under conditions of air superiority, the three Ju 87As proved very successful.

Early in 1938, a standard Ju 87A-1 was taken from the Dessau production line, fitted with a 1,000 hp Jumo 211A engine, and redesignated Ju 87 V6. This was followed by a more extensively modified machine, the Ju 87 V7, intended as the forerunner of the Ju 87B production aircraft. The machine had an entirely redesigned cockpit canopy, enlarged vertical tail surfaces, spats in place of trouser fairings, and an additional MG 17 gun in the port wing.

Ten pre-production Ju 87B-0s were produced later in 1938, followed by the generally-similar B-1. Four variants of the basic model were produced: the standard Ju 87B-1/U1, the B-1/U2 with alternative radio equipment, the B-1/U3 with additional armour protection, and the B-1/U4 with skis in place of the standard wheeled undercarriage. The Ju 87B-1/Trop was fitted with desert survival equipment.

A Ju 87B-1 of III./St.G 2 after nosing over during a gale. (*J. Zazvonil*)

The Ju 87B-1 was replaced on the production line late in 1939 by the improved B-2 which was powered by the 1,200 hp Jumo 211Da engine with direct fuel injection. The machine had hydraulically-operated radiator cooling gills and modified undercarriage legs and could carry a 1,000 kg (2,200 lb) bomb load. The Ju 87B-2/U1, U2, U3 and U4 were, respectively, similar modifications to those of the B-1 described earlier.

With the introduction of the Ju 87B, production of the machine was transferred from Dessau to the Weser-Flugzeugbau GmbH at Berlin-Tempelhof, and later Bremen-Lemwerder; Junkers remaining responsible for the development of new sub-types. During 1937 and 1938 only 395 Ju 87s were built, production being increased to 557 in 1939 and 611 in 1940.

One of the features of the Ju 87 was the siren mounted in a fairing in the upper leading edge of each undercarriage leg. These were initially a simple structure operated by air passing through them during a high-speed dive. Later a more elaborate system was introduced where the sirens were driven by small airscrews mounted in the nose of the special fairing. The purpose of these sirens was to add to the psychological effect of the dive-bomber, proving particularly menacing in the terror bombing of civilians.

The Ju 87C was a special conversion of the dive-bomber intended for operation from the aircraft carrier *Graf Zeppelin* which was under construction at Kiel. A batch of Ju 87C-0 pre-production aircraft left the Weser factory during the summer of 1939. This variant was fitted with a jettisonable undercarriage, was stressed for catapulting and carried an arrester hook forward of the tailwheel. A small number of Ju 87C-1s with electrically-folding wings were laid down later in the year, but were converted to B-2 standard when work on the *Graf Zeppelin* was temporarily abandoned.

In October 1938, five of the first production Ju 87B-1s were sent to Spain and proved even more successful than the Ju 87A-1s which had preceded them. In December 1938, a Staffel was formed in readiness for operations from the aircraft carrier *Graf Zeppelin*. Designated 4.(Stuka)/186, the Staffel was initially equipped with the Ju 87A and based at Kiel-Holtenau. In May 1939, it was re-equipped with the Ju 87B-1 and eventually received a few Ju 87C-0s. It took part in the Polish campaign and was expanded to Gruppe strength on 16 September, 1939.

The final production variant based on the B-series airframe was the Ju 87R long-range anti-shipping variant. The airframe was modified to take an extra 150 litre (33 Imp gal) tank in each wing plus points for two 300 litre (66 Imp gal) drop tanks beneath the wings. The Ju 87R-1 had a range of 1,410 km (876 miles) as compared with 550 km (342 miles) of the Ju 87B-1, and other variants included the Ju 87R-2, R-3, and R-4, which differed only in equipment.

When German forces invaded Poland on 1 September, 1939, all nine of the Luftwaffe's Stukagruppen took part. I./St.G 1, II., and III./St.G 2 and 4.(St)/186 operated in the north, the remaining six being based in the south. With little or no aerial opposition, the Ju 87 was able to wreak havoc on Polish troops and communications, much to the satisfaction of its protagonists. Only thirty-one Ju 87Bs were lost during the campaign, and the myth of the Stuka was born.

The Luftwaffe's next major operation was the invasion of Norway and Denmark on 9 April, 1940. Only one Stukagruppe, I./St.G 1, equipped with the Ju 87R, based at Kiel and later Stavanger, was assigned to the operation. During one notable bombing attack on the Vigra radio station, mid-way between Bergen and Trondheim, on 15 April, a Ju 87R rammed one of the aerials, putting the transmitter out of action.

Before the Norwegian campaign was complete, Hitler launched his invasion of France and the Low Countries. Taking part were nine Stukagruppen, comprising 320 Ju 87Bs and 38 Ju 87Rs operating mainly under the control of Generalfeldmarschall Wolfram von Richthofen's

VIII. Fliegerkorps. I./St.G 76 was attached to St.G 2 and IV.(St)/LG 1 came under the control of St.G 77, these units striking at Allied troop concentrations and operating in close co-operation with the Panzer units.

The majority of Netherlands and Belgian Air Forces' aircraft were destroyed on the ground, and the largely obsolescent machines of the Armée de l'Air were unable to provide any effective opposition to the Luftwaffe. It is some measure of the inadequacy of the Allied air defence system that only fourteen Ju 87s were lost during the first four days of the campaign.

Less than two weeks after the invasion, forces from the British Expeditionary Force were preparing to withdraw from the encircled port of Dunkirk. The Luftwaffe was given the task of preventing the evacuation, but for the first time its supremacy was challenged by RAF fighter squadrons operating from airfields in southern England. Although the Ju 87s bombed the beaches during breaks in the RAF cover, they suffered heavily when confronted by Hurricanes and Spitfires. By 5 June, 1940, the evacuation was complete, and Luftwaffe forces transferred southwards to assist in the crossings of the Marne, Seine, and Loire.

The campaign against the British Isles opened with isolated bombing of coastal shipping, but it was not until 8 August, 1940, that the first major Ju 87 sortie was made against a convoy. Three separate waves of Ju 87s attacked, escorted by Messerschmitt Bf 109Es, but losses were severe, one formation being scattered before it could reach the target. On 13 August a force of Ju 87s from VIII. Fliegerkorps attempted to bomb the RAF airfield at Middle Wallop. They were intercepted by Spitfires from No. 609 Squadron and the havoc wreaked on the German formation led to the day being noted as the 'glorious 13th' in the Squadron's records.

At this time VIII. Fliegerkorps had 220 Ju 87Bs operational, drawn from I. and II./St.G 1, I. and II./St.G 2 and St.G 77. In addition, II. Fliegerkorps had 60 aircraft on hand from III./St.G 1 and IV.(St)/LG 1. On 15 August, 1940, forty Ju 87s with heavy fighter escort attacked RAF airfields at Hawkinge and Lympne and severely damaged the latter. Next day, St.G 2 bombed Tangmere, but suffered heavy losses. Three days later St.G 77 bombed the Poling radar station, but lost 12 aircraft. This was virtually the last straw, and the Stukagruppen were withdrawn to the Pas de Calais area to prevent further destruction.

Early in January 1941, I./St.G 1, II./St.G 2 and Stab/St.G 3 were transferred to Trapani in Sicily with the intention of making a surprise attack on the British Mediterranean convoys. On 10 January, the two Gruppen bombed and all but sank the carrier *Illustrious*, and next day II./St.G 2 under Maj Enneccerus sank the cruiser *Southampton*. A few days later, I./St.G 1 under Hptm Werner Hozzel bombed the damaged *Illustrious* in Valletta harbour, but 2.Staffel lost all its pilots apart from the Staffelkapitän.

On 6 April, 1941, Germany struck at Greece and Yugoslavia. Three Stukagruppen were transferred from France for the operation, I. and

III./St.G 2 under Oberst Oskar Dinort and I./St.G 3 under Oblt Heinrich Eppen. St.G 77 later joined the forces of VIII. Fliegerkorps in the Balkans, and, on 27 April, Athens fell. Less than a month later, the Luftwaffe attacked Crete, St.G 2's Ju 87Bs operating against the Royal Navy and sinking the cruiser *Gloucester* and several destroyers.

Germany's most ambitious operation, and the one that was perhaps to contribute more than any other to its downfall, was Operation Barbarossa, the invasion of the Soviet Union. Seven Stukagruppen were placed at the disposal of II. and VIII. Fliegerkorps, II. and III./St.G 1 with 70 aircraft, I. and III./St.G 2 with 83 aircraft, and the whole of St.G 77 with 122 aircraft. In addition, IV.(St)/LG 1 was operational in northern Norway with forty-two Ju 87Bs.

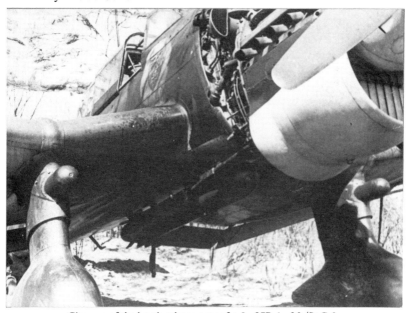

Close-up of the bomb-release gear of a Ju 87B-1 of 3./St.G 2.

Early operations on the Russian front were to prove as successful for the Ju 87 as those in Poland and France. The Soviet Air Force had been largely destroyed in attacks on its airfields and was unable to put up any effective opposition. Some measure of the Luftwaffe's success on the first day of the campaign can be gauged by the fact that it claimed the destruction of 1,811 Soviet aircraft for the loss of 35. The Russians have subsequently admitted the loss of 1,200 aircraft up to noon on 22 June, 1941.

One of the most notable operations carried out by the Stukagruppen on the Eastern Front was against the Russian battleships *Marat* and *October Revolution*. On 23 September, 1941, units I. and III./St.G 2 based at Tyrkowo bombed the vessels at Kronstadt, a 1,000 kg (2,205 lb) bomb dropped at almost 90 deg˙ by Oblt Hans Ulrich Rudel sinking the *Marat*.

385

Another attempt was made to sink the *October Revolution* on 4 April, 1942, when bombers from KG 4 and St.G 2 attacked. Code-named Operation Ice Thrust, the attack only succeeded in damaging cruisers and harbour installations, and the giant battleship remained intact.

Previously, in February 1942, IV.(St)/LG 1 operating in northern Norway was redesignated I./St.G 5. Commanded by Maj Karl Stepp, the unit was equipped with the Ju 87B and operated against the Murmansk railway which was used to transfer from the Arctic ports to the whole of the eastern front urgently needed supplies from Britain and the United States.

In December 1941, Luftflotte 2 was transferred to the Mediterranean with the object of destroying Malta as a base and driving British forces from North Africa. At its disposal were fifty-three Ju 87s from I. and II./St.G 3 plus a further 12 aircraft from the Einsatz-Staffel of Erg./St.G 1. A third Gruppe was added to St.G 3 during the spring of 1942 and the unit took part in the bombing of Tobruk on 20 June, 1942. Ten days earlier the Ju 87 had played a major part in the capture of Bir Hakim from Free French forces.

A formation of Ju 87Ds.

During the spring of 1940, an extensive redesign of the basic Ju 87 had been undertaken to make use of the 1,400 hp provided by the new Jumo 211J engine. The Ju 87D, as the new variant was designated, was given more refined nose contours, achieved by moving the oil cooler from atop the engine to below it, and simultaneously shifting the oil coolant radiator to below the wings, inboard of the undercarriage legs. The cockpit canopy was extensively redesigned, being tapered towards the rear, and tankage was similar to the Ju 87R. The aircraft carried more extensive armour, and the defensive 7·9 mm MG 15 machine-gun in the cockpit was replaced by a twin MG 81Z of similar calibre.

A snow-camouflaged Ju 87D-3 in Russia. The Luftwaffe made considerable use of temporary paint finishes to match various types of terrain. (*R. C. Seeley*)

Offensive armament of the Ju 87D was considerably increased, provision being made for a 1,800 kg (4,000 lb) bomb under the fuselage and either four 50 kg (110 lb) or two 500 kg (1,100 lb) weapons beneath the wings. In practice the 1,800 kg bomb was rarely carried, most aircraft using the 1,400 kg (3,085 lb) armour-piercing weapon or the 1,000 kg (2,200 lb) general-purpose bomb. Provision was also made for a WB 81 or WB FF weapon container beneath each wing, housing respectively six MG 81 machine-guns and two 20 mm MG FF cannon.

The prototypes for the D-series were the Ju 87 V21 (c/n 0536) and V22 (c/n 0540), both of which flew for the first time in February 1941. Because of delays with the new Jumo 211J engine, the third prototype, the Ju 87 V23 (c/n 0542) did not fly until April. The V24 (c/n 0544) joined the

flight of three Ju 87D-5s over Russia. During operations the undercarriage spats of the Ju 87 were often removed for ease of maintenance. (*R. C. Seeley*)

387

programme in May 1941, the last D-series prototype, the Ju 87 V25 (c/n 0538), being used for tropical trials.

The first production models were the Ju 87D-1 and D-1/Trop with desert equipment. Both these and the Ju 87D-2, with a strengthened tail-wheel and glider towing hook combination, had the wing of the B-2. The Ju 87D-3 was a specially designed ground attack variant with heavy armour to protect both the engine and the crew from ground fire. The Ju 87D-4 was basically similar to the D-3 but could carry a torpedo. The D-4 variant never saw service, and the few machines completed were eventually reconverted to D-3 standard.

Until the appearance of the Ju 87D-5, the wing span had remained constant at 13·8 m (45 ft $3\frac{1}{2}$ in), but this model had a new wing with a span of 15 m (49 ft $2\frac{1}{2}$ in). This aircraft was intended solely for the ground-attack rôle and had the jettisonable undercarriage first introduced on the Ju 87C-0. The dive-brakes were not fitted.

The Ju 87D-6 was similar to the D-5, but the D-7 and D-8 had large flame-damping tubes over the exhaust system, and the 1,500 hp Jumo 211P engine. Intended for use by the night ground attack groups, the Ju 87D-7 and D-8 were converted from the D-3 and D-5 respectively by the Menibum company at Hamburg. Apart from the new engine, these variants had the two forward-firing MG 17 machine-guns replaced by two 20 mm MG 151/20 cannon.

The Ju 87D-1 began to replace the Ju 87B-2 in service at the end of 1941, during which year production of the aircraft dropped to 476 machines. The new variant resulted in an upsurge in production, 917 Ju 87s being built in 1942, 1,844 in 1943 and 1,012 up to September 1944 when construction finally came to a halt.

One of the first units to receive the Ju 87D-1 was I./St.G 2 based near Leningrad, followed in February 1942 by St.G 1, and in April by St.G 77. St.G 3 under Oberst Walter Sigel received its first examples of the Ju 87D-1/Trop in May 1942, using their aircraft to assist in the capture of Bir Hakim. When the Allies launched the second battle of El Alamein, the Ju 87s were heavily engaged in an attempt to stem the Eighth Army's advance. By 15 November, the Geschwader's strength had been reduced to 30 aircraft and shortly afterwards I./St.G 3 was withdrawn from operations.

Probably the most famous of all dive-bomber units was St.G 2, the Immelmann-Geschwader, commanded by Oberst Paul-Werner Hozzel at the time of its re-equipment with the Ju 87D. I./St.G 2 was led by Hptm Hans Ulrich Rudel who later became the only pilot to be awarded the Knight's Cross with Golden Oakleaves.

By January 1943, the Luftwaffe's ground attack formations were in a rather parlous state. Owing to failure to produce a satisfactory replacement for the Ju 87, the aircraft was forced to remain as the Luftwaffe's main ground attack machine. The one aircraft that had been designed to supplement the Ju 87, the Henschel Hs 129, was by no means an unqualified

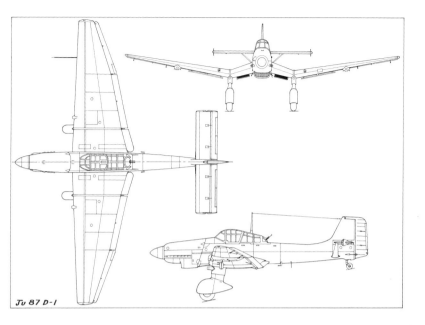

Ju 87 D-1

success, and it was not until the Focke-Wulf Fw 190F and G series appeared that the situation improved.

After the surrender of the German Sixth Army at Stalingrad, a great proportion of the Luftwaffe in the east was assembled in an attempt to hold the Donetz line. Ju 87D units brought into the assault were put under the control of Fliegerdivision Donetz and included II./St.G 1 (operating under II./St.G 2), the whole of St.G 2, plus I. and II./St.G 77. In addition, the newly-formed Störkampfstaffeln were brought into action, but serviceability was extremely low, and the Luftwaffe's ground attack units failed to halt the Russian advance which crossed the Donetz on 5 February, 1943.

Luftflotte 4's operations greatly increased from 20 February, 1943, and on 15 March Kharkov was recaptured. Use was made for the first time of the Ju 88C-6 equipped Eisenbahnstaffeln, 9./KG 3, 14./KG 27 and 9./KG 55, to attack Soviet rail communications, and the Ju 87 units were again heavily employed against Soviet armour and troop concentrations. Operations began to tail off on the Donetz front after the beginning of April, the Luftwaffe turning its attentions to the Kuban Peninsula. Despite the large number of aircraft employed, the offensive proved a failure, and Luftwaffe forces moved north to occupy positions on either side of the Russian salient at Kursk.

The Allied offensive against Rommel re-opened on 15 January, 1943, and on the 23rd, Tripoli fell. Luftwaffe ground attack forces comprised II. and III./St.G 3 with the Ju 87D-1/Trop, I./Sch.G 2 with similar equipment, and 8./Sch.G 2 with the Henschel Hs 129B. Losses from Allied fighters were severe, and by May all Luftwaffe units had been withdrawn to

Sicily, Italy and Sardinia. St.G 3 took no further part in operations and arrived in Russia shortly afterwards.

On 5 July, 1943, the Germans launched their last great offensive of the war, code-named Operation Citadel. Ground attack forces comprised the whole of St.G 2 and St.G 77 plus III./St.G 3 with the Ju 87D, I. and II./Sch.G 1 with the Fw 190, 4. and 8./Sch.G 2 with the Hs 129B plus the Störkampfstaffeln. The Hs 129B and the newly-arrived Ju 87G were directed against the massed Soviet armoured divisions, whilst Ju 87D sorties were directed against Soviet communications, playing a major part in clearing the way for Wehrmacht advances in the Belgorod area.

On 5 October, 1943, an order was issued to rationalize the Luftwaffe's ground attack formations. All dive-bomber, ground attack and fast bomber groups were incorporated into new ground attack wings. In addition to this new command, the General der Schlachtflieger was established under Oberst Hubertus Hitschold. Much attention was given to the replacement of the Ju 87D with the new Focke-Wulf Fw 190F and G ground attack aircraft. In February 1944, II./SG 2 was re-equipped with the Fw 190, and during March II./SG 77 began to receive the aircraft but it was not until August 1944 that the replacement of the Ju 87D was completed within the majority of the Stukagruppen.

This was not the end of the Ju 87D however. The now rather ancient aircraft continued to be used in Staffel strength until the last days of the war, and even in April 1945 the machine was to be seen in service with NSGr 1 and 2 in the West, NSGr 4, 8, and 10 in the East, and NSGr 9 in northern Italy. The aircraft were thrown in to try to check enemy tank thrusts and block convoy movements, but with overwhelming air superiority and improved anti-aircraft weapons to cope with, these sorties were little short of suicidal.

The Ju 87D was by no means the last variant of the basic design to see service. An experimental model to be known as the Ju 87F was proposed, with oversized tyres and the 1,750 hp Jumo 213 engine, but the final Service variant was the Ju 87G. Developed towards the end of 1942, the Ju 87G marked the end of the aircraft as a dive-bomber. Intended specifically for the anti-tank rôle, the Ju 87G-1 and G-2 were basically Ju 87D-3 and D-5 airframes fitted with two 37 mm Flak 18 cannon, one slung under

The ungainly Ju 87G-1 which entered service on the Eastern Front in October 1943.

Close-up of a Ju 87G-1 anti-tank aircraft showing a 37 mm BK 3·7 cannon underwing.
(*J. Zazvonil*)

each wing outboard of the undercarriage legs. The shells had a special tungsten centre which exploded only when they had passed through the tank's armour plating.

The pre-production model, the Ju 87G-0, was extensively tested both at Rechlin and Tarnewitz and, although being extremely unwieldy in the air, proved to have an excellent tank-destroying potential. Hptm (later Oberst) Hans Ulrich Rudel took part at the Rechlin armament trials and in May 1943 took a Ju 87G with him to the Crimea. He first used it in action against Soviet armour in the Krymskaya and Temryuk areas, but the Ju 87G's first real operational blooding came during Operation Citadel.

On 5 July, 1943, Rudel attacked a column of 12 of the potent Soviet T-34 tanks. Always aiming for the tank's lightly-protected rear which housed the engine and fuel, he was able to claim destruction of all 12 tanks single-handed. This and similar successes led to the construction of the Ju 87G-1 and improved G-2 production models and to Rudel being asked to form a special Panzerstaffel within St.G 2.

Designated 10.(Pz)/St.G 2, the unit was equipped with the Ju 87G-1 and proved most successful. Consequently III./St.G 2, which, after the death of Hptm Walter Krauss in a Russian Po-2 raid on 17 July, 1943, was commanded by Hptm Rudel, was re-equipped with the aircraft. II. Gruppe (soon to be re-equipped with the Fw 190) commanded by Maj Kurt Kennel was given the unenviable task of protecting Rudel's expert pilots.

The Ju 87G was no novice's aircraft, and, although extremely potent in

391

the hands of pilots such as Rudel and his Gruppe, could prove equally dangerous to an inexperienced pilot. Therefore, only one Gruppe and four Staffeln were ever equipped with the machine. These were III./SG 2 and 10.(Pz)Staffel of SG 1, SG 2, SG 3, and SG 77. Eventually, the Staffeln from SG 1 and 3 were redesignated as I.(Pz)/SG 9, but the remaining units operated the Ju 87G until the end.

Late in 1940, the Ju 87B-1/Trop was delivered to the Regia Aeronautica, being operated by the 96th, 97th, 101st, and 121st Gruppi Tuffatori. The Royal Rumanian Air Force received the Ju 87D-1 and D-5 which equipped its 3rd and 6th Dive Bomber Wings. Following the Rumanian coup d'état on 23 August, 1944, the 3rd Dive Bomber Wing transferred its allegiance to the Russians and operated *against* German forces.

A few Ju 87B-2s were delivered to Bulgaria and Hungary in 1942, but the only Royal Hungarian Air Force unit to operate the machine, 102/1 Zuhanóbombázó Század (dive-bomber squadron), was equipped with the Ju 87D-5. It was formed in May 1943 under the command of Capt Jenö Korossy and its first operations were flown in August from Gomel against partisans. In September, Capt Gyözö Levay took over command and up until October the squadron flew over 1,000 sorties. It returned to the frontline in June 1944, and often operated in company with the aircraft of SG 77. Finally, in August 1944 it was re-equipped with the Focke-Wulf Fw 190. The Ju 87D-7 was also delivered to the Slovakian Air Force.

The last production model of the Junkers dive-bomber was the Ju 87H dual-control trainer. Essentially similar to the Ju 87D, the few completed Ju 87H-1, H-3, H-5, H-7, and H-8 trainers, were in fact converted from D-series airframes. The dive-brakes were removed and transparent blisters fitted to the rear of the cockpit canopy to improve the instructor's view.

The original Ju 87F proposal was abandoned mainly because it offered insufficient increase in performance over the standard Ju 87D. In the spring of 1941, a more extensive redesign was undertaken, with a wing of increased span, a fully retractable undercarriage, a 1,776 hp Jumo 213A engine, two forward-firing MG 151/20 cannon, and a dorsal barbette containing an MG 151 cannon and an MG 131 machine-gun. The design, which was completed in the summer of 1943, received the RLM designation Ju 187, but as it offered only a marginal increase in performance over the Ju 87D it was abandoned.

Perhaps the most interesting experiments carried out with the Ju 87 were those conducted by the Graf Zeppelin research institute at Ruit near Stuttgart. A standard Ju 87D-3 was fitted with two large overwing pods to carry two men each. Mounted on each wing at almost centre-span, the huge non-jettisonable pods had large transparent windows to assist the pilot's sideways vision. Despite extensive tests, the scheme, which was to enable agents to be dropped behind the Allied lines, was not adopted.

Early in May 1945, Oberst Hans Ulrich Rudel led the remnants of his once proud Geschwader on its final mission. Comprising three Ju 87G-1s

The Ju 87D-3 experimentally fitted at the Graf Zeppelin research institute with two overwing personnel pods each carrying two men.

and four Fw 190s, the formation set course for the American-occupied airfield at Kitzingen. One by one the aircraft landed, each running into the other at the end of the runway, thus destroying themselves and providing, by this act of defiance, a fitting obituary to the story of the Ju 87.

*Wartime operational units:* IV.(Stuka)/LG 1, I., II. and III./St.G 1, I., II. and III./St.G 2, I., II. and III./St.G 3, I./St.G 5, III./St.G 51, I./St.G 76, I., II. and III./St.G 77, I., II. and III./SG 1, I., II. and III./SG 2, I., II., III. and 10.(Pz)/SG 3, I./SG 5, I., II., III. and 10.(Pz)/SG 77, 4.(Stuka)/186, NSGr 1, 2, 4, 9 and 10.

Ju 87A-1: Span 13·8 m (45 ft 3⅓ in); length 10·8 m (35 ft 5¼ in); height 3·9 m (12 ft 9½ in); wing area 31·9 sq m (343·3 sq ft).
Empty weight 2,300 kg (5,071 lb); loaded weight 3,400 kg (7,497 lb).
Maximum speed at 4,000 m (13,124 ft) 320 km/h (199 mph); maximum range 1,000 km (621 miles).

Ju 87B-2: Span 13·8 m (45 ft 3⅓ in); length 11 m (36 ft 1 in); height 3·9 m (12 ft 9½ in); wing area 31·9 sq m (343·3 sq ft).
Empty weight 2,750 kg (6,063 lb); loaded weight 4,250 kg (9,321 lb).
Maximum speed at 4,000 m (13,124 ft) 380 km/h (237 mph), at sea level 340 km/h (211 mph); cruising speed at 4,600 m (15,092 ft) 280 km/h (174 mph); service ceiling 8,000 m (26,248 ft); maximum range (with bomb load) 600 km (372 miles).

Ju 87D-7: Span 15 m (49 ft 2½ in); length 11·5 m (37 ft 8¾ in); height 3·9 m (12 ft 9½ in); wing area 33·6 sq m (362·6 sq ft).
Empty weight 3,940 kg (8,687 lb); maximum loaded weight 6,600 kg (14,553 lb).
Maximum speed at 4,800 m (15,745 ft) 400 km/h (248 mph); cruising speed at 5,000 m (16,405 ft) 300 km/h (187 mph).

There is a Ju 87B in the Museum of Science, Chicago, and the Royal Air Force has the Ju 87D-4 c/n 494085.

393

The Junkers Ju 88 V1 which flew for the first time on 21 December, 1936. (*H. Redemann*)

# Junkers Ju 88

Originally conceived as a high-speed bomber for the Luftwaffe, the Junkers Ju 88 was adapted for a wide variety of additional rôles. Besides serving as a bomber and reconnaissance aircraft on all fronts to which German armed forces were committed, it operated as an intruder over the British Isles, a torpedo-bomber in the Mediterranean and Norway, a night fighter in Germany, in the anti-tank rôle on the Russian steppes, and finally, as the war drew to its conclusion in 1945, as a missile. It was undoubtedly the Luftwaffe's most used bomber aircraft, being built in numbers that equalled the total of all other German medium bombers.

The Ju 88 was first mooted early in 1934 as a result of a requirement issued to the German aircraft industry for a Kampfzerstörer or multi-purpose aircraft. Three companies produced designs: Focke-Wulf the Fw 57, Henschel the Hs 124, and Junkers the Ju 85/88. After some consideration, the RLM revised the specification to call purely for a Schnellbomber or high-speed bomber. The new requirement, drawn up early in 1935, was issued to four companies: Focke-Wulf, Henschel, Junkers, and Messerschmitt. Focke-Wulf refused to participate in the new competition, but the other three companies produced respectively the Hs 127, the Ju 85/88, and the Bf 162.

Two parallel studies were produced by the Junkers design team, W. H. Evers, and Alfred Gassner, an American, both of whom had considerable experience of lightweight stressed metal skin aircraft construction. Work began on the projects on 15 January, 1936, the first, designated Ju 85, had twin fins and rudders, and the second, designated Ju 88, a single fin and rudder. After some deliberation, the RLM decided on the Ju 88 project, and construction of the first prototype was begun in May 1936.

Because of excessive structural weight, only one prototype of the Focke-Wulf Fw 57 was completed. (*R. C. Seeley*)

The Ju 88 V1, D-AQEN, made its first flight at Dessau on 21 December, 1936, piloted by Flugkapitän Kindermann. The aircraft was an attractive cantilever low-wing monoplane with an oval-section fuselage and extensively glazed pilot's cabin in the nose. The three-seat aircraft was built of metal with flush riveted stressed-skin covering and was powered by two 1,000 hp Daimler-Benz DB 600A engines in annular cowlings. The electrically-operated backwards-retracting mainwheels had twin oleo legs, and a small retractable tailwheel was fitted. Only limited flight testing was carried out before the prototype crashed, after which it was replaced by t<sup>L</sup>e generally similar V2, D-AREN, on 10 April, 1937.

The Ju 88 V3 D-ASAZ, which made its first flight on 13 September, 1937, was the first Ju 88 to have the 1,000 hp Junkers Jumo 211A, the reliable twelve-cylinder liquid-cooled engine, cowled in circular nacelles with annular radiators, which was to provide the power for all subsequent A-series production aircraft. The Ju 88 V3, with a redesigned cockpit canopy similar to that later to be fitted to the production variant, was

Although possessing an excellent performance, the Henschel Hs 127 was abandoned in favour of the Junkers Ju 88.

395

extensively tested at the experimental station at Rechlin, and the results of these trials were so encouraging that they led to the abandonment of its two rivals, the Hs 127 and the Bf 162.

The fourth prototype followed on 2 February, 1938, with increased length and loaded weight, a 'beetle's eye' glazed nose and provision for a fourth crew member. The V4 also had a ventral gondola with provision for a 7·9 mm MG 15 machine-gun. The Ju 88 V5, D-ATYU, which first flew on 13 April, 1938, was originally similar to the V4 but powered by two 1,200 hp Jumo 211B-1 engines. It was later modified by the removal of the ventral gondola, the lowering of the cockpit roof line and the fitting of a streamlined unglazed nose for record-breaking purposes. Widely publicized as the Ju 85S, the machine, piloted by Ernst Siebert and Kurt Heintz, established a new closed-circuit record in March 1939, carrying a 2,000 kg (4,410 lb) payload over a distance of 1,000 km (621·37 miles) at an average speed of 517 km/h (321·25 mph). Four months later, the machine, with the same crew, achieved an average of 500 km/h (310·6 mph) over a 2,000 km (1,242·74 miles) closed circuit.

The Ju 88 V6 which was fitted with four-blade propellers and acted as forerunner of the A-series production aircraft.

Five further prototypes were ordered during this time, the first of which, the Ju 88 V6, D-ASCY, with single oleo undercarriage legs and four-blade airscrews, served as the prototype for the Ju 88A-0 pre-production aircraft. The Ju 88 V7 which flew on 27 September, 1938, was similar, later being fitted with two 20 mm MG FF cannon and two 7·9 mm MG 17 machine-guns in an unglazed nose as prototype for the Ju 88C Zerstörer.

The Ju 88 V8 and V9, which flew respectively on 3 and 31 October, 1938, were fitted with dive-brakes to meet an RLM requirement that the aircraft should be capable of being used as a dive-bomber. The Ju 88 V10, which flew on 3 February, 1939, was fitted with external bomb racks. Many more Ju 88s were allocated Versuchs numbers, the last recorded being the Ju 88 V102 used in connection with the Ju 88B programme.

A pre-production batch of ten Ju 88A-0s were completed for Service trials by Erprobungskommando 88 early in 1939, being essentially similar

A Ju 88A-4 of 8./KG 51, with a similar aircraft of 7.Staffel beyond. (*H. Obert*)

to the Ju 88 V10. In August 1938, Ernst Udet laid down the Takt system of construction for all large state-owned firms such as Junkers and Arado. Tools and jigs for the Ju 88 were produced at the Junkers Schönebeck plant, and the wing and tail sections were constructed respectively at Halberstadt and Leopoldschall. The fuselage was originally built in two complete shells which were then brought together at Aschersleben, but later the fuselage was broken down into many small parts. This method was to play a major part in the endless versions of the Ju 88 that were produced.

Sixty Ju 88A-1 production aircraft were produced by the end of 1939. By 1940, the rate had risen to 300 aircraft per month and was to remain more or less constant throughout the war. Flight testing of the aircraft was carried out at Berneburg. Dornier at Wismar, Arado at Brandenburg, Heinkel at Oranienburg, Henschel at Schönefeld, and the Volkswagen plant at Wolfsburg, all provided components for the aircraft.

The Ju 88A-1 was generally similar to the A-0 apart from having three-blade VDM airscrews. The aircraft was capable of either dive- or level-bombing attacks, the latter being made with the aid of a Lotfe periscopic bomb sight. Diving attacks were made at a 60 deg angle, the pilot placing the target within the illuminated circle on his sight. Bombs were usually released at 1,500 m (3,300 ft) immediately after which the elevators were automatically placed in the full-up position, bringing the aircraft out of its dive and into a climb. Early in the life of the Ju 88, limitations were placed on high-speed manoeuvres as the aircraft was so highly stressed that the first ten Arado-built machines all suffered undercarriage failures on landing.

The Ju 88A-2 was essentially similar to the A-1, but was fitted with rocket-assisted take-off equipment; the Ju 88A-3 was a dual-control trainer variant; and the A-5, which preceded the A-4, had increased span and a strengthened undercarriage.

397

A Ju 88A-4 of 4./KG 77 undergoing routine maintenance. (*H. Thiele*)

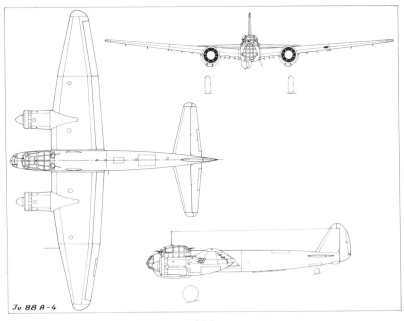

Ju 88 A-4

By far the most important variant of the series was the Ju 88A-4 which had the new wing introduced on the A-5 and 1,340 hp Junkers Jumo 211J-1 or J-2 engines. The new wing was increased in span from 18·37 m (60 ft 3¼ in) to 20 m (65 ft 7½ in) and had all-metal ailerons in place of the fabric-covered type. Defensive armament varied considerably, a typical combination comprising one 7·9 mm MG 81 machine-gun in the nose, one 13 mm MG 131 machine-gun or a twin MG 81Z installation firing forward, two MG 81s in the rear of the cockpit, and an MG 131 or MG 81Z in the rear of the ventral gondola. Bomb load comprised ten 50 kg (110 lb) SC 50 bombs internally and four 250 kg (550 lb) SC 250 or two 500 kg (1,100 lb) SC 500 bombs externally. With no internal load, the A-4 could carry four SC 500 bombs.

The undercarriage of the Ju 88A-4 was also strengthened and provision made for increased armour protection, especially for the pilot. The Ju 88A-4/Trop was a tropicalized variant with provision for sun blinds, water containers, and other desert survival equipment, and tropicalized variants of the A-1 and A-5 were also converted by Luftwaffe maintenance units.

The Ju 88A-6 was generally similar to the A-5 but fitted with a special balloon-cable fending device. To compensate for the bulk of this structure, a special counterbalance weight of 60 kg (132 lb) was installed in the tail. The Ju 88A-6 proved extremely unwieldy and most that saw service had the balloon fending structure removed. The Ju 88A-6/U was a special three-seat long-range maritime reconnaissance bomber without ventral gondola but with FuG 200 Hohentwiel search radar.

The Ju 88A-7 was a dual-control trainer version of the A-4, while the A-8 was similar to the A-6 but had the fuselage of the A-4 and balloon-cable cutters in the wings. The Ju 88A-9, A-10, and A-11 were the respective designations of the Ju 88A-1/Trop, A-5/Trop, and A-4/Trop modified from the outset for desert operations. The Ju 88A-12 was a dual-control trainer with wider cockpit but without the ventral gondola and dive-brakes.

The Ju 88A-13 was a heavily-armoured ground attack variant which could carry up to sixteen 7·9 mm MG 17 machine-guns, six of which were mounted in each of two pods carried beneath the ETC 500 bomb racks. The Ju 88A-14 was essentially an improved version of the A-4 designed mainly for the anti-shipping rôle. Armament was increased by the installation of a 20 mm MG FF cannon in the ventral gondola, but there was no bomb sight. The Ju 88A-15 had a bulged wooden bomb bay which enabled it to carry up to 3,000 kg (6,600 lb) of bombs. The Ju 88A-16 was a dual-control trainer version of the A-14. The final production model of the A-series was the A-17 torpedo-bomber. Instead of the four underwing ETC 500 racks there were two PVC racks, each of which could carry an LT F5b torpedo.

In August 1939 the experimental Ju 88 test unit at Rechlin, Erprobungskommando 88 under Hptm Pohl, was redesignated I./KG 25.

The Ju 88A-15 which was fitted with a bulged wooden bomb bay. (*H. Redemann*)

In September 1939, I./KG 25 was renamed I./KG 30, the unit's first operation taking place on 26 September when it took-off from Westerland/Sylt to bomb British warships in the Firth of Forth. Gefr Karl Francke was credited with sinking the aircraft carrier *Ark Royal*, but in fact no damage was suffered by any British ship.

I./KG 30's next notable operation was on 16 October, 1939, when nine aircraft took-off again to bomb warships in the Firth of Forth. The attack was intercepted by Spitfires from Nos. 602 and 603 Squadrons from Turnhouse, and the leading aircraft, piloted by Hptm Pohl, was shot down. The second machine, piloted by Oblt von Riesen, scored a near miss on the destroyer *Mohawk*, but was chased out to sea by Spitfires, eventually landing at Westerland with one engine out of action. Some damage was caused to the warships, but two aircraft were lost and the others severely mauled. It was an early warning of what was to come.

Hptm Doench replaced Pohl as commander of I./KG 30, and two further Gruppen were established respectively on 17 November, 1939, and 1 January, 1940. Following the complete establishment of KG 30, the famous Eagle Wing, the Ju 88A-1 was delivered to LG 1, KG 51 Edelweiss, and Aufklärungsgruppe 122.

All three Gruppen of KG 30, plus 1.(F)/122, took part in the invasion of Norway and Denmark on 9 April, 1940, operating from Westerland and Hamburg-Fuhlsbüttel respectively. KG 30, with semi armour-piercing SD 1000 bombs, operated mainly against Royal Navy vessels often acting upon sighting reports provided by 1.(F)/122.

When Germany invaded France and the Low Countries in May 1940, the Luftwaffe possessed eight Gruppen equipped with the Ju 88A-1. The aircraft saw limited service during the campaign, offensive bombing mainly being done by the Heinkel He 111. It was not until the Battle of Britain that the aircraft's first major test came. Isolated attacks were made by aircraft from LG 1 and KG 51, but the first major assault came on 11 August, 1940, when He 111s and Ju 88s bombed Weymouth and Portland.

Next day, sixty-three Ju 88A-1s from KG 51 and KG 54 bombed

400

Portsmouth, fifteen aircraft diverting to attack the radar station at Ventnor in the Isle of Wight. Parts of Portsmouth were heavily damaged and the radar station was put out of action for 11 days. On 'Eagle Day'*, 13 August, 1940, KG 54 attacked the aerodromes at Odiham and RAE Farnborough but was broken up by RAF fighters. Largescale Luftwaffe attacks followed during the afternoon, with the loss of 45 aircraft.

On 15 August, fifty Ju 88A-1s from I., II. and III./KG 30 from Aalborg attacked the Bomber Command aerodrome at Driffield in Yorkshire. Ten Whitleys were destroyed on the ground for the loss of six Ju 88s. Late that afternoon, twelve Ju 88s from I./LG 1 under Hptm Kern bombed Middle Wallop, and 15 aircraft from II./LG 1 under Maj Debratz took-off to attack Worthy Down. I./LG 1 destroyed several Spitfires on the ground; but II./LG 1 was less successful, only three aircraft reached their target; and no less than five aircraft from 4./LG 1 were shot down. Only the Staffelkapitän, Hptm Joachim Helbig, and one other crew survived.

On 16 August, two Ju 88s attacked the aerodrome at Brize Norton and destroyed 46 training aircraft. Two days later, Ju 88s bombed Gosport and caused damage to airfield installations. Operations continued against airfield targets until, on 7 September, the Luftwaffe switched its attentions to the bombing of London and brought some relief to the hard-pressed pilots of RAF Fighter Command.

The operations that followed resulted in severe losses for the German Air Force. Prior to the Battle of Britain, Luftwaffe fighter and bomber units had never trained together and this resulted in poor co-operation between them. Consequently, RAF fighters broke through the escort and took heavy toll of the bombers, although the high speed of the Ju 88 helped to prevent such severe losses as suffered by the He 111 and Do 17.

From October 1940, daylight raids by the Luftwaffe in force began to tail off and, during the winter of 1940–41, the Luftwaffe turned its attentions to the night bombing of the British Isles. These missions were often

* 'Eagle Day' was the code name for the day on which the proposed German invasion of the British Isles was to begin.

A standard production Ju 88A-1 after a slight accident. (*J. Zazvonil*)

401

fraught with danger, not from prowling fighters, but because of the poor condition of many of the French airfields. Many of these were improved for daylight operations during the Battle of Britain but were ill-suited for use at night. In addition, many of the more experienced crews had been killed during the summer and their replacements were not used to flying the Ju 88A-1 at night, a somewhat difficult machine to handle.

By the end of 1940 the Ju 88A-4 had begun to replace the A-1 on the production lines. The increase in span was to prove a great advantage, and the type also had its defensive armament increased, this having been proposed by Ernst Zindel (chief of Junkers design and construction) early in 1940 but vetoed by Udet and Göring until after the Battle of Britain.

At an early stage in the development of the Ju 85 and Ju 88, the Junkers design team had proposed a variant of the basic designs with a more extensively glazed nose which eliminated the stepped windscreen. This was initially thought by the RLM to be much too radical, but in 1939 the proposal was re-examined, and consideration was given to powering the aircraft with 1,500 hp Jumo 213A or 1,550 hp BMW 139 engines then undergoing Service trials.

Three production variants were proposed: the Ju 88B-1 level- and dive-bomber, the B-2 two-seat destroyer, and the B-3 two-seat reconnaissance aircraft. The initial prototype was the Ju 88B V1, D-AUVS, which flew early in 1940 and was basically an A-1 airframe with the new nose. It was powered by two 1,600 hp BMW 801MA radials, this engine having supplanted the BMW 139 some time earlier. The Ju 88B V1 was followed by a batch of ten Ju 88B-0 pre-production aircraft which differed in having the increased wing span of the A-5 and a fuselage length increase of 70 cm (2 ft $3\frac{1}{2}$ in). Armament comprised six 7·9 mm MG 81 machine-guns, and maximum bomb load was 2,500 kg (5,510 lb).

In the event, no production of the Ju 88B was undertaken, but several of the B-0s were delivered to a Staffel of the Aufklärungsgruppe of the Oberbefelshaber der Luftwaffe. Alternatively known as Kommando Rowehl, the unit operated a mixture of Ju 86P-2s and Ju 88B-0s from Bucharest and Cracow and systematically mapped the western part of the Soviet Union in preparation for the forthcoming German invasion.

As previously described, the Ju 88 V7 was modified as the prototype of the proposed Ju 88C heavy fighter. The aircraft possessed a maximum speed of 502 km/h (312 mph), similar to that of the Messerschmitt Bf 110C which was then entering service. In addition, the Junkers product had almost three times the range of the Bf 110, and early in 1939 the RLM ordered it into production. During July and August, a small batch of Ju 88C-0s were converted from early production A-1s and used operationally during the Polish campaign by the Zerstörerstaffel of KG 30.

The Ju 88 destroyer was proposed in two variants: the C-1 with 1,600 hp BMW 801MA air-cooled radials, and the C-2 with the liquid-cooled 1,200 hp Jumo 211B-1. Because of the decision to channel early BMW

402

801 production to the new Focke-Wulf Fw 190 fighter, the C-1 and proposed radial-engined C-3 and C-5 were abandoned. Thus the first production model was the Ju 88C-2 which carried an armament of one 20 mm MG FF cannon and three 7·9 mm MG 17 machine-guns.

In May 1940, the RAF began to attack Germany by night and it was at once realized that the Flak units, to whom the defence of Germany had been entrusted, were unequal to the task. Therefore, on 20 July, 1940, Göring ordered Gen Kammhuber to set up a night-fighter force. I./NJG 1 had been formed in June from I./ZG 1, and it was joined in July by II./NJG 1 formed from the Zerstörerstaffel of KG 30 and III./NJG 1 formed from IV.(N)/JG 2.

II./NJG 1, which became operational at Amsterdam-Schiphol, was basically an intruder Gruppe mainly equipped with the Ju 88C-2 and commanded by Hptm Karl Heyse. The Gruppe moved to Gilze Rijen in August and began night-intruder operations against Bomber Command stations in Yorkshire, Lincolnshire, and East Anglia, acting on reports provided by the German radio interception network. On 11 September, 1940, the unit was redesignated I./NJG 2, and on 10 December, 1940, mainly at Kammhuber's instigation, Göring promised to expand the unit to full Geschwader strength. This proposal was strongly resisted by Gen Hans Jeschonnek, German Chief of Air Staff, who commented, 'at this rate the night fighters will absorb the whole of the Luftwaffe'.

Consequently, the Gruppe never had many more than 20 aircraft operational at one time, a hopelessly inadequate number to cope with the ever-increasing threat posed by Bomber Command. Despite these limitations, the unit was very successful, maintaining almost nightly patrols over British aerodromes.

On 13 October, 1941, Hitler ordered that further intruder operations should cease immediately and that I./NJG 2 be transferred to the Mediterranean. There is little doubt that had these operations been expanded, they could have substantially reduced the effectiveness of RAF night raids. The British bombers were at their most vulnerable during take-off and landing, and the failure of the Luftwaffe to exploit this to the full must be considered a great tactical error.

Despite the abandonment of intruder operations, development of the fighter versions continued with the Ju 88C-4. This was similar to the C-2, but had the increased span and other improvements introduced on the A-4. The Jumo 211B-2 engines were retained initially but were replaced by the 1,340 hp Jumo 211J-1 and J-2 units, under the designation Ju 88C-4/R. Other improvements included more armour protection for the crew and an extra 7·9 mm MG 15 machine-gun in the rear of the ventral gondola.

The first major fighter variant was the Ju 88C-6 introduced in 1942. It was powered by two Jumo 211J engines and had three forward-firing 7·9 mm MG 17 machine-guns, a single 20 mm MG FF/M cannon in the nose plus a further pair of MG FF/M weapons in the nose of the gondola. The

A Ju 88C-6a day fighter. This aircraft had the standard 'beetle eye' nose painted on in order to deceive enemy pilots into thinking it was a standard bomber variant. (*H. Redemann*)

Ju 88C-6a was a day fighter; the C-6b differed in having full radar equipment for use as a night fighter. Initially FuG 202 Lichtenstein BC was carried, but by the autumn of 1942 this was replaced by the simplified FuG 212 Lichtenstein C-1.

The Ju 88C-7a was an intruder with provision for an internal 500 kg (1,100 lb) SC 500 bomb and a jettisonable ventral gun pack; the C-7b had underwing racks for a total of 1,500 kg (3,300 lb) of bombs; and the C-7c was a night fighter powered by two 1,600 hp BMW 801MA radial engines. Little production was undertaken before the variant was replaced by the Ju 88R series.

The Ju 88R-1 was basically a C-6 powered by two 1,600 hp BMW 801MA or BMW 801C engines. Armed with three MG 17 machine-guns, two MG FF and one 20 mm MG 151/20 cannon, it used a similar radar system to that of the C-6b. The Ju 88R-2 was powered by two 1,700 hp BMW 801D engines and carried FuG 217 Neptun R tail warning radar. In addition, some machines had FuG 350 Naxos Z passive radar, which homed on to the emissions produced by both the British and American H2S systems.

The Ju 88R-1 night fighter differed from the C-6b purely in having BMW 801 radial engines. (*H. Redemann*)

404

Initially, the Luftwaffe's reconnaissance units had to make do with a conversion of the standard production Ju 88A-1, pending the introduction of a specialized photographic-reconnaissance aircraft. Designated Ju 88D, the definitive conversion was basically a Ju 88A-4 airframe fitted with an Rb 50/30 and an Rb 20/30 camera in the rear fuselage. It had extra fuel tanks in place of the forward bomb bay, but no dive-brakes.

The Ju 88D-0 was powered by 1,200 hp Jumo 211B-1 engines, although it was proposed to fit the more powerful Jumo 211J units in the D-1 production model. In the event, these failed to materialize until later, and consequently the first model to enter service was the Ju 88D-2 powered by Jumo 211B-2, G-1 or H-1 engines. Both models were fitted with four ETC bomb racks, the inboard racks being used to carry long-range drop tanks. The Ju 88D-1/Trop and D-2/Trop (later respectively redesignated Ju 88D-3 and D-4) carried desert survival equipment, and the Ju 88D-5 carried one Rb 50/30 and two Rb 75/30 cameras.

As previously described, several of the ten Ju 88B-0s completed were delivered to the Aufklärungsgruppe of the Ob.d.L. The remaining machines were retained by Junkers for test purposes, one aircraft being fitted with BMW 801C engines and a power-operated dorsal turret, under the designation Ju 88E-0. The turret contained a single 13 mm MG 131 machine-gun, and two additional weapons of similar calibre were mounted in the nose and in the rear of the cockpit. No production of the Ju 88E-0 was undertaken, but following disappointing progress with the Ju 288, the RLM ordered Junkers to develop the aircraft into the Ju 188.

With operations against the British Isles beginning to tail off, the Luftwaffe switched its attention to the attack on Greece, code-named Operation Marita. At 18.00 hr on 6 April, 1941, III./KG 30 took-off from Gerbini to mine the approaches to Piraeus harbour. The aircraft of 7./KG 30 led by Hptm Hajo Herrmann carried both bombs and mines and came in to the attack at low level. Herrmann's aircraft released its bombs on the freighter *Clan Frazer* which, unbeknown to the German crew, still had 250 tons of high explosives on board. With a shattering explosion of almost nuclear proportions, the ship blew up, destroying in the holocaust ten other vessels and making the port of Piraeus unusable for many weeks. The defences were temporarily shattered, and then one anti-aircraft gun suddenly opened fire, putting Herrmann's port engine out of action. With great skill, Hermann managed to land his aircraft at Rhodes which had recently fallen to the Italians.

With the capture of Greece, Germany turned to the capture of Crete. On 20 May, the Luftwaffe launched a huge airborne armada against the island, and two days later large forces from the British Mediterranean Fleet were spotted to the north. They were attacked by Ju 87s from St.G 2 and later by Dornier Do 17s from KG 2 and Ju 88s from Hptm Cuno Hoffmann's I./LG 1 from Eleusis. The cruisers *Naiad* and *Carlisle* were damaged, and shortly afterwards the battleship *Warspite* received a direct hit. Three and a half hours later, the cruiser *Gloucester* was sunk by bombs from St.G 2 and I. and II./LG 1. It was further proof of the vulnerability of unescorted naval vessels to air attack.

At 03.15 hr on 22 June, 1941, Germany launched Operation Barbarossa, the invasion of the Soviet Union. Operations began with a strike against Russian airfields in an attempt virtually to destroy the Soviet Air Force on the ground. The airfields were so widely dispersed that it was only possible to allocate three bombers to attack each. Many of the Ju 88s and Do 17s carried 2 kg (4½ lb) SD 2 and 10 kg (22 lb) SD 10 fragmentation bombs, the latter being dropped from high altitudes in bundles of four. These proved extremely effective against personnel and aircraft but had an unfortunate habit of failing to release from the aircraft's bomb racks. The bombs would become fused and a slight jolt would cause them to detonate and blow the aircraft to pieces.

The initial attack on Soviet airfields was followed by the bombing of Moscow, by Ju 88s from KG 3 and KG 54 and Heinkel He 111s from III./KG 26, part of KG 28, KG 53, KG 55, and KGr 100. One hundred and twenty-seven bombers took part in the raid, which resulted in the dropping of 104 tons of high explosive and 46,000 incendiary bombs. On 23 June, 1941 Moscow was attacked by 115 bombers and on the next night by 100 aircraft. After that, the raids rapidly dwindled in number and strength and by the end of 1941 the average number of aircraft taking part in an attack was seven.

Perhaps the most notable of Ju 88 operations were those directed against the PQ series of Arctic convoys. These convoys were engaged in bringing urgently needed supplies to the Soviet ports of Murmansk and Archangel. In addition to having to cope with action by German forces, the convoys also had to face some of the worst weather in the world.

The first 12 convoys proceeded with virtually no hindrance from the Luftwaffe, but at the end of March 1942 PQ 13 was attacked by Ju 88s from III./KG 30 under Hptm Hajo Herrmann based at Banak, when only two ships were sunk. The next convoy, PQ 14, had to return to Iceland because of fog and ice floes, but PQ 15 lost three ships to the torpedo-bombers of the Luftwaffe.

The first real effort came on 25 April, when PQ 16 was spotted from Blohm und Voss Bv 138s of 2./Kü.Fl.Gr 406 and Focke-Wulf Fw 200s from I./KG 40. Sighting reports of the 34-ship convoy were relayed to the forward headquarters of Luftflotte 5 at Banak, and one hundred Ju 88s from KG 30 at Banak and He 111s from I./KG 26 at Bardufoss swept in to the attack. After the first onslaught, the convoy scattered, but the attacks continued for five days, the ships coming within range of the Ju 87s of I./St.G 5 on 30 April. Despite the huge effort involved, only seven ships were sunk.

On 27 June, 1941, convoy PQ 17 sailed from Iceland in thick fog. On 2 July it was spotted by U-boats and continuously shadowed by Focke-Wulf

A Ju 88A-4 fitted with a pair of L 10 glider torpedoes, after its port undercarriage leg collapsed.

Fw 200s from I./KG 40. The ships were attacked by U-boats and by Heinkel He 115 torpedo floatplanes, but it was not until 5 July that the first really devastating attack was made. The three Gruppen of KG 30 under Maj Erich Blödorn attacked successively under their respective Kommandeurs, Hptms Kahl, Stoffregen and Herrmann. The first victim was the freighter *Peter Kerr*, sunk by Lt Clausener, and this was followed by the sinking of the *Washington, Pan Kraft, Fairfield City, Bolton Castle*, and *Zaafaran*. Yet again the convoy scattered, but this time to little effect. The final aerial attack was made on 10 July when Ju 88A-4s from 5. and 6./KG 30 severely damaged the *Hoosier* and *El Capitan*.

On 12 July, Generaloberst Stumpff, commander of Luftflotte 5, claimed the destruction of all 34 ships that comprised convoy PQ 17. His claim was based on the fact that no ships were to be found in the White Sea area, but in actual fact the survivors were hiding along the coast of Novaya Zemlya. It was not until several weeks later that the last of 11 survivors limped into Archangel. Even though Stumpff's claims were exaggerated, it was not until September that the Allies again attempted to mount another Arctic convoy operation.

Convoy PQ 18 sailed from Loch Ewe for the North Russian ports on 2 September, 1942. Ju 88 forces in Northern Norway at this time comprised 1.(F)/22 at Bardufoss, III./KG 26, I., II. and III./KG 30, plus the Ergänzungs-Staffel of the latter unit at Banak. These were supported by the He 111s from I./KG 26 at Banak and several naval reconnaissance units. The convoy was sighted on 8 September by a Blohm und Voss Bv 138 from Kü.Fl.Gr 406 near Jan Mayen Island. It comprised 39 freighters, three tankers, a rescue ship, and many destroyers and corvettes.

Then, on the 9th, Luftflotte 5 headquarters were shocked to receive reports of a second group of ships, six destroyers, a cruiser, and, most worrying of all, the carrier *Avenger*, with the Hurricanes of Nos. 802 and 883 Squadrons aboard. The first attack came on 13 September when the convoy was bombed by Ju 88s from KG 30. They were pursued by the Hurricanes, the Fleet Air Arm aircraft eventually claiming the destruction of five Luftwaffe aircraft, with a further 17 badly damaged. Despite further strikes by KG 26, convoy PQ 18 reached Archangel in good order. Thirteen ships were lost, but these losses were not nearly so bad as those suffered by PQ 17. PQ 18 was the last Arctic convoy to be attacked by Luftwaffe forces until just before the war ended. Early in November 1942, KG 26, KG 30, and the newly-formed I./KG 60, were transferred to the Mediterranean area.

Four RZ 65 rocket-launchers beneath a Ju 88A-4. (*H. Redemann*)

On 28 November, 1941, Generalfeldmarschall Kesselring's Luftflotte 2 was transferred from central Russia to the Mediterranean. Luftflotte 1 units were combined with formations from the Second Air Fleet to form Luftflotte Ost which for a time controlled the whole of northern and central Russia.

In December 1941, Kesselring initiated the campaign which was aimed at the final destruction of Malta. The island had long been an irritant to the Axis powers, and the final jab came in November when 12 transports, totalling 54,900 tons, were sunk by British ships and aircraft. Five bomber Gruppen, I./KG 54, II. and III./KG 77, KGr 606 and KGr 806, all equipped with the Ju 88A-4, were transferred to Sicily. In addition, the Ju 88C-equipped Staffeln of I/NJG 2 were moved there to begin intruder operations against Malta. At first only scattered attacks were carried out, and Luftwaffe losses were quite severe.

Then, on the night of 20/21 March, a large Ju 88 formation escorted by Messerschmitt Bf 110s from III./ZG 26 attacked Takali airfield. Some aircraft carried 1,000 kg (2,200 lb) PC 1000 RS rocket bombs in an attempt to destroy a possible underground hangar. The attack was followed next morning by a further assault, and on 22 March other airfields were bombed.

On 23 March, the Luftwaffe diverted its effort against Malta to bomb a convoy of four transports, four cruisers, and 18 destroyers attempting to bring supplies to the beleaguered island. Eventually all four transports were sunk, but not before some 5,000 tons of supplies were unloaded at Valletta. The Luftwaffe then concentrated on bombing the dock installations around Valletta, and in April the Royal Navy destroyers were obliged to depart.

In mid-April, 47 Spitfires were flown in to Malta from the carriers *Eagle* and *Wasp*, but Luftwaffe bombers managed to destroy several of them on the ground before they could be re-armed and fuelled. On 11 May, 1942, the four destroyers of Capt Poland's flotilla left Alexandria in an attempt to intercept an Axis convoy off Benghazi. At 15.30 hr the ships were attacked by I./LG 1 based at Heraklion under Hptm Joachim Helbig and *Lively* sank after a near miss. This attack was followed by one from II./LG 1 based at Eleusis under Hptm Kollewe, and then, at 17.00 hr, I./LG 1's Ju 88s struck again. *Kipling* sank almost immediately, followed eventually by the *Jackal*, and only Capt Poland's flagship, *Jervis*, returned to Alexandria intact.

On 13 June, a British convoy comprising six transports escorted by a battleship, two aircraft carriers, three cruisers and 17 destroyers was sighted by a reconnaissance aircraft. From the following day, the convoy was continually attacked, and by the time it reached Malta, only two transports remained. The last convoy to operate under these conditions passed through the Straits of Gibraltar on 9/10 August. It comprised 14 merchant vessels escorted by three aircraft carriers, a battleship, six cruisers, and 24 destroyers. The convoy was continuously attacked by Ju 88s from Catania, Gerbini and Comiso in Sicily, and eventually nine of the 14 transports were sunk.

During the summer of 1942, a Ju 88C-4 was experimentally fitted with a Nebelwerfer rocket launcher. This weapon comprised six revolving barrels firing a WGr 21 or 28 missile, and the modified version of the aircraft was known unofficially as the Ju 88N. Trials with the Nebelwerfer as an aircraft weapon were soon abandoned in favour of the specialized Ju 88P series of ground attack aircraft.

The Ju 88P V1 was modified from a Ju 88A-4, with a very large fairing beneath the fuselage housing a 75 mm KwK 39 armoured-car cannon. This forward-firing weapon was supplemented by a twin MG 81Z installation in the rear. Trials against captured Soviet T-34 tanks at Rechlin-Roggentin were relatively successful, it being found that the aircraft could fire two shells during each pass. These trials resulted in the construction of a small number of Ju 88P-1 production aircraft. These differed in having the nose of the Ju 88C, armour protection for the engines, and the improved 75 mm PaK 40L anti-tank gun. This weapon was semi-automatic, one of the three crew members being employed to complete the loading process.

Several Ju 88P-1s were delivered to the Versuchskommando für Panzerbekämpfung in 1943 for operational tests, and the aircraft was also issued to Panzerjäger-Staffel 92 and 6./KG 3, which experimented with the aircraft as a 'train-buster'. The machine proved extremely unwieldy in the air and was very vulnerable to fighter attack.

The Ju 88P-2 was fitted with a pair of 37 mm BK 3·7 Flak 18 cannon with the barrels offset to port. The Ju 88P-3 was similar but had increased armour protection for the crew. An attempt was made by Erprobungskommando 25 to use the aircraft as a destroyer against USAAF bomber formations, but it was found to be completely unsuitable. The small number of aircraft completed were delivered to NSGr 1, 2, 4, 8, and 9 and used operationally during 1944.

The Ju 88P-2 which was fitted with two 37 mm BK 3·7 guns in a large ventral housing.

The final variant of this series was the Ju 88P-4 which was fitted with a single 50 mm BK 5 cannon in a smaller gondola than that of the first three sub-types. Other projected weapons for the Ju 88P included the 88 mm Düka 88 U-boat gun, several types of flame-throwers, and the RZ 65 solid-fuel rocket. A plan existed for fitting the Ju 88P-4 with a 22-shot magazine launcher for this rocket, and one machine was actually completed and tested.

The Ju 88C series was never used in large numbers by the Nachtjagdgeschwader, which operated the Messerschmitt Bf 110 until the middle of 1944 when the Ju 88G began to appear. Late in 1943, one of the few Ju 88C-5s completed was fitted, as the Ju 88G V1, with FuG 212 Lichtenstein C-1 radar and no less than six MG 151/20 cannon. The Ju 88C was followed by a batch of Ju 88G-0 pre-production aircraft which differed in having the square tail fin used on the Ju 188, FuG 220 Lichtenstein SN-2 radar and reduced armament of four MG 151/20 cannon. Both types were powered by 1,700 hp BMW 801D radials and carried a rearward firing 13 mm MG 131 machine-gun.

The Ju 88G-1, which was placed in production in the spring of 1944,

The 'toasting fork' aerial array used in conjunction with the Lichtenstein SN-2 radar equipment is clearly visible in this view of a Ju 88G-1 (c/n 714811). (*USAF*)

was generally similar to the G-0. The Ju 88G-2 was to have been produced by Henschel, who ceased production of the bomber variants in April 1944. The G-3, G-4, and G-5 were projects only, and the Ju 88G-6a was similar to the G-1 but was powered by two 1,700 hp BMW 801G engines. The Ju 88G-6b carried additional radio equipment, two MG 151/20 cannon in a Schräge Musik obliquely upward-firing gun installation, and enlarged fuel capacity. The Ju 88G-6c was similar but was powered by two 1,750 hp Jumo 213A engines.

The final production variant of the G-series was the Ju 88G-7 which was powered by two Jumo 213E engines, which, with MW-50 power boosting, produced 1,800 hp for take-off. The Ju 88G-7a carried FuG 220 Lichtenstein SN-2 radar, and the G-7b had FuG 218 Neptun V equipment with Hirschgeweih 'toasting fork' aerials or with the Morgenstern array in which the elements were enclosed by a pointed wooden nose cone. The G-7c, of which only ten were completed before the end of the war, carried FuG 240 Berlin N-1s centimetric radar with a scanner enclosed in a plywood nose cone.

The Ju 88H was an ultra-long-range reconnaissance aircraft based on a combination of Ju 88D-1 and G-1 components. The fuselage was similar to the Ju 88D, but there was no ventral gondola and the length was increased to 17.75 m (57 ft 10¾ in) by the insertion of two additional sections. The wings and engines were taken from a Ju 88G-1, and the aircraft had a maximum range of 5,150 km (3,200 miles). Two variants

Luftwaffe aircrew prepare a Ju 88G-7a of I./NJG 100 for a sortie. (*R. C. Seeley*)

411

were built, the Ju 88H-1 reconnaissance aircraft with FuG 200 Hohentwiel search radar and three cameras, and the H-2 destroyer with the radar and cameras replaced by six 20 mm MG 151/20 cannon.

The Ju 88H-3 and H-4 were respectively similar to the H-1 and H-2 but were powered by two 1,776 hp Jumo 213A-12 engines, which could be boosted to provide 2,240 hp with MW-50 water-methanol injection. The fuselage length was increased by a further 3 m (9 ft 10 in), the span of the tailplane was also increased and Ju 188 vertical tail surfaces were used. The few aircraft completed were adapted as the lower components for Mistel combination aircraft. The Ju 88G-8 was similar to the G-7 but with the fuselage of the H-2, the G-10 was similar but was used in connection with the Mistel programme, and the G-12 was developed into the Ju 188R series.

Early in 1943, a standard production Ju 88A-4 airframe was fitted with two 1,700 hp BMW 801D radials and a smooth, rounded, glazed nose in place of the 'beetle's eye' type of the earlier model. Intended as the prototype of the proposed S-series, the machine received the alternative designations Ju 88 V93 and S V1. This aircraft was 65 km/h (40 mph) faster than its predecessor, but the increase was not sufficient for the RLM, who urged Junkers to produce an aircraft capable of escaping fighter interception. The Ju 88S-0 however, was similar to the V93, carrying an armament of one 13 mm MG 131 and three 7·9 mm MG 81 machine-guns.

During the late autumn of 1943, the Ju 88S-1 appeared on the production lines. It was powered by two BMW 801G-2 engines with GM-1 power boosting which increased the output of each engine to 1,730 hp. The GM-1 system, which involved the injection of nitrous oxide into the superchargers where it provided additional oxygen for combustion, was first tested by the Ju 88 V55 in April 1943. The one snag with the GM-1 system was that the nitrous oxide was held under pressure in three tanks aft of the bomb bay, and a single hit in one of these tanks was sufficient to blow the aircraft to pieces.

The Ju 88S-1 had no ventral gondola, less armour, defensive armament

One of the fastest versions of the Ju 88 was the S-1 which could be distinguished by its smoothly-glazed nose.

The Ju 88S-1 entered service with I./KG 66 early in 1944. (*H. Redemann*)

confined to one rearward-firing MG 131 machine-gun, and a crew of three. No dive-brakes or automatic pull-out device were fitted, and normal offensive load comprised two 1,000 kg (2,205 lb) SD 1000 bombs carried on racks beneath the wing centre section. The Ju 88S-2 was powered by 1,810 hp BMW 801TJ engines with exhaust driven turbo-superchargers and was fitted with a bulged wooden bomb bay similar to that of the Ju 88A-15. The final development was the Ju 88S-3, which was basically an S-1 airframe powered by two 1,776 hp Jumo 213A-12 engines. The power from these engines could be temporarily increased to 2,125 hp by the addition of GM-1. Maximum speed with the GM-1 system was 615 km/h (382 mph) at 8,500 m (27,900 ft).

A photographic reconnaissance version of the Ju 88S, designated Ju 88T, was produced in parallel with the bomber. The Ju 88T-1 was similar to the Ju 88S-1 but carried an Rb 20/30 and either an Rb 50/30 or Rb 75/30 camera installation in the rear fuselage. Defensive armament was restricted to a rearward firing MG 131 or twin MG 81Z machine-gun, and a crew of three was carried. The Ju 88T-3 was similar to the S-3, but plans for largescale production of the machine at Henschel's Schönefeld factory were abandoned in favour of the Ju 88G-2 night fighter.

As may be imagined, the Ju 88 was used in connection with many experimental devices. In December 1944, an FLA 103Z remote-controlled barbette housing two MK 103 cannon was tested beneath a Ju 88, this weapon being intended for the Ju 388J. The 50 mm MK 214A cannon was fitted to a Ju 88, as was the Kurt spherical bomb which featured rocket braking in a separate base and underwent trials at Travemünde and Leba in 1944. A Ju 88A-5 acted as testbed for the 800 kg (1,760 lb) thrust BMW 003A-1 turbojet, the engine being carried below the forward fuselage to one side of the ventral gondola.

A proposal was also made to install two BMW 003A-1 turbojets under the wing racks of the Ju 88H-1, the engines being used to boost the aircraft's performance when over the target area. The proposed variant was to have had two 1,800 hp BMW 801TG engines as main powerplants, and estimated maximum speed was 718 km/h (446 mph) at 9,000 m (29,500 ft) with all four engines in operation.

In order to test the Junkers 109-004 turbojet in flight, an early production engine was attached beneath the fuselage of a Ju 88A-5. (*H. Redemann*)

In addition to serving widely with the Luftwaffe, the Ju 88A-4 was also delivered to several of Germany's allies. In March 1943, the Finnish Air Force bomber unit, PLeLv 44, was transferred to Germany and equipped with 23 ex-Luftwaffe Ju 88A-4s. The aircraft saw service both against the Russians and, after the peace treaty of 4 September, 1944, against German forces which remained in Finland.

A similar situation developed with the Ju 88A-4 and D-1 aircraft delivered to the Rumanian forces. Initially operating against Soviet forces in southern Russia, the aircraft were used against the Germans following the Rumanian coup d'état of 23 August, 1944. The Ju 88A-4 also saw service with the 4/III Bomber Group of the Hungarian Air Force and was delivered to the 51st Gruppo Bombardamento Terrestre of the Regia Aeronautica in August 1943. The Italian Air Force's 9th Stormo also operated a small number of Ju 88D-1 reconnaissance aircraft.

By early 1943, operations by the Kampfgeschwader had slumped to an average of 39 per day. Most Ju 88s equipped bomber groups in the Mediterranean area, although a number were in service on the Eastern Front and in Norway. Eleven reconnaissance groups were equipped with the Ju 88D and three units operated the Ju 88C-6b night fighter in Germany and the Mediterranean area. One destroyer unit, V./KG 40 at Bordeaux-Mérignac, was also operational with the Ju 88C-6a.

V./KG 40 had been formed in September 1942 in an attempt to combat the operations of RAF Coastal Command against German U-boats. The unit saw little action until March 1943, and in fact only 27 aircraft from the unit were sighted by RAF patrols during the whole period. After March, frequent skirmishes between V./KG 40 and the Mosquitos, Beaufighters, and, in one notable case, a Sunderland of RAF Coastal Command, were reported. During the winter of 1943/44, V./KG 40 was redesignated as the third I./ZG 1, the unit being joined a little later by the newly-formed III./ZG 1. Groups I. and III./ZG 1 remained operational with their Ju 88C-6as until June 1944 when the Allied landings made their bases untenable, I./ZG 1 having only three operational aircraft on 20 June. Both units were disbanded, their personnel being absorbed by fighter units which were then in the process of formation or expansion.

Ju 88 operations in the Mediterranean were mainly confined to the night bombing of ground targets in the battle area during March and April 1943, although even these were made difficult by heavy Allied attacks on their Sardinian airfields towards the end of March. Eventually the units were withdrawn to Sicily and Italy, and, when the Allies landed in Sicily on the night of 9/10 July, 1943, the only Ju 88 unit remaining on the island was 2.(F)/122 at Trapani.

By this time, the only two Ju 88 bomber groups were left on the Eastern Front. Five groups had been transferred to Italy, KG 51 had been withdrawn to Illesheim for re-equipment with the Messerschmitt Me 410A, and KG 6 was divided between the Mediterranean and Western Fronts. On 3 September the Allies landed at Reggio, and seven days later at Salerno, and after a period of frantic operations the campaign entered a static phase.

On 21 January, 1944, the Allies landed at Anzio in an attempt to resolve the deadlock on the Italian front. The only Ju 88 bomber units able to oppose the landings were I. and III./LG 1, part of KG 30 and I./KG 76. Based in northern Italy, these units struck at ground targets but were rarely able to mount sorties of over 15 aircraft. Luftwaffe bomber forces were steadily withdrawn from February 1944, and, when the Allies landed in Normandy in June 1944, no Kampfgruppe remained near the beachhead.

In December 1943, several Ju 88 units were withdrawn from Italy and transferred to France to join forces with other bomber units placed under the command of Gen Maj Dietrich Pelz, who had been given the title Angriffsführer England (Attack Leader England) and had been charged with the 'reprisal' bombing of British cities. Under his command were seven Ju 88A-4 equipped bomber Gruppen: I., II. and III./KG 6, II./KG 30, I. and II./KG 54 and I./KG 76, although the latter unit returned to Italy following the Anzio landings.

Pelz knew that his crews lacked the training of those that had struck at England some three years before and therefore decided to use the pathfinder unit, I./KG 66, to lead the attacks. The first operation was on 21 January, 1944, when virtually every available bomber on the Western Front struck against London. Some indication of their effectiveness can be gauged from the fact that of the 500 tons of bombs dropped, only 30 fell on London. Another attack was carried out two days later, but the results were little better. In the two attacks no less than 57 Luftwaffe aircraft were shot down by night fighters and anti-aircraft fire.

During this period the first Ju 88S-1s were delivered to I./KG 66, and this type began to replace the now rather ancient A-4 variant. Attacks continued against British cities throughout February, March, and April, although the number of aircraft employed dwindled rapidly. Accuracy improved somewhat, although during one attack on Bristol no bombs fell on the city, the majority hitting Weston-super-Mare, some 20 miles away.

It was not until the last week of April that Peltz turned his attention to the bombing of British ports. The Allies had begun to assemble shipping in the southern ports in preparation for the forthcoming D-Day landings. On 23 April, 1944, one hundred sorties were flown against Portsmouth, and two days later 130 aircraft bombed the Poole/Swanage areas. Little success was achieved in these or succeeding attacks, and by the end of May they had been virtually abandoned.

Two partially stripped Ju 88s in a Luftwaffe hangar. (*R. C. Seeley*)

During the middle of 1944, the Ju 88G-1 began to enter service with the night fighter units, the aircraft rapidly replacing the Messerschmitt Bf 110. By August 1944, the Ju 88 had been delivered to NJG 1 (who were also equipped with the Heinkel He 219), NJG 2, 3, 4, 5, 6, I./NJG 7 and I./NJG 100. On 13 July, 1944, the first Ju 88G-1 fell into Allied hands when 4R-UR of 7./NJG 2 landed by mistake at Woodbridge in Suffolk. The aircraft was fitted with both FuG 200 Lichtenstein SN-2 and FuG 227 Flensburg which homed on to the emissions of the British 'Monica' tail warning radar. The Allies were able to examine both devices, with the result that the 'Monica' set was removed from all Bomber Command aircraft and a new type of 'Window' introduced to jam SN-2 radar.

By August 1944, the Luftwaffe's bomber force was all but finished. The only Ju 88 equipped units that remained were I. and II./LG 1, II./KG 6, II./KG 30, I./KG 54 and I./KG 66 in the West, I. and II./KG 26 in Italy and 14.(Eisenbahn)/KG 3 in central Russia. KG 1 had been equipped with the Heinkel He 177 in May 1944, KG 76 was receiving its first Arado Ar 234 jet bombers, and KG 6, KG 30, and KG 54 were being slowly withdrawn with the intention of re-forming them as day fighter units. In the event, only I./KG(J) 54 became operational with the Messerschmitt Me 262, the other units slowly converting to the Messerschmitt Bf 109 and Me 262 when the war ended. In December 1944, only I. and II./LG 1 under Oberst Joachim Helbig remained in the West with I. and II./KG 26 in northern Norway. This unit was equipped with the Ju 88A-17 torpedo-bomber and operated against the Arctic convoys. Its only success came on 23 February, 1945, when it sank the freighter *Henry Bacon*.

In contrast to the demise of the Ju 88 as a bomber, the aircraft was now equipping virtually the whole of the night fighter force. The Ju 88G became the mount of many of the Luftwaffe's night fighter aces. Perhaps the most famous was Oberst Helmut Lent, Kommodore of NJG 3, with 102 night victories, but others included Hptm Heinz Rökker of 2./NJG 2 with 62 kills, Maj Paul Zorner of II./NJG 100 with 59, Hptm Martin Becker of IV./NJG 6 with 58, Hptm Gerhard Raht of I./NJG 2 with 58 and Hptm Heinz Strüning of 9./NJG 1 with 56.

As a final gesture of defiance, an attempt was made to resume intruder operations over the British Isles on 3 March, 1945. About 100 aircraft succeeded in penetrating British defences, attacking aerodromes and shooting down 22 bombers. A small follow-up sortie was attempted during the next night, but the Luftwaffe lost 20 machines during the attacks, and the operations were abandoned. It was during the second attack that the last enemy aircraft to be brought down on British soil was claimed by the defences. This was the Ju 88G-6 coded D5-AX of 13./NJG 3 which crashed at Elvington near Pocklington aerodrome, Yorkshire, at 01.51 hr.

*Wartime operational units:* 3.(F)/10, 2., 3. and 4.(F)/11, 4.(F)/14, 1., 2. and 3.(F)/22, 1. and 3.(F)/33, 2., and 3.(F)/100, 1.(F)/120, 1., 3. and 4.(F)/121, 1., 2., 3., 4. and 5.(F)/122, 1., 2., 3. and 6.(F)/123, 1.(F)/124, 1. and 2./Nachtaufklärungsstaffel, 1., 2., 3. and 4./Aufkl.Gr.Ob.d.L., NAGr 12, the meteorological reconnaissance squadrons, I. and III./ZG 1, III. and IV./ZG 26, II., III. and IV./NJG 1, I., II., III. and IV./NJG 2, I., II., III. and IV./NJG 3, I., II. and III./NJG 4, I., II., III. and IV./NJG 5, I., II., III. and IV./NJG 6, I./NJG 7, NJGr 10, I. and II./NJG 100, I. and II./NJG 200, Nachtjagdstaffel Norwegen, (also used in small numbers by NJG 101 and 102), NSGr 30, KG 1, I./KG 2, KG 3, III./KG 4, KG 6, I./KG 25, KG 26, 30, II. and V.(Z)/KG 40, KG 51, 54, I./KG 60, I. and III./KG 66, KG 76, 77, II. and III./KG 100, KGr 101, 106, 506, 606 and 806, LG 1, Versuchsverband Ob.d.L., II. and Versuchskommando/KG 200, Panzerstaffel 92 and various test Kommandos.

Ju 88A-4: Span 20 m (65 ft 7½ in); length 14·4 m (47 ft 2¾ in); height 4·85 m (15 ft 11 in); wing area 54·5 sq m (586·63 sq ft).

Empty weight 9,860 kg (21,737 lb); normal loaded weight 12,100 kg (26,680 lb); maximum loaded weight 14,000 kg (30,870 lb).

Maximum speed at 5,300 m (17,390 ft) 470 km/h (292 mph), at 6,000 m (19,685 ft) 450 km/h (280 mph); cruising speed at 5,300 m (17,390 ft) 370 km/h (230 mph); climb to 5,400 m (17,716 ft) 23 min; service ceiling 8,200 m (26,900 ft); normal range 1,790 km (1,112 miles); maximum range 2,730 km (1,696 miles).

Ju 88G-7b: Span 20 m (65 ft 7½ in); length 15·58 m (51 ft 1½ in); height 4·85 m (15 ft 11 in); wing area 54·5 sq m (586·63 sq ft).

Loaded weight 13,100 kg (28,885 lb).

Maximum speed at 9,000 m (29,529 ft) 626 km/h (389 mph); initial rate of climb 500 m/min (1,640 ft/min); service ceiling 10,000 m (32,810 ft); normal range 2,250 km (1,398 miles).

Ju 88S-1: Span 20 m (65 ft 7½ in); length 14·85 m (48 ft 8⅔ in); height 4·8 m (15 ft 8½ in); wing area 54·5 sq m (586·63 sq ft).

Empty weight 8,300 kg (18,300 lb); loaded weight 13,800 kg (30,430 lb).

Maximum speed at 8,000 m (26,250 ft) 559 km/h (341 mph), at 8,000 m (26,250 ft) 610 km/h (379 mph) with GM-1; cruising speed 465 km/h (289 mph); service ceiling 10,500 m (34,450 ft), or 11,500 m (37,730 ft) with GM-1.

The Royal Air Force has the Ju 88R-1 c/n 360043.

# Junkers Ju 90

The Luftwaffe, unlike the air powers of the two western Allies, was never to possess a strategic bomber force. This was undoubtedly one of the major reasons why Germany lost the Second World War for, had it been able to strike at Atlantic convoys bringing urgently needed supplies to Britain and to destroy Soviet production centres, the outcome of the conflict might well have been different.

It is not widely known that a strategic bomber force for the Luftwaffe

After the abandonment of the Junkers Ju 89 bomber, the aircraft was developed into the Ju 90 airliner for Lufthansa. (*R. C. Seeley*)

was proposed as early as 1935, mainly by Generals Wever and Milch, respectively Chief of Staff and Secretary of State for Air. Contracts were placed with Dornier and Junkers for the construction of four-engined strategic bombers resulting in the Do 19 and the Ju 89 designs. The former possessed none of the agility usually attributed to Dornier aircraft and was seriously underpowered.

The Ju 89, which was designed by Dipl Ing Ernst Zindel, was a much more sophisticated machine, having a maximum speed of 390 km/h (242 mph) compared with only 320 km/h (199 mph) of the Do 19. The Ju 89 V1, D-AFIT (c/n 4911), made its first flight from Dessau in December 1936 and bore some resemblance to the Ju 86. It was followed by a generally similar second prototype (c/n 4912), and proposed armament was to have comprised three 20 mm MG FF cannon and two 7·9 mm MG 15 machine-guns.

The Junkers Ju 90 V1, D-AALU, which was adapted from the Ju 89 V3 and crashed during flutter trials on 6 February, 1938.

Even as these prototypes were undergoing trials, it was obvious that the whole strategic bomber programme was about to be abandoned. The first major setback came when Gen Wever was killed in an air crash on 3 June, 1936, and a growing distrust between Göring and Milch led to the latter being deprived of many of his powers including the directorship of the RLM's technical department early in 1937.

Realizing that the Ju 89 would soon be abandoned, Junkers asked if they could use the major components of the third aircraft as the basis of a transport for Lufthansa. The RLM granted permission for this, provided that an alternative engine to the 960 hp Daimler-Benz DB 600 could be found for subsequent machines. Therefore, the wings, tail assembly, and engines of the Ju 89 V3 (c/n 4913) were married to an entirely new fuselage, the aircraft being redesignated the Ju 90 V1.

The Ju 90 V1, D-AALU *Der Grosse Dessauer*, made its first flight on 28 August, 1937, but crashed during flutter tests on 6 February, 1938. The aircraft was a neat low-wing monoplane with twin fins and rudders and a fully retractable undercarriage. The fuselage was a rectangular-section

419

monocoque structure built mainly of duralumin but with some steel components. Similar materials were used for the wing, which was built in five sections and had marked sweepback to the leading edge. The ailerons and flaps formed the typical Junkers double-wing, a similar principle being used for the elevators and rudders. Apart from the rudders and the rear part of the elevators which had corrugated covering, the aircraft had a smooth duralumin skin with flush riveting.

The Ju 90 V5, D-ABDG *Württemberg*, in service with Lufthansa during 1939. (*Lufthansa*)

Provision was made for 40 passengers who could be accommodated in various cabin layouts. The Ju 90 V1 was powered by four Daimler-Benz DB 600A engines, but the V2, D-AIVI *Preussen* (c/n 4914), had four 830 hp BMW 132H air-cooled radials. The V2 aircraft was the forerunner of the proposed Ju 90B production series, but, with the BMW engines, proved somewhat underpowered. Consideration was given to the design of a heavier aircraft, the Ju 90S, to be powered by four 1,550 hp BMW 139 radials.

Meanwhile, development of the Ju 90 continued, the V3, D-AURE *Bayern* (c/n 4915), entering service on Lufthansa's Berlin–Vienna route in the summer of 1938. The Ju 90 V4, D-ADLH *Sachsen* (c/n 4916), preceded a batch of ten production Ju 90B-1s which were allocated the c/ns 90-0001 to 90-0010 and also received the Versuchs numbers V5 to V14. Thus, the first production Ju 90B-1, D-ABDG *Württemberg*, received the alternative designation Ju 90 V5.

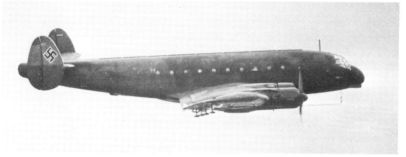

A Ju 90B-1 production aircraft. (*H. Redemann*)

The Ju 90 V6, D-AEDS *Preussen*, replaced the second prototype which had crashed during tropical trials at Bathurst in November 1938. The Ju 90 V8, D-AQJA *Baden*, and the generally similar V9 were to have been delivered to South African Airways under the designation Ju 90Z-2. They were to have been powered by Pratt & Whitney SC3-G Twin Wasp engines and receive the registrations ZS-ANG and ZS-ANH; although the machines were completed in the summer of 1939, they were never delivered to the South African airline.

Four further standard production Ju 90B-1s were completed: the V10, D-ASND *Mecklenburg*, the V12, D-ATDC *Hessen*, the V13, D-AJHB *Thüringen*, and the V14, D-AVMF *Brandenburg*. Only a few of these machines were delivered to Lufthansa, and the war prevented them from being introduced into full-scale passenger service. In 1940, they were impressed into the Luftwaffe as transports and used operationally for the first time during the Norwegian campaign. Eventually the Ju 90 V4 and V6 were returned to Lufthansa, but the remaining machines were retained by the Luftwaffe.

These aircraft were later delivered to the Viermotorige Transportstaffel (Four-engine Transport Squadron) which was formed on 2 January, 1943. The squadron had six Ju 90B-1s plus the Ju 90 V4, two Ju 290s, a Ju 252 and a Focke-Wulf Fw 200B. After being redesignated LTS 290, it

The Ju 90 V7 which was later delivered to the Luftwaffe. (*H. Redemann*)

421

operated supply missions over Stalingrad, then was transferred to the Mediterranean. The Ju 90s remained operational until the autumn of 1943, the squadron having been redesignated Transportstaffel 5 at the end of April. The Ju 290 developed from the Ju 90 is described on page 442.

Ju 90B-1: Span 35·02 m (114 ft 10¾ in); length 26·3 m (86 ft 3½ in); wing area 184 sq m (1,980·55 sq ft).
Empty weight 16,000 kg (35,274 lb); loaded weight 23,000 kg (50,706 lb).
Maximum speed at 2,500 m (8,202 ft) 350 km/h (217 mph); cruising speed at 3,000 m (9,842 ft) 320 km/h (199 mph); landing speed 109·4 km/h (68 mph); service ceiling 5,500 m (18,044 ft); normal range 1,247 km (775 miles); maximum range 2,092 km (1,300 miles).

The second Junkers Ju 60, D-2400, just after take-off. (*Lufthansa*)

# Junkers Ju 160

During the early 1930s, Swissair bought a number of Lockheed Orion high-speed airliners. To compete with these aircraft, Lufthansa commissioned the design of a somewhat similar machine, the Junkers Ju 60.

The Ju 60 was a cantilever low-wing monoplane with an oval-section fuselage in both sides of which were four square cabin windows for the six passengers. The crew of two were seated beneath a raised canopy positioned just behind the radial engine. All-metal construction was used throughout and, although the wings, fin, rudder and elevators had the normal Junkers corrugated skin, the fuselage and tailplane was covered in smooth duralumin sheet.

As far as is known, only two aircraft were built, both in 1932. These were the Ju 60a with a fixed undercarriage and the Ju 60ba 1, D-2400

One of the Junkers Ju 160A-0s, D-UQOR (c/n 4209), which saw service on several of Lufthansa's internal routes. (*Lufthansa*)

(c/n 4201), with a forwards-retracting unit. Both aircraft were powered by a 600 hp BMW Hornet C engine enclosed by a NACA cowling. The Ju 60ba 1 was later re-registered D-UPAL and the first aircraft eventually carried the letters D-URIM.

An improved version of the Ju 60 was produced in 1934 under the designation Ju 160. Essentially similar to the previous design, the Ju 160 had a new wing with a swept leading and straight trailing edges and three passenger windows on either side of the fuselage. Smooth metal sheet covering was used overall. The prototype, the Ju 160 V1 D-UNOR (c/n 4202) was named *Luchs* (*Lynx*) and was powered by a 660 hp BMW 132E radial driving a two-blade metal airscrew. All Ju 160s had inwards-retracting mainwheels, and the Junkers double-wing formed both ailerons and flaps.

The first production model was the Ju 160A which was similar to the prototype apart from having a tailwheel, in place of a skid, and a modified rudder. An improved version was also built, the Ju 160D-0.

Forty-eight Ju 160s were constructed, at least 20 of these entering service with Lufthansa during 1935–36. Apart from operating a large number of domestic services, the aircraft also flew on the Breslau–Prague–Munich route. Most Ju 160s were commandeered by the Luftwaffe after the beginning of the Second World War and were widely used in the communications and training rôles.

Ju 160A: Span 14·32 m (46 ft 11¾ in); length 12 m (39 ft 4½ in); wing area 34·8 sq m (374·5 sq ft).

Empty weight 2,320 kg (5,114 lb); loaded weight 3,450 kg (7,606 lb).

Maximum speed 340 km/h (211 mph); cruising speed at 2,000 m (6,562 ft) 315 km/h (196 mph); landing speed 100 km/h (62 mph); service ceiling 5,200 m (17,060 ft); endurance 3 hr 12 min.

This view of the Ju 188E-1 clearly shows the extended wingtips introduced by the Ju 188 series. (*H. Redemann*)

# Junkers Ju 188

In July 1939 the technical department of the RLM issued the ill-fated Bomber B specification which called for a twin-engined replacement for the Heinkel He 111 and Junkers Ju 88. Junkers were ordered to proceed with all possible speed with their competitor for the requirement, the Ju 288, while radical development of the basic Ju 88 airframe was strictly forbidden. Nevertheless, Junkers continued work on the Ju 188 as a private venture, and subsequent events were to prove the wisdom of their decision.

Development of the Ju 88E-0 airframe led, in September 1941, to the Ju 88 V27, D-AWLN, forerunner of the proposed Ju 188. The aircraft was basically a Ju 88E, being powered by two 1,600 hp BMW 801MA radials, but with new pointed wingtips and the span increased by 2 m (6 ft 6¾ in). In addition to the modified wing, the Ju 88 V27 was fitted with an EDL 131 dorsal turret housing a single 13 mm MG 131 machine-gun. The first real prototype for the Ju 188 was the Ju 88 V44, which, although basically similar to the V27, was fitted with new square vertical tail surfaces and a larger tailplane in an attempt to cure the instability problems suffered with the Ju 88E-0.

By October 1942, the RLM had realized that the Ju 288 would at best be seriously delayed, and they began to show interest in the Ju 188 as a temporary measure pending the introduction of the more radical design into service. The official recognition of the Ju 188 programme led to the Ju 88 V44 being redesignated Ju 188 V1, construction of a second prototype being initiated at the Bernburg factory. This machine joined the test programme in January 1943, and the following month the first Ju 188E-0s appeared.

The Ju 188E-0 and E-1 differed from the prototypes in being powered by

1,600 hp BMW 801ML engines, although later production aircraft were fitted with the 1,700 hp BMW 801D and G. A maximum bomb load of 3,000 kg (6,615 lb) made up of various combinations could be carried. The Ju 188E-2 was a torpedo-bomber which could carry two 800 kg (1,764 lb) LT1b or two 765 kg (1,686 lb) LT F5b torpedoes under the wing, and provision was made for FuG 200 Hohentwiel search radar.

During the summer of 1943, the first Ju 188E-1s were delivered to Erprobungskommando 188, a unit formed specially for introduction of the aircraft into operational service. In August 1943, Erprobungskommando 188 was redesignated as the 4th Staffel of I./KG 66 under Maj Helmut

The Junkers Ju 188E-0 which later served as a transport aircraft for Gen Erhard Milch. (*H. Redemann*)

Schmidt. I./KG 66 had been formed in April 1943 at Chartres from 15./KG 6 and operated a mixed collection of Dornier Do 217s, Ju 188s, and Ju 88Ss on pathfinding duties. The Gruppe's first operation with the Ju 188 over the British Isles was on 18 August, 1943, when Lt Hans Altrogge led three aircraft to bomb the Ruston and Hornsby factory at Lincoln.

In September 1943 a number of Ju 188s were delivered to the specially-formed Erprobungsstaffel of KG 6, and I.Gruppe of the Geschwader completed its conversion to the aircraft in October. KG 6 lost its first Ju 188E-1 on the night of 8/9 October when 3E-KF (c/n 260204) was

The Ju 188E was the first variant of the bomber to see service. (*H. Redemann*)

425

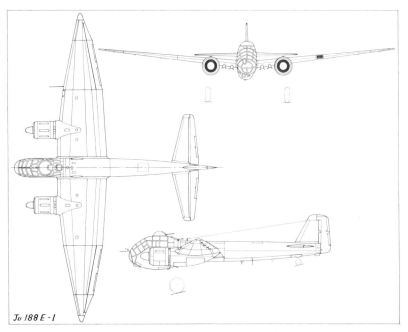

Ju 188 E-1

shot down by a Mosquito. The Ju 188s of I./KG 66 normally carried two 500 kg (1,100 lb) SC 500 high explosive bombs, and eighteen 50 kg (110 lb) LC 50 marker bombs which burned with a green, white, or yellow flame for about four minutes.

The Ju 188 initially caused some confusion among the British defences as its pointed wings bore some resemblance to those of the Mosquito, and, in a few unhappy cases, the British machine was attacked in error. In September 1943, the specialized Ju 188F-1 reconnaissance aircraft was delivered to 3.(F)/121 in southern Russia. Produced in parallel with the Ju 188E, the Ju 188F-1 was powered by two 1,700 hp BMW 801Ds and carried two Rb 50/30 or two Rb 75/30 cameras for daylight photography and two NRb 40/25 or NRb 50/25s for night missions. The Ju 188F-2 was similar, but was powered by two 1,700 hp BMW 801Gs and fitted with FuG 200 search radar. By January 1944, three other units, 3.(F)/22 in northern Russia, 3.(F)/122 in France and 4.(F)/11 in central Russia, were equipped with the aircraft.

At an early stage in the development of the Ju 188, the RLM had asked that the aircraft should be capable of being powered either by the BMW 801 radial or the Junkers Jumo 213A liquid-cooled engine. The 1,776 hp Jumo 213A powered bomber was designated Ju 188A, the first pre-production examples of which left the Bernburg assembly lines shortly after the first E-0s. The Ju 188A-0s also differed from the E in that they had no dive-brakes or automatic pull-out gear and the MG 131 machine-gun in the dorsal turret was replaced by a 20 mm MG 151/20 cannon.

426

Other defensive armament comprised a fixed, forward-firing MG 151/20, an MG 131 in the rear of the cockpit, and a twin MG 81Z installation in the ventral position.

In January 1944, the Ju 188A-2 began to appear on the production lines. This model was powered by two 1,776 hp Jumo 213A-1 engines, the power from which could be boosted to 2,240 hp for take-off by the addition of MW-50 water injection. The Ju 188A-3 was a torpedo-bomber variant similar to the E-2 and was used in small numbers by III./KG 26 towards the end of 1944. The Ju 188C-0 was an experimental version of the A-1 fitted with an FA 15 tail barbette housing two 13 mm MG 131 machine-guns. This remote controlled installation was aimed by means of a PVE 11 periscope but proved extremely unreliable.

A Ju 188F-1 photographic-reconnaissance aircraft. (*F. Selinger*)

The Ju 188D-1 was a photographic reconnaissance variant of the Ju 188A, with a camera installation similar to that of the Ju 188F. There was no forward-firing MG 151/20 cannon, and the crew was reduced to three. The Ju 188D-2 was similar, but had provision for FuG 200 search radar. Eventually, the Ju 188D and F reconnaissance aircraft were delivered to 17 Staffeln, including: 4.(F)/11, 4.(F)/14, 1. and 3.(F)/22, 1. and 3.(F)/33, 2.(F)/100, 1.(F)/120, 3. and 4.(F)/121, 3., 4., 5. and 6.(F)/122, 1. and 6.(F)/123 and 1.(F)/124. The last-mentioned unit. based at Kirkenes in Arctic Norway, often provided sighting reports for the torpedo-bomber operations of KG 26.

By the end of 1943, Hitler was becoming more and more concerned at the build-up of the Allied strategic bombing offensive and ordered the

Luftwaffe bombing force to strike back. By January 1944, a force of nearly 400 medium and heavy bombers had been collected together for Operation Steinbock, the code name for the attack on London. The main components of the force were Ju 88s and Do 217s, although Ju 188s were in service with II./KG 2 and elements of I./KG 6 and I./KG 66. During the spring of 1944, the Ju 188 was delivered to the Stab/KG 6, and by July, I. and II./KG 2 at Gilze Rijen and Achmer, and II. and III./KG 6 at Brétigny and Villarouche were partially equipped with the aircraft.

The Ju 188G-01 which was fitted with a manually-operated tail turret housing two MG 131 machine-guns. (*H. Redemann*)

Other projected variants of the basic airframe included the Ju 188G bomber and the Ju 188H reconnaissance aircraft. The Ju 188G-01, which in fact was rebuilt from the Ju 188 V2, was fitted with a manually-operated tail turret which housed two MG 131 machine-guns, but the extremely small dimensions of the turret led to its abandonment. The production variant, the Ju 188G-2, were to have been fitted with the FA 15 barbette, and were to have had a large ventral pannier capable of carrying a 3,300 kg (7,275 lb) bomb load. The Ju 188H-2 was similar, also being powered by 1,700 hp BMW 801G-2 engines, but was a photographic reconnaissance aircraft.

The Ju 188R-0, of which three machines were completed, was an experimental night fighter variant of the Ju 188E. The first two aircraft carried an armament of four 20 mm MG 151/20 cannon, but the third machine, the Ju 188R-03, was fitted with two 30 mm MK 103 weapons. The Ju 188R offered no advantage over the standard Ju 88G and was abandoned. The Ju 188J, K and L were redesignated Ju 388J, K and L.

The final variants were the Ju 188S and T, fast, high-altitude versions of the Ju 188A, with an entirely new and much slimmer glazed nose and a pressurized nose section. No defensive armament was carried, the aircraft relying solely on its high speed to escape interception. Both versions were powered by two 1,750 hp Jumo 213E-1 engines with three-speed two-stage superchargers and induction coolers. The power could be boosted to no less than 2,168 hp for take-off with the addition of GM-1 injection. The Ju 188S-1 could carry a bomb load of only 800 kg (1,764 lb) but had a

428

maximum speed of 686 km/h (426 mph). The Ju 188T-1 reconnaissance variant attained a speed of 700 km/h (435 mph). Few Ju 188S-1s were completed before production was abandoned. Several of the completed machines were fitted with armour and a 50 mm BK 5 cannon as the Ju 188S-1/U close-support aircraft.

As has previously been described in the Ju 88 history, the nitrous oxide for the GM-1 system was held under pressure in three bottles carried in the rear of the fuselage. Initially, these bottles were extremely vulnerable to enemy fire, but the problem was tackled by Prof Lutz of the DFL at Brunswick who designed a bullet-proof container. The new bottle was completely bullet-proof, and consisted of an inner and outer shell, similar to a vacuum flask, with the nitrous oxide between the two bottles, the vapour serving as an elastic buffer.

Although the Ju 188 proved extremely popular with its crews, only 1,076 were completed before production terminated early in 1944. The aircraft had disappeared from bomber service by the autumn of 1944, but the 570 or so reconnaissance aircraft continued in service until the end of the war.

*Wartime operational units:* 4.(F)/11, 4.(F)/14, 1. and 3.(F)/22, 1. and 3.(F)/33, 1. and 2.(F)/100, 1.(F)/120, 3. and 4.(F)/121, 3., 4., 5. and 6.(F)/122, 6.(F)/123, 2. and 4./Nachtaufklärungsstaffel, Sonder-Aufkl.Sta/Ob.d.L., FAGr 1, 2 and 3, Versuchsverband Ob.d.L., I. and II./KG 2, I., II. and III./KG 6, III./KG 26, I./KG 66, 1., 2. and 6./KG 200, Erprobungskommando 188.

Ju 188E-1: Span 22 m (72 ft 2 in); length 14·95 m (48 ft 0½ in); height 4·44 m (14 ft 6¾ in); wing area 56 sq m (602·778 sq ft).
Empty weight 9,854 kg (21,737 lb); loaded weight 15,508 kg (31,989 lb).
Maximum speed at 6,000 m (19,686 ft) 500 km/h (310 mph); cruising speed at 5,000 m (16,405 ft) 375 km/h (233 mph); climb to 6,000 m (19,686 ft) 17·6 min; service ceiling 9,300 m (30,513 ft); normal range 1,950 km (1,211 miles).

# Junkers Ju 252

By early 1939 it was becoming obvious to Deutsche Lufthansa that the venerable Ju 52/3m, although an efficient and reliable aircraft, was now being surpassed both in Britain and America by new and more advanced designs. Therefore, they requested Junkers to design a new aircraft, to combine the best qualities of the Ju 52 with a much improved performance.

The resultant aircraft, the Ju 252, was of the same general layout as the Ju 52/3m but had smooth instead of corrugated metal skinning, a retractable undercarriage, and a pressurized cabin. Three aircraft were ordered,

Developed as an airliner for Lufthansa, the Junkers Ju 252 V1 first flew in October 1941.

each to be powered by three 1,340 hp Junkers Jumo 211F liquid-cooled engines. The Ju 252 V1, D-ADCC, which made its first flight from Dessau in October 1941, could carry 21 passengers. The Ju 252 V2 and V3 followed in 1942.

Twenty-five Ju 252s had been ordered by Lufthansa, but following unfavourable reports from the war fronts, it was decided to cut the order to 15 and deliver these to the Luftwaffe for transport duties. Therefore, the Ju 252 V4 was fitted with a power-operated gun turret above and just behind the pilot's cabin, with provision for carrying a 13 mm MG 131 machine-gun. In addition to this, the machine was fitted with a large ventral

One of a batch of Ju 252A-1 production aircraft delivered to the Luftwaffe in 1943.

loading ramp which, when lowered, raised the rear of the fuselage to a level position so that a military vehicle could be loaded.

Several Ju 252A production aircraft were also allocated Versuchs numbers, these aircraft being essentially similar to the fourth prototype, powered by three 1,400 hp Jumo 211J engines. Three further variants were projected but not built. The Ju 252B was to have been fitted with increased armament, the Ju 252C powered by three Bramo 323 radials, and the Ju 252D fitted with floats.

The first aircraft to be delivered to the Luftwaffe was the Ju 252 V5 which entered service with Lufttransportstaffel 290 (LTS 290) in January 1943. Based at Berlin-Tempelhof, the unit, commanded by Hptm Braun, also possessed a number of Ju 90s, Ju 290s, and a Focke-Wulf Fw 200. The Ju 252 V5 was destroyed by Allied action after LTS 290 transferred to Grosseto in Italy in March 1943, and two months later the unit was redesignated Transportstaffel 5. The Ju 252 V3 was used as a troop transport in August 1943, and the V4 and several of the Ju 252As served with Transportstaffel 5 and I./KG 200.

Ju 252 V5: Span 34·09 m (111 ft 10⅓ in); length 25·1 m (82 ft 4¼ in); height 6·6 m (21 ft 8 in); wing area 121·5 sq m (1,307·87 sq ft).
Empty weight 13,100 kg (28,885 lb); loaded weight 22,000 kg (48,510 lb).
Maximum speed at 6,000 m (19,686 ft) 439 km/h (273 mph); maximum cruising speed at 5,700 m (18,701 ft) 418 km/h (260 mph); initial rate of climb 225 m/min (738 ft/min); service ceiling 6,850 m (22,674 ft); normal range 4,000 km (2,485 miles); maximum range 6,600 km (4,101 miles).

# Junkers Ju 287

In November 1943, Oberst Siegfried Kneymeyer, became Germany's new Chief of Technical Air Armament (Chef TLR/E). His qualifications included Luftwaffe service, studies in physics and aerodynamics, and the distinction of making the first high-altitude reconnaissance sortie over North Africa in a Ju 86P-2. From April 1943 he was technical officer to Gen Pelz (then Angriffsführer England) and, from July 1943, was Göring's personal consultant on technical matters. Although he was not heeded at first, Kneymeyer proposed the abandonment of all conventionally-powered bombers (except the Ju 88) and a concentration on jet fighters and bombers. He considered that a speed superiority margin of 150 km/h (93 mph) was theoretically possible and that it was essential for Luftwaffe aircraft to have this margin in order to make up for numerical inferiority. Such a speed margin over the best Allied aircraft had already been proved feasible with such aircraft as the Messerschmitt Me 262 fighter, but what of similar possibilities for the bomber? The prototype of

431

The Junkers Ju 287 V1 (RS-RA) was a flying testbed for the radical sweptforward wing planned for the Ju 287 jet bomber. Where possible, components from other aircraft were adapted in order to speed the construction of the testbed. (*USAF*)

the world's first turbojet bomber, the Arado Ar 234 V1, had, in fact, already flown on 15 June, 1943, but this aircraft was very small for a bomber (only marginally larger than the Me 262) and its unswept wing limited its speed to about that of the best Allied aircraft.

Kneymeyer therefore became interested in a bomber project which a team under Dipl Ing Hans Wocke had been studying at Junkers from about June 1943. This bomber project envisaged the use of more turbojet power than hitherto and a wing sweep of some 25 deg in order to allow a heavy bomber to exceed Mach 0·8 in level flight. At this time, wings with marked sweep on both leading and trailing edges had not been flown, although Prof A. Busemann had suggested such wings at a 1935 conference in Rome. For some time after this, the sweptback wing was seen as the only practical way of reaching high Mach numbers by postponing the drag rise caused by compressibility. Although there was a certain minimum structural depth for a wing of a given chord, the aerodynamic thickness/chord ratio could still be made progressively less with increasing wing sweep. The investigation of wing sweep therefore formed a part of the research programmes of the Luftfahrtforschungsanstalt (LFA), Deutsche Versuchsanstalt für Luftfahrt (DVL) and other institutes and, although it was ascertained that a sweptback wing would be good at high speeds, it was also ascertained that there would be certain stability problems which would prove most troublesome at low speeds.

Dr Wocke proposed that the new bomber would not only use a greater wing sweep angle than before but would be likely to benefit by having the wing swept forward instead of backward. He reasoned that, without losing the essential high speed feature of an aerodynamically reduced thickness/ chord ratio conferred by wing sweep, the radical forward-swept wing would also give other advantages. Stability problems would become most troublesome, not at low speeds, but at high speeds, when it was hoped they would be more easily and safely dealt with. The wingtips would be the last sections to stall due to the lower lift coefficient here so that aileron control would still be available when the main wing section had stalled. Shock waves which originated at the wing root would be unable to spread out to the wingtips. Since wingtip leading-edge slots and washout would not be

432

necessary to maintain aileron control at high angles of attack, the associated drag penalty was avoided. Apart from these and other aerodynamic benefits (which were confirmed by wind-tunnel tests), there was another incidental but significant benefit in that the wing spars could easily be arranged to avoid the space needed for the fuselage bomb bay, thereby allowing the maximum bomb load to be carried internally without resorting to drag-producing external bomb loads. On the debit side, it was foreseen from the start, and proved in later flight tests, that axial twisting of the wing had to be avoided as far as possible by suitable structural design, which meant there should be the minimum number of cutouts in the wing skin.

This view clearly shows the unorthodox configuration of the Ju 287 V1.

In March 1944 the RLM ordered prototype development of the bomber, the designation Ju 287 was issued, and detail design work began under Dipl Ing Ernst Zindel. Because of the wing's radical nature, it was decided to flight test this on a jet aircraft of similar proportions to the proposed Ju 287 but quickly built from whatever parts could be adapted. Nevertheless, this flying testbed was designated Ju 287 V1. Its fuselage, adapted from a Heinkel He 177A, was ready by April 1944, and the fitting of the new wings began. Other adaptations included Ju 388 tail components, Ju 352 mainwheels and captured Consolidated B-24 Liberator nosewheels. Since initial flights were primarily aimed at low-speed evaluation, a non-retractable undercarriage sufficed, and this was of the tricycle type with twin, separated nosewheels and wheel spats. Although more power was planned for subsequent aircraft, four Junkers Jumo 109-004B-1 turbojets each of 900 kg (1,980 lb) static thrust were sufficient for the Ju 287 V1. These engines were attached one at each side of the forward fuselage and one beneath the trailing edge of each wing. The all-metal wing had two spars with heavy, taper-machined cap sections, and the wing section was of a special Junkers reverse-camber laminar form. Since the wing roots were to be the first to stall, the inner wing leading edges were provided with slots to delay the stall. For landing, the wing trailing edge could be cambered along its entire clear length by drooping the ailerons 23 deg and by lowering the flaps up to 40 deg. A tail parachute was fitted for braking.

The Ju 287 V1 with ciné-camera near the fin to film movement of the wool tufts on the wing and wing/fuselage areas.

Five months after detail design began, the Ju 287 V1 (RS-RA) made its first flight on 16 August, 1944, with Flugkapitän Siegfried Holzbauer at the controls. Because the runway at Junkers' Dessau plant was of insufficient length, the aircraft was transferred for this and further flights to Brandis, and it was from there and at the same time that the equally revolutionary Messerschmitt Me 163B Komet rocket-powered interceptors were making their first operational sorties. Despite the longer runway, the Ju 287 V1 still needed the additional power of a Walter 109-501 jettisonable rocket unit of 1,000 kg (2,200 lb) thrust fitted beneath each turbojet. The take-off must, therefore, have been a very noisy, smoky affair.

For the low-speed trials, a camera was mounted forward of the fin in a streamlined fairing to record the movements of wool tufts attached to the wing upper surfaces. Apart from some engine failures, the aircraft proved very pleasant to fly and required little trimming for differing conditions. There were, however, some bad effects caused by the sweptforward wing. When the aircraft was yawed, the trailing wing gained lift which produced a rolling tendency. A more serious problem arose when the aircraft was put into tight turns at high speed, when the flexing of the wings tended to tighten the turn, and extra elevator loads were needed to counteract this. A similar effect could be encountered if a gust struck the wing, when the

434

flexing of the wing would tend to increase the applied force further, unlike a sweptback wing where the reverse happens.

Since there was little possibility of further structurally stiffening the wing, the notion of mass balancing the wing by mounting the engines forward of the wing main spar was arrived at. This arrangement was planned for the Ju 287 V2, for which two engines were to be mounted beneath each wing and one on each side of the forward fuselage. For this aircraft, and for the planned Ju 287A-0 pre-production and Ju 287A-1 initial production aircraft, six BMW 109-003A-1 turbojets each of 800 kg (1,760 lb) static thrust were to be fitted. The Ju 287 V2 was designed from the start as an all-new aircraft and was intended for high-speed flight testing up to the designed limit. Only the wing was basically the same as the V1 prototype, and the new fuselage had a bulged and fully glazed nose and was to accommodate the retracted undercarriage wheels. The upper sections of the main oleo legs, which were attached to the wing main spar, retracted into the wings.

When, in July 1944, bombers were generally abandoned in favour of fighters, official backing for the Ju 287 development was dropped, although construction of the Ju 287 V2 had been started. Junkers continued work, however, at a slower pace, and the Ju 287 V1 produced valuable data during the course of some 17 flights. The RLM then mysteriously again took an interest in the development and in March 1945 ordered the Ju 287 into production. Construction then continued with the Ju 287 V2 at a dispersed Junkers factory near Brandis. Work also started on the Ju 287 V3, which was to have a pressure cabin for a crew of three, accommodation for a 4,000 kg (8,820 lb) bomb load, a remote-controlled

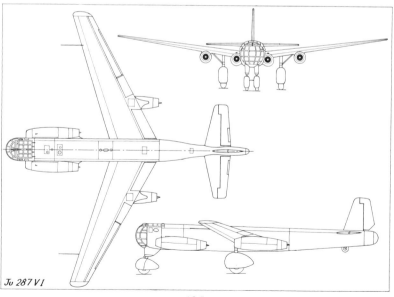

Ju 287 V1

435

tail barbette and other operational equipment, to act as the prototype for the Ju 287A-0. Since the arrangement of using six BMW 109-003 or similar turbojets was aerodynamically unsound, project studies were made of the aircraft powered by fewer, but more powerful, engines. In the Ju 287B-1, power was to be provided by four Heinkel-Hirth 109-011A-1 turbojets each of 1,300 kg (2,866 lb) static thrust, while the Ju 287B-2 was to be powered by either two Junkers Jumo 109-012 turbojets each of 2,780 kg (6,130 lb) static thrust or two BMW 109-018 turbojets each of 3,400 kg (7,497 lb) static thrust. Although none of these engines were ready by the war's end, the BMW design was of special interest since it was intended to operate at altitudes up to 16,500 m (54,120 ft).

By the end of the war, Soviet forces had captured the Ju 287 V1 (which had suffered bomb damage after its transference to Rechlin test and evaluation centre) and the unfinished Ju 287 V2. These aircraft, together with Dr Bruno Baade (formerly of Junkers' Dessau factory) and other German engineers, were transferred to Podberezhye in the USSR. At this centre the Ju 287 programme was continued under Baade and began with flights of the Ju 287 V1 from Nikolovdskoye airfield with the German test pilot Kapitän Dülgen at the controls. The Ju 287 V2 was then completed but in a modified form using sweptback wings. This aircraft was flown with various German engines and developments of these and is said to have flown at about 1,000 km/h (621 mph) before the programme was ended by about 1948. Interestingly enough, the post-war Hamburger Flugzeugbau HFB 320 Hansa executive jet aircraft with sweptforward wings is evidence that Dipl Ing Hans Wocke persisted with his ideas in post-war years since he presided over the design of that aircraft.

Ju 287 V-1: Span 20·11 m (65 ft 11¾ in); length 18·3 m (60 ft 0½ in); wing area 58·3 sq m (627·3 sq ft).

Empty weight 12,510 kg (27,557 lb); maximum loaded weight 20,000 kg (44,100 lb).

Maximum level speed at 6,000 m (19,685 ft) 559 km/h (347 mph); maximum diving speed 650 km/h (404 mph); landing speed 190 km/h (118 mph); stalling speed 170 km/h (105 mph); service ceiling 10,800 m (35,425 ft); maximum range 1,500 km (932 miles).

Ju 287 V3 (including estimated data): Span 20·11 m (65 ft 11¾ in); length 18.6 m (61 ft 0¼ in); wing area 58·3 sq m (627·3 sq ft).

Empty weight 11,930 kg (26,278 lb); maximum loaded weight, including 4,000 kg (8,820 lb) bomb load, 21,520 kg (47,450 lb).

Maximum level speed at 5,000 m (16,400 ft), without bomb load, 865 km/h (537 mph); cruising speed at 7,000 m (22,960 ft) 792 km/h (493 mph); initial rate of climb 880 m/min (2,887 ft/min); service ceiling 12,000 m (39,360 ft); maximum range, with 50 per cent bomb load, 2,125 km (1,320 miles), with full bomb load 1,585 km (985 miles).

The Junkers Ju 288 V2, D-ABWP, was flown in comparative trials with the Junkers Ju 88 V16, D-ACAR, at the end of 1941. (*H. Redemann*)

# Junkers Ju 288

When, by late 1937, the Junkers Ju 88 prototypes had eliminated possible rivals for a production contract, Junkers were already considering a replacement for this aircraft. Their most favoured design for a new medium bomber went under the project designation of EF 73, and its advanced features included a pressurized cabin and remote-controlled defensive armament. Submitted to the RLM, the EF 73 project did not itself obtain a development contract but was used as a basis for formulating the so-called Bomber B specification which was issued late in 1939 to Arado, Dornier, Focke-Wulf, and Junkers. Originally, major requirements were that the B medium bomber type should have a maximum speed of 600 km/h (373 mph) and carry a 4,000 kg (8,820 lb) bomb load to any part of the British Isles from French or Norwegian bases. For power, there were to be two engines of the twenty-four cylinder liquid-cooled type, such as the Junkers Jumo 222 or Daimler-Benz DB 604, being developed for the 2,500 hp class.

Under the guidance of Heinrich Hertel, Junkers' original design was then brought up to date and then modified again in accordance with the wishes of the RLM technical department. By the end of May 1940, cockpit and fuselage mockups had been inspected at Dessau and a contract was issued for the construction of prototypes under the designation Ju 288. (Unusually, this designation did not connect the type in any way with the Ju 88 or the later developments, Ju 188, 388, or 488.) Already, in February 1940, however, Junkers had begun the construction of the Ju 288 V1 with an optimism born out of being instrumental in formulating the official specification.

The other designs competing with the Ju 288 were the Focke-Wulf Fw 191 which later received a development contract, the Dornier Do 317 which was put on low priority development, and the Arado Ar 340 which was eliminated. Of the four designs, the Ar 340 was the most radical in appearance: twin tail booms extended from the engine nacelles but were not connected at the rear by a tailplane; instead, each boom had its own vertical fin and rudder with a half-tailplane attached to the outside. This left a central fuselage with a clear rear field of fire for the armament. Another aircraft, which was developed at first unofficially to the Bomber B specification, was the Henschel Hs 130C.

The elegantly proportioned all-metal Ju 288 was straightforward in layout, being a twin-engined shoulder-wing monoplane with twin fins and rudders, but it had many ingenious features. Typically German was the accommodation of the three crew members in close proximity in a glazed nose cabin, this being pressurized and enclosed beneath a bulged, glazed framework. Since the specification called for dive-bombing ability, dive-brakes were fitted to the upper and lower surfaces of the wing trailing edges, and it was proposed to fit an evaporative engine cooling system in the leading edges of the wing outer panels. The planned armament comprised a rear-firing remote-controlled single-gun barbette on each side of the fuselage. Each main leg of the fully-retractable tailwheel undercarriage had twin wheels and the main legs retracted backwards into the engine nacelles.

In the spring of 1940, the Ju 88 V2, D-AREN, and Ju 88 V5, D-ATYU, were modified to flight test components for the Ju 288 such as the nose section, vertical tail surfaces, dive-brakes, wing leading-edge coolers, and also ducted airscrew spinners. A Ju 288 static test airframe was also available in the same year. Finally, the Ju 288 V1, D-AOTF, made its first flight in January 1941. It was powered by two 1,600 hp BMW 801MA air-cooled radial engines, because the more powerful designated engines were not ready, and had a revised layout of gun barbettes, there being one

First prototype of the Ju 288 to be fitted with Junkers Jumo 222 engines was this Ju 288 V5 which flew in October 1941. The ducted spinners were unsuccessful. (*H. Redemann*)

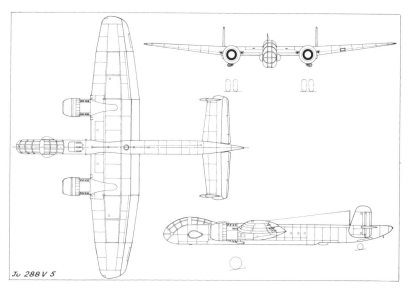

Ju 288 V 5

just behind the cabin and one below the rear fuselage, but the barbettes were dummies. This prototype was joined by the Ju 288 V2, D-ABWP, in the early spring of 1941, and the Ju 288 V4, D-AACS, in the summer. All these prototypes were powered by BMW 801 engines (as were the first prototypes of the Focke-Wulf Fw 191 competitor early in 1942), and it was not until 8 October, 1941, that the Ju 288 V5 was flown with the first available Junkers Jumo 222 engines, although these were not developing their full power. Each engine drove a four-blade airscrew with a ducted spinner extending to the diameter of the engine nacelle, but these spinners proved unsuccessful. At the end of 1941, the Ju 288 V2 was flown in comparative trials with the Ju 88 V16, D-ACAR. Up to this stage, the purpose of the prototypes had been development of the Ju 288A production aircraft, which was to carry a bomb load of 5,000 kg (11,025 lb), but, although the prototypes were giving high performance, various faults and bad handling characteristics indicated that a redesign was needed.

Thus, the planned Ju 288A was abandoned in favour of the Ju 288B production version, which had increased span and wing area, an enlarged tail assembly and a larger cabin for a crew of four, but, because of increases in structural and equipment weights, it was necessary to reduce the bomb load to 3,000 kg (6,615 lb). The first prototype with the new wing for the Ju 288B was the V6, which flew in November 1941; the V7, although it also had the bigger wing, differed in using again the BMW 801 radial engine. The Ju 288 V8 had the smaller wing planned for the Ju 288A but the taller fins planned for the Ju 288B and was flown with Junkers Jumo 222 engines. The first full prototype for the Ju 288B was the Ju 288 V9 (VE-QP) which flew in May 1942. This prototype had Junkers

Jumo 222 engines and dorsal and chin barbettes but no armament. Armament, in the form of a single 15 mm MG cannon, was fitted in a remote-controlled tail barbette for the Ju 288 V3 in the summer of 1942, but this prototype, like the V2, suffered an undercarriage failure. With the lagging development of the Junkers Jumo 222 engine and the abandonment in 1942 of the Daimler-Benz DB 604 engine, prototypes continued to be flown with other engines. The Ju 288 V10 appeared with two 1,810 hp BMW 810TJ radials with exhaust-driven superchargers, while the V11 appeared with two 2,600 hp Daimler-Benz DB 606 twenty-four cylinder liquid-cooled engines. The DB 606 consisted of a coupled pair of DB 601 engines and was an interim solution to the problem of providing more than 2,000 hp from one unit for one airscrew. Three more prototypes for the Ju 288B were flown, and sufficient Junkers Jumo 222 engines were obtained for these, but before the end of 1942 this planned production version had been abandoned in favour of the Ju 288C production version.

First flown in the spring of 1943, the Ju 288 V103 (DE-ZZ) had Daimler-Benz DB 610 engines and was a prototype for the Ju 288C. Development of the Ju 288 bomber was eventually cancelled but some of the prototypes were issued for service. (*H. Redemann*)

The Ju 288C was designed specifically for the DB 606 engine, since it offered the requisite power and some hope of sufficient deliveries. Some structural strengthening of the aircraft was also undertaken, and the planned armament comprised a remote-controlled barbette at the fuselage chin, forward dorsal and aft ventral positions. By about August 1942, the first two prototypes for the Ju 288C, the Ju 288 V101 and V102, were ready. All the barbettes were fitted to the Ju 288 V103 (DE-ZZ) which flew in the spring of 1943, and this prototype had the more powerful (2,900 hp rating) DB 610 engines as did the next three prototypes flown in the summer of 1943. The DB 610 was of the same configuration as the DB 606 but consisted of a coupled pair of DB 605 engines. Serving as a test bed for the Ju 288 programme, the Heinkel He 177 V11 had been fitted with a pair of DB 610 engines and was flown at Dessau. Although used in the Heinkel He 177 bomber, the various coupled engines worked on by Daimler-Benz had reduced power-to-weight ratios and reliability and were but a stop-gap solution for the Ju 288. In any event, by mid-1943, the whole Bomber B programme had been cancelled because of difficulties and an unwillingness to commit effort and scarce material to a new bomber at a time when thoughts were turning more towards defence.

Although the Ju 288 prototypes had a bad record in terms of accidents and development difficulties, the type had been steadily improved and was giving a high performance by the time the contract was cancelled. Thus, Junkers considered it worthwhile to complete two more of the partially-built prototypes for research purposes, and these, the Ju 288 V107 and V108, were flown from July 1943. By the summer of 1944, when flight testing finished because of strict control on fuel supplies, only a small number of the Ju 288 prototypes were still serviceable but some of these were issued for operational use. Each aircraft had special armament in the form of a single 50 mm BK5 (KWK 39) cannon in a pod beneath the fuselage. This large weapon had a weight of 540 kg (1,190 lb), a barrel length of 3·04 m (9 ft 11⅝ in) and could, theoretically, empty its 22-shell magazine in half a minute. Thus equipped, the Ju 288s were probably intended as bomber-destroyers.

Even larger guns were proposed for the Ju 288 during 1940–41 to enable the aircraft to attack warships. An early proposal was to fit the Düka or Düsenkanone 280 in the lower fuselage, and the single 280 mm shell, with the assistance of the aircraft's velocity, was expected to penetrate 200 mm (7⅞ in) armour steel. Before firing, the gun barrel would have extended in front of the nose, but, upon firing, the whole gun would have recoiled back inside the fuselage to a position just past the wing main spar, and the barrel would have telescoped to about a third of its length. This scheme was abandoned in favour of others, one of which was to fit the Gerät 104 Münchhausen. This gun was extended forward hydraulically and returned under the firing recoil and was expected to penetrate up to 400 mm (1 ft 3¾ in) armour steel with its single 355·6 mm shell, or Panzergranate, having a combined muzzle and aircraft velocity of 405 m/sec (1,329 ft/sec).

Ju 288C-1: Span 22·657 m (74 ft 4 in); length 18·15 m (59 ft 6¼ in); wing area 65 sq m (699·4 sq ft).

Empty weight 13,400 kg (29,547 lb); fuel 4,915 kg (10,838 lb); bomb load 3,000 kg (6,615 lb); normal loaded weight 21,390 kg (47,165 lb).

Estimated performance with two 2,950 hp Daimler-Benz DB 610 engines—maximum speed at 6,800 m (22,300 ft) 655 km/h (407 mph); cruising speed 518 km/h (322 mph); landing speed 150 km/h (93 mph); initial rate of climb 490 m/min (1,607 ft/min); service ceiling 10,400 m (34,112 ft); maximum range 2,600 km (1,615 miles).

The Junkers Ju 90 V7 which acted as a development aircraft for the Ju 290 programme and later saw Luftwaffe service. (*H. Redemann*)

# Junkers Ju 290

Early in 1939 the Junkers Ju 90 V5, D-ABDG *Württemberg*, was withdrawn from service and completely rebuilt for the Ju 90S programme. It was fitted with an entirely new wing with parallel centre section, and a reinforced undercarriage, and had, in addition, enlarged oval fins and rudders. The newly developed Trapoklappe hydraulically-operated loading ramp was installed and this enabled army vehicles to be driven directly into the aircraft from the rear and the dropping of large stores by parachute.

Later in 1939, design work for the Ju 90S was transferred to Prague, Dipl Ing Kraft being appointed chief designer for the project. Detail design work and the production of mockups was entrusted to the Letov factory at Letnany, production of the machine being switched from Dessau to the Junkers plant at Bernburg.

Although it had been proposed to power the Ju 90S with the BMW 139 radial, development of this engine had been abandoned in June 1939 in favour of the BMW 801MA. Early in 1940, the Ju 90 V4 was re-engined with these units which developed 1,600 hp for take-off. Later in the year, the Ju 90 V5 was also fitted with four BMW 801 engines and used for blown-flap trials, but these proved unsuccessful.

The second development machine for the Ju 90S (now redesignated Ju 290) programme was the Ju 90 V7, D-ADFJ *Baden*. This had an increase of 2 m (6 ft $6\frac{3}{4}$ in) in fuselage length which helped to cure the instability problems suffered by the two previous BMW 801 powered machines. The Ju 90 V8 was similarly modified and was fitted with an underfuselage gondola containing a forward firing MG 151/20 cannon and a rearward firing MG 131 machine-gun. Two further MG 151/20 cannon were carried, one in a hydraulically-operated dorsal turret, the other in the tail, and provision was made for MG 131 machine-guns in the beam positions.

The final development machine for the Ju 290 was the Ju 90 V11,

442

The Junkers Ju 90 V11 which was redesignated Ju 290 V1. (*H. Redemann*)

D-AFHG *Oldenburg*, which was redesignated Ju 290 V1. Intended as a transport machine for the Luftwaffe, the Ju 290 V1 had increased span, new angular fins and rudders and square fuselage windows. It made its first flight in August 1942, and was followed by two generally similar Ju 290A-0s (c/ns 10150 and 10151).

Five Ju 290A-1s (c/ns 10152 to 10156) were completed late in 1942, being generally similar to the A-0 but having the armament introduced in the Ju 90 V8. The production Ju 290A-1 was powered by four 1,600 hp BMW 801L air-cooled radials. Two aircraft were delivered to Luft-Transportstaffel 290 (LTS 290) which had been formed at Tempelhof on 2 January, 1943, under Hptm Heinz Braun. Other equipment used by the unit included the Ju 90 V4, six Ju 90B-1s, the Ju 252 V5 and a Focke-Wulf Fw 200B-0. LTS 290 operated directly under the Luftwaffe's High Command until March 1943, when it was transferred to Grosseto as a supply unit for the Mediterranean area.

During the spring of 1943, the basic design was adapted for use as a maritime reconnaissance aircraft to replace the Focke-Wulf Fw 200C, which was becoming more and more vulnerable to enemy action. The aircraft, which received the designation Ju 290A-2, were basically similar to the A-1 apart from additional radio equipment, FuG 200 Hohentwiel search radar and a second HDL 151 dorsal turret. Three aircraft were

The Ju 290 V1 which was destroyed on 13 January, 1943, while taking-off on a supply flight to Stalingrad. (*H. Redemann*)

443

The first Ju 290A-3 (c/n 10160) which was later delivered to FAGr 5. (*H. Redemann*)

built (c/ns 10157 to 10159), being delivered to Fern-Aufklärungsgruppe 5 (FAGr 5) which had been formed on 1 July, 1943.

The Ju 290A-3 was similar to the A-2 but had a low-drag rear dorsal turret and 1,700 hp BMW 801D engines in place of the 1,600 hp BMW 801Ls. Five aircraft (c/ns 10160 to 10164) were completed and delivered to FAGr 5. The Ju 290A-4, of which five aircraft (c/ns 10165 to 10169) were completed, was similar to the A-2 apart from having two low-drag dorsal turrets.

1./FAGr 5 became operational at Mont de Marsan on 15 October, 1943, being joined a month later by 2.Staffel. The aircraft operated widely over the Atlantic, providing sighting reports for both U-boats and the Focke-Wulf Fw 200s of KG 40. Early in 1944 the first of eleven Ju 290A-5s (c/ns 10170 to 10180) reached FAGr 5. This had improved armour protection, two MG 151/20 cannon in place of the beam-mounted MG 131 machine-guns, and carried a crew of nine.

The next aircraft (c/n 10181) was completed as the prototype of the Ju 290A-7. It was similar to the V5, but was fitted with a new bulbous glazed nose housing a further 20 mm MG 151/20 cannon. Offensive armament in the shape of three Henschel Hs 293 or three Fritz X missiles could be carried on ETC racks, one beneath each wing, and one under the fuselage. A batch of twenty Ju 290A-7s (c/ns 10186 to 10205) were ordered, but only 13 of these were completed.

The Ju 290A-9, of which three aircraft were completed (c/ns 10182 to 10184), was an ultra-long-range reconnaissance aircraft with substantially reduced armament. The Ju 290A-6 (c/n 10185) was developed as a 50-seat transport for use by the Führer-Kurierstaffel, Hitler's personal transport

Delivered in the spring of 1944, the first production Ju 290A-7 (c/n 10181) was fitted with a new bulbous nose housing a gun turret. (*H. Redemann*)

444

unit commanded by Flugkapitän Heinz Baur. The aircraft was eventually delivered to 1./KG 200 at Finsterwalde and flown to Barcelona by Hauptmann Braun on 26 April, 1945. It was later used by the Spanish Air Force until the mid 'fifties when it was finally scrapped through lack of spares.

The Ju 290A-8, of which ten (c/ns 10211 to 10220) were proposed but only one completed, was basically similar to the A-7, but had increased armament. No less than ten MG 151/20 cannon were carried, one being mounted in each of four dorsal turrets. The partly completed Ju 290A-8 (c/n 10212) and part of a Ju 290B-2 were discovered at Ruzyne Airport near Prague after the war. They were transported to the Letov factory and completed in 1946 as the L 290 Orel 48-seat transport aircraft.

The second Ju 290A-8 (c/n 10212) which was completed at the Letov factory in Czechoslovakia as the L 290 Orel. (*J. Zazvonil*)

Late in 1943, work began on the Ju 290B-1 high-altitude bomber. This machine dispensed with the Trapoklappe for the first time and had nose and tail MG 131V turrets each containing four 13 mm machine-guns, two dorsal turrets each housing two MG 151/20 cannon, and a ventral barbette with a further pair of MG 151/20s, and was to have been fully pressurized, but the aircraft was abandoned in favour of the Ju 290B-2 which had 20 mm beam guns, a twin MG 151/20 tail turret, but no pressurization. No Ju 290B-2 was completed before the end of the war.

In the spring of 1944 three aircraft from FAGr 5 were transferred to Finsterwalde and modified to carry no less than 23,800 litres (5,238 Imp gal) of fuel. Flying from Odessa and Mielec, the aircraft made several flights to Japanese-occupied Manchuria, carrying aero-engines and other special cargoes. Return flights were made with raw materials such as rare metals and crude rubber.

An effort was made to add a fourth Staffel to FAGr 5, but few Ju 290s reached the unit, equipped in the main with Heinkel He 111s and Dornier Do 217s. Finally, FAGr 5 was withdrawn from France in August 1944 and disbanded, its aircraft being transferred to I./KG 200 commanded by Maj Gartenfeldt and based at Finsterwalde. I./KG 200 was joined early in 1945 by Transportstaffel 5 under Hptm Braun, the unit having been redesignated from LTS 290 in April 1943. The combined unit was responsible for evacuating important Nazi leaders as the Allies advanced.

Several developments of the Ju 290 were proposed. The Ju 290B MS was to have carried a magnetic-mine degaussing ring, the Ju 290C was a long-range reconnaissance project, and the Ju 290D and E were bomber projects. The C- and D-series were similar projects, with four 2,000 hp BMW 801E engines, and a redesigned loading ramp to carry Henschel Hs 293 control equipment. The Ju 290E was to have had an internal bomb bay capable of carrying no less than 18,400 kg (40,572 lb) of bombs. The proposed production model was to have been powered by four 2,500 hp Junkers Jumo 222A/B engines.

*Wartime operational units:* FAGr 5, LTS 290, Transportstaffel 5, 1./KG 200.

Ju 290A-5: Span 42 m (137 ft 9$\frac{1}{2}$ in); length 28·64 m (93 ft 11$\frac{1}{2}$ in); height 6·83 m (22 ft 4$\frac{3}{4}$ in); wing area 205·3 sq m (2,191·53 sq ft).

Normal loaded weight 41,000 kg (90,405 lb); maximum loaded weight 45,000 kg (99,225 lb).

Maximum speed at 6,000 m (19,686 ft) 440 km/h (273 mph); cruising speed 360 km/h (224 mph); climb to 1,000 m (3,280 ft) 4·2 min; service ceiling 6,000 m (19,686 ft); maximum range 6,150 km (3,820 miles).

# Junkers Ju 322 Mammut (Mammoth)

The Junkers Ju 322 was designed late in 1940 as a very large transport glider to fulfil the same specification as the Messerschmitt Me 321 Gigant glider. However, whereas Messerschmitt were asked to use a tubular-steel structure in their glider, the RLM required Junkers to produce an all-wooden design. At first named Goliath and, later, equally aptly re-named Mammut, the Ju 322 was a huge aircraft with a wing span and area exceeding even that of the Me 321 and the payload was to be 20,000 kg (44,100 lb) comprising, for example, either a tank or more than 100 fully-equipped troops.

Working at Merseburg, a design team under Heinrich Hertel submitted their design by the end of October 1940, although the order had already been given to both Junkers and Messerschmitt to put their gliders into production. Using ideas embodied in such designs as the Junkers-G 38 and EF 94, the Ju 322 carried practically all of its payload inside the wing. The outer panels of the multi-spar wing had dihedral on their undersurfaces, were of equi-taper planform and attached to a centre section of increased thickness/chord ratio. The leading edge of the centre section was the nose of the glider and incorporated a large curved loading door which hinged upwards. To the port side of the loading door, and on top of the centre section, was a raised, glazed gondola enclosing the cockpit. A tail boom led from the centre section trailing edge to support a tall, angular fin and rudder, the fin carrying at its base a braced tailplane.

A rare picture of the only Junkers Ju 322 Mammut transport glider. (*H. Redemann*)

The control surfaces were conventional but, with an aircraft of this size, servo operation was considered necessary. Armament planned for production gliders was to comprise three turrets each mounting a single MG 15 7·9 mm machine-gun; turret dispositions were two above the wing centre-section leading edge and one above the forward section of the tail boom. For take-off, the Ju 322 used a large trolley constructed of lattice girders and running on eight pairs of large-diameter wheels. This trolley was connected to the glider's four separate, sprung, landing skids and released as the glider became airborne.

During construction of the Ju 322 V1, many problems with the wooden construction came to light mainly as a result of Junkers' lack of experience with this type of construction, and the use of unsuitable materials. By this time, payload had been reduced to about 16,000 kg (35,280 lb) and then, following loading trials, reduced further to 11,000 kg (24,255 lb). This latter payload reduction was largely a result of fitting a stronger cargo floor after a tracked vehicle had broken through the floor of the Ju 322 V1 during the loading trials.

A special unit, Sonderkommando Merseburg, began preparations for flight testing during March 1941 and, in the following month, the Ju 322 V1 made its maiden flight using the Ju 90 V7 as a towing aircraft. Following take-off, the Mammut's trolley was destroyed when it fell back to the runway while the glider itself showed severe spiral instability on the tow-line. A disaster was narrowly avoided when the glider rose above the Ju 90, threatening to force the latter's nose into the ground, but both aircraft became controllable once the towline was released and the Ju 322 V1 made a smooth landing near to the village of Blösien. A pair of tanks later towed it back to Merseburg.

Despite enlargement of the vertical tail surfaces (to cure the spiral instability) and other modifications, the Ju 322 was considered an inherently bad design and was abandoned on orders from the RLM in May 1941. The V1 prototype made a few more test flights prior to this but was eventually cut up for fuel together with the completed Ju 322 V2 and partially-completed airframes for 98 other gliders. This, of course, left the field clear for the Messerschmitt Me 321 Gigant.

Ju 322 Mammut: Span 62 m (203 ft 5 in); length 30·25 m (99 ft 3 in); wing area 925 sq m (9,952 sq ft) approx; payload 11,000 kg (24,255 lb); gliding angle 1 : 50. No other data available.

One of the ten Junkers Ju 352A-0s completed between September 1943 and February 1944. (*Smithsonian Institution*)

# Junkers Ju 352 Herkules (Hercules)

By 1943, the German aircraft industry had begun to suffer from a lack of light metal alloys, and it was decided that in all aircraft, apart from actual combat types, as little use of these materials as possible should be made. One of the larger non-combatant types at this time was the Junkers Ju 252 which was redesigned to make use of mixed wood and steel construction with fabric covering. The resultant aircraft was the Ju 352 Herkules which, although similar in outline to the Ju 252, had new angular vertical tail surfaces and square in place of semi-circular cabin windows.

The Ju 352 was fitted with the Trapoklappe hydraulically-operated loading ramp, which, when lowered, raised the tail of the aircraft off the ground. The ramp was positioned below the rear fuselage and was hinged at the front to allow a Kübelwagen scout car to be driven directly into its

A Ju 352A-1 was rebuilt in Czechoslovakia after the war and flew to Moscow in 1946 with Russian markings. (*J. Zazvonil*)

hold. The centre part of the ramp incorporated a stairway and the aft edge provided an auxiliary skid in the event of a belly landing.

The prototype Ju 352 V1 flew for the first time on 1 October, 1943, from the Junkers factory at Fritzlar. This aircraft and the Ju 352 V2 were each powered by three 1,000 hp Bramo 323R-2 air-cooled radials which could be boosted to 1,200 hp by water-methanol injection. The two prototypes were followed by ten Ju 352A-0 pre-production aircraft which also bore the experimental numbers V3 to V12. The aircraft had one 20 mm MG 151/20 cannon in the EDL 151 dorsal turret and provision for two 13 mm MG 131 machine-guns firing through the cabin windows. A total

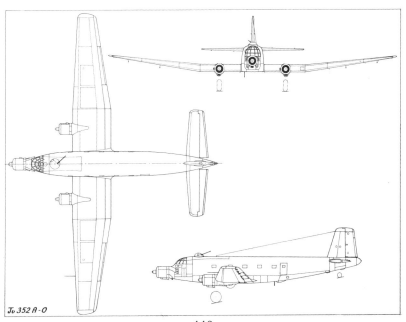

Ju 352 A-0

449

of thirty-three Ju 352A-1 production aircraft were delivered between April and September 1944. The projected Ju 352B-1 and B-2 with 1,800 hp BMW 801 radials were not built.

Apart from use by the agent-dropping I./KG 200, the only unit to receive the aircraft in numbers was the special Ju 352 Gruppe under Maj Günther Mauss, ex-commander of I./TG 5. Mauss' unit operated supply missions over East Prussia, Kurland and Schleswig-Holstein, and at the end of the war was based at Tutow, south-east of Rostock.

Ju 352A-1: Span 34·2 m (112 ft 2½ in); length 24·2 m (79 ft 4¾ in); height 6·6 m (21 ft 8 in); wing area 121·5 sq m (1,307·8 sq ft).

Empty weight 12,500 kg (27,562 lb); loaded weight 19,520 kg (43,041 lb).

Maximum speed at 4,000 m (13,124 ft) 330 km/h (205 mph); cruising speed 240 km/h (149 mph); service ceiling 6,000 m (19,686 ft); normal range 1,800 km (1,119 miles); maximum range 2,980 km (1,852 miles).

# Junkers Ju 388

During 1943, when the war in the air reached a new peak of ferocity, the Luftwaffe was holding its own at least in German skies, and aircraft production was reaching new levels. The air war was, however, very much one of attrition, so there was official reluctance to countenance the loss of production associated with bringing new types of aircraft into service, despite the fact that the Luftwaffe was losing ground in the performance of its aircraft. Thus, the practice of modifying and improving aircraft currently in production was much in favour, and the RLM enthusiastically selected aircraft for development from a range of Junkers' proposals based on the Ju 188. There was an urgent need to improve both speed and altitude of all classes of aircraft, and this led to development of the Ju 188S and T high-altitude intruder and reconnaissance aircraft, described on pages 428–29.

Also selected for parallel development with these two types were the Ju 188J night and bad-weather fighter, the Ju 188K bomber and the Ju 188L reconnaissance aircraft, all three being designed for high-altitude operation and, as far as possible, to have common airframes with equipment differing only to suit their different rôles. These three types were considered especially important and were therefore redesignated Ju 388J, K, and L in September 1943 for development in a programme code-named Hubertus. The Ju 388K and L were similar to the Ju 188S and T, and had similar pressurized nose sections, but for the Ju 388J a new design of pressurized cabin was necessary because of the nose-mounted radar equipment. One of the new features planned for all Ju 388s was the fitting of a remote-

450

Three views of DW-YY. This was a Junkers Ju 388L-0, the pre-production version of the Ju 388L high-altitude reconnaissance aircraft which was descended from a long line of Ju 88 derivatives. (*H. Redemann*)

451

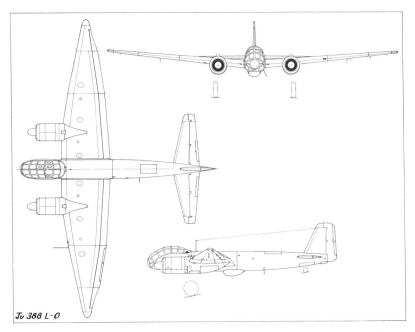

Ju 388 L-0

controlled FA 15 tail barbette mounting two 13 mm MG 131 machine-guns, this being the sole armament in the case of the Ju 388 K and L.

It was planned to use for all three models the Junkers Jumo 213E-1 engines (as for the Ju 188S and T), but, because of a doubtful supply situation, the 1,800 hp BMW 801TJ air-cooled radial engine with turbo-supercharger was selected instead.

Late in 1943, the Ju 388 V1 was built from a Ju 188T airframe as the prototype for the Ju 388L reconnaissance machine, and this was followed in January 1944 by the Ju 388 V3 as the prototype for the Ju 388K bomber. Later still, the Ju 388 V2 was the prototype for the Ju 388J Störtebeker* fighter. Successful trials with these prototypes led to plans for production despite difficulties in the development of the remote-controlled armament being tested in a Ju 188C-0. The Jägerstab, which radically revised the production programmes for aircraft, had its Programme 226 accepted on 8 July, 1944, and called for a monthly output of between 300 and 400 of the Ju 388s compared with only 180 of the Ju 88 night-fighters and 50 Heinkel He 219s per month. These figures reflect considerable faith in the Ju 388 and, although by then Hitler was being persuaded to abandon conventional bombers, the Ju 388K bomber still went ahead.

By July 1944, the first of ten Ju 388K-0 pre-production bombers were leaving the Dessau plant, although no tail barbettes were available for them. Only five production Ju 388K-1s were built before production had

* Named after a 15th century German pirate.

452

to stop early in 1945, but these aircraft did receive the FA 15 tail barbette. The bomb load for this type was carried beneath the fuselage but was enclosed by a large wooden ventral fairing. Although up to 3,000 kg (6,610 lb) of bombs could be carried, a more conventional load was about 2,000 kg (4,410 lb) of bombs, *e.g.* one SC 1800 Satan or two SC 1000 Hermann bombs. Further planned versions of the Ju 388K were the K-2 with Junkers Jumo 213E-1 engines and the K-3 with Junkers Jumo 222E engines.

Responsibility for the Ju 388L reconnaissance aircraft was given to the Allgemeine Transportanlagen GmbH (ATG) at Merseburg near Leipzig where the first ten pre-production Ju 388L-0s were built from Ju 188S-1 airframes. By August 1944, the first of these were being despatched to Erprobungskommando 388 for Service evaluation and, by October, the first production Ju 388L-1s were being completed. Once again, the FA 15 barbette was not available for the pre-production machines, which were fitted with fixed twin 7·9 mm MG 81 machine-guns firing aft from a ventral housing. Although the FA 15 barbette was fitted to the production L-1s, it was still under-developed and was therefore later supplemented by another 13 mm MG 131 in the rear of the cabin glazing. An extra, fourth, crew member was needed to operate this gun, and the modified aircraft was redesignated Ju 388L-1b.

The Ju 388L-1 had a large wooden ventral fairing (similar to the Ju 388K) in which were carried two day or night cameras of the same type used with the Ju 188F. A jettisonable auxiliary fuel tank could also be carried in the fairing to give a total maximum fuel capacity of 4,830 litres (1,063 gal), and FuG 217 Neptun tail-mounted warning radar was fitted. A few Ju 388L-3s were built which differed in having Junkers Jumo 213E-1 engines with MW-50 boosting. Before Ju 388L production stopped in December 1944, the Weser-Flugzeugbau joined in with ATG but only succeeded in producing ten examples. Although the Ju 388L was issued to the Luftwaffe, it never became fully operational with the conventional long-range reconnaissance units. The special Versuchsverband Ob.d.L. operated three Ju 388Ls, one of which was coded T9-DL.

A Ju 388L-1b (RT-KE). The majority of Ju 388s built were high-altitude reconnaissance versions but high-altitude fighter and bomber versions were also planned.

453

While the Ju 388J Störtebeker fighter was increasingly the most needed version, work on it proceeded the most slowly, due to the extra work involved in developing the different fuselage nose and pressure cabin sections, and only four examples, including the prototype, were produced. The prototype (Ju 388 V2) was the only one of the four machines to receive the tail barbette, but the forward-firing armament of all four machines was the same. This comprised two 20 mm MG 151 and two 30 mm MK 103 cannon in an offset ventral fuselage fairing. An aerial array was mounted on the nose for FuG 220 Lichtenstein radar equipment, and a crew of four was carried. The tail barbette, omitted from the three Ju 388J-1s built, was to have been fitted to subsequent machines beginning with the J-2. The first major modifications were planned for the Ju 388J-3, which was to have Morgenstern radar equipment with much shorter aerials slightly protruding from a pointed, wooden nose cone, and also two extra MG 151 cannon in an oblique dorsal Schräge Musik (Jazz Music) mounting. It was also hoped later to equip J-3s with Junkers Jumo 213E-1 engines in place of the BMW 801TJs. The Ju 388J-4 was planned to have the very heavy armament of two 50 mm BK5 cannon in a ventral fuselage pod, giving an installation weight of about 1,200 kg (2,646 lb) excluding ammunition. Single guns of this type were used by other aircraft such as the Ju 88P-4 and Ju 288.

The Ju 388 was used in tests with the Henschel Hs 298 and, later, the very promising Ruhrstahl X-4, both these air-to-air missiles being scheduled for use with the Ju 388. (They are described on pages 692 and 700.) Because of its high performance, many rôles were planned for the Ju 388, and it was one of the aircraft proposed to tow an unpowered Messerschmitt Me 328 glider fighter up to altitude or to Mistel-tow a powered Me 328B bomber to the target area. The proposed Ju 388M-1 was to be similar to the K-1 type but with an ETC 2000 rack instead of the ventral bomb housing to enable a Blohm und Voss L10 Friedensengel torpedo to be carried. The L10 consisted of a normal LT 950 torpedo fitted with wings and tail unit to enable drops to be made at greater altitudes than normal. Some Ju 388M-0s were under construction, but these, together with the projects, were too late, and by the time the war ended only a small number of Ju 388L reconnaissance machines had seen any operational service. In all the various rôles planned for it, the Ju 388 would have been a good match for most Allied aircraft, but only about 75 operational examples were built, the majority of which were for reconnaissance.

*Wartime operational units:* 3./Versuchsverband Ob.d.L., Erprobungskommando 388.

Ju 388J-1: Span 22 m (72 ft $2\frac{1}{8}$ in); length, excluding aerials, 14·95 m (49 ft $0\frac{5}{8}$ in); wing area 56·6 sq m (609 sq ft).
Empty weight 10,565 kg (23,296 lb); fuel 2,175 kg (4,796 lb); oil and sundries 350 kg (772 lb); crew 400 kg (882 lb); ammunition 275 kg (606 lb); loaded weight 13,765 kg (30,352 lb).

Maximum speed at 12,000 m (39,360 ft) 580 km/h (360 mph); cruising speed 450 km/h (280 mph); landing speed 180 km/h (112 mph); initial rate of climb 380 m/min (1,246 ft/min); service ceiling 13,000 m (42,640 ft); range 2,000 km (1,242 miles).

Ju 388L-1: Span 22 m (72 ft $2\frac{1}{8}$ in); length 14·95 m (49 ft $0\frac{5}{8}$ in); wing area 56·6 sq m (609 sq ft).

Empty weight 10,345 kg (22,811 lb); maximum fuel 3,775 kg (8,324 lb); oil and sundries 300 kg (661 lb); crew 300 kg (661 lb); ammunition 50 kg (111 lb); maximum loaded weight 14,770 kg (32,567 lb).

Maximum speed at 12,000 m (39,360 ft) 615 km/h (382 mph); initial rate of climb 400 m/min (1,312 ft/min); service ceiling 13,000 m (42,640 ft); maximum range with auxiliary fuel 3,460 km (2,149 miles).

A Ju 388K is held by the Smithsonian Institution.


# Junkers Ju 390

The United States declaration of war in December 1941 finally forced the German Air Ministry to consider seriously the several proposals already made for a bomber capable of attacking New York from European bases. The specification called for a six-engined design and resulted in the Focke-Wulf Ta 400, the Messerschmitt Me 264B and the Junkers Ju 390.

Of the three designs, the Junkers machine was by far the easiest to produce, making use as it did of a large number of Ju 290 components.

The Ju 390 V1. (*H. Redemann*)

The Junkers Ju 390 V1 six-engined transport which made its first flight in August 1943.

Compared with the Ju 290, the Ju 390 V1 had increases in both fuselage length and wing span, the latter allowing the installation of an extra pair of 1,700 hp BMW 801D radial engines. The Ju 390 V1, which was built at Dessau, flew in August 1943, followed two months later by the V2 which was assembled at Bernburg.

The second prototype had a still longer fuselage and carried FuG 200 Hohentwiel search radar, five 20 mm MG 151/20 cannon and three 13 mm MG 131 machine-guns. The aircraft was delivered to FAGr 5 at Mont de Marsan in January 1944 for operational evaluation, and during one of its test flights it approached within 20 km (12 miles) of New York and returned successfully.

Construction of a third aircraft was begun, the machine eventually being converted as prototype for the proposed Ju 390A-1 bomber/reconnaissance aircraft. This machine, which was designed mainly for use by the Japanese Army Air Force, carried an armament of eight MG 151/20 cannon, two in each of three turrets, and one in each beam position. Four MG 131 machine-guns were mounted in both nose and tail turrets, and a 1,800 kg (3,960 lb) bomb load or a Fritz X, Hs 293 or Hs 294 missile could be carried externally. In the event, the Ju 390 V3 was never completed, and only two examples of this very large aircraft ever flew.

Ju 390A-1*: Span 50·3 m (165 ft 1 in); length 34 m (112 ft 2½ in); height 6·9 m (22 ft 7⅔ in); wing area 253·69 sq m (2,729·73 sq ft).

Empty weight 36,900 kg (81,364 lb); loaded weight 75,500 m (146,477 lb).

Maximum speed at 6,000 m (19,686 ft) 505 km/h (314 mph); maximum range 9,700 km (6,027 miles).

* Weights and performance estimated.

456

# Junkers Ju 488

By 1944, the Luftwaffe was still virtually without a heavy strategic bomber, since the Heinkel He 177s in service were completely unreliable in their under-developed state and the prospects of bringing other types, such as the Junkers Ju 390A and Messerschmitt Me 264B, into production were remote in view of the war situation. A proposal therefore came from Junkers' to produce quickly a four-engined heavy bomber with the minimum of new jigs and tools, by using components from their numerous Ju 88 series plus parts from the Ju 288, the latter having been abandoned with the Bomber B programme. This Junkers proposal was given approval, and the projected bomber, which was planned for operational service by mid-1945, was designated Ju 488.

The hybrid Ju 488 was to incorporate components of previous designs in the following way. The pressurized forward fuselage of the Ju 388K and the rear fuselage of the Ju 188E were to be married with new fuselage sections and fuel tanks, while a wooden ventral bomb bay was to be formed from the ventral panniers of the Ju 388K and Ju 88A-15. Wings from the Ju 388K were to be fitted to a new parallel wing centre section which also carried the two extra engine nacelles complete with two extra main undercarriage units, giving four main undercarriage members (of a well-established design), each retracting rearwards into its own nacelle. Finally, the twin-finned tail unit was adopted from the Ju 288C.

Two prototypes, the Ju 488 V401 and V402, were quickly got under way, with the fuselages and new wing centre sections being built in France at the former Latécoère factory at Toulouse, the other flying surfaces and components being built at Junkers' Dessau and Bernburg plants. Each of these two prototypes was to be powered by four 1,800 hp BMW 801TJ fourteen-cylinder air-cooled radial engines and were to be used as flight test aircraft without armament or military equipment. All the parts were completed for the Ju 488 V401 and V402, but the fuselages and wing centre sections, which were about to be sent to Germany for final assembly, were sabotaged beyond repair at Toulouse on the night of 16/17 July, 1944. By 22 August, the Germans had evacuated the Toulouse area in the face of the advancing Allies.

However, even while the first two Ju 488 prototypes were under construction, a reappraisal of the aircraft led to a redesign to economize on materials in short supply and to increase the fuel and bomb load. This work concentrated on a new, enlarged, fuselage having a welded steel-tube structure with metal sheet and fabric covering. Only the Ju 388K pressurized nose section for the crew of three was retained from the original fuselage design. The increased depth of the new fuselage enabled the previous ventral bomb pannier to be dispensed with. The normal fuel capacity was increased by 150 per cent to 10,400 litres (2,288 Imp gal) and the maximum bomb load more than doubled to 5,000 kg (11,025 lb). For defensive armament, it was planned to install two remote-controlled barbettes, one in the dorsal position with two 20 mm MG 151 cannon and one in the tail position with two 13 mm MG 131 machine-guns. To deal with the increased weight of the aircraft, it was planned to fit four Junkers Jumo 222A-3 twenty-four cylinder liquid-cooled four-row radial engines, which had been developed originally for the 2,500 hp class but, after protracted development, were probably delivering only about 2,200 hp for take-off.

The redesigned bomber was planned for production as the Ju 488A, and, for this, four development prototypes were begun as the Ju 488 V403 to V406 inclusive. This work did not proceed far, however, because the Ju 488 programme was cancelled in November 1944, by which time the deterioration in the war situation for Germany made the building of any large new aircraft, especially strategic bombers, ludicrous.

Ju 488A *: Span 31·28 m (102 ft 7¼ in); length 23·24 m (76 ft 3 in); wing area 88 sq m (947 sq ft).

Empty weight 21,000 kg (46,305 lb); normal fuel and oil 9,100 kg (20,066 lb); ammunition and sundries 600 kg (1,323 lb); maximum bomb load 5,000 kg (11,025 lb); crew of three 300 kg (661 lb); loaded weight 36,000 kg (79,380 lb).

Maximum speed at 7,000 m (24,600 ft) 690 km/h (429 mph); cruising speed 480 km/h (298 mph); initial rate of climb 550 m/min (1,804 ft/min); service ceiling 11,500 m (37,720 ft); maximum range with normal fuel load 3,400 km (2,111 miles).

* Figures are estimates.

A radial-engined Klemm L 25, D-2397, fitted with skis and operated by the Deutscher Luftsport-Verband (German flying training school). (*F. Selinger*)

# Klemm Lightplanes

After the end of the First World War, Dr Ing Hans Klemm began the design of lightplanes for the Daimler aircraft company at Stuttgart. In 1919, he produced the L 15 glider, and a modified version, powered by a 12 hp Harley-Davidson engine, was constructed. The L 20 low-wing monoplane powered by a 20 hp Mercedes engine followed in 1924 and two years later Klemm founded his own company at Böblingen near Stuttgart, the Klemm Leichtflugzeugbau GmbH.

The first aircraft produced by the new company was the L 25 low-wing monoplane which flew for the first time in 1927 powered by a 20 hp Mercedes engine. About 600 Klemm L 25s were built powered by various and progressively more powerful engines. Several aircraft were fitted with floats and the type saw some service with the Luftwaffe in its early days.

A larger L 25 development was produced under the designation L 26, the L 27 had a bigger forward cockpit, and the three- and four-seat Kl 31 and Kl 32 cabin monoplanes were built during 1933. The Klemm Kl 33 single-seat ultra-light high-wing monoplane powered by a 40 hp Argus engine was only built in small numbers.

One of the most important Klemm designs was the Kl 35, designed, like all other types produced by the company, for private ownership. The prototype, the Kl 35a, flew for the first time in 1935 powered by an 80 hp Hirth HM 60R four-cylinder inverted air-cooled engine. It was an attractive low-wing monoplane built of wood with mixed wood and fabric covering. The design had an inverted gull wing with a fixed undercarriage and two tandem seats. The mainwheels were partly enclosed by neat spats.

459

The Klemm Kl 32b-XIV three-seat sports and liaison aircraft.

The second prototype, the Kl 35b was followed by the Kl 35B production series powered by the 105 hp Hirth HM 504A-2 four-cylinder inverted air-cooled engine. During 1938, the Kl 35BW was produced with wood or metal floats, this type establishing several records in its class. The Kl 35 was later exported to Czechoslovakia, Hungary, Rumania and Sweden, and was also built under licence by Sweden for use by her air force in the training rôle.

In 1938 the improved Klemm Kl 35D was produced, designed to serve as a trainer with the Luftwaffe. The Kl 35D differed in being powered by an 80 hp Hirth HM 60R engine and had a braced and strengthened undercarriage with the spats removed. Apart from the standard wheel undercarriage, the Kl 35D was also fitted with floats and skis. This variant saw considerable service with the Luftwaffe's pilot training schools during the Second World War.

Two versions of the Kl 36 cabin monoplane were designed for the 1934 Circuit of Europe, the Kl 36A with a 220 hp Hirth HM 508F eight-cylinder inverted-vee air-cooled engine and the Kl 36B with a 150 hp Bramo Sh 14A nine-cylinder air-cooled radial. In 1938, Klemm produced the Kl 105 ultra-light monoplane to be powered by a 50 hp Zündapp Z 9-092 four-cylinder air-cooled engine or the 50 hp Hirth HM 515 unit of similar configuration.

The Kl 106 was a development of the Kl 35D powered by a 100 hp

The Klemm Kl 35D was experimentally fitted with mockups of two overwing personnel containers by the Graf Zeppelin research institute.

460

Hirth HM 500 four-cylinder inverted air-cooled engine and the Kl 107 was a cabin version of the Kl 105 with a 105 hp Hirth HM 500A-1 engine. Twenty aircraft were ordered, but only six were completed, all during 1940. The final Klemm design was the Kl 151 four-seat cabin tourer to be powered by a 240 hp Argus As 10C eight-cylinder inverted-vee air-cooled engine.

Kl 35D: Span 10·4 m (34 ft 1½ in); length 7·5 m (24 ft 7¼ ft); height 2·05 m (6 ft 8¾ in); wing area 15·2 sq m (163·61 sq ft).
Empty weight 460 kg (1,014 lb); loaded weight 750 kg (1,654 lb).
Maximum speed at sea level 212 km/h (132 mph); cruising speed 190 km/h (118 mph); landing speed 78 km/h (48 mph); rate of climb 180 m/min (591 ft/min); service ceiling 4,350 m (14,272 ft); normal range 665 km (413 miles).

# Lippisch DM-1

In 1942, Dr Alexander Lippisch withdrew from the Me 163 development programme at Messerschmitt's Augsburg plant, and then led a new research programme at the Luftfahrtforschungsanstalt Wien (LFA). He worked on high-speed aerodynamic problems and a delta-wing aircraft programme, and, with increasing co-operation between the LFA and the Deutsches Forschungsinstitut für Segelflug (DFS), he received data on ram-jets in exchange for aerodynamic data. Lippisch had, of course, worked at the DFS before moving to Messerschmitt.

The marriage of the new conceptions of delta-wing and ramjet power-plant promised exciting possibilities for a new, fast interceptor aircraft, and, accordingly, the design of the LP-13a interceptor was begun by Lippisch late in 1944, this project being discussed further on page 631. In order to confirm the low-speed handling of the design and to obtain more data, it was decided to build an experimental test glider of similar form and dimensions to the projected fighter. This test glider was designated DM-1 because it was developed by the Flugtechnische Fachgruppe at the Darmstadt and Munich universities in accordance with the designs of Lippisch. The Flugtechnische Fachgruppe, formerly the Akademische Fliegergruppen or Akaflieg, was an independent association of students of aircraft construction and similar faculties, who supplemented their studies by building and flying aircraft. When the facilities at Munich and Darmstadt were bombed, the group moved to Prien and was in a position to begin construction of the DM-1 in November 1944.

The DM-1 was a delta-wing aircraft with large delta fin which extended almost to the apex of the wing, symmetrical elliptical sections being used for both fin and wing. The distribution of pressure of the main profiles was to be such that in passing Mach 1 the compression shock at the leading and trailing edges of the profiles would occur at the same time and thereby result in no moment change on the aircraft, although, of course, the DM-1 was to fly at subsonic speeds. Wing and fin sections were of a thickness that enabled the pilot to occupy a sitting position, partly in the fin and partly in the wing. The leading-edge root of the fin was therefore glazed for visibility in normal flight and the underside of the wing's nose was also glazed. This latter feature was possible because no ramjet intake was fitted but was also considered most advantageous because, during landings, high angles of attack were anticipated as a feature of the wing with its 60 deg sweepback and low aspect ratio of 1:2. The wing had no twist or dihedral, and two outer control surfaces operated differentially to give longitudinal and lateral control. There were, in addition, two inner surfaces at the trailing edge, for trimming only, and a normal rudder attached to the fin. Wing and fin were of two-spar wooden construction with plywood skinning, and there was a tubular metal nosewheel undercarriage. The three undercarriage members retracted, not by folding but by being drawn in through holes.

The plan was that the DM-1 should be carried to altitude mounted above a modified Siebel Si 204 as a Huckepack or Mistel combination and then

This Lippisch DM-1 delta-form glider was built to gain data on the lower-speed range for a radical, projected, ramjet-powered interceptor. (*Smithsonian Institution*)

462

The DM-1 was completed and taken to the United States after the war for evaluation. This view shows the underside nose glazing and the holes through which the undercarriage members were drawn.

released to examine the low-speed handling qualities. Higher speeds up to 560 km/h (350 mph) were to be examined by diving and, possibly, at a later stage, by fitting a rocket unit to give speeds up to 800 km/h (500 mph). The DM-1 was almost complete by the end of the war when discovered by the Americans. At their request, it was completed and then towed away behind a rebuilt Douglas C-47 (Dakota), also found at Prien, and eventually flight-tested in the United States before passing to the Smithsonian Institution.

There were also two other similar test aircraft planned for Lippisch's programme, these being the DM-2 and DM-3. The DM-2 was to be powered by a turbojet to examine effects on engine and airframe at speeds between 800 and 1,200 km/h (497 to 745 mph), while the DM-3 was to be rocket-powered to attain a maximum speed of 2,000 km/h (1,242 mph). Such high speeds were to be flown at high altitude, and there was, allegedly, the even faster DM-4 design for which no details are available.

DM-1: Span 5·92 m (19 ft 5$\frac{1}{8}$ in); length 6·6 m (21 ft 7$\frac{7}{8}$ in); height 3·18 m (10 ft 5$\frac{1}{4}$ in); wing area 20 sq m (215 sq ft); wing sweepback 60 deg; maximum wing profile thickness 16·6 per cent at 45 per cent chord; maximum fin profile thickness 19·2 per cent at 45 per cent chord.

Empty weight 297 kg (655 lb); loaded weight 460 kg (1,015 lb).

Typical release altitude 8,000 m (26,240 ft); maximum speed 560 km/h (350 mph) in an unpowered dive; landing speed 72 km/h (45 mph); maximum permissible sinking speed at landing 6 m/sec (20 ft/sec).

463

A Messerschmitt Bf 108 Taifun with automatic airscrew pitch-change mechanism.

# Messerschmitt Bf 108 Taifun (Typhoon)

The Messerschmitt Bf 108 four-seat cabin low-wing monoplane was one of Messerschmitt's most successful designs to the extent that it was still being developed long after the end of the war, and not only its derivatives but some of the early examples are still flying, more than 38 years after the original design was produced. The designer of this aircraft, Dipl Ing Willy Messerschmitt, had a long background of designing gliders and then single-engined high-wing monoplanes, and had founded the Messerschmitt Flugzeugbau in 1925 at Bamberg in Bavaria. By 1927, this concern was collaborating with the Bayerische Flugzeugwerke AG (BFW) at Augsburg and, the following year, Messerschmitt was one of the managers of the company. After going through a period of financial struggle BFW was recovering by the time Messerschmitt became a director in 1933.

In 1933, BFW received a contract from the RLM for an aircraft to participate in the 4th Challenge de Tourisme Internationale, of 1934. The resulting design had the works' designation of M 37 (following on from the previous M 36 transport) and the official designation Bf 108. Of generally advanced design, the Bf 108 was a complete break with previous Messerschmitt design lineage and was the first aircraft of its size to use all-metal stressed skin construction. The wing was a patented single-spar design and had trailing-edge flaps and automatic leading-edge slots which opened on approaching the stall. The main undercarriage legs pivoted near the wing roots to retract outwards into wells where they were almost totally enclosed. Six aircraft were built by 1934, these being prototypes and Bf 108As, and each was powered by a single 225 hp Hirth HM 8U or 210 hp Argus As 17 air-cooled inline engine. A feature of these aircraft was that all control surfaces were hinged at their leading edges without any dynamic balancing.

Beginning with the first prototype, D-ILIT, flight tests started in the spring of 1934 and were very satisfactory. The aircraft proved most pleasant to fly, was fast, safe, and had excellent low-speed qualities, while the design of the metal structure made maintenance easy. Nevertheless, despite all the excellent attributes of the aircraft, the antagonism that various people had for Messerschmitt almost caused a setback at the beginning. When one Bf 108 crashed during a training flight for the Challenge de Tourisme Internationale, the German team manager, Theo Osterkamp, did his best to have the aircraft withdrawn from the contest, but his attempt was over-ruled by Maj Loeb. Most of the contest successes of the Bf 108 occurred in 1938, when it won first place in two German international races and first place in the Belgian international Queen Astrid race. It also won second place in the 1937 Oases rally in Egypt and the 1938 Raduno del Littorio in Italy. In July 1939 the Bf 108 set a new altitude class record of 9,075 m (29,766 ft).

This crash-landed Bf 108B was in Luftwaffe service. (*H. Redemann*)

During 1935 an improved version, the Bf 108B, was produced with a 270 hp Argus As 10 eight-cylinder inverted-vee air-cooled engine. Modifications included a revised fin shape, dynamic balancing of elevator and rudder, removal of the tailplane upper bracings and the fitting of a tail-wheel in place of the previous skid. Only a small number of these aircraft were built at Augsburg, but, by the time BFW had become Messerschmitt AG in July 1938, production had been transferred to the new Regensburg plant and over 500 aircraft had been completed by 1942. In that year, production was again transferred, this time to the SNCA du Nord factory at Les Mureaux in France.

The Bf 108B, which became known, in modified form, as the Taifun (Typhoon), was popular everywhere and gained publicity for Messerschmitt by being flown all over the world by Luftwaffe officers before the war. In German wartime service, the Luftwaffe used the type for fast communication duties and such work as ferrying pilots and personnel. The Luftdienst (Air Service), which was run chiefly by civilians and undertook various duties such as target towing, rescue and supply operations, also employed the Taifun in considerable numbers. Over fifty Bf 108Bs in

465

A Bf 108B of the Luftdienst which, run chiefly by civilians, used many of these aircraft for various duties. (*R. C. Seeley*)

all were exported, numbers going to Bulgaria, Hungary, Japan, Rumania, Switzerland, the USSR, and Yugoslavia. Altogether, 885 Messerschmitt Bf 108s were built before the end of the war.

A special record-breaking version, the Bf 108C, was proposed in 1941 with the more powerful 400 hp Hirth HM 512 twelve-cylinder inverted-vee engine, but the next version which was to have been proceeded with was the Me 208. This was similar to the Taifun but had a retractable nosewheel undercarriage. Two prototypes of the Me 208 (the V1 being coded GK-RZ) were built at the Les Mureaux plant before the war ended, but one was destroyed in a bombing raid.

Post-war French development of the Taifun was quite prolific. Production of the Bf 108 continued as the Nord 1001 Pingouin (Penguin) with a 240 hp Renault 6Q-10 engine and the Nord 1002 Pingouin II with a Renault 6Q-11 engine, some 285 of these types being built. There was also

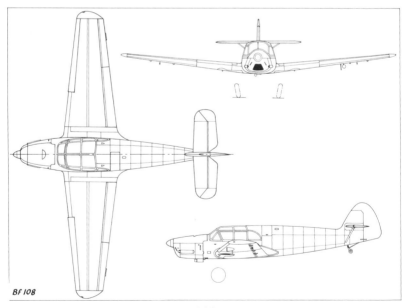

Bf 108

the Nord 1003 with a 240 hp Potez 6D engine and the Nord 1004 with a 305 hp Potez engine. The Me 208 was also continued for the French forces as the Nord 1101 Ramier (Wood Pigeon) and for civil use as the Nord 1101 Noralpha, again with 240 hp Renault engines, and development continued up to about 1950 with various types such as the Nord 1204/02 and Wassmer Super 4/21 with Continental and Lycoming engines respectively, although by then the original aircraft had changed considerably in equipment. On occasions, these post-war derivatives of the Taifun (which had in its design the embryo of the Bf 109) are used in 'popular' films to represent the Bf 109.

Bf 108A (with 225 hp Hirth HM 8U engine): Span 10·31 m (33 ft 9$\frac{7}{8}$ in); length 8·06 m (26 ft 5$\frac{3}{8}$ in); wing area 16 sq m (172·16 sq ft).
Empty weight 560 kg (1,235 lb); fuel and oil 172 kg (380 lb); pilot and three passengers 300 kg (660 lb); loaded weight 1,032 kg (2,275 lb).
Maximum speed 291 km/h (181 mph); cruising speed 250 km/h (155 mph); landing speed 63 km/h (58 mph); range 700 km (435 miles). This version was similar to the first prototypes.

Bf 108 Taifun (with 240 hp Argus As 10C engine): Span 10·62 m (34 ft 10$\frac{1}{8}$ in); length 8·29 m (27 ft 2$\frac{3}{8}$ in); wing area 16·4 sq m (176·46 sq ft).
Empty weight 880 kg (1,941 lb); fuel and oil 172 kg (380 lb); pilot and three passengers 300 kg (660 lb); loaded weight 1,352 kg (2,981 lb).
Maximum speed 303 km/h (188 mph); cruising speed 265 km/h (165 mph); landing speed 85 km/h (53 mph); initial rate of climb 360 m/min (1,180 ft/min); take-off distance 240 m (788 ft); landing distance 230 m (755 ft); service ceiling 5,000 m (16,400 ft); maximum range 1,000 km (621 miles). This was the principal version employed by the German wartime services.

# Messerschmitt Bf 109

Without doubt the Bf 109 can be claimed as the most famous German aircraft of all time. Synonymous with the name of Messerschmitt, the little fighter was built in larger numbers than any other aircraft excepting one, the Russian Ilyushin Il-2. It gained its fame as the arch-enemy of the Spitfire during the Battle of Britain and continued an intense rivalry with the British fighters until the close of the Second World War. Even after the end of that conflict, the Bf 109 remained in service in various guises with foreign air arms for almost 20 years.

In 1933, Willy Messerschmitt and Rakan Kokothaki, directors of Bayerische Flugzeugwerke AG, signed a contract with a Rumanian company for the construction of the M 36 transport aircraft. This resulted in complaints being received from Obstlt Wilhelm Wimmer, an influential official in the technical department of the RLM, that BFW were concentrating on producing aircraft for foreign countries. Messerschmitt countered these charges by explaining that Wimmer's office had failed to place any development contract with BFW, and that the firm had been forced to solicit outside orders to enable it to survive.

The result of this disagreement was the placing of a contract for a new high-speed fighter monoplane with BFW and three other companies, Arado, Focke-Wulf and Heinkel. The four firms produced, respectively, the Bf 109, the Ar 80, the Fw 159 and the He 112.

The BFW Bf 109 was a cantilever low-wing monoplane built of metal with flush-riveted duralumin skin. The fuselage was a beautiful oval-section monocoque structure with an enclosed cockpit. The single-spar wing was fitted with automatic leading-edge slots and the inboard portions of the trailing edge carried slotted flaps. The narrow-track undercarriage retracted outwards into the wing, but the tailwheel was fixed.

The first prototype, initially designated Bf 109a, D-IABI (c/n 758), made its first flight from Augsburg during the middle of September 1935 piloted by Flugkapitän 'Bubi' Knötsch. The design owed much to that of the earlier Messerschmitt lightplanes such as the M 23 and Bf 108. Although designed around the 610 hp Junkers Jumo 210A twelve-cylinder inverted-vee liquid-cooled engine, the Bf 109 V1, as the prototype was later redesignated, was in fact powered by an imported 695 hp Rolls-Royce Kestrel V engine.

The four types competed in trials held at Travemünde in October 1935, and it was quickly established that the Heinkel and BFW designs were far superior to the other two. The Ar 80 suffered from the drag of its fixed undercarriage, and undercarriage retraction problems beset the Fw 159, which was unusual in having a parasol wing layout. Many observers considered that the He 112 was superior to the Bf 109, so that it came as

The Focke-Wulf Fw 159 competed with the Arado Ar 80, Heinkel He 112 and Messerschmitt Bf 109. D-INGA was the second Fw 159 prototype, which crashed after undercarriage failure.

468

The attractive Arado Ar 80 V3 fighter, D-IPBN, failed because of its high structural weight and sluggish performance.

something of a surprise when development contracts were awarded for ten prototypes of both designs.

The Bf 109 V2, D-IUDE (c/n 809), joined the test programme in January 1936 and differed from the first prototype in being powered by a Jumo 210A engine in place of the Rolls-Royce Kestrel. Provision was made for two 7·9 mm MG 17 machine-guns above the engine cowling, this armament being intended for the proposed Bf 109A production model. The Bf 109 V3, D-IHNY (c/n 810), first flew in June 1936 and was generally similar to the V2.

By this time, the RLM was beginning to revise its ideas on fighter armament, and the Bf 109A was replaced by the Bf 109B, which was to carry three MG 17 machine-guns, with the third weapon firing through the airscrew boss. It was eventually intended to replace this with a licence-built 20 mm Oerlikon cannon (the MG FF) as soon as this weapon became available in quantity. Consequently, the Bf 109 V4, D-IOQY (c/n 878), was fitted with three machine-guns, the MG FF eventually replacing the third weapon.

The Bf 109 V5 and the V6, D-IHHB, reverted to the armament of three MG 17 machine-guns and were forerunners of the proposed Bf 109B production model. The Bf 109 V7, D-IALY, was generally similar but was fitted with full operational equipment and a Jumo 210B engine. A small batch of Bf 109B-0 pre-production aircraft, similar to the V7, were delivered to the Luftwaffe in the spring of 1937. The Bf 109B-1 differed in being powered by a 635 hp Jumo 210D engine, and the Bf 109B-2 was fitted with a 640 hp Jumo 210E which drove a two-blade licence-built Hamilton variable-pitch metal airscrew in place of the old wooden type of Schwarz manufacture. Relatively few Jumo 210E engined Bf 109B-2s were completed before a switch was made to the 670 hp Jumo 210G.

469

The prototype for the Messerschmitt Bf 109E-3 was the V17, D-IWKU, which crashed during a test flight.

The first Bf 109B-1s were delivered to I./JG 132 Richthofen at Döberitz-Elsgrund. JG 132, which was led by Oberst von Massow, was a direct descendant of the famous JG 1 Richthofen of the First World War. Bf 109Bs and Cs were eventually delivered to I./JG 131 at Jesau, JG 132, JG 134 Horst Wessel at Dortmund, JG 135 (later JG 233) at Bad Aibling, JG 136, I./JG 137 (later I./JG 231), JG 141 at Pardubitz, I./JG 232 Loerzer at Bernburg, JG 234 Schlageter at Cologne, and Küsten-Jäger-Gruppe 136 at Sylt.

The Bf 109 V1 was first publicly revealed at the 1936 Olympic Games, held in Berlin, but the fighter's first real impact on the aviation world came during the international flying meeting held at Zürich between 23 July and 1 August, 1937. Five BFW aircraft took part, including two Bf 109B-1s, a B-2, and the Bf 109 V10 and V13. The last two aircraft, respectively D-ISLU and D-IPKY, were both fitted with early examples of the 950 hp Daimler-Benz DB 600 engine and had exceptional performance. The international circuit of the Alps race was won by the Bf 109B-2 piloted by Maj Seidemann, after Ernst Udet crashed the V10 after an engine failure. The climb and dive competition was won by Dipl Ing Francke flying the Bf 109 V13; the speed event was taken by a Bf 109B-2; and the team race was won by Bf 109Bs flown by Hptm Restemeier and Lts Trautloft and Schleif.

Even as these impressive victories were taking place, a small batch of twenty-four Bf 109B-2s was being delivered to 1. and 2./Jagdgruppe 88 based in Spain as the fighter component of the Condor Legion. Some time earlier, in December 1936, the Bf 109 V4 had been evaluated in Spain, followed shortly afterwards by the V5 and V6. The BFW fighter immediately proved its superiority over all other fighters taking part in the Spanish Civil War, including the much-vaunted Polikarpov I-16 being used by the Republicans.

The operations of Jagdgruppe 88 led to the development of new fighter tactics which were to stand the Luftwaffe in good stead during future operations. Prior to the Spanish Civil War, the Jagdgruppen had been using the close formation of three aircraft; ideal for formation aerobatics,

470

but very restrictive in combat. It was pilots like Werner Mölders that developed the tactical formation known as the Schwarm (swarm). This comprised four aircraft, made up of two sections of two, known as the 'Rotte', positioned like the tips of the fingers when spread out flat. The aircraft were positioned about 200 metres (650 feet) apart and were controlled with the aid of FuG 7 radio-telephones. This loose formation, which enabled one fighter to protect another's tail, was found to be ideal for aerial combat, and was eventually adopted as standard practice throughout the world.

One of a batch of forty Bf 109Bs delivered to Jagdgruppe 88 of the Condor Legion in Spain. (*H. Obert*)

Although the MG FF cannon had been tried on the Bf 109 V4, the weapon caused severe vibration when fired, and experiments were made with other methods of augmenting the aircraft's armament. The Bf 109 V8 was fitted with four MG 17 machine-guns, two of the weapons being mounted in the wing roots. The Bf 109 V9 was fitted with two 20 mm MG FF cannon in the wings, but severe vibration led to the temporary abandonment of this layout.

Development of these prototypes led to the Bf 109C-0, which was similar to the B-2 apart from having the armament of the V8. The Bf 109C-1 was similar, but the C-2 was fitted with a total of five MG 17 machine-guns. The proposed Bf 109C-3 was to have carried the armament tested by the V9, and the C-4 was to have been fitted with an engine-mounted MG FF/M cannon, but neither variant was completed.

As already mentioned, the Bf 109 V10 had been fitted with an early example of the Daimler-Benz DB 600 engine, and this was followed by the Bf 109 V11 and V12 fitted with production 960 hp DB 600A engines and capable of a maximum speed of 520 km/h (323 mph). The Bf 109 V13, which had taken part in the contest at Zürich, was re-engined with a specially boosted DB 601 engine which could produce 1,650 hp for short periods. Flown by Dr Wurster, the machine captured the world speed record for landplanes with a speed of 610·55 km/h (379·38 mph) on 11 November, 1937.

The Daimler-Benz DB 600 engined prototypes were the predecessors of the Bf 109D production model. The Bf 109D-0 was fitted with a 960 hp

DB 600Aa engine and an armament of two MG 17 machine-guns and an engine-mounted MG FF/M cannon. The Bf 109D-0s, which were converted from Bf 109B airframes, were followed by a small number of D-1 production aircraft, but this version was soon abandoned in favour of the Bf 109E.

On 11 July, 1938, the Bayerische Flugzeugwerke AG were renamed Messerschmitt AG. Even after this change, the Bf 109 retained its original designation in all official German publications and documents, and Me 109 was used only by unofficial sources.

The first really major production version of the fighter was the Bf 109E which differed in being powered by a 1,100 hp Daimler-Benz DB 601A engine. This powerplant was based on the earlier DB 600, but was fitted with direct fuel injection, in place of a carburettor, and improved superchargers. The fuel injection system proved to be a great asset in combat, as the engine did not cut out under conditions of negative gravity. The first prototype for the E-series was the Bf 109 V14, D-IRTT, which appeared during the summer of 1938 and had two MG FF cannon in the wings and two engine-mounted MG 17 machine-guns. The Bf 109 V15, D-IPHR, was similar, but armament was reduced to a single 20 mm MG FF/M cannon.

A Bf 109E-3 of the Luftwaffe. (*R. C. Seeley*)

The Bf 109E-0 had four MG 17 machine-guns, and the first aircraft were delivered to JG 132 at Düsseldorf in December 1938. The Bf 109E-1 was similar, and the E-1/B could carry four 50 kg (110 lb) SC 50 or a single 250 kg (550 lb) SC 250 bomb. The Bf 109E-2 had two MG 17s and two MG FF cannon, and the E-3, which reached the Luftwaffe during the early summer of 1940, four MG 17s and an engine-mounted MG FF/M cannon.

When the Luftwaffe went to war in September 1939, its fighter units had no less than 1,060 Messerschmitt Bf 109s of various sub-types. Some indication of the build-up of Bf 109 strength can be gained from the fact that a year earlier, on 26 September, 1938, the Luftwaffe had only 171 Messerschmitt fighters, the remaining fighter units' strength consisting of 640 Arado Ar 68 biplanes.

In addition to the single-engined fighter units, ten élite destroyer Gruppen were formed in 1938 with the eventual intention of equipping them with the Bf 110. At the outbreak of war, only three units had received

A Bf 109E-3 of I./JG 1 at De Kooy, 1941. (*H. Obert*)

the twin-engined machine; the others were equipped with a mixture of mainly obsolescent Bf 109 variants. II./ZG 1 had the Bf 109E-1, I./ZG 2 the Bf 109D-1, ZG 26 the Bf 109C and D, and I./ZG 52 and II./ZG 76 the Bf 109D-1. The naval fighter units, 5. and 6./Trägergruppe 186 were equipped with a mixture of Bf 109Bs and Es.

A Staffel of Bf 109E-3s preparing for take-off. (*H. Redemann*)

473

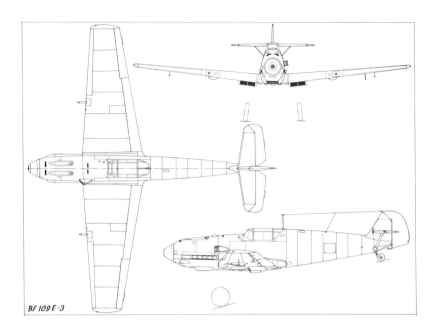

The cockpit of the Bf 109E. The Revi C 12/C reflector gunsight can be seen just behind the windscreen. (*H. Redemann*)

This Bf 109E-4, piloted by Uffz Hans Schubert of 3./JG 1, nosed over after a tyre burst at De Kooy in May 1941. (*H. Obert*)

The German attack on the Low Countries and France proved to be virtually a repeat of the previous successful campaign against Poland. Only one French fighter, the Dewoitine D.520, was capable of meeting the Bf 109E on anything like equal terms, but due to mismanagement this aircraft never reached l'Armée de l'Air in any numbers. The RAF had six Hurricane squadrons in France and these were joined by another four by 12 May, 1940. Although fighting bravely, the British squadrons were unable to combat the well-organized Luftwaffe units successfully, and by 28 May they had all been withdrawn to southern England. On the previous day, over the beaches of Dunkirk, Spitfires clashed with Bf 109s for the first time, showing that at last an aircraft had appeared which was at least the equal of the German fighter.

Operations against the British Isles began early in July 1940 when Oberst Johannes Fink was given the task of clearing the Straits of Dover of British shipping. In addition to his own KG 2, Fink had under his command two Stuka Gruppen plus the Bf 109Es of JG 51 and III./JG 3. As the battle progressed, the Bf 109 found itself increasingly opposed by the Spitfire. The Hurricane, although an excellent fighter, could not meet the Messerschmitt on equal terms, and, recognizing this, the British commanders switched the Hawker fighter to bomber-interception duties.

As regards the relative merits of the Spitfire and the Bf 109, there was little to choose. The former was slightly faster, was definitely more manoeuvrable, but performance at altitude was inferior. There was also little to choose between the pilots of the Luftwaffe and the RAF, although the latter had the advantage of fighting over their own country in defence of their loved ones, feeling that only they stood between them and Nazi domination. Other vital factors in the eventual defeat of the Luftwaffe in the day battle over the British Isles was the superb radar and reporting network employed by the RAF and the restricted range of the Bf 109E. It had always been intended that the Bf 110 should take on the rôle of long-

475

This Bf 109E-4 (c/n 1361) carried an SC 250 bomb beneath the fuselage in connection with the development of fighter-bomber tactics. (*H. Thiele*)

range bomber escort, but this machine proved unable to defend even itself against the fighters of the RAF.

Development of the Bf 109E continued with the E-4 model which was similar to the E-3 but did not have the engine-mounted cannon. The Bf 109E-4/B was a fighter-bomber variant similar to the E-1/B, and the E-4/N was powered by a 1,200 hp DB 601N engine. The Bf 109E-5 and E-6 were both reconnaissance variants with defensive armament reduced to two MG 17 guns. The former was powered by a DB 601Aa, the latter by the more powerful DB 601N. The Bf 109E-7 was generally similar to the E-4/N apart from having attachment points for a drop-tank, and the E-7/U2 was a heavily-armoured ground attack variant. The Bf 109E-7/Z had GM-1 power boosting, the E-8 was powered by a 1,300 hp DB 601E engine, and the E-9 was a reconnaissance variant with an Rb 50/30 or two Rb 32/7 cameras.

A Bf 109E-4/N of 1./JG 27 at Ain El Gazala with a camera pod fitted beneath the fuselage, June 1941. (*R. C. Seeley*)

476

The Bf 109E-4 experimentally fitted with overwing fuel tanks by the Graf Zeppelin research institute at Stuttgart-Ruit in 1942.

A Bf 109E-7 of JG 5 over Finland, 1942.

A Bf 109E-8 experimentally fitted with skis and a jettisonable three-wheel take-off trolley.

477

Perhaps the most interesting conversion of the Bf 109E was the Bf 109T series of carrier-borne fighters intended to operate from the aircraft carrier *Graf Zeppelin*. Conversion of ten Bf 109T-0s was undertaken by Fieseler at Kassel during 1939–40, the machines having increased span, manually folding outer wings, wing spoilers, arrester hooks and catapult spools. Sixty Bf 109T-1s were built by Fieseler during 1940–41, the machines being generally similar to the T-0 but powered by a DB 601N engine. The Bf 109T-2 was a conversion of the T-1 in which the arrester hooks and catapult spools were removed.

Early in 1941, fifty or so Bf 109T-1s were delivered to I./JG 77 at Drontheim in Norway. The aircraft operated quite successfully from the tiny windswept airfield, but after a short time I./JG 77 was redesignated IV./JG 51, and the aircraft handed over to Einsatz-Staffel Drontheim. This was not the last operational use of the Bf 109T, however. On 10 April, 1943, Jagdstaffel Heligoland was equipped with sixteen Bf 109T-2s. The unit was given the task of helping to combat USAAF raids against Kiel, Bremen and Emden, being redesignated 11./JG 11 on 30 November, 1943. Finally, on 10 April, 1944, its few remaining aircraft were handed over to IV./JG 5, and the Staffel was disbanded.

With the conclusion of the daylight offensive against the British Isles, the activities of the Luftwaffe's fighter units declined considerably. Experiments had been made by 3./Erpr.Gr 210 and II.(S)/LG 2 with the Bf 109E-1/B during the battle, and Göring ordered that a Staffel from each Jagdgeschwader be equipped for fighter-bomber duties. The pilots were given an extremely cursory insight into the tactics of bomb aiming, trajectories, and the other mysteries of dropping bombs accurately from a fast, sensitive fighter aircraft. It was of little wonder that the Staffeln concerned felt that the whole thing was a waste of time.

During the spring of 1940, a standard Bf 109E airframe (c/n 5604) was fitted with a DB 601E engine in a new symmetrical cowling. Modifications were also made to the supercharger and radiator intakes, and the machine was fitted with a new cantilever tailplane. The aircraft made its first flight on 10 July, 1940, and development led to the Bf 109F series. In addition to the modifications previously enumerated, the Bf 109F-0 featured new rounded wingtips, a smaller rudder and a fully-retractable tailwheel.

The first production model was the Bf 109F-1, which was powered by a DB 601N engine and had an engine-mounted 20 mm MG FF/M cannon and two MG 17 machine-guns. The Bf 109F-2 had the MG FF/M weapon replaced by the faster-firing 15 mm MG 151, and the Bf 109F-2/Z used GM-1 power boosting. The Bf 109F-3 switched to the 1,300 hp Daimler-Benz 601E engine, and the F-4 had the 15 mm MG 151 replaced by a 20 mm MG 151/20 weapon. The Bf 109F-4/B was a fighter-bomber, the F-4/R1 had a pair of underwing MG 151/20 cannon, and the F-2 and F-4/Trop were tropicalized variants of the basic models. The F-5 and F-6 were both photographic reconnaissance variants, armament being reduced to two MG 17s in the former and deleted altogether in the latter.

The Bf 109F-1 was not produced in any numbers, the first model to enter service with the Luftwaffe being the Bf 109F-2, a number of which were delivered to III./JG 26, under Maj Gerhard Schöpfel, in May 1941. The Bf 109F proved to be an excellent fighter, having superior performance at altitude to the new Spitfire V, although its reduced armament caused some controversy amongst the leading Luftwaffe pilots. Werner Mölders, an excellent shot, considered that the single centrally-mounted gun was ideal, but Adolf Galland stressed that a heavy-cannon armament would be much more effective, especially in the hands of the less-expert pilot. Maj Walter Oesau of III./JG 3 even refused to fly the Bf 109F, until lack of spares finally forced him to exchange his E-4 for the newer variant.

At 03.15 hr on 22 June, 1941, Germany launched Operation Barbarossa, the massive attack against the Soviet Union over a 2,000-mile front by three army groups and four Luftflotten. The Luftwaffe's fighter force comprised JG 3 under Maj Günther Lützow equipped with the Bf 109F; II. and III./JG 27 under Maj Wolfgang Schnellmann with the Bf 109E; JG 51 under Mölders with the Bf 109F, II. and III./JG 52 under

The pilot of a Bf 109F of I./JG 51 prepares for take-off. (*H. Redemann*)

479

During his period in command of III./JG 2, Hptm Karl Heinz Greisert flew this Bf 109F-2. (*R. C. Seeley*)

Maj Hans Trübenbach with the Bf 109E; JG 53 under Maj Günther von Maltzahn with the Bf 109F; JG 54 under Maj Hannes Trautloft with the Bf 109F; and JG 77 under Maj Bernhard Woldenga with the Bf 109E. In addition, I.(Jagd.)/LG 2 was operational under Hptm Herbert Ihlefeld, this unit being redesignated as the new I./JG 77 on 24 January, 1942.

The opening attacks were directed mainly against Soviet aircraft on the ground, many Bf 109s carrying 2 kg ($4\frac{1}{2}$ lb) SD 2 fragmentation bombs. During the first day of the campaign, the Luftwaffe claimed the destruction of no less than 1,811 Soviet aircraft for the loss of 32 of its own machines. Success followed success, and on 30 June, 1941, JG 51 claimed its 1,000th victim. JG 53 brought its total of enemy aircraft to 1,000 on 31 July, followed by JG 54 on 1 August and JG 3 on 15 August.

Luftwaffe fighter units in the West had been reduced to two Geschwader, JG 2 under Maj Walter Oesau and JG 26 under Obstlt Adolf Galland, both equipped with the Bf 109E-7, F-2 and F-4. Hptm Rolf Pingel, commander of I./JG 26, was forced to belly-land his F-2 near Dover on 10 July, 1941. This was the first Bf 109F to fall into Allied hands, it was quickly repaired and test-flown by the RAF but completely destroyed in a crash soon afterwards.

A Bf 109F-4 prior to delivery to the Luftwaffe in 1941.

480

In August 1941, the first Focke-Wulf Fw 190A-1 was delivered to II./JG 26, and gradually this superb fighter began to supplant the Bf 109s in service with JG 26, although it was not for some time that JG 2 received its first Focke-Wulfs. Also operational in the West and equipped with the Bf 109F was JG 1 under Obstlt Carl Schumacher. This unit provided the sole daylight defence of the German homeland.

During the early autumn of 1941, I./JG 27 under Hptm Eduard Neumann was transferred to North Africa to supplement the small Luftwaffe force operating in that area under X.Fliegerkorps. The unit was still equipped with the Bf 109E-4/Trop and was based at Ain-el-Gazala. On 24 September, Lt Hans Marseille of 3./JG 27 claimed the destruction of five enemy aircraft, and he was shortly to become the most celebrated German pilot of this war theatre. By the end of 1941, the other two Gruppen of JG 27 had been transferred to North Africa, the Geschwader now being equipped with the Bf 109F-4/Trop.

A Bf 109F-4/Trop of II./JG 27 at Sanyet, September 1942. In the background can be seen another Bf 109F and a Ju 88A of LG 1. (*R. C. Seeley*)

A major German operation in February 1942 was the transfer of the battlecruisers *Scharnhorst* and *Gneisenau* from Brest to the safety of Wilhelmshaven. Code-named Operation Cerberus, the passage of the ships was to be protected by over 200 fighters drawn from JG 1, JG 2 and JG 26, operating in shifts. The majority of the fighters were Bf 109F-2s and F-4s, although JG 26 had re-equipped with the Fw 190A. During the operation, only four German fighters were lost for which the Luftwaffe claimed the destruction of 49 British aircraft.

On 10 March, 1942, Gen Hugo Sperrle, commander of Luftflotte 3, issued a directive calling for the setting up of two fighter-bomber Staffeln within JG 2 and JG 26. This only served to legalize the two units,

10.(Jabo)/JG 2 and JG 26, which had been formed in November 1941. Both units were equipped with the Bf 109F-4/B fitted with racks for a 250 kg (550 lb) SC 250 bomb. Unlike the earlier fighter-bomber units of the Luftwaffe, which attacked at high altitude with little attempt at accuracy, these two Staffeln flew in at low level in an attempt to evade the radar defence.

Often taking advantage of poor visibility, the aircraft would take-off from the well-defended bases at Abbeville, Ligescourt, Poix, or St Omer, hug the ground and streak over the Channel. Favourite targets were ports and gasholders along the south coast of England, Dover, Brighton, Folkestone, Worthing, and Newhaven receiving special attention. JG 2, based to the south around Évreux and Caen, concentrated its attacks on isolated vessels in the Channel. JG 26, based further north, attacked Dover and nearby towns along the coast. The form of attack was hurried, but it did serve to keep the RAF fighter defences at constant readiness. Up to 26 July, 1942, 10.(Jabo)/JG 2 claimed the sinking of 20 ships totalling some 63,000 tons. 10.(Jabo)/JG 26 was similarly successful, claiming the destruction of eight railway installations, eight barracks, six ships, five factories, two gasholders, and two harbour installations.

The early months of 1942 proved most successful for JG 27 in North Africa. Opposed only by obsolescent Hawker Hurricanes and Curtiss Tomahawks, the Bf 109F-equipped unit was able to destroy a large number of Allied aircraft. In addition to JG 27, JG 53 Pik-As was also in the Mediterranean at this time, based variously in Greece, Crete and Sicily and operating in the main against Malta.

A large variety of experimental versions of the Bf 109F were produced. One aircraft was fitted with a BMW 801 radial for comparative trials with the Fw 190, and another was fitted with a Junkers Jumo 213 in an annular cowling. A Bf 109F-4 (c/n 14003) was fitted with butterfly tail surfaces, which were found to bestow improved flight characteristics on the design but were not proceeded with because of RLM pressure to produce more and more aircraft without interrupting the construction programme. Another project to fall by the wayside was the Bf 109F fitted with boundary-layer fences in place of leading-edge slots.

Several Bf 109Fs were also used in connection with the development of the Messerschmitt Me 209A and Me 309 fighters. A Bf 109F-1 (c/n 5603) was fitted with a fixed nosewheel undercarriage for both the Me 309 and Me 262 programmes, and the Bf 109 V24 (c/n 5604) was used to test various cooling systems in the Göppingen wind-tunnel. The Bf 109 V30 (c/n 5716)—a converted F-1—and the V30a (c/n 5717)—converted from an F-4—were both fitted with pressurized cabins. Altitudes of over 12,000 m (39,372 ft) were achieved during the test programme, but the earlier aircraft suffered from icing of the cockpit glazing and ineffective cabin sealing. The Bf 109 V31 (c/n 5642) was fitted with an inward-retracting undercarriage of wide track similar to that later applied to the Me 209A and Me 309.

Early in 1943, work began on a high-altitude development of the F-series, the Bf 109H. The Bf 109H V1 was converted from a standard Bf 109F by the addition of a 2 m (6 ft 6½ in) wing section and the bracing of the tailplane. The machine underwent development trials at Rechlin and was later transferred to the Daimler-Benz factory at Stuttgart-Echterdingen where it was destroyed in an air raid in August 1944. A small batch of Bf 109H-0 pre-production aircraft was followed by a small number of Bf 109H-1 machines. This variant was powered by a 1,300 hp DB 601E engine and had one 30 mm MK 108 cannon and two MG 17 machine-guns.

Several developments of the basic design were proposed, including the Bf 109H-2 and H-3 with a Jumo 213 engine installed as a 'power egg', and the Bf 109H-5 fitted with a DB 605L engine. The Bf 109H series was proposed in two major variants, one fitted with three MK 108 and two MG 151/20 cannon, the other unarmed but carrying an Rb 50/30 or Rb 75/30 camera.

A small number of Bf 109Hs was delivered to a reconnaissance unit on the Channel coast in April 1944. The unit is reported to have been 3.(F)/121 based at Bernay under the command of Hptm Heinzel. In addition to the Bf 109H which could attain an altitude of 13,500 m (44,293 ft), the unit is also reported to have operated a captured Republic P-47 Thunderbolt.

The next, and major, production version of the Messerschmitt fighter was the Bf 109G—known as the Gustav. The Bf 109G was basically an F-series airframe fitted with the new DB 605A engine. This engine was similar to the DB 601E but had an increase in compression ratio which raised its maximum output to 1,475 hp. Externally, the Gustav could be distinguished from the Bf 109F only by two small features. These were the addition of two tiny intakes aft of the spinner and the disappearance of the small triangular windows below the windscreen.

Because of shortage of DB 605 engines, the twelve Bf 109G-0s retained

A Bf 109G-2 of I./JG 77 in the Mediterranean area. (*R. C. Seeley*)

Two Bf 109G-2s of the Rumanian Air Force with an Me 323E-2 in the background. (*R. C. Seeley*)

the DB 601E and were armed with two MG 17 machine-guns and a single MG 151/20 cannon. The machines also had some structural strengthening, and provision was made for a pressurized cockpit. The Bf 109G-1 was fitted with the 1,475 hp DB 605A-1 engine, the power from which could be increased by the addition of GM-1 nitrous-oxide injection. The Bf 109G-1/Trop was fitted with tropical filters and had the MG 17 weapons replaced by two 13 mm MG 131 guns. These necessitated large fairings over the breech blocks and were responsible for the Bf 109G's other nickname, the Beule (Bump).

The Bf 109G-2 was an unpressurized version of the G-1, and the G-2/R1 was a fighter-bomber variant with provision for an under-fuselage bomb rack and two underwing drop tanks. An unusual feature of the G-2/R1 was a third, jettisonable, mainwheel positioned below the rear fuselage to provide ground clearance for the bomb during take-off. The G-3 was similar to the G-1, but employed FuG 16Z radio equipment in place

The Bf 109G-2/R1 long-range fighter-bomber fitted with an extra undercarriage leg which was jettisoned after take-off. (*H. Redemann*)

A Bf 109G-6/R2 of 9./JG 3 with 210 mm WGr 21 rocket tubes underwing. (*R. C. Seeley*)

of FuG 7A. The Bf 109G-4 was an unpressurized version of the G-3. The G-5 was powered by the DB 605D engine with MW-50 water-methanol injection which increased maximum power to 1,800 hp for short periods. This variant also had a new enlarged wooden fin and rudder and a lengthened tailwheel oleo leg in an attempt to cure the fighter's characteristic take-off swing.

Most important of all Gustavs was the Bf 109G-6 which could be powered by the DB 605AM, AS, ASB, ASD or ASM engine. This version had two MG 131 machine-guns, a single 30 mm MK 108 cannon firing through the spinner, and two underwing MG 151/20 weapons. This combination was ideal for bomber interception but severely reduced the machine's efficiency in fighter-versus-fighter combat. The Bf 109G-6/U4 carried two MK 108 cannon in place of the MG 151/20s, and the

Maintenance work being undertaken on a Bf 109G-6/R2 of 9./JG 3 during the spring of 1944. (*R. C. Seeley*)

485

G-6/U4N was fitted with FuG 350 Naxos homing radar. The G-6/R1 was a fighter-bomber with an ETC 250 or ETC 500 bomb rack, and the G-6/R2 carried two WGr 21 Dödel rocket tubes. The Bf 109G-7 was a proposed variant to incorporate all the improvements introduced by the G-6 but was not built.

The first Bf 109Gs were delivered to 11./JG 2 Richthofen during the summer of 1942. This Staffel, which had been formed in May, undertook high-altitude interception missions with the Bf 109G-1.

By February 1943, the following units were equipped with the Bf 109G: I./JG 1 operating in the defence of Germany; JG 3 under Maj Wolf-Dietrich Wilcke and JG 52 under Maj Hannes Trautloft in southern Russia; JG 5 under Obstlt Günther Scholz in Norway and Finland; JG 27 under Obstlt Eduard Neumann; JG 53 under Maj Günther von Maltzahn; and JG 77 under Maj Joachim Müncheberg in the Middle East; and III./JG 54 under Maj Reinhard Seiler in France.

III./JG 54 had been transferred from Russia to strengthen the Luftwaffe units attempting to combat the growing menace of the USAAF daylight bombing offensive. Day fighter forces in Germany were further strengthened on 1 April, 1943, by the formation of JG 11. Commanded by Maj Anton Mader, JG 11 was formed from a nucleus provided by I. and III./JG 1 and equipped with a mixture of Bf 109Gs and Fw 190s.

Operations proved that it was extremely difficult to destroy a Boeing B-17 Fortress with the early variants of the Bf 109G which were lightly armed, and consequently much thought was given to the development of powerful anti-bomber weapons. Perhaps the most novel was the brainchild of Lt Heinz Knocke of 5./JG 1, which is described in his book *I flew for the Führer*. This involved the dropping of a 250 kg (550 lb) SC 250 bomb, equipped with a time fuse, from a Bf 109G onto the American formation. Knocke himself achieved the first success with this weapon on 22 March, 1943, but the experiment saw little operational use. Another novel form of armament was the 210 mm WGr 21 rocket tube used operationally by Staffeln of JG 1, JG 3, JG 26 and JG 27.

One of the most important actions in which the Luftwaffe participated on the Eastern Front was Operation Citadelle, a major attempt by Germany to regain the initiative in the area. Eight fighter Gruppen took part, including II. and III./JG 3 with the Bf 109G; I., III., and IV./JG 51 with the Fw 190; I. and III./JG 52 with the Bf 109G; and III./JG 54 with the Fw 190. On 5 July, 1943, the first day of the campaign, these units claimed the destruction of 432 Soviet aircraft, of which II./JG 3 under Maj Kurt Brändle destroyed 77 including 62 bombers.

Nine Gruppen, all equipped with the Bf 109G, were operational in July 1943 in the Luftflotte 2 area. These included II. and III./JG 27, II./JG 51, JG 53 and JG 77. All units were heavily engaged during the Allied invasion of Sicily, but later in July, II./JG 27 was withdrawn to Wiesbaden-Erbenheim to join I. Gruppe in the defence of Germany. Previously, in April 1943, IV./JG 27 had been formed in Greece under Oblt

A woman mechanic at work on the Daimler-Benz DB 605 engine of a Bf 109G.
*(Messerschmitt)*

Alfred Burk, and this unit was joined by the newly-established I./JG 4 in July. These two units intercepted the first USAAF raid on the Ploesti oil-fields on 1 August, 1943, a raid in which 54 American bombers were lost.

A IVth Gruppe was added to Jagdgeschwader 5 early in 1943, the Geschwader operating mainly in northern Norway and Finland equipped with the Bf 109G-2 and G-6. In February 1943, IV./JG 5 was re-equipped with the Fw 190A, and I. and II./JG 5 were withdrawn to northern Russia in January 1944 and then to the Western Front at the time of the Allied invasion. Both Gruppen were eventually disbanded, being incorporated into the newly-established JG 4 and JG 6.

Late in July 1943, five further Jagdgruppen were withdrawn from bases in southern Russia and Italy to Germany to supplement the forces of JG 1, JG 2, JG 11, JG 26, III./JG 54 and ZG 26 then engaged in the defence of Germany. II./JG 27 under Hptm Werner Schroer was transferred from Vibo-Valentia in Italy to Wiesbaden; II./JG 51 under Maj Karl Rammelt, from Sardinia to Neubiberg near Munich; and the entire Jagdgeschwader 3 under Obstlt Wolf-Dietrich Wilcke, from southern Russia. On 21 July, two new Gruppen were formed, JGr 25 under Maj Herbert Ihlefeld and JGr 50 under Maj Hermann Graf. These were equipped with specially boosted Bf 109Gs and were intended to combat RAF Mosquito raids which were becoming more and more troublesome. A few interceptions were attempted, but the Messerschmitt fighter proved incapable of catching the British aircraft.

487

On 27 June, 1943, a new Jagdgeschwader was set up under the command of Maj Hajo Herrmann, a former bomber pilot with III./KG 30. Designated JG 300, the unit operated Wilde Sau (Wild Boar) sorties, a system of free-lance night defence using single-engined fighters operating with the aid of searchlights. JG 300's first major sortie was on the night of 17/18 August, 1943, when it attempted to intercept a force of RAF bombers attacking the Peenemünde research establishment. Operations by the Geschwader were so successful during the summer months of 1943 that two new units were formed: JG 301 under Maj Helmut Weinrich and JG 302 under Maj Ewald Janssen. Of these three Geschwader, I. and III./JG 300, I. and III./JG 301 and I./JG 302 were equipped with the Bf 109G. Only one Gruppe in each Geschwader had its own aircraft, the other machines being shared between a day and night fighter unit, examples being III./JG 11 with II./JG 300 and II./JG 27 with I./JG 302.

Development of the Messerschmitt fighter continued with the Bf 109G-8 high-speed reconnaissance aircraft which carried two MG 131s and one MG 151/20 cannon plus two Rb 12·5/7 or Rb 32/7 cameras. Many reconnaissance Staffeln were equipped with the aircraft, perhaps the most notable being NAGr 13 under Maj Schulz-Moderow based in the vicinity of Chartres. This unit, which operated in conjunction with 3./NAGr 12, undertook many important missions during the Allied invasion of Normandy, being particularly active around the Caen area.

A Bf 109G-10/U4 prior to take-off. (*R. C. Seeley*)

The fastest of all Gustav variants was the Bf 109G-10, which attained a maximum speed of 690 km/h (428 mph) at 7,500 m (24,607 ft). It was powered by a DB 605G engine with MW-50 water-methanol injection and carried an armament of one MK 108 cannon and two MK 131 machine-guns. The Bf 109G-10/U4 carried two MK 108 cannon in an under-fuselage tray which could be replaced by a non-jettisonable Irmer Behälter auxiliary fuel tank. The Bf 109G-10/R2 and R6 had the enlarged tail surfaces introduced on the G-5/R2 as standard and carried FuG IFF equipment. Several Gustav variants beginning with the G-6 were fitted with a specially modified cockpit canopy known as the Galland hood which

This Bf 109G-10/U4 was captured by US forces at the end of the war. (*R. C. Seeley*)

considerably reduced the cockpit framing and provided the pilot with a much-improved view.

The Bf 109G-12 was a tandem two-seat training version of the standard G-series airframe, many of which were converted by Luftwaffe maintenance units. This variant saw service with many of the Jagdgeschwaderschulen, of which there were 13, designated JG 101 to JG 110 and JG 114 to 116. Several of these became operational towards the end of the war, including JG 102 in Norway and JG 104 which took part in Operation Bodenplatte (*see* page 491).

The Bf 109G-14 was a fighter-bomber similar to the G-6 carrying an armament of one MG 151/20 cannon firing through the spinner and two MG 131 machine-guns. Two further MG 151/20s or two WGr 21 rocket tubes could be carried beneath the wing, and the aircraft normally carried an ETC 250 bomb rack. The G-14/R2 had the enlarged wooden tail surface, and the G-16 was a heavily-armoured ground attack variant which failed to see operational service.

The Bf 109H has been described previously: there was no Bf 109I, and the Bf 109J was the German designation for a proposed variant to be built

The prototype Bf 109G-12 two-seat trainer modified from a G-5 airframe.

489

A Bf 109G-14/U4 of a Croatian fighter squadron which was surrendered by its pilot at Falconara, Italy, in April 1945. (*USAF*)

under licence in Spain. The next, and final, production series was the Bf 109K which entered service late in 1944. The Bf 109K-0 was similar to the G-10, being powered by a DB 605D engine with GM-1 injection. The Bf 109K-2 and K-4 were powered by the 1,500 hp DB 605ASCM/DCM engine with MW-50, which increased maximum output to 2,000 hp for a short period. Both versions were armed with two 15 mm MG 151s and a single 30 mm MK 103 or MK 108 cannon; the K-4 differing solely in that it had a pressurized cabin. The Bf 109K-6 was similar to the K-2 but had three MK 103 cannon and two MG 131 machine-guns. The final production variant was the Bf 109K-14, which was powered by a DB 605L engine with MW-50 and had two MG 131 machine-guns and a single MK 108 cannon. Only two Bf 109K-14s saw service, these being delivered to the Stab of II./JG 52 under Maj Wilhelm Batz in the late spring of 1945.

Many other modifications of the basic Bf 109 airframe were proposed. The Bf 109L was a variant in which the DB 605 engine would have been replaced by a 1,750 hp Junkers Jumo 213E unit. Maximum speed was

A Bf 109K-2, probably of I./JG 51, spring 1945. (*J. Zazvonil*)

490

estimated at 763 km/h (474 mph). The Bf 109S was projected with blown flaps to improve handling characteristics at low speeds, and a Bf 109G (c/n 110039) was fitted with servo-assisted elevators and rudder tabs.

The Bf 109Z Zwilling (Twin), of which one prototype was completed late in 1942 but never flown, comprised two F-series airframes joined together by new wing and tail sections. The pilot would have sat in the port fuselage, and the proposed armament of the first variant was five MK 108 cannon. The Bf 109Z-2 was similar, but armament would have been reduced to two MK 108s and a bomb load of 1,000 kg (2,205 lb) would have been carried. The span of both variants was 13·27 m (43 ft 6½ in) and the loaded weight 6,000 kg (13,200 lb). The Bf 109Z-3 and Z-4 were respectively modifications of the Z-1 and Z-2, to have been powered by two Jumo 213 engines. Progressive development of the Bf 109Z led eventually to the Me 609 project.

The Jumo 211F powered CS 199 two-seat trainer developed from the Bf 109G in Czechoslovakia after the war. (*J. Zazvonil*)

Certainly the most radical of all variants of the Messerschmitt fighter was the Bf 109TL project. Conceived in January 1943, the project was for a twin-jet fighter to make use of as many Bf 109 components as possible. It was planned to use a standard Bf 109 fuselage with the wing assembly of the Me 155 project and the nosewheel of the Me 309. The aircraft was to be powered by two 850 kg (1,874 lb) static thrust Junkers Jumo 109-004B turbojets and carry an armament of one MG 151/20 and two MK 103 cannon. Estimated maximum speed was 840 km/h (522 mph) at sea level, and it was anticipated that the aircraft would attain a service ceiling of 11,400 m (37,415 ft). After only two months, the Bf 109TL project was abandoned, as it was realized that the Me 262A-0 Schwalbe (Swallow) would soon be leaving the production lines and the project would only serve to divert effort from it.

The final desperate attempt by the Luftwaffe to gain superiority in the West was made on New Year's Day 1945 under the code name of Operation Bodenplatte. This was an all-out attack by no less than 750

Luftwaffe fighters against Allied airfields in Holland, Belgium and Luxembourg. For the first time the Bf 109K-2 and K-4 were used operationally, each Gruppe being led by a flight of Junkers Ju 88G night fighters.

The final major operation by a Bf 109 equipped unit was made on 7 April, 1945, by a special unit known as Rammkommando Elbe. Formed at the instigation of Oberst Hajo Herrmann, commander of IX.Fliegerdivision, the unit was equipped with 150 Messerschmitt Bf 109Gs piloted in the main by students. Of the 120 aircraft that took off to intercept a USAAF raid, only 15 returned.

*Wartime operational units:* 2. and 4.(H)/12, 1.(H)/13, 2.(H)/14, 2.(H)/21, 1.(H)/32, 1.(F)/33, 1.(F)/100, 1.(F)/120, 1.(F)/121, 1., 2. and 3.(F)/122, 1., 3., 4. and 5.(F)/123, 1.(F)/124, 3./Aufkl.Gr.Ob.d.L., NAGr 1, 2, 3, 4, 5, 8, 9, 10, 11, 12, 13, 14 and 15, 7.(F) and 9.(H)/LG 2, JG 1, JG 2, JG 3, JG 4, JG 5, III./JG 6, III./JG 7 (small numbers during formation only), JG 11, I./JG 20, I./JG 21, JGr 25, JG 26, JG 27, JGr 50, JG 51, JG 52, JG 53, JG 54, I./JG 70, I./JG 71, I. and III./JG 76, JG 77, JGr 200, JG 300, JG 301, JG 302, I.(Jagd)/LG 2, II.(Jagd)/Träg Gr 186, KG(J) 6, KG(J) 55, II. and III./ZG 1, I./ZG 2, ZG 26, I./ZG 52, II./ZG 76, III. and IV./NJG 1, NJGr 10, NJG 11, I./NJG 100, II.(Sch)/LG 2, I. and II./Sch.G 1, I./Sch.G 2, Erprobungsgruppe 210, SKG 210, IV./KG 200, 1./Versuchsverband Ob.d.L., Rammkommando Elbe, Erprobungskommando 25.

Bf 109E-3: Span 9·85 m (32 ft 4¼ in); length 8·63 m (28 ft 4 in); height 3·4 m (11 ft 2 in); wing area 16·17 sq m (174 sq ft).
Empty weight 2,005 kg (4,421 lb); loaded weight 2,505 kg (5,523 lb).
Maximum speed at 3,800 m (12,463 ft) 570 km/h (354 mph); climb to 5,000 m (16,405 ft) 6·2 min; service ceiling 11,000 m (36,091 ft); absolute ceiling 11,500 m (37,731 ft); normal range 663 km (412 miles).

Bf 109F-3: Span 9·92 m (32 ft 6½ in); length 8·86 m (29 ft 0¾ in); height 3·4 m (11 ft 2 in); wing area 16·05 sq m (172·75 sq ft).
Empty weight 1,960 kg (4,321 lb); loaded weight 2,750 kg (6,063 lb).
Maximum speed at 6,000 m (19,686 ft) 630 km/h (391 mph); service ceiling 12,000 m (39,370 ft); normal range 710 km (440 miles).

Bf 109G-6: Span 9·92 m (32 ft 6½ in); length 9·02 m (29 ft 7 in); height 3·4 m (11 ft 2 in); wing area 16·05 sq m (172·75 sq ft).
Empty weight 2,700 kg (5,953 lb); loaded weight 3,150 kg (6,945 lb).
Maximum speed at 7,000 m (22,967 ft) 623 km/h (387 mph), at sea level 544 km/h (338 mph); climb to 6,000 m (19,868 ft) 6 min; service ceiling 11,750 m (38,551 ft); absolute ceiling 12,100 m (39,700 ft); normal range 725 km (450 miles); maximum range 990 km (615 miles).

Bf 109K-4: Dimensions as Bf 109G-6. Loaded weight 3,370 kg (7,438 lb); maximum speed at 6,000 m (19,686 ft) 728 km/h (452 mph) and 607 km/h (377 mph) at sea level; climb to 5,000 m (16,405 ft) 3 min, to 10,000 m (32,811 ft) 6·7 min; service ceiling 12,500 m (41,012 ft); normal range 590 km (366 miles).

Numerous examples of the Bf 109 still exist including CASA HA 1112s built in Spain.

A Messerschmitt Bf 110 bearing the wasp insignia of Zerstörergeschwader 1.

# Messerschmitt Bf 110

During the late 1930s, attempts were made by many of the major air powers to produce a long-range twin-engined fighter with the performance of a single-engined interceptor. Germany's major foray into the field was the Messerschmitt Bf 110 design. Although proving unable to meet single-engined interceptors on anything like equal terms, the Bf 110 was to provide the Luftwaffe with a most valuable night fighter which was to remain in service until the close of the war in Europe.

The Bf 110 was conceived in 1934 as a result of a Luftwaffe specification calling for a long-range strategic fighter. The machine was a cantilever low-wing monoplane built of metal with duralumin flush-riveted stressed skin. The fuselage was an oval-section monocoque structure with an elongated and extensively glazed canopy enclosing the crew of three. The tailplane was mounted above the rear of the fuselage with endplate fins and rudders and the wing was a single-spar structure which incorporated leading-edge automatic slots and trailing-edge slotted flaps. The main undercarriage members retracted backwards into the engine nacelles and the tailwheel folded into the rear of the fuselage.

The aircraft was designed around two Daimler-Benz DB 600 twelve-cylinder inverted-vee liquid-cooled engines, which were just making their appearance. The first prototype, the Bf 110 V1, made its maiden flight on 12 May, 1936, from Augsburg-Haunstetten airfield. Although proving very fast, the Bf 110 exhibited an ominous lack of manoeuvrability.

Two further prototypes followed, respectively on 24 October and 24 December, 1936, the former, the Bf 110 V2, being delivered to Rechlin for Luftwaffe acceptance trials on 14 January, 1937. The success of these tests led the RLM to place a contract for four Bf 110A-0 pre-production aircraft. These were completed between August 1937 and March 1938

493

The Henschel Hs 124 V1 was designed to the same specification as the Messerschmitt Bf 110 and Focke-Wulf Fw 57 high-speed fighter-bombers.

but, because of slow deliveries of the DB 600 engine, were powered by Junkers Jumo 210Bs, which only provided 610 hp for take-off. The Bf 110A-0 had four 7·9 mm MG 17 machine-guns in the nose and a single 7·9 mm MG 15 in the rear of the cockpit.

On 19 April, 1938, the first of two Bf 110B-0s made its initial flight. Both aircraft were powered by 670 hp Junkers Jumo 210G engines, but, following quantity deliveries of the DB 600A during the summer, the aircraft were fitted with this powerplant. The Bf 110B-0s were followed by the generally similar B-1 production model. This aircraft had similar armament to the A-0 but carried two 20 mm MG FF cannon in the nose in addition to the four MG 17 machine-guns. The Bf 110B-2 was similar, and the B-3 was a two-seat trainer.

Relatively few Bf 110Bs were completed before the machine was replaced on the production lines by the improved C-series. The new sub-type differed in being powered by two 1,100 hp Daimler-Benz DB 601A engines with direct fuel injection in place of conventional carburettors. The

A pair of early production Messerschmitt Bf 110C-1s of I.(Z)/LG 1 operating in Poland, September 1939. (*R. C. Seeley*)

first Bf 110C-0s were delivered to the Luftwaffe in February 1939, followed shortly afterwards by the C-1 production aircraft.

Late in 1938 Göring initiated the formation of the Zerstörergeschwader which were rapidly staffed with some of the Luftwaffe's most experienced fighter pilots. This was to cause some dissension within the Jagdflieger, who felt they were losing their best people. When originally formed, the Zerstörergruppen were equipped with the Bf 109C and D, pending the largescale introduction of the Bf 110. The first unit to be equipped with the Bf 110C-1 was I./(Zerstörer) Gruppe of the technical development unit, Lehrgeschwader 1, based at Greifswald. By September

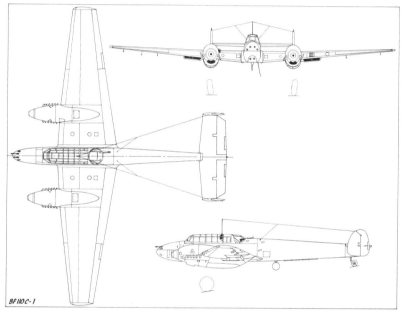

BF110C-1

1939, two further Gruppen were equipped with the Bf 110, I./ZG 1 under Maj Joachim-Friedrich Huth and I./ZG 76 under Hptm Reinecke.

The campaign against Poland opened with a mass attack on Polish Air Force aerodromes, the Bf 110s from the three previously mentioned Gruppen flying as escorts to Luftwaffe bomber units. The German fighters proved more than a match for the high-wing monoplanes of the Polish Air Force and served to strengthen the belief that the Luftwaffe was invincible.

The Bf 110 first saw action against the RAF on 18 December, 1939, when twenty-two Wellingtons attempted an armed reconnaissance of the Heligoland Bight. Sixteen Bf 110s from I./ZG 76 and thirty-four Bf 109s intercepted, and the fray developed into a long running battle. Only ten Wellingtons succeeded in regaining British shores and two of these crashed on landing. Not for another three years did a large Allied bomber formation enter German airspace in daylight.

During the winter of 1939/40, Luftwaffe operations were confined to armed reconnaissance and border defence. It was not until 9 April, 1940, that German forces were again committed to a largescale campaign— Operation Weserübung, the invasion of Norway and Denmark. Only three fighter Gruppen were assigned to support the invasion, two of these, I./ZG 1 at Barth and I./ZG 76 at Westerland, equipped with the Bf 110C.

On the day of the invasion, 1. and 2./ZG 1 were given the task of escorting the bombers of KG 4 attacking Copenhagen; 3./ZG 1 and 2./ZG 76 operated over Aalborg; and 3./ZG 76 strafed Sola Airport, Stavanger. 1./ZG 76 was to protect the landing of paratroops at Oslo's Fornebu Airport, but because of bad weather these failed to arrive. Finally, 1./ZG 76 became the first unit to land at Oslo, followed shortly afterwards by the Junkers-Ju 52/3ms from KGrzbV 103.

Several further variants of the Bf 110C were produced. The Bf 110C-1/U1 was a glider tug for the Messerschmitt Me 321, and the C-2 differed from the C-1 in having revised electrical systems and FuG 10 and FuG 111aU radio equipment. The Bf 110C-2/U1 was fitted with remote control barbettes similar to those later used on the Me 210, and the C-3 and C-4 were similar to the C-1 and C-2 apart from having improved MG FF cannon. The Bf 110C-4B was a fighter-bomber and the C-5 was a reconnaissance aircraft with a camera replacing the MG FF cannon, the C-6 had a pair of 30 mm MK 101 cannon in a ventral fairing and the C-7 was a fighter-bomber with two ETC 500 racks.

The Bf 110D, which entered service in the spring of 1940 with V.(Z)/LG 1, was a specialized long-range fighter variant. The D-0 had a large 1,050 litre (231 Imp gal) 'Dackelbauch' (Dachshund belly) non-

A Bf 110C-4 of a Luftwaffe training unit, which crashed at Prague-Ruzyne. (*J. Zazvonil*)

496

The long-range Bf 110D-0 which was fitted with the 'Dackelbauch' auxiliary fuel tank.
(*K. Ries*)

jettisonable fuel tank beneath the fuselage and was without the two MG FF cannon. The non-jettisonable fuel tank took the form of a huge ventral 'blister' covered by a fairing constructed of plywood and fabric. The Bf 110D-1/R1 did not have the under-fuselage tank but was equipped with two 900 litre (198 Imp gal) underwing drop tanks.

The Bf 110D-1/R2 was similar to the D-0, and the D-1/U1 and proposed D-4 production model were night fighters with provision for an infra-red sensing device (Spanner Anlage) in the nose. Used in conjunction with a 'Q Rohr' sighting screen, the device proved too sensitive and was abandoned. The Bf 110D-2 was a fighter-bomber with two ETC 500 racks, the D-2/Trop had tropical equipment and the D-3 could carry both bombs and drop tanks.

On 15 May, 1940, RAF Bomber Command had begun to attack Germany by night. At this time, the night fighter defence of Germany was left solely to the flak units, but they soon proved unequal to the task. Consequently on 20 July, 1940, Göring ordered Oberst Josef Kammhuber to set up a night fighter force. I./ZG 1, with the Bf 110, under Hptm Günther Radusch had been renamed as I./NJG 1 late in June, and by the end of July, Nachtjagdgeschwader 1 contained three Gruppen.

On 6 July, 1940, I./ZG 52 was redesignated II./ZG 2, and a special fighter-bomber unit designated Erprobungsgruppe 210 was established under Hptm Walter Rubensdörffer. When the Battle of Britain began in earnest, it soon became clear that the fast but unmanoeuvrable Bf 110 was no match for the single-engined fighters of the RAF. On 11 August, 1940,

Two Bf 110D-3s of III./ZG 26 in flight over the Mediterranean coast, summer 1941.

ten Bf 110s were lost, and two days later five aircraft from a force of 23 from V.(Z)/LG 1 were destroyed and many others seriously damaged. Next day, six Bf 110s from I./ZG 76 at Stavanger were lost, followed in the afternoon by six from an attacking force of 15 from Erpr Gr 210, including the aircraft of the Kommandeur, Hptm Rubensdörffer.

Eventually it was realized that the Bf 110 could no longer operate in daylight without fighter escort, but, because of the shortage of single-engined fighters, the machine continued to operate alone. When attacked, a formation of Bf 110s would form a defensive circle in an attempt to protect each other's rear. This largely nullified the aircraft's one advantage of a high maximum speed and rendered it extremely vulnerable to the highly manoeuvrable fighters of the RAF. The final fighter-bomber attack on the British Isles by Erpr Gr 210 came on 27 September, 1940, when, escorted by I./ZG 26, it attacked Bristol. Again the unit suffered heavy losses, the new Kommandeur, Hptm Martin Lutz, falling to Hurricanes of No. 504 Squadron.

With the close of the daylight offensive over the British Isles, the Luftwaffe turned its attention to night bombing. At the end of 1940, the Germans sent a small force to the Middle East to support Mussolini's struggling armies. Included among the German forces were two Bf 110 equipped units, I./NJG 2 at Gela and III./ZG 26 at Palermo.

The next major action undertaken by German forces was the assault on the Balkans. Among the attacking forces were Stab, I. and II./ZG 26, under Obstlt Johann Schalk, equipped with Bf 110s. During 22 May, 1941, Royal Navy units were reported to be in positions north and west of Crete. ZG 26's Bf 110s, based at Argos, in company with Bf 109s from I.(J)/LG 2 and II. and III./JG 77, escorted the bombers and dive-bombers of VIII Fliegerkorps as they attacked the British ships. The cruisers *Gloucester* and *Fiji* were sunk, and during the next few days several destroyers were lost.

Development of the Bf 110 continued, the next production variant being the Bf 110E fighter-bomber. The Bf 110E-0 and E-1 were similar to the E-1/R2 but were powered by DB 601N engines, and the E-3 was a recon-naissance variant.

The Bf 110F-0, F-1 and F-3 were respectively similar to the E-0, E-1, and E-3, but were powered by 1,300 hp DB 601E engines. The Bf 110F-2 was equipped with two 210 mm WGr 21 underwing rocket tubes, and the F-4 was a night fighter with provision for an additional pair of 30 mm MK 108 cannon under the fuselage. The F-4/U1 was similar but had two 20 mm MG FF guns in a Schräge Musik installation.

At first the Luftwaffe's night fighters attacked their quarry visually and with the aid of searchlights, but this system proved extremely vulnerable to weather conditions. Kammhuber soon introduced the Himmelbett system

The 'Dobbas' collapsible freight container experimentally fitted beneath a Bf 110E.
(*H. Thiele*)

of ground-controlled interception, which comprised a chain of radar stations from Denmark to the Swiss border. Each station comprised two of the giant Würzburg radar sets, one to track the fighter, the other the bomber. Fighter controllers radioed instructions to the pilot of the interceptor and directed him on to the target.

The Bf 110 proved by far the most successful of the early German night fighters, and by June 1941 four of the five Nachtjagdgruppen were equipped with the aircraft. In addition to being more manoeuvrable than the larger Dornier Do 17/215 and early Junkers Ju 88 night fighters, the Bf 110 was also considerably cheaper.

On 22 June, 1941, Germany launched Operation Barbarossa—the invasion of the Soviet Union by three army groups and four air fleets. The Bf 110 was now equipping only one Zerstörergeschwader, ZG 26 Horst Wessel. In addition, the newly formed Schnellkampfgeschwader 210 was operational with the Bf 110E-1.

The fuselage bomb racks fitted to the Bf 110E.

The Bf 110 units in Russia were engaged mainly in fighter-bomber operations, striking at Soviet Air Force units on the ground and combating enemy troop movements. Late in 1941 the two Geschwader were joined by II./ZG 1 which had been tentatively equipped with the Me 210. Early in 1942 a Zerstörerstaffel was added to Jagdgeschwader 5 in northern Norway and Finland and eventually became 13.(Z)/JG 5. Two new Bf 110 equipped night fighter units were also formed late in 1941, bringing NJG 3 up to full strength.

By the end of 1941, it was becoming clear that the Me 210, which had been intended as a replacement for the Bf 110, was totally inadequate. Consequently the Luftwaffe was forced to make do with a new version of the Bf 110 with more powerful engines—the G-series.

The two initial sub-types, the Bf 110G-0 and G-1, were both powered by DB 601E engines but were quickly abandoned in favour of the Bf 110G-2 fighter-bomber. Powered by two 1,475 hp DB 605B engines this variant had four 7·9 mm MG 17 machine-guns and two 20 mm MG 151/20 cannon in the nose and either one 7·9 mm MG 15 or a twin MG 81Z installation in the rear cockpit. Two ETC 500 racks, mounted below the fuselage, could each carry a 500 kg (1,100 lb) bomb, and four ETC 50/VIII racks under the wings could each carry a 50 kg (110 lb) bomb.

The Bf 110G-2/R1 had a 37 mm Flak 18 cannon with 72 rounds beneath the fuselage, the G-2/R2 had GM-1 power boosting and increased armour, and the G-2/R3 had two 30 mm MK 108 cannon in place of the four MG 17 machine-guns. The Bf 110G-2/R4 was similar but had the Flak 18 gun, and the G-2/R5 had the GM-1 installation. The Bf 110G-3 was a reconnaissance aircraft with armament reduced to four MG 17 machine-guns, and the G-3/R3 had two 30 mm MK 108 cannon.

The most widely used night-fighter variant was the Bf 110G-4, which was produced initially in parallel with the F-4. It was powered by two 1,475 hp DB 605B-1 engines, and the basic aircraft had an armament of four MG 17 machine-guns and two MG 151/20 cannon. A large number of sub-variants were produced, designated Bf 110G-4/U1 to U8 and G-4/R1 to R8. The Bf 110G-4/U series of modifications were mainly concerned with GM-1 power boosting equipment and radar installations. The R-series of conversion packs were mainly concerned with additional armament.

Perhaps one of the most interesting of these was the Bf 110G-4/R8, which had provision for two 20 mm MG FF cannon in a Schräge Musik installation. This comprised two MG FF cannon mounted behind the rear cockpit bulkhead and arranged to fire forwards and upwards at an angle of between 70 and 80 degrees. The system was invented by an armourer, Paul Mahle, of II./NJG 5, and was first used successfully on 17 August, 1943, when Gefr Hölker of 5./NJG 5 shot down two bombers. He was followed by Lt Peter Erhardt who shot down four bombers within half an hour using the device, and by the end of 1943 the installation was widely used.

Although the Himmelbett ground control system worked well on moon-lit nights, it was realized that it would not be effective in the dark. Consequently Kammhuber asked the Telefunken company to produce a radar set suitable for installation in a night fighter and, in August 1941, the Lichtenstein BC underwent its operational flight trials. The radar had a maximum range of two and a half miles and was introduced into service in February 1942. By the autumn, the majority of Luftwaffe night fighters were fitted with this or with the simplified Lichtenstein C-1.

In addition to the designations described earlier, the Bf 110G-4 carried four letter-suffixes indicating the type of radar carried. The Bf 110G-4a carried FuG 212 Lichtenstein C-1 radar with a four-pronged radar array; the G-4b carried both FuG 212 and FuG 220b Lichtenstein SN-2 radar; and the G-4c was similar but without the FuG 212. The Bf 110G-4d, of which 45 were completed in March 1945, was fitted with FuG 277 Flensburg radar which homed on to the British Monica tail-mounted warning set. Total production of the Bf 110 was 5,873 aircraft.

The Bf 110F-4 and G-4 were produced for some time in parallel; for example, in December 1943, thirty F-4s and thirty-seven G-4s were completed. At the end of 1942 the German night fighter force comprised 389 aircraft of which the majority, at least 300, were Bf 110s. During that year the RAF lost 1,291 bombers in night attacks on targets in German-occupied territory, an estimated two-thirds to fighters. Considered as a failure during the Battle of Britain, the Bf 110 was proving a very uncomfortable thorn in the side of Bomber Command.

A Bf 110G-4a/R1 of 3./NJG 6 at Mainz-Finthen, April 1944. (*K. Ries*)

Shortly before midnight on 24 July, 1943, reports reached 2 Flieger-division's operations room at Stade that a formation of RAF bombers was approaching north of the Elbe estuary. Bf 110 night fighters from NJG 3 were immediately sent to intercept, when suddenly the operators of the huge Würzburg radar sets saw, instead of several distinct traces, a whole mass of echoes. What had happened? The answer was simple and effective. One thousand strips of aluminium foil measuring 30 cm by 1·5 cm comprised one bundle of 'window'; it cost about the same as a box of matches. Each of the 791 attacking aircraft dropped one such bundle per minute causing a whole cloud of echoes to cover the screens of both the Würzburg and Lichtenstein radars and render them virtually useless.

The paralyzing of the Himmelbett system led to the evolution of new tactics under the code names Wilde Sau and Zahme Sau (respectively Wild Boar and Tame Boar). The former tactics were used mainly with single-engined fighters and involved making free-lance interceptions over the target itself. Zahme Sau tactics, propounded by Oberst von Lossberg, involved the use of Bf 110 night fighters getting into the bomber stream as it approached or left the target and attacking visually.

The Luftwaffe first used Zahme Sau tactics on 17 August, 1943, when 597 bombers attacked the V-weapons research establishment at Peenemünde. It was a bright moonlit night, ideal for the new German tactics, but because of equally brilliant RAF tactics, few bombers were lost.

From July 1943 daylight attacks on Germany by USAAF heavy bombers began to increase rapidly in intensity. By the end of August, no less than 12 fighter Gruppen had been transferred to the defence of the Reich, including I. and II./ZG 1 and III./ZG 26 from southern Italy. Soon afterwards, I./ZG 1 became I./ZG 26, and a second Gruppe was established to bring the Horst Wessel Geschwader back to full strength. In October 1943 a new ZG 76 was established, and the resurrected destroyer force then comprised II./ZG 1 under Hptm Egon Albrecht; I., II. and III./ZG 26 under Maj Karl Boehm-Tettelbach; and I. and II./ZG 76 under Oberst Theodor Rossiwall. A IIIrd Gruppe was added to ZG 76 in November, the Kommandeur being Hptm Johannes Kiel, ex-Staffelkapitän of 7./ZG 26.

As yet the American bombers were operating without long-range fighter escort, and the Bf 110s of the various Zerstörergruppen were able to wreak havoc with their heavy calibre cannon and WGr 21 rockets. The Gruppen of ZG 26 were distributed between Wunstorf, Quakenbrück and Hildesheim, ZG 76 operating from bases in southern Germany. Both units only attacked when they were outside the penetration range of the escorting American fighters.

It was not until the beginning of January 1944 that the USAAF again attacked in strength. They were attacked by Bf 110s from the Zerstörergruppen, who fired their 210 mm rockets into the box-like formations with devastating results. As the American formation broke up, they were assailed by Bf 109s and Focke-Wulf Fw 190s from the Jagdgeschwader, and again the USAAF lost 60 bombers.

On 16 March, 1944, a bomber formation from the USAAF attacked Augsburg. It was intercepted by forty-three Bf 110s from ZG 76. At first the Luftwaffe fighters struck successfully, but then the American escort pounced. Unable to survive in combat with the Spitfires and Hurricanes of 1940 vintage, the Bf 110s were cut to pieces by the Mustangs and Thunderbolts. No less than 26 German fighters were lost, approximately 60 per cent of the attackers. Shortly afterwards, III./ZG 76 was disbanded, and re-equipment of the other Zerstörergruppen with the Me 410 was made a priority.

By June 1944 eight Zerstörergruppen were operational, but only one of these, II./ZG 1 based at Wels in Austria, was equipped with the Bf 110.

A Bf 110G-4b/R3 fitted with Lichtenstein SN-2 radar and two MK 108 cannon in an underfuselage pack.

One of the last operations undertaken by this unit took place on 2 July, 1944. In company with Me 410s from I./ZG 76 and Bf 109Gs from II./JG 27, it intercepted a large American bomber force over Budapest. The three Gruppen claimed the destruction of 45 aircraft, of which 34 were four-engined bombers. Shortly afterwards, II./ZG 1, still under the command of Hptm Egon Albrecht, became III./JG 76 and was re-equipped with the Bf 109G.

This was by no means the end of the Bf 110 in Luftwaffe service however. During the light summer nights of 1943, the visual search tactics employed by the Nachtjagdgruppen had proved very successful, but they were no more than a stop-gap pending the introduction of new equipment able to operate in spite of 'window' jamming. At the end of 1943 three devices entered service in the German night fighter force to assist the crews to find their targets: the FuG 220 Lichtenstein SN-2, FuG 350 Naxos, and FuG 277 Flensburg.

The FuG 220 Lichtenstein SN-2 was a completely new radar set which worked on a frequency not jammed by 'window' then in use by the RAF, and was often used together with FuG 212 Lichtenstein C-1, because of the poor resolution of the SN-2 at close range; FuG 350 Naxos homed on to the emissions from the British H2S radar and simultaneously provided warning of the approach of British centimetric radar equipped night fighters; FuG 277 Flensburg homed on the emissions of the British Monica tail warning set.

With the introduction of these new electronic devices, the German night fighter force was once again able to work effectively on the darkest nights. This allowed new tactics to be formulated, aimed at setting up long-running battles.

So it was that the German defenders were able to inflict serious losses on the raiders during the first months of 1944. On 21 January, 1944, fifty-five bombers were lost out of a force of 648 attacking Magdeburg, and a week later 43 were shot down out of 683 attacking Berlin. On 19 February no less than 78 bombers were lost from a force of 823 attacking Leipzig. The greatest night battle, in fact the greatest air battle of all time, occurred on 30 March, 1944. The force of 795 bombers attacking Nuremberg was engaged by 20 Staffeln of twin-engined night fighters, about 200 aircraft. In the slaughter that followed, 94 bombers were shot down.

At this time it is of interest to examine the composition of the German night fighter force. There were no less than 25 night fighter Gruppen operational. Of these, about 60 per cent were equipped with the Bf 110, a total of nearly 320 aircraft.

From the liberation of France until the end of the war, the story of the German night fighter force was one of unremitting decline. First the capture of France punched a great hole in the German air reporting network, seriously reducing the warning time available to the defenders. Then the RAF started to jam the FuG 220 Lichtenstein SN-2 radar and removed the Monica tail warning devices from their aircraft, which rendered the Flensburg radar useless.

During the autumn of 1944 German fuel reserves began to drain away, as one by one the refineries and storage depots were bombed or captured. On 31 December, 1944, the German night fighter force had 913 aircraft on strength, but only 150 of these were Bf 110s. The new Junkers Ju 88G and Heinkel He 219 night fighters were rapidly replacing the Messerschmitt design, but many of these were grounded through lack of fuel.

From the beginning of 1945 to the end of the war, many night fighter units were called upon to operate in the ground attack rôle. Night ground attack sorties were a particularly hazardous business and losses were consequently high. Another hazard were the de Havilland Mosquito night fighters of No. 100 Group Fighter Command, which operated against the German night fighters. The night fighter organization, perhaps the most efficient in the Luftwaffe, had finally collapsed.

*Wartime operational units:* 3.(H)/10, 2.(F)/11, 3.(H)/12, 3.(H)/13, 2.(F)/14, 3.(F)/22, 2.(H)/31, 2. and 4.(H)/33, 3. and 4.(F)/121, 1., 2., 3., 4. and 5.(F)/122, 1., 2. and 3.(F)/123, 1.(F)/124, 1./Aufkl.Gr.Ob.d.L., 7.(F)/LG 2, NAGr 1, 5, 6, 8, 13, 14, 15 and 16, the meteorological reconnaissance squadrons, ZG 1, ZG 2, ZG 26, I./ZG 52, ZG 76, I.(Z) and V.(Z)/LG 1, NJG 1, I., II. and III./NJG 2, NJG 3, NJG 4, NJG 5, NJG 6, NJGr 10, NJG 200, Nachtjagdstaffel Norwegen, Erprobungsgruppe 210, SKG 210, (also used in small numbers by the staff flights of the various Stukagruppen).

Bf 110C-4: Span 16·2 m (53 ft 4¾ in); length 12·1 m (39 ft 8½ in); height 3·5 m (11 ft 6 in); wing area 38·5 sq m (413 sq ft).
Empty weight 5,200 kg (11,466 lb); normal loaded weight 6,750 kg (14,884 lb).
Maximum speed at 7,000 m (22,967 ft) 560 km/h (349 mph), at sea level 470 km/h (294 mph); cruising speed at 7,000 m (22,967 ft) 480 km/h (301 mph), at sea level 420 km/h (263 mph); service ceiling 10,000 m (32,811 ft); normal range 775 km (481 miles); maximum range 910 km (565 miles).

Bf 110G-4b/R3: Span 16·2 m (53 ft 4¾ in); length 12·65 m (41 ft 6¾ in); height 4 m (13 ft 1½ in); wing area 38.5 sq m (413 sq ft).
Empty weight 5,100 kg (11,245 lb); normal loaded weight 9,400 kg (20,727 lb); maximum loaded weight 9,900 kg (32,830 lb).
Maximum speed at 7,000 m (22,967 ft) 550 km/h (342 mph), at sea level 500 km/h (311 mph); service ceiling 8,000 m (26,248 ft); maximum range, with external fuel tanks, 2,100 km (1,305 miles).

Only one Bf 110 is known to survive, this is a Bf 110G held by the Royal Air Force.

# Messerschmitt Bf 161 and Bf 162

Early in 1935 the RLM issued the requirement for a Schnell bomber, or fast bomber, which led to the adoption of Junkers' famed Ju 88. This aircraft had two competitors, the Henschel Hs 127 and the Messerschmitt Bf 162, both of which were unsuccessful.

The Bf 162, which was unofficially named Jaguar, was designed to use two 960 hp Daimler-Benz DB 600A twelve-cylinder liquid-cooled engines and was closely based on the Bf 110 fighter in order to assist development and the hoped-for production. The Bf 162 V1, D-AIXA, first flew in the spring of 1937, several months after the first flight of the Bf 110 V3 which it closely resembled. By comparison with the latter, the Bf 162 V1 had widened fuselage centre and nose sections, a very much shorter cockpit canopy, a shorter and glazed nose and a small fuselage bomb bay. Accommodation was for three crew members, and the widening of the cockpit permitted one seat to be placed almost alongside the pilot's seat. A bomb load of 1,000 kg (2,205 lb) could be carried, but about half of this load had to be on inboard underwing racks supplementing the small internal bomb bay.

The first prototype was joined by the Bf 162 V2, D-AOBE, which first

The Messerschmitt Bf 162 V2, which first flew in September 1937, as D-AOBE and was designed as a fast bomber.

flew in September 1937, and by the Bf 162 V3, D-AOVI, which flew on 20 August, 1938. The V2 prototype is believed to have had two MG 15 machine-guns and to have flown at 480 km/h (298 mph), but remarkably little data are known for the type in general. The only three prototypes built were finally employed for general research and development work, and the RLM '8' number of 162 was later re-issued for Heinkel's Salamander turbojet fighter.

The Messerschmitt Bf 161 V2 with nose glazed for reconnaissance work. No production was undertaken of either the Bf 161 or the Bf 162 bomber.

A parallel development with the Bf 162 was the Bf 161, which was intended as a fast reconnaissance aircraft but which could be used for bombing if necessary. The Bf 161 was powered similarly to the Bf 162 (but with two DB 601 engines), the principal difference between the types being that in the Bf 161 a crew of two was carried, and the nose was altered for the reconnaissance rôle, being more extensively glazed, slightly longer, of a blunted shape, and housed the photographic equipment. Because of its lower priority, the Bf 161 V1, D-AABA, first flew about a year after the Bf 162 V1, while the Bf 161 V2 first flew in the autumn of 1938. A distinguishing feature of the V2 was that the upper half of its glazed nose was extended further forward than the lower half. Only three prototypes of the Bf 161 were built, and, as with the Bf 162, no production was undertaken.

Bf 162 V2: Span 17·16 m (56 ft 3⅝ in); length 12·75 m (41 ft 10 in); height 3·58 m (11 ft 8 in).
Normal loaded weight: 5,800 kg (12,789 lb).
Maximum speed 480 km/h (298 mph); initial rate of climb 540 m/min (1,771 ft/min); normal range 780 km (485 miles).

The Me 163 V21. About thirty-one pre-production Me 163B-0s were issued with V-numbers and used in a testing and operational evaluation programme during 1942. (*Messerschmitt AG*)

# Messerschmitt Me 163 Komet

The first tailless aircraft to become operational, the rocket-powered Messerschmitt Me 163B Komet interceptor, was placed high on the list of Germany's Wunderwaffen (wonder weapons), and few would dispute that it was one of the most dramatic and revolutionary aircraft of the Second World War. The Me 163 stemmed from the work of Dr Alexander Lippisch, whose first tailless glider, known as the Storch (Stork), was built in 1926 and flown the following year. This glider was progressively developed and eventually fitted with an 8 hp engine driving a pusher propeller to become the Storch V, which made its first powered flight on 17 September, 1929. Lippisch, always pursuing the tailless theme, was particularly keen on a delta-wing planform, and he therefore turned his attention to the design of a glider of this layout, having obtained some private financial support. This glider, known as the Delta I, began flying in the summer of 1930 and was later fitted with a 30 hp engine to fly, early in 1931, at speeds up to 145 km/h (90 mph). It is said that the Horten brothers were inspired to begin their work on tailless aircraft as a result of seeing a flight of the Delta I, but official reaction was quite the reverse, and, because the aircraft had no tail, no airworthiness certificate was issued!

By 1932, however, Lippisch had received an order for his Delta III design which had to be built by Focke-Wulf, and he was also collaborating with Gerhard Fieseler at the latter's works to build the Delta III Wespe (Wasp). This radical aircraft had two engines driving a pusher and a tractor airscrew, two seats in tandem and a small foreplane, but its flight characteristics were very poor and eventually cost a pilot his life.

508

By 1933, Lippisch and his design team were established at the DFS at Darmstadt where modification and development of the Delta III and IV aircraft was continued, but, after both aircraft had crashed within the same fortnight, an RLM order banned further development of tailless aircraft. This ban was later removed due to the efforts of Dr W. Georgii (then director of the DFS) and work continued with the modification of the Delta IVa design into the Delta IVb, which received the RLM designation DFS 39. The reconstructed aircraft had a modified wing planform, twin vertical surfaces instead of wingtip anhedral, and a 75 hp engine driving a tractor airscrew. In this form, the aircraft received an airworthiness certificate as a two-seat sports aeroplane, and, in 1937, an RLM order came for a second DFS 39, which, it was eventually revealed, was to be powered by a top-secret rocket motor.

The DFS 40 was built for research into tailless flight. From this and other work, Lippisch concluded that the wingtip rudders should be replaced by a central, vertical surface when considering high-speed flight.

This was the beginning of Project X or DFS 39 for which the DFS was to build the wing and Ernst Heinkel AG was to build the rest of the airframe because they had full manufacturing facilities and were already working on their own rocket aircraft, the He 176. Although the RLM had selected the DFS 39 for rocket power and stipulated a modest speed of up to 350 km/h (217 mph), Lippisch began work on the DFS 40 and DFS 194, which were both originally intended to have conventional propulsion for research work. With the aid of model flights and wind-tunnel tests at the AVA, Göttingen, Lippisch concluded that the DFS 39's wingtip rudders would be a source of flutter on the sweptback wing and that future designs required a central fin and rudder for improved control. A fin and rudder was not omitted altogether (as in the case of the Horten designs) because of the need to balance the effects of the fuselage nose, which extended beyond the wing contour.

The division of construction work, together with the strict security curtain, seriously hampered work on Project X, and Lippisch was able to have the programme transferred from Heinkel and the DFS into one unit at Messerschmitt AG, Augsburg, where he and his team of 20 formed Section L on 2 January, 1939. Attention then turned to modifying the more promising DFS 194 design to use rocket instead of piston-engine power, and the airframe, which was transferred from the DFS, was completed at Augsburg soon after war started and then sent to Peenemünde-West early in 1940. There, a Walter RI-203 rocket motor was fitted, being of similar design to that fitted in the He 176 but calibrated to give a reduced thrust of 300 kg (660 lb) for a longer running time; as before, the motor worked on the cold principle using T-Stoff and Z-Stoff propellants. Thus equipped, the DFS 194 was test-flown by Lippisch's test pilot, Heini Dittmar, and, despite development problems with the rocket motor, the aircraft was flown at speeds of up to 500 km/h (342 mph).

During this time, work was proceeding at Augsburg on the next stage of development in the shape of the aircraft designated Me 163. This work had been carried on with low priority, probably because of official disenchantment with the He 176, which had flown in June 1939, but, with the successful flights of the DFS 194, an official spur was given, and the first prototype, the Me 163 V1, was completed during the winter of 1940–41. The design of this aircraft, and that of the Me 163 V2 which followed, was generally similar to the DFS 194 in appearance but embodied important new features, the most obvious being an enlarged fin and rudder, an increase in wing trailing-edge sweepback which reduced wing area, and a more rounded fuselage and canopy profile. The wing, which retained the feature of compound sweepback on the leading edge, had aerofoil sections designed by Lippisch to give stability previously accomplished by the drag-producing method of wingtip washout. To avoid elevon control reversal, the DFS 194 had automatic leading-edge slots near the wingtips to ensure that the centre section stalled first, but, for the new aircraft, Lippisch replaced these with special fixed slots. These fixed slots, which were to be a feature of all subsequent Me 163 designs, had low drag under normal conditions, achieved by ensuring equal pressure at each end of the slot and hence no flow through it.

In the spring of 1941, the Me 163 V1 made its first unpowered flights from Lechfeld, followed by further gliding from Augsburg. On these flights, the aircraft, piloted by Heini Dittmar, was towed by a Bf 110 to heights between 4,000 and 8,000 m (13,120 and 26,240 ft) and achieved excellent gliding angles of 1 : 20 in normal flight and was dived at speeds up to 850 km/h (528 mph). The flying qualities were very good, with the exception of control surface flutter which was gradually cured by careful balance adjustments. The whole programme received increased support at this time due to the favourable impression it had made on Ernst Udet.

The Me 163 V1, having been fully tested, was sent to Peenemünde-West in the summer of 1941, where a Walter RII-203 rocket motor was fitted for powered flights. The new motor, which still used T-Stoff and Z-Stoff propellants on the cold principle, had a new feature of throttle control which allowed thrust variation in steps between 150 and 750 kg (330 and 1,650 lb). All was not well with this motor, however, which proved unreliable, a major problem being that the jets became clogged with

Inside this small rocket exhaust nozzle, some $1\frac{1}{2}$ tons of thrust could be released against the small airframe of the Me 163.

particles of calcium permanganate catalyst, while, if too little catalyst was supplied, the thrust fluctuated violently and induced risk of explosion. Many serious accidents, and deaths, did in fact occur during development. On one occasion, an entire building at Peenemünde was demolished, and at the rocket station at Trauen-Fassberg a similar accident occurred. Despite these tribulations, powered flights with the Me 163 V1 began, and Dittmar soon broke the world speed record and built up to speeds of 915 km/h (568 mph), the limit being set by the available 1,200 kg (2,640 lb) of propellants carried, which were consumed in about $2\frac{1}{4}$ minutes at full thrust. To conserve fuel for a purely level flight, therefore, the Me 163 V1 was towed on 2 October, 1941, by a Bf 110 to a height of 3,600 m (11,810 ft) and, after casting off, was accelerated to a speed of 1,004·5 km/h (623·8 mph). At this speed, Dittmar had to cut out the rocket motor

An Me 163B-0 showing the skid extended with the jettisonable take-off trolley fitted.

511

because the compression shock occurring at the wingtips induced negative lift, vibration, and a sudden dive. Although a safe landing was made once the controls reacted again, this remarkable flight was shrouded in secrecy, but the RLM was impressed and followed it up on 1 December, 1941, by ordering prototypes of an operational aircraft, the Me 163B.

The first of the new prototypes, the Me 163 V3, was ready in April 1942, but the new Walter motor designed for it was still under development at Kiel. The most obvious differences of the new design from the Me 163 V1 and V2 were the constant sweepback of the wing leading edge, an entirely redesigned and enlarged fuselage with pointed nose and fully blown cockpit canopy, and an almost full-length ventral fairing which housed the extendable landing skid and tailwheel. Space for propellants was increased, and provision was made for operational armament, radio, and armour. The previous system of jettisonable take-off wheels was retained. While awaiting the rocket motor, the Me 163 V3 was glide-tested and exhibited excellent handling qualities, but it was at this time that Lippisch withdrew from the programme. From Augsburg he went to direct the Luftfahrtforschungsanstalt Wien, this move being prompted allegedly because of mounting friction between himself and Willy Messerschmitt.

Nevertheless, the ground-work had been laid, and work continued with the construction of 70 pre-production Me 163B-0s at Messerschmitt's Regensburg factory, while the Wolf Hirth-Werke constructed ten Me 163A gliders, with similar airframes to the Me 163 V1, intended for training purposes.

By the early autumn of 1942, the first examples of the new Walter 109-509A-0-1 rocket motor were considered sufficiently developed for flying. This was the first Walter unit to use the hot system and regenerative cooling of the combustion chamber. The propellants were T-Stoff (80 per

One of the first Messerschmitt Me 163B-0s to have its Walter rocket motor fitted. A structural tube and feed pipes led back to the combustion chamber at the end of the fuselage. (*Messerschmitt AG*)

512

This Me 163 V13, one of the original test programme Me 163B-0s, was found damaged at the airfield in Poltzen (near Leipzig) which was captured by combat Command A, 9th Armoured Division, 1st US Army. (*US Army*)

cent hydrogen peroxide and 20 per cent water) as before, but with C-Stoff (hydrazine hydrate, methyl alcohol, and water) to give a higher specific impulse. The thrust could be controlled in steps from 300 to 1,500 kg (660 to 3,300 lb), but the unit was very susceptible to cavitation in the pumps and would start very hard. With this motor, the powered test programme began with the Me 163 V3 in August at Peenemünde-West, but, early in the programme, Heini Dittmar suffered a severe spinal injury in a rough landing, this being the first of many similar injuries which Me 163B pilots were to receive. The test programme continued, the principal pilots being Wolfgang Späte and Rudolf Opitz. About 31 of the Me 163B-0s were used in the programme and issued with V-numbers, while an improved motor, the Walter 109-509A-2, was introduced which almost eliminated hard starts and had air ejectors to prevent pump cavitation. T-Stoff and C-Stoff were again the propellants, but maximum thrust was increased to 1,700 kg (3,740 lb). Before the availability of this improved Walter motor, BMW were requested to design an alternative motor for the Me 163B; the result was the BMW 109-510 rocket motor which used M-Stoff (methanol) and SV-Stoff (nitric acid) propellants to give infinitely variable thrust from 300 kg (660 lb) to 1,500 kg (3,300 lb). Protracted development problems arose with the pumping system, however, and this motor was not fully developed by the end of the war.

The programme entered a new phase early in 1943, when the remaining Me 163B-0s were each fitted with a pair of MG 151 20 mm cannon and redesignated Me 163Ba-1 for use by a new unit, the Erprobungs-kommando 16 (EK 16) at Peenemünde-West. This unit was led by Späte who had under him Hptm Toni Thaler, Oblt Pöhs, Lt Herbert Langer, and Oblt Kiel, all experienced pilots. Their principal work was to investigate the operational use of, and train pilots for, the Me 163B Komet, and generally advise and liaise between Augsburg, the RLM, and the Luftwaffe. Out of this work sprang what might be called the Späte plan for a string of Komet bases connecting the north and south of Germany and over which Allied bombers had to pass, the Komet bases being about 150 km (93 miles) apart so that the short ranges of the Komets slightly overlapped.

The training of Komet pilots had not begun by July 1943, but, in that month, EK 16 was moved to Bad Zwischenahn because of the attention Peenemünde was beginning to receive from Allied bombers. By the autumn of 1943, however, the first 30 selected Luftwaffe pilots had begun their elaborate training. This training began with flying straightforward gliders but continued on various Habicht gliders, having progressively shorter wing spans, with consequent higher landing speeds. The next stage started with flying an unpowered Me 163A, followed by a powered Me 163A (fitted with a Walter RII-203 rocket unit), and then an unpowered Me 163B until, finally, a flight in a powered Me 163Ba-1 was made. This cautious programme was necessary because of the quite different characteristics of the Komet, its one-chance-only landing at high speed (220 km/h or 137 mph), and the fact that a pilot under training always had to fly solo. Very much later, when the need for pilots became pressing, a two-seat trainer, the Me 163S, was developed and at least one was built, but it is unlikely to have been used. The Me 163S was an Me 163B airframe without fuel tanks, rocket motor or armament, but with a second raised cockpit and canopy for the instructor behind the standard cockpit and with the addition of water ballast tanks.

When the training programme was well advanced, Späte, the key man in the whole programme, was inexplicably transferred to the Russian front to

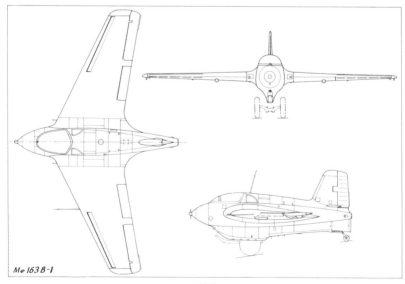

Me 163B-1

514

become Gruppenkommandeur of IV./JG 54, and his place in EK 16 was taken by Thaler. Plans also moved ahead for the establishment of an operational Komet-Geschwader, JG 400, the first element of which began forming at Wittmundhaven under Oblt Olejnik in May 1944, but their first work was confined to that of the weapons test programme taken over from EK 16. This was the beginning of 1./JG 400, and it was followed by 2./JG 400 and 3./JG 400 forming at Venlo, these three Staffeln making up I./JG 400 which, along with EK 16, found itself based at Brandis (near Leipzig) by June 1944. The task of the Komets at Brandis, which had nothing like the requisite facilities, was to defend the Leuna oil refineries 90 km (55 miles) to the southwest, a distance which used up much of the Komet's range. This concentration of Komets at one base reversed the progress made on the Späte plan.

An operational Komet of 1./JG 400. The apparent nonchalance of the pilot belies the great nervous strain that was involved in operating and flying the interceptor. At least one pilot and fuelled Komet was always on standby for instant action should enemy bombers fly within range.

The aircraft then being issued were production Me 163B-1as which were not built at Regensburg but in dispersed factories under the overall supervision of the Klemm company. This plan, where manufactured sections were brought together for final assembly, did not work well initially. Much trouble arose, such as bad fairings between wing and fuselage, and supervision and development work was eventually handed to the more experienced Junkers firm. The Me 163B-1a was generally similar in appearance to the Me 163Ba-1 but was now fully equipped, as standard, with two MK 108 30 mm cannon in the wing roots, containers for 120 rounds of ammunition, a Revi 16B gunsight, a 90 mm armoured glass flat screen beneath the Plexiglas canopy, light and medium armour steel plate protection for the pilot's head, shoulders, and back, and an armoured steel nose cone. The cockpit afforded excellent visibility but was unpressurized and, even during the Komet's short flight, a pilot often suffered from

515

Sequence from a ciné film showing an Me 163 Komet taking-off. The take-off trolley can be seen falling away in the last three views. Once free of this trolley, a Komet accelerated rapidly and was usually put into a very steep climb.

extreme cold due to high operating altitudes. On each side of the pilot's seat was a small self-sealing T-Stoff tank of 60 litres (13·2 Imp gal) capacity, aft of the cockpit was the main T-Stoff tank of 1,040 litres (229 Imp gal) capacity, and behind this the Walter 109-509A-2 rocket motor. The fuselage, which was of semi-monocoque stressed-skin metal construction with central load-transmission frame, was of basically circular cross section, but this was actually distorted by the large fairings between wings and fuselage, the fairing aft of the canopy and the ventral skid fairing. Mounted on the nose of the aircraft was a small propeller which drove a generator for the electrical supply. The wings, which contained the C-Stoff tanks totalling 500 litres (110 Imp gal), were of wooden construction with main and auxiliary spars and plywood skinning and bolted to short stubs at the fuselage. At the trailing edge were fabric-covered elevons and, inboard, large trimming surfaces. The flaps were positioned forward of the trimming surfaces, at about mid-chord. The wing root had a reverse camber section of 14 per cent thickness ratio and a 3 deg angle of incidence, while the wingtip had a symmetrical section of 9 per cent thickness ratio and a structural washout of 5 deg. The special Lippisch-designed leading-edge fixed slots took up about half the outboard span of each wing. One Komet had been tested with up-turned elevons instead of the wingtip washout, but flight characteristics were almost identical to those with the standard wing.

On 16 August, 1944, Komets from Brandis made their first contact with Allied bombers, Boeing B-17 Fortresses, though without success. In fact, although II. and III./JG 400 were also formed by the end of the year and some 300 Komets were manufactured in all, only nine kills, including two probables, are recorded for JG 400 in its entire period of action.

The reasons for this lack of success are many. To begin with, fuel shortages, bad facilities, Allied bombing and delayed training hampered operations before they started. The Walter motors were still temperamental, though most troubles came from leaking propellant pipe joints which at the least filled the cockpit with choking steam but could, and did, cause explosions. During take-off the directional control was very poor on the narrow-tread wheels, and there was the possibility of the jettisoned main wheels rebounding from the runway to hit the aircraft, while a rocket malfunction during the climb was not uncommon. If the bomber stream was then found, a pilot would streak above it and then make a high-speed gliding dive on to a selected target but, as so often happened, his troublesome MK 108s could jam (the average stoppage rate was about one in every 100 rounds) or the Komet would exceed its critical Mach number and go into a dive. Once safely away from the combat area, a pilot could enjoy the pleasant characteristics of his aircraft during the glide back to base, but not for long because great dangers still awaited him. Allied piston-engined fighters lurking near the airfield found the gliding Komet, which could do nothing but land straight away, an easy target. Furthermore, a Komet's landing could fracture the pilot's spine in the event of a jammed landing skid, or it could easily overturn if it ran on to soft ground, whereupon there was either an explosion or the pilot was burnt by fuel ullage spill. The only safety feature the aircraft had was an emergency fuel dumping system for use in cases of rocket malfunction, but it is interesting to note that the percentage of landing accidents, though high, was not as high as that for the Messerschmitt Bf 109.

The armament problem was seen as one of the most frustrating because, even when the MK 108s did not jam, scoring hits at the high speeds was virtually impossible even for very experienced pilots, and some pilots even reduced speed to score hits with the result that they themselves became vulnerable targets. Although there was the possibility of using R4M unguided rockets (which had been tested with a powered Me 163A), these still presented aiming problems. A very promising armament was therefore evolved by a Dr Langweiler and known as the SG 500 Jagdfaust (Fighter fist). This equipment consisted of five vertically-firing tubes in each wing root, each tube containing a single 50 mm shell, and the equipment fired in salvo fashion when actuated by the shadow of a bomber passing over a light cell. The armament was tested by Lt Hachtel of EK 16 using first a Focke-Wulf Fw 190 and then an Me 163B-1a, and it was shown to be feasible for a Komet to score a hit simply by flying at full speed beneath a bomber. Only 12 Komets were actually fitted with SG 500 armament and these were not issued for operations. However, Lt Fritz Kelb of EK 16 used one such aircraft and shot down a B-17G Fortress.

Efforts were also made to improve the rocket motor, and the Walter concern conducted experiments with the first two-chamber motor, the

A pilot prepares to enter an Me 163B Komet for a test flight. (*H. Redemann*)

109-509B. In this design, overall efficiency was increased by having a large chamber for take-off and climb and a small chamber for cruising and level flight. The outcome of this work was the 109-509C motor which had a main chamber giving a step-controlled thrust up to 2,000 kg (4,400 lb) and an auxiliary chamber giving a fixed thrust of 200 kg (440 lb), the greatly improved efficiency and reduced consumption of the auxiliary chamber offering increased flight time. The new motor was ready for production in February 1945, but only a few pre-production examples became available, and two were fitted to the V6 and V18 examples of the Me 163B-0. On 6 July, 1944, the Me 163 V18 attained the remarkable speed of 1,130 km/h (702 mph) at low altitude, but, although a safe landing was made, the rudder was torn away when flutter developed. BMW also worked on a new rocket motor, the 109-708, for the Komet; as with their earlier 109-510 design, the new motor used SV-Stoff (nitric acid) oxidant, but the fuel was changed to R-Stoff or Tonka self-igniting fuel. The 109-708 was designed to give a controlled thrust up to 2,500 kg (5,500 lb), but, again, the BMW work was started too late to see application. There was also some consideration given to conserving thrust during take-off by using a solid-fuelled ATO rocket. Using 500 kg (1,100 lb) and 1,000 kg (2,200 lb) thrust ATO rockets, various tests were made with an Me 163B-0

518

at Bremen, Augsburg and then Brandis, but the scheme was not applied operationally.

The next development was to design the Me 163C to use the Walter 109-509C motor. In the Me 163C, the great advantage of a pressurized cockpit was introduced and there was a redesigned, lengthened fuselage with a bubble canopy and increased fuel tankage. Only a few pre-production Me 163C-0s were manufactured although probably not flown, but it was anticipated that the eight minute endurance of the Me 163B-1a would have been improved by 50 per cent. The final development of the Komet, the Me 163D, is dealt with separately on page 547 under the heading Me 263.

By the end of 1944, Späte had returned to become Geschwader-Kommodore of the whole of JG 400, but, although it was finally agreed to use his plan for a string of Komet bases by the spring of 1945, by then the Komet units were being forced from one base to another by encroaching Allied forces. Disbandment of the units began in February 1945, and only II./JG 400, led by Opitz, remained at the end and found itself at Husum.

The Komet and the sensations of a pilot flying it were characterized by the unit emblems painted on its nose, such emblems depicting a rocket-propelled flea in the case of 1./JG 400 and the legendary Baron Münchhausen riding on a cannon ball in the case of 2./JG 400. Nevertheless, despite the aircraft's high performance and the excellent calibre of its pilots, the Me 163 failed, for the various reasons mentioned, to benefit Germany in any way, although theoretically it was well suited to the Luftwaffe's defence problems. Faced with similar defence problems to that

Moving a Komet into its take-off position. (*H. Redemann*)

of Germany, Japan acquired manufacturing rights and built adaptations of the 109-509A rocket motor to power the Mitsubishi J8M1 Shusui (Swinging Sword) interceptor based broadly on the Me 163B. By the end of the war, five of these aircraft had been built, but only one flew although over 50 of the externally-similar MXY 8 Akigusa (Autumn Grass) training gliders had been built, some of which were used.

519

DFS 194: Span 9·3 m (30 ft 6⅛ in); length 5·38 m (17 ft 7¾ in); wing area 17·55 sq m (188·84 sq ft).
Loaded weight 2,100 kg (4,620 lb).
Maximum speed at sea level 550 km/h (342 mph).

Me 163A (glider version): Span 9·3 m (30 ft 6⅛ in); length 5·42 m (17 ft 9⅜ in); loaded weight 2,300 kg (5,060 lb).

Me 163B-1a: Span 9·32 m (30 ft 7 in); length 5·69 m (18 ft 8 in); wing area 19·62 sq m (211 sq ft).
Empty weight 1,905 kg (4,191 lb); weight of propellants 2,005 kg (4,411 lb); weight allowance for ammunition and pilot 200 kg (440 lb); loaded weight 4,110 kg (9,042 lb).
Maximum speed at sea level 830 km/h (515 mph); maximum speed at 3,000 m (9,840 ft) 960 km/h (596 mph); limiting Mach number 0·82; landing speed 220 km/h (137 mph); initial rate of climb 3,600 m/min (11,810 ft/min); rate of climb at 10,000 m (32,800 ft) 10,200 m/min (33,470 ft/min); time to service ceiling of 12,100 m (39,690 ft) 3·35 min; maximum powered endurance 8 min; approximate operational range 80 km (50 miles).

Me 163C: Span 9·8 m (32 ft 2 in); length 7·035 m (23 ft 1 in); wing area 20·7 sq m (223 sq ft).
Empty weight 2,500 kg (5,500 lb); weight of propellants 2,425 kg (5,335 lb); weight allowance for ammunition and pilot 200 kg (440 lb); loaded weight 5,125 kg (11,275 lb).
Maximum speed at 4,000 m (13,120 ft) 950 km/h (590 mph); initial rate of climb 4,200 m/min (13,775 ft/min); service ceiling 16,000 m (52,480 ft); maximum powered endurance (making use of motor cruise chamber) 12 min; approximate operational range 125 km (78 miles).

About a dozen Me 163s still exist in museums and collections in Australia, Britain, Canada, and Germany.

# Messerschmitt Me 209 V1 to V4

In the last few years before the Second World War, Hitler became very anxious to demonstrate to the world the supposed superiority of his Third Reich. This suited the German aircraft industry very well since, by the successful attainment of international aviation records, its development programmes could be advanced together with a boost in prestige. For their part, Messerschmitt at Augsburg began work on the P.1059 project in 1937 for the purpose of gaining a new absolute world speed record, and, in the same year, three prototypes were begun under the official designation Me 209.

The Me 209 was a small low-wing monoplane designed around a specially-produced Daimler-Benz DB 601ARJ twelve-cylinder inverted-vee liquid-cooled engine which gave 1,800 hp and could be boosted to 2,300 hp for short bursts. The airframe was kept as small as possible

The Messerschmitt Me 209 V1 which gained the absolute speed record on 26 April, 1939. Its speed was not officially surpassed by a piston-engined aircraft until 16 August, 1969.

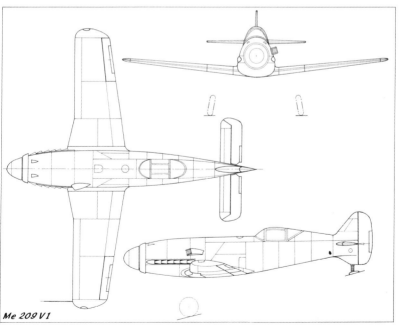

Me 209 V1

521

and equipment reduced to the minimum, the pilot's cockpit was set well aft, the fin had a substantial ventral section and the tailplane and elevators were of very small area. Also of minimum area were the tapered wings and, although no data are available, the wing loading was said to be very high for its time. The wide-track undercarriage consisted of two main members (which retracted inwards into the wing and its centre section) and a skid attached to the bottom of the ventral tail fin. Of special interest was the engine evaporative cooling system, designed to dispense with the normal drag-producing radiators. After passing around the engine, the water was piped out to the wings, where it was cooled by partial evaporation through holes in the skin and then passed back into circulation. This system naturally entailed a constant loss of water, the consumption varying between 4·5 litres (0·99 gal) and 7 litres (1·54 gal) per minute depending on engine speed. Although the engine could not be run for more than 30 minutes at a time, at least 200 litres (44 gal) of cooling water had to be carried even for making up losses on a flight interspersed with high-speed runs.

Such an aircraft looked promising from the speed point of view but very much of a handful from the pilot's point of view, and this latter worry was confirmed with the first test flights. The Me 209 V1, D-INJR, which was initially fitted with a normal DB 601A engine, made its first flight on 1 August, 1938, in the hands of Dr J. H. Wurster, then both chief test pilot and chief engineer at Augsburg. Among the aircraft's less endearing characteristics were its tendency to nose down without warning or apparent reason, its generally unstable flight and its heavy unwieldy controls. During the landing approach, the high sinking speed resulted in a very heavy touch-down, and, even on the runway, the aircraft would suddenly swerve at the slightest provocation.

The second aircraft, the Me 209 V2, D-IWAH, made its first flight on 8 February, 1939, but crashed on 4 April, 1939, when it was being flown by Flugkapitän Fritz Wendel (who had assumed the job of chief test pilot, leaving Dr Wurster to concentrate on engineering). During the landing approach, the engine seized and the aircraft almost fell out of the sky. Although the V2 was wrecked, Wendel escaped unhurt and went on to set a new record in the same month flying the V1 prototype re-engined with the special DB 601ARJ.

Painted dark blue and trailing a long plume of white steam from its cooling system, the Me 209 V1 must have looked impressive flying around a marked course to gain a new absolute speed record of 755·138 km/h (469·22 mph) on 26 April, 1939. This speed exceeded by only a small margin the previous record set up only 27 days before by Hans Dieterle in the Heinkel He 100 V8, but the Me 209 V1 record for piston-engined aircraft stood for over 30 years. (On 16 August, 1969, in the USA Darryl G. Greenamyer beat the Me 209 V1 record by flying his Grumman F8F-2 Bearcat, *Conquest I*, at an average speed of 776·449 km/h (482·533 mph). His highest speed was actually 820·824 km/h (510·031 mph) and

Following the absolute speed record gained by the Me 209 V1, the Me 209 V3 shown here was used for experimental purposes. A major alteration was the fitting of a ventral radiator.

the engine power of his modified aircraft was 3,100 hp). At the end of May 1939, the Me 209 V3, D-IVFP, was flown but was used only for experimental purposes and, with the coming of war in September that year, the question of new international records no longer arose.

There was, however, a fourth aircraft built, the Me 209 V4, D-IRND, military-coded CE-BW in 1940, first flown on 12 May, 1939. It is rather remarkable that, in this V4 aircraft, an attempt was made to produce the prototype for a fighter from a design which had absolutely nothing to commend it for any rôle except high speed. The principal changes made for the Me 209 V4 were the fitting of a standard DB 601 engine and a new wing, the latter in the hope of improving the flight and landing characteristics. The new wing was increased in span by 1·49 m (4 ft 10⅝ in) to give a total of 9·29 m (30 ft 5¾ in), with consequent increased area, and was fitted with automatic leading-edge slots. Armament was planned as two MG 17 guns in the nose upper cowling, one MK 108 firing through the propeller shaft, and two MG 17s in the wings, but the last two weapons could not be fitted because of lack of space inside the wings. For the first eight flights, an evaporative cooling system was used but could not be developed to a standard suitable for Service use. Thus, progressively larger under-wing radiators were fitted, and, because control was still difficult, wing span was again increased, first by 0·40 m (1 ft 3¾ in) and then by another 0·35 m (1 ft 1¾ in). Each of these modifications was accompanied by a decrease in performance until the aircraft's only attribute, its speed, was little better

The Me 209 V4, illustrated, was hopefully put forward as a fighter development of the record-breaking aircraft. Progressively larger radiators were fitted until it lost its only attribute, speed. (*H. Redemann*)

than the Luftwaffe's Bf 109F fighter, and this naturally brought about its final demise.

Much abuse has been heaped upon the experimental Me 209 and, in this connection, snatches of Fritz Wendel's remarks probably sum the aircraft up '. . . the 209 was a brute. Its flying characteristics still make me shudder. . . . In retrospect, I am inclined to think that its main fuel was a highly volatile mixture of sweat from my brow and the goose pimples from the back of my neck!' Nevertheless, the Me 209 V1 did put up a remarkable record performance and it is fortunate, in view of the destruction wrought in Germany, that some parts of this aircraft at least survive today. Its airframe (minus wings and engine) was removed by the Polish Army and is now stored at the Polish National Aircraft Museum, Crakow. The RLM '8' number of 209 was re-issued for an entirely different design, this being done in several cases when experimental aircraft were scrapped.

Me 209 V4 (in final form): Span 10·04 m (32 ft 11¼ in); length 7·24 m (23 ft 9 in). Loaded weight 2,800 kg (6,174 lb).
Maximum speed at 6,000 m (19,680 ft) about 600 km/h (373 mph); cruising speed at 5,000 m (16,400 ft) 500 km/h (311 mph); maximum rate of climb 1,125 m/min (3,690 ft/min); service ceiling 11,000 m (36,080 ft).

# Messerschmitt Me 209A

When, in mid-1943, any idea of developing the Me 309 (*see* page 553) into a new piston-engined fighter was abandoned, Messerschmitt produced a new design still in the hope of providing a successor to the Bf 109. For this, the RLM re-issued the designation Me 209, although, to avoid confusion with the previous Me 209 V1 to V4 aircraft, the first prototype of the new design was designated Me 209 V5 while the first production aircraft, if any, were to be designated Me 209A.

In the interests of saving time and to ensure the minimum slowing down in fighter production, the new Me 209 was designed to embody a large proportion of Bf 109G components, including rear fuselage. The most obvious departures from the Bf 109G were the use of a more powerful 1,750 hp Daimler-Benz DB 603A-1 engine with an annular radiator and driving a large three-blade airscrew, a wide-track inwards-retracting undercarriage, a pressurized cockpit with the type of hood later used on the Bf 109K, enlarged vertical tail surfaces, and a wing of increased span and area. The new design had a 25 per cent higher wing loading than the Bf 109G and, in terms of overall aerodynamics and moments, was in fact much closer in conception to its later competitor, the Focke-Wulf Fw 190D-9.

On 3 November, 1943, the first prototype, the Me 209 V5 (SP-LJ) made its maiden flight and was followed by the second prototype (probably the Me 209 V6) making its first flight on 22 December, 1943. Although the performance of these machines was excellent, it was decided in that month to begin construction of the third prototype with a 1,750 hp Junkers Jumo 213E twelve-cylinder inverted-vee liquid-cooled engine (still with an annular radiator) in view of a shortage of DB 603 engines. This third aircraft, which was eventually designated Me 209A-2, began flying in May 1944, but at about the same time the Fw 190 V17/U1 (prototype for the Fw 190D) began flying, and this was also successful. Although there was little to choose between the overall performance of the Me 209A-1 and the Fw 190D, the latter aircraft required less reorganization of the production lines, and the Messerschmitt development was therefore abandoned by the time the first production Fw 190D-9s went into operation with III./JG 54 in the autumn of 1944. At the same time, the Me 262 turbojet fighter began entering service, and Messerschmitt gave up any ideas for new piston-engined interceptors. Before conceding defeat in this sphere, however, a fourth prototype designated Me 209H V1 was constructed and began flying in June 1944. This aircraft was powered by a DB 603G engine and had an enlarged wing to give a higher service ceiling. The Me 209A prototypes were finally used as flying testbeds.

Me 209A-2: Span 10·95 m (35 ft 11 in); length 9·62 m (31 ft 6¾ in); wing area 17·15 sq m (184·53 sq ft).

Empty weight 3,475 kg (7,662 lb); loaded weight 4,200 kg (9,261 lb).

Maximum unboosted speed at 6,000 m (19,680 ft) 660 km/h (410 mph); cruising speed 490 km/h (305 mph); service ceiling 13,000 m (42,650 ft).

The Messerschmitt Me 210 V1, D-AABF, in its original form with twin fins and rudders.

# Messerschmitt Me 210

The Messerschmitt Me 210 was projected in 1937 as a multi-purpose twin-engined aircraft to replace the Messerschmitt Bf 110, which even then was showing some shortcomings. An RLM specification was later issued to cover the design, calling for a twin-engined multi-purpose fighter with remote-controlled defensive armament. Besides the Me 210, two other designs were projected: the Ago Ao 225 and the Arado Ar 240. The Ao 225 was an extremely advanced design with a large centrally-mounted engine driving both airscrews via extension shafts, but owing to its advanced nature and the financial troubles being experienced by the company, the machine was abandoned. The Arado and Messerschmitt designs were both accepted, the unusual step being made of ordering a thousand Me 210s off the drawing board.

Some indication of the success of this design can be gauged by the fact that, at one stage of the war, Göring was heard to remark that his epitaph would read: 'He would have lived longer if the Me 210 had not been produced.'

The Me 210 V1, D-AABF (c/n 2345), was a low-wing monoplane somewhat similar in appearance to the Bf 110 and powered by two 1,100 hp Daimler-Benz DB 601Aa engines. It made its first flight on 2 September, 1939, but proved to possess such marked longitudinal instability that the twin fins and rudders were replaced by a large single vertical surface. Comparative trials with the V2, initially fitted, like the V1 and V3, with twin fins and rudders, proved that the single surface marginally improved flight characteristics. Several modifications were later made to the V2 and V3 including the provision of the single fin and rudder assembly, the fitting of a new cockpit canopy with bulged sides and mockups of the FDL 131 remote-controlled barbettes. Despite the improvements introduced by the Me 210 V2, the aircraft crashed during flutter trials on 5 September, 1940.

The Me 210 V2, WL-ABEO, was fitted with single fin and rudder.

Although unsatisfactory results were achieved with the prototypes, a batch of Me 210A-0 pre-production aircraft was delivered to Erprobungsgruppe 210 towards the end of 1940. The unit had been formed with the intention of introducing the new Messerschmitt fighter-bomber into service, but all its operations were in fact carried out with Bf 109s and Bf 110s.

Early in 1941 the first of two major production sub-types was delivered. The Me 210A-1 was a destroyer with an armament of two 20 mm MG 151/20 cannon and two 7·9 mm MG 17 machine-guns. The A-2 was a fighter-bomber which could carry two 1,000 kg (2,205 lb) bombs on underwing racks, but its normal offensive load comprised two 500 kg

An Me 210A-1 of Versuchsstaffel 210 based at Soesterberg in the Netherlands, August 1942. (*R. C. Seeley*)

(1,102 lb) bombs carried internally and two 250 kg (550 lb) weapons externally. The Me 210B-1, of which four were built, was a photographic reconnaissance aircraft with provision for two cameras but without the two MG 17 guns. The Me 210C-1, C-2 and D-1 were respectively conversions of the A-1, A-2 and B-1, but powered by 1,475 hp DB 605B engines. The C-2 was to have had provision for a single 1,800 kg (3,970 lb) SC 1800 bomb.

The first active use of the Me 210 was made by II./ZG 1 based on the Eastern Front. The unit converted to the aircraft late in 1941 but could rarely muster more than a third of its total strength for operations. Perhaps the least desirable trait of the Me 210 was its tendency to spin at the slightest provocation, especially at high angles of attack. Numerous modifications were introduced on the production line in an attempt to cure the troubles, the most important being a $1 \cdot 09$ m (3 ft $6\frac{3}{4}$ in) increase in fuselage length.

Despite these modifications, the toll of accidents continued unabated, and on 14 April, 1942, production, already slowed by the many modifications introduced to the basic design, was finally brought to a halt. The temporary halt in the Me 210 programme led to a loss to the German war effort of over 600 aircraft and a financial loss of at least 30 million RM to Messerschmitt.

Finally, in July 1942, a decision was made to fit the Me 210 with leading-edge slots, and this substantially improved the aircraft's flight characteristics. The modification was fitted retrospectively to all Me 210s and assembly was resumed in August 1942, ninety-five being delivered during the year, eighty-nine in 1943 and seventy-four in 1944. Many of

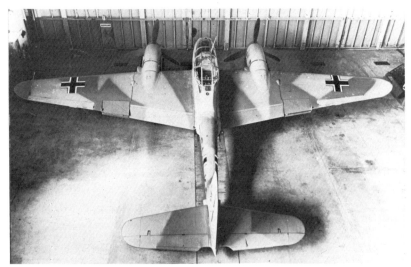

An early production Me 210A-2 fighter-bomber showing the 'splinter' type camouflage pattern used on many German aircraft. (*H. Redemann*)

Close-up of the Me 210A-0 (c/n 063) fitted with external bomb racks.

these never reached front-line units, and a large proportion were converted to Me 410 standard.

The task of re-introducing the Me 210 into Luftwaffe service was entrusted to an experimental unit designated Versuchsstaffel 210 based at Soesterberg in central Holland. Late in August 1942, the unit became operational under Luftflotte 3 as 16.Staffel/KG 6.

The Me 210 made its operational début over the British Isles early in September 1942, the first losses occurring on the 6th of the month when two aircraft were shot down by RAF Hawker Typhoons over Yorkshire. In November 1942, a number of Me 210As were delivered to III./ZG 1 at Trapani in Sicily, and in January 1943 a few were received by 2.(F)/122, also at Trapani, and 10./ZG 26 in Tunisia. Apart from some desultory use by the Nachtjagdverbände, no other Luftwaffe unit was equipped with the Me 210. III./ZG 1 and 2.(F)/122 began conversion to the Me 410 in May 1943. The Me 210 was also built under licence by Duna Repülögépgyár at Budapest and used by the Hungarian Air Force's 102 Fast Bomber Group.

*Wartime operational units:* 2.(F)/122, II. and III./ZG 1, III./ZG 26, Versuchsstaffel 210.

Me 210A-1 (early production): Span 16·4 m (53 ft 7¾ in); length 11·2 m (36 ft 8¼ in); height 4·3 m (14 ft 0½ in); wing area 36·2 sq m (389·6 sq ft).

Loaded weight 8,100 kg (17,857 lb).

Maximum speed 620 km/h (385 mph); service ceiling 7,000 m (22,967 ft); normal range 2,400 km (1,491 miles).

529

The Messerschmitt Me 261 V2 (BJ-CQ), seen here with airscrews and some cowling removed, was flown in the spring of 1941 to provide long-range flight data.

# Messerschmitt Me 261

This specialized long-range monoplane was projected in 1937 for the sole purpose of gaining prestige by making new record flights, and, as a start, it was hoped it would fly the Olympic Torch nonstop from Berlin to Tokyo for the 1940 Olympic Games. Such prestige aircraft had been much in vogue since the German aircraft industry was reinstated, and the P.1064, as the project was designated, received the particular interest of Hitler with the result that three prototypes were eventually ordered under the designation Me 261. Because of Hitler's interest, those concerned with the development of the aircraft later nicknamed it the Adolfine.

Since the main parameter of the Me 261 design was long range, the aircraft was to carry a crew of five and have the greatest possible fuel capacity with very limited payload. The crew members comprised a pilot, co-pilot, radio operator, navigator, and flight engineer, and the slender fuselage had room for crew bunks. A considerable quantity of fuel was carried by sealing the maximum internal volume of the single-spar wing to act as tanks, the strength of the wing being augmented by the use of stressed metal skin and a thick profile section. For power, two 2,700 hp Daimler-Benz DB 606A/B twenty-four cylinder engines were chosen to drive two 4·6 m (15 ft 1⅛ in) diameter, four-blade airscrews. Each DB 606 engine derived its considerable power by virtue of coupling, side by side, two DB 601 twelve-cylinder liquid-cooled engines with drive gears connected to the single airscrew shaft. Thus, each DB 606 engine was mounted in a flattened nacelle, having two separate oil coolers underneath and two separate radiators mounted outboard beneath the wing trailing edge. The heavily-loaded Me 261 required not only powerful engines but large-diameter mainwheels, and these were turned through 90 deg when retracted back into the wings. The tailwheel was also retractable.

By the spring of 1939, the Augsburg factory had the construction of prototypes under way at a low priority, but this work stopped just before the outbreak of war. However, because it was felt that interesting data could be gained from the special qualities of the Me 261, work on it resumed in 1940 when labour could be spared, and the Me 261 V1 (BJ-CP) made its first flight on 23 December, 1940. This aircraft was joined by the Me 261 V2 (BJ-CQ) the following spring, and both aircraft were flown by Karl Baur and Fritz Wendel to provide long-range flight performance data. The V2 differed from the V1 in having a dorsal fuselage clear-view dome instead of a rear fuselage glazed step.

The final prototype, the Me 261 V3 (BJ-CR), was flown early in 1943. This aircraft was similar in appearance to the V2 prototype but had increased accommodation for seven crew members and used more powerful 2,950 hp Daimler-Benz DB 610 engines, each engine being a coupled pair of DB 605s housed in a modified nacelle. One notable flight of 10 hr duration was made by Karl Baur with this aircraft on 16 April, 1943, and, although such flights pointed to the possibility of long-range reconnaissance, the Me 261 was rejected for this rôle on the grounds that the extra weight of necessary operational equipment could be carried only by sacrificing some of the fuel, thereby reducing the range. Nevertheless, after a damaged undercarriage had been repaired in May 1943, the Me 261 V3 was employed for long-range reconnaissance by the Aufklärungsgruppe/ Ob.d.L. The other two prototypes were eventually written-off after Allied air attack in 1944.

Me 261 V3: Span 26·87 m (88 ft $1\frac{7}{8}$ in); length 16·69 m (54 ft $9\frac{1}{8}$ in); height 4·72 m (15 ft $5\frac{7}{8}$ in); approximate wing area 76 sq m (817·76 sq ft).

Maximum speed at 3,000 m (9,840 ft) 620 km/h (385 mph); economic cruising speed 400 km/h (248 mph); service ceiling 8,250 m (27,060 ft); range at economic cruising speed 11,000 km (6,831 miles).

Empty and loaded weights are unknown.

# Messerschmitt Me 262

When the Messerschmitt Me 262 entered service during the autumn of 1944, it was the first turbojet aircraft to do so and thereby opened a new era in aerial warfare. Allied leaders, already anxious about the newly-operational Me 163B rocket interceptor, became further alarmed at the latest threat to their bomber streams and the only immediate, albeit inadequate, answer to the problem was to rush out the hybrid Republic P-47M Thunderbolt escort fighter. Although this piston-engined aircraft was specially prepared to achieve a maximum level speed of about 755 km/h (470 mph), it was still some 113 km/h (70 mph) slower than the best level speed of the Me 262 fighter, and other factors, such as better manoeuvrability, could not always make up for this deficiency.

Fortunately for the Allies, only a small proportion of the 1,430 Me 262s manufactured were employed operationally, and their effects were diffused over various rôles, ranging from day and night interception to reconnaissance and bombing, and, although good results could be, and were, obtained in all these rôles, many tactical errors were made, and the final total operational tally was not outstanding. Although Germany's leaders made many mistakes which resulted in the greatly delayed service introduction of jet aircraft, the first Me 262s were still put into service some six months before the turbojet engines were fully developed. Also, given that many Me 262s were wasted in ground attack work (and this is by no means certain in view of the vast numbers of Allied aircraft packed on continental airfields at the time), there is a strong case for believing that fighter versions of the Me 262 were also tactically misused. Many German tacticians believed that the rôle of the Me 262 fighters should be to fly from a string of bases stretching from the Netherlands to northern France with the purpose of engaging Allied bomber escort fighters, leaving the bombers to fly on alone to be attacked later by the Luftwaffe's conventional fighters. Jet fighter tactics in general were, however, still being worked out, and the wisdom of the tactics mentioned was not realized until too late when all the satellite bases were over-run.

Despite the lost opportunities and administrative bungling, the Germans did get jet aircraft operational before anyone else, and considerable kudos must go to certain officials in the RLM's technical department for initiating the necessary development programmes at an early date, because, despite achievements of the technicians, directives for the procurement of specific new weapons had to come from official departments.

By the end of 1938, Hans A. Mauch and Helmut Schelp of the power-plant development group of the technical department were working on the plans for an official jet engine programme. At about this time, Hans M. Antz joined the airframe development group and set about organizing a complementary official programme for jet and rocket airframes, and part of this programme was to lead to the introduction, for example, of the Me 163B Komet interceptor in addition to the Me 262. Antz's programme, although opposed by older RLM officials, was rapidly set up, and one of his first moves was to interest Messerschmitt in the possibilities of jet propulsion, with the result that the company's chief of development, Robert Lusser, set about making a basic investigation. Before the end of 1938, a formal order was issued to Messerschmitt for the development of a turbojet fighter for which Antz merely specified an endurance of one hour at 850 km/h (528 mph) and (presumably for the sake of speed) only limited armament. Estimated data concerning the weights and dimensions expected for turbojet engines was calculated by Schelp and used in Messerschmitt project studies for the fighter. These studies were headed by Woldemar Voigt and were chiefly concerned with the many possible

An Me 262A-1a Schwalbe fighter.

arrangements of both single- and twin-engined layouts. Much difficulty was anticipated with the ducts for a fuselage-mounted engine (later confirmed in the Heinkel He 178), while it was foreseen that any single-engined layout, being inflexible from the c of g point of view, would be problematical without precise engine details. Thus, a twin-engined layout crystallized under the designation P.1065, the engines being mounted inside the wings, because with that layout varying engine designs could be more easily accommodated to give the correct c of g position.

The basic design of the P.1065 was completed by June 1939, and a wooden mockup was inspected by RLM officials on 1 March, 1940. An order for three prototypes followed, and the design of the Me 262, as the aircraft was now officially designated, was undertaken primarily by Rudolf Seitz. This design phase ended in mid-May and resulted in the engines being planned for underwing mounting instead of inside the wings, in order to simplify spar design. (It is interesting to note that, in Britain, Glosters designed the Meteor jet fighter with the centrifugal turbojets mounted integral with the wing and, although these engines resulted in a cowling of considerably greater frontal area than those for the Me 262's axial engines, there was little to choose between them from the point of view of drag. Nevertheless, taking the complete airframe, the Me 262 was considerably cleaner and had less drag than the Meteor.) The design of the Me 262, although radical in nature, was quite conservative in its aims in order to ensure success, and it was estimated that the requisite performance could be obtained with engines of 680 kg (1,496 lb) static thrust each. An all-metal stressed-skin structure was used with formers and stringers for the fuselage, ribs and stringers for all flying surfaces and sheet-metal covering overall. The moderately sweptback wing (18 deg 32 min on the leading edge) was low-mounted and had long-span ailerons, plain flaps inboard of the engines and full-length automatic leading-edge slots. A triangular fin carried at about mid-height the tailplane and a two-piece elevator. Trim tabs were provided for ailerons, rudder and tailplane. The fuselage, which had a rounded triangular cross section, carried the fuel tanks fore and aft of the cockpit, which was provided with a framed canopy having a hinged centre section for access. Guns and ammunition were to be carried in the fuselage nose. Curiously, the aircraft was provided with a tailwheel undercarriage which brought the rear of the turbojet nacelles very close to the ground. For retraction, the main undercarriage members swung inwards while the tailwheel retracted rearwards.

The Messerschmitt Me 262 V1 (PC-UA) which initially flew with a piston engine and airscrew because the turbojets were not ready. (*H. Redemann*)

By early 1941 the three prototypes of the Me 262 were completed, but no turbojets were available. To gain some idea of the aircraft's characteristics, it was initially planned to fit two Walter liquid-fuelled rocket motors, but this plan had to be abandoned because units of sufficient thrust were not then ready. The Me 262 V1 (PC-UA) was therefore fitted with a single 1,200 hp Junkers Jumo 210G piston engine and airscrew, and it flew in this form on 18 April, 1941, with Flugkapitän Fritz Wendel at the controls. Prior to this, on 2 April, the Heinkel He 280 (later competitor of the Me 262) had flown on the power of two Heinkel HeS 8 (109-001) turbojets, and two examples of this engine were later used to attempt the first jet-powered flight of the heavier Me 262, but, with each engine developing only about 500 kg (1,100 lb) of thrust, the aircraft could not take-off.

In the meantime, development work was going ahead at a low priority on other turbojet engines. With the opposition of Eisenlohr (head of

534

powerplant development) counteracted by the support of Udet, Mauch launched his turbojet development programme in August 1938 by requesting engine firms to make surveys of jet propulsion. Initially, only BMW and Junkers showed any enthusiasm at all for the idea, and Heinkel were already working in this field on their own. In the summer of 1939, contracts were issued to BMW and Junkers for the development of turbojets, the only official requirement being that a static thrust of 680 kg (1,496 lb) should be achieved, so that, for a start, the Me 262 could be powered. BMW's contract was originally for a counter-rotating axial-flow engine (the 109-002), and, although this was later abandoned as being too difficult a starting point, a straightforward axial-flow engine was also begun in 1939 to provide data. It was this second engine (the P.3302) which BMW-Spandau developed into the 109-003 and which first ran in August 1940 but gave only 150 kg (331 lb) of thrust. In the summer of 1941, the 109-003 engine began flight tests beneath a Bf 110, and, on 25 November, 1941, an attempt was made to fly the Me 262 V1 (with piston engine retained) on the power of two 450 kg (992 lb) thrust 109-003 engines. This attempt failed because of turbine failures at take-off power, although the thrust was almost certainly too low anyway. It was not until mid-1943 that the static thrust was raised to 800 kg (1,760 lb) in the 109-003A-0 pre-production engine, and not until mid-1944 did production 109-003A-1 engines begin appearing, but by then the RLM had decided to reserve most of the BMW engines for the Heinkel He 162.

Junkers' turbojet development was, in the event, of more importance to the Me 262, and their engine, the 109-004, began development under Anselm Franz as a conservatively-designed engine which was to achieve production status speedily and, if necessary, at the expense of performance. (The RLM later concurred with this policy and decided that the potentially more advanced BMW 109-003 should undergo a longer development as a later replacement.) The first Junkers 109-004A was bench running in November 1940, but all the major problems were not solved until January 1942, the first flight of the engine being made on 15 March, 1942, under a Bf 110 test-bed. In the early summer of 1942, the first pilot-production 109-004A-0 engines were ready, and two of these were fitted to the Me 262 V3 (PC-UC) without any piston engine. This aircraft made the first all-jet Me 262 flight, on 18 July, 1942, with 840 kg (1,848 lb) static thrust from each engine but was badly damaged in August during a take-off at Leipheim with the Rechlin pilot Dipl Ing Beauvais at the controls. Although the aircraft was subsequently rebuilt and rejoined the test programme, it crashed and was destroyed after a few flights and killed the test pilot Ostertag.

Soon after the first flight of the V3, the similarly-powered Me 262 V2 (PC-UB) joined the test programme with its maiden flight on 2 October, 1942, and this was followed by an order for forty-five Me 262s to supplement the 15 already on order by then. In this month also, the design of the production 109-004B engine was completed, and the first 109-004B-0s were delivered in January 1943. Two of these engines, which had the same thrust as the A model, were fitted to the Me 262 V1, which was then flown again on 2 March, 1943.

The Me 262 V4 (PC-UD) joined the test programme in April and, on the 22nd of that month, was flown by Gen Lt Adolf Galland. This flight was of some importance for the Me 262 (and German jets in general) since it was part of the plan to convince the non-technical Luftwaffe and official personnel of the desirability of jets. After his flight, Galland enthused greatly over the Me 262 and organized a meeting at the RLM soon after, when it was decided to transfer most of Messerschmitt's production from the Bf 109 to the Me 262. Although the aircraft was ordered into production on 5 June, 1943, much delay ensued, not least of which was the destruction of various jigs on 17 August, 1943, when the Regensburg factory was bombed, followed by the transfer of the development programme from Augsburg to Oberammergau. The suicide, in November 1941, of Ernst Udet (who had usually favoured radical developments) had already been a blow, and, since then, decisions on aircraft production were taken by Erhard Milch, who favoured impressing Hitler with large production figures for old aircraft and cared little about jets. Milch, therefore, did very little to facilitate new production lines.

On 26 June, 1943, the Me 262 V5 (PC-UE) made its first flight. Unlike the previous machines, which had tailwheel undercarriages, this aircraft had a fixed nosewheel giving greatly improved ground-view and take-off attitude. Also, fitted beneath the rear fuselage, were two Rheinmetall-Borsig 109–505 solid-fuelled ATO rockets each giving 500 kg (1,100 lb) thrust for 6 seconds. The turbojet intakes were fitted with mesh intake guards,

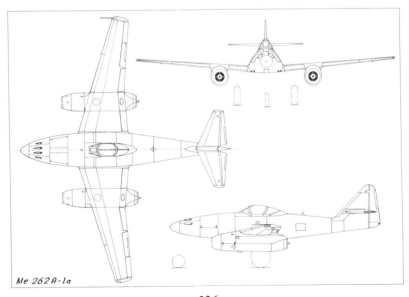

Me 262 A-1a

intended to prevent the ingress of debris from runways and during combat but, although they allegedly did not affect performance, they were not fitted in later production aircraft. With the appearance of the Me 262 V6, VI-AA (c/n 130 001), a fully-retractable nosewheel undercarriage was introduced, and this aircraft was the first to have 109-004B-1 production turbojets, which had an increased thrust of 900 kg (1,980 lb). The B-1 model had been put into production around June 1943 and flew in the V6 in October, but difficulties with the turbine were not overcome until December.

In November 1943, the situation for production began to look more hopeful. In that month Col Siegfried Kneymeyer, who had front-line experience of the way the Luftwaffe was beginning to suffer, became head of the development section (TLR/FL-E) of technical air armament. Kneymeyer realized that, in view of the Luftwaffe's numerical inferiority, a striking superiority in aircraft performance was essential, and he proposed to abandon all bombers and concentrate on jet aircraft, especially the Me 262. Although Göring agreed with him, Bormann and Goebbels persuaded Hitler to continue the existing aircraft programme in order to continue small-scale bombing raids on England. Thus, when Hitler saw the Me 262 V6 flown by Gerd Linter at Insterburg on 26 November, he declared that it was just the thing for carrying a 500 kg (1,100 lb) bomb load to England, and, although hardly anyone could agree that the order was reasonable, an extensive modification programme was begun. Nevertheless, development and production plans for the fighter version went ahead simultaneously, since Göring was keen to try the fighter in service.

In November 1943, the Me 262 V7 (VI-AB) flew with a pressurized cockpit, whilst the V8 (VI-AC) was the first to have armament fitted, this consisting of four 30 mm MK 108 cannon in the upper nose synchronized to reduce vibration. Although potentially an excellent cannon, the MK 108 was prone to about one stoppage in a hundred in its underdeveloped state. When first tried in the Me 262, the MK 108 ammunition threw so much debris on the windscreen that the pilot could not see, but when the ammunition propellant was altered, the guns flashed violently and a long conical flash eliminator had to be developed. The Me 262 V9 (VI-AD) appeared in January 1944 to test various radio installations. It was not until May, or six months after the bomber development was begun, that the Me 262 V10 appeared with bomb pylons beneath the nose for high-speed bombing tests. The previous month, a bottleneck in engines began to disappear as the 109-004B-1 turbojet began true mass production.

By April 1944 thirteen pre-production Me 262A-0 fighters had been manufactured in addition to some 12 development prototypes, and, although Hitler still wanted the bomber version, he had finally agreed to accept the fighter also. The situation, however, was still far from perfect for Germany as shown by programme No. 225 (fighter production) issued by the Jägerstab. Although this programme called for sixty Me 262s in May 1944, for example, it also called for a total of 2,580 Messerschmitt

Bf 109 and Focke-Wulf Fw 190 piston-engined fighters from all factories combined in the same month. So far as Messerschmitt was concerned, these figures were quite unrealistic, since the large Regensburg factory had been heavily bombed in February and most of the tools and jigs destroyed.

The initial production aircraft was the Me 262A-1a Schwalbe (Swallow) armed with four MK 108 cannon. Ing Josef Helmschrott was in charge of all constructional problems, and the requisite high degree of accuracy was obtained by special attention to detail manufacture, especially ribs which were produced from metal dies, and, although the Me 262 was never fully tooled-up, there was progressively less inspection and more reliance on assembly jigs as tooling progressed. The actual man-hours taken for each Me 262 airframe in production was 9,000-10,000; the planned figure of 6,000 man-hours per airframe was never reached because of transport and supply difficulties. In the early stages of construction, no special attention was paid to the accuracy of aileron and elevator shrouds, but, following troubles on flight tests, these were later closely controlled.

The outer sections of the wing leading-edge automatic slots were never satisfactory since these opened about 25 mm (1 in) and increased drag at high speeds due to deflections. Aileron oscillation occurred initially at Mach 0·8, aeroelastic deformation produced pronounced nose-down pitching moments at high speed, and the elevator became heavier due to a change of pressure distribution. The precise characteristics varied from one aircraft to another, according to manufacturing accuracy, but, once the above troubles were diminished by careful testing and adjustment of control surfaces, an Me 262 was permitted the final design speed of 1,000

An Me 262A-1a fighter of JG 7 Nowotny showing R4M rockets installed beneath the wing. (*H. Redemann*)

538

Close-up of R4M rockets fitted beneath wing of an Me 262A-1a fighter. (*H. Redemann*)

km/h (621 mph) in a dive. It is interesting to note that, although the rocket-powered Me 163B Komet had a far greater climb rate, that aircraft's critical Mach number of 0·82 could be exceeded by the Me 262 at Mach 0·86 in a dive, because the latter aircraft was held stable by much larger tail-unit moments, especially in pitch.

The maximum level speed of an average Me 262 at 7,000 m (22,880 ft) was 868 km/h (536 mph) in winter, or 820 km/h (508 mph) in summer, the difference being caused by as much as 30 per cent difference in engine thrust caused by the variation in air temperature. The best level speed attained by an Me 262—probably the special Me 262 V12, VI-AG (c/n 130 007), was 930 km/h (578 mph) when up-rated 109-004B-4 turbojets were fitted. Although the B-4 late-production model had the same thrust as the B-1 model, the engines used in the experimental flight were undoubtedly up-rated to about 1,000 kg (2,205 lb) static thrust each by allowing greater combustion chamber temperature. The principal new feature of the B-4 engine was its use of hollow, air-cooled turbine blades instead of the previous solid type, but the B-4 engine was to be run in service at the same temperature and thrust as the previous B-1 engine so that the advantages of increased durability and reliability could be gained. One of the major drawbacks of German operational turbojets in general was the fact that they had a tendency to flame-out at altitude and suffer compressor stall at high speeds and altitude, and these troubles very often imposed a limit of about 8,000 m (26,240 ft) on the aircraft. It was planned to overcome the problem by the development of duplex fuel burners and an improved compressor, but this work was never completed.

With very careful nursing, however, one Me 262 reached an altitude of 12,700 m (41,656 ft) on the power of its 109-004 engines.

During the summer of 1944, the first Me 262A-0s were delivered to Erprobungsstelle Rechlin for testing in all aspects of air worthiness, performance, and equipment, pending acceptance by the Luftwaffe. The standard procedure was, however, speeded up by using extra aircraft, and also, from July, the 1st Staffel of the Versuchsverband Ob.d.L., followed by the 3rd Staffel, began experimenting with the Me 262 on carefully selected or clandestine missions.

Having due regard to its idiosyncrasies, the excellent characteristics of the Me 262 reported by Messerschmitt test pilots were confirmed in these trials. In many ways it was easier to fly than the Bf 109, although it could not turn as sharply. Also, acceleration and deceleration in level flight were less than with typical piston-engined fighters. The Me 262 could, however, dive with great rapidity, and its top level speed by far outclassed that of any piston-engined aircraft.

A number of versions of the standard aircraft were now being prepared, starting with the Me 262A-1a/U1 fighter, which differed from the A-1a version in having two MK 108, two MK 103 and two MG 151/20 guns in the nose. The Me 262A-1a/U2 was a bad-weather fighter, with FuG 125 radio supplementing the standard equipment. An unarmed reconnaissance version, the Me 262A-1a/U3, had two vertical Rb 50/30 cameras.

The production bomber variant was designated Me 262A-2a Sturmvogel (Stormbird) and had, in addition to the standard armament, racks to carry either a single 1,000 kg (2,205 lb), two 500 kg (1,100 lb) or two 250 kg (550 lb) bombs. In the Me 262A-2a/U1, two of the MK 108 cannon were removed to make room for a TSA bomb sight. The Me 262A-2a/U2 had the more extensive modification of an enlarged, partly-glazed nose section to accommodate a prone bomb-aimer and standard Lotfe 7D

An Me 262A-2a (c/n 110 813) Sturmvogel bomber with two 500 kg bombs beneath its nose. This was the bomber version ordered by Hitler.

Rare picture of the Me 262A-2a/U2 (being towed) which was fitted with a new, glazed, nose section for a prone bomb-aimer.

level-bombing sight, but only one prototype of this design was produced. In the Me 262A-3a, extra armour protection was intended to make the aircraft suitable for ground attack in addition to interception work. The projected Me 262A-4a unarmed reconnaissance machine with two Rb 50/30 cameras was abandoned in favour of the Me 262A-1a/U3, already mentioned, and the Me 262A-5a with a similar camera installation became an armed reconnaissance version with two MK 108 cannon and two drop tanks.

The first semi-operational Luftwaffe jet fighter unit was known as Erprobungskommando 262 (EK 262) and, after a period of evaluating the Schwalbe, EK 262 finished its work in September 1944 when a new fighter unit, Kommando Nowotny, was formed. The new unit had two Staffeln of about twenty Me 262A-1as based at Achmer and Hesepe and became operational on 3 October, 1944, against USAAF bombers. Initial operations were rather poor. A number of jets were shot down because their pilots had great difficulty in scoring hits at high speed, and elected to slow down, thereby losing their only advantage. Further losses were incurred through undercarriage, turbojet, and structural failures. The undercarriage failures, one of the biggest problems, were caused by the high-speed landings on stationary wheels, the resulting shocks causing structural damage and tyre failure. A series of trials were therefore conducted under Stabsingenieur Fitjer at Rechlin, and it was considered that about 75 per cent pre-spinning of the landing wheels was essential if an improvement was to be effected; aerodynamic means of pre-spinning the wheels was therefore tried on a Siebel Si 204, an Arado Ar 234 and an Me 262 (c/n 130 168), but the final results were never satisfactory.

When, on 8 November, 1944, Maj Walter Nowotny was killed flying an Me 262A-1a, part of his unit was used as the foundation for a new fighter wing, JG 7, which was named in his honour. Other pilots from the defunct Kommando Nowotny unit were used to form a fighter training unit designated III./Ergänzungsjagdgeschwader 2 which was based at Lechfeld with Me 262B-1a two-seat trainers. Since, from about September 1944, the first Me 262A-2a bomber units had been formed, there was also a bomber training unit designated IV./(Erg)/KG 51. The first bomber units were Kommando Schenk (commanded by Maj Wolfgang Schenk), formed from a detachment of KG 51 Edelweiss, and an experimental bomber unit known as Kommando Edelweiss.

This Me 262A-1a fighter (c/n 112 385) served with the third Staffel of JG 7 Nowotny. The numeral 8 and rear fuselage band were yellow. This aircraft was one of many found intact by the 5th Armoured Division of the US 9th Army when it captured an airfield between Stendal and Borstel, Germany, on 15 April, 1945. (*USAF*)

When JG 7 Nowotny (only the III.Gruppe and Geschwader-Stab of which ever became fully operational) began operations, first from Brandenburg and then mainly from Parchim, some attempt was made to overcome the problem of attacking at high speed. Maj Sinner, commander of III./JG 7, instigated tests with 55 mm R4M unguided rocket armament which yielded slightly better results. In operations, twelve R4M rockets were carrried in a wooden rack under each wing of a modified Schwalbe designated Me 262A-1b. Included in other armament being developed was the Ruhrstahl/Kramer X-4 guided missile (*see* page 700).

In October 1944, tests began with an Me 262A (c/n 130 056) as a night

An Me 262A (c/n 130 056) experimentally fitted with SN-2 Lichtenstein radar equipment for night-fighter tests, October 1944.

An Me 262B-1a/U1 (c/n 111 980) night fighter fitted with drop tanks under its nose. The aircraft was 'red 12' of Kommando Welter which was assigned to the defence of Berlin in March 1945. (*USAF*)

fighter fitted with SN-2 Lichtenstein radar equipment, flown by Oberst Hajo Herrmann, of Jagddivision 30, who reported excellent results. Consequently, the conversion of the Me 262B-1a two-seat model as an interim two-seat night fighter was made, resulting in the Me 262B-1a/U1 with very extensive radar and radio equipment. The only drawback with this model was that the antler-type antennae at the nose reduced speed by some 60 km/h (37 mph). Only one prototype of the proposed production night fighter was flown before the war ended: this was the Me 262B-2a with extended fuselage for extra fuel tankage and two extra MK 108s firing obliquely upwards from a Schräge Musik installation behind the cockpit section. A second similar aircraft was ready for flight testing, which, by virtue of its centimetric radar not needing the large antenna array, promised to reduce normal speed by only 11 km/h (7 mph). The first experimental jet night-fighter unit was known as Kommando Stamp and, when later redesignated Kommando Welter, had the job of defending Berlin with about 10 aircraft. In April 1945, this unit became the 10th Staffel of NJG 11 as a special jet Wilde Sau night-fighting Staffel.

During December 1944, a special short-range reconnaissance unit was formed, Sonderkommando Braunegg, with the Me 262A-1a/U3, and the

Me 262B-1a/U1s and other Me 262s photographed on 6 June, 1945. (*USAF*)

543

aircraft was used in its most successful rôle thanks to its virtual immunity to attack when flown fast and without diversion. The following spring the unit formed the Gruppen-Stab and 2nd Staffel of NAGr 6, which also had some Me 262A-5as on hand. With the increasing phasing-out of German piston-engined bombers in 1944, bomber pilots became available for re-training, and the following new Me 262 fighter units appeared early in 1945: KG(J)6, KG(J)27, and I./KG(J)54 which were formed from the respectively numbered Kampfgeschwader although only the latter unit became operational.

While operations with the Me 262 were proceeding, experiments and development work were being undertaken with a view to adding the spectacular climb rate and ceiling of the rocket interceptor (Me 163B) to the endurance of the turbojet fighter. On 27 February, 1945, a prototype designated Me 262C-1a (c/n 130 186) made its first flight with a Walter 109-509A-2 rocket unit fitted to exhaust from a modified tail, standard turbojets being retained. The rocket unit, which was of the same type as that used in the Me 163B, used T-Stoff and C-Stoff propellants to give a step-controlled thrust up to 1,700 kg (3,740 lb), which enabled the fighter to climb to 11,700 m (38,400 ft) in $4\frac{1}{2}$ min from a standing start.

By this time, the BMW 109-003A turbojet was in production and the firm had pressed on with the development of the first combination turbojet/rocket engine, the 109-003R. This was a standard 003A turbojet to which was added a specially-designed BMW 109-718 rocket unit burning SV-Stoff (concentrated nitric acid) with R-Stoff (Tonka self-igniting fuel) to give a thrust of 1,000 kg (2,205 lb) for 3 min. The propellant pumps were electrically coupled, when required, to an extension drive from the turbojet, and, in the case of twin-engined aircraft, both rockets were automatically cut off in the event of one failing. Although not fully developed, two 109-003R units were fitted to an Me 262C-2b (c/n 170 078), and a single test flight was made by Flugkapitän Karl Baur, the same pilot having flown the Me 262C-1a. Although this flight appears to have been made without incident, the performance obtained is unknown. However, by turning the rockets on at 700 km/h (435 mph) at sea level, an initial climb rate of 5,100 m/min (16,728 ft/min) was expected, with an altitude of 10,000 m (32,800 ft) being reached in 1 min 55 sec, and an altitude of 13,000 m (42,640 ft) being reached in 2 min 20 sec, with a maximum level speed of 900 km/h (559 mph) at 9,000 m (29,520 ft). Ultimately, it was decided to proceed with the simple arrangement of a jettisonable Walter 109-509A-2 rocket unit and propellant tanks slung beneath the fuselage, and this arrangement was to have been used in the Me 262C-3a, but the only prototype was not completed in time.

A more unusual method of boosting the Me 262's rate of climb and ceiling, by adding ramjets, was also proposed but not put into effect. The ramjets were to be of the long, subsonic type which Dr Eugen Sänger began developing at the DFS, Ainring, from mid-1941. Although Sänger wanted to use an Me 262 to advance the flight tests and experiments already begun with ramjets mounted above a Dornier Do 17Z and Do 217E, Messerschmitt decided to consider the proposed experiment in the light of an operational application. In the event, lack of fuel prevented an experimental flight, but, with a ramjet duct measuring 1·13 m (3 ft 8½ in) in diameter and 5·90 m (19 ft 4¼ in) in length mounted over the wing above each turbojet, the following performance was expected: the time to reach 10,000 m (32,800 ft) altitude would be 6 min, the maximum speed would be about 1,000 km/h (621 mph), and an increase of nearly 4,000 m (13,120 ft) in operational ceiling would result. On the other hand, the ramjets were also to use the same J2 fuel as the turbojets, and, for a given fuel load, use of the ramjets would result in the radius of action and endurance being reduced to one third of the normal.

One of the four Me 262A-1as experimentally fitted with a single 50mm MK 214A cannon. The blinding flash from this weapon discouraged salvo firing but results were good in tests.

There was also considerable further thought being given to alternative armament for bomber destruction. In each of four Me 262A-1as, a single 50 mm MK 214A cannon was fitted in the nose, giving a total installed weight of 710 kg (1,562 lb) and a large proportion of the 2·82 m (9 ft) long barrel projecting. Because the blinding flash was even greater than that experienced with early MK 108 installations, firing in salvoes was not usually attempted but, even so, results in firing trials were very good, with far greater ranges than conventional armament. Armament was also proposed similar to the vertically-firing SG 500 Jagdfaust (successfully tested in the Me 163B), and there were plans to double the number of R4M missiles being carried by installing a further 24 in the nose. Of the great many other Me 262 projects, special mention may be made of the three-seat bad-weather night fighter which had a lengthened fuselage, enlarged wings with increased sweepback, and was to be powered by two Heinkel-Hirth 109-011 turbojets; and the Aufklärer II which had greatly increased fuselage depth to accommodate internally an extra 1,450 litre (319 Imp gal) fuel tank for longer-range reconnaissance.

The Luftwaffe made its last big effort on New Year's Day 1945, when all available aircraft attacked Allied airfields. After this the decline was rapid and soon the jets were among the few Luftwaffe aircraft still flying, the Me 262s usually being forced to operate from autobahn 'runways'. By the end of the war, only the third Gruppe of JG 7 Nowotny at Fassberg and the famed Jagdverband 44 remained operational with Me 262s. JV 44 was formed by Gen Lt Adolf Galland as a last-ditch effort to concentrate the cream of the Luftwaffe's fighter pilots together with the best available fighter aircraft into a single unit. Formed from 12./JG 54 on 10 February, 1945, at Brandenburg-Briest, JV 44 began operations on 31 March from Munich-Riem with about twenty-five Me 262s and 50 pilots (including Späte, Lützow, Barkhorn, Steinhoff, and Schnell). A month later, all surviving Me 262s (except those of III./JG 7) were being flown from disintegrated units to JV 44's base, so that this unit finally had a surfeit of almost 100 jet fighters, but, after transferring to Salzburg-Maxglam, the unit was finally forced to surrender on 3 May, 1945. In its brief period of just over a month's operations, JV 44 turned in an impressive record for a new unit and showed what the Me 262 was capable of by destroying some 45 Allied aircraft while having an average of only six Me 262s serviceable at a time.

When the Me 262 first began to enter service at the end of 1944, the Allies were greatly alarmed. This alarm sprang from the fact that no immediate counteraction was to hand, rather than from what the Me 262 actually did, although when successful sorties were made these were sometimes devastating. For the bombers, escorting fighters and bomber gun-turrets were too slow for protection, and the loss of the 100 or more Me 262s shot down was usually caused by the jets slowing down to attack or to land.

After the war there were plenty of Me 262s left for Allied testing and examination, and some assembly was also undertaken by the Research Institute for Aerodynamics at Letnany in Czechoslovakia, where the Me 262A-1a was designated S-92 and the two-seat Me 262B-1a the CS-92. Today there are fewer than ten Me 262s preserved in various parts of the world, which compares with about the same number for the Me 163B.

*Wartime operational units:* 2./NAGr 6, I., II. and III./JG 7, I./KG(J) 54, Jagdverband 44, 10./NJG 11, I. and II./KG 51, III./EJG 2, 1./Versuchsverband Ob.d.L., Erprobungs-kommando 262, Einsatzkommando Braunegg, and Schenk, Kommando Edelweiss, Nowotny, Stamp and Welter. (KG(J) 6, 27, 30 and 55 were in the process of forming with the Me 262 at the end of the war).

Me 262A-1a Schwalbe with two Junkers Jumo 109-004B-1 or B-4 turbojets each of 900 kg (1,980 lb) static thrust: Span 12·5 m (41 ft 0⅛ in); length 10·605 m (34 ft 9½ in); height 3·830 m (12 ft 6¼ in); wing leading-edge sweepback 18 deg 32 min; wing area 21·68 sq m (233·3 sq ft).

Empty weight 4,000 kg (8,820 lb); pilot 100 kg (220 lb); ammunition 185 kg (408 lb); fuel 2,490 kg (5,490 lb); loaded weight 6,775 kg (14,938 lb).

Maximum level speed at 7,000 m (22,880 ft) 868 km/h (536 mph); limiting Mach number 0·86; landing speed 175 km/h (109 mph); initial rate of climb 1,200 m/min (3,936 ft/min); approximate service ceiling 11,000 m (36,080 ft); range at 6,000 m (19,680 ft) 845 km (525 miles); range at 9,000 m (29,560 ft) 1,050 km (652 miles).

# Messerschmitt Me 263

The shortcomings of the Messerschmitt Me 163B have already been described, and, since they were not overcome as well as they could have been in the Me 163C design, work was started by Messerschmitt on another redesign early in 1944. This redesign was begun as the Me 163D but then, when Junkers took it over and completed the work under the guidance of Prof H. Hertel, redesignated Ju 248. The designation was changed yet again, to Me 263, in August 1944 when the first prototype was completed at Junkers' Dessau factory.

Extensive redesign of the Messerschmitt Me 163B Komet's fuselage produced this Me 263 for the chief purpose of increasing the rocket interceptor's endurance.

The design of the Me 263 was primarily concerned with providing increased fuel capacity and improved ground-handling characteristics, thereby giving greater endurance and range and also decreasing accidents and saving ground-handling time. An entirely new fuselage was provided, longer and of increased diameter, which housed the hydraulically-retractable nosewheel undercarriage. The cockpit, enclosed by a bubble canopy, was pressurized with air drawn in through a small intake just below the nose and compressed by a compressor driven by a small three-blade propeller at the nose; this system maintained a cockpit altitude of 8,000 m (26,250 ft) up to flight-levels of 15,000 m (49,200 ft). The same pressure was piped into the three fuselage T-Stoff tanks and helped to prevent cavitation in the tanks, which were interconnected and regulated to prevent adverse flow and C of G movement during a steep climb. Despite the increased fuselage length, no tailplane was fitted. The fin and rudder were substantially the same as those of the Me 163B, as was the wing, but enlarged redesigned wing stubs were fitted, and it is thought that automatic leading-edge slots replaced the previous fixed slots.

Two MK108 30 mm cannon were again to be used but with ammunition

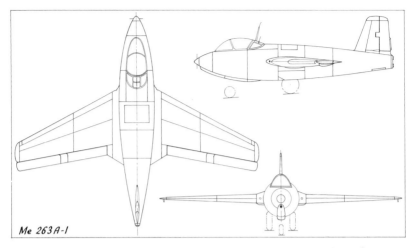

Me 263A-1

increased to a total of 150 rounds, and a complete redesign of armour protection eliminated the previous armoured nose-cone. Power was provided by a Walter 109-509C rocket motor, and, by using the cruising chamber of this motor, endurance could be increased to 15 min, some 50 per cent more weight of propellant being carried than in the Me 163B.

Using the Me 263 V1, Junkers conducted only gliding trials before handing the aircraft over to Messerschmitt late in 1944 for powered flight tests. Since it was heavier than the Me 163B but used similar wings, the Me 263 had a reduced safe-load factor. Furthermore, flight and wind-tunnel tests showed that the aircraft's centre of pressure moved rapidly at about Mach 0·8, which was lower than the Me 163B's limiting Mach number of 0·82. Thus, the Me 263 could not be safely dived at a speed much higher than its maximum level speed, and consideration was being given to the design of a tailplane. Another disappointment was that the great improvement in ground handling expected from the tricycle undercarriage was not obtained, due to the narrow track of the main wheels (little more than the fuselage diameter), and the previous wingtip skids were still to be seen on the Me 263. To shorten the landing run, a mesh parachute of 3·5 m (11 ft 6 in) diameter for release from the fuselage was designed, but it is not certain if this was tested. For the benefit of increased endurance alone, the new aircraft was considered worth the effort, but the plans to mass-produce the Me 263A-1 were too late for realization.

Me 263A: Span 9·5 m (31 ft 2 in); length 7·88 m (25 ft 10½ in); wing area 17·91 sq m (192·6 sq ft).

Empty weight 2,000 kg (4,400 lb); weight of propellants 3,000 kg (6,600 lb); allowance for ammunition and pilot 300 kg (660 lb); loaded weight 5,300 kg (11,660 lb).

Maximum speed at 3,000 m (9,840 ft) 950 km/h (590 mph); limiting Mach number 0·80; initial rate of climb 4,200 m/min (13,808 ft/min); service ceiling approximately 16,000 m (52,480 ft); maximum powered endurance (making use of motor cruise chamber) 15 min; operational range approximately 160 km (100 miles).

548

The Messerschmitt Me 264 V1 (RE-EN) made its first flight in December 1942 as an aerodynamic test aircraft. Construction was speeded up by fitting Junkers Ju 88A-4 engine nacelles.

# Messerschmitt Me 264

At an early stage in the war, the RLM's technical department requested the aircraft industry to provide feasibility studies for a bomber capable of flying nonstop to the United States and back, although the possibility of that country joining in the war against Germany was, at that time, considered remote. Bomber designs brought forth by this request were versions of the planned Focke-Wulf Fw 300 airliner and Junkers Ju 290 modified for ultra-long-range bombing, but the Messerschmitt Me 264 was a completely new design. The large amount of fuel for the envisaged missions was to be carried at the expense of bomb load and by dispensing with defensive armament. The Me 264 was planned on the basis of carrying an 1,800 kg (3,969 lb) bomb load to New York with the hope that speed and altitude would provide the bomber's defence.

Although there was no official requirement for an Amerika-Bomber, as the Me 264 became unofficially known, the influential Willy Messerschmitt managed to obtain an order to construct three prototypes on a low-priority basis, and work began at Neu-Offing, near Ulm, in 1941. In December 1942, the first prototype, the Me 264 V1 (RE-EN), made its first flight. This machine was considered an early aerodynamic test aircraft, and its construction had been accelerated by using four Junkers Jumo 211J-1 liquid-cooled engines, complete with Ju 88A-4 type nacelles and radiators.

The Me 264 was a very clean all-metal aircraft with a cigar-shaped, circular-section monocoque fuselage and a high aspect ratio finely tapered wing. The rounded glazed nose enclosing the crew compartment was followed by a parallel fuselage section, the lower half of which contained the

549

bomb bay and the upper half a galley, a walkway (to the rear-fuselage observation positions), and a crew rest area, essential in view of the possible 45-hr flight duration. The wing, which had a sweptback leading edge and straight trailing edge, had a single main spar and an auxiliary spar, and the loads were transmitted through the main spar and two auxiliary bulkheads into the fuselage. Control surfaces were conventional, including split flaps on the inner wing sections, but the tailplane, with its twin fins and rudders, was electrically adjustable during flight. Electro-hydraulic operation was provided for the flaps, bomb doors and retractable nose-wheel undercarriage, the latter being then unusual for a large aircraft. All fuel was carried in the wings, only the main oil tank being inside the fuselage. Originally, it was planned to develop the Me 264 as a pressurized aircraft, but this was later abandoned, and only oxygen masks and heating were provided for the crew. Particular attention was paid to obtaining a smooth exterior finish by filling all joints with putty before applying the first coat of aviation varnish.

By the time the Me 264 V1 was flying, the United States had declared war on Germany and the RLM's technical department looked more carefully into the requirements of an Amerika-Bomber, with the result that a larger, six-engined, aircraft with a greater bomb load was called for. To meet this new demand, proposals for the Junkers Ju 390, Focke-Wulf Ta 400, and a six-engined Me 264B were put forward, the Ju 390 being chosen because it could use certain components already in production for the Ju 290. The Me 264 was not, however, abandoned, and the two pending prototypes were ordered to be completed as development prototypes for the Me 264A ultra long-range reconnaissance aircraft.

The Me 264 V1 flying in December 1942. By about this time, the development of an Amerika-Bomber had become more of a possibility. (*F. Selinger*)

The extensive redesign needed for the Me 264A was not completed until mid-March 1943, and, although the basic structure was little changed, the design was simplified for production. Although studies were made to use four Daimler-Benz DB 603 or four Junkers Jumo 213 engines, the final choice was for four 1,700 hp BMW 801G fourteen-cylinder radial engines, partly because they were more fully developed for Service use and were also air-cooled. For these engines (which could later be the more powerful BMW 801Es) GM-1, or nitrous oxide injection, was provided to boost the bomber's speed when under attack. The GM-1 unit, with about a

Close-up of the Me 264 V1 which went for a time to Transportstaffel 5. Work on the ultra-long-range Me 264 programme, in all its various aims, stopped by the end of 1944.

25 min supply of nitrous oxide was housed in the bomb bay and could be switched on at an altitude of 8,300 m (27,224 ft) to produce a speed increase of about 95 km/h (59 mph). Also housed in the bomb bay were marker flares, radio buoys and three Rb 50/30 ciné cameras. Apart from the standard armour around the engines, a further 1,000 kg (2,205 lb) of armour was strategically positioned, and there was an elaborate defensive armament of four single 13 mm MG 131 machine-guns and two 20 mm MG 151 cannon. For 30 per cent of the 25,250 litres (5,555 Imp gal) of fuel in the wings, self-sealing tanks were provided, the balance being in rubber bags with quick-draining cocks. The remaining space in the bomb bay could be used to carry up to 3,000 kg (6,615 lb) of either extra fuel or bombs, but, in this condition, an extra, jettisonable, wheel had to be fitted to each main undercarriage leg. Alternatively, extra fuel could be carried within the bomb bay in two jettisonable tanks each of 6,400 litres (1,408 Imp gal) capacity, but this load required two extra, jettisonable, wheels for each main undercarriage leg. Under these overload conditions, up to six Walter ATO rocket units each of 1,000 kg (2,205 lb) thrust could be fitted beneath the wings, and both rocket units and the single auxiliary wheels deployed parachutes when jettisoned. Electrical de-icing equipment was included for the wing and tail unit and chemical de-icing for the airscrews. The final modification for the Me 264A was an increase in span from the 38·90 m (127 ft 7½ in) of the V1 prototype to 43 m (141 ft 1 in), by fitting new wingtips.

Late in 1943, the Me 264 V2 was being prepared for its first ground tests when it was destroyed in an Allied bombing raid but this prototype had no armament or operational equipment fitted. Work continued on the Me 264 V3 which was intended as a complete production prototype for the A-series. In the meantime, the Me 264 V1 was put into service with Transportstaffel 5 (which also operated other large aircraft such as the Junkers Ju 290, Arado Ar 232, Junkers Ju 252, and Piaggio P.108T), but it is doubtful whether the aircraft did much more than stand idle. There was a plan for the V1 to act as a flying test-bed for an aircraft steam turbine being planned by Osermaschinen GmbH from August 1944, but its ultimate fate was destruction on the ground in an air raid.

By the end of 1944, the Me 264 programme was finally recognized as the pipe-dream it was. In view of the extensive use of duralumin in this large aircraft and the shortage of such metal, the programme was shut down, and the Me 264 V3 was probably never completed. A special version of the Me 264A was being planned which could perform long-range reconnaissance and also carry fifteen passengers over long distances. The modifications for this version included fitting seats in the former bomb bay and removing or re-siting the equipment previously installed there, reducing the armament to two guns in the two dorsal turrets, and omitting the armour and de-icing systems.

There were many other versions of the Me 264 planned or projected. For boosting speed, there were projects to fit it with either two Junkers Jumo 109-004 or two BMW 109-018 turbojets in addition to the normal engines, while another project envisaged the use of two BMW 109-028 propeller-turbines only. A version was proposed, using four turbojets, paired beneath the wings, and a new tailplane mounted at the top of a single fin to clear the jet efflux. Two final examples of Me 264 projects are the studies to use Ritz heat exchangers to increase range substantially, and the plan for one able to tow an Me 328A pulse-jet fighter for protection. This fighter protection was probably studied because the service ceiling of the Me 264 had not proved to be outstanding.

Me 264 V3 (or A): Span 43 m (141 ft 1 in); length 20·9 m (68 ft 6⅞ in); wing area 127·7 sq m (1,370 sq ft); aspect ratio 14·5.

Empty equipped weight 23,360 kg (51,509 lb); crew of six 540 kg (1,191 lb); normal fuel 19,700 kg (43,438 lb); oil 1,260 kg (2,778 lb); nitrous oxide 680 kg (1,500 lb); normal loaded weight 45,540 kg (100,416 lb); maximum auxiliary fuel and tanks 10,500 kg (23,152 lb); maximum overloaded weight 56,040 kg (123,568 lb); jettisonable take-off equipment 4,300 kg (9,481 lb).

Maximum speed at 34,500 kg (76,072 lb) at 8,300 m (27,224 ft) 470 km/h (292 mph) without boost; maximum speed at 34,500 kg (76,072 lb) at 8,300 m (27,224 ft) 565 km/h (351 mph) with GM-1 boost; average cruising speed 350 km/h (217 mph); landing speed 160 km/h (99 mph); take-off run, at normal load and with ATO 1,500 m (4,920 ft); initial rate of climb at normal load 138 m/min (453 ft/min); service ceiling 8,000 m (26,240 ft); maximum range 15,000 km (9,315 miles); maximum endurance 45 hr.

# Messerschmitt Me 309

At the beginning of 1941, the question of a replacement fighter for the Messerschmitt Bf 109 was being looked into at Messerschmitt's Augsburg factory. The chief drawback with the latest Bf 109F-1, which was entering service by May 1941, was that its range was adequate for little more than local operations and, in this respect, the first Focke-Wulf Fw 190As, which were entering service by November, were only marginally better. Compared with these types, therefore, the new design was planned to have about 85 per cent more range and 25 per cent greater speed, the desirability of such increases being reinforced by Battle of Britain experience. For the desired range, some 770 litres (169·4 Imp gal) of fuel was to be carried without recourse to external fuel tanks, while aids to increased speed included thin wings and a ventral radiator which could be progressively retracted as the airspeed rose. This latter feature was chosen as another means of reducing drag after disenchantment with evaporative engine-cooling methods used on the Me 209 V4 and its predecessors. Although contemporary service ceilings were to be only slightly improved upon, the pilot's comfort was to be catered for by a pressurized cockpit, and an increase in armament was also planned. The design of such items as the retracting radiator, tricycle undercarriage nose-member and pressurized cockpit were tested on Bf 109F aircraft before the first prototype of the Me 309, as the new design was designated, was built.

The Messerschmitt Me 309 was superficially similar in appearance to the American Bell P-39 Airacobra, but, although considerably more advanced than this aircraft, the Me 309 was never to enjoy the same success. It was an all-metal single-seat low-wing monoplane although the wing was not quite flush with the bottom of the fuselage. The wing had a tapered planform with rounded tips and considerable dihedral and was fitted with automatic leading-edge slots and large plain flaps which extended from the wing roots to the inboard ends of the ailerons. The tailplane was attached at the base of the fin, both elevators and rudder being dynamically balanced. The fuselage, with its oval cross-section, carried the fuel and had the cockpit set well back in line with the trailing edge of the wing. A raised cockpit canopy gave all-round vision and had a hinged centre section for access. The large, retractable, ventral radiator was situated beneath the fuselage in line with the wing and the engine air intake was positioned on the port side of the nose cowling. The main undercarriage units retracted inwards into the wing and the nosewheel rearwards into the fuselage, the nosewheel and part of its leg turning through 90 deg to lie flat beneath the engine.

On 27 June, 1942, the Me 309 V1 (GE-CU) began taxi-ing trials, which revealed a disconcerting tendency towards nosewheel shimmy and directional instability, while in flight snaking at high speeds indicated the need for redesign of the vertical tail surfaces. After some modifications, including improvement of the cooling system, the V1 made a short first flight on 18 July, 1942, but the undercarriage hydraulic-retraction system proved too weak, and engine overheating occurred. Further flights revealed more shortcomings including instability, and a succession of modifications were made in an effort to improve the aircraft. These included alterations to the tailplane, ailerons, nosewheel leg and undercarriage hydraulic system; but the aircraft was still unsatisfactory and Messerschmitt's chief test pilot, Fritz Wendel, had formed the opinion that the type offered few advantages over the Bf 109 and would be difficult for Service pilots to handle, primarily because of the high wing loading. Despite the liberal use of automatic leading-edge slots and trailing-edge flaps, the landing speed was uncommonly high also. In its undeveloped state, the Me 309 V1 was sent to be flown by E-Stelle Rechlin's test pilot, Beauvais, on 20 November, 1942, and his report confirmed Wendel's opinions and also stated that the aircraft's control forces were too high and that it would probably run into trouble with its nosewheel undercarriage on operational airfields. A later flight comparison with a standard Bf 109G showed, as expected, that that aircraft could turn inside the Me 309.

Thus, plenty of justifiable criticism was heaped on the Me 309, which the authorities were never very enthusiastic about because of their reluctance to stem the flow of fighters already in mass production, and at some time the original order for nine experimental aircraft was cut back to only four. This proved to be a difficulty for Messerschmitt since, in view of the obvious need for a great deal of development, a considerable amount of redesign was planned for each experimental aircraft. Subtle but extensive aerodynamic differences were planned, such as alterations in the incidence and profiles of the flying and control surfaces, while at least five quite different fin shapes were designed.

On 28 November, 1942, the Me 309 V2 (GE-CV) made its first and last flight, since its nosewheel leg collapsed on landing and the aircraft swerved on its nose and broke almost in two. A similar, though not fatal, failure occurred with the first prototype, but this machine carried on the programme at a low tempo and had its original 1,750 hp Daimler-Benz DB 603A-1 engine replaced by a 1,450 hp DB 605B engine. In 1943, this aircraft was joined by the Me 309 V3 (GE-CW) in the spring and the Me 309 V4 (probably GE-CX) in the summer, the V4 being fitted with four MG 131, two MG 151/20 and two MK 108 guns in the wings and fuselage.

By mid-1943, if not before, the Me 309 was regarded as little more than an experimental flying test-bed, and its actual development as a fighter had been abandoned in view of its shortcomings in this direction and the greater promise of Messerschmitt's Me 262 turbojet fighter. Some of the planned variants of the Me 309 were as follows. The basic fighter variant was to be armed with one MG 151 and two MG 131 guns, while a fighter-bomber variant was to be similarly armed but carry two 250 kg (550 lb) bombs in addition, these versions probably being designated Me 309A-1 and B-1 respectively. A third version was to carry three MG 151 and four MG 131 weapons in the Zerstörer rôle. All versions were planned with auxiliary fuel drop tanks, but a special version was to carry a single 1,000 kg (2,205 lb) bomb under the starboard wing and a drop tank under the other wing. Somewhere among the many variants the designation Me 409 was issued (about which details are lacking), and the Me 609 was to be formed by joining two Me 309s together with a new parallel-chord wing centre section and a parallel-chord tailplane connecting the fins in the same type of layout as the Bf 109Z. The Me 609 was projected for the Zerstörer and Schnellbomber rôles, carrying up to 2,000 kg (4,410 lb) bomb load in the latter rôle.

Me 309 V1 (with DB 603A-1 engine): Span 11·04 m (36 ft 2⅝ in); length 9·46 m (31 ft 0¾ in); wing area 16·55 sq m (178·08 sq ft).
Empty weight 3,530 kg (7,784 lb); pilot 100 kg (220 lb); fuel and oil 620 kg (1,367 lb); loaded weight 4,250 kg (9,371 lb).
Maximum speed at 8,500 m (27,880 ft) 733 km/h (455 mph); cruising speed at 6,000 m (19,680 ft) 665 km/h (413 mph); landing speed 177 km/h (110 mph); climb to 8,000 m (26,240 ft) 10·1 min; service ceiling 12,000 m (39,360 ft); approximate range, without auxiliary fuel tanks, 1,400 km (870 miles).

# Messerschmitt Me 321 Gigant (Giant)

The design of the large Messerschmitt Me 321 high-wing monoplane glider was begun in 1940 in competition with the even larger Junkers Ju 322 Mammut (Mammoth). Later to be aptly named Gigant, the V1 prototype of the Me 321 made its first flight from Messerschmitt's Leipheim factory aerodrome in March 1941, being towed behind a Junkers Ju 90. The smooth, almost floating, landing of an Me 321, reminiscent of a small sports glider, belied the fact that without power-operated controls it was hard work for the pilot to control it. Nevertheless, the aircraft was put into production as the Me 321A, which was similar to the Me 321 V1 in having the pilot as the sole crew member.

The Gigant had a structure of welded steel tubing and wood with a mixed covering chiefly of fabric and wood. The rectangular-section fuselage was tall and cavernous at the forward section but, aft of the wing, tapered sharply towards the tail. Perched on top of the fuselage and on a level with the wing leading edge was the pilot's cabin, the fuselage nose sweeping down sharply in front of the cabin to permit a reasonable view. Loading was through large clamshell nose doors or through smaller doors

An Me 321 Gigant glider with four Walter ATO rocket units operating and being towed off by a Junkers Ju 290 at Augsburg. (*H. Redemann*)

on each side of the rear fuselage. The thick-section high-mounted wing was braced to the bottom of the fuselage and had a tapered planform, slight dihedral on the outer panels and auxiliary-wing type ailerons (similar to Junkers' designs) occupying most of the trailing edge. There was a very tall fin, and the tailplane, which was braced above and below, carried an elevator in two halves, both elevators and rudder being dynamically balanced. Since the glider was of relatively light construction, the weight was spread over a multi-wheel bogie undercarriage although these wheels were replaced in later Me 321B models by two large-diameter wheels fitted to the fuselage at the point of the wing bracing attachment. Another change introduced with the Me 321B was the increase in the crew from one to three and the fitting of four 7·9 mm MG 15 machine-guns. For all models, the payload could consist, for example, of either 22 tons of freight, a company of soldiers, an 88 mm Flak gun, or a small tracked vehicle.

The Gigant was towed either by a single Junkers Ju 290A-1, a trio of Messerschmitt Bf 110Cs (known as a Troika-Schlepp) or, ideally, by a single Heinkel He 111Z Zwilling (Twin). Such towing power was not

Rare picture of a Heinkel He 111Z Zwilling towing a Messerschmitt Me 321 Gigant glider. (*H. Thiele*)

always sufficient on bad terrain when the glider was fully loaded, and ATO units could be fitted in the following combinations of Walter rocket units which were jettisoned after use and recovered by parachute: eight 109-500s (*e.g.* on Me 321A-1) each giving 500 kg (1,102 lb) thrust for 30 sec, four 109-501s each giving 1,000 kg (2,205 lb) thrust for 42·5 sec, or four 109-502s each giving 1,500 kg (3,307 lb) thrust for 30 sec. There were also various schemes, some of which were tested only, for fitting multiple arrangements of Argus 109-014 pulse-jets, of the type employed in the Fieseler Fi 103 (V1) flying bomb, intended to extend the range of the glider once released from its tow.

In May 1941, the first Luftwaffe unit received the Gigant. This was the Grossraumlastensegler unit Me 321 based at Leipheim and commanded by Fritz Morzik. The unit comprised three Staffeln of six Me 321A-1s and a Motorstaffel with four trios of Bf 110Cs for towing. Ferrying material during the proposed invasion of the United Kingdom was probably set as one of this unit's duties, but it was disbanded in December 1941. The principal work of the Gigant then became ferrying material to the Eastern Front. Another unit known to have used the Me 321A-1 (*e.g.* W6-SW) was the Grossraumlastensegler-Kommando 2 (abbreviated to (GS)Kdo2), which was based at Obertraubling in January 1943 and used He 111Z towing aircraft. Altogether, about two hundred Me 321s were built at the Messerschmitt Leipheim and Obertraubling (Regensburg) factories, and in France.

Me 321B: Span 55 m (180 ft 5⅛ in); length 28·15 m (92 ft 4¼ in); wing area 300 sq m (3,228 sq ft).
Empty weight 12,000 kg (26,460 lb); loaded weight 34,000 kg (74,970 lb).
Minimum safe towing speed 160 km/h (99 mph).

# Messerschmitt Me 323 Gigant (Giant)

Early in 1941, a Messerschmitt team headed by a Dipl Ing Degel began redesign of the Me 321 glider to produce a new powered military transport aircraft. The principal modifications included structural strengthening and the provision of wing mountings for four piston engines, and, although a new twin-finned tail assembly was proposed, the single large fin and rudder of the Me 321 was retained. The first aircraft, designated Me 323 V1, was produced by modifying an Me 321 (c/n 456), which was fitted with four 1,140 hp Gnome/Rhône 14N 48/49 supercharged air-cooled radial engines and began flight tests in April 1942. Intended as prototype for the Me 323C (the A and B sub-series being used by the Me 321), the under-powered Me 323 V1 was quickly followed by the six-engined Me 323 V2. Ten other six-engined Me 323D-0s followed, being powered by the 1,140

The Messerschmitt Me 323 V2 was the first German aircraft to be fitted with six engines. (*H. Redemann*)

hp Gnome/Rhône 14N 48/49 radial, but the first major production type was the Me 323D-1. This appeared in September 1942 and had six 1,140 hp Gnome/Rhône 14N radial engines and was armed with five 7·9 mm MG 15 machine-guns in the nose and upper fuselage, and between eight and ten 7·9 mm MG 34 infantry machine-guns in the fuselage sides. The Me 323D-2, which was tested in 1943, was generally similar to the D-1 but had increased fuel capacity and two-blade wooden airscrews in place of the former three-blade metal units.

In December 1942, the improved Me 323D-6 appeared with modified engine cowlings and a revised armament of five 13 mm MG 131 guns. (Previously, in February 1942, there had been a proposal to increase the power of the Me 323 by using six 1,600 hp BMW 801A engines, but this was not taken up.) The D-6 had a crew of five and could carry 130 troops on two decks, although a great many more troops were crammed in under emergency conditions such as evacuations. Alternative flooring could also be fitted to carry loads varying from oil drums to a small tracked vehicle.

Like its namesake, the Me 321 glider, the Me 323 had clamshell nose doors and fuselage doors for loading, but all Me 323s appear to have retained the ten-wheeled bogie-type undercarriage. The Me 323 was also hard pressed to take-off under adverse ground conditions, and towing assistance was sometimes obtained from the same types of aircraft used for the Me 321. ATO units, such as eight Walter 109-500 cold-type rockets each giving 500 kg (1,102 lb) thrust for 30 sec, could be fitted as an alternative. Once in the air, the Me 323 was even more difficult to handle than its glider predecessor, and to equalize the engine powers the assistance of two flight engineers was required.

The first unit to be equipped with the Me 323 was I./KGrzbV 323 which was formed during the first ten days of November 1942. It had nine aircraft and became operational in the Middle East, where a second unit, II./KGrzbV 323, was formed in March 1943. These units operated between North Africa and Trapani, Sicily, supplying Rommel, and used mainly the Me 323D-6. Although the aircraft flew most of the time un-

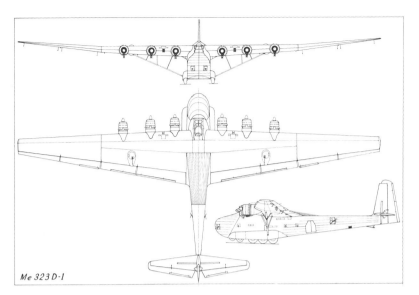

Me 323 D-1

escorted, and were formidably armed, on 22 April, 1943, there was a disastrous loss when 21 loaded Me 323s were shot down. This disaster occurred because the aircraft were ferrying fuel, and many went down in flames. In another instance a Martin Marauder of No. 14 Squadron, RAF, shot down an Me 323 in July 1943. This attack took place north-west of Cap Corse on the northern tip of Corsica, and, although the Me 323 flew on at sea level after three engines were knocked out, it was finally shattered with its full load of troops against the Corsican coastal foothills.

During 1943, the Leipheim factory produced 19 examples of a new version, the Me 323E-1. This version had six Gnome/Rhône 14R radial engines with the increased power of 1,200 hp each, and the aircraft length was increased by 0·45 m (1 ft 5¾ in). The armament was increased by adding two HDL 151 gun turrets with a 20 mm MG 151/20 gun in each and the crew was increased to seven. The Me 323E-2 was similar to the E-1 but had a low-drag EDL 151 gun turret. A major redesign occurred with the Me 323E-2/U1, which had six 1,340 hp Junkers Jumo liquid-cooled engines with nacelles similar in form to those of the Heinkel He 111. Furthermore, there was another power turret with an MG 131 gun fitted in

An early production Me 323D (possibly the V12).

A standard Me 323E-2 transport dwarfs the Bf 108 beneath its wing.

the nose and an MG 131 in the rear of each inboard and outboard engine nacelle, while MG 131s were standardized as the fuselage side guns.

January 1944 saw the I. and II./TG 5 placed under the command of the general transport force on the Eastern Front with a few Ju 52/3ms supplementing the Gigant force. Other transport aircraft were gradually acquired and, by March 1944, I./TG 5 was supplementing its Me 323Es with Arado Ar 232s and Italian Savoia Marchetti S.M. 82s, while II./TG 5 had Ju 52/3ms in addition to its Me 323Ds and Es.

During this early 1944 period, Messerschmitt had to divert its major effort to the production of the Me 262 turbojet aircraft, and Degel's team therefore transferred to the Zeppelin factory at Friedrichshafen to continue Gigant development. Here, a few Me 323E-2s were modified to take six 1,350 hp Junkers Jumo 211R engines, and these aircraft were redesignated Me 323F-1. Through gradual development, the empty and normal loaded weights of the Me 323 had been increased by 13·5 per cent and 25·5 per cent respectively when comparing the F-1 with the earlier D-1 version. The projected ZMe 323G had six 1,320 hp Gnome/Rhône 14R 4/5 radial engines, and a version of this type with a butterfly tail was projected jointly by Zeppelin and the French Sud-Ouest concern under the designation ZSO 523. Other projected variants were the ZMe 423, based on the Me 323F-1, and the ZMe 323H, based on the Me 323E, with a greatly increased payload obtained at the expense of speed and range. Although production was planned into 1945, it gradually fell off and stopped in April 1944, and the Me 323s were increasingly replaced by other transport aircraft. Total production amounted to 198 machines. So far as is known, the Me 323 story ended in June 1944 when the TG 5 Gruppen disappeared from the records, after transferring to Luftflotte 4 control in May 1944.

Me 323D-6: Span 55 m (180 ft 5$\frac{3}{8}$ in); length 28·15 m (92 ft 4$\frac{1}{4}$ in); wing area 300 sq m (3,228 sq ft).

Empty weight 27,330 kg (60,260 lb); normal loaded weight 43,000 kg (94,815 lb).

Maximum speed at sea level 285 km/h (177 mph); cruising speed at sea level 218 km/h (136 mph); initial rate of climb 216 m/min (708 ft/min); range 1,100 km (683 miles).

# Messerschmitt Me 328

Although the Messerschmitt Me 328 was never destined to become operational or even technically successful, it is of interest as one of the few piloted aircraft to fly solely on pulse-jet power, and, in view of its early lack of promise, the diversity of design proposals is surprising.

The basic design was first started by Messerschmitt late in 1942 as a cheap and simple high-speed aircraft for low-level bombing and possibly also for the emergency day-fighter rôle. Also considered by the Messerschmitt engineers was work done the previous year by the DFS, in which various layouts of the Messerschmitt design study P.1079 (which proposed various jet engine installations in a single-seat aircraft) were examined for their possible application as parasite or hook-on components of larger aircraft.

It was not until the beginning of 1943, when the fortunes of the Luftwaffe were declining on all fronts and when Allied landings in Europe were obviously imminent, that serious development began. This was handed in March to Jacob Schweyer Segelflugzeugbau which worked in co-operation with both the DFS and Messerschmitt. Final construction of the Me 328 was planned to be largely of wood, but, for the first test airframes, various composite construction methods were tried.

The general layout of the Me 328, which in overall size was even smaller than the Heinkel He 162, was that of a mid-wing aircraft, the circular-section fuselage having a raised cockpit canopy with a rear fairing extending back and down to the base of the fin. The tailplane was mounted

Before fitting pulse-jet units to the Messerschmitt Me 328 fighter-bomber prototypes, gliding trials were conducted. A cable-type catapult is the method of launching here. Points of interest are the take-off wheels falling away and the extended, leading-edge, slots. Curiously, the pilot appears to be wearing a trilby hat and trench coat!

halfway up the fin, and the equi-tapered wing had leading-edge slots and inboard landing flaps. Provision was made to alter the span of the wings, for test purposes, by means of detachable tips and, since the pulse-jet powerplants could provide no auxiliary drives, electrical power was obtained from wing-mounted air-driven generators. Self-sealing fuel tanks were housed in the rear fuselage and in the nose, and the pilot was protected by some armour plate and a bullet-proof windscreen. An extendible skid sufficed for landing gear.

This Me 328 prototype (RL-TY) has two pulse-jet units fitted to exhaust beyond the airframe but, although acoustic effects were minimized, vibration effects on pilot and airframe were still bad. (*USAF*)

While construction was proceeding at the Jacob Schweyer works, tests with models were made in the Messerschmitt wind-tunnel at Augsburg to determine the best positions for the proposed two Argus pulse-jet power plants. Initially, these were to be mounted on short outriggers, one on each side of the fuselage, with the ends of the tailpipes passing beneath and beyond the tailplane; this arrangement would have obviated the acoustic effects of the pulse-jets on the airframe, but, apparently, physical vibration made the design of suitable attachment mountings difficult. Of various wing positions investigated, one was settled upon where the pulse-jets were below the wings at quarter-span, the tailpipes to terminate in front of, and below, the tailplane. In this position, the design of vibration-absorbing mountings was easier to resolve, but the rear fuselage and tail assembly were later to receive the detrimental effects of the pulsating efflux. Later tests were made using two or four pulse-jets in the hope of minimizing these effects, and, in these cases, the tubes were to be mounted two on each side of the rear fuselage beneath the tailplane to exhaust aft of the tailplane. This, surely, was the best way of utilizing the powerplant and the principle of having the tailpipe extending beyond the airframe was exactly that applied to the Fieseler Fi 103 (V 1) flying bomb.

The main criterion guiding the Me 328 programme was to produce a cheap rapidly-built aircraft in large numbers, and there appears to have been little concerted effort towards designing for a specific mission. It was estimated from actual specimens that approximately four Me 328 could be built for every Focke-Wulf Fw 190 or Messerschmitt Bf 109

An Me 328 prototype at the DFS for trials with early models of the Argus pulse-jet. Acoustic effects from the exhausts of the pulse-jet damaged the rear fuselage and tail unit.

this being largely due to the very much simpler power units of the Me 328.

The two basic versions, the Me 328A and Me 328B, were initially intended as day fighter and low-level bomber respectively. The DFS and Jacob Schweyer produced between them ten test aircraft in all (V1 to V10), and the V1 was mounted, without pulse-jet ducts, above a Dornier Do 217E (JT-FL) for tests. For the first flights, forces acting upon the Me 328 were measured while it was attached to the Dornier carrier, but later it was released for its first gliding trials, at Hörsching in Austria. Releases were made at altitudes varying from 3,000 m (9,840 ft) to 6,000 m (19,680 ft), and testing was performed at speeds of 145 km/h (90 mph) to 745 km/h (465 mph). Although these tests showed the aircraft to be aerodynamically poor, its supposed overall merit was considered sufficient to proceed with the work; thereafter, however, the aircraft was seen more as an expendable piloted missile from which the pilot baled out after aiming at important precision targets, such as ships or formations of day-bombers.

Early powered flight trials did nothing to enhance the reputation of the Me 328 or, for that matter, the pulse-jet, since several accidents occurred as a result of structural failures in the rear of the airframe caused by the pulse-jet acoustics. The powered aircraft was assisted on take-off by either a three-wheeled Lippisch-Latscherwagen with the Madelung KL-12 cable-type catapult or by an Rh B rocket-propelled rail carriage, and landings were made upon an extendible skid. The two methods of air launching were from a rig above the carrier aircraft or from a towing pole at its rear.

As a pure fighter, where bomber protection or increased radius of action was the aim, pole-towing was favoured and, in this case, the fighter was to make a ground landing rather than a reconnection to the parent aircraft.

563

The Me 328A-1 was to use two wing-mounted pulse-jets while the Me 328A-2 was to use four fuselage-mounted pulse-jets. Two projected towed hook-on fighters were the Me 328A-1 and A-2, intended to be used with the Heinkel He 177 or Messerschmitt Me 264 as protection on long-range bomber sorties, but, as the powered tests with the Me 328 showed, the pulse-jet was of little use to a fighter, because its power fell off rapidly with altitude and its operational ceiling was below that of Allied aircraft. With this disenchantment came proposals to use Junkers Ju 88s and Ju 388s to tow unpowered glider-fighter versions of the Me 328 into combat positions.

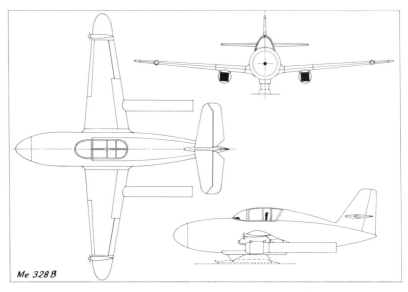

Me 328 B

Thus, the A-series was abandoned and reworked into fast bomber projects designated the B-series; at a time when fighters were urgently needed to defend Germany, the impetus for fast bomber projects came from Hitler's obsession with attack. When carried to the target zone by a carrier aircraft, the final run-in was to be made at low level or, alternatively, the Me 328B's bomb could be of the stand-off type and launched from a distance in cases where the carrier aircraft was unable to approach close enough to the target. Proposed carrier aircraft varied from the Junkers Ju 388 to the Heinkel He 177 and were to carry the Me 328B in the Mistel arrangement. Operations were even foreseen where the Me 328B might return to the carrier aircraft after the bombing sortie, refuel and then be operated in the fighter protection rôle.

Since the problems brought about by the pulse-jets were never fully resolved, the whole Me 328 programme was in danger of being written off. To guard against this possibility, a further version was proposed, designated the Me 328C, which was to be powered by a Junkers Jumo 004B turbojet installed in the fuselage. In this case, of course, the aircraft partially lost its only virtues—cheapness and simplicity.

Finally, the unpowered version of the Me 328B was adopted by 5./KG 200 for use as a piloted glider bomb. Following completion of the gliding tests, a production order was placed in April 1944 with a factory in Thuringia, but no aircraft materialized and the attention of 5./KG 200 turned to the piloted V1 (Fieseler Fi 103R). After release from its parent aircraft, the Me 328B bomb would have glided for the requisite range and then steepened its gliding angle to 12 to 1 for the attack run, when the speed would have reached 710 km/h (441 mph).

Me 328A-1 (with two wing-mounted pulse-jets): Total pulse-jet thrust at sea level 600 kg (1,320 lb).
Span 6·4 m (21 ft); length 6.83 m (22 ft 4$\frac{7}{8}$ in); height 2·1 m (6 ft 10$\frac{5}{8}$ in); wing area 7·5 sq m (80·7 sq ft).
Loaded weight 2,200 kg (4,840 lb); fuel weight 290 kg (638 lb).
Maximum speed at sea level 755 km/h (470 mph); landing speed 165 km/h (103 mph); rate of climb at 4,000 m (13,120 ft) 16 m/sec (3,150 ft/min) ; radius of action 770 km (480 miles).
Armament two MG 151/20.

Me 328A-2 (with four fuselage-mounted pulse-jets): Total pulse-jet thrust at sea level 1,200 kg (2,640 lb).
Span 8·5 m (27 ft 10$\frac{5}{8}$ in); length 8·63 m (28 ft 2$\frac{5}{8}$ in); height 2·1 m (6 ft 10$\frac{5}{8}$ in); wing area 12 sq m (129·1 sq ft).
Loaded weight 3,800 kg (8,360 lb); fuel weight 1,520 kg (3,345 lb).
Maximum speed at sea level 920 km/h (572 mph); landing speed 145 km/h (90 mph); rate of climb at 4,000 m (13,120 ft) 25 m/sec (4,920 ft/min); radius of action 1,400 km (870 miles).
Armament two MK 103.

Me 328B-1*: Total pulse-jet thrust at sea level 600 kg (1,320 lb).
Span 6·4 m (21 ft); length 6·83 m (22 ft 4$\frac{7}{8}$ in); height 2·5 m (8 ft 2$\frac{3}{8}$ in); wing area 7·5 sq m (80·7 sq ft).
Loaded weight 2,700 kg (5,940 lb); fuel weight 290 kg (638 lb); bomb load 500 kg (1,100 lb).
Maximum speed at sea level 680 km/h (423 mph); landing speed 165 km/h (103 mph); radius of action 630 km (392 miles).
Armament two MG 151/20.

Me 328B-2*: Total pulse-jet thrust at sea level 800 kg (1,760 lb).
Span 8·5 m (27 ft 10$\frac{5}{8}$ in); length 8·63 m (28 ft 2$\frac{5}{8}$ in); height 2·5 m (8 ft 2$\frac{3}{8}$ in); wing area 12 sq m (129·1 sq ft).
Loaded weight 4,730 kg (10,405 lb); fuel weight 1,520 kg (3,345 lb); bomb load 1,400 kg (3,080 lb).
Maximum speed at sea level 590 km/h (370 mph); landing speed 142 km/h (88 mph); radius of action 800 km (497 miles).
Armament two MK 103.

*The Me 328B-1 and B-2 were to have been powered by two pulse-jets or four providing the same total power. Figures for radius of action include an allowance for the parasite portion of a mission.

The Messerschmitt Me 210 V13 made its first flight on 17 April, 1941, and acted as a development aircraft for the proposed Me 310.

# Messerschmitt Me 410 Hornisse (Hornet)

When it became obvious that the Messerschmitt Me 210 would never be a success, Messerschmitt proposed a new high-altitude development with more powerful engines and a pressurized cockpit, the Me 310. The aircraft was to be powered by two 1,750 hp Daimler-Benz DB 603A engines driving four-blade airscrews and to have a span of 18 m (59 ft 0$\frac{2}{3}$ in). It had been anticipated that the Me 310 would have a maximum speed of 675 km/h (419 mph) at 11,000 m (36,091 ft), but it was abandoned in favour of the Me 410.

A much less radical design, the Me 410 Hornisse was essentially an Me 210 incorporating all the latter's modifications but with DB 603A engines. The installation of these units necessitated a 20 cm (8 in) increase in the length of the cowlings, but apart from this the Me 410 was almost indistinguishable from its predecessor. During 1942, six Me 210As were taken from the assembly lines and converted to Me 410 standard, and following successful tests the first real prototype was completed. Towards the end of 1942, the Me 410 V1 (DI-NW) made it first flight and the RLM placed a large order for the type.

The first production model was the Me 410A-1 light bomber with a defensive armament of two MG 17 machine-guns, two MG 151/20 cannon and an MG 131 machine-gun in each FDL 131 remote-controlled barbette. Internal bomb load could comprise two 1,000 kg (2,205 lb) SD 1000 bombs, but the more usual combination was eight 50 kg (110 lb) SC 50 bombs internally and an additional four SC 50s under the wing centre section.

The Me 410A-1/U1 was a photographic-reconnaissance variant without the two MG 151/20 cannon and having provision for an Rb 20/30, Rb 50/30 or Rb 75/30 camera in the bomb bay. The A-1/U2 was a destroyer

566

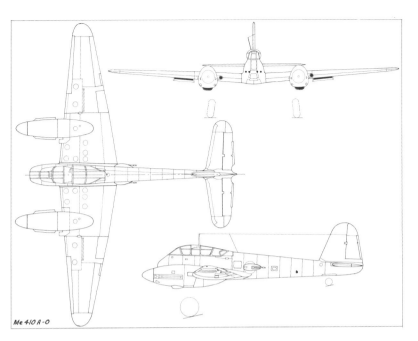

Me 410 A-0

with a bulged wooden container, known as the WB 151A, installed in the bomb bay, mounting two extra MG 151/20 weapons. The Me 410A-1/U4 was a specialized bomber-destroyer with a 50 mm BK 5 gun beneath the fuselage. Adapted from the L/60 weapon carried by the Sd.Kfz 234 series of armoured cars, the gun weighed some 900 kg (1,984 lb), severely reducing manoeuvrability, carried 21 rounds and is reputed to have had a recoil pressure of some seven tons.

The Me 410A-2 was a destroyer with the two MG 17 machine-guns replaced by two 30 mm MK 103 cannon mounted in the bomb bay. The A-2/U1 was similar to the A-1/U1, the A-2/U2 was a night fighter having radar equipment, and the A-2/U4 was similar to the A-1/U4. The Me 410A-3 was a reconnaissance variant with provision for three cameras but without the MG 17 weapons.

An Me 410A-1 of the Luftwaffe. (*R. C. Seeley*)

Me 410As were delivered simultaneously in May 1943 to three Luftwaffe units: 5./KG 2 at Lechfeld, 2.(F)/122 at Trapani and III./ZG 1 at Gerbini. The two latter units had previously been equipped with the Me 210A, but 5./KG 2 converted from the Dornier Do 217. The Staffel was later combined with the remnants of II./KG 40 (which had also operated the Do 217) to form the Me 410 equipped V./KG 2.

The Messerschmitt 410A-1s of V./KG 2 (which comprised Staffeln 14, 15, and 16) operated mainly at night against targets in the British Isles. The fast new fighter-bomber provided the RAF night-fighter crews with a tough adversary, the first loss being recorded on 13 July, 1943, when U5-KG (c/n 238) was shot down by a Mosquito. The type was later to play a significant part in the bombing of London during the early months of 1944.

The second bomber unit to equip with the Me 410 was I./KG 51 Edelweiss, which withdrew from Russia to Illesheim in May 1943 to exchange its Junkers Ju 88s for the new aircraft. It received its first Me 410As late in June but was not recorded as fully operational until December 1943 at Beauvais. The unit operated some fighter-bomber sorties over the British Isles, and was later very active against the Allied landings in Normandy. During the autumn of 1944 the unit was withdrawn from operations and re-equipped with the Me 262 jet bomber.

In April 1944 the first Me 410Bs were delivered. The Me 410B-1 and B-2 were basically similar to the A-1 and A-2 apart from being powered by two 1,900 hp Daimler-Benz DB 603G engines. The Me 410B-2/U1, B-2/U2 and B-2/U4 carried similar additional weapons to those of the

Close-up of the nose of an Me 410B-6 fitted with FuG 200 Hohentwiel radar. (*H. Thiele*)

568

A-series conversions. A variety of R-series field conversion packs were also developed for the Me 410B, most being concerned with additional armament.

The Me 410B-3 was a reconnaissance aircraft similar to the A-3 apart from the more powerful engines, and the Me 410B-5 was a torpedo-bomber which could carry two 400 kg (882 lb) BT 400 or two 200 kg (441 lb) BT 200 torpedoes. With the weapons-bay fuel tank removed, the Me 410B-5 could carry a 900 kg (1,984 lb) LT 5b torpedo. The Me 410B-6 was a specialized anti-shipping aircraft carrying FuG 200 Hohentwiel search radar and a forward-firing armament of two 20 mm MG 151/20 cannon, two 30 mm MK 103 guns and two 13 mm MG 131 machine-guns. The final projected B-series aircraft were the Me 410B-7 and B-8, respectively day and night reconnaissance aircraft, but neither was built.

Further projected variants included the Me 410C high-altitude fighter. Powered by two 2,000 hp Daimler-Benz DB 603JZ engines in annular cowlings, the Me 410C was to have been fitted with the high aspect ratio wing originally proposed for the Me 310. The Me 410C was replaced by the Me 410D before the former could be built, the latter aircraft having wooden outer wing panels in the quest to conserve strategic materials. The Me 410D, which was also projected with 1,810 hp BMW 801TJ radials and 1,800 hp Junkers Jumo 213E/JZ engines, both with turbo-superchargers, was not built.

A proposed interim model, the Me 410H, was also projected in 1944. This was to have a new centre section which would increase overall span to 23 m (75 ft 5$\frac{1}{2}$ in) and be powered by 1,900 hp DB 603G engines. Armament was to have comprised two 30 mm MK 103, two 30 mm MK 108 and two 20 mm MG 151/20 cannon, with the 13 mm MG 131 machine-guns retained in the fuselage gun barbettes. The Me 410H was abandoned in September 1944 when production of all other variants of the Hornisse ceased. Total production was 1,160 aircraft.

*Wartime operational units:* 3.(F)/22, 1.(F)/33, 1. and 4.(F)/121, 1., 2. and 5.(F)/122, FAGr 1 and 3, II. and III./ZG 1, I., II., III. and IV./ZG 26, I., II. and III./ZG 76, I./NJG 1, I./NJG 5, V./KG 2, I. and II./KG 51, Erprobungskommando 25.

Me 410A-1/U2: Span 16·4 m (53 ft 7$\frac{3}{4}$ in); length 12·4 m (40 ft 8$\frac{1}{2}$ in); height 4·3 m (14 ft 0$\frac{1}{2}$ in); wing area 36·2 sq m (389·6 sq ft).

Empty weight 6,150 kg (13,560 lb); loaded weight 10,650 kg (23,483 lb).

Maximum speed at 6,700 m (21,982 ft) 625 km/h (388 mph); climb to 6,700 m (21,982 ft) 10·7 min; service ceiling 10,000 m (32,810 ft); maximum range 2,330 km (1,447 miles).

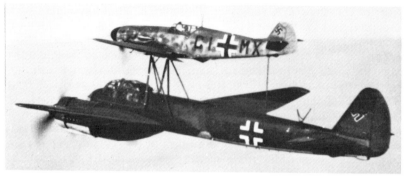

A Messerschmitt Bf 109F (CI-MX) connected to a Junkers Ju 88A-4. Testing with this Mistel combination was begun by the DFS in July 1943.

# Mistel (Mistletoe) Composite Aircraft

During the Second World War, various ways were found of employing whole bomber aircraft as large bombs. The major effort in this field was made by the Germans, but, before discussing this, mention must be made of some of those used by other countries. The earliest guided bomber appears to have been used by the Italians, who used a Savoia Marchetti S.M.79 bomber, packed with explosives and fitted with radio-control equipment, against British warships off the Algerian coast on 13 August, 1942. The aircraft was set on course by a pilot, who then baled out, but the mission failed due to a radio fault. In August 1944, the Americans used old Boeing B-17 Flying Fortresses containing nine tons of explosives and napalm to blast what was left of the massive concrete A4 rocket bunkers on the French coast, these operations being more in the nature of experimental demolition work. In a very much more sombre vein, the Japanese used pilot-guided bombers in their early Kamikaze operations, which began on 13 October, 1944.

The fundamental difference of the German method of using guided bombers was that a guiding pilot sat in a separate aircraft attached above the unmanned bomber, guided the composite aircraft towards the target and at the last minute detached his aircraft from the bomber. The lower component of such composite aircraft became known in general as Mistel (Mistletoe) aircraft while the whole combination was known unofficially as Vater und Sohn (Father and Son). The development of such aircraft was shared primarily by the DFS (Deutsches Forschungsinstitut für Segelflug) and Junkers.

In 1940, the DFS began studying the problem of coupling one aircraft to another in flight so that one could tow the other. The incentive for this work was the desire to provide escort fighters on long-range missions when

570

a fighter could detach from an aircraft under attack and, after the action, recouple and refuel. This work had its unsuccessful outcome in the Messerschmitt Me 328. Another application was that a heavily-loaded aircraft could have fuel pumped into it from a tanker-aircraft after take-off. The first experiments to couple aircraft in flight were made in the spring of 1940 when a Heinkel He 46 was used to tow a Gotha Go 150. Later, a Junkers-Ju 52 towed a Focke-Wulf Fw 58 Weihe. The results of these experiments were handed over to Junkers, who made their own tests with a Ju 90 towing an Fw 58 Weihe, and the DFS finalized their work in the summer of 1941.

DFS then turned its attention to the problem of towing heavier loads, and, in January 1942, the Mistel concept (which had been projected earlier by Department F of the DFS) was adopted for development. Proposals at this time, made chiefly by the Junkers test pilot Flugkapitän Siegfried Holzbauer, that old Ju 88 aircraft should be converted into Mistel components for offensive use, failed to interest the RLM. Nevertheless, practical experiments began in 1942 under Fritz Stamer of the DFS, and a DFS 230 glider was used as the lower component with a Klemm Kl 35, Focke-Wulf Fw 56 Stösser, and, later, a Messerschmitt Bf 109E aircraft mounted above. It should be noted that experiments at this time were still investigating the problems of air-towing loads, but their success led the RLM to order early in 1943 a prototype combination of a Ju 88A-4 and a Bf 109F to investigate the problems of using the Mistel in an attack rôle.

The DFS then designed suitable connecting structures for the two

A Mistel 1, comprising a Junkers Ju 88A-4 guided by a Messerschmitt Bf 109F-4. Final tests of the hollow-charge warhead had been made by April 1944.

aircraft whereby the main forces acting on them were transmitted to the main spars. Coupling links could be explosively or mechanically disconnected, but, although the mechanical type could be used many times, they needed considerable manufacturing time, the first set taking ten weeks from March to May 1943. The task of developing a guidance and control system was tackled jointly by Junkers, Patin and the DFS. The firm of Patin actually produced the guidance equipment under the direction of the DFS, which also did the testing. Testing of the prototype Ju 88A-4/Bf 109F-4 (CI-MX) combination began at the end of July and was successfully completed by October 1943, by which time 15 more Mistel combinations of the same aircraft types were on order from Junkers under the weapon code-name Beethoven.

The steering and control system operated as follows. A master compass, S-compass, and Askania or Patin three-axes autopilot, were installed in the rear of the bomber and this equipment steered the combination in normal flight with the fighter's controls remaining free. The fighter pilot had two thumb-operated control buttons connected with the equipment in the bomber, the button on the control column operating the bomber's rudder and ailerons simultaneously, and the button on a new centre panel operating the bomber's elevators. There was also a second control method, for use during take-off and for making more rapid course alterations, whereby the normal controls of the fighter operated in unison the control surfaces of both aircraft. Either control method could be selected as required by operating a switch. One advantage which became clear early with the Mistel method, as opposed to towing, was that it was easier for the pilot during a long flight.

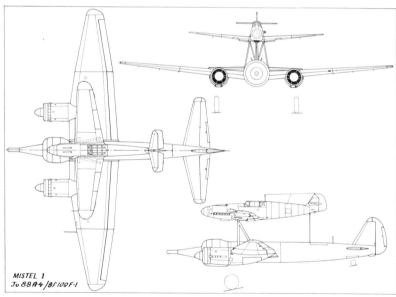

MISTEL 1
Ju 88A-4/Bf 109F-1

From the conversion point of view, most of the considerable amount of work had to be done on the bomber component. There was no need to strengthen the fighter, except for a small section at the tail, but the bomber required considerable double-skinning, additional formers plus steel channels. There was then the removal of most of the internal equipment, complete re-wiring, fitting the new control equipment, attachment of superstructure, extra fuselage fuel tanks, and new engines. Ju 88 aircraft converted for Mistel use were first produced with a fairly standard nose section, attached by quick-release bolts, and the bare essentials to accommodate two crew for flight testing and/or training. To prepare the aircraft for operations, the nose section was replaced by a warhead using the same attachment points, crew accommodation was removed and final internal connections made. The 3,500 kg (7,715 lb) warhead was of the hollow-charge type containing 1,725 kg (3,800 lb) of high explosive (70 per cent Hexogen and 30 per cent TNT) and an impact fuse which was primed about three seconds after the aircraft separated. The 1,000 kg (2,205 lb) steel core of this warhead had a theoretical armour penetration of 7·5 m (24 ft 7¼ in); in actual tests, this core burst through some 18·5 m (60 ft 8⅜ in) of concrete. Successful tests with hollow-charge warheads had been made against the French battleship *Oran* late in 1943, and the final Mistel warhead tests were made in April 1944.

At about the same time a unit comprising about five pilots and designated 2./KG 101 was formed under the command of Hptm Horst Rudat and this unit transferred to Junkers at Nordhausen for instruction. For this training, Ju 88A-4/Bf 109F-4 combinations from the prototype batch were used in their Mistel S1 training form, the operational form being designated Mistel 1. The instructors were Siegfried Holzbauer and Flugkapitän Horst Lux, and the first aiming trials were made by Rudat against the Danish island of Moen. With the instruction completed, Rudat set up a training base with five Mistels at Kolberg in the Baltic.

On 16 April, 1944, the Operations Staff of the Luftwaffe completed its top secret paper covering the operational possibilities of the Mistletoe, in which it was deduced that worthwhile targets would include the major fleet anchorages of Gibraltar, Scapa Flow, and Leningrad. Gibraltar and Leningrad were partially ruled out, however, because of the extreme range of the former and the improbability of launching a surprise attack on the latter. Although Scapa Flow was heavily defended and no fighter escort could be provided because of extreme range, it was considered that this target could be attacked provided the Mistels had the element of surprise. The base of operations was to be Grove airfield in Denmark, 772 km (480 miles) from Scapa Flow, and the Mistels were to fly at low altitude, guided to the target by 'Funkboje Schwan' radio buoys previously laid down in the North Sea.

While such plans as these were being considered, however, the D-Day landings enforced the transference of 2./KG 101's aircraft to St Dizier from where five Mistels made the first sortie on the night of 24/25 June,

1944, to attack invasion shipping in the Seine Bay. For this sortie, an escort of Bf 109G-6s was provided by I./JG 301 and the first Mistel attack was made by Feldwebel Saalfeld. German sources state that four Mistels hit ships but the other failed and had to be jettisoned due to the impracticability of landing a fully-loaded Mistel combination. Incidentally, because of their lack of defence, all Mistels were operated at night. The combination could be flown on the power of two or three engines (using fuel from the bomber only) according to the speed and range required.

On 9/10 August, Mistels attacked shipping in the English Channel but without success. One Ju 88 lower component crashed at Binley, near Andover, and was completely destroyed, although RAF Intelligence gathered some information from the pieces. At about this time, Mistels were flown to Grove for the Scapa Flow attack, and 2./KG 101 was redesignated III./KG 66 with the addition of Beleuchter- and Ergänzungsstaffeln (illumination and replacement). In October 1944, five Mistels took off for the Scapa Flow attack, but three crashed in the Teutoburger Wald and the remaining two failed to find the target.

Operational Mistel 1 combinations being prepared for action. (*A. Price*)

Another redesignation was made on 10 November when III./KG 66 became II./KG 200 with three Staffeln as follows: 5.(Bel)/KG 200 with the Ju 88S and the Ju 188A and E; 6./KG 200 under Oblt Walter Pilz with the Mistel 1 and 3; and 7.(Erg)/KG 200 with the Mistel S1 and S2. Also on hand were a certain number of Bf 109 and Fw 190 escort fighters.

The Mistel 2 comprised the combination Ju 88G-1/Fw 190F-8 (or A-6). Seventy-five examples of the Mistel 2 were ordered initially, and then, in December 1944, a further 50 were ordered.

In November, the Scapa Flow attack plan was finally abandoned and Unternehmen Eisenhammer (Operation Iron Hammer) to destroy Soviet power stations, was planned. In view of the fact that the USSR had little radar defence, this plan was considered feasible with about 100 Mistels having drop tanks to increase their range. Warhead tests were made at E-Stelle Udetfeld, and it was decided that two Mistels could destroy a small power station and six Mistels a large one. Originally it was planned to fly from airfields in East Prussia, but Oranienburg, Parchim, Lärz, Marienehe and Peenemünde airfields had to be substituted later.

A Mistel 2 (Ju 88G-1/Fw 190F-8) of KG 30 at Oranienburg in April 1945. The so-called Elefantenrüssel (Elephant's trunk) fuse nose has been removed from the warhead. Fuel drop tanks for both aircraft can be clearly seen. The pilot in the fighter is running up the bomber's engines.

For II./KG 200 to undertake Unternehmen Eisenhammer, a special training programme was launched with the planned completion date of 1 February, 1945. As already mentioned, Mistels were first prepared in a form suitable for testing and training, so there was no lack of training aircraft. In the training rôle, a safety bumper was fitted above the bomber to prevent the nose of the fighter touching during separation, because the datum line of the fighter was inclined about 15 deg towards the bomber and produced problems for the trainees.

New versions of the Mistel, which appeared during this period, were the Mistel 3A (Ju 88A-4/Fw 190A-8), Mistel 3B (Ju 88H-4/Fw 190A-8) and Mistel 3C (Ju 88G-10/Fw 190F-8), and the large Junkers factory on Bernberg airfield was producing them from new aircraft.

A modification which had appeared by this time was the addition of a third, jettisonable, mainwheel unit which was attached to heavily-reinforced cover plates below the fuselage of the Ju 88. This addition became necessary because a number of burst tyres had resulted from the overloaded combinations during take-offs.

On 9 March, 1945, four Mistels and five Ju 188s from II./KG 200 attacked the Görlitz bridges over the Neisse. One Mistel crashed in flames over Belzig, the pilot baling out. At 10·06 hr, one Mistel hit the south bridge but a second one missed. The fourth Mistel then hit the north bridge, and one Ju 188 was shot down by flak. The night of 25/26 March saw four Mistels attacking the Rhine bridges with unknown results, and considerably more Mistels were used against bridges over the Vistula.

575

This Mistel S 3C trainer (Ju 88G-10/Fw 190F-8) was found by a Cavalry group of the US Ninth Army on an airfield between Stassfurt and Bernburg on 16 April, 1945. The Ju 88G-10 had c/n 450066. Note the safety bumper fitted below the nose of the Fw 190.
(*US Army*)

Although some 82 Mistels were ready for use on 26 March, these were soon whittled down to 56 in bridge attacks by the time Unternehmen Eisenhammer was to be finally launched on 28/29 March, 1945. Eisenhammer never happened, however, because all efforts on the Eastern Front had by then to be directed to halting the rapid advance of the Red Army. To assist in this, therefore, Mistel aircraft were used in the rôle of bridge-destroyers as the aircraft became available, and there were never sufficient available for a largescale attack.

A Mistel from KG 30 (part of which joined with II./KG 200 in April 1945) together with a Ju 88S from I./KG 66 and an He 111 from I./KG 4 successfully attacked a bridge target on the night of 7/8 April. On the following night, another five Mistels from KG 30 were sent to attack a target near Warsaw, but four were shot down and one pilot was lost. The next day saw the destruction by USAAF bombers of the Mistel base at Rechlin-Lärz, but Mistel bridge attacks continued from other bases. On 11/12 April, bridges over the Bober and Quais rivers were attacked; on 12/13 April, bridges over the Oder and Küstrin; and on 14/15 April, bridges over the Oder again. In the attack on the Küstrin bridges, Mistels were flown from Peenemünde led by Lt Hans Altrogge who flew ahead in a Ju 88S as pathfinder. On this particular occasion, the Fw 190s strafed the flak positions after separating from the Mistels, but there were no successes. The final Mistel attack took place on 16 April when the composites were used along with Henschel Hs 293 missiles (possibly from Versuchs-kommando KG 200) against Soviet bridgeheads.

Given that a Mistel formation reached its target area without mishap (there were, for example, four out of a formation of six Mistels shot down by Mustangs on 3 February, 1945, southeast of Hamburg), it was by no means certain that hits would be achieved on the target, this fact having been already illustrated. Being aware of this soon after Mistel operations started, the RLM's technical department requested that the DFS look into the question of controlling the Mistel component to the target after separation. The DFS then took their Ju 88A-4/Bf 109F test combination and proceeded to fit wire-link control equipment similar to the Dortmund/Duisburg (FuG 207/237) equipment designed for Henschel Hs 293B air-to-ground missiles. Because the low-frequency control impulses were nearly the same as those for the three-axes autopilot, however, a special instrument had to be developed for the Ju 88. This work was being done by Institute C of the DFS, but, although nearly complete by about April 1945, the test aircraft combination was burned out at Hörsching. For more precise target control, Institute S and Department H worked on the assembly of a television guidance system (similar to that designed for the Henschel Hs 293D) whereby a camera was to be fitted to the Ju 88 and a picture of the target transmitted to a television screen in the fighter aircraft.

Junkers also played a part in further development of the Mistel system and new composites were tested during 1945. These included a long-range pathfinder version of the Mistel 3B (known as a Führungsmachine, in which the upper Fw 190A-8 fighter component could be launched for protection if necessary) and an attack Mistel consisting of a Junkers Ju 88G-7 and a Focke-Wulf Ta 152H. Two interesting fast Mistel projects were the Mistel 4 (Ju 287/Me 262) and Mistel 5 (Ju 268/Me 262 or He 162).

Arado also projected Mistel arrangements which included the combinations Ar 234C/Fi 103, Ar 234C-3/E.377, and Heinkel He 162/Arado E.377A. The Arado E.377 was projected as a simple, pilotless, mid-wing monoplane with either a 2,000 kg (4,410 lb) warhead or a modified SC 1800 bomb in the nose. It had no control surfaces, being merely aimed by the parent aircraft beneath which it was carried. The whole combination was to take-off on a special Rheinmetall-Borsig 20-ton trolley. In the case where the small Heinkel He 162 was to be the parent aircraft, the E.377A, fitted with two BMW 109-003A turbojets of its own, was to be used.

To mention three final examples of Mistel, there were the combinations of Dornier Do 217K V3/DFS 228 (reconnaissance), Focke-Wulf Ta 154/Fw 190 (attack) and Siebel Si 204/Lippisch DM-1 (planned for research).

In this section it has been discussed how the air-towing method evolved into the Mistel combination to ease the problem of carrying heavy loads. During 1944, the DFS looked further into these methods because they were inefficient due to aerodynamic interferences, structure drag, and airscrew wash, and devised a method of side-by-side attachment. In this method, the wingtips of two aircraft were to be attached, one towing the other, and no problems were expected because the necessary control equipment had already been developed for Mistel use. For initial tests, two Klemm Kl 35 aircraft were to be connected to make take-offs and landings, but, although the towing Kl 35 was modified at Prien and was ready to fly, tests were not begun.

Mistel 3C (Ju 88G-10/Fw 190F-8)*: Span 20·08 m (65 ft 10½ in); length, including nose of warhead, 18·538 m (61 ft 9⅞ in); combined wing area 72·8 sq m (783·6 sq ft).

Fuel carried in Ju 88 wings and fuselage 6,130 kg (13,515 lb); fuel carried by Fw 190, including two 540 litre (118 Imp gal) overwing tanks and one 300 litre (66 Imp gal) drop tank, 1,064 kg (2,345 lb); explosive content of warhead 1,725 kg (3,800 lb); maximum take-off weight 23,600 kg (52,038 lb).

Maximum speed approximately 550 km/h (342 mph); cruising speed at sea level 320 km/h (199 mph), at 4,000 m (13,120 ft) 340 km/h (211 mph); typical impact speed of lower component after a dive at about 15 deg 595 km/h (370 mph); maximum range with 8,190 litres (1,800 Imp gal) of fuel 4,100 km (2,545 miles).

Mistel 5 (Ar 234C-3/Ar E.377)*: E.377 unpowered lower component: Span 12·2 m (40 ft); wing area 25 sq m (269 sq ft).

Airframe weight 2,000 kg (4,410 lb); warhead 2,000 kg (4,410 lb); ballast or incendiary weight 500 kg (1,105 lb); fuel 4,500 kg (9,920 lb); flying weight 9,000 kg (19,845 lb); flying weight of 'Father' Ar 234C-3 11,000 kg (24,255 lb); combination take-off weight less Rh-B trolley 20,000 kg (44,100 lb); combination weight at target at maximum range 13,750 kg (30,315 lb); no other details available.

\* Most figures are estimated.

# Siebel Fh 104 Hallore and Si 204

In 1934 Hans Klemm set up a new factory at Halle (Saale) for the production of all-metal military aircraft. The factory, known as the Flugzeugbau Halle GmbH, was ready in 1936 and took on the work of producing the Klemm Kl 104, a five-seat light transport aircraft designed at Klemm's Böblingen factory to the same specification as the Ago Ao 192 and Gotha Go 146. The Kl 104 was redesignated Fh 104 and later became

The Siebel Fh 104 V2, D-IMCH, light transport prototype. The original design was by Klemm. (*R. C. Seeley*)

An Fh 104 Hallore (GM-AG) about to air-tow an auxiliary fuel tank. Most of the small number of Fh 104s were employed by the Luftwaffe on communication and liaison duties.

known as the Hallore.* The prototype Fh 104, D-IQPG, made its first flight in 1937 and became known as the Siebel Fh 104 in that year, when Klemm handed over the Halle factory to Fritz W. Siebel at the earliest opportunity and went back to his light aircraft work at Böblingen.

Presenting clean lines and a neat appearance, the Fh 104 had a fuselage and tail unit of duralumin construction, the cabin having a short, rounded nose, a stepped windscreen and side windows. The low-mounted tapered wing had a wooden two-spar structure covered with plywood and housed two fuel tanks. Flaps were fitted and there were trim tabs on the rudder and two-piece elevator. Hydraulic power was used to retract the undercarriage, the main members of which swung back into the lower part of the two engine nacelles. The Fh 104 V1 and V2 (D-IMCH) prototypes were each powered by two 270 hp Hirth HM 508C air-cooled, inverted-vee engines with two-blade airscrews. The principal difference between these two prototypes was that the second machine had a redesigned cockpit screen and single, instead of twin, undercarriage oleo legs.

By 1938, the Fh 104 was gaining a reputation for itself by winning the main trophy and other prizes in the Italian Littorio Rally and, in September 1938, by flying 6,200 km (3,850 miles) in the Europa-Rundflug competition. These successes brought about the order for small-scale production which was started in 1938. In March 1939, the Fh 104 flew some 40,000 km (24,840 miles) in a round-Africa flight, and, that year, the first eleven Fh 104A production aircraft were built. The production aircraft differed from the prototypes by having 280 hp Hirth HM 508D engines with two-blade variable-pitch airscrews. The undercarriage could be fitted with skis, including a small tail ski, instead of wheels.

By May 1942, production of the Fh 104A had ceased, with only 46 built. Most of these were employed by the Luftwaffe on communication and liaison duties, one Fh 104 being used, for example, by Kesselring in France during 1940. For some years after the end of the war, an Fh 104A was still being flown as the personal aircraft of Gen Vicherek, commander-in-chief of the Czechoslovak Air Force.

With the phasing out of the Fh 104, Siebel put in hand a considerably enlarged development of this aircraft known as the Si 204. This was, in

* Hallore is the name for a person born in Halle.

An early Si 204D without automatic airscrew-pitch governors.

fact, a completely new design having an all-metal structure, a single-spar wing, and a dihedral tailplane with twin fins and rudders at its tips. The tailplane incidence was adjustable, and electrically-operated trim tabs were fitted. The main undercarriage members retracted backwards into the twin engine nacelles. The aircraft could carry a crew of two and eight passengers and was to fulfil the duties of instrument, radio, radar and navigation training.

The Si 204A first flew in 1941, powered by two 360 hp Argus As 410 engines and fitted with a stepped cockpit similar to the Fh 104. In the following year the Si 204D appeared, with a shorter, fully-glazed, unstepped nose, and powered by two 600 hp Argus As 411 twelve-cylinder engines driving two-blade airscrews with pitch-changing vanes in front of the spinners.

Principal production of the Si 204 was in France where the SNCAC concern was producing five aircraft a month by the end of 1942. An example of an Si 204A in Luftwaffe service is the one coded OM-HP used by Flugzeugführerschule FFS(B) 9. Pilots agreed that the Si 204 was a very pleasant aircraft to fly, and its usefulness warranted continued production after the war. SNCAC continued to build the Si 204A (as the NC 702) and Si 204D (as the NC 701), total post-war numbers reaching more than 300. Both versions bore the type-name Martinet and were powered by 590 hp Renault 12S-00 engines. A freighter version of the NC 702 could carry up to 800 kg (1,763 lb) of payload. In Czechoslovakia also, post-war production of the Si 204D was taken up under the designation C-103, and Argus As 411 engines were fitted.

The Si 204D supplanted the Fh 104 in service and took on more duties. (*H. Lächler*)

580

This Si 204D is armed with a machine-gun turret and external bomb load. (*J. Zazvonil*)

Fh 104A: Span 12·06 m (39 ft 6¾ in); length 9·5 m (31 ft 2 in); height 2·64 m (8 ft); wing area 22·3 sq m (240 sq ft).
Empty weight 1,510 kg (3,329 lb); loaded weight 2,350 kg (5,181 lb).
Maximum speed at sea level 350 km/h (217 mph); cruising speed at 2,500 m (8,200 ft) 335 km/h (208 mph); climb to 1,000 m (3,280 ft) 1·9 min; service ceiling 6,600 m (21,648 ft); range 920 km (570 miles).

Si 204D: Span 21·33 m (69 ft 11¾ in); length 11·95 m (39 ft 2½ in); height, to tip of radio mast, 4·25 m (13 ft 11⅜ in); wing area 46 sq m (495 sq ft).
Empty weight 3,950 kg (8,710 lb); loaded weight 5,600 kg (12,348 lb).
Maximum speed at 3,000 m (9,842 ft) 364 km/h (226 mph); cruising speed 340 km/h (211 mph); climb to 1,000 m (3,280 ft) 3·3 min; service ceiling 7,500 m (24,600 ft); range 1,800 km (1,118 miles).

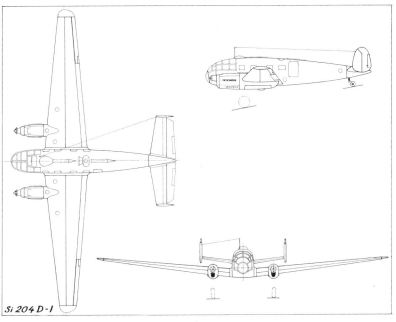

Si 204 D-1

The Skoda-Kauba SK 257 V 1, D-EZWA, prototype was designed as an intermediate fighter trainer. (*J. Zazvonil*)

# Skoda-Kauba SK V1-V8 and SK 257

Early in 1942, the Austrian aeronautical engineer, Otto Kauba, was able to interest the RLM in his proposal for a flying bomb, and, on the strength of this, the Skoda-Kauba Flugzeugbau design bureau was established in Prague with the intention of having its designs manufactured by other companies. The total number of employees of this bureau never exceeded about 120, but, led by Otto Kauba, its designs were certainly prolific although none were to achieve production status.

The layout of the flying bomb was tested in the first aircraft built, designated SK V1A, which was a light monoplane with tractor airscrew, but with unique control elevons attached on booms some distance behind the wing trailing edges. At a later date it was proposed that the cockpit should be replaced by an explosive charge, the power unit should be a pulse-jet or athodyd, and guidance should be similar to that of the Fi 103 (V1). However, this aircraft was deliberately crashed by its Czechoslovak pilot (who escaped unharmed), and, although two other modified aircraft were built, the SK V1 and SK V2, the project was abandoned by the end of 1943 because of the promise shown by the Fi 103.

The next design built, the SK V3, was merely a stubby, light sports aircraft but it was followed by a much more serious and successful type, the SK V4. This was a single-seat low-wing monoplane fighter-trainer with very clean lines and powered by a 240 hp Argus As 10C-3 engine with tractor airscrew. Flight trials with the SK V4 showed such promise that an RLM contract was issued for the similar but more powerful SK 257.

The need for a fighter-trainer with just the right qualities, leading

582

towards the tricky Messerschmitt Bf 109, was rather a pressing one for the Luftwaffe, and it had to make do with a varied collection of mainly foreign aircraft, such as captured Dewoitine D.520s, for the intermediate training rôle. Four prototypes of the SK 257 were built at the Avia plant near Prague and their excellent handling and performance met the Luftwaffe's requirement and quantity-production was ordered.

The aircraft had very clean and aesthetic lines and was powered by a 485 hp Argus As 410 engine with a two-blade tractor airscrew. The fuselage consisted of a welded steel-tube structure with plywood skinning, and the wings were generally of wooden construction with a single box spar. Of particular importance were the wide-track undercarriage for

The Skoda-Kauba SK V8 primary trainer, seen here fitted with skis, flew late in 1944.
(*J. Zazvonil*)

ground stability and the electrically-actuated variable incidence tailplane for quick trim changes. Mass production was entrusted to a factory at Trenčín in Slovakia, but only five aircraft were built and with such poor workmanship that they were rejected upon inspection.

Although, with this setback, the SK 257 faded from the scene, a great deal of other design work was undertaken, including the SK V5 piston-engined fighter to replace the Focke-Wulf Fw 190 and the SK P 14 ramjet interceptor. The last designs for which any metal was cut, however, were the experimental SK V6 single-seat twin-boom monoplane with pusher airscrew, the small SK V7 research aircraft with canard layout and pusher airscrew (which was not completed) and the SK V8 two-seat primary trainer which flew late in 1944.

SK V1: Span 6 m (19 ft 8$\frac{1}{4}$ in); length 4·5 m (14 ft 9$\frac{1}{8}$ in); loaded weight 600 kg (1,320 lb); estimated maximum speed 250 km/h (156 mph).

SK V4: Span 7·6 m (24 ft 11$\frac{1}{4}$ in); length 5·6 m (18 ft 4$\frac{1}{2}$ in); height 2·9 m (9 ft 6$\frac{1}{8}$ in); wing area 8·4 sq m (90·4 sq ft).
Empty weight 1,000 kg (2,205 lb); loaded weight 1,250 kg (2,750 lb).
Maximum speed 420 km/h (261 mph); initial rate of climb 612 m/min (2,008 ft/min); service ceiling 7,500 m (24,600 ft); range 900 km (560 miles).

SK 257: Span 7·6 m (24 ft 11$\frac{1}{4}$ in); length 7·1 m (23 ft 3$\frac{1}{2}$ in); height 1·8 m (5 ft 10$\frac{7}{8}$ in); loaded weight 1,030 kg (2,266 lb); maximum speed 350 km/h (218 mph).

# ROTARY-WING AIRCRAFT

INTRODUCTION
During the 1920s when the autogyro emerged and was generally taken up
and developed, there was little interest shown in Germany in rotating-wing
aircraft, but, during the 1930s, interest began to grow and some work was
done on the autogyro. Although a most useful machine, however, the
autogyro can retrospectively be seen as merely a stepping-stone towards
the far more useful helicopter, and it was Juan de la Cierva's development
of the articulated autogyro rotor which was one of the prime factors
assisting this step. Thus, for Germany, work on rotating-wing aircraft
really began when the swing was towards helicopter development, and, in
this field, great strides were made until the end of the Second World War,
designs ranging from the huge projected Focke Achgelis Fa 284 flying
crane down to the Austrian-designed diminutive Baumgartl Heliofly III
and NR54 V2 portable helicopter.

Despite the great range of the work, one characteristic was common to
virtually all German and Austrian designs, and this was that rotor systems
always either lacked, or inherently counteracted, rotor torque effects. In
other words, the small tail rotor method of counteracting main rotor
torque (which was successfully developed by Igor Sikorsky, beginning
with his VS-300 helicopter in 1939) was virtually ignored by the Germans,
and, yet, despite German successes, the Sikorsky layout is the principal one
in use today. In Doblhoff's jet helicopters we see the elimination of rotor
torque altogether, but the most successful German designs, namely those
of Heinrich Focke and Anton Flettner, used twin-rotor systems to counteract torque. Other designs had counter-rotating co-axial rotors or airscrew-
driven rotors, and only Flettner's early Fl 185 helicopter had separate
airscrews on outriggers to counter rotor torque. Probably the two most
revolutionary designs mentioned in this section are the projected Focke
Achgelis Fa 269 convertiplane and the Focke-Wulf Triebflügel or thrust-
wing VTOL fighter; both forms were pursued after the war, but, whereas the
convertiplane and its derivatives are very much with us still, the airscrew-
driven VTOL fighter became obsolete even before it was fully developed.

Heinrich Focke introduced his side-by-side twin-rotor helicopter layout
on the Fa 61 and so much publicity attended the successful career of this

machine that it is still sometimes thought to be the world's first successful helicopter. In fact, the first successful helicopter (certainly in Europe at least) was the French Breguet-Dorand 'Gyroplane Laboratoire' which first flew on 26 June, 1935, but had very little publicity. The performance of the French machine was impressive and, interestingly, owed much to its two contra-rotating co-axial rotors. Focke's finest achievement with his rotor system lay in the Fa 223 Drache (Kite), largest of the German helicopters built, which could lift a payload of at least 1,280 kg (2,820 lb), this being more than any other contemporary helicopter could lift. Anton Flettner introduced his unique intermeshing twin-rotor system on the Fl 265 and went on to design the similar Fl 282 Kolibri (Humming-bird), which was the most developed of the German helicopters.

A man who was close to German helicopter development programmes throughout the war was Dr Kurt Hohenemser. His chief interest was in theoretical work, although he was familiar with mechanical and constructional detail, and he did much investigation into problems which arose, particularly with the Fa 223, Fl 282, and Doblhoff WNF 342 helicopters.

On the operational side, the Fa 223 and Fl 282 helicopters, together with the Fa 330 gyro kite, were the only machines which saw some limited service, and these types are given most space in this section. Most of the duties which are undertaken by the helicopter today were, however, being performed or investigated. The prime rôles were seen as assisting troops (the Wehrmacht being ever keen on mobility), and reconnaissance and anti-submarine work for the Kriegsmarine. Unfortunately, details of operations are scarce and various first-time uses of the helicopter may never be known. In trying to assess this aspect, it should be remembered that the Allies too had helicopters in limited use during the war; the type they used was the Sikorsky R-4 or Hoverfly which carried out rescue and convoy protection work. There can be little doubt that German helicopters were intended to be employed in a variety of rôles in considerable numbers, and this plan was thwarted only by the fact that the factories set up for helicopter production received considerable attention from bombing. This could have been part of the general offensive or could indicate that the Allies attached considerable importance to the part enemy helicopters could play in the war.

# AEG Helicopter

As early as the First World War, consideration was given to more convenient means of aerial observation than captive balloons. Many of these new ideas centred around rotating-wing aircraft, the most noteworthy in this sphere being the Hungarian Petroczy-Karman design for a captive helicopter having three engines driving two contra-rotating co-axial rotors.

R. Schmidt worked along similar lines from about 1933 for the large German electrical concern, Allgemeine Elektrizitäts-Gesellschaft (AEG), and this work was finalized in 1940 in the shape of a tethered electric helicopter for use as an aerial observation or support post for the army.

The AEG helicopter had two two-blade rotors mounted co-axially, one being attached to the shaft and one to the shell of a 200 hp electric motor, thus giving contra-rotation. Three fixed arms were attached above the upper rotor, and these arms not only supported the cabin below but served as the cable attachment points for tethering. The three tethering cables were, in fact, also used to feed power to the motor from a ground source via the control panel located in the special launching and transporting truck. The observer could make an emergency escape by using a parachute which was explosively blown into the air. Despite successful trials, the AEG helicopter does not appear to have been adopted for military use, probably because of the impracticability of always having to find a considerable electric current supply.

AEG helicopter: Rotor diameter 7·925 m (26 ft); loaded weight 1,225 kg (2,700 lb); ceiling 1,000 m (3,280 ft).

# Baumgartl Heliofly III

The Austrian engineer, Paul Baumgartl, concerned himself during the Second World War with the design of small single-seat helicopters, in the suburbs of Vienna. It is not certain whether his work was sponsored by the German Government, but his machines were in the same category as those of Nagler-Rolz, described on page 610. Baumgartl's first product was the Heliofly I of 1941, which was little more than a strap-on autogyro glider for sporting use.

Resulting from the previous work was a design in 1942 for a strap-on helicopter. This was the Heliofly III-57, which had a rotor consisting of two co-axial contra-rotating single blades, each of which was to be driven by its own 8 hp Argus As 8 engine, which also acted as a counterbalance. When it became apparent that the Argus engines could not be readily obtained, the helicopter was redesigned in 1943 as the Heliofly III-59 to be powered by a single 16 hp engine. In this design, the engine drove and counterbalanced the lower blade and, through gearing, also drove the upper blade, so that torque was still counterbalanced by contra-rotation. A weight, instead of an engine, counterbalanced the upper blade, and the flapping rotor system had cyclic pitch control.

Heliofly III-59: Rotor diameter 6·1 m (20 ft); length 6·i m (20 ft); empty weight 35 kg (77 lb); loaded weight 120 kg (265 lb) approx.

The Doblhoff/WNF 342 V4, one of the prototypes of the world's first jet-driven helicopter. (*USAF*)

# Doblhoff/WNF 342

Under the designation WNF 342, the world's first jet-driven helicopters were built by the Wiener Neustadter Flugzeugwerke (WNF) in the suburbs of Vienna, four machines being built representing progressive experimental steps in a research programme instituted in October 1942. This programme was directed by Friedrich von Doblhoff, who had decided to develop a jet-driven helicopter in preference to a mechanically-driven one because of the attraction of simplicity, lack of rotor torque and transmission gear.

The operating principle was to use a conventional piston engine driving a compressor to provide a compressed air supply, which, after mixing with fuel, was fed as a combustible mixture up through the rotor hub and out through the three hollow rotor blades to be burnt in tip-mounted combustion chambers, thereby generating thrust. Each of the first three machines (V 1, V 2, and V 3) was provided with only a small rear propeller to blow air at the tail surfaces for steering, but the last machine (V 4) had a second propeller mounted co-axially to provide thrust for forward flight when clutched to the compressor motor. Thus, by gradual development, the rotor jets (which had a high fuel consumption) were only used for take-off, hovering and landing, and the rotor blades turned by autorotation for forward flight in the manner of an autogyro.

For the first three machines, although flapping and dragging rotor hinges were provided, no blade pitch-change arrangement was made since this was not required for early tests, vertical control being provided simply by varying the rotor speed. By the time the WNF 342 V4 was built, however, a most ingenious control method had been devised to provide both collective and cyclic pitch control. Each rotor blade was connected to the rotor head by means of a flexibly-coupled tube flanked by steel-strip leaf-type spring straps connected to an upper aluminium alloy casting. This upper casting rotated in a lower fixed casting, a seal being provided between the two, and fuel mixture flowed into this hollow assembly to be piped out to each blade. Passing up through the casting was a hollow fixed shaft which carried a bearing for the upper casting and which was flexibly connected to the helicopter framework. Inside this hollow shaft, a solid shaft rotated in a spherically-seated bearing to carry the blade pitch control spider at its head. Thus, angular displacement of this solid shaft tilted the spider to give appropriate cyclic pitch control. For collective pitch control, the spider was connected to the solid shaft by means of a pressure regulator connected to the upper casting (containing the pressurized fuel mixture) by a pipeline. The spider was given a vertical movement according to the mixture pressure opposed by springs within the regulator. In addition, collective pitch was governed by the torsional stiffness of the centrifugally-loaded spring straps. When the pilot moved the throttle control, a rapid increase (for example) of mixture pressure and jet thrust followed by an increase in collective pitch ensued, while the rotor rpm remained constant.

The WNF 342 V1 was built and first flown in the spring of 1943 but was superficially damaged the following year during an air raid on Vienna, whereupon the test programme was moved a short distance away to Obergraffendorf. Here, the 60 hp Walter Mikron engine was replaced by a 90 hp Walter Mikron engine, and general modifications were made to the extent that the machine was redesignated WNF 342 V2. It should be emphasized that the fluid design of the WNF 342 was such that modifications, as dictated by empirical experiment, could be readily catered for. Thus, the basic framework was of all-tubular construction with no refinements, such as fairings, appearing as semi-permanent fittings until the V4 machine, although this machine was by no means intended as the final design. Starting with the V3 machine, increases were made in rotor diameter, and both the V3 and V4 used the extra power of the 140 hp BMW-Bramo Sh 14A engine to drive the compressor. In all designs, an Argus As 411 supercharger was adapted as a compressor. Before the end of the war, consideration was being given to replacing the compressor system with rotor-mounted pulse-jets or even miniature turbojets.

Within their limited performance, the V1 and V2 machines flew smoothly enough, but serious vibration manifested itself in the V3 machine and eventually destroyed it. These troubles were eliminated in the last example which behaved well and was very smooth, but although it was hovered for a total of 25 hours, it was not tested in forward flight above 40 to 48 km/h (25 to 30 mph) before the programme had to be halted. In 1945, Soviet troops approaching Vienna caused Doblhoff's team to withdraw hastily to Zell am See where the V2 and V4 machines were captured by United States' forces. The WNF 342 V4 has been preserved by the Smithsonian Institution, Washington. Bearing in mind the constant modifications made, the following salient data are given where known.

WNF 342 V1: Single-seater. Rotor diameter 9 m (29 ft 6 in); disc area 59·7 sq m (642 sq ft); disc loading 7·55 kg/sq m (1·54 lb/sq ft); empty weight 227 kg (500 lb); loaded weight 450 kg (990 lb).

WNF 342 V2: Single-seater. Rotor diameter 9 m (29 ft 6 in); disc area 59·7 sq m (642 sq ft); empty weight 235 kg (740 lb).

WNF 342 V3: Single-seater. Rotor diameter 9·75 m (32 ft); disc area 74·8 sq m (805 sq ft); disc loading 7·33 kg/sq m (1·5 lb/sq ft); loaded weight 550 kg (1,210 lb); useful thrust per rotor jet 13·1 kg (28·8 lb); rotor rpm 300.

WNF 342 V4: Two-seater. Rotor diameter 10 m (32 ft 9½ in); disc area 78·6 sq m (845 sq ft); disc loading 8·17 kg/sq m (1·67 lb/sq ft); empty weight 431 kg (950 lb); loaded weight 640 kg (1,410 lb); useful thrust per rotor jet 13·3 kg (29·3 lb); rotor rpm 305; maximum forward speed tested to 48 km/h (30 mph).

The Flettner Fl 265 (TK-AN). Following successful military evaluation, the Fl 265 was ordered into production in 1940 but Flettner was ready with an improved helicopter, the Fl 282.

# Flettner Fl 265

Through a gradual process of working on various rotating-wing schemes, Anton Flettner arrived at his celebrated scheme of intermeshing rotors first employed in the Fl 265 helicopter. This scheme, though viewed with suspicion by many at the time, dominated Flettner's helicopter work a couple of years prior to, and then throughout, the war. When, in 1930, Flettner first turned his attention to helicopter problems, he designed a helicopter having a single, torqueless, rotor, the absence of torque being achieved by applying the drive directly at the rotor, two 30 hp Anzani engines driving small airscrews, being attached to the rotor blades. This helicopter was unfortunately destroyed in 1933 during tethered tests when it was overturned by a gust of wind.

Flettner then turned to the design of a straightforward two-seat autogyro, the Fl 184. This machine was scheduled to carry out trials with the German Navy to ascertain its suitability for reconnaissance and anti-

Sole prototype of the Flettner Fl 184 autogyro, D-EDVE, which caught fire and crashed.

submarine work, such a machine offering distinct advantages over naval fixed-wing aircraft which required catapult-launching and special recovery procedures. The Fl 184 had a fully-enclosed fuselage and tail surfaces, and the 12 m (39 ft 4½ in) diameter rotor employed cyclic pitch control. At the nose was mounted a 140 hp Siemens-Halske Sh 14 radial engine driving a two-blade wooden propeller. During 1936, before this design could be evaluated, the only prototype, D-EDVE, caught fire in flight and was completely destroyed.

In the next design, the Fl 185, the machine was arranged to act as a helicopter when the rotor was powered or act as an autogyro when the rotor autorotated in forward flight. A 140 hp Siemens-Halske Sh 14A engine was mounted in the nose and was provided with a cowl and frontal fan for cooling. Behind the engine was a gearbox from which the drive was taken to the rotor and to two variable-pitch airscrews mounted on outrigger arms extending from the fuselage sides. When the rotor was powered, to counteract torque the airscrews provided thrust in opposite directions, but, when the rotor was freely autorotating, the pitch of the air-screws was altered to give thrust for forward flight when they also took up the full power of the engine. Again, only one prototype, D-EFLT, was built, and this was only given a few tests near the ground before being abandoned.

During 1938, the German Navy placed a contract for six Fl 265s, the design of which Anton Flettner had begun in 1937 as the first to use intermeshing contra-rotating synchronized rotors. The single-seat Fl 265 had a very similar fuselage and tail surfaces to the earlier Fl 185, and, once again, the engine was mounted at the nose with a cowl and cooling fan. The 160 hp Bramo Sh 14A radial engine provided the power for the two two-blade rotors, which had inclined shafts mounted close together and had an inertia-damping system to reduce the vibration reaching the control column.

The Fl 265 V1, D-EFLV, made its first flight in May 1939, and its first autorotative descents were made the following August, but this machine was eventually destroyed in flight when the rotor blades struck each other. Because of this accident, the Fl 265 V2 was the first to be used in a series of naval trials in the Baltic and Mediterranean in which Fl 265s operated from platforms fitted to cruisers and even made landings on U-boat decks. Despite the fact that one Fl 265 was lost due to its refuelling being overlooked, the trials were a great success and augured well for the machine's place in naval reconnaissance and anti-submarine work. Other rôles were also evaluated when an Fl 265 was used in exercises with Wehrmacht troops and performed such work as towing dinghies across a river and lifting bridge sections during construction. Although the Fl 265 had performed its duties well, had flown in adverse conditions and had no trouble going into and out of autorotation, natural doubts were expressed concerning its vulnerability to aerial attack. Consequently, a test was made in which a Messerschmitt Bf 109 and a Focke-Wulf Fw 190 fitted with camera guns made determined simulated attacks on an Fl 265 for 20

Sole prototype of the Flettner Fl 185 helicopter, D-EFLT, with anti-torque/forward thrust airscrews on outriggers. This machine was soon abandoned.

591

Only six prototypes of the Flettner Fl 265 helicopter were built, the design being Flettner's first with his intermeshing rotors. This Fl 265 (TK-AN) is seen in the Chalais-Meudon wind-tunnel in France. (*F. Selinger*)

minutes but failed to score one hit because of the helicopter's manoeuvrability. During the war, German fighters made similar but genuine attacks on a British rotorcraft but with the same lack of success.

The outcome of all these successes was that Flettner received instructions in 1940 to proceed with quantity production of the Fl 265, but, by that time, the design of a more advanced two-seat derivative of the Fl 265, the Fl 282, had been completed and the programme was switched to the new type. Thus, only the six prototypes of the Fl 265 were completed.

Fl 265: Diameter of each rotor 12·3 m (40 ft 4¼ in); disc area 123 sq m (1,325 sq ft); disc loading 8·17 kg/sq m (1·67 lb/sq ft); empty weight 800 kg (1,764 lb); loaded weight 1,000 kg (2,205 lb); maximum speed 160 km/h (99 mph).

# Flettner Fl 282 Kolibri (Humming-bird)

The Flettner Fl 282 Kolibri was designed from the outset as a two-seater, so that, at the expense of range, an observer could be carried, with obvious benefits in the rôles of army and navy spotting and anti-submarine work. The observer was to be accommodated in a seat facing rearwards and positioned behind the rotor shafts, and the design provided for a permissible c of g travel which allowed the helicopter to fly with or without the

592

observer without trim changes. The design was finalized by about July 1940 and work began on 30 prototypes and 15 pre-production machines at Flettner's Johannisthal and Bad Tölz factories. For early flight trials, which began in 1941, the first three Fl 282 prototypes were built as single-seaters and had enclosed Plexiglas-panelled cabins, but subsequent machines were built as open two-seaters.

Departing from previous Flettner practice, the 160 hp BMW-Bramo Sh 14A radial engine was mounted in the centre of the fuselage, thus providing the pilot with an excellent forward view. Cooling air for the enclosed engine was drawn in through openings beneath the fuselage by a wooden fan, and a high-pressure air tank was connected to the engine cylinders through a distributor for starting. On the forward end of the engine crankcase was mounted a transmission unit which changed the direction of drive from horizontal to upward and aft by 65 deg. A drive-shaft with universal joints then took the drive from the engine transmission unit to the upper transmission unit, which consisted of gears and shafts connecting the two rotor shafts. The final cross-shaft between the two rotor shafts was fitted with a free-wheeling unit to disconnect the engine drive, and also with a rotor brake. On the drive-shaft from the engine, a friction disc clutch was fitted which was used for running up the rotors until there was no slippage, when a positive dog-type clutch, on the same shaft, was then engaged. Total reduction through all the transmission units was 12·2 : 1.

The two two-blade rotors, which were synchronized to be parallel in the 45 deg position, were mounted on shafts having an included angle of 24 deg between them and an inclination forward of 6 deg. The rotor blades consisted of wooden ribs mounted on tubular steel spars with a covering of plywood followed by fabric. Flapping and dragging hinges were fitted, the latter having friction dampers. A centrifugally-operated blade-pitch governor held the rotor rpm within prescribed limits, the governor being driven through clutches from the rotor transmission. In order to ensure that power-off autorotation was not lost, the governor was set for a minimum rotor speed of 160 rpm. With the use of his collective-pitch lever, the pilot could over-ride the governor but only to increase rpm. Under certain conditions, self-excited oscillations could occur in the rotor; this phenomenon happened in flight on one occasion when an Fl 282 was being flown with a high collective pitch and the low rotor speed of 140 rpm (compared with the recommended 175 rpm). Vibration became so severe that the pilot prepared to bale out, but, before he could do so, the machine went into autorotation and the vibration ceased.

At the rear end of the fuselage, a horizontal stabilizer was provided for trimming purposes and a fin and rudder of very generous area. This large area was necessary because much of it was ineffective due to the poor aerodynamic shape of the fuselage causing rearwards flow separation and turbulence. Steering of the Fl 282 was by a combination of the rudder and differential collective pitch change on the two rotors, but only the rudder could give steering during autorotation since collective pitch was then ineffective (another reason for the large rudder area).

The fuselage consisted of a welded tubular-steel structure with metal panelling enclosing the centre (engine) section and fabric the rear section and vertical surfaces. The undercarriage was of the non-retractable tricycle type with the nosewheel connected to the rudder pedals for steering.

The Flettner Fl 282 V6 operating from a German warship, 1943/44. The most developed of German helicopters, the Fl 282 was going into small-scale service by 1943 and, the following year, mass production was planned. (*F. Selinger*)

The Fl 282 was more highly developed and flew more hours than any other German helicopter, and very extensive tests and measurements were made of all flight aspects. Most of this test work was done by Flettner's chief pilot, Hans E. Fuisting, who also undertook blind flying and trained many of the 50 pilots who learned to fly the Fl 282. Some new pilots ran into trouble when flying near the ground, because, as they turned with the wind, they lost lift and struck the ground. One new pilot had a fatal accident when flying his Fl 282 blind in cloud, and the assumed cause of the accident was that the machine had been dived and the controls then pulled back so violently that the blades were forced into each other or into the tail. The diving speed thereafter was restricted to 175 km/h (109 mph). On occasions, the Kolibri was landed autogyro fashion and without the use of collective pitch. This was done by descending vertically, diving nose-down and then pulling back on the controls to land, but, on one occasion at least, the tail hit the ground and was damaged.

594

Extremely manoeuvrable and very stable, even in gusty conditions, the machine could be flown hands-off in forward flight above 60 km/h (37 mph) for indefinite periods by making an adjustment to neutralize the loads on the controls. However, in forward flight at speeds below 60 km/h (37 mph) there was some longitudinal instability which reached a maximum at about 40 km/h (25 mph). Another slight criticism of the Fl 282 was that it vibrated rather badly while the rotor was running up on the ground, but this vibration decreased upon lifting off, although there was still a certain amount of vibration transmitted to the control column, which was sluggish and tended to overshoot the requisite amount of movement. Although many of the mechanical components were unnecessarily complicated and heavy, the general design and workmanship were of excellent quality, and, as an endurance test, one machine was flown 95 hours in all without replacements or repairs. The engine, which had a long development history, was said to be capable of 400 hours between overhauls.

Beginning in 1942 with the Fl 282 V5, the German Navy held a series of trials in the Baltic, the machine behaving well under the worst weather conditions. The Fl 282s in these trials operated from a platform mounted on one of the gun turrets of the cruiser *Köln*, and, on at least one occasion, a landing was made in very heavy seas. By 1943, twenty Fl 282s had been built and some were used for convoy protection in the Mediterranean and Aegean. Unfortunately, little is known of the operational employment of the machine, although it is known that Luft-Transportstaffel 40, based at Ainring in April 1945, had at least three Fl 282s (and also three Focke Achgelis Fa 223s) at its disposal. It was possibly one of this unit's Fl 282s that flew Gauleiter Hanke out of besieged Breslau just before the capture of that city.

The great success of the Kolibri, which was even better than the Fl 265, resulted in a production order for 1,000 machines being given in 1944 to the Bayerische Motorenwerke (BMW), which prepared the requisite tooling-up only to have production forestalled by Allied bombing of the Munich and Eisenach works. The Flettner Johannisthal factory was also bombed, and, by the end of the war, this concern had completed only 24 prototypes in all. Of these, only three were discovered by the Allies in a serviceable condition for testing, the Fl 282 V15 and V23 being taken to the USA and a third machine to the USSR. Examples known to have survived are the Fl 282 (c/n 28368) at the Cranfield Institute of Technology, and the Fl 282 V23 at the United States Air Force Museum, Dayton, Ohio.

During 1944, when the Fl 282 was considered fully developed, Anton Flettner turned to the design of the Fl 339, using all the experience gained with the Fl 282. The Fl 339, which never got beyond the project stage, was to have been a much larger helicopter weighing some 3,000 kg (6,615 lb) empty, carrying about 20 passengers and being powered by a single engine.

Fl 282B: Rotor diameter 11·96 m (39 ft 2¾ in); fuselage length 6·56 m (21 ft 6¼ in); height 2·2 m (7 ft 2½ in); disc area 119 sq m (1,281 sq ft).

Disc loading 8·41 kg/sq m (1·72 lb/sq ft); empty weight 760 kg (1,675 lb); loaded weight 1,000 kg (2,205 lb).

Maximum speed at sea level 150 km/h (93 mph); maximum diving speed 175 km/h (109 mph); maximum sideways speed approximately 24 km/h (15 mph); vertical rate of climb at loaded weight at sea level 91·5 m/min (300 ft/min); rate of autorotative descent at loaded weight 475 m/min (1,560 ft/min); hovering ceiling approximately 300 m (985 ft); service ceiling 3,292 m (10,800 ft); absolute ceiling with minimum load 4,100 m (13,450 ft); range, with pilot only, 300 km (186 miles); range, with two crew and reduced fuel, 180 km (112 miles).

The Focke Achgelis Fa 61 helicopter showed signs of Cierva Autogiro influence but with the main difference of having twin rotors. (*Smithsonian Institution*)

# Focke Achgelis Fa 61

Using as a starting point the experience gained from 1932 by Prof Heinrich Karl Focke in the licence building of Cierva Autogiros, the Focke Achgelis company began a series of helicopter experiments and model tests which culminated in the design of the Fa 61. Although a helicopter, the Fa 61 showed signs of having been influenced by the Cierva C.19 Autogiro, but its most strikingly obvious difference was its twin rotors mounted side by side. This layout of the rotors was to prove so successful in the helicopter field that Focke pursued it throughout the war (during which time nations such as Britain, the USA, and the USSR also produced helicopters with similar rotor mountings), and his rotor designs were further characterized by their exceptionally high disc loadings for the time.

The fuselage of the Fa 61 was no more than that of a conventional light aircraft with horizontal stabilizer attached to the top of the fin and rudder, a single open cockpit, a nose-mounted 160 hp Bramo Sh 14A radial engine with a small two-blade cooling propeller, and a tail-sitting undercarriage. To prevent nosing-over, there was a small wheel fitted beneath the nose. Extending from either side of the forward part of the fuselage were two tubular-steel outrigger structures, which terminated in the rotor heads. A system of gears and shafts transmitted the engine power out to the two rotors, which revolved in opposite directions, each rotor having three articulated and tapered blades with cyclic pitch for longitudinal and directional control. Differential operation of the cyclic pitch gave lateral control by inducing asymmetric rotor lift.

With the test pilot Ewald Rohlfs at the controls, the Fa 61 made its first flight, of 28 seconds, on 26 June, 1936, and made its first autorotative landing in May the following year. Once developed, the great success of the machine was demonstrated by the series of new FAI world rotorcraft records it established until the start of the war, when official recording became impossible. On 25 June, 1937, with Rohlfs at the controls, the Fa 61 established an altitude record of 2,439 m (8,000 ft) and an endurance record of 1 hr 20 min 49 sec. The following day, the same pilot and machine established a straight-line distance record of 16·4 km (10·18 miles), a closed-circuit distance record of 80·604 km (50·05 miles) and a straight-line speed record of 122·553 km/h (76·1 mph) over a 20 km course. On 25 October, 1937, the straight-line distance record was broken by Hanna Reitsch, who flew the Fa 61 helicopter 108·974 km (67·67 miles) between Bremen and Berlin, and she also flew the machine indoors in the Deutschlandhalle, Berlin, in February 1938 to demonstrate the Fa 61's ease of control and sensitivity. The straight-line distance record was broken yet again by the Fa 61 on 20 June, 1938, when Karl Bode flew it 230·348 km (143·05 miles), and he established a new altitude record of 3,427 m (11,240·5 ft) with the machine on 29 January, 1939, this being the last official record obtained by a German rotorcraft of pre-1945 vintage.

Despite the great success of the Fa 61 and the large amount of publicity its noteworthy flights received, it was in reality no more than an experimental machine to put Prof Focke's ideas to the test. There was, however, to have been a two-seat sports version of the Fa 61, designated Fa 224, which would have had performance augmented by use of the more powerful 270 hp Argus As 10C engine, but this was shelved with the advent of war. By 1938, design was already under way of a far more ambitious and useful helicopter, the Fa 266 (otherwise Fa 223).

Fa 61: Rotor diameter 7·01 m (23 ft); disc area 38·6 sq m (415 sq ft).

Disc loading 24·6 kg/sq m (5·1 lb/sq ft); empty weight 800 kg (1,760 lb); loaded weight 953 kg (2,100 lb).

Maximum speed at sea level 123 km/h (76·4 mph); cruising speed 100 km/h (62 mph); inclined rate of climb 220 m/min (720 ft/min); service ceiling 2,410 m (7,900 ft); range 230 km (143 miles).

A Focke Achgelis Fa 223 in flight. Originally designed for Deutsche Lufthansa as the world's first genuine transport helicopter, the Fa 223 was then developed for military use. (*Smithsonian Institution*)

# Focke Achgelis Fa 266 Hornisse (Hornet) and Fa 223 Drache (Kite)

The Focke Achgelis Fa 266 Hornisse resembled an enlarged version of the Fa 61 and was designed for Deutsche Lufthansa as a six-seat civil transport, which gained it the distinction of being the world's first genuine transport helicopter. The prototype was completed late in 1939, but, because war had started, it was decided to develop it for military use. After 100 hours' ground running, and tethered hovering tests, the Fa 266 made its first free flight in August 1940, by which time it was redesignated Fa 223 Drache.

The operational rôles planned for the Fa 223 Drache were those of anti-submarine patrol, reconnaissance, rescue, cargo transport and pilot training. The machine was to be tested in these rôles using 30 pre-production Fa 223s, which the RLM ordered from the Focke Achgelis Bremen factory.

The fuselage of the Fa 223 was divided into four compartments, these being the extensively-glazed nose cockpit which afforded an excellent view for the pilot and observer, the load compartment with starboard entrance door and self-sealing fuel and oil tanks, the engine compartment and, last, the tail section. The fuselage structure was of welded steel tubes, and fabric

598

covering was used except for the metal panelling of the engine compartment. The engine was a 1,000 hp BMW-Bramo 323 Q3 Fafnir (later redesignated BMW 301R) with a supercharger and cooling fan and, together with a gearbox, was mounted as one unit in two rings, which in turn were attached to the four longitudinal fuselage members by adjustable cables. Struts prevented fore and aft movement of the engine. The front fireproof bulkhead of the engine compartment was separated from the rear wall of the load compartment by a 0·20 m (8 in) gap. This gap was open at the top and sides of the fuselage, with a wire mesh covering, and engine-cooling air was drawn in through this gap and exhausted from an annular opening behind the rear edge of the compartment panelling. Engine exhaust was piped out through the fuselage roof and ejected aft.

Tubular-steel outriggers extended from the fuselage sides to support the two rotor heads. Power from the engine was transmitted via a friction plate clutch to the gearbox and then by long hollow shafts to the rotor head gears, the lower end of the starboard shaft having a rotor brake and both shafts having a stabilizing friction clutch at their centres to damp any tendency to whip. The total reduction between engine and rotors was 9·1 : 1, the normal speed of the rotors being 275 rpm.

The rotor axes were inclined inwards by about $4\frac{1}{2}$ deg and slightly forwards, and each rotor head had a free-wheel device to allow the rotors to revolve in the event of the drive transmission jamming. Flapping and dragging hinges were provided for the rotor blades, the drag hinges having friction dampers, and inertia dampers reduced vibration in the cyclic pitch control. Each blade consisted of wooden ribs attached to a conically-drawn high-tensile steel tube, the covering being a mixture of plywood and fabric.

The orthodox fin and rudder was surmounted by a strut-braced tailplane which was adjustable for longitudinal trimming only. Hydraulic brakes, operated from the rudder pedals, were fitted to the mainwheels only, and the nosewheel was self-centring and could turn through 360 deg.

Control of the Fa 223 was in the following manner. The control column was used to give longitudinal control by equal cyclic-pitch change of the rotor blades, and lateral control by differential collective-pitch change of the rotor blades. The rudder pedals were used to give yaw control by differential cyclic-pitch change of the rotor blades, the control effect being increased by use of the rudder during forward flight. A trimmer wheel was provided for tailplane adjustment, and all control links were by cables. Two machines (numbered 13 and 16) were experimentally fitted with a separate collective-pitch lever next to the throttle, and a throttle governor to maintain a constant engine speed, but this arrangement was under development only. On all other machines, the pilot had a lever with only two positions for collective pitch, one for powered setting and one for autorotation. In addition, an automatic device adjusted the tailplane and altered the blade pitch from the powered setting to the autorotation setting

599

for a glide landing in the event of a power failure, but the pitch could not be reset in the air. Thus, apart from pitch adjustments for attitude control, the rotors must be regarded as having had a fixed pitch, the lift being controlled by the engine throttle. This fact reduced the safety, handling, and performance characteristics and, in order to maintain a constant rotor speed during a climb, progressive engine throttling was necessary and this cancelled out the benefits of an engine supercharger. Considerable skill and experience was also necessary during hovering and low-speed flight because of the very sluggish lift control; more than one Fa 223 was lost when making downwind turns at low level.

Most of the equipment required for the various rôles the Fa 223 was to perform could be fitted to or removed from the basic machine, the various equipment being as follows. For all rôles except training, an FuG 17 radio, FuG 101 radio altimeter, nose-mounted MG 15 machine-gun, and an observer's seat were fitted. Additional equipment required was a rescue cradle, winch and electric motor operating through the fuselage floor, for reconnaissance and rescue; a hand camera pointing through the cockpit floor, for reconnaissance and anti-submarine duties; a jettisonable 300 litre (66 Imp gal) auxiliary fuel tank, for reconnaissance; fuselage racks and two 250 kg (550 lb) bombs for anti-submarine work. For cargo transport a load-carrying beam was used to carry heavy or bulky loads suspended beneath the helicopter by cable, which had a pilot-operated, electric quick-release mechanism at its lower end. The maximum load actually carried by an Fa 223 by this method was 1,280 kg (2,820 lb), which was greater than by any other contemporary helicopter. However, carrying loads suspended by cable proved tiring for the pilot on long flights, and, during troop-supplying trials, stabilizing surfaces fitted to the loads were found to give some improvement. The remaining equipment which could be fitted was a Luftwaffe dinghy stowed in the tail section, respirator racks and, for training purposes only, dual controls.

Of the 30 pre-production Fa 223s ordered from Bremen, only ten were completed before the factory was bombed, destroying other machines in various stages of construction. The firm then moved to Laupheim, near Stuttgart, where seven more Fa 223s were built. Early in 1942, the Fa 223 was considered ready for operational testing, and trials began, although by July 1942, because of constant losses and setbacks caused by bombing, only two machines had actually flown. Successful trials with the Fa 223, primarily in the assistance of troops, resulted in the ordering of 100, but only eight were test flown, and six of these were destroyed by bombs in July 1944 at Laupheim. Once again a new production factory was established, in Berlin, with a production capacity of 400 aircraft a month, but only one was completed by the end of the war.

Despite all these efforts, only ten or eleven Fa 223s were actually flown, and in total they flew about 400 hours, including about 9,985 km (6,200 miles) of cross-country flying. The maximum flying time, in Germany, on any one machine was about 100 hours. The fate of one Fa 223 (No. 12) is perhaps particularly interesting; this helicopter, after completing a long cross-country flight from Germany, was flown to Mont Blanc to perform a mountain rescue of 17 people trapped in the snow. Unfortunately, a mechanical link failure resulted in a rotor disintegrating, and, although the machine touched down on its wheels, it was hurled against an embankment and the crew was killed.

Although the Fa 223 was particularly effective in the rescue rôle, details of its use or trial in this or other rôles are few, but it is known that the few machines available were used on a small scale in general transport and communication work, Luft-Transportstaffel 40 having three Fa 223s on hand at Ainring in April 1945. It was probably these three machines which were the only ones serviceable at the end of the war, and one of these was finally destroyed by its pilot. The remaining two (Nos. 14 and 51) were taken over by American Forces at Ainring in May 1945 for evaluation. One Fa 223 (No. 14), which had first flown in July 1943, was flown by its German crew (consisting of the pilot H. Gersenhauer, the engineer H. Zelewski, and the mechanic F. Will) to England and made history by being the first helicopter to cross the English Channel. It arrived at Brockenhurst, Hampshire, in September 1945 and began flight trials but was destroyed the following month, having had a flying life of 170 hours. The accident occurred when the automatic pitch change mechanism malfunctioned and switched the rotors to the autorotation condition. Since this occurred when the Fa 223 was hovering only about 20 m (65 ft) from the ground, it had neither the altitude nor the forward speed for an autorotative landing.

An operational Fa 223 (DM-SO). Only a few were built in time for Service use, some going to Luft-Transportstaffel 40. (*R. C. Seeley*)

Although the few Fa 223s built saw little service, the design was capable of fulfilling to a remarkable extent most of the rôles for which post-war helicopters were designed. As for the shortcomings in performance and production already mentioned, it seems fairly certain that these would have been remedied had not the constant bombing harassment interfered. After the war, development of the Fa 223 was continued in France and Czechoslovakia. In France the new development, in which Prof Focke assisted, was designated SE 3000 and made its first flight on 23 October, 1948. In Czechoslovakia, a start was made on helicopters in the autumn of 1945 by reconstructing two Fa 223s from salvaged parts, the resulting machines being more or less standard.

After the war, France and Czechoslovakia worked on the Fa 223. A Czechoslovak example, probably constructed chiefly from salvaged parts, is seen here. (*J. Zazvonil*)

Fa 223E; Rotor diameter 12 m (39 ft 4½ in); distance between rotor centres 12·5 m (41 ft 0⅛ in); span over rotors 24·5 m (80 ft 4⅝ in); disc area 226 sq m (2,435 sq ft); fuselage length 12·25 m (40 ft 2¼ in); height 4·36 m (14 ft 3⅝ in).

Maximum operational disc loading 19·07 kg/sq m (3·9 lb/sq ft); empty weight 3,180 kg (7,000 lb); normal loaded weight 3,860 kg (8,500 lb); maximum operational loaded weight 4,315 kg (9,500 lb); maximum permissible loaded weight in sea level tests 5,000 kg (11,000 lb).

Maximum speed 176 km/h (109 mph) but limited to 120·5 km/h (74·8 mph) to avoid rotor vibrations; cruising speed 120·5 km/h (74·8 mph); maximum backward speed 10·4 km/h (6·5 mph); initial rate of climb at normal loaded weight 244 m/min (800 ft/min), vertical, or 335 m/min (1,100 ft/min) with forward speed; rate of auto-rotative descent 1,235 m/min (4,050 ft/min); service ceiling at normal loaded weight 2,010 m (6,600 ft) with vertical climb, or 4,880 m (16,000 ft) with forward speed; range with auxiliary fuel tank 700 km (435 miles).

Using the fuselage of a DFS 230 assault glider, this Focke Achgelis Fa 225 rotaglider was built to give a short landing but did not go into service.

# Focke Achgelis Fa 225

During the first half of the Second World War, the assault glider was of considerable importance in the rapid landing of troops and supplies, but its use was dependent on the availability of sufficient landing area. Where the landing area was restricted by natural or artificial obstacles, the glider's landing run could be shortened by nose braking rockets, although the landing approach remained unaltered. The idea therefore arose of exploiting the almost vertical or very steep descent to be obtained from rotary wings in autorotation, and in 1942 the fuselage of a DFS 230 glider had its fixed wings replaced by an Fa 223 three-blade rotor mounted on a structural pylon. To take the increased landing load, a braced undercarriage replaced the normal skid. This hybrid rotaglider, designated Focke Achgelis Fa 225, was towed behind a Junkers-Ju 52/3m in tests, during 1943, and could land within a distance of 18 m (59 ft). It was not, however, put to operational use, probably because of changing operational requirements, and possibly because its advantages were counterbalanced by the fact that the towing speed was considerably lower than that of the standard DFS 230, and it would have been more vulnerable to attack with its slower assault approach speed.

Fa 225: Rotor diameter 12 m (39 ft 4½ in); disc area 113 sq m (1,217 sq ft); disc loading 17·7 kg/sq m (3·63 lb/sq ft); loaded weight 2,000 kg (4,410 lb); maximum towed speed 190 km/h (118 mph).

603

# Focke Achgelis Fa 269

By 1943 it was considered that sufficient experience had been gained in the field of helicopters to undertake the bold project of an experimental convertiplane which would combine the vertical landing and take-off characteristics of the helicopter with the higher cruising speed and economy of the fixed-wing aircraft, the resulting design being the Focke Achgelis Fa 269.

The layout was that of a mid-wing cantilever monoplane with oval-section fuselage, large-area tailplane, and single fin and rudder. The wing leading edge had slight sweepback and the trailing edge compound taper.

Two engines were to have been mounted on the wings beyond mid-span and these would have driven very-large-diameter pusher propellers. For level flight these propellers would have been used in the orthodox position but for take-off and landing they would have pivoted downward and forward through about 85 deg. Actual propeller diameter would have been

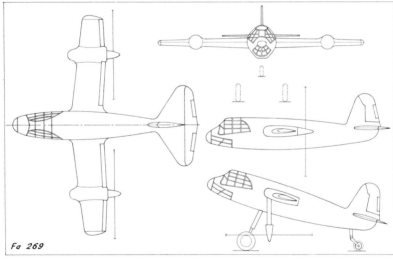

Fa 269

approximately equal to the aircraft's semi-span. At the front of each engine there was a special pivoting gearbox, from which a drive shaft passed back between the engine cylinder banks to drive its propeller aft of the wing trailing edge. The whole of each shaft could be pivoted at the wing leading edge and out of the recess in the engine and wing, to swing its propeller beneath the wing. In the fully-down position, the plane of the propellers was almost parallel with the ground when the aircraft was at rest, and a very long tailwheel undercarriage, which retracted into the fuselage, was necessary because of the length of the drive shafts. Considerable development would have been needed for the special engines, gearboxes, drives and power-pivoting mechanisms, not to mention the propeller pitch-control system for use when landing and taking-off (when the conventional control surfaces would be ineffective). The project, apparently, did not have sufficient priority for development to be undertaken at this stage of the war, and no prototype was built. The only known data for the Fa 269 is that the design horizontal speed was 600 km/h (373 mph).

# Focke Achgelis Fa 284

The Fa 284 was probably the world's first helicopter design for the specific rôle of a flying crane. The machine was extremely large and ambitious and was to employ once again Focke's side-by-side layout of twin rotors. Much of the fuselage was of open framework construction with tail surfaces at the rear. A central two-seat enclosed cockpit afforded a good view, through the forward open framework, of the suspended load below. Extending sidewards from the front of the fuselage were the two outrigger structures for the rotors, and housed in each outrigger was a 1,600 hp BMW 801 engine with a main undercarriage member immediately below.

Although some parts of the Fa 284 may have been manufactured, the design was abandoned (probably late in 1943) for an adaptation of the Fa 223, which would have kept the production of new parts to a minimum.

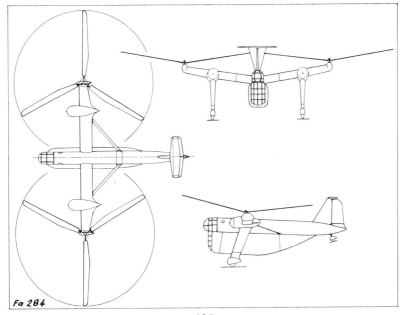

Fa 284

The plan was to build a four-rotor helicopter by combining two Fa 223s with the fuselages in line and joined by a new centre section. There is a possibility that the designation Fa 284 was transferred to the twin Fa 223, but, although the centre section was manufactured at Laupheim, a complete machine did not materialize. The data below refer to the original Fa 284 project.

Fa 284: Rotor diameter 17·83 m (58 ft 6 in); distance between rotor centres 19·47 m (63 ft 10½ in); span over rotors 37·3 m (122 ft 4½ in); length 13·72 m (45 ft).
Empty weight 8,100 kg (17,860 lb); maximum loaded weight 12,000 kg (26,460 lb).
Cruising speed 208 km/h (129 mph); absolute ceiling 6,350 m (20,828 ft); range 400 km (248 miles).

# Focke Achgelis Fa 330 Bachstelze (Water Wagtail)

Early in 1942, Focke Achgelis at Laupheim were asked to design a simple single-seat gyro kite which surfaced U-boats could tow aloft to extend the observer's range of view. At this time, the U-boats were being forced away from the dense shipping areas around the coasts of Britain and the United States to hunt further out into the Atlantic where there was greater safety, but where their low position in the water made searching for, and shadowing, the spread-out convoys a very difficult task unless a bosun's chair could be attached to the periscope.

The gyro kite, designated Fa 330 Bachstelze, was seen as some sort of solution and ingenuity was shown in its design. The machine could be easily assembled or dismantled in a few minutes and stowed through a U-boat hatch. The body structure consisted of two main steel tubes, one horizontal and one vertical. On the horizontal tube was mounted the pilot's seat with controls and a small instrument panel, and landing skids, and, at the rear end, a simple tailplane, fin and rudder. The vertical tube, behind the pilot's seat, formed a pylon for the rotor.

The freely-rotating rotor had three blades, each of which consisted of a tubular-steel spar with plywood ribs and thin plywood and fabric covering. Each rotor blade had flapping and dragging hinges with adjustable dampers. Blade pitch could only be adjusted, with screws, on the ground before take-off. The best results were normally obtained with the blade pitch as coarse as possible, although starting was then more difficult. In addition to the flapping and dragging dampers, there were also inter-blade connecting cables and blade-droop cables, the latter being attached to the blades and to an inverted tripod extending upward from the rotor hub. The rotor axis was slightly ahead of the machine's c of g, and the towing cable attachment point was slightly ahead and below the c of g.

The Focke Achgelis Fa 330 Bachstelze gyro kite was towed by a surfaced U-boat to extend the range of view. (*Smithsonian Institution*)

Movement of the control column tilted the rotor head in the appropriate direction for longitudinal and lateral control, and operation of the rudder pedals gave directional control. The tailplane was not adjustable. The Fa 330 was launched from the deck of the surface-running U-boat by giving the machine a slight backwards tilt once the rotor was revolving. If there was a wind, a push by hand sufficed to get the rotor moving, but otherwise a pull-rope was wound around a grooved drum on the rotor hub. In case this rope did not slip off when the rotor started, an over-ride mechanism was fitted.

Pilot training was given in a wind-tunnel at Chalais-Meudon near Paris, and the kite was very easy to operate and could be flown hands-off for up to 10 seconds. It is believed that two or three crew members of each Fa 330 equipped U-boat learned to fly it.

Having 150 m (492 ft) of towing cable available, it was possible to maintain an altitude of 120 m (394 ft) thereby extending the possible range of vision very usefully to 40 km (25 miles) compared with only 8 km (5 miles) on the U-boat deck. In an emergency, the pilot, who had telephone contact with the U-boat, pulled a lever over his head which jettisoned the rotor and released the towing cable. As the rotor flew away and up, it pulled out a parachute mounted behind the pylon. At this stage, the pilot, attached to the parachute, unfastened his safety belt to allow the remainder of the Fa 330 to fall into the sea while he made a normal parachute descent. In a normal descent, the kite was winched in to the deck and, upon landing, the rotor brake applied.

Although designed by Focke Achgelis, the Fa 330 was built by the Weser-Flugzeugbau at Hoykenkamp, near Bremen. This particular factory manufactured Focke-Wulf .Fw 190 fuselages, a few Fa 223 helicopters

607

and about two hundred Fa 330s. Variations made in the basic design were an increase in rotor diameter to 8·53 m (28 ft) on late machines and the option of adding simple landing wheels to the skids. There was also a proposal, designated Fa 336, to build a powered version of the Fa 330 with landing wheels and a 60 hp engine.

The principal U-boat class to use the Fa 330 was the ocean-going Type IX which had a surface displacement of 740 tons, a surface speed of 18 kt and a submerged speed of 7·5 kt. Among the operational U-boats of the Kriegsmarine, only the Type IX-D/2 supply U-boat had a faster surface speed of 19·2 kt, and this type possibly used the Fa 330 also. Little is known of actual operations with the kite, or how many were issued, but there is no doubt that the use of the gyro kite was unpopular, because, in an emergency, the U-boat had either to delay its dive in order to pick up the kite's pilot, or dive and hope to pick him up later. The advantages of a self-propelled machine seem clear. The first Fa 330s were probably issued in mid-1942 but were used in the South Atlantic only on rare occasions. From June 1942, the harried U-boat forces swung their main effort from the Atlantic to the Gulf of Aden and the Indian Ocean, where more use of the gyro kite was made. U-861, for example, used her kite on a patrol in the Indian Ocean off Madagascar. However, the new theatre of operations provided opportunities to exchange the Fa 330 for, in the eyes of the commander, something more usable. At Penang, Malaya, the Japanese had permitted the establishment of a U-boat base in the summer of 1943, and it was here that an Fa 330 was exchanged for a small Japanese floatplane. On another occasion, at the Surabaya (Java) U-boat base, a gyro kite was exchanged for a Japanese floatplane to supplement the two Arado reconnaissance aircraft which kept watch over the harbour.

More Fa 330s survive today than any other examples of German rotary-wing aircraft, not only because they were built in by far the greatest numbers, but probably also because their small size does not make great demands on valuable preservation space.

Fa 330: Rotor diameter 7·315 m (24 ft); disc area 41·85 sq m (450 sq ft); length 4·42 m (14 ft 6 in).

Disc loading with 68 kg (150 lb) pilot 3·5 kg/sq m (0·73 lb/sq ft); weight without pilot 82 kg (180 lb).

Typical airspeed 40 km/h (25 mph); minimum airspeed to maintain flight approximately 27 km/h (17 mph). Typical rotor speed 205 rpm.

# Focke-Wulf Triebflügel (Thrust-wing)

Although only a project, the Focke-Wulf Triebflügel (Thrust-wing) fighter, designed in September 1944, was a most interesting study in rotary-wing flight and embodied several radical features. The fighter was to be a tail-sitting, vertical take-off aircraft deriving its lift and thrust from three wings which rotated around the fuselage at a point approximately one-third of the fuselage length from the nose. No torque was transmitted to the fuselage from the rotating wings, since these were driven by three tip-mounted ramjets, the wings being revolved up to the ramjet operating speed by three 300 kg (660 lb) thrust rockets.

Each ramjet was 0·68 m (2 ft 3 in) in diameter, gave about 840 kg (1,850 lb) of thrust and was developed from the experiments conducted from 1941 by Otto Pabst in Focke-Wulf's gas dynamics department, at Bad Eilsen. Principally by the development of special fuel burners and the method of air compression, Pabst had succeeded in evolving a basic design of ramjet in which the total length was no more than $2\frac{1}{2}$ times the ramjet diameter, which made the type suitable for rotary motion. Successful tests of the Pabst ramjet were made in the LFA (Brunswick) wind tunnel at speeds up to Mach 0·9.

The Triebflügel fighter was to stand vertically on the ground, supported by its four tail fins, each of which had a small outrigger wheel at its tip. The main landing load was to be taken on a single main wheel at the base of the fuselage, and during flight all wheels were enclosed by streamlined

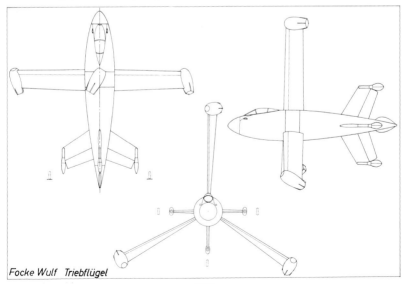

Focke Wulf Triebflügel

tulip-shaped pods. The pilot was accommodated conventionally in a nose cockpit with bubble hood, and the nose-mounted armament was to consist of two 30 mm MK 103 cannon with 100 rounds plus two 20 mm MG 151 cannon with 250 rounds.

The rotating untapered wings had a gradually decreasing pitch from root to tip in the manner of an airscrew, and no control method, apart from rpm adjustments, appears to have been intended for adjusting the wing characteristics. Control of the aircraft was by means of the control surfaces at the trailing edges of the tail fins. Thus, for flying in a horizontal path, the tail would be depressed slightly to direct part of the thrust force into a lift force.

After the war, some development of this type of VTO fighter was resumed, notably in the United States where experiments were made with aircraft using turbine-driven nose-mounted contra-rotating airscrews to counteract torque.

Fw Triebflügel: Rotating wing diameter 11·5 m (37 ft 8¾ in); length 9·15 m (30 ft); total wing area 16·5 sq m (176·5 sq ft); disc area 80 sq m (860·8 sq ft).

Empty weight 3,200 kg (7,056 lb); ramjet and rocket fuel 1,590 kg (3,506 lb); ammunition 285 kg (628 lb); pilot 100 kg (220 lb); loaded weight 5,175 kg (11,410 lb).

Maximum speed at sea level 1,000 km/h (621 mph), at 11,000 m (36,080 ft) 840 km/h (522 mph); rate of climb 7,500 m/min (24,600 ft/min) at sea level or 1,200 m/min (3,936 ft/min) at 11,000 m (36,080 ft); climb to 8,000 m (26,240 ft) 1·8 min, to 15,000 m (49,200 ft) 11·5 min; service ceiling 14,000 m (45,920 ft); range at 925 km/h (575 mph) at sea level 650 km (404 miles); maximum range of 2,400 km (1,490 miles) obtained at 675 km/h (419 mph) at 14,000 m (45,920 ft).

# Nagler-Rolz NR 55 and NR 54

The Austrian Bruno Nagler began work in the rotary-wing field in 1929 when, with Raoul Hafner, he built his RI Revoplane near Vienna. This was a single-seat machine with a rotor driven by a 45 hp engine and had a vertical torque-balancing surface acting in the rotor downwash. This machine, and also the generally similar RII machine of 1932, was successfully tested in Great Britain. In 1934, Nagler brought out his Helicogyro which had a 90 hp Pobjoy radial air-cooled engine, a two-blade rotor and a pusher propeller. The engine could drive the rotor for hovering, when torque was balanced by a vertical surface, or the propeller could be driven for forward flight leaving the rotor to generate lift by autorotation. This single-seat aircraft was tested in Great Britain in 1937. With the outbreak of war, Nagler joined with Franz Rolz to form the Nagler-Rolz Flugzeugbau, which was subsidized by the German Government to undertake development of small single-seat helicopters.

In 1940 the first machine from the new concern appeared as the NR 55, which had the unusual feature of a single-blade rotor. This rotor blade was counterbalanced by a 40 hp engine which applied to it a torqueless drive by means of two small airscrews which pulled it round at about 135 rpm. The rotor diameter was 10·67 m (35 ft), and the machine weighed about 340 kg (750 lb) loaded, but, although a cruising speed of 96 km/h (60 mph) was thought feasible, only hovering tests were undertaken because the machine was built purely for testing the rotor system, which proved satisfactory.

Development of the NR 55 concept continued in 1941 with the generally similar NR 54 V 1, in which considerable reductions were made in size and weight. The engine power was reduced to 24 hp and the rotor diameter to 7·92 m (26 ft). Empty and loaded weights were 80 kg (176 lb) and 177 kg (390 lb) respectively, and the cruising speed was 88 km/h (55 mph).

The NR 54 V2 produced in 1941 was the world's first portable helicopter. By development, the simplest possible single-seat helicopter had been produced, which flew on remarkably little power. The rotor consisted of two single blades, each of which had an 8 hp motor driving a small airscrew to give a torqueless drive, and the pilot's controls consisted of two levers, one to alter rotor blade pitch and the other to control the engines. Four of these machines were built for development, but, for unknown reasons, production was not initiated.

NR 54 V2: Rotor diameter 7·92 m (26 ft); empty weight 36·5 kg (80 lb); loaded weight 140 kg (310 lb); cruising speed 80 km/h (50 mph); rate of climb with forward speed 152 m/min (499 ft/min); ceiling 457 m (1,499 ft); range 48 km (29·8 miles).

611

# FIXED-WING AIRCRAFT PROJECTS

INTRODUCTION

Limitations of space prevent complete coverage of the great many German aircraft projects of the Second World War, but the examples chosen for brief discussion give a general picture of the trends in German aircraft design during the latter part of the conflict. Various projected developments of aircraft actually built have been mentioned in this work under the appropriate headings, and so projects in this section do not, for the most part, bear any relation to aircraft actually constructed.

From 1943 onward, German technicians and designers were increasingly absorbed with the production of defensive weapons, which to the aircraft industry meant missiles, fighters, and interceptors, and discussion of the last two categories form the main portion of this section. Much of the advanced nature of these projects revolved around the latest developments in jet and rocket power units, and the resultant great increases in speed led to every kind of new aerodynamic problem. German designers tackled these problems vigorously, and the incorporation of some form of wing sweep, to delay compressibility effects, became universal where speeds above Mach 0·8 were attempted. Most common was the sweptback wing, but the sweptforward wing was also favoured, notably by Junkers, Blohm und Voss and Heinkel. At Blohm und Voss, where the most esoteric of designs could be found, wings combining both sweepback and sweepforward were studied, while, going still further, there was the projected Bv P.202 fighter. In this design, the tapered wing was to be at right angles to the fuselage for optimum take-off and landing performance, but, for high-speed flight, the wing was to pivot so that the port wing had sweepback and the starboard wing sweepforward! One would have thought that the resulting stability problems would have exceeded the mechanical problems of the more conventional variable-sweep wing known today.

Following the successful work of Horten and Lippisch, there was a widespread vogue in designing tailless and delta-wing aircraft for all rôles. It is worth remembering that the de Havilland D.H.108, which on 9 September, 1948, became the first turbojet-powered aircraft officially to exceed Mach 1, was a sweptback tailless aircraft although it had a fin and rudder.

612

Despite the Germans' grasp of the general requirements of high-speed flight, they were, like everyone else, in the dark regarding many of the aerodynamic details which are necessary for high-speed flying. Although they were in possession of some of the finest wind-tunnels and other research equipment in the world, such equipment could give very misleading information because of scale effect. To correct this situation, a supersonic research aircraft was needed from which data could be obtained to calibrate high-speed wind-tunnels, and just such an aircraft, the DFS 346, was being planned. On the important detail side, for instance, much effort was put into the development of landing aids for high-speed aircraft, and even the problem of increasing turbojet air-intake duct efficiency, by bypassing or sucking off the boundary layer, was being tackled in some aircraft designs such as the Junkers EF128 and Messerschmitt P.1110.

The proliferation of known German aircraft projects may give the impression that the German aviation industry was superior to any other, but, although it was advanced in many spheres, one cannot judge an industry from projects alone. As Prof Junkers put it, 'Ideas are as cheap as blackberries!' To an idea must be added practicality, money, and time, and the last commodity was very scarce during the desperate period in which most of the projects discussed here were conceived. One must also bear in mind that, whereas the details for a great proportion of German work were eventually generally released, details of the work of the victorious powers are not so easily found for comparison, although any

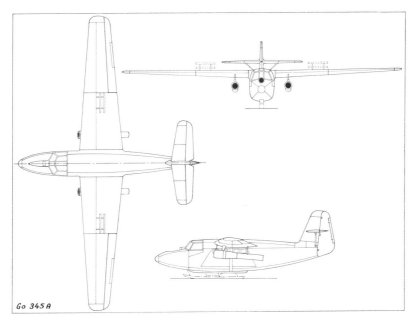

Go 345A

A description of this Gotha Go 345A appears on page 219.

healthy industry continuously plans future developments. In the planning of such future developments, as far as the acquisition of specific aircraft (or weapons) is concerned, some sort of directive must usually come from Government departments. This leads, of course, to the issuing of specifications for competition, and a great many varied and conflicting aircraft specifications were issued by the ever-changing and vacillating military and political leaders of the Third Reich.

# Miniature Fighter Competition

During November 1944, the RLM issued a requirement for the simplest possible type of fighter which could be more rapidly produced than the Heinkel He 162 Salamander (Volksjäger) then being built. The design was not, however, to be a semi-expendable weapon in the manner of the Bachem Ba 349 Natter, because conventional landings and take-offs were to be made. Much had already been done in the Volksjäger (People's Fighter) competition to simplify airframes, so attention now turned towards simplifying the power unit, though without losing too much in the way of performance. Thus, the power unit was to be the simple pulse-jet as produced by Argus for the Fieseler Fi 103 (V1) flying bomb, although it had been shown with the ill-starred Messerschmitt Me 328 that the acoustics of the pulse-jet had bad effects on both airframe and pilot. The Miniaturjäger (Miniature Fighter) was to employ the minimum of strategic materials, dispense with refinements such as electronic equipment and, by virtue of quick production, increase the chances of intercepting the enemy by flying in large numbers. The use of the pulse-jet would save something like 450 man-hours of manufacturing time per engine compared with the turbojets then in use. The problem of supplying all the new pilots was common to both Miniatur- and Volksjäger programmes whichever was adopted. Only three firms, which also participated in the Volksjäger competition, put forward Miniaturjäger projects, Blohm und Voss, Heinkel and Junkers.

# Blohm und Voss P.213

For the Blohm und Voss P.213, wood construction was to be employed for wings and tail surfaces and the unique fuselage was to consist of left and right halves pre-formed from armoured steel sheet. A boom led from the fuselage to support an inverted butterfly tail, beneath which the tube of the 300 kg (660 lb) thrust pulse-jet passed. The pulse-jet was fed with air from a fuselage nose intake but the resulting long intake duct would have required careful design in order not to lose the beneficial ram-effect to the pulse-jet. A bubble canopy was provided for the pilot, and the proposed armament was a single MK 108 30 mm cannon in the nose. Mounted on top of the fuselage, just behind the cockpit, was the wing which had a straight leading edge, sweptforward trailing edge and slight dihedral. The initial boost for take-off was to be provided either by catapult or rockets, and the nosewheel undercarriage retracted into the fuselage. Although this design had various ingenious features, its estimated performance fell below that of the competing Junkers EF 126, and, for that matter, the best German piston-engined fighters, but this was to be expected in view of the small power unit selected.

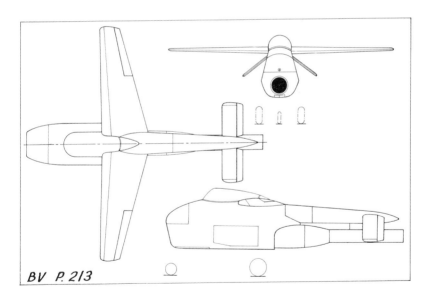

BV P.213

P.213: Span 6 m (19 ft $8\frac{1}{4}$ in); length 6·2 m (20 ft $4\frac{1}{8}$ in); height 2·28 m (7 ft $3\frac{3}{4}$ in); wing area 5 sq m (53·8 sq ft).

Loaded weight 1,560 kg (3,435 lb).

Maximum speed at sea level 700 km/h (435 mph); maximum speed at 9,000 m (29,520 ft) 450 km/h (280 mph); initial rate of climb 1,200 m/min (3,936 ft/min); ceiling 10,000 m (32,800 ft); approximate range 150 km (93 miles).

# Heinkel He 162B

For their entry in the Miniaturjäger competition, Heinkel took the short cut of offering their standard He 162A fitted with either one or two pulse-jets instead of the standard BMW 109-003E turbojet. Either a single Argus 109-044 (He 162B-2) or two Argus 109-014 (He 162B-1) pulse-jets were fitted in a position further aft than the previous turbojet mounting, the twin pulse-jets being mounted side by side. Further description of these aircraft is unnecessary, since they differed as little as possible from the He 162A, but it should be noted that they were to be heavier because of the greater fuel load to be carried.

He 162B-1 with two pulse-jets giving a total thrust of 670 kg (1,475 lb): Span 7·2 m (23 ft 7¾ in); length 9 m (29 ft 8½ in); height 2·55 m (8 ft 4⅜ in); wing area 11·15 sq m (120 sq ft).
Loaded weight 3,300 kg (7,260 lb).
Maximum speed at sea level 810 km/h (503 mph); initial rate of climb 1,098 m/min (3,600 ft/min); ceiling 8,000 m (26,240 ft); range 410 km (255 miles).

He 162B-2 with one pulse-jet of 500 kg (1,100 lb) thrust: Dimensions as for the B-1.
Loaded weight 2,900 kg (6,380 lb).
Maximum speed at sea level 710 km/h (441 mph); initial rate of climb 720 m/min (2,360 ft/min); ceiling 6,500 m (21,320 ft); range 380 km (236 miles).

# Junkers EF 126 Elli

The Junkers EF 126 was to be built with a metal fuselage and wooden flying surfaces largely to resemble the Fieseler Fi 103 (V1) in layout, a single Argus 109-044 pulse-jet of 500 kg (1,100 lb) thrust being fitted above the fuselage and cropped fin, and the pilot seated well forward beneath a bubble canopy. A retractable nosewheel undercarriage was fitted, on which the aircraft took-off with the assistance of two solid-fuelled rockets. It was foreseen that, with the pulse-jet's typical falling-off of performance with altitude, the EF 126 would be at a disadvantage under certain conditions, and so it was also planned to use the aircraft in the ground-attack rôle. Therefore, in addition to the two MG 151/20 20 mm cannon in the nose, with 180 rounds of ammunition, provision was made to carry an auxiliary ground-attack load of 400 kg (880 lb) beneath the wings. This auxiliary load could consist, for example, of two AB 250-3 containers each holding 108 SD2 (Butterfly) anti-personnel bombs, which were scattered by an air-burst fuse.

616

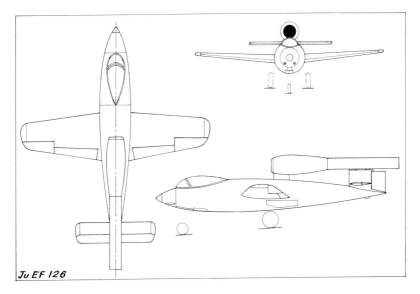

Ju EF 126

Although no EF 126 flew during the war, a mockup was built at Dessau, and, after the war, the Russians were sufficiently interested to have a prototype built. This unpowered prototype was test-flown after being towed to height by another aircraft but was completely destroyed upon landing, killing the pilot.

EF 126 Elli: Span 6·65 m (21 ft 9$\frac{7}{8}$ in); length 7·6 m (24 ft 11$\frac{1}{4}$ in); wing area 8·9 sq m (95·8 sq ft).

Empty weight 1,100 kg (2,426 lb); pilot 100 kg (220 lb); ammunition 100 kg (220 lb); fuel 1,100 kg (2,426 lb); auxiliary load 400 kg (880 lb); maximum loaded weight 2,800 kg (6,172 lb).

Maximum speed at sea level 780 km/h (485 mph) without auxiliary load or 680 km/h (422 mph) with auxiliary load; initial rate of climb with auxiliary load 480 m/min (1,575 ft/min); endurance 23 min at maximum speed or 45 min on 60 per cent power; range 300 km (186 miles) at maximum speed or 350 km (218 miles) on 60 per cent power.

# Emergency Fighter Competition

During 1943, details became available of the Heinkel-Hirth 109-011 turbo-jet of 1,300 kg (2,866 lb) static thrust, which was being developed as a second-generation engine to replace the less-powerful Junkers and BMW turbojets then going into service. Aircraft firms, particularly Focke-Wulf and Messerschmitt, therefore began planning projects for single-engined aircraft which could equal or surpass the performance of twin-engined jet aircraft such as the Messerschmitt Me 262. For some time, no official requirement was issued for such new aircraft, because there was full confidence in the superiority of existing jet aircraft, and, in any case, development of the 109-011 engine was very protracted. Towards the end of the war, however, the failure of aircraft powered by BMW 003 and Junkers 004 turbojets to operate reliably above about 11,000 m (36,080 ft) was seen as a shortcoming which could nullify the introduction of German jets. The problem became all the more urgent for the Me 262 fighter with the imminent appearance of Allied jet aircraft, and, in any event, it was considered that a service ceiling of at least 13,000 m (42,640 ft) was necessary to combat such Allied aircraft as the Boeing B-29 Superfortress, de Havilland Mosquito, Lockheed Lightning and Republic Thunderbolt.

The OKL (High Command of the Luftwaffe) therefore insisted that an improved fighter was urgently needed and, at the end of 1944, an Emergency Fighter Competition was instigated by Col Siegfried Kneymeyer, Chief of Technical Air Armament (Chef/TLR). The specification issued to all the main aircraft companies required that the new fighter be powered by a single Heinkel-Hirth 109-011A turbojet, have a level speed of about 1,000 km/h (621 mph) at 7,000 m (22,960 ft), operate at altitudes up to 14,000 m (45,920 ft) and be armed with four MK 108 30 mm cannon. By February 1945, two projects had been received from Focke-Wulf, three from Messerschmitt, and one each from Heinkel, Junkers, and Blohm und Voss, both Focke-Wulf and Messerschmitt showing particular interest in the proposal after their lack of enthusiasm for the earlier Volksjäger and Miniaturjäger competitions. On 27 and 28 February, an official meeting was held to make a decision about these projects, and Focke-Wulf's first proposal was selected in mid-March for development and production under the designation Ta 183. The eight projects described in the following are only those which were ready in time for the official selection, and most of the data are based on those given at that time and are arranged as far as possible to allow ready comparison. Because of bad communications at that late stage of the war, much difficulty was experienced in preparing and collecting the various project estimates, and the usual comparative report of the DVL Institute could not be obtained in full.

# Blohm und Voss P.212

The Blohm und Voss P.212 project was of very unorthodox design. It was a tailless mid-wing monoplane to be powered by a Heinkel-Hirth 109-011A turbojet. The wing was sweptback 40 deg at quarter chord, was untapered and had marked dihedral. There were full-span leading-edge slats, and wide-span trailing-edge flaps with, outboard, very-short-span ailerons. The structure was of metal with steel skin. At the rear of each wingtip was a low aspect ratio fin and rudder and outboard of these structures were downswept tapered surfaces, the rear sections of which acted as elevators and, to some extent, additional rudders and ailerons.

The fuselage was quite deep and extended well aft of the trailing-edge roots with the tailpipe almost in line with the trailing edge of the rudders. The pressurized cockpit had a bubble canopy and was positioned above the curved tubular-steel duct which led from the nose air intake to the engine and formed part of the fuselage structure. The nosewheel undercarriage retracted forward into the fuselage and in the nose were two MK 108 30 mm cannon (100 rpg) with provision for another three MK 108s (60 rpg).

The fuselage fuel tank and wing integral tanks provided a total capacity of 1,500 litres (330 Imp gal).

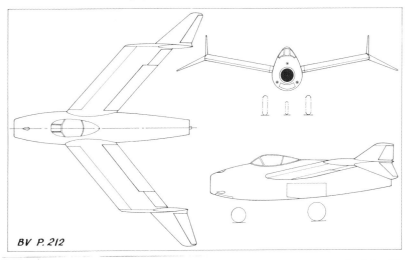

BV P.212

P.212: Span 7 m (22 ft 11⅝ in); length 7·55 m (24 ft 9¼ in); wing area 14 sq m (150·7 sq ft).
Empty weight 2,700 kg (5,954 lb); pilot 100 kg (220 lb); fuel 1,250 kg (2,757 lb); ammunition 120 kg (264 lb); loaded weight 4,170 kg (9,195 lb).
Maximum speed at sea level 910 km/h (565 mph); initial rate of climb 1,280 m/min (4,200 ft/min); take-off distance 840 m (2,757 ft); landing speed 177 km/h (110 mph); landing distance 608 m (1,986 ft); service ceiling 12,500 m (42,000 ft); range 1,125 km (699 miles).

# Heinkel P.1078C

The Heinkel P.1078 was originally projected in three versions designated P.1078A, B, and C, but only the C version was submitted. The P.1078A was similar to Messerschmitt's P.1101 entry, but the P.1078B was a tailless version with a similar wing but a totally new fuselage. The new fuselage, which no longer needed the tail boom, had the nose section divided into two 'gondolas', that to port for the pilot and the starboard 'gondola' for the armament, a rectangular air intake being set well back between the two. Although the B version offered improved performance over the A version, it was considered that the air intake might cause difficulties and, in any case, the pilot's view to starboard was restricted. Some consideration was then given to various asymmetrical arrangements, but, finally, the more conventional P.1078C design was adopted.

The P.1078C was a tailless aircraft with the wing swept back 40 deg at quarter-chord, the wingtips having marked anhedral. This aircraft was estimated to have an altitude advantage of about 900 m (2,950 ft) and a sea-level speed advantage of 48 km/h (30 mph) over the P.1078A. Also the structural weight was reduced by about 150 kg (330 lb). The anhedral wingtips were adopted because it was felt that these would, compared with vertical fins, have less influence on the critical Mach number of the wing and also give better roll damping. Constructional details were not settled but it is likely that the P.1078C would have had an all-metal structure except for wooden outer wing panels. The fuel capacity of 1,450 litres (320 Imp gal) would have been provided in the wing, and the air intake duct was to have been flattened to provide space above for the cockpit and below for the retracted nosewheel. The mainwheels would have retracted forwards and inwards into the fuselage, and the two MK 108 30 mm cannon (100 rpg) would have been mounted one each side of the cockpit. Power was provided by a 1,300 kg (2,866 lb) thrust Heinkel-Hirth 109-011A turbojet.

P.1078C: Span 9 m (29 ft 6$\frac{3}{8}$ in.); length 6 m (19 ft 8$\frac{1}{4}$ in); wing area 17·82 sq m (191·6 sq ft).

Empty weight 2,450 kg (5,403 lb); pilot 100 kg (220 lb); fuel 1,200 kg (2,646 lb); ammunition 120 kg (264 lb); loaded weight 3,870 kg (8,533 lb).

Maximum speed at sea level 1,025 km/h (636 mph), at 7,000 m (22,960 ft) 990 km/h (615 mph); initial rate of climb 1,255 m/min (4,018 ft/min); take-off distance 700 m (2,298 ft); landing speed 183 km/h (114 mph); landing distance 640 m (2,100 ft); ceiling 12,900 m (42,312 ft); maximum range 1,500 km (932 miles).

# Junkers EF 128

The Junkers EF 128 was another tailless design but, unlike the Blohm und Voss P.212 and Heinkel P.1078C, had the important difference of having air intakes at the fuselage sides under the wing at about the mid-chord position, these intakes being arranged to divert the boundary-layer flow to a vent outlet aft of the cockpit fairing. The wings, of two-spar, all-wood construction, were shoulder-mounted, swept back 45 deg at quarter-chord and had twin vertical fins and rudders on the trailing edge at about mid-span and extending above and below, and the trailing edges of the wings had ailerons and elevators. There was a small ventral fin at the rear of the fuselage. 540 litres (119 Imp gal) of fuel were contained in the wings, and a further 1,025 litres (226 Imp gal) were contained in a fuselage tank. Like the Heinkel design, the pressurized cockpit was provided with an ejector seat and armour protection. The nosewheel undercarriage retracted backwards into the fuselage, and the twin MK 108 30 mm cannon (100 rpg) were installed in the sides of the nose, with provision for a further two. Power was provided by a 1,300 kg (2,866 lb) thrust Heinkel-Hirth 109-011A turbojet.

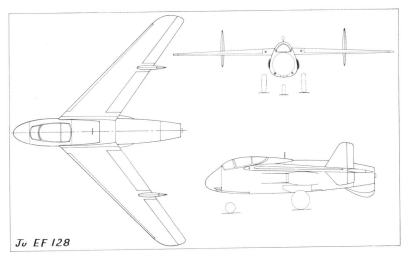

Ju EF 128

EF 128: Span 8·9 m (29 ft 2¾ in); length 7 m (22 ft 11⅝ in); wing area 17·6 sq m (189·5 sq ft).

Empty weight 2,600 kg (5,733 lb); pilot 100 kg (220 lb); fuel 1,250 kg (2,757 lb); ammunition 120 kg (264 lb); loaded weight 4,070 kg (8,974 lb).

Maximum speed at 96 per cent thrust: at sea level 900 km/h (559 mph), at 7,000 m (22,960 ft) 990 km/h (615 mph); initial rate of climb 1,370 m/min (4,500 ft/min); take-off distance 700 m (2,298 ft); landing speed 186 km/h (116 mph); landing distance 665 m (2,180 ft); ceiling 13,750 m (45,100 ft); range 1,300 km (808 miles).

# Messerschmitt P.1101

Design of the Messerschmitt P.1101 was begun early in 1944 and, on the company's own initiative, the construction of a prototype started around July 1944. This prototype was to ascertain the best sweepback angle for the wings, which could be varied on the ground between 35 deg and 45 deg. For the competition entry, the P.1101 was submitted in the following form: The wing, swept back 40 deg at quarter-chord, was shoulder-mounted and had steel spars with wooden ribs and skin. Wing leading-edge slots and plain camber-changing flaps were provided as well as conventional aileron, elevator and rudder controls, all tail surfaces being swept. The barrel-like fuselage had a slender tail-boom aft of the tailpipe, a pressurized cockpit set well forward, and a nose air intake, the turbojet exhausting beneath the tail boom. Armour plate gave the pilot protection against 12·7 mm fire from the front and 20 mm fire from the rear. The nose-mounted armament consisted of either two or four MK 108 cannon (100 rpg). The nosewheel retracted with a 90 deg turn into the space beneath the air intake, and the main undercarriage wheels retracted rearwards and inwards. Three fuselage fuel tanks, totalling 1,565 litres (345 Imp gal) capacity, were installed behind the cockpit above the wing spars.

The development of this aircraft was the main task for Messerschmitt engineers at Oberammergau during the latter stage of the war. Construction of the prototype, which had a Junkers 109-004B turbojet because the

The sole Messerschmitt P.1101 jet fighter, construction of which began around July 1944.

The uncompleted P.1101 was taken to the United States after the war. Here it is seen used as mockup with an Allison J-35 turbojet fitted, but the Germans had planned to use the Heinkel-Hirth 109-011A turbojet eventually.

Heinkel-Hirth engine was not ready, was about 80 per cent complete when it was transferred to the Tyrol mountain area where it was discovered by the Americans. The P.1101 was then taken to the USA and, together with the detail drawings, given to the Bell Aircraft Corporation for examination. This resulted in the Bell X-5 research aircraft, which, although superficially similar to the P.1101, was an entirely new aircraft. The most important difference was that the wing sweepback could be varied in flight from 20 deg to 60 deg. New fuselage profiles were created to accommodate alternative American turbojets and changes were made in the tail surfaces.

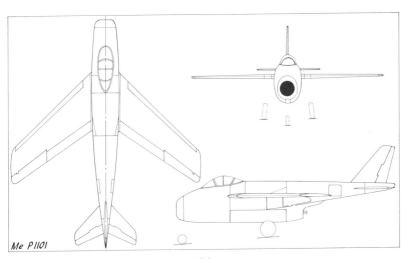

Me P1101

623

This work was begun late in 1948, and, on 20 June, 1951, the first of two X-5s made its maiden flight piloted by 'Skip' Ziegler from Edwards Air Force Base, California.

P.1101: Span 8·24 m (27 ft 0⅜ in); length 9·25 m (30 ft 4⅛ in); height 2·8 m (9 ft 2¼ in); wing area 15·86 sq m (170·6 sq ft).

Empty weight 2,600 kg (5,733 lb); pilot 100 kg (220 lb); fuel 1,250 kg (2,757 lb); ammunition 120 kg (264 lb); loaded weight 4,070 kg (8,974 lb).

Maximum speed at sea level 885 km/h (550 mph), at 7,000 m (22,960 ft) 981 km/h (609 mph); initial rate of climb 1,335 m/min (4,380 ft/min); take-off distance 720 m (2,361 ft); landing speed 172 km/h (107 mph); landing distance 570 m (1,869 ft); ceiling 13,800 m (45,265 ft); range 1,500 km (932 miles).

# Messerschmitt P.1110

The Messerschmitt P.1110 had a similar wing to the P.1101 but an entirely new fuselage and tail layout. All-metal construction was used throughout, and the elimination of a nose air intake made possible a slender fuselage of roughly circular cross-section. Initially, the air intakes were to be rectangular openings at the fuselage sides just forward of the wing trailing-edge fillets (P.1110/I), but these were to be replaced by an annular intake surrounding the fuselage at the same point (P.1110/II). A suction fan, driven from the turbojet engine, was to draw in the boundary-layer air from the forward part of the fuselage through slots in the air intake. In the P.1110/I design, a single vertical fin with a sweptback

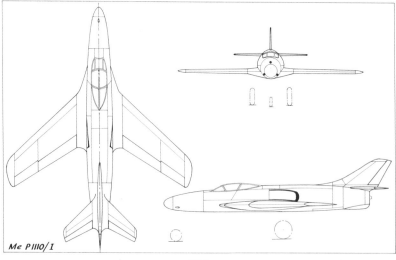

Me P1110/I

tailplane at its base was provided, the unit being of rubber and wood construction, but this was to be changed in the P.1110/II design to a butterfly tail unit. The pressurized cockpit had a canopy of very low profile and the usual armour protection. In front of the cockpit were three MK 108 cannon (two with 70 rpg and the third with 100 rpg) grouped in the nose, and there was provision for a further two MK 108s in the wing roots. The nosewheel retracted into the lower portion of the gun compartment, and the main undercarriage members retracted forwards into the wing roots. The aircraft was powered by a 1,300 kg (2,866 lb) thrust Heinkel-Hirth 109-011A turbojet.

P.1110/I: Span 8·24 m (27 ft 0¾ in); length 9·25 m (30 ft 4⅛ in); wing area 15·86 sq m (170·6 sq ft).

Empty weight 2,800 kg (6,174 lb); pilot 100 kg (220 lb); fuel 1,250 kg (2,757 lb); ammunition 145 kg (319 lb); loaded weight 4,295 kg (9,470 lb).

Maximum speed at 96 per cent thrust: at sea level 900 km/h (559 mph), at 7,000 m (22,960 ft) 1,000 km/h (621 mph); initial rate of climb 1,289 m/min (4,230 ft/min); take-off distance 790 m (2,590 ft); landing speed 179 km/h (111 mph); landing distance 610 m (2,000 ft); ceiling 13,100 m (42,968 ft); range 1,500 km (932 miles).

# Messerschmitt P.1111

The Messerschmitt P.1111 design was for a tailless aircraft, powered by a 1,300 kg (2,866 lb) thrust Heinkel-Hirth 109-011A turbojet, the wings being swept back 45 deg at the quarter-chord line. The wings were of wide chord to form a near-delta planform but with considerable trailing-edge sweepback, and a single sweptback vertical fin and rudder extended beyond

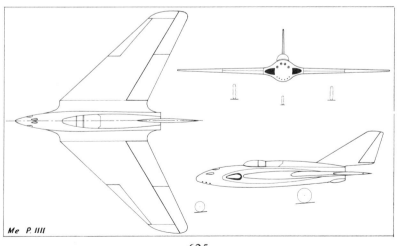

Me P. IIII

the rear of the fuselage. The wing-mounted controls consisted of elevons, inboard split flaps and outboard leading-edge slats. There were air intakes in the wing roots, and slightly curved ducts passed either side of the cockpit to the turbojet. Each wing contained three fuel tanks, the total capacity being 1,565 litres (345 Imp gal). The canopy for the pressurized cockpit had a long fairing extending to the base of the fin, and armour was similar to that in the other Messerschmitt designs. Four MK 108 cannon were installed in the nose, these having 100 rpg. The wide-track tricycle undercarriage had the nosewheel mounted well forward, the mainwheels retracted inwards into the wing roots and the nosewheel retracted rearwards into the bottom of the gun compartment.

P.1111: Span 9·16 m (30 ft 0⅝ in); length 6·50 m (21 ft 3⅞ in); wing area 28·03 sq m (301·39 sq ft).

Empty weight 2,750 kg (6,064 lb); pilot 100 kg (220 lb); fuel 1,250 kg (2,757 lb); ammunition 220 kg (485 lb); loaded weight 4,320 kg (9,526 lb).

Maximum speed at 96 per cent thrust: at sea level 900 km/h (559 mph), at 7,000 m (22,960 ft) 995 km/h (618 mph); initial rate of climb 1,423 m/min (4,668 ft/min); take-off distance 600 m (1,968 ft); landing speed 155 km/h (96 mph); landing distance 450 m (1,476 ft); range 1,500 km (932 miles).

# Focke-Wulf Ta 183

Beginning in 1942, a Focke-Wulf team headed by Hans Multhopp made a series of aerodynamic studies for turbojet fighters. These studies culminated in a fighter project study known at Focke-Wulf as Huckebein (a raven which traditionally made trouble for others). From this project study, two similar designs were put forward as entries in the Emergency Fighter Competition and one was later designated Ta 183. Purely for convenience, the two designs are called Fw Project I and II in the following.

Fw Project I: This was an aircraft with stubby fuselage, mid-mounted wings swept back 40 deg at quarter-chord and a long, slender fin swept back 60 deg with the dihedral tailplane mounted at its apex. The wing had a tapered main spar constructed from two dural I-beams with steel flanges to form a torque box, the spar attachment at the fuselage centreline being by means of a single bolt. Bonded wooden ribs and plywood skinning built up the wings around the main spar, and each wing panel contained six fuel compartments totalling 1,565 litres (345 Imp gal) capacity. Forged fittings, welded to the main spar, and steel root ribs were used, and the two wings could be interchanged since they had the same profile over the entire span and no camber, twist or dihedral. The fin and tailplane comprised laminated wood torsion-box beams with wooden ribs and formers covered with plywood. Control was by means of wing elevons and the rudder, the

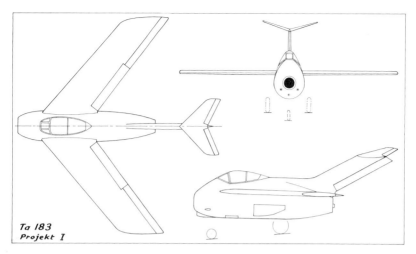

Ta 183
Projekt I

control surfaces on the tailplane being used only for trimming. Trimming was electrically actuated, but there was hydraulic operation of the flaps and also the nosewheel undercarriage which retracted into the fuselage. The fuselage was divided longitudinally into two main sections, the upper section being the primary structure designed to take up the forces from the wings, tail assembly, engine and undercarriage. This upper section contained the pressurized cockpit, positioned well forward and with frontal armour protection. The lower section housed the turbojet, with a cylindrical air duct passing directly back from the nose intake, and two nose-mounted MK 108 cannon (100 rpg). This armament could be increased to four MK 108s, but total ammunition was then 320 rounds. The turbojet was a 1,300 kg (2,866 lb) thrust Heinkel-Hirth 109-011A. A semi-monocoque mixed construction making extensive use of spot-welded light-

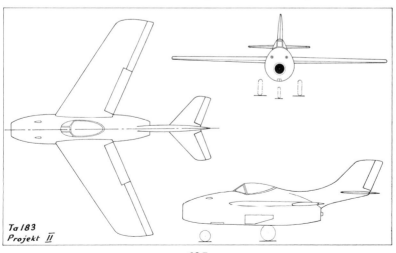

Ta 183
Projekt II

metal skinning was to be used for the fuselage. Steel, wood and duralumin respectively accounted for 40, 23 and 21 per cent of the airframe structure weight, and the production of a complete aircraft with engine and including final pre-flight inspection was estimated at only 2,500 man-hours, based on a production rate of 300 aircraft per month and working two shifts a day.

Following the February 1945 conference at which the Emergency Fighter projects were finally considered, the OKL decided to have Focke-Wulf's Project I developed, and this was accordingly ordered in March under the designation Ta 183. With the greatest possible speed, the Focke-Wulf concern co-ordinated its offices at Bremen, Bad Eilsen, and Detmold with a view to detail-designing the Ta 183. Preceding mass production there were to be 16 Versuchs aircraft, comprising the Ta 183 V1 to V3, powered by Junkers 109-004B turbojets (pending delivery of the Heinkel-Hirth 109-011A engines), the Ta 183 V4 to V14 as 0-series pre-production aircraft, and the Ta 183 V15 and V16 as static test aircraft. Detail design work was never completed, however, and no aircraft were built, since, by April, all factories suitable for production were over-run by Allied troops.

Provision was made in the original project for the aircraft to have the extra power of a 1,000 kg (2,205 lb) thrust rocket motor to enhance the interception performance. The rocket fuel for a 200-sec burn was to be contained in underwing drop-tanks, and the extra equipment weighed about 150 kg (330 lb). Alternatively, for use as a fighter-bomber, it was planned that a bomb load of up to 500 kg (1,100 lb) could be carried in the equipment space in the bottom of the fuselage. Loaded in this manner, the bomb would have protruded about halfway out of the fuselage. The following data relate to the aircraft in the fighter configuration without rocket equipment or bomb load.

Project I (Ta 183): Span 10 m (32 ft 9¾ in); length 9·4 m (30 ft 10 in); wing area 22·52 sq m (242·2 sq ft).

Empty weight 2,830 kg (6,241 lb); pilot 100 kg (220 lb); fuel 1,250 kg (2,756 lb); ammunition 120 kg (264 lb); loaded weight 4,300 kg (9,481 lb).

Maximum speed at sea level 871 km/h (541 mph), at 7,000 m (22,960 ft) 955 km/h (593 mph); initial rate of climb 1,225 m/min (4,020 ft/min); take-off distance 658 m (2,160 ft); landing speed 165 km/h (102 mph); landing distance 508 m (1,665 ft); ceiling 14,000 m (45,920 ft).

Project II: This design was similar in layout and equipment to Project I but was aerodynamically less radical. A slimmer fuselage was designed and wing sweepback was only 32 deg at quarter-chord. The wing was also set further back from the fuselage nose. A fin of wider chord carried the tailplane near its base, and the method of control was the same as for Project I. The nose-mounted armament of two MK 108 cannon (100 rpg) could be supplemented by a third cannon at the expense of the forward-fuselage fuel tank.

Project II: Span 9·5 m (31 ft 2 in); length 8·75 m (28 ft 8½ in); wing area 20·02 sq m (215·28 sq ft).

Empty weight 2,650 kg (5,844 lb); pilot 100 kg (220 lb); fuel 1,250 kg (2,756 lb); ammunition 120 kg (264 lb); loaded weight 4,120 kg (9,084 lb).

Maximum speed at sea level 905 km/h (562 mph), at 7,000 m (22,960 ft) 963 km/h (598 mph); initial rate of climb 1,390 m/min (4,560 ft/min); take-off distance 659 m (2,160 ft); landing speed 166 km/h (103 mph); landing distance 512 m (1,680 ft); ceiling 13,500 m (44,280 ft).

Other projects designed to meet the Emergency Fighter specification, which were too late for official consideration, included the Messerschmitt P.1116 and Henschel P.135, which differed widely in layout. The Me P.1116 design had a 40 deg sweptback wing and a cockpit mounted well aft along the fuselage just forward of a butterfly tail unit. There was a nose air intake leading to the engine bay which was beneath the fuselage nose-section and which ended at the rear of the wing roots, so that the jet exhaust passed beneath the rear fuselage. The Henschel P.135, on the other hand, was a stubby aircraft with slim, semi-delta wings having slightly upturned tips. The canopy of the centrally-mounted cockpit was faired back into the base of a single vertical fin and rudder, which projected aft of the rear of the fuselage, and there was a central nose air intake.

# Ramjet Fighters

Systematic experiments with ramjet power units were first begun in Germany by H. Walter KG at Kiel around 1937 and were followed, beginning in 1938, by the work of Dr Wolf Trommsdorf on ramjet-accelerated artillery shells. Work that was more nearly to see its outcome in aircraft powered by ramjets was done by Dr Eugen Sänger at the DFS, starting in 1941, and under Dr Otto Pabst at Focke-Wulf's gas dynamics department. Other men, such as Dr Alexander Lippisch, also made their own basic ramjet calculations.

Up to the end of 1943, however, there was little official interest shown in the ramjet, despite its attractions of simplicity and promise of high speeds. There were many reasons for this lack of enthusiasm, such as the ramjet's needing to be boosted up to its self-operating speed and its high fuel consumption, but there was also the fact that no aircraft had been flown solely on ramjet power, unlike the equally new turbojet and rocket power forms. Only Sänger's ramjets had been, rather unimpressively, air-towed above Dornier test beds. Ramjet work, then, remained unco-ordinated and out of the limelight for some time. The situation began to improve, when, in November 1944, it was decided at a meeting of the Chef/TLR that the ramjet was of importance and that experience with it should be shared as quickly as possible and on a large scale. The development of subsonic ramjets was stressed. Although full official subsidy was now available for the work, it should be said that, in view of the then critical shortage of aviation fuels, exaggerated hopes were held in official circles of using non-strategic solid fuels such as foam coal. In fact, however, any serious aircraft design that followed, discreetly made provision for the carrying of liquid fuel even if the design initially called for solid fuel. Details are given here of four projects either considered or worked on in various stages to use a ramjet powerplant.

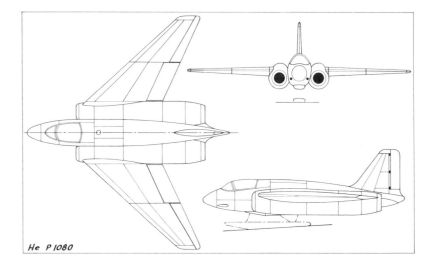

He P.1080

# Heinkel P.1080

Shortly before the end of the war, Heinkel received data on ramjets from the DFS and, with an official order, designed a tailless fighter. This project, the P.1080, envisaged the use of two 900 mm (2 ft 11½ ft) diameter ramjet ducts mounted one on each side of the fuselage and with their outer surfaces faired into the wing, the greater proportion of the ducts being exposed to the airstream for cooling purposes. To cut down on design time, the sweptback wings with the elevon controls were based on those for the Heinkel P.1078 but a single orthodox fin and rudder was used in place of wingtip anhedral. The pilot's cockpit was placed well forward, sufficient space being left in the nose for a radar unit and two MK 108 30 mm cannon. The rear fuselage housed a fuel tank. For take-off, boosting power was provided by four solid-fuel rockets each of 1,000 kg (2,205 lb) thrust. A jettisonable undercarriage was to be used, and the landing was to be made on an extendible skid.

P.1080: Span 8·9 m (29 ft 3⅜ in); length 8·15 m (26 ft 8⅞ in); wing area 20 sq m (215·2 sq ft).

The sea-level thrust expected from each ramjet was 420 kg (926 lb) at 500 km/h (311 mph), and 1,560 kg (3,440 lb) at 1,000 km/h (621 mph). No other details known.


# Lippisch LP-13a

Stemming from his research programme into high-speed delta-wing aircraft design at the LFA, Vienna, Dr Alexander Lippisch projected a ramjet-powered interceptor late in 1944. This design, the LP-13a, was for an aircraft having a pure delta wing completely enclosing a centrally-mounted ramjet duct, and a triangular dorsal fin, the latter containing the cockpit with a glazed leading-edge section. The wings had a leading-edge sweepback of 60 deg, the elliptical-form profile having a thickness ratio of 16·6 per cent, while the thickness ratio of the fin was some 19·2 per cent. Scale-model experiments in a DVL high-speed wind-tunnel indicated that the structure of the LP-13a had outstanding stability up to the maximum tested speed of Mach 2·6, and no unfavourable characteristics were indicated in the subsonic range. Less promising aspects of the design were that powdered coal fuel was to be used, and it is not clear how the duct was to be cooled. A liquid-fuelled rocket motor was planned for take-off and boosting to operating velocity when the coal was to be ignited by an oil burner which had, in turn, been ignited by a gas flame. The test glider, Lippisch DM-1, which was to ascertain the low-speed characteristics of the LP-13a, is described on page 461.

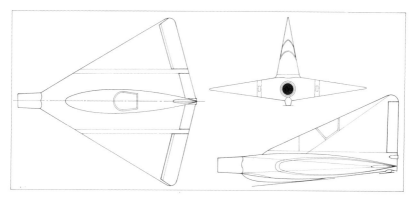

LP-13a: Span 5·92 m (19 ft 5⅛ in); length 6·7 m (21 ft 11¼ in); height 3·18 m (10 ft 5¼ in); wing area 20 sq m (215 sq ft).
Loaded weight 2,300 kg (5,072 lb).
Maximum speed at high altitude 1,650 km/h (1,025 mph); maximum duration 45 min, for which an estimated 800 kg (1,760 lb) of solid fuel was required.

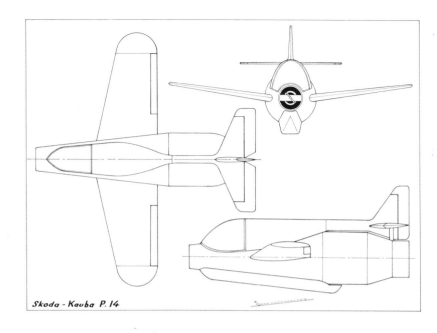

Skoda - Kauba P. 14

# Skoda-Kauba SK P.14

At the beginning of 1945, the Skoda-Kauba Flugzeugbau in Prague issued a work order to the DFS for the design of a subsonic interceptor with ramjet propulsion. How the design work was divided between the two concerns is uncertain, but Skoda was to build the aircraft. The SK P.14 had a centrally-located ramjet duct with a diameter of 1,500 mm (4 ft 11 in) and a length of 9,500 mm (31 ft 2 in). This duct formed an integral part of the fuselage structure, but the walls of the constant-diameter section (the combustion chamber) and the exhaust nozzle were exposed to the airstream for cooling. The pilot, who occupied a prone position beneath a canopy, together with a fuel tank, tail unit and an MK 108 cannon, were all situated along the top of the duct. All flying surfaces were of tapered planform, the wings being mounted on the duct centreline and the tailplane occupying a high position. Take-off and boost rockets were provided, the take-off run being made on a jettisonable tricycle undercarriage and the landing on an extendible skid. Fuel for the ramjet was planned as foam coal initially, but the design made provision for switching to liquid fuel if this became available. Data for the SK P.14 are more detailed than for most of the ramjet projects, and the following details are believed to have come from the construction manual.

SK P.14: Span 7·9 m (25 ft 11 in); length 9·5 m (31 ft 2 in); height 4·2 m (13 ft 9⅜ in); wing area 12·5 sq m (135 sq ft).

Empty weight 1,480 kg (3,264 lb); pilot 100 kg (220 lb); fuel 1,200 kg (2,646 lb); ammunition and oxygen 70 kg (154 lb); loaded weight 2,850 kg (6,284 lb).

Maximum speed at sea level 1,000 km/h (621 mph); initial rate of climb 810 m/min (2,657 ft/min); take-off distance 200 m (656 ft); landing speed 150 km/h (93 mph); landing distance 150 m (492 ft); service ceiling 18,500 m (60,680 ft); time to service ceiling from standing start 12·7 min; optimum operating time 45 min at 640 km/h (398 mph) at 13,000 m (42,640 ft). The ramjet was expected to give a thrust of 4,400 kg (9,702 lb) at sea level and Mach 0·83, or 1,350 kg (2,878 lb) at 10,000 m (32,800 ft) and Mach 0·815.

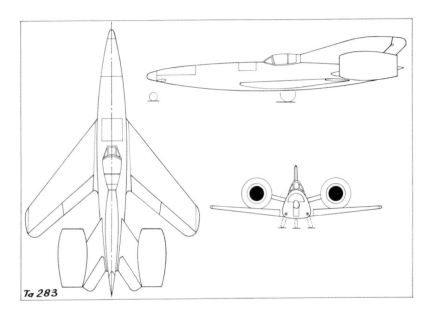

Ta 283

# Focke-Wulf Ta 283

Under the designation Ta 283, Focke-Wulf instituted the design of a fighter to be powered by two unusually bulbous ramjet units. These units, more promising in various respects than Sänger's long ramjet ducts, were based on the work of Pabst and were of the type designed for the Focke-Wulf Triebflügel project described on page 609. Trial units had been tested in an LFA wind-tunnel up to Mach 0·9 with some success. To avoid any disturbance of the airflow, the ramjets for the Ta 283 were mounted at the tips of the sharply sweptback tailplane while the low-set wings had a leading-edge sweep of 45 deg and split flaps. The fin and rudder had more the appearance of a dorsal spine and was faired into the cockpit canopy. The wings and cockpit were set well back, resulting in a long slim nose in which the armament was installed. The aircraft sat very low on a retractable nosewheel undercarriage and take-off was to be achieved by the use of a Walter rocket motor.

Ta 283: Span 7·97 m (26 ft 1¾ in); length 11·81 m (36 ft 5⅝ in).
Loaded weight 5,380 kg (11,863 lb).
Maximum speed at service ceiling 1,125 km/h (699 mph) or Mach 1·05; climb to 3,000 m (9,840 ft) 2·5 min; service ceiling 10,000 m (32,800 ft); range 690 km (429 miles).

# Rocket-powered Aircraft

Since the Germans had developed rocket motors to the stage where they could be, and were, successfully used in aircraft and missiles, there were naturally a good many projects planned for this form of power where duration could be sacrificed for speed, rate of climb and ceiling. The competition for a piloted, rocket-powered aircraft, intended to combine the virtues of interceptor aircraft and missile, was won by Bachem's Ba 349 Natter in August 1944, and this is described on page 55. There was also the similarly-powered Focke-Wulf Volksjäger project submitted, not very seriously, as a competitor to the Heinkel He 162A Salamander. Selected from a long list of such projects, two having widely differing aims are described here, the first was for operational use and the second for pure research.

# Arado E.381

By December 1944, Arado had worked out in some detail the projected E.381 rocket-powered interceptor which differed from previously mentioned designs in that it was to be carried to the combat zone beneath an Arado Ar 234C turbojet aircraft thereby minimizing the usual handicap of limited duration. The small E. 381 had a fuselage with a rounded glazed nose, and simple rectangular wings which were positioned halfway along the fuselage and just above the centreline. Just forward of the wing leading edge, the top of the fuselage was increased in height with a rounded step which led straight back to the tail unit. This consisted of a rectangular tailplane, mounted just above the wake of the wing, and almost-square endplate fins. Control surfaces comprised full-span ailerons, a one-piece full-span elevator and twin rudders. The underside of the final fuselage section was cut away in a step for the egress of the rocket exhaust. Because of limited ground clearance beneath the Ar 234C, the fuselage cross-section of the E.381 was kept to the minimum, which in turn meant a prone position for the pilot. Furthermore, in order to clear the undercarriage of the carrier aircraft, the E.381 had to be suspended well aft of the carrier aircraft's centre of gravity, and this meant that its wings had to give full support from the start of the mission. During coupled flight, the pilot of the fighter received instructions from the carrier pilot regarding trim changes, which were effected by altering the longitudinal angle of the fighter relative to the carrier. Release of the fighter was made as high above the enemy formation as possible and the rocket motor switched on only to maintain a high speed and for climbing for a second attack. The fighter returned to base, making use of its considerable gliding range, landed on a skid and released its braking parachute. If necessary, the fighter could be dismantled into units of wing, fuselage, and tail unit, which were light enough for manual handling.

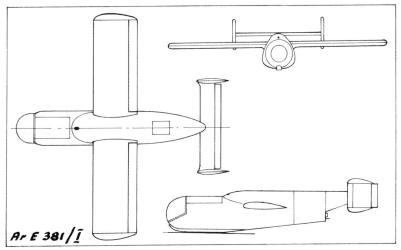

Ar E 381/I

The fuselage nose section was formed from a 5 mm armour-steel tube into a pear-shaped cross-section with a Plexiglas nose fairing, inside which was a 140 mm ($5\frac{1}{2}$ in) armour glass screen for protection. Access to the cockpit was by means of a front, upper armoured hatch. Alongside the pilot's legs were two C-Stoff containers and behind his feet was the T-Stoff tank, all suitably protected. The rear section of the fuselage housed the controllable Walter 109-509A-2 rocket unit which exhausted its 1,700 kg (3,740 lb) thrust beneath the short tail section. The single MK 108 cannon was installed in the top of the fuselage above the wing, had 45 rounds of ammunition and fired over the cockpit section. All flying surfaces and the rear of the fuselage used sheet-steel construction, the wing having a tubular steel spar, and the spaces inside the flying surfaces were filled with light metal as a protection against aerial mines. For high-altitude flight, the pilot appears to have been provided only with oxygen equipment and, from the carrier aircraft, with hot air heating.

635

Ar E.381: Span 5 m (16 ft $4\frac{7}{8}$ in); length 4·95 m (16 ft $2\frac{7}{8}$ in); wing area 5·5 sq m (59·18 sq ft).

Empty weight 890 kg (1,963 lb); pilot 100 kg (220 lb); C-Stoff fuel 52 kg (115 lb); T-Stoff oxidizer 150 kg (330 lb); ammunition 28 kg (62 lb); loaded weight 1,220 kg (2,690 lb).

Maximum speed at 8,000 m (26,240 ft) 900 km/h (559 mph).

# DFS 346

The first part of the DFS research programme in which the subsonic DFS 228 was used to test the pressure cabin, emergency pilot-rescue equipment and rocket unit at high altitudes where it was considered supersonic flight could be most easily achieved at a later stage, was described on page 97. The second part of this programme had the aim of determining the characteristics of various wing forms before proceeding to the programme's third part, supersonic flight tests. In order to flight-test various wings therefore, the DFS acquired the designs for Heinkel's projected P.1068 (which preceded Heinkel's projected He 343A four-engined jet bomber) and modified it to give five versions as follows: P.1068—with 25 deg swept-back wing; P.1068A—with 35 deg sweptback wing; P.1068B—with unswept wings but with propulsion; P.1068C—with 35 deg sweptback wings and propulsion; P.1068D—with 35 deg sweptback wings with laminar profile.

Where used, propulsion was to be by means of up to four Walter 109-509A-1 rocket units having a maximum thrust of 1,500 kg (3,300 lb) each. All versions could be fitted with mockup nacelles for turbojets and had slots and Fowler flaps, only the P.1068D having additional nose flaps. The

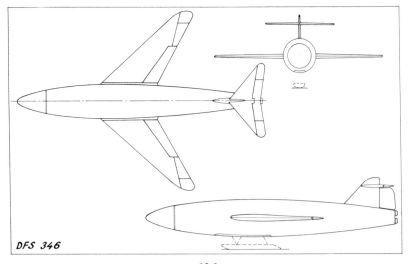

DFS 346

636

planning office of the Wrede company in Freilassing was requested to assist in the construction planning, and the drawings for the P.1068, P.1068A and B, as well as most of the drawings for the D version, were finished. Static tests of the undercarriage were necessary before the C version was started. For all versions, the cockpit, front fuselage, instrumentation and control surfaces were common and had only to be built once, but the centre fuselage and wings had to be built anew for each version. The firm of Wrede was to build all the aircraft, with the DFS only delivering certain difficult parts and fitting the test equipment. Construction of the P.1068 was nearly completed, the requisite parts of the P.1068A were 50 per cent complete, and parts of the P.1068C were begun, but all material, together with some of the drawings, was destroyed by fire at the Wrede factory near the end of the war.

The third part of the DFS supersonic programme was the planned construction of the DFS 346 based on the previous experiments. Both the DFS and the RLM were anxious to speed up the development of this supersonic aircraft, and agreement was reached that the Siebel Flugzeugwerke at Halle should build the aircraft according to DFS direction. Preliminary tests were made in the DFS wind-tunnel at Darmstadt, and a further scale model was being constructed for high-speed tests by the DVL in Berlin. In November 1944, Siebel received the drawings for the DFS 346, which was to be built in the following manner.

The aircraft was of all-metal semi-monocoque duralumin construction, the fuselage having an unbroken cigar-shaped profile with mid-mounted wings swept back 45 deg and a short broad fin and rudder unit supporting a sweptback tailplane near its top. The circular cross-section fuselage had a maximum diameter of 1·62 m (5 ft $3\frac{3}{4}$ in) and accommodated the pilot in a prone position in the pressurized nose-section, there being a pointed, full-glazed nose cone. The nose section was to be pressurized to an equivalent altitude of 8,000 m (26,240 ft) up to at least 30,000 m (98,400 ft), and contained all the instrumentation. In an emergency, the pilot and instruments were to be saved by jettisoning the whole nose section by firing explosive attachment bolts, a parachute then automatically deploying from the nose section at the appropriate time. The centre section of the fuselage housed the C-Stoff and T-Stoff propellants for the two Walter 109-509B or C tail-mounted rocket units, each being calibrated to give a maximum thrust of 2,000 kg (4,410 lb).

One unusual feature was that the ailerons and elevators were constructed in two parts, either one or two parts being used. The inner control surfaces had the largest area, were hinged at about 50 per cent of their chord to give aerodynamic balance and were effective at subsonic speeds. The outer control surfaces were smaller but extended into more of the aerofoil depth; these surfaces had no aerodynamic balance, were hinged at their leading edges and were effective at supersonic speeds by protruding out of the stern shock waves. The attachment of the wings was such that forces in all directions and the movement of the centre of pressure could be

637

measured, whilst the forces in every individual control system were to be measured.

For launching, the DFS 346 was to be carried above another aircraft to about 10,000 m (32,800 ft) starting altitude. Initially, gliding tests were to be made up to about 900 km/h (559 mph) and any necessary refinements made before using rocket power. Gradually the speed and altitude were to be built up until Mach 2 was reached above 20,000 m (65,000 ft). Incidentally, the aircraft had sufficient thrust to climb vertically, and Dr Felix Kracht considered that eventually Mach 2·6 could be reached at an altitude of 35,000 m (114,800 ft).

Although the Siebel personnel had all the materials and rocket units available to construct the DFS 346, they were, apparently, more interested in their first priority of Junkers' aircraft construction and nothing had materialized by the end of the war. The Russians, however, took the project over and had set German engineers to work on it by about 1946 at Podberezhye in the USSR. The first DFS 346 airframe was constructed there and final assembly with the Walter rocket units and instruments was undertaken at Toplistan airfield near Moscow. Unpowered, towed flights were then made with the aircraft by the German test pilots Rauschen and Motsch. In the meantime, the former Siebel test pilot Wolfgang Ziese trained for the powered test of the DFS 346 by piloting, in a prone position, converted German gliders such as the Kranich and Grunau IIB. For its maiden flight from Toplistan, the DFS 346 was carried up to about 10,000 m beneath a Boeing B-29 Superfortress which the Russians had kept after its forced landing near Vladivostok in 1944. After release, Ziese switched on the rocket power and accelerated the DFS 346 to 1,100 km/h (683 mph) which, if the release altitude was maintained, took the aircraft beyond Mach 1. Although a safe landing was made on the aircraft's central skid, it is known from the meagre details of this flight that slight vibration occurred in the DFS 346 at the top speed which indicates that the German performance data given below was estimated optimistically. The flight described may be the one connected with the Russian claim to have exceeded Mach 1 in May 1947. Success with the first DFS 346 was followed by something of a farce with two other examples which the Russians secretly built on their own in order to practise what they had learned from the Germans. Both of these aircraft were destroyed during their first launchings from the B-29 due to a recurring fault in the release gear, one pilot being killed. In view of the Russian claim of May 1947 it is worth recording that the rocket-powered Bell XS-1 piloted by Capt C. E. Yaeger first exceeded Mach 1 on 14 October, 1947, using the same type of flight pattern laid down for the DFS 346.

DFS 346: Span 8·9 m (29 ft 2¾ in); length 11·65 m (38 ft 2⅝ in); height 3·5 m (11 ft 5⅞ in); wing area 20 sq m (215·2 sq ft).

Maximum speed at 20,000 m (65,600 ft) 2,125 km/h (1,320 mph) or Mach 2, at 35,000 m (114,800 ft) 2,765 km/h (1,717 mph) or Mach 2·6; absolute ceiling 35,000 m (114,800 ft).

# Bombers

During 1943 the OKL sought a new long-range heavy bomber to replace the troublesome Heinkel He 177, and various jet bomber projects, including the Blohm und Voss P.188, were studied by the RLM's technical department. In the event, the Junkers Ju 287 turbojet-powered heavy bomber was the only one of which construction was begun before the war ended. There was, of course, construction work in hand for small turbojet attack aircraft such as the Arado Ar 234 and Henschel Hs 132. Although the official policy by July 1944 was togive up conventional bombers, the industry still worked on projects at least up to the end of 1944, although, long before then, the construction of large bombers bordered on absurdity, particularly as very little wood and other non-strategic materials could be used. The range of designs was varied, and most evolved around the large, new, third and fourth generation turbojets either projected or in early stages of development. There were also, although mostly of an earlier vintage, many projects planned around multiple arrangements of the current BMW 003 and Junkers 004 turbojets and up-rated versions of these types.

# Blohm und Voss P.188

Under the designation P.188 Blohm und Voss made four studies around the same projected bomb load and wing. The proposed wing is of special interest since it was of W planform having sweptback inner sections and sweptforward outer sections intended to combine the advantages of the sweptforward wing (adopted on the Ju 287) and the sweptback wing. Another radical feature of the project in general was the plan to provide the wing with variable-incidence to improve landing characteristics. The engines were to have been four Junkers Jumo 109-004C turbojets uprated to give 1,000 kg (2,205 lb) static thrust each, these engines being slung beneath the inboard wing sections either paired in common nacelles or separately. The fuselage centre section was designed as an armoured steel shell to contain fuel, the fore and aft sections being bays for the tandem twin mainwheels, stabilization being provided by small outrigger wheels housed between the engines. Crew accommodation was in a nose cabin, the glazing of which was flush with the fuselage profile except in the case of the P.188.02 which had the glazing bulged upwards. Another variation in the

639

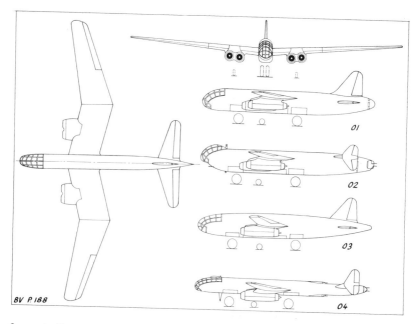

four studies was that the P.188.01 and 03 had a single vertical fin and rudder, while the P.188.02 and 04 had twin fins and rudders at the tailplane tips.

P.188.01: Span 27 m (88 ft 7 in); length 17·425 m (57 ft 2 in).
Loaded weight 24,200 kg (53,361 lb) including 2,000 kg (4,410 lb) bomb load.
Maximum speed at 8,000 m (26,240 ft) 873 km/h (542 mph); ceiling 13,000 m (42,640 ft); range 2,285 km (1,420 miles).

# Focke-Wulf Bomber Projects

Focke-Wulf made basic project studies during 1944 to ascertain the best layout for a bomber powered by two Heinkel-Hirth 109-011A turbojets each of 1,300 kg (2,866 lb) static thrust. As a basis for comparison of these studies (for which no project number is known), it was assumed that a 1,000 kg (2,205 lb) bomb load should be carried at 1,000 km/h (621 mph) on an action radius of 1,000 km (621 miles), which, of course, gave rise to the appellation, the 1000 × 1000 × 1000 Bomber-Projekt. Three studies were made, two of which were similar. These two each had swept-back wings, fin and tailplane, with conventional controls and the engines carried beneath the wings. In the second of these two studies, the wings and tailplane were of parallel chord, the fuselage was deepened and the engines

640

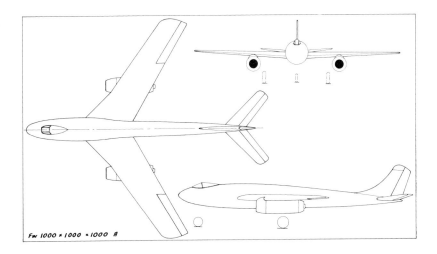

Fw 1000 × 1000 × 1000 A

were on underwing pylons to increase the mass-balance effect and also turned out of line to enhance single-engine controllability. The third study was completely different. This was a delta-wing design which had a pressurized cockpit pod extending forward from the delta apex. The wing centre section was of increased depth to accommodate the fuel and bomb load. At the rear of the centre section were housed the two engines side by side and they received air from two leading-edge wing-root intakes. Wing trailing-edge sweepback was provided only on the wing outer panels, and the wingtips were bent vertically downwards. Conclusions drawn from these studies are unknown. Messerschmitt also made a bomber study, designated P.1108, to fulfil the same $1000 \times 1000 \times 1000$ requirements, but, for some obscure reason, this aircraft was projected with four 109-011A engines. The P.1108 had moderately sweptback

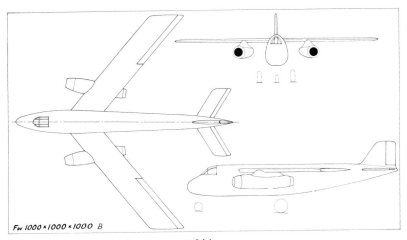

Fw 1000 × 1000 × 1000 B

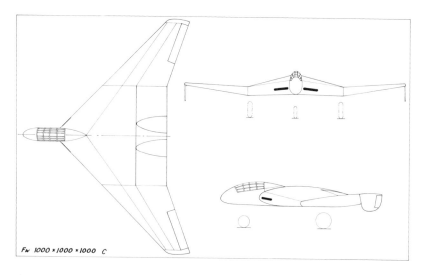

Fw 1000 x 1000 x 1000 C

wings and a butterfly tail; the engines were mounted in pairs extending
beyond the wing trailing edges, and, although each engine had its own
nacelle, a common rectangular underwing intake was provided for each
pair.

Focke-Wulf delta bomber: Span 14 m (45 ft $11\frac{1}{4}$ in); length 5·8 m (19 ft $0\frac{3}{8}$ in); height
2·75 m (9 ft $0\frac{1}{4}$ in); wing area 55 sq m (591·8 sq ft).
Empty weight 4,200 kg (9,621 lb); loaded weight 8,100 kg (17,860 lb).
Maximum speed at 10,000 m (32,800 ft) 1,000 km/h (621 mph); ceiling 15,000 m
(49,200 ft); range 2,500 km (1,552 miles).

# Henschel P.122

The Henschel P.122 design was for an all-wing bomber in the sense that it
had no tailplane, but there was a conventional fuselage which supported a
vertical fin and rudder at its rear. The cigar-shaped fuselage had, in the
nose, a pressurized cockpit, the glazing of which faired in unbroken lines
with the fuselage profile. The low-mounted sweptback wings had double
elevon controls. A single BMW 109-018 turbojet of 3,400 kg (7,497 lb)
static thrust was to have been carried directly beneath each wing at mid-
span. The projected bomb load is unknown.

P.122: Span 22·48 m (73 ft 9 in); length 12·4 m (40 ft $8\frac{1}{8}$ in).
Loaded weight 15,100 kg (33,295 lb).
Maximum speed at 10,000 m (32,800 ft) 935 km/h (581 mph); ceiling 17,000 m
(55,760 ft); range 2,000 km (1,242 miles).

# Horten XVIII B

The Horten XVIII B design was of all-wing configuration with very high aspect ratio and a kinked trailing edge where the sweptforward trailing edge of the centre section met the sweptback outer wing panels. Furthermore, there was a large delta-shaped, vertical fin and rudder (an unusual Horten departure), and the crew was accommodated in the forward, glazed base of this fin. A remote-controlled gun barbette was mounted beneath the rear of the fin which extended beyond the wing trailing edge. Six Junkers 109-004D turbojets were grouped under the wing centre section, these engines being almost standard but uprated to 1,050 kg (2,315 lb) static thrust each. A bomb load of 4,000 kg (8,820 lb) was to be carried.

Ho XVIII B: Span 42 m (137 ft 9½ in); length 19 m (62 ft 4 in); wing area 195 sq m (2,098·2 sq ft).
Loaded weight 44,000 kg (97,020 lb).
Maximum speed at 6,000 m (19,680 ft) 900 km/h (559 mph); range 9,000 km (5,590 miles).

# Junkers EF 130

The Junkers EF 130 design was for a bomber slightly larger than the company's Ju 287 and of completely different layout. The EF 130 was a true all-wing aircraft of all-metal construction, the wing having a high aspect ratio. Apart from a very small trailing surface near each wingtip, there were no vertical surfaces, control being by means of outboard ailerons and long-span inboard elevators. The crew was accommodated in a leading-edge gondola. The four BMW 109-003E turbojets were grouped side by side above the rear of the wing centre-section. The projected bomb load is uncertain but is thought to have been about 3,000 kg (6,615 lb).

EF 130: Span 24 m (78 ft 8⅞ in); wing area 120 sq m (1,291·2 sq ft); loaded weight 38,000 kg (83,790 lb); maximum speed at 6,000 m (19,680 ft) 990 km/h (615 mph); range 5,900 km (3,665 miles).

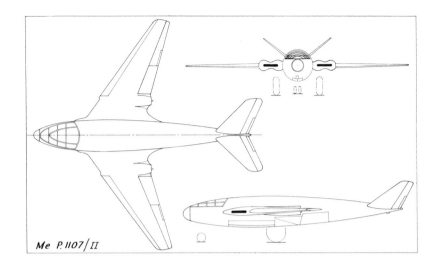

Me P.1107/II

# Messerschmitt P.1107

In its final form, the Messerschmitt P.1107/II, this projected bomber was similar to the P.1108 mentioned on page 641, but with four BMW 109-018 turbojets. The P.1107/II had a circular-section cigar-shaped fuselage, the lines of the nose being unbroken by the cockpit glazing. Mounted on the fuselage centre-line was a sweptback tapered wing having bulged roots to accommodate the four turbojets of 3,400 kg (7,497 lb) static thrust each. Thus, the engines were mounted as close to the fuselage sides as possible and had their air intakes in the wing leading edge. Instead of having recourse to a high-mounted tailplane to clear the engine exhaust streams, a butterfly tail unit was adopted. Control devices consisted of ailerons, flaps and leading-edge slots on the wings and differential control surfaces on the tail unit. The lower part of the fuselage accommodated the bomb bay and the retractable undercarriage, the latter having two large-diameter mainwheels and twin nosewheels. All-metal construction was used. Previously, in the P.1107/I layout, the engines were beneath the wings, and the lower exhaust line permitted the use of conventional tail surfaces instead of the butterfly tail unit. The P.1107/II had a span of 17·37 m (57 ft), a loaded weight of 30,700 kg (67,693 lb) which included a 4,000 kg (8,820 lb) bomb load and a maximum speed of 880 km/h (547 mph), these being the only known details.

# MISSILES

This section does not purport to deal with all German missiles since this would require a separate book. Instead, the salient points of the more developed missiles are given with the intention of portraying a general picture of German efforts in this field, which was becoming an increasingly important extension of the aircraft industry. Missiles of minor importance are included where these relate to a main-stream development or are of special interest. Not all the missiles described were being developed as direct instruments of war; some formed part of a missile development programme or were for pure research. It should be noted that, leaving aside minor unguided solid-fuelled rockets of the type generally used by the belligerents, only six missile types were ready in time to see operational service with German forces in the Second World War. These were the ground-to-ground A4 (V2), Fi 103 (V1) and Rheinbote, the air-to-ground Fritz X and Hs 293A and, on a very minor scale, the anti-tank X-7 missile. On the question of data for each missile type, it will be noted that direct comparisons are not always possible because it has been necessary to leave out certain figures or present these in varying forms according to availability, for example, speed may be given in terms of all-burnt velocity, final velocity or limiting Mach number.

# A-series of rockets and Peenemünde (HVP)

During the 1920s and early 1930s, widespread unsponsored experiments with rockets were carried on in Germany by men who ranged from the gifted to the eccentric. The defeat of Germany in the First World War had shackled the military with the Versailles Treaty which prohibited the manufacture or development of contemporary weapons of major size and this restriction was particularly felt in the German Army with regard to long-range offensive guns. In casting around for a possible alternative, some hope was seen in rockets, and the task of investigating this field fell to Reichswehr Capt Walter Dornberger in 1929. He began by sponsoring the apparently more promising of the rocket amateurs and eventually, in 1932, set up a test station at the Army's Kummersdorf-West proving ground, south of Berlin. Here, men such as Wernher von Braun, Walter Riedel and Heinrich Grünow began the dangerous work which eventually led to their first complete experimental rocket, the Aggregat 1 or A1 of 1933.

# A1, A2 and A3

The A1 rocket was approximately 1·395 m (4 ft 6⅞ in) long by 0·3 m (11⅞ in) diameter and was provided with a rocket motor, burning liquid oxygen and alcohol, to give a thrust of 300 kg (660 lb) for 16 sec. To stabilize the rocket, it was decided to use an electric motor to rotate the nose section to produce a gyroscopic effect but, when all modifications were completed, the weight of the rocket was about 149 kg (329 lb), it was nose heavy and was never launched. However, the rocket was redesigned as the A2, the principal change being to move the rotating stabilizer from the nose to the centre section, and in December 1934, from the island of Borkum, two of these A2s were launched with some success to about 2,500 m (8,100 ft).

As the scope of the work expanded and larger rockets were contemplated, it became obvious that a more suitable and larger testing range would be needed, Borkum having been only an interim alternative to the unsuitable Kummersdorf range. In April 1936, therefore, the Heereswaffenamt (Army Ordnance Board) and the RLM (Air Ministry) jointly purchased the northern peninsula of the Baltic island of Peenemünde, providing some 450 km (290 miles) of launching range along the waters off the southern Baltic coast. There were also the small, off-lying islands of Ruden and Greifswalder Oie which could be used in the work. The Peenemünde establishment, eventually the largest of its kind in the world, was to become the clearing house for all German rocket work and was divided into two sections. The east section, designated Heeresversuchsanstalt Peenemünde (HVP), consisted of test beds and manufacturing facilities for the Army and was commanded by Col Leo Zanssen, Dornberger being the head of Weapon Test Section 11 and von Braun the technical director. The west section consisted of the Luftwaffe airfield and facilities for the testing of aircraft missiles, ATO units and rocket aircraft, and was known as Erprobungsstelle Karlshagen, commanded by Maj Henckelman.

Tests on a new experimental rocket, the A3, which had been developed at Kummersdorf, were begun at HVP in 1937. The A3 design incorporated important innovations, not least of which was a gyro-stabilized unit which controlled molybdenum rudders operating in the exhaust stream. The nose contained instruments, and there was a parachute recovery arrangement. Performance of the previous A2 rockets had not been spectacular due largely to a lack of aerodynamic refinement. For the A3, therefore, aerodynamic data was supplied by work in the small 10 by 10 cm wind-tunnel of the Technische Hochschule at Aachen. The resulting streamlined body had four slender tail fins extending beyond the base of the body and surrounded by a ring for structural strength. The rocket weighed 750 kg (1,654 lb) and had a total length of approximately 7·6 m

(24 ft 11¼ in) and a body diameter of 0·75 m (2 ft 5½ in), and had a motor burning liquid oxygen and alcohol to give a thrust of about 1,500 kg (3,300 lb) for 45 sec. From the first launching of an A3 on 6 December, 1937, a series of failures occurred which were attributed to inadequate stabilizing power in anything more than a gentle breeze.

# A5 and A4 (V2)

These setbacks with the A3 necessitated the shelving of actual design work on the military A4 rocket, which was under way, in order to conduct further research. It had been obvious early on that the small Aachen wind-tunnel and others like it would be inadequate for research on large super-sonic missiles. Thus, it was in 1936 that Dornberger commissioned a Dr Hermann to organize the construction of a larger 40 by 40 cm wind-tunnel at Peenemünde to form part of a new research division known as the Forschungslabor. By 1943, this division had various wind-tunnels and could simulate velocities up to Mach 4·5. Initially, the work of the Forschungslabor was supported by other institutions in Germany and by both rocket-powered and free-flight test models; this work produced, in

To obtain aerodynamic data for the A5 research rocket (itself providing data for the military A4 rocket), small-scale A5 models were dropped from aircraft. Here, a Heinkel He 111 is the carrier.

An A4 (V2) ground-to-ground rocket mounted on a Meilerwagen mobile launcher at Peenemünde. Once moved to the vertical position, the rocket could be fuelled.

1937, data for a new research rocket, the A5, which was introduced as a step towards the A4.

The A5 used the same motor as the A3 together with gas rudders, since the main problems were of stability and aerodynamics. Much was learned by dropping small-scale A5 models from aircraft and, gradually, stabilizing and steering gear was perfected to give successful A5 flights of up to 17 km (11 miles) range ending in parachute descents.

With these successes to build on, design of the A4 began again, but, whereas the A5 had measured some 6·85 m (22 ft 1$\frac{3}{8}$ in) in length by 0·67 m (2 ft 2$\frac{3}{8}$ in) in diameter and weighed around 900 kg (1,980 lb), the A4 was to be 14·036 m (46 ft 0$\frac{5}{8}$ in) long by 1·65 m (5 ft 5 in) in diameter and have an operational weight of 12,840 kg (28,250 lb). To lift this vastly greater weight, a new rocket motor had to be developed which eventually gave a thrust of 25,000 kg (55,125 lb) for 68 sec.

The development of this motor, which was more powerful than any other before the war, or for some time after, was supervised by Dr Walter Thiel until his death in an air raid in 1943. As with previous motors, liquid oxygen and alcohol were still chosen as the propellants. First, both these liquids were already in largescale commercial production at a reasonable price; furthermore, liquid oxygen promised a minimum of problems in atomization, mixing and ignition, because of its purity and because its combination with alcohol could keep combustion temperatures down with obvious benefit. Alcohol was, in any case, excellent as an external coolant, and, by mixing 25 per cent water to 75 per cent alcohol, temperature and safety margins could be increased without much detriment to performance. To ensure adequate supplies of liquid oxygen, a plant for its production was established at Peenemünde.

A vast amount of work was done and many different designs of motor were tested before the basic A4 motor emerged. To obtain the requisite performance, 129 kg (284·4 lb) per sec of propellant was required to be fed to the combustion chamber, and, since the previous system of pressurizing the propellant tanks with nitrogen was not, by itself, suitable on this scale, a new and advanced pumping system had to be devised. This system consisted of a turbine operated by steam released from hydrogen peroxide by a calcium permanganate catalyst to give 675 to 680 hp at around 5,000 rpm to drive liquid oxygen and alcohol feed pumps from a common shaft. (Such a system was essentially that originated at H. Walter KG, Kiel.) The propellants were introduced into the combustion chamber through eighteen injection and mixing cups. The sequence of starting the motor was to light a pyrotechnic igniter inside the combustion chamber and then open the propellant valves to allow fuel to flow to the motor under nitrogen pressure in the tanks alone. With this reduced flow, a thrust of only 6,800 kg (14,960 lb) resulted, which was insufficient for lift-off but provided a check that the motor was functioning satisfactorily. If this was the case, hydrogen peroxide was allowed to flow to produce steam for the pump turbine, and the resultant increased propellant flow enabled the requisite lift-off thrust to be generated.

As for cooling the motor, it was no longer sufficient to build one of the propellant tanks around it as before, and it was found necessary to provide regenerative cooling by surrounding the motor with a jacket, inside which alcohol flowed on its way to the injectors. In addition, film cooling was also required whereby a small proportion of alcohol from the jacket was allowed to penetrate the inner motor wall.

Static firing tests of the basic motor intended for the A4 began at Peenemünde on 21 March, 1940, and a pilot factory was planned to explore techniques for the mass production of the A4, which was optimistically hoped to begin at the end of 1941. However, it was not until 18 March, 1942, that the first complete A4 rocket was statically tested, only to result in an explosion. Subsequent tests and actual launchings also met with various failures, and only one really successful launching took place before the end of 1942. Nevertheless, there seemed little doubt that the rocket would eventually attain its planned range of 250 km (155 miles).

Dornberger's biggest battle in fostering the A4 programme was not with the military but with Hitler, who viewed the whole thing more in the light of an interesting technical triumph for Germany rather than as a military weapon. However, with the support of Armaments Minister Albert Speer, the plans for mass production were finally endorsed by Hitler on 22 December, 1942, and given much increased priority.

These plans were set back by shortages of men and materials (notably graphite for the gas rudders) and the RAF bombing attack on Peenemünde on 17 August, 1943, in which many personnel were killed, among them Dr Thiel. Even so, a further step towards the operational use of the A4 was taken by setting up a training centre at Peenemünde under the code name of Heimat-Artilleriepark 11 or HAP 11. Also, work forged ahead on the production both of huge storage and launching bunkers and the equipment for mobile launching batteries, while new factories were planned for propellant production.

The process of persuading the missile to deliver its 975 kg (2,150 lb) high explosive warhead with reasonable accuracy required several factors to be taken into account. Although an inclined launch would have been ideal, the size of the rocket, together with the need to minimize structural weight, made it necessary for a filled rocket to stand in the vertical position. The flight of an A4, therefore, had to start with a vertical launching, followed at altitude by a gradual tilt of 49 deg from the vertical, immediate propellant cut-off (Brennschluss) at an exact speed, depending on the requisite range, and coasting flight up and down a parabolic curve to the target. Remote radio control was discarded early in the development stage because of the risk of interference from Allied jamming and other influences, and a self-contained control system was developed, which left only the signal for cutting the motor to be effected from the ground. Contained behind the warhead of the rocket was a unit incorporating two gyroscopes, one sensing roll and yaw errors and the other sensing pitch errors, and these initiated signals to the servo-motors which operated the graphite exhaust rudders and the aerodynamic rudders in unison for corrections. With this system, the prevention of roll was essential if alignment of the rocket's fins with the target, and hence accuracy, was to be obtained. The gradual tilting of the rocket on to the desired trajectory was programmed automatically by a pre-set rotating drum device, and a telemetry link with the ground gave the velocity when the cut-off signal could be sent. After early operations with the A4, the process of measuring the velocity and cutting the motor was undertaken within the rocket, dispensing with the radio link. To do this, a pre-set gyroscopic integrating accelerometer, known as the I-Gerät, was used, and this was later replaced by an electrolytic integrator. (The I in I-Gerät stood for the river Isar in Bavaria.)

Another important electronic feature of the rocket concerned the fusing arrangement for the warhead. A central exploder tube extended from within the warhead to form the extreme point of the nose, where a radio device was fitted. This radio sent out signals and received them back from the ground and was set to initiate an electrical fuse (also in the exploder tube) at a height of about 3 m (10 ft) from the ground before impact. Connected in the circuit with the radio device, fuse and batteries, was a complex device known as a Sterg unit. The function of the Sterg, among other things, was to cut off the electrical supply to the fuse in the event of a rocket failing to lift off, and in this capacity it acted as a safety device.

Despite unfavourable comparisons in official circles between the A4

A4 (V2) rockets in operational camouflage, being set up and launched. When used, the stabilizing wires up to the nose were removed once the rocket was fuelled.

rocket and the Luftwaffe's Fieseler Fi 103 flying bomb, also being developed at Peenemünde, good performance by the A4 and poor performance by the then undeveloped Fi 103 in front of high officials during May 1943 kept the A4 programme going. Furthermore, because of the deteriorating war situation, Hitler gave it the highest priority rating of DE 12. From pilot production at Peenemünde, production was intended to reach up to 950 rockets a month at Henschel's Rax works and the Zeppelin works at Friedrichshafen. However, these factories were bombed in the summer of 1943, and production lines were therefore set up underground in the Harz mountains near Nordhausen. From this vast manufacturing centre, which was given the cover name of Mittelwerke GmbH, eighty-six A4s were delivered in July 1944, and from September a steady output of over six hundred A4s a month was achieved. Before this, in the summer of 1943, production of rocket components had begun at widely dispersed factories throughout occupied Europe, the most difficult component, the pump turbine, being undertaken by Heinkel's Jenbach factory. The organization of this dispersed production was undertaken by a special A4 committee presided over by Gerhard Degenkolb.

While rockets were being stockpiled, the first training and testing battery from HAP, number 444, was set up at Köslin and then moved near Blizna in Poland. Here it undertook actual test shots in November 1943, only to reveal weaknesses in the mass-produced rockets, causing one break-up after another. The main trouble, that of the rocket snapping round upon re-entering the denser atmosphere and breaking in two, was virtually remedied by August 1944 by simple reinforcing of a section of the rocket's skin.

On 1 December, 1943, a new Army Corps, the 65th, was commissioned under the command of Field Marshal von Rundstedt, and Lt Gen Erich Heinemann became the Corps' first GOC. This was a special OKW formation with headquarters at Saint-Germain and was staffed by both Army and Luftwaffe personnel for control of all secret weapon formations, which included, of course, A4 rocket and Fi 103 flying bomb activities.

With the final technical problems overcome, German rocket troops were deployed in the following areas: near the Hague, two batteries of Mobile Artillery Section 485, commanded by Col Hohmann; near Liège, two batteries of Mobile Artillery Section 836, commanded by Maj Weber, plus the original battery, number 444, in the same area. It was the 444th which launched the first A4 offensive shot on 5 September, 1944, aimed at Paris. This was followed on 9 September by Mobile Artillery Section 485 firing the first two A4s at London from a range of 322 km (200 miles), the first falling in Chiswick at 18.43 hr. By the end of the month, although launchings were far below expectation, due to various manufacturing problems, the A4 was being heralded with great enthusiasm in official circles as Vergeltungswaffe 2 (V2) (Retaliation Weapon 2), after the previous protracted difficulties.

The massive concrete installations at Watten, Siracourt and Wizernes, forming fixed firing batteries and constructed under the Todt organization with enormous man-power, never opened fire thanks to regular poundings by Allied aircraft in Operation Crossbow, and the installations were virtually finished off by Boeing B-17 Flying Fortresses, packed with explosives, remotely guided into them during August 1944. In contrast, the mobile Army units, who fired their rockets from constantly changed sites, carried out their assignments with great efficiency despite the radical nature of the weapons, and almost a thousand A4s were launched against London in the first ten weeks of action.

Although about six thousand A4s were constructed, only about half this number was launched by the Germans, 1,054 falling in Britain plus about 60 falling off the coast and 1,675 falling on the Continent. Although London, or Target 42 as it was known, had originally been the prime target, it was Antwerp which eventually received the hardest blow from the A4 since it received 1,265 hits compared with 517 hits on London. Numbers of A4s have been preserved as Museum exhibits.

Performance of an average production A4 with a range of 305 km (189 miles) was:

Maximum velocity 5,580 km/h (3,466 mph); impact velocity 2,900 km/h (1,800 mph); trajectory height 97 km (60 miles); total flight time 3 min 40 sec. The rocket weighed 12,900 kg (28,380 lb) complete, including alcohol 3,770 kg (8,300 lb), liquid oxygen 4,900 kg (10,780 lb), other fuels 160 kg (352 lb), and warhead (60 per cent amatol and 40 per cent metal) 975 kg (2,145 lb). Total fuel capacity 11,375 litres (2,500 Imp gal).

Transporting an A4b, designed to increase the range of the A4 (V2) and used to test Wasserfall missile components. This A4b has had its fin controls removed while on the Meilerwagen transporter.

# A4b and A9

Once the A4 was sufficiently developed to go into action, von Braun and the teams at Peenemünde were able to devote more attention to further rocket developments. The prime aim was to obtain rockets with greater range whereby, for a start, coverage could be given to all of Britain. From the beginning of work on the A4, the idea of fitting wings to the rocket to increase its range by decreasing its rate of descent was envisaged and projected under the designation A9. The first positive step towards such a rocket was taken by fitting sweptback wings to standard A4 rockets and redesignating them A4b. The first A4b was launched on 27 December, 1944, but crashed soon after lift-off due to a guidance failure. Neither was the second and last A4b launching a success on 24 January, 1945, because, although the rocket reached a height of 78 km (48·5 miles) and successfully attained supersonic speed, the wings could not withstand the strain when re-entering the denser atmosphere and the intended range of 435 km (270 miles) was not attained.

A6 and A8 were design studies for long-range rockets while the A7 was to be a winged version of the A5 for study purposes; none of these designs was built.

# A9/A10

The final project in the A-series of rockets was that designated A9/A10, although, again, this project had early origins, in fact as early as the summer of 1940. The idea was to obtain greater range by launching to a greater height either an A4 type or winged A9 mounted above a new A10 booster stage. The design of this two-stage rocket has been heralded as the first for an ICBM (Inter-Continental Ballistic Missile), since the range of a winged final stage was calculated to be some 4,800 km (2,980 miles), or sufficient to carry a standard-weight warhead as far as various cities in the United States. A complete A9/10 combination would have measured approximately 26 m (85 ft $3\frac{5}{8}$ in) in height by 4·75 m (15 ft 7 in) in maximum diameter for a total weight of about 100 tons. For power, it was hoped to employ a new rocket motor intended for the A4. This motor was planned to give 30,500 kg (67,100 lb) of thrust (20 per cent more than the standard A4 motor), using Visol and nitric acid as propellants. The A9 would have had one of these motors and the A10 boost section would have had a group of six. Thus, the combination was to lift off with a combined booster thrust of 183,000 kg (402,600 lb) maintained for some 50 sec, and the A9 stage was to ignite and separate at a velocity of 4,280 km/h (2,660 mph) and reach a final velocity of 7,680 km/h (4,770 mph).

Yet another ambitious scheme for attacking the USA with rockets was the plan to tow A4s behind U-boats to within range and then fire them from special containers. Each container was virtually a simplified, small submarine displacing some 500 tons submerged and was cigar shaped with a rounded nose and stabilizing tail fins. Manned by a small crew, a container would be trimmed to run at the requisite depth or tilt into a vertical position in the manner of a fishing float. In this position, the serviced A4 would be launched through the opened nose doors. Up to three of these containers could have been towed by a U-boat and, in addition to the towing cable, a pipe-line and cables were to allow extra fuel to be drawn from the containers and electric power and commands to be drawn from the U-boat.

Since the main effort of the Army at Peenemünde had been put into the A4, other projects saw little headway before the end of the war. From the time of the first bombing attacks on Peenemünde, prudent measures were taken to gradually evacuate and disperse the personnel and facilities. Nevertheless, even to the end of the war, much of the establishment was kept running, particularly the development and pilot works section which was known by 1945 as the Elektromechanische Werke. The prime function of this section was, by then, the development of anti-aircraft missiles in addition to further development of the A4.

The last test A4 rocket was launched from Peenemünde's Prüfstand VII

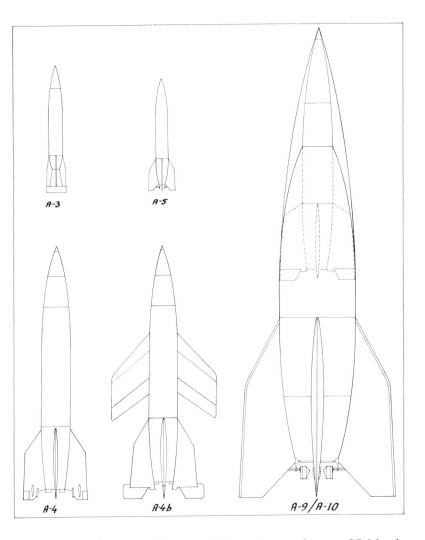

A-3    A-5

A-4    A-4b    A-9/A-10

(Test Stand VII) on 14 February, 1945, and soon after, on 27 March, 1945, the last operational A4 of the war was launched. This rocket, aimed at London, fell on Orpington in Kent.

A4s continued to be used after the war for research work, most of them being fired from the White Sands Proving Ground, New Mexico, from where a purely altitude shot yielded a record A4 height of 183·5 km (114 miles). The last A4, albeit modified, was fired in the summer of 1951 from White Sands.

# Elektromechanische Werke (EMW)

Towards the end of 1942, it was becoming obvious to the Germans that the ever-increasing stream of high-flying Allied bombers could not be effectively hampered by the guns of the Luftwaffe's Flak regiments, and such work could not be left to fighter aircraft which could not be everywhere at once. Once official interest began in the so-called Flak rockets (or, more correctly, Flak-Raketen), a development programme was planned by Gen Walter von Axthelm, Inspector-General for Flak defences, although both at Peenemünde and in other parts of Germany project studies had already been made.

One of the prime functions of the Elektromechanische Werke at Peenemünde became the development of anti-aircraft missiles and, of these, the types known as Wasserfall (Waterfall) and Taifun (Typhoon) had their origins with the Peenemünde establishment where a special command, subordinated to HAP 11, was established to co-ordinate the work.

# EMW Wasserfall (Waterfall)

By early 1943, the Forschungslabor was working on the aerodynamics of Wasserfall, and the basic body shape of the larger A4 rocket was adopted, because this was the only sizeable body which had successfully flown at speeds up to Mach 5 without difficulty. This was the prime reason why the Army establishment was asked to develop a proposed Luftwaffe missile.

The original specification required that the missile should start from zero, attain a height of 20 km (12·42 miles), a final speed of 2,860 km/h (1,775 mph), be controllable from the ground up to a 50 km (31 mile) range, and describe certain minimum curves in order to follow an enemy aircraft. Based on static tests, it was decided to allow a load factor of 12 for the missile, which would well exceed the load factors for aircraft, assumed to be between 6 and 8 in the case of fighters and dive-bombers down to between 2 and 3 for other bombers and transport aircraft. To provide the requisite control, the body was fitted with four small wings of symmetrical section at approximately the centre of gravity (which unfortunately moved as the propellants were depleted) and, at the tail, four fins which each had a control surface. As in the case of the A4, control had to be supplemented at lift-off by four rudders operating in the rocket exhaust.

Destruction of aircraft was to be accomplished not by direct hit but by maximum blast effect and, therefore, a single warhead containing a massive 235 kg (517 lb) of high explosive (possibly liquid) was originally designed for, but later this charge was divided into 145 kg (319 lb) for the warhead and 90 kg (198 lb) for a self-destruction charge. This destruction charge was intended to slash the rocket to pieces with the aid of the so-called Nipolit filaments to ensure that only small pieces fell on home territory whether or not a hit was achieved.

Wasserfall was designed for operation on the Rheinland control system in which the missile was guided by signals from the ground station to fly along the 'line' between the station and the target. There were several variations of this equipment, but basically the target was tracked by a radar unit, the Flaksichtgerät, and its position transmitted to another unit, the Flakflüggerät, which compared the angular difference between the lines of sight to the target and to the missile. Thus informed, the operator used a joystick control to initiate command signals from a ground transmitter to the missile receiver. Operation of the missile fuse was to be signalled by various methods from the ground, but since the inaccuracies here were greater than the lethal range of the warhead, these methods were to be supplemented by a proximity fuse.

Dr Thiel, who had been instrumental in the design of the A4 motor, began the design of a new motor for Wasserfall, and experimental models of it, the P.IX, were being run on Prüfstand II from March 1943, followed by tests on a more developed motor on Prüfstand VI by July 1943. The following month, Dr Thiel was killed and the motor development was then led by Dr M. Schilling.

Liquid oxygen and alcohol, as used in the A4, were unsuitable for the new motor since the value of this combination was far outweighed by its unsuitability in a missile, which might have to wait, fully-fuelled, for as much as six months and then be ready for firing. Many experiments were made with fuels, but they all came within the overall categories of Visol and Salbei which applied to various combinations of hydrocarbon fuels and mixed acid oxidizers respectively. These propellants gave automatic ignition when brought together and, although the exact types were never finally settled, they would probably have been vinylethylether (with 10 to 15 per cent aniline added to promote rapid ignition) for the Visol and 90 per cent nitric acid plus 10 per cent sulphuric acid for the Salbei.

To deliver the propellants to the motor, the complex turbine and pump arrangement was replaced by the simpler method of pressurizing the propellant tanks, since these were within the size limit for this method. Inside the tanks, swinging feed pipes stayed with the fuel regardless of forces on the missile or its position, and, incidentally, this arrangement afforded an extra 4 km ($2\frac{1}{2}$ miles) of range. When explosive starter valves were operated, compressed nitrogen was released to pass through a regulating valve, whereupon metal discs were ruptured and the nitrogen passed into the propellant tanks. The propellants, in turn, were forced into the feed pipes to rupture further metal discs and flow to the injection head, the

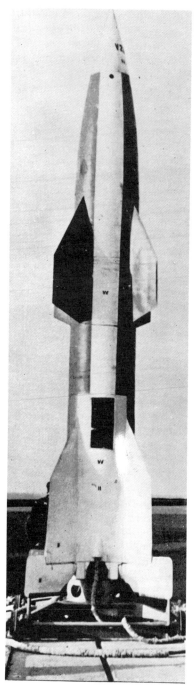 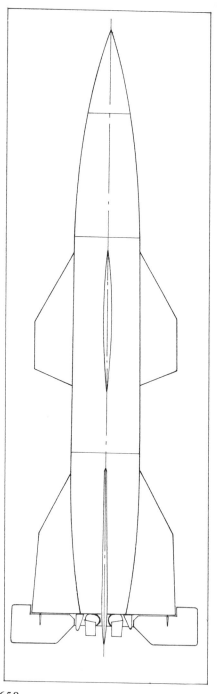

Salbei flowing around a motor cooling jacket before injection. For the purpose of filling and storing for long periods, over-sized propellant tanks were to be fitted to allow for losses, and various metals for the tank construction were tried, from chrome-nickel steel to mild steel with an aluminium lining.

In firing the missile, safety arrangements had to be different from those for the A4 because of the difference in propellants and the method of forcing them into the motor. First, the final bursting discs in the pipe-lines were made so that the one in the oxidant line ruptured at a lower pressure; this ensured that, initially, an excess of oxidant was in the combustion chamber to avoid a fuel-rich explosion. Second, the first explosive starter valve, which released pressurizing nitrogen, could be explosively closed again and the pressure in the tanks allowed to vent to the atmosphere if the appearance of the exhaust flame indicated danger prior to lift-off. Actual ignition did not occur for about five seconds after the firing button was pressed.

Since Wasserfall was intended to stand in the open in all weathers, it was originally intended to anchor it with four explosive bolts, these being sheared just prior to full thrust being reached. However, in later trials, one or two mishaps occurred due to one or more of the bolts failing to explode, and the method was abandoned; it was then found quite safe for the missile to stand unbolted in wind velocities up to 60 km/h (37 mph). To further the knowledge of weather resistance and long storage, all essential components were tested for 24 hr in containers filled with pure oxygen at a pressure of 25 atmospheres—taken to be equivalent to one year's storage.

Although launchings of Wasserfall were scheduled to start before the end of 1943, these plans were frustrated because the limited personnel available was further reduced by von Braun's need for more people on A4 work. In this he was fully backed by the much higher priority rating of the A4 programme. The A4's top priority, which affected the entire German missile and aircraft programmes in various measures, was also felt by Wasserfall where scarce materials were commonly needed by both, for example, graphite for the exhaust gas rudders. Although these rudders were only needed in Wasserfall for about 15 sec from lift-off, they were by then badly burnt and gave asymmetric effects to the rocket exhaust. Thus, in addition to experimenting with alternative materials such as silicon carbide, consideration was also given to jettisoning the rudders once they had done their job.

From March 1944, modified A4 rockets were fired to test Wasserfall components and control methods. (There had even been an earlier proposal to use a redesigned A4 as a flak rocket.) Following the explosion of the first Wasserfall missile, the first successful launch took place with the second

◀ An EMW Wasserfall ground-to-air test missile. Late development and complexity prevented its use against Allied bombers.

missile at Peenemünde on 29 February, 1944. The programme continued with an unrecorded number of successful launchings, plus several accidents since the design was far from settled and constant experimentation was undertaken. About 35 Wasserfalls were actually launched.

Pilot production of Wasserfall was planned to take place in what was to have been the biggest underground factory of all, at Bleicherode, but in fact even the factory was never started. Production was due to begin in October 1945 with 50 missiles and gradually rise to 900 a month by March 1946.

Various conflicting views were held and nothing was settled as to how Wasserfall (and other missiles) were to be deployed in the defence of the Reich. Such deployment had to be decided, ideally, at an early stage in the case of Wasserfall, for, although it appeared as mobile a weapon as the A4 and could if necessary use an A4 type launching trailer, it required a fixed and more specialized launching pad. For instance, it had to be possible for any spillage of the dangerous automatically-igniting fuels to be quickly dispersed and diluted, and for each site the more complicated ground control system had to be set up. The first Wasserfall site, it was estimated, could have been ready by November 1945, and a total of about 20 could have been ready four months later with about 100 missiles available for each site.

Bearing in mind that the missile was still very much in the development stage, the following data are for the Wasserfall C-2 8/45, the production design:

Length 7·835 m (25 ft 8 in); body diameter 0·88 m (2 ft 10⅝ in); main fin span 1·89 m (6 ft 2⅜ in); tail fin span, including rudders, 2·51 m (8 ft 3 in).

Starting weight 3,500 kg (7,700 lb); all-burnt weight 1,525 kg (3,355 lb); Visol weight 425 kg (935 lb); Salbei weight 1,550 kg (3,410 lb); nitrogen weight 70 kg (154 lb); high explosive weight 235 kg (517 lb).

Total propellant capacity 1,525 litres (335 Imp gal); motor thrust 8,000 kg (17,160 lb) for 40 sec.

Minimum velocity for adequate control 1,370 km/h (850 mph); maximum operational height 17·7 km (11 miles); maximum operational range 26·5 km (16½ miles). Note that range could be sacrificed for altitude and vice versa; the figures given are maximum values of each and could be influenced by the amount of manoeuvring performed. Note also that up to 15 per cent of propellant could remain in the tanks after a full flight.

# EMW Taifun (Typhoon)

Towards the end of 1944 many people (aware of both Germany's needs and industrial capacity) were in favour of cancelling the extravagant A4 programme in favour of the protective Wasserfall and other flak rockets. Going even further than this was a Peenemünde range officer, Dipl Ing Scheufeln, who was concerned in the firing trials of Wasserfall but became increasingly dissatisfied with the programme and considered that without a homing device, for which there was little prospect, Wasserfall was too large, uneconomic and of poor quality. Scheufeln therefore favoured scrapping Wasserfall and started work, on his own initiative, on the design of a small, cheap, unguided flak rocket. This was the beginning of Taifun, submitted to the RLM in September 1944, and the following month the project was accepted and Scheufeln put in charge of its development at the EMW.

At this time, most German flak specialists considered that contact fusing in shells was superior to time fusing, in view of the increasing size of Allied bombers and their formations, and this theory was being confirmed by results. Of course, with a direct hit, a much smaller charge of explosive could be used to ensure aircraft destruction than in the case of a blast weapon such as Wasserfall. Having ascertained that the explosive weight should be 0·5 kg (1·1 lb) and the operational height 15 km (9·3 miles), it was decided, after trials with a solid-fuelled Taifun design, to develop a model burning Salbei and Visol propellants, as for Wasserfall. The resultant design was a small, non-guided, fin-stabilized, high-speed missile having slow rotation.

The Salbei was contained in an inner tubular tank and the Visol in the annular space between it and the body tube wall. Forward of the tank section was a unit containing a cordite cartridge for pressurizing the propellant in the tanks, the cartridge being ignited electrically by induction coils supplied from an external electrical source. Projecting into the top of this cartridge was the contact fuse for the warhead so that the missile would destroy itself if it failed to reach its target.

Once pressurized, the propellants ruptured metal discs at the rear end of the tanks and entered the combustion chamber through simple straight jets to impinge on the chamber walls and self-ignite upon mixing. An ingeniously simple device was fitted to obtain quick ignition and to ensure maximum thrust, for high initial acceleration and accuracy, as the missile left its rail. This device was an expendable valve which partially blocked both the Salbei inlet from the central tank and the motor nozzle throat. On firing, therefore, a fuel-rich mixture entered the chamber, giving insufficient thrust to move the missile but allowing the chamber pressure to build up. When the pressure was high enough, the valve in the throat blew out and simultaneously opened the Salbei inlet fully. The time between firing the cartridge and the missile taking flight was only 11/100th of a second. This method of starting Taifun was a prime reason for its exceptional accuracy, and dispersion was so small that care had to be taken with the launching rails to ensure sufficient spread of fire from a salvo. Because burning time was so short, a simple heat-absorbing combustion chamber sufficed.

Two types of contact fuse were developed and tested in Taifun, varying in the method of arming the fuse after launching. The first type was armed simply by acceleration in the manner of a gun shell; the second type was far more ingenious. Here, a condenser was charged by the ionization of the gas stream and fired the fuse by discharging through a nose rod contacting the target.

Taifun F, the production version, was in production at EMW during January 1945, and some 600 rounds were completed. Although the projectors were also in production at this time, it is doubtful whether any rounds were operationally tested. Production was intended to continue when most of the EMW evacuated to the Mittelwerke, Nordhausen, but time ran out. Definitive versions of the projector were intended to be rapid conversions of 88 mm gun mountings, each to carry thirty missiles. Compared with the hopeless prospects for Wasserfall batteries, it was likely that some 400 batteries of 12 projectors each could have been in action by September 1945, this number being worked up to from around March.

Taifun F: Length 1·93 m (6 ft 4 in); diameter 100 mm (4 in).

Operational weight 21 kg (46·2 lb); explosive weight 0·5 kg (1·1 lb); weight of propellants 11 kg (24·2 lb); pressurizing cordite weight 175 gm (6·2 oz).

Thrust 840 kg (1,848 lb) for 2·5 sec.

Maximum velocity 3,600 km/h (2,235 mph); maximum operational height 15 km (9·3 miles).

An interesting comparison can be made between Taifun F and the British 76·2 mm (3 in) unrotated anti-aircraft rockets, which are credited with being the first to bring down aircraft. These rockets burned a solid propellant and each had a 0·91 kg (2 lb) warhead fused with a standard gun shell fuse (later photo-electric fuses were used). Operational weight was 14·5 kg (32 lb), and a thrust of 680 kg (1,500 lb) was obtained for 1·6 sec. Velocity and ceiling are not known but were less than for Taifun F.

Four other versions of Taifun were developed or projected as follows, the numbers being given arbitrarily, because actual designations are not known:

Taifun (1): Similar to Taifun F but with thrust increased to 1,400 kg (3,080 lb) for a shorter burning time of 1·5 sec. Statically tested only.

Taifun (2): Similar to Taifun (1) but with thrust increased to 3,000 kg (6,600 lb) for a further decreased burning time of about 0·9 sec. Flight trials had been made.

Taifun (3): Similar performance to Taifun (1) but of smaller size and weight, this was considered the best design but was never built. Diameter was to be 70 mm ($2\frac{3}{4}$ in).

Taifun (4): This was a small model measuring 1·5 m (5 ft 3 in) by 50 mm (2 in) diameter, intended for short-range work. Statically tested only.

Taifun was the last project undertaken at Peenemünde, and, by February 1945, the evacuation of even the EMW section began in earnest, because of the nearness of the Red Army which was eventually to capture the establishment.

# Blohm und Voss Bv 143

Blohm und Voss, with its interests in both the marine and aviation fields, was well equipped to consider safer and more effective methods of delivering a torpedo attack on a ship. Under the leadership of Dr Ing Richard Vogt, work was undertaken on the Bv 143 winged torpedo, which it was intended to release from an aircraft at an altitude and range impossible for conventional torpedoes. The missile had a cigar-shaped body with very simple square-tipped wings and a cruciform tail unit, and it was kept on a fixed course by means of a gyroscopic device which adjusted the control surfaces. These control surfaces consisted of a divided elevator, a divided rudder and ailerons of the detached, auxiliary wing type. Considerable

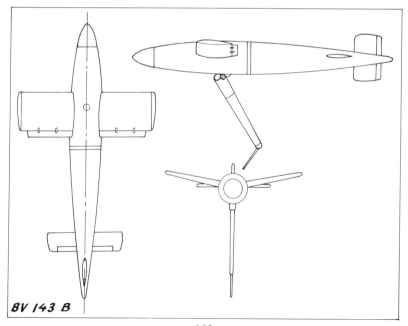

BV 143 B

stability was given by wing dihedral. After release from the carrier aircraft at a set distance from the target, the missile was designed to make its approach in a flat glide, and, when 2 m (6 ft 7 in) from the sea's surface, a feeler arm hanging from the fuselage was moved by the sea to switch on a rocket motor. The boost and acceleration provided by this motor was intended to bring the missile into level flight, when it would speed into the target just above the waterline.

To power the Bv 143, H. Walter K.G. at Kiel designed a rocket unit to fit inside the fuselage, the unit being based on their 109-501 and 109-502 ATO rocket units. The propellants used were T-Stoff (hydrogen peroxide) and Brennstoff (petrol), while B-Stoff (hydrazine hydrate) was injected to initiate combustion and Z-Stoff to decompose the T-Stoff in an effort to obtain more complete combustion between the T-Stoff and petrol by freeing oxygen. Starting was obtained by the feeler arm closing a switch to ignite electrically a small powder charge, which ruptured a membrane to allow air pressure to the propellant tanks. Valves allowed the correct sequence of flow for the propellants, but, since there was no air pressure reducing valve, the thrust dropped from the full 1,500 kg (3,300 lb) down to 700 kg (1,540 lb) during the 40-sec running time.

During 1943, four missiles were assembled and tested, and the full weakness of the project shown up, since the height available for changing to level flight proved quite insufficient, the limitation being imposed by the feeler arm. Because of this the project was shelved in the hope that a suitable electrical altimeter device might later become available, although the official opinion then was that the weapon was of no tactical value. At a later date, the Bv 143 was to be used in tests of the Hamburg infra-red homing device, but none was installed.

Bv 143A: Span 3·13 m (10 ft 3¼ in.); length 5·98 m (19 ft 7½ in); wing area 2·45 sq m (26·36 sq ft); maximum fuselage diameter 0·58 m (1 ft 10¼ in).

Operational weight 1,055 kg (2,321 lb); total propellant weight 170 kg (375 lb); explosive weight 180 kg (396 lb).

Maximum speed 415 km/h (288 mph).

# Blohm und Voss Bv 246 Hagelkorn (Hailstone)

Work at Blohm und Voss continued at low priority on various aerial torpedoes and other missile projects, but the next missile of any significance produced was the Bv 246 Hagelkorn glider bomb which, until ordered into production at the end of 1943, was designated Bv 226. The idea was to attack targets safely and cheaply by releasing the Bv 246 at considerable range and allowing it to glide to the target.

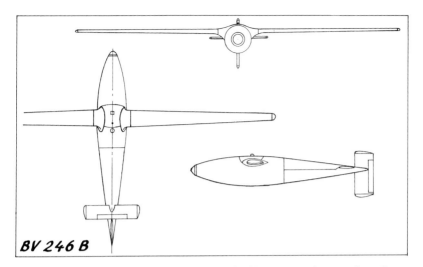

**BV 246 B**

Aerodynamically, the unpowered Bv 246B possessed very clean lines. The fuselage was cigar-shaped, tapering finely towards the rear where a cruciform tail unit was fitted, the tailplane being forward of the fins. A noteworthy feature was the high-mounted wing which had the high aspect ratio of 25·5 and an average loading of 515 kg/sq m (102 lb/sq ft). This wing gave the bomb a gliding angle of 1 : 25, which allowed an aircraft to attack a target at, for example, a distance of 210 km (130 miles) if the bomb was released at an altitude of around 10,500 m (34,440 ft). A shorter-range version, the Bv 246A, was also designed but not pursued.

To control and guide the bomb, a gyroscope gave control signals to the rudder, and these signals were, in turn, modified by a direction-finding device tuned to a radio beam from the parent aircraft, *e.g.* Heinkel He 111 or Junkers Ju 88. However, there was little official interest in such a scheme, because by then German radio navigational aids were being effectively countered and even put to use by the British; interest revived when it was proposed that the direction-finding device in the Bv 246B should be tuned to the transmitters in southern England which were providing navigational aids to the Allied bombers pounding Germany. Thus it was hoped that attacks could be made on these important targets which were too small for the inaccurate V-weapons and too well guarded for conventional bombing.

On 12 December, 1943, series production began of the Bv 246B but was cancelled on 26 February, 1944, due to enforced pruning of the German missile programme in general. Nevertheless, many hundreds of the bombs had already been stockpiled, and these were used in a test programme from the early summer of 1944 until December. This programme was carried out from Karlshagen with the Focke-Wulf Fw 190G-8 and other types, as carrier aircraft. There is a possibility that this programme was undertaken by IV./KG 101. An air attack on the airfield on

665

17 July, 1944, destroyed 29 of the missiles, but further stocks were procured and testing continued.

A number of versions of the Bv 246 had been planned, including types for carrying war gases and others acting as targets for flak rockets and air-to-air missiles, but, of the 1,100 manufactured, most were of the Bv 246B type and none was used on operations. Final tests with the weapon were made early in 1945 when it was used in tests with the Radieschen (Radish) ultra-short wave passive homing device developed by the German Post Office and designed by Dr Ing Kleinwächter for use against ground transmitters. The Radieschen was fitted in the missile's modified nose and acted on the gyroscopic control equipment for the rudder and elevator. Ten Bv 246s thus equipped were launched over the Unterlüss artillery ranges. Due to the gyroscopic equipment being still under development, all but two missiles failed, but those two were driven within a few yards of the target transmitter.

Bv 246B: Span 6·41 m (21 ft); length 3·53 m (11 ft 6¼ in); wing area 1·47 sq m (15·82 sq ft); maximum fuselage diameter 0·54 m (1 ft 9⅜ in).
Operational weight 730 kg (1,606 lb); explosive weight 435 kg (957 lb).
Velocity at target 450 km/h (280 mph).

# Fieseler Fi 103 (V1)

Although given the RLM designation of Fieseler Fi 103, this never-to-be-forgotten ground-to-ground medium-range flying bomb was also known to the Luftwaffe as FZG 76 (Flakzielgerät 76 or anti-aircraft aiming device 76), for deception purposes and in official circles under the code name Kirschkern (Cherrystone), and later as the V1. The Fieseler company developed only the airframe; equally important parts were played by the firms of Walter, Argus and Siemens in the development of the catapult, propulsion and guidance systems respectively.

The first person in Germany to take an interest in and make an effort to

Possibly the best-preserved Fi 103 (V1) flying bomb, now in Canada. (*National Aeronautical Collection – Ottawa*)

develop the pulse-jet engine for aeronautical use was the fluid dynamicist Paul Schmidt. This work, started in 1928, was done with difficulty purely as a sideline, and after a failure to obtain official backing in 1934 for a proposal for a VTO aircraft, Schmidt was advised by a friend to work out pulse-jet applications of a more obviously military nature. Thus, he submitted proposals for a flying bomb, an interceptor fighter, and a light bomber to the then new RLM. The flying bomb had stubby wings and tail surfaces, the pulse-jet engine being incorporated as an elongation of the rear fuselage with air intake slots and valves in a flush band around the middle of the fuselage aft of the wings. The estimated speed was 800 km/h (497 mph) at an altitude of 2,000 m (6,560 ft), but the RLM rejected the proposal as technically dubious and tactically uninteresting.

Matters improved, however, when, in 1935, Dornberger, von Braun and various eminent scientists sponsored Schmidt, and the RLM and Heereswaffenamt took an active interest in the idea of a flying bomb and granted considerable development funds for the so-called Schmidtrohr engine. By 1940, Schmidt's pulse-jets were giving up to 500 kg (1,100 lb) thrust in stationary operation and, by 1942, this had been uprated to 750 kg (1,650 lb) with take-off accelerations in mind. The results obtained were good but progress very slow, due, it seems, to the RLM's unwillingness to give sufficient backing to enable development tempo to be increased. Schmidt's work continued for much of the war on a low priority, but his pulse-jets never took to the air. The last gesture made to him was in 1943 when the engine for the Fi 103 was officially designated as an Argus-Schmidtrohr.

In fact, the RLM had already decided in 1939 to ask the Argus-Motoren-Gesellschaft in Berlin to develop the pulse-jet, and this work was begun under the leadership of Dr Ing Fritz Gosslau. Argus had established all the basic principles before they were allowed to view Schmidt's work in March 1940, and, although they partially adopted the Schmidt valve system, they retained their own methods for other features, particularly fuel/air mixture formation.

A small Argus pulse-jet of 120 kg (265 lb) static thrust was rapidly developed and flew for the first time, suspended beneath the Gotha Go 145 D-IIWS on 30 April, 1941. During the summer of 1941, cargo gliders fitted with the Argus pulse-jet proved the unit's low speed capabilities and also, incidentally, were the first flights to be made on this type of power alone. Doubts existed, however, about the high speed capabilities of the pulse-jet. These doubts were forcibly expressed when Fritz Gosslau's close collaborator, Dr Dietrich, left Argus after he thought he had proved that the pulse-jet could perform no useful work above 600 km/h (375 mph).

Despite all the unknown factors concerning the flying bomb, the RLM eventually decided to take a chance on its feasibility and accordingly ordered the missile on 19 June, 1942. The development of the airframe was placed in the hands of Gerhard Fieseler's aircraft firm at Kassel, H.

Walter KG began work on the catapult, and Siemens took over an Askania autopilot for development into the guidance system.

Within a short time, early models of the Argus 109-014 pulse-jet were ready, the system having been tested by mounting units above Dornier Do 17 and Junkers Ju 88 carrier aircraft. It is interesting to note here that the rhythmic exhaust explosions near the exhaust outlet of the tube, with the attendant large variations in pressure, caused considerable damage to the carriers' airframes. The airframe of the flying bomb was to be protected against this by mounting the pulse-jet so that the end of the exhaust tube extended aft of the tail. Because of detrimental effects on the compass guidance system, the lowest possible vibration was also necessary; the pulse-jet was therefore mounted with a pivoted fork at the front and a singly pinned lug at the rear, but, despite the additional aid of rubber bushes and dampers, considerable vibration was still transmitted.

The initial Fieseler airframe design was designated P.35, but little is known of this. The airframe which was evolved had a fuselage made largely of pressed steel sheet with an aluminium alloy nose fairing. The fin and tailplane had control surfaces and there was a simple wing of plywood construction with a single steel-tube spar.

Briefly, the bomb was controlled in the following manner. A gyroscopic unit initiated signals to the air-operated rudder and elevator which stabilized the bomb in all three axes, while directional information was obtained from a compass pre-set before launching. Further information to maintain altitude, within certain limits, derived from an aneroid capsule. Finally, an air log, driven by a small nose airscrew, measured a pre-set distance after which the bomb dived into its target.

Early in December 1942, Gerhard Fieseler flew in a Focke-Wulf Fw 200 over Peenemünde to release the first Fi 103 airframe on an unpowered test flight. On Christmas Eve of the same year, the first Fi 103 was catapulted from Peenemünde-West to achieve the initial modest flight aim of about 1,000 m (1,100 yd). It soon became apparent, however, that all was not well since the bombs were consistently crashing. Due to the urgency of the programme, all the elements of the bomb had to be tested as a whole unit before they were fully developed, and so faults were difficult to isolate, especially as bombs were launched out to sea and were not retrievable. An early form of telemetry (FuG 23) was therefore adopted whereby a cheap transmitter was installed in the bomb to send information on seventeen variables to an aircraft flying alongside, but this was not of much use if the bomb crashed immediately after leaving the catapult. Pressure for rapid development was great, particularly as the Luftwaffe chiefs were becoming worried that the Army's A4 rocket would eventually take over the job of aerial bombardment. Much of the technical trouble was traced to the engine air intake and its fuel system, and, when these were improved, something like a usable weapon was ready. Then, in comparing the simplicity of the Fi 103 with the A4, it was the turn of the Army to worry.

As with the A4, production of the Fi 103 was dispersed over many factories, but Volkswagen and Fieseler were the main producers. Production was already under way while trials were still being conducted, since a large stockpile was required before operations began. As a result of the Allied attack on Peenemünde in August 1943, all Fi 103 trials were moved to East Prussia, where catapults were installed to face the sea at the naval base at Brüsterort.

On 1 July, 1943, Col Max Wachtel was posted to an experimental unit known as the Lehr- und Erprobungskommando Wachtel, which had its headquarters at Zempin near Peenemünde, and had the task of working out firing drills for the Fi 103. This unit formed the basis for a new Luftwaffe Flak-Regiment commissioned on 16 August, 1943, the erroneous term Flak being retained throughout in a feeble attempt to mislead Allied Intelligence. The number of Züge (platoons) in this regiment determined the number of flying bomb sites which could be manned, and the regiment composition was probably intended to be as follows: four platoons in each battery, four batteries in each section, four sections in the Regiment, making sixty-four platoons in all. However, indications are that there were only forty-eight platoons and thirteen batteries, the strength of a platoon being about eighty men. Other units looked after transport and site defence. Until September 1943, firing drill research, and also air launching tests, had to be done without fully-developed bombs, but then improved specimens were received and progress made.

Soon, catapult launching sites were being constructed in Picardy, Artois and Normandy. Unlike the A4 rocket, the Fi 103 could only be launched from fixed sites, each of which was an elaborate affair. The Walter catapult, essential for launching, consisted of an inclined track about 48 m (150 ft) long beneath which was a slotted tube containing a piston, which engaged with a lug on the flying bomb. In a chamber at the end of the tube, 100 kg (220 lb) of hydrogen peroxide was decomposed by a potassium permanganate catalyst to drive the piston forward, the tube slot being closed by a tubular sealing strip as the piston travelled. The catapult track was shielded on each side by walls of concrete blocks and there were concrete access roads, test and assembly houses, explosion-proof shelters and a compass swinging platform. Such sites were very vulnerable to air attack and so simplified sites were also built (using a tenth of the labour) which had only the catapult, concrete roads and a substantial protective test wall, the shelters being of log and earth construction.

Most sites were placed within a dense growth of tall trees which had only their lower branches removed to provide clearance for the emerging bomb. At one site, bombs were launched across a public road but it is not known if this road was closed.

As already mentioned in the A4 section, all secret weapon formations came under the control of the new 65th Army Corps from 1 December, 1943, but the attack on London (the prime target) could not begin for another six months due to incessant modifications on the production line

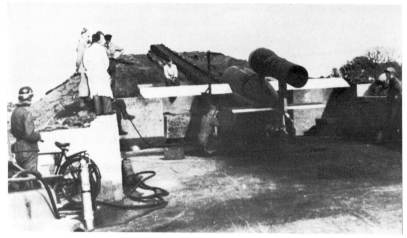

Preparing to test-launch a Fieseler Fi 103 (V1) ground-to-ground flying bomb. Best known of all German missiles, more than 30,000 V1s were produced. (*H. Redemann*)

and Allied bombardment. Thus, D-Day (6 June, 1944) came and went without Allied preparations being interfered with, another intended objective of the Fi 103.

Finally, in the early hours of 13 June, 1944, almost three months before the first A4 fell on London, the first ten Fi 103s were catapult-launched at the capital, a figure which fell far short of the planned mass launching. Four crashed immediately, two failed to make landfall and three exploded around London; the tenth was the first to explode on England which it did at 04.18 hr near Gravesend. French observers were of the opinion that about a third of the bombs launched failed to fly correctly and, in some cases, bombs had even turned 180 deg, to crash behind the launching site! In any event, the protective installations show that launching operations were hazardous.

After strenuous efforts, the Germans managed to have over 40 catapults operational by 15 June, and the first mass attack took place that night. Up until noon on 16 June, 244 bombs were launched of which 45 crashed immediately after launching. By 29 June, the 2,000th Fi 103 had been launched.

On 7 July, the first air-launched Fi 103s were used operationally when III./KG 3, Blitz-Geschwader, attacked Southampton using Heinkel He 111s as carriers. The damage caused was very small, and there appears to have been little enthusiasm for this sortie.

Fi 103 attacks on London reached their zenith on 2 August, 1944, when a landfall of 107 bombs was recorded, for which 316 had been launched from 38 catapults. Twenty-five of these bombs crashed immediately after launching.

As Allied forces moved across France and over-ran the launching sites, so this method of attacking London diminished until, finally, all units were moved back to central Holland from where the main target was to be Antwerp. Commensurate with this move, in October 1944, the Flak Regiment 155 (W) was disbanded to be re-formed as the 5th Flak Division, still with Col Wachtel in command.

With the French launching sites gone, the only method of attacking England with Fi 103s was by air-launching them. III./KG 3, which had been engaged sporadically on this type of operation from Gilze Rijen in Holland, was renamed I./KG 53, and two other Gruppen eventually followed from other decimated or dispersed bomber units. By early October, the first part of KG 53 Legion Condor had begun its operations against London from various bases in Germany. During these sorties, each He 111 carried a single Fi 103 beneath the starboard wing inboard of the engine, the actual launching taking place at night at about 450 m (1,475 ft) over the North Sea. Roughly 1,200 bombs in all were thus launched by all units, but only about 65 ever reached London, plus about 150 which were scattered elsewhere on land. Furthermore, this small percentage was paid for heavily in terms of some 77 bombers lost due to accidents and the RAF defence, and air-launchings ceased by 14 January, 1945.

Meanwhile, the new Netherlands-based catapults were stepping up their bombardment of Antwerp in concert with A4 bombardment, and this action was intensified in December to coincide with the German Ardennes offensive which only just failed.

From the start of the Fi 103 and A4 programmes, the Nazi party organization had striven by constant interference to obtain direct control of these programmes, and this was finally achieved by January 1945, when the entire V-weapon offensive came under the direction of SS Gen Kammler, with consequent disruption of the previous chains of command and further mixing of Luftwaffe and Army elements. Situtations even arose where the Army operated Fi 103s with Luftwaffe personnel, and the Waffen SS operated them alone.

The last Fi 103 (and the last V-weapon) hit London on 29 March, 1945, and the last hit Antwerp in the same month: 2,419 hits were recorded on London and 2,448 on Antwerp, but, to achieve these hits, roughly four times the number of bombs had to be launched. There were, of course, other less heavily bombarded cities in Britain, France and the Netherlands. These figures do not appear so uneconomic when compared with the A4 rocket, which cost about 50 times as much as the Fi 103 but only carried about the same weight of explosive (although it was delivered in a more penetrating manner). Altogether, more than 30,000 Fi 103s were produced during the war.

In some respects the pulse-jet propulsion system failed the Fi 103. First, it did not provide that extra margin of speed, and nothing like sufficient altitude, required to render it invulnerable to the best Allied fighters and less vulnerable to the good anti-aircraft defences for which it was an almost ideal target. Second, a small fault (the remedy of which was eventually

671

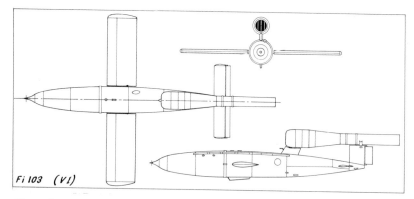

Fi 103 (V1)

effected) caused the fuel-starved motor to cut out upon commencement of the bomb's dive; this power cut provided both warning to those below to take cover and also minimized the penetration effect of the warhead. In contrast to the Fi 103, the A4 arrived at supersonic speed and was only heard after it had reached the target. The British Army made plans for destroying A4s by anti-aircraft fire but A4 attacks ceased before authorization was given to attempt their destruction.

Standard Fi 103s appear to have had two types of wing but no other apparent differences; one wing was of tapered planform with a span of 4·87 m (16 ft), the other was of parallel chord and 5·3 m (17 ft 4⅝ in) span. The standard warhead of Trialen explosive was sometimes supplemented by the addition of, for example, twenty-three 1 kg (2·2 lb) B2 incendiary bombs released from a metal grid, and the explosive could be replaced by various war-gases. Some Fi 103s were modified for increased range by reducing the warhead weight in order to carry extra fuel.

Proposals for improving Fi 103 performance included replacing the 109-014 pulse-jet with the more powerful 109-044 pulse-jet of 500 kg (1,100 lb) static thrust, a Porsche 109-005 turbojet of the same thrust, or some undefined ramjet, when any of these units were ready. These proposals were in addition to work done to improve the thrust of the pulse-jet by nitrous oxide injection and other refinements. Furthermore, there were plans for an Fi 103 to be air-towed or carried by an Arado Ar 234C jet bomber. With this plan in mind, extensive tests were made at Rechlin using an Ar 234B to tow an engineless Fi 103. Details of the frustrated plans to use the Fi 103 as a piloted suicide bomb have already been described on page 149. Nearly a score of Fi 103s still exist including one in the Imperial War Museum and one in the Science Museum in London.

Fi 103: Span, tapered wing, 4·87 m (16 ft), or parallel wing, 5·3 m (17 ft 4⅝ in); length 7·9 m (22 ft 7⅜ in); body diameter 0·838 m (2 ft 9 in).

Operational weight 2,180 kg (4,796 lb); explosive weight 850 kg (1,870 lb); fuel weight 515 kg (1,133 lb).

Launching velocity from Walter catapult 105 m/sec (345 ft/sec); catapult launching time approximately 1 sec.

Static thrust of 109-014 at sea level 350 kg (770 lb); approximate efficient life of 109-014 inlet valves 20 min; pulse frequency 47 cycles/sec constant.

Maximum operational speed 645 km/h (400 mph); range 240 km (149 miles); ceiling 3,000 m (8,840 ft).

In tests, the maximum speed reached by a non-operational Fi 103 before the war ended was 793 km/h (493 mph).

# Henschel Hs 293

The claim can be made for Henschel that their work in the missile field was the most concentrated and prolific of all the German firms, and a fair measure of success in operational application was achieved. Of course, no firm did work on its own in this field but usually took and incorporated from other specialists (in such fields as electronics and propulsion) what was currently possible and moulded these elements into a missile system. At Henschel a team had been established, by 1939, to carry out such work, a bold step for a firm that had been in the aviation business only since 1933 although their heavy engineering experience was of long standing. Research work on the control of unmanned aircraft had been undertaken by DVL, Siemens, Askania and the Schwarz Propeller Werke from 1937, which resulted in models being built by Schwarz. These models were aerodynamically unsuccessful, but the RLM urged Henschel to continue the work in 1939 with an eye to future missile developments. This, then, was the beginning of missile experience for the team who were joined in January 1940 by the man who was to direct their work, Prof Dr Herbert A. Wagner, previously of Junkers. Other members of the team were Josef Schwarzmann (electrics), Reinhard Lahde and Otto Bohlmann (aeronautics), Wilfried Hell (engineering), and Dr Henrici (project study).

At an early date it was decided by the RLM that the Henschel effort should be directed towards an air-to-ground missile which could be remotely guided onto the target from some distance away. For attacks on shipping the RLM had suggested a missile which would level out just above the water (a lead later followed by Blohm und Voss) and also another which would enter the water, but Henschel decided these would be too ambitious with no experience to draw upon, and work was therefore started on a straightforward glider bomb, the Hs 293.

The first design was designated Hs 293V-1 but was not built. (Note that V numbers refer to a design and many examples of the same design were often built, unlike aircraft where only one example of each V model was built.) The first model built was the Hs 293V-2 and examples of this were used in control tests from Karlshagen. This version was designed in February 1940, had no engine or warhead, and was later given the cover code of FZ 21.

By July 1940, a new design, the Hs 293V-3, was being tested, but there was still no rocket motor and the minimum release altitude was 1,000 m (3,280 ft). By the end of 1940, the Hs 293A-0 had been produced with further refinements and an underslung rocket motor pod, which allowed an advantageously low release altitude of 400 m (1,315 ft) with an acceptable target range being maintained. The first of this new design was launched on 16 December, 1940, but control failed. Two days later a successful launch was made and testing continued throughout the year. Of the three designs mentioned so far, 1,900 examples were built purely for experiment and modification in the Hs 293 development programme, which lasted until early 1944; 1,700 of these were Hs 293A-0s which formed the basis of the production model, the Hs 293A-1, now described.

Attached to the warhead of an SC 500 bomb were two wings behind which was the fuselage rear section carrying instrumentation and a tail-plane mounted above the wake of the wing. At the point where the tailplane was attached, the fuselage was flattened to form low aspect ratio ventral and dorsal fins, the fabricated structure in general being of duralumin. Conventional ailerons operated by electromagnets and an elevator operated by a screw and electric motor were used to alter the bank and pitch angles under the radio control of the bomb aimer. No rudder was provided since any tendency towards lateral instability was over-ridden by the remote control. Since the warhead was that of an SC 500 thin-walled demolition bomb, the missile was suitable for attacking only non-armoured ships and similar targets.

All aerodynamic surfaces were symmetrical, the airframe being designed for inexpensive precision machining with the aid of a digital computer and gauges. Inaccuracies in the elevator deflection had to be less than $0.1$ deg and so, to avoid having to make the radio control more accurate, an impact pressure plate was fitted. This plate influenced the elevator actuating system and adjusted the amount of elevator deflection according to air density and missile velocity. The airframe limiting Mach number was $0.85$, and a conical drag body trailing behind each wingtip could be fitted to limit speed to between Mach $0.75$ and $0.8$.

The single underslung pod contained a Walter 109-507B liquid propellant rocket unit operating on T-Stoff (hydrogen peroxide) and Z-Stoff (sodium permanganate) with air-pressurized tanks. This motor provided 600 kg (1,320 lb) thrust for ten seconds, which added about 195 km/h (120 mph) to the speed of the missile to drive it ahead of the carrier aircraft, where the bomb aimer could see it, and to decrease the rate of descent if required. Final speed of the missile varied between 435 km/h (270 mph) and 900 km/h (560 mph) depending on the launching height and release distance from the target, which varied between 400 m (1,315 ft) and 2,000 m (6,560 ft) for height and $3.5$ km ($2.2$ miles) and 18 km ($11.2$ miles) for range. In practice, maximum speeds were not attained because weather conditions at Karlshagen prevented high launchings during tests, and enemy ship radar made only medium and low altitude attacks possible in later sorties. Because of this, the Mach limiting drag bodies mentioned were not necessary.

Radio control of the missile was by means of a Knüppel (joystick) control box, Kehl transmitter and Strassburg superhet receiver which, with minor variations, were elements common to all of the German radio command systems. Development and manufacture was primarily the responsibility of Telefunken (transmitters) and Stassfurter Rundfunk (receivers). To ensure a fast response to the bank-angle orders without over-riding, the missile had in its control system a gyroscopic autopilot. The control equipment could operate on any of eighteen channels (48 to 50 mc/sec) thus enabling up to eighteen aircraft to launch their missiles simultaneously in the same area.

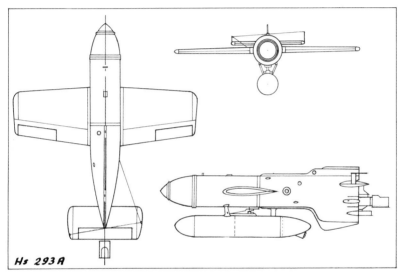

Hs 293A

At an early stage of the radio control development, modifications were considered to render the system safe from jamming. Accordingly, the Kehl/Strassburg system (FuG 203/230) was adapted as the Dortmund/Duisburg system (FuG 207/237). This was an audio frequency system where the link between control aircraft and missile was by means of two wire transmission lines, which unwound from bobbins on the aircraft with a payout of 12 km (7·5 miles) and also from bobbins on the missile wingtips with a payout of 18 km (11·2 miles), giving a possible maximum wire link of 30 km (18·7 miles). One hundred Hs 293A-1s were modified to operate on wire link and were designated Hs 293B, but this designation was later dropped since all IIs 293A-1s were manufactured to operate on either remote or wire-link control.

During 1941, selected Luftwaffe personnel received initial training on indoor missile control simulators and then each trainee controlled three actual Hs 293A launchings. To ascertain the methods and effectiveness of using the Hs 293A in service, the 13th Staffel of KG 100 was disbanded and re-formed as Erprobungs- und Lehrkommando 36 in July 1943. Later in the year, I./KG 50 was withdrawn from Stalingrad to be trained on the Hs 293A when it was redesignated II./KG 40 in October 1943. Mass production of the Hs 293A-1 had already begun in January 1942.

The procedure for using the Hs 293A-1 in action was that during the flight to the target, the missile was heated by warm air supplied through hoses from the carrier aircraft to minimize the effects of the considerable drop in temperature possible on long flights. Such a drop in temperature affected the internal humidity of the bomb, lowered the potential of its battery and iced up the pipes in the Walter unit because of the compressed-air propellant feed. As the target zone was approached, the transmitter and receiver were electrically connected for sequencing, the various sets heated up, and the missile gyroscope was run up to speed. After selecting the target, the carrier aircraft usually took up a course to port of the target ship, the bomb aimer being in the starboard side of the aircraft. When the aimer pressed the release button on his bomb sight, the electrical systems in the bomb were disconnected from the aircraft electrical supply and connected to their own battery, the release mechanism operated and the day or night flares in the tail of the bomb ignited. A thermic relay prevented control of the bomb for one second after release to prevent possible collision and then, at the operator's discretion, the rocket motor was started. The aimer then used his control stick to maintain the bomb on his line of sight to the target, the bomb usually following a series of arcs as corrections were made.

This line-of-sight method of guidance eliminated any need for complex electronic processes for predicting the future position of a target but was uneconomic of potential range and demanded excessive manoeuvres from the missile towards the end of the flight.

The Hs 293A-1 went into action for the first time on 25 August, 1943, when II./KG 100, based at Cognac with Dornier Do 217E-5s, attacked destroyers in the Bay of Biscay with uncertain results, but, two days later, the Gruppe sank the corvette *Egret* with the missile. The following month, II./KG 100 transferred to Istres, near Marseilles, for attacks on Mediterranean shipping which, from September 1943, they performed at night using flare light.

Meanwhile, the missile attack on shipping in the Atlantic was to continue, particularly since, by October 1943, sea-going U-boats were being lost at a rate of 30 per cent, and this percentage was rapidly rising in a quickly diminishing fleet. Thus, after completing their training, II./KG 40 (previously I./KG 50) transferred to Bordeaux-Mérignac on 25 October, 1943, with Heinkel He 177A-5s. Their first major operation with the Hs 293A-1 took place on 21 November, 1943, when, under the control of Fliegerführer Atlantik, with twenty aircraft, they attacked an Atlantic convoy. This action was something of a failure due to bad weather, and

II./KG 40 transferred their operations to Mediterranean attacks in support of KG 100. The Hs 293 continued to be used sporadically in the Atlantic by III./KG 40, which had some of its Focke-Wulf Fw 200C-3 Condors modified and redesignated Fw 200C-6 to carry two missiles each. These aircraft were used for the first time on 28 December, 1943, when four Condors attacked British naval units, the one missile-carrying aircraft being forced to ditch.

A generally more successful time was had in the Mediterranean until 26 November, 1943, when II./KG 40 lost half its attacking force during and after an attack on a convoy off the Algerian coast (Bougie). II./KG 100 made a final attack off the Algerian coast (Oran) on 10 January, 1944. By that time, attacks had to be made at night, and by 21 January, 1944, all the units in southern France were moved to northern Italian airfields to oppose the expected Allied landings in Italy. The landings at Anzio proved a great test for the missiles, and many aircraft thus equipped were put into operation alongside conventional bombers. These sorties continued until March but most were flown with the armour-piercing Fritz X missile (described on page 696) which had most successes. Missile attacks gradually became less effective, partly due to launchings at excessive range and partly due to unsuspected Allied jamming.

The Hs 293A continued to be used, however, one of the last units equipped with it being the Stab and III. Gruppe of KG 100, which were based at Toulouse-Francazal during the summer of 1944 with special Dornier Do 217Rs, the units finally disbanding in August for retraining as fighter pilots. Final operations with the Hs 293 (and with any missiles) were undertaken by a special unit of KG 100 formed to attack bridges across the Oder, which the Red Army was approaching. These sorties were undertaken with some success using Dornier Do 217s in April 1945.

In addition to *Egret* and numerous escort vessels and transports, the following warships were sunk by Hs 293A missiles: the destroyers *Inglefield, Boadicea, Intrepid* and *Dulverton*, and the Greek destroyer, *Vasilissa Olga*.

Aircraft used on operations with the Hs 293, and also the Fritz X (the principal modification being the installation of the radio equipment in the aircraft), included the Heinkel He 111H-12, He 177A-3/R3, He 177A-3/R4, He 177A-5/R2; Focke-Wulf Fw 200C-6, Fw 200C-8; and Dornier Do 217E-5, Do 217K-2, Do 217K-3, Do 217M-11 and Do 217R. Also modified to carry these missiles but not used in this rôle were a few Junkers Ju 290A-7s and Heinkel He 277B-5/R2s.

The number of Hs 293A-1s produced is not known, but a proportion of the 1,700 Hs 293A-0s were probably converted to Hs 293A-1 standard.

Because of the icing troubles already mentioned with the Walter 109-507B rocket unit, two other motors were developed for intended use with the Hs 293. The first was the BMW 109-511 of 600 kg (1,320 lb) thrust using M-Stoff (methanol) and SV-Stoff (nitric acid) propellants and utilizing a proportion of the combustion gases to give a propellant pressure feed. The second was the WASAG 109-512 of 1,200 kg (2,640 lb) thrust employing solid diglycol propellant. The latter unit was tested and was to have been adopted but is unlikely to have seen action, since neither this nor the BMW unit were fully developed.

Hs 293A-1: Span 3·1 m (10 ft 3⅝ in); length 3·82 m (11 ft 8⅞ in); wing area 1·92 sq m (20·66 sq ft); fuselage diameter 0·47 m (1 ft 6⅞ in).

Operational weight 1,045 kg (2,304 lb); total propellant weight (for 109-507B) 63·5 kg (140 lb); explosive weight 295 kg (649 lb).

# Henschel Hs 294

Early in 1940, work was begun on developing missiles which could be guided into the sea to strike a ship below the waterline. With design experience gained on the Henschel Hs 293, bringing the missile near the water surface was not difficult, but for it to be able to make the actual entry at a shallow angle without unacceptable course deflections proved to be a major problem.

Extensive tests were begun by using Hs 293A fuselages with entirely new noses, and resulted in an experimental series of missiles designated Hs 293C-1, C-2, C-3, and C-4. From these were developed, during 1943, the larger Hs 294A and Hs 294B, which were intended for attacks on armoured ships below the waterline. The B version differed from the A in being equipped for wire-link control.

The warheads of these missiles were of a slender, conical shape having ogive noses. Part of the underwater stability problem was solved by allowing the wings and rear fuselage structure to break away at specially weakened points as the missile impacted with the water, a small ridge on the upper side of the warhead's nose curving its underwater path up towards the ship. The angle of entry into the water was between 15 deg and 30 deg with an optimum angle of 22 deg, and the warhead would travel under its own momentum for an underwater distance of some 45 m (148 ft). A further benefit was that proximity fuses, similar to those used in conventional marine torpedoes, could be used, but, in fact, it was the delayed development of just this part of the equipment which made the Hs 294 too late for service, although contact fuses could have been used.

An RLM contract called for 1,130 Hs 294A-0s, and maximum production was to be 50 per month, but the number actually constructed is not known. A further contract called for 300 Hs 294V-2s, which were similar to the A-0 version but with trailing-edge wing-spoiler controls, and at least 56 of these were built. Twenty-five Hs 294A-0 airframes were in the

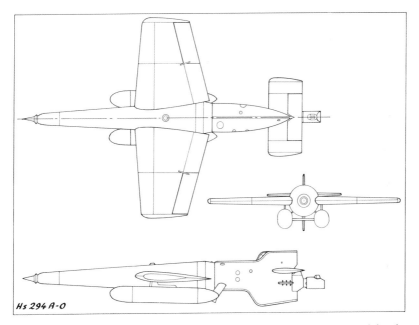

Hs 294 A-0

process of being converted to have a television camera mounted in the forward end of the right hand rocket pod, this system being the same as that for the Hs 293D, described below.

The Hs 294A-0 was powered by two underslung Walter 109-507D rocket units giving a total of 1,300 kg (2,860 lb) thrust for ten sec. Two BMW 109-511 units were probably projected for the Hs 294V-1 but in fact it was used only for underwater tests. There was also a proposal to fit a single BMW P.3375 (RII 301) rocket giving 1,500 kg (3,300 lb) thrust for ten sec, but this plan did not materialize.

Hs 294A-0: Span 4·025 m (13 ft 2½ in); length 6·12 m (20 ft 0⅞ in); wing area 5·3 sq m (57·03 sq ft); fuselage diameter 0·65 m (2 ft 1⅝ in).
Operational weight 2,170 kg (4,774 lb); explosive weight 656 kg (1,443 lb).
Maximum speed 860 km/h (535 mph); target range 4 to 14 km (2·49 to 8·7 miles); release altitude 800 to 5,500 m (2,625 to 18,040 ft).

# Henschel Hs 293D

Probably the most interesting of Henschel's developments in guided bombs was the Hs 293D, in which a radical departure was made in the guidance system. This missile was a standard Hs 293A-1 with an extended nose and fuselage centre section to .carry television equipment, enabling the bomb

679

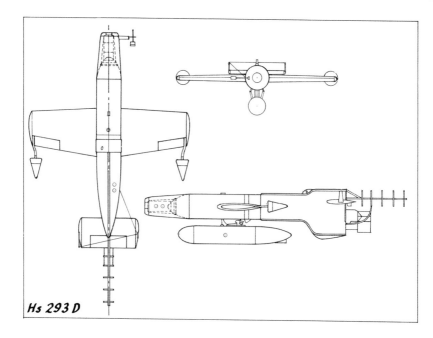

*Hs 293 D*

aimer to sight the target on a screen in the carrier aircraft. This equipment was developed because of the disadvantages inherent in line-of-sight guidance, namely the necessity for the carrier aircraft to maintain a fixed course, for the aimer to have unobstructed view, and the diminishing definition of target and missile with increasing range and poor weather conditions. Thus, with the television equipment, the carrier aircraft was free to take evasive action, and the aimer's view grew clearer as the missile approached the target.

The length of a converted Hs 293A-1 was increased by 0·68 m (2 ft 2¾ in) with the installation of the Tonne A nose camera and the converter and power set in the fuselage. The standard length was further increased by 0·56 m (1 ft 10⅛ in) with the installation of a Yagi aerial at the rear of the bomb, and the total weight of all the new equipment was 110 kg (242 lb). Attached to the camera nose fairing was a wind vane which adjusted the optical axis of the camera independently of the varying angle of attack of the missile, and a clear sight screen, heated to prevent condensation and icing, was fitted in the nose.

Television transmissions from the bomb were received by a further Yagi aerial on the carrier aircraft, a picture being given on a graduated screen by a Seedorf receiver mounted above the standard control box at the aimer's position.

The complete television equipment, known as K11, was developed by Fernseh GmbH in collaboration with Dr Weiss of the Reichpost-Forschungsanstalt. Since, with targets such as ships, the best resolution was required horizontally, the picture lines were posed vertically, 224-line pictures being screened at a frequency of 50 pictures per second.

For testing, two Heinkel He 111s and a Dornier Do 217 were converted and fitted with the necessary equipment. Test flights from Karlshagen in early 1944 were made with about seventy Hs 293D missiles against a wreck lying off the coast. The aimer's view was rather unnerving, since, just before the missile hit the target, because of the 13 deg wide angle view camera lens the screen image appeared to explode in front of him.

The tests were not altogether successful at this early development stage, although (as proved by modern missiles) the scheme was perfectly feasible and a potential improvement on line-of-sight guidance. Professor Wagner was at the controls of the carrier aircraft for most of the tests but has frankly stated that he was inexperienced. In addition, the lack of indoor simulators, the general pressure of work, and lack of official impetus hindered the development programme. Nevertheless, plans for the mass production of equipment to convert standard missiles were under way, although they did not come to fruition. Ranges and release altitudes were similar to the Hs 293A-1, but the reception of a clear television picture could not be obtained over 4 km (2·5 miles) range. Further developments were in hand to reduce equipment weight and provide wire links for the television equipment (50 lines only) to obviate jamming.

# Henschel Hs 293E, F, G, H and I

Hs 293E was the designation given to twenty Hs 293A-0 airframes which were being modified (and may have been completed) to take the Hs 293A-1 warhead and to test the control system of the Hs 293C-2 which dispensed with potentiometers; the type was later abandoned.

The Hs 293F was a highly experimental missile designed to carry the same payload and have similar operating characteristics to the Hs 293A-1. The principal aim was to simplify construction and save critical materials, and this gave rise to several interesting features. A delta wing was employed and there was no tail unit, the trailing edge of each wing having three separate controls. Elevation was controlled by inboard spoilers, roll was controlled by central spoilers, and small wingtip ailerons controlled the yaw effect of spoiler control. These spoilers, known as Wagner bars after their designer, were unusual in that they were located immediately behind the wing trailing edge. Each spoiler had a curved surface in order to maintain a constant and small clearance between itself and the wing as it swung above or below the trailing edge as required for control. Two Schmidding SG33 rocket units, burning diglycol solid fuel, each giving 1,855 kg (4,081 lb) thrust for 3·5 sec, were slung beneath the fuselage.

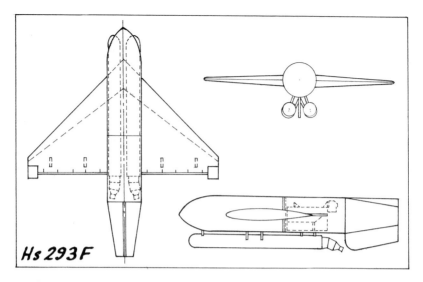

**Hs 293 F**

The extent of progress with this design is unknown, but development was shelved early in 1944 pending a decision of the RLM to issue a development contract for 50 missiles.

Hs 293F: Span 1·6 m (5 ft 3 in); length 3·2 m (10 ft 6 in); wing area 1·92 sq m (20·66 sq ft); fuselage diameter 0·47 m (1 ft 6½ in).
Total propellant weight 72 kg (159 lb); explosive weight 295 kg (649 lb).

In an attempt to add some of the advantages of the Fritz X guided bomb to the Hs 293A, the Hs 293G was produced, capable of either near vertical or horizontal attacking flight paths. A special gyroscopic unit was fitted which could be swivelled 90 deg from the horizontal to the vertical axis as required, and a WASAG 109-512 solid diglycol fuelled rocket motor was fitted. Full details of the Hs 293G design are lacking; only ten examples were produced in 1942, and work was eventually stopped in favour of Fritz X.

During 1943–44, a small number of Hs 293A-0 airframes were modified into an experimental series of Hs 293H missiles. These were for use with control equipment possessing a fifth transmission frequency, for a detonation signal to be given when the missile was air-launched into bomber formations. The intention was not to hit individual enemy aircraft but to use the missile as a blast weapon on the whole formation; the detonation signal could be given from the carrier aircraft or, better still, from a fighter which could make a closer approach to the enemy.

Since this missile was to operate at high altitudes, a rocket motor was specially developed by Schmidding which would operate within the temperature ranges of +70 deg C to −60 deg C. This motor, the 109-513, operated on M-Stoff (methanol) and A-Stoff (oxygen), the latter being, unusually, in gaseous form, to give a thrust of 610 kg (1,342 lb) for 11 sec in the production model. No propellant pumps were used, and series production of the rocket motor began in March 1944.

The Hs 293HV-1 was the first experimental model, the primary purpose of which was to conduct tests on night steering equipment on moving air targets, although actual details of the equipment are unknown. Further development on detonation and control was undertaken with the Hs 293HV-2 and HV-6 models; the Hs 293HV-6 was the first model to have a barometric fuse installed to ensure no missile returned to the ground unexploded. A television camera was fitted to the Hs 293HV-3 to improve guidance and the aimer's timing of warhead detonation. The Hs 293HV-7 was similar to the HV-2 but was equipped with some type of infra-red proximity fuse. The Kakadu proximity fuse, which was a high frequency type using Doppler effect, was intended for test in the Hs 293HV-4.

Carrier aircraft envisaged were the Dornier Do 217K-2, U-1 and M types, but the Hs 293HV-5 was designed for use with fast carriers such as the Arado Ar 234.

Finally, the designation Hs 293H-1a was reserved for the production model, but developments were discontinued in favour of air-to-air missiles designed for the purpose from the outset. The missile was intended to be released at a target range of between 0·5 and 4 km (0·31 and 2·5 miles) and at an altitude of between 800 m (2,625 ft) below the target to 4,000 m (13,120 ft) above it.

Hs 293H-1a: Span 3·1 m (10 ft 3⅝ in); length (without proximity fuse) 3·82 m (11 ft 8⅞ in); wing area 1·92 sq m (20·66 sq ft); fuselage diameter 0·47 m (1 ft 6⅞ in). Operational weight 980 kg (2,156 lb); total propellant weight 36·8 kg (81 lb); explosive weight 295 kg (649 lb).
Maximum speed 900 km/h (560 mph).

Hs 293I was the designation applied to an Hs 293A redesigned for an increased explosive weight of about 500 kg (1,100 lb). Other details are unknown, but it was probably a preliminary step towards the Hs 295 design.

# Henschel Hs 295

This series was a redesign of the basic Henschel missile to give greater explosive effect plus armour piercing ability but without submarine capability. The aft fuselage and the control method were as the Hs 293A-1, and the wing was that of the Hs 294. The warhead bulged to a greater diameter than the fuselage, and balance was maintained by the insertion of

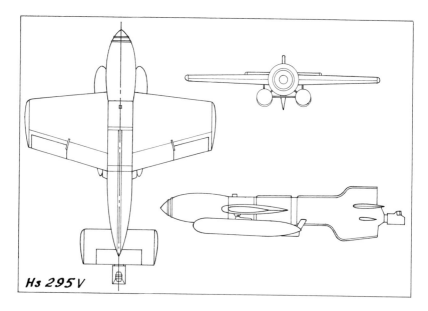

Hs 295V

an extra fuselage section. A pair of underslung Walter 109-507D (Hs 295V-2) or 109-507B (Hs 295D) rocket pods were fitted.

Design work started in early 1942 and flight tests began with the Hs 295V-1 in 1943. This was followed by the manufacture of some 50 test models of the further development, the Hs 295V-2. The incorporation of television equipment and a camera in the nose of the starboard rocket pod of the Hs 295V-1 produced the Hs 295D model, which was in the trials stage in April 1944. Tests on this series were not completed, and no quantity production was started.

Hs 295V-2: Span 4·025 m (13 ft 2½ in); length 4·952 m (16 ft 3 in); maximum body diameter 0·553 m (1 ft 9¾ in).

Operational weight 2,080 kg (4,576 lb); total propellant weight 127 kg (280 lb); explosive weight 580 kg (1,276 lb).

All-burnt velocity 725 km/h (450 mph); limiting Mach number 0·625.

Hs 295D: Span 4·625 m (15 ft 2 in); length 5·443 m (17 ft 10⅛ in); maximum body diameter 0·553 m (1 ft 9¾ in).

Operational weight 2,100 kg (4,620 lb); total propellant weight 127 kg (280 lb); explosive weight 580 kg (1,276 lb).

Maximum speed 860 km/h (535 mph); launching height 500 m to 8,000 m (1,640 ft to 26,240 ft); launching range 4 km to 14 km (2·5 to 8·7 miles).

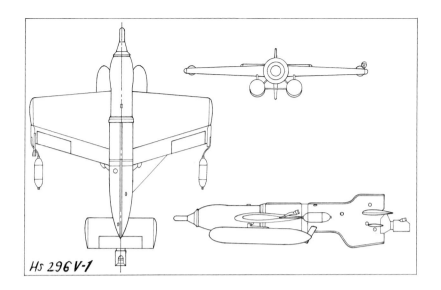

Hs 296 V-1

# Henschel Hs 296

Henschel only produced one model of the Hs 296 series, the Hs 296V-1, and this design amalgamated the rear fuselage and wing of the Hs 294, the control system of the Hs 293 and a similarly enlarged warhead to that of the Hs 295. The design of this type was started concurrently with the Hs 295, but production and testing details are unknown. There are some indications that this missile could be launched horizontally or near-vertically in the manner of the Hs 293G.

# Henschel GT 1200

The design of the Henschel GT 1200 series was intended for air-to-underwater attacks in the same manner as the Hs 294 series, though some major rethinking was done and there was less adoption of previous elements than before.

The first model, the GT 1200A, was constructed so that the wings and aft-fuselage broke away upon entry into the water, but, unlike the Hs 294, the warhead was provided with underwater propulsion and steering. Because velocity was added to the warhead during the final part of its trajectory, it is possible (though not confirmed) that rocket units for the aerial trajectory were not fitted, although this would have presented no

685

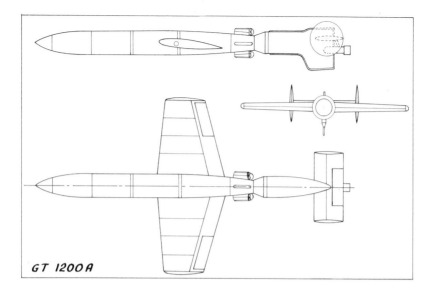

GT 1200A

problems and would have increased the range. The underwater rocket unit
was exposed and ignited when the aft-fuselage broke away, and the unit
was probably of the Schmidding 109-573 type fuelled with solid diglycol
propellant to give a thrust of 100 kg (220 lb) for six seconds.

The fuselage of the GT 1200A was of parallel section from the pointed
nose to just aft of the wings, where it tapered into a sharp waist and then
out again to the tail fairing. The wings were of roughly equi-taper planform, and there was a rectangular tailplane (Hs 294) with new circular
end-plates or fins. Total length, including flare unit, was 7·325 m (24 ft
$0\frac{3}{8}$ in), the wing span was 3·975 m (13 ft $0\frac{1}{2}$ in), and fuselage diameter was
0·525 m (1 ft $8\frac{5}{8}$ in). Aerial control was by means of conventional ailerons
and elevator, without rudders, and underwater steering was by means of a
cruciform arrangement of four rudders situated behind the wings where the
aft-fuselage broke away.

The next development, the GT 1200B, had a decrease in overall length
to 6·825 m (22 ft $3\frac{3}{4}$ in) which was made possible by mounting the control
equipment in two streamlined nacelles extending from the wing leading
edges. There was also considerable narrowing of the aft-fuselage.

The final development, the GT 1200C, was the last Henschel development in the air-to-underwater (or ground) missile field. It was longer than
the two previous designs, the total length being 7·350 m (24 ft $1\frac{3}{8}$ in) but
was basically the same. The control gear or target-seeking device was
presumably installed in the nacelle beneath the nose, which supplanted the
wing nacelles, and the aft-fuselage was made as parallel-sided as possible.
For this missile, it was proposed to use the Blohm und Voss Bv 142 as a
launching aircraft.

No other details of the GT 1200 series are known.

# Henschel Zitterrochen (Torpedo Fish)

All Henschel air-to-ground missiles were subsonic, but the question of future supersonic missiles had been taken up by Henschel's Dr Voepl, who made design studies and also model tests up to Mach 1·5 in one of the Göttingen wind-tunnels. This work resulted in a basic configuration in the form of a model known as Zitterrochen which represented a tailless mono-wing missile, the thin wings having a triangular planform and the so-called Wagner bar controls or spoilers at the trailing edges. A missile developed from this was envisaged as having an underslung tailplane attached to a ventral fin, and two underslung rocket pods.

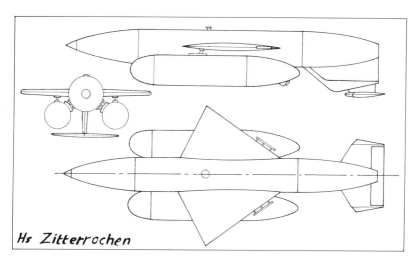

*Hs Zitterrochen*

The Wagner bar controls, already mentioned on the Hs 293F, were virtually spoilers moved back to the trailing edge with similar effect and control. Such controls were tested on some of the Hs 293Cs for roll control and in 1943–44 for pitch control on the Hs 293V-4. This work led to a simplified control scheme in 1944, when bar controls were used exclusively in the Hs 293A-2. The Zitterrochen was ready for production but was cancelled by the RLM; however, the work was not wasted, because the control methods were adapted for the Hs 298 and Hs 117 missiles.

Loading a Henschel Hs 117 Schmetterling guided missile on to a modified gun mounting for a test launching. This ground-to-air missile was close to operational use, albeit in small numbers at first, when the war ended.

# Henschel (Hs 297) Hs 117 Schmetterling (Butterfly)

During 1941, Henschel's first studies in the ground-to-air field of missiles were made, which resulted in some conservative flak rocket projects. One of these was originally designated Hs 297 but, when a development order was received in 1943, was redesignated Hs 117 Schmetterling.

This subsonic missile was shaped like a small aircraft with sweptback wings and a cruciform tail unit. The nose was asymmetric and divided into the warhead extension on the starboard side and a shorter extension for a generator propeller on the port side. Aerodynamic control was by means of solenoid-operated Wagner bars at the trailing edges of the wings and tailplane, and no rudder was required.

Launching was from a modified 37 mm gun mounting, which formed two crutches upon which the wings rested. For take-off boost, one Schmidding 109-553 solid diglycol-fuelled rocket unit was fitted above the fuselage and another beneath it, each boost unit giving 1,750 kg (3,850 lb) thrust for four seconds to accelerate the missile to 1,100 km/h (680 mph). Once expended, the boosters fell away to ignite the sustainer motor installed in the rear fuselage, and the speed rapidly fell to about Mach 0·77, that is, some 950 km/h (590 mph) at sea level. Automatic means were employed to ensure that the missile flew below its critical Mach number and that the set airspeed remained constant, in order to assist guidance and make the design of the controls easier. The Mach number was maintained by thrust regulation, whereby the propellant valves were adjusted according to the difference between static or barometric pressure and total or ram pressure, these varying with altitude and speed. It is interesting to note that in later tests with the Hs 117H (basically the same as the Hs 117), the Mach regulation equipment was not used, and speeds of Mach 0·05 higher than wind-tunnel predictions were realized. Wind-tunnel tests had been made at both the DVL and Göttingen.

Most examples of the Hs 117 were powered with the BMW 109-558 rocket motor, which used R-Stoff (Tonka or a composition, self-igniting, fuel) and SV-Stoff (Salbei or concentrated nitric acid) propellants to give an initial thrust of 375 kg (825 lb) for 33 sec falling to 60 kg (132 lb) over the last 24 sec. A gas pressure propellant feed was used, and the propellant

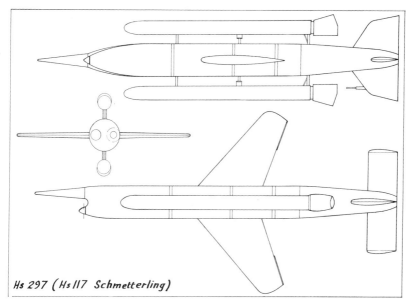

Hs 297 (Hs 117 Schmetterling)

valves were electrically adjusted via gear wheels. A powder squib-ruptured membrane was used for starting, followed by spontaneous ignition.

An alternative sustainer motor was the Walter 109-729. This was essentially the same in performance, design and weight as the BMW 109-558, but used SV-Stoff oxidizer, Br-Stoff (petrol) as fuel and a small quantity of furfural alcohol to initiate combustion with the acid.

Since the Hs 117 was intended for low- and medium-altitude interceptions, it was anticipated that visual line-of-sight guidance would suffice, using available equipment in order to get the missile operational in the shortest time. The missile was sighted visually, using a 10X telescope. Two operators were needed, one to search and set the telescope in the approximate direction given by the standard optical flak predictor and the other to control the missile onto the line-of-sight using a joystick control. The

689

control link was along similar lines to the Kehl/Strassburg system and was code-named Parsival. A separate frequency for the detonation signal was available, pending the introduction of suitable proximity fuses. No remote control of the launching mounting was necessary, and only rough corrections were required.

Under blind conditions it was hoped to use the Mannheim Riese ground radar apparatus, whereby both target and missile were indicated on cathode ray tubes, and the operator applied control to achieve coincidence.

Testing of the Hs 117 began in May 1944 at Karlshagen, and, by September, twenty-two launchings had been made including some from a Heinkel He 111 aircraft. The first blind tests were simulated with Würzburg radar equipment when the missile was released from an He 111 and control was applied from the ground, with satisfactory results, according to the pilot's observations. Other tests were made, from September 1944, by the Luftwaffe's Flak LET 700, which had the task of evaluating the flak missiles and formulating methods for their employment.

Mass production of the Hs 117 was ordered in December 1944 and planned to start in March 1945, with 150 per month rising to a steady 3,000 a month by November that year. The first launching site was planned for March 1945, with 60 sites to be ready by November plus ten a month after this. Although the Hs 117 came closest of all German ground-to-air missiles to being operational, the overall plans were quite unrealistic, and no missiles went into service.

A special supersonic version of the Hs 117 was under construction but not completed; this missile was intended to have a speed of between 1,335 and 1,435 km/h (830 and 890 mph).

Hs 117 Schmetterling: Span 2 m (6 ft 6$\frac{1}{4}$ in); length (including proximity fuse) 4·29 m (14 ft 0$\frac{7}{8}$ in); fuselage diameter 0·35 m (1 ft 1$\frac{3}{4}$ in).

Approximate starting operational weight 420 kg (924 lb) including 170 kg (374 lb) for two 109-553 boosters; total liquid propellant weight 72 kg (158·5 lb) for BMW 109-558 or 81 kg (178 lb) for Walter 109-729; total solid booster propellant 80 kg (176 lb); standard explosive weight 23 kg (50·6 lb).

Operational speed below Mach 0·77; ceiling 10,000 m (32,800 ft) at a range of 32 km (19·87 miles).

# Henschel Hs 117H

At an early stage in the Henschel Hs 117 Schmetterling development, a version, designated Hs 117H, was designed for the air-to-air rôle. This missile was something more than a stop-gap design (unlike the unaccepted Hs 293H) and, together with the Ruhrstahl X-4 missile, remained in active development until the end of the war. It must be said, though, that a prime reason why it was not cancelled in the cut-backs of January 1945 was that

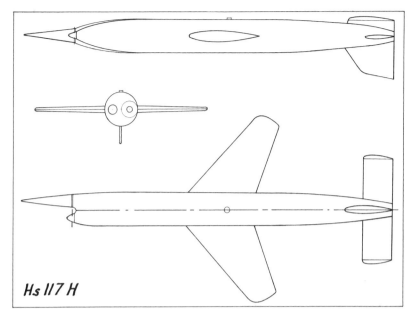

**Hs 117 H**

its development was running parallel to the badly needed Hs 117 Schmetterling flak rocket.

Unlike the Ruhrstahl X-4 and Hs 298 air-to-air missiles (*see* pages 700 and 692), the Hs 117H was intended for use at considerable range and was therefore to be used by piston-engined aircraft, such as the Junkers Ju 188 and Ju 388, which, being easier to shoot down or pursue, could benefit from the safer launching range.

Apart from some modification of the tail unit, differences from the Hs 117 were small, and, again, the BMW 109-558 rocket motor was internally installed during tests, although it was possible, for production models, to install the WASAG 109-512 solid fuelled rocket. No booster rockets were required for the air-launching.

Sighting of the missile was by the standard Revi reflector sight, and no telescopic sight was intended because of vibration effects. Guidance to the target was then performed with the conventional radio-link control, line-of-sight fashion. Detonation was to be by radio signal initially but later by proximity fuse, and pure homing was an eventual goal. The range of attack was to be between 6 and 10 km (3·7 and 6·2 miles), depending upon visibility, and up to 5,000 m (16,400 ft) above the parent aircraft. In the event, no operations were undertaken with the Hs 117H.

Hs 117H: Span 2 m (6 ft 6¾ in); length (without proximity fuse) 3·69 m (12 ft 1¼ in); fuselage diameter 0·35 m (1 ft 1¾ in).

Approximate starting operational weight 325 kg (823 lb); total propellant weight 72 kg (158·5 lb) for BMW 109-558; explosive weight 100 kg (220 lb).

Maximum velocity 900 km/h (560 mph).

# Henschel Hs 298

The Hs 298 was the first Henschel missile designed specifically for the air-to-air rôle and the first such to receive prolonged development. It was also Henschel's smallest missile and was developed around a similar specification to the Ruhrstahl X-4, though of lower performance.

The first model, the Hs 298V-1, resembled a small aircraft with a vertically asymmetric fuselage, the upper and longest extension of the nose holding the warhead and fuse, and the lower and shortest having a small generator propeller. The mid-mounted wings were sweptback by 30 deg at quarter chord, and a rectangular tailplane had square fins at the tips. Wagner-bar controls were fitted at the wing and tailplane trailing edges. The radio link was by means of a Kehl transmitter and Colmar receiver with the usual frequency for a fuse-ignition signal, pending the availability of a suitable proximity fuse. Also to be fitted were the usual impact fuse and a self-destruction fuse. Later plans envisaged the use of a wire-link control system.

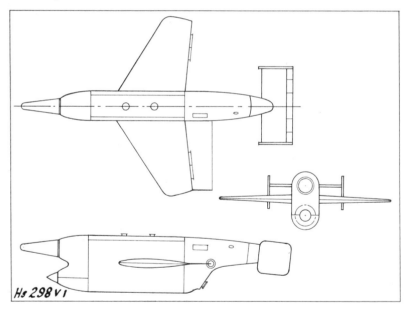

Hs 298 V 1

Further development led to the Hs 298V-2 design which differed in having a new wing sweptback 38 deg at quarter chord, new circular fins and the warhead moved to the lower position with the generator propeller in the top position.

The power unit for the Hs 298 was the Schmidding 109-543 two-stage, solid-diglycol fuelled rocket motor. Upon ignition this unit gave an acceleration thrust of 150 kg (330 lb) for 5·5 sec, followed by a sustainer thrust of 50 kg (110 lb) for 20 sec.

The first experimental missile was fired in May 1944, and over 300 of the experimental series were manufactured. Aircraft intended to use the Hs 298 included the Junkers Ju 88G-1, Ju 388 and Focke-Wulf Fw 190, but, although mass production was planned for the beginning of 1945, development was not finalized, and the missile was cancelled in favour of concentration on the Ruhrstahl X-4. The range of attack was to be between 0·5 and 2·5 km (0·31 to 1·55 miles) with launchings from 1,000 m (3,280 ft) below to 2,000 m (6,560 ft) above the target.

Hs 298V-1: Span 1·29 m (4 ft 2¾ in); length, including fuse nose, 2·003 m (6 ft 6⅞ in); wing area 0·42 sq m (4·52 sq ft); fuselage depth 0·415 m (1 ft 4⅜ in).
Operational weight 95 kg (209 lb); propellant weight 6·5 kg (14·3 lb); explosive weight 25 kg (55 lb).
Maximum speed 940 km/h (585 mph).

Hs 298V-2: Span 1·274 m (4 ft 2⅛ in); length 2·545 m (8 ft 4¼ in); fuselage depth 0·415 m (1 ft 4⅜ in).
Operational weight 125 kg (275 lb); propellant weight 6·5 kg (14·3 lb); explosive weight 48 kg (105·6 lb).
Maximum speed 680 km/h (425 mph).

# Messerschmitt Enzian (Gentian)

The Messerschmitt Enzian subsonic ground-to-air missile was designed to fulfil a similar rôle to the Henschel Schmetterling but, unlike the latter, was intended as a blast weapon. Although employing much wood in its construction, Enzian was also a much heavier missile and of entirely different aerodynamic design. Its design was undertaken at Messerschmitt by Dr Hermann Wurster early in 1944, and the airframes were intended to be mass produced by Holzbau-Kissing KG at Sonthofen, Allgäu.

Based on similar aerodynamic principles to the Me 163 interceptor-fighter, the missile had a circular section low aspect ratio fuselage with ventral and dorsal fin but no tailplane. The mid-mounted wings had considerable sweepback and full-span trailing-edge elevons which operated in unison or differentially to control pitch and roll and thus direction.

To launch and boost the missile, four Schmidding 109-553 solid-diglycol fuelled rocket units were grouped symmetrically around the fuselage to give a combined boost thrust of 7,000 kg (15,400 lb) for four sec. The launch rails were 6·80 m (22 ft 3¾ in) in length and were mounted on a modified 88 mm gun platform; in fact, a point launching would have sufficed, since the speed when leaving the rails was too low for the controls to be effective.

693

A Messerschmitt Enzian ready for the second test flight on 29 April, 1944. When the missile programme was pruned in January 1945, this ground-to-air guided missile was abandoned.

Enzian E-1, E-2, and E-3, the test models, were designed to have the Walter RI-210B sustainer rocket motor in the rear fuselage. This motor used SV-Stoff (mixed acid) and Br-Stoff (petrol) for propellants, with a small quantity of furfural alcohol to initiate combustion with the acid. T-Stoff (hydrogen peroxide) was also carried to provide catalyst-released steam for a turbine driving both propellant pumps. Compressed air, released by an electrically-operated explosion valve, forced the T-Stoff into the catalyst chamber and thus began operation, but, since no air-reducing valve was used, a constant reduction in pressure caused a constant reduction in turbine speed and thrust. Thus, the thrust fell from an initial 2,000 kg (4,410 lb) to a final 1,000 kg (2,205 lb) over the 70 sec burning time, this being intentional to prevent the missile from exceeding its limiting Mach number of between 0·8 and 0·9.

About 15 of these Walter motors were manufactured and at least ten of them used in Enzian launchings at Karlshagen from April to September 1944.

Control of the missile was by means of a Kehl/Strassburg or Kogge/Brigg radio link with joystick control and line-of-sight guidance. In the first test flights, the missiles ran very badly out of control, not because of electronic failure but because the importance of accurate alignment of the thrust line in relation to the centre of gravity was not appreciated.

The operational versions of Enzian were to be the E-4, flying up to Mach 0·9 and, later, the redesigned supersonic E-5, flying up to Mach 2.

694

For these versions new rocket motors were designed by Dr Konrad and Dr Beck of the Deutsche Versuchsanstalt für Kraftfahrzeug- und Fahrzeug-Motoren (DVK) at Berlin and Dresden. These motors used S-Stoff (nitric acid) and Visol for propellants, with a compressed-air feed. Starting was by use of bursting discs, and a simple air pressure regulation scheme still allowed a gradual falling off of thrust. The motor for E-4 gave an initial thrust of 2,000 kg (4,410 lb), which fell to 1,000 kg (2,205 lb) at the end of the 70 sec burning time; the motor for the E-5 gave an initial thrust of 2,500 kg (5,512 lb), which fell to 1,500 kg (3,307 lb) at the end of the 56 sec burning time.

In all, 38 Enzian missiles were tested, some of these being the E-4 version, but no E-5s were built, and the whole Enzian programme was another casualty of the January 1945 cancellations, largely because the work was at such an early stage.

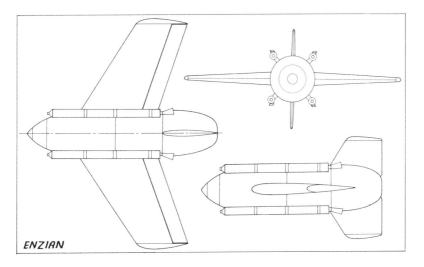

ENZIAN

Enzian E-4, (production version): Span 4 m (13 ft 1½ in); length 2·4 m (7 ft 10½ in); fuselage diameter 0·88 m (2 ft 10⅝ in).

Approximate starting operational weight 1,800 kg (3,969 lb) including 340 kg (750 lb) for four Schmidding 109–553 boosters; total liquid propellant weight 600 kg (1,323 lb); total solid booster propellant 144 kg (317 lb); explosive weight, including self-destruction charge, 300 kg (661 lb).

All-burnt velocity 975 km/h (605 mph); velocity at target 910 km/h (565 mph); maximum range was obtained at a height of 2,500 m (8,200 ft) and was 24·5 km (15·2 miles) without manoeuvring allowance; ceiling was 12,500 m (41,000 ft) when maximum range was reduced to 9·9 km (6·15 miles) without manoeuvring allowance.

# Ruhrstahl/Kramer X-series Missiles

Although covering widely differing sizes and purposes, the X-series of missiles all had one thing in common, which was the use of tail-mounted spoilers for control. In 1938, Dr Max Kramer was the first to make actual application of the spoiler when he conducted experiments at the Deutsche Versuchsanstalt für Luftfahrt (DVL). In these experiments, radio-controlled spoilers were fitted to the tails of 250 kg (550 lb) bombs to control their trajectories, and tests were made from the Adlershof airfield near Berlin.

## X-1 (Fritz X)

In 1940, the RLM became interested in Kramer's work and accordingly chose the PC 1400 bomb warhead for use with a controlled free-fall weapon for attacking armoured ships. Development was entrusted to Ruhrstahl AG in Westfalen under Dr Kramer's guidance and the new missile designated PC 1400X (code name Fritz X) by the military and X-1 by the company. (The missile has also been referred to as Fx 1400 and simply as Fx.)

Fritz X had four centrally-mounted, plain cruciform fins forming the aerodynamic pivotal points for control, which was effected during free fall in the pitch and yaw planes by tail-mounted spoilers. Further spoilers in the tail roll-stabilized the missile automatically under the commands of a single gyroscope. The structure surrounding the four tail fins formed an air-brake ring to limit the final velocity. The thick-wall, armour-piercing warhead was of either cast or forged steel and was capable of piercing 130 mm ($5\frac{1}{8}$ in) of armour plate when the missile was dropped from an altitude of 6,000 m (19,680 ft). The warhead fuse was a type AZ 38B electrical micro-delay, and a second fuse, type AZ 80, destroyed the control unit in the event of a missile failing to explode.

Each of the six spoilers was located between boundary-layer fences and was operated by an electro-magnet situated in the thickest part of the appropriate tail fin. Unlike the pivoted Wagner-bar controls of certain Henschel missiles, these spoilers passed through, and were operated directly by, the electromagnetic coils and projected alternatively out of one side of the fin or the other. Despite the fact that a spoiler produces a rippled airflow and drag, the device was chosen on the grounds of cheapness and minimum power requirements. Also, simplification of the control system was possible, since the spoilers could oscillate back and forth with a time-lag on one side or the other for control, as dictated by the radio signals.

A DVL test-drop of a Ruhrstahl/Kramer X-1 (Fritz X) controlled-trajectory bomb, showing the tail flares. The weapon later scored noteworthy military successes.

The rear section of the missile contained the electronics, the radio link being the Kehl/Strassburg system, and the receiving antenna was built into the tail shroud. A battery provided power for the gyroscope and receiver generators and supplied all other circuits direct. Later transmitters, starting with type Kehl IV, could be used for either Fritz X or Henschel Hs 293 missiles. In line with Hs 293 developments, wire-link control was developed for Fritz X and designated Düren/Detmold (FuG 208/238). This was a simple direct-current system and two wire transmission lines unwound from bobbins in the tail of the missile only, the payout being 8 km (5 miles). Later, due to diminishing industrial capacity, the wire-link equipment was discontinued for Fritz X.

697

An experimental series of the missile was begun in February 1942, and testing began soon after from Karlshagen, but, since a minimum dropping altitude of 4,000 m (13,125 ft) was necessary, the test programme was moved during April 1942 to Erprobungsstelle Süd at Foggia, in southern Italy, where more favourable weather conditions prevailed. The only significant problems encountered were with spoilers jamming; as an alternative to electro-magnetic power, pneumatic power was tried, using a tail-mounted air intake, but this scheme ran into temperature troubles. The problems were largely overcome in the end in a DVL wind-tunnel and the electromagnets retained. During tests, 50 per cent of the missiles released impacted within a 5 m (16·4 ft) square, the aimer being assisted by a flare unit housed in the blunt end of the missile's body.

To determine the operational use and possibilities of Fritz X, the Erprobungs- und Lehrkommando 21 was formed in September 1942 at Garz/Usedom and began testing. Although the missile was simpler than the Henschel Hs 293A, it took longer to develop, but time was regained during its introduction into service because of the Luftwaffe testing groups' experience with the Hs 293A. Thus, both types were operational at about the same time, and, by July 1943, III./KG 100 was based at Istres near Marseilles with Fritz X carrying Dornier Do 217K-2s and executed their first operation over the Mediterranean on 29 August, 1943. The first, and best known, success with the Fritz X occurred on 9 September, 1943, when the bulk of the Italian fleet, comprising the battleships *Roma*, *Italia*, and *Vittorio Veneto*, together with six cruisers and 13 destroyers, steamed out of Spezia and Genoa for the agreed surrender to the Allies. Between Corsica and Sardinia the fleet was attacked by III./KG 100, the *Roma* being hit and sunk, after catching fire, and the *Italia* also being hit.

With Allied landings on Italian beaches now obviously imminent, the anti-shipping guided bomb assumed great importance, especially since the Italian Navy no longer existed and German U-boats had little hope of running safely through the Bay of Biscay to the Mediterranean. The Salerno landings began on 9 September, and, in the holocaust of the following week, III./KG 100 scored hits or near misses on the cruiser USS *Savannah* and several transport ships, while a night attack produced confusion in which the cruiser HMS *Uganda* was damaged in collision with HMS *Delhi*. The real success, however, was on 16 September when HMS *Warspite* was hit by Fritz X missiles, the severe damage necessitating its being towed to Malta, with the *Delhi* having to be used as escort. Other warships which received the attentions of the Fritz X included the destroyer HMS *Janus* and cruiser HMS *Spartan*, which were sunk, and the cruiser USS *Philadelphia*, which was damaged, but, by the end of September, Allied air defences were making Fritz X sorties prohibitive, because bombers launching this missile had to attack their targets at a relatively short horizontal distance, because the missile had no gliding properties. Furthermore, the bombers had to slow to their minimum speed by the use of the flaps, as for a landing approach, to avoid overshooting the

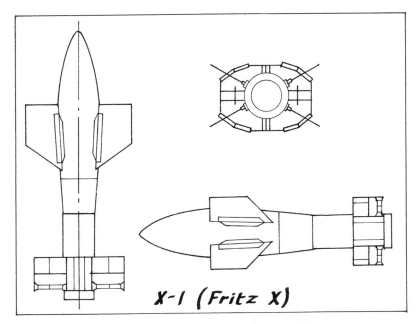

**X-1 (Fritz X)**

line-of-sight of the bomb aimer. Added to these conditions was the necessity of maintaining a steady course during the guidance phase, from which it can be seen that the carrier bombers made easy targets. This led to Fritz X being eventually abandoned; final sorties with the missile were against land targets.

Although plans had been made to produce 750 missiles a month, the total number of Fritz X missiles manufactured between April 1943 and December 1944 was 1,386, of which 602 were consumed in tests, training and operations. Further developments of the guided bomb were undertaken at Ruhrstahl AG but failed to receive production contracts. These developments included the Peter-X, X-2 and X-3 designs, in which aerodynamic refinements and, in the case of Peter-X designs, between 25 and 40 per cent increase in capacity were made. In addition, there were the X-5 armour-piercing and X-6 high explosive designs, which each had a total weight of 2,500 kg (5,512 lb). The most interesting innovation was introduced in the X-3 design, in which the anti-roll spoilers of the Fritz X were dispensed with and the missile allowed to roll, this system being applied later to the X-4 air-to-air missile.

X-1 (Fritz X): Span across fins 1·352 m (4 ft 5$\frac{1}{8}$ in); length 3·262 m (10 ft 8$\frac{3}{8}$ in); body diameter 0·562 m (1 ft 10 in).

Operational weight 1,570 kg (3,454 lb); explosive weight 320 kg (704 lb).

Maximum speed 1,035 km/h (630 mph) after 8,000 m (26,240 ft) drop; minimum dropping altitude of 4,000 m (13,125 ft) gave a range up to 4·5 km (2·8 miles); maximum dropping altitude of about 8,000 m (26,240 ft) gave a range of up to 9 km (5·6 miles).

699

A Ruhrstahl/Kramer X-4 air-to-air guided missile developed particularly for use with German jet fighters. (*US Army*)

# X-4

Work on the X-4 guided air-to-air missile began early in 1943 and the weapon received the RLM number 8-344. Although its development was parallel to that of the Henschel Hs 298, it was of higher performance and suitable for use with high-speed aircraft, notably the Messerschmitt Me 262. Air-to-air missiles with ranges greater than aircraft guns received official interest when the growing efficacy of bomber armament was foreseen, but the missiles were also needed for another reason in the case of the Me 262. This aircraft, in common with all German jet aircraft, began snaking at high speed and made aiming with guns and unguided rockets (R4M) unpromising in the short attack times. The single missile with relatively large warhead which could be guided after release was therefore one answer to the problem.

The X-4 had a cigar-shaped body with four centrally-mounted swept-back fins and four small tail fins. Two of the opposing central fins held streamlined pods for the wire-control bobbins, and a spoiler control was fitted in each of the four tail fins, giving two pairs of spoilers for pitch and yaw control only. In order to compensate for manufacturing inaccuracies and to dispense with roll control, the missile was encouraged to spin at about one revolution per second by offsetting, and fitting trim tabs to, the main fins. Because of the spinning, it was necessary to fit a small gyroscopic unit to switch the control signals to the spoilers as the missile rotated through each appropriate position ($\pm 45$ deg), *e.g.* yaw signals were only switched to spoilers within 45 deg limits of the vertical.

The wire-link control system used the Düsseldorf (FuG 510) transmitter and Detmold (FuG 238) receiver and operated on similar lines to the wire-control equipment for Fritz X. Pitch commands were given by switching the direct-current polarity, and the yaw commands by altering the current intensity. Total payout of the wires was some 5·5 km (3·5 miles), and the fighter pilot had the usual joystick control unit, initially aiming by standard gunsight followed by line-of-sight guidance.

In addition to an impact fuse, there was to be fitted either a Kranich or Meise acoustic proximity fuse to detonate the warhead, and, in the event of a miss, self-destruction occurred at the end of the motor burning time. The acoustic fuses, although far from perfect proximity fuses, were chosen for their simplicity and small size. The Kranich was made by Ruhrstahl and employed a membrane and wire, tuned to vibrate and close an electrical contact at a distance of about 7 m (23 ft) from the target; the Meise was made by Neumann und Borm and used a resonance microphone and two-stage amplifier tuned for initiation at a range of about 15 m (50 ft).

The component parts of the X-4 all had the quality of maximum compactness as their keynote, and, in this respect, the BMW 109-548 rocket motor was specifically tailored to the X-4 shape and requirements with considerable ingenuity. The design had to be both simple and insensitive to violent manoeuvres in all directions. Thus, the propellants were contained within tubes which were spirally wound inside the profile of the missile's central body. The inner spiral tank contained R-Stoff or Tonka fuel and a resilient piston of chrome leather, while the outer spiral tank contained SV-Stoff or Salbei (nitric acid) oxidizer and an aluminium-coated piston. These

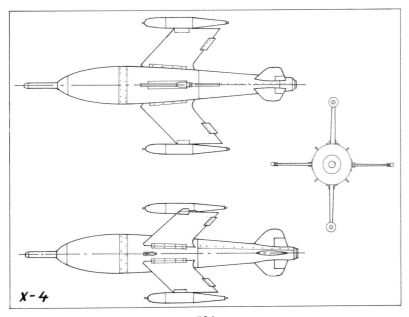

X-4

pistons not only took up the compressed-air pressure but ensured maximum propellant discharge. Self-igniting, the propellants produced a thrust of 140 kg (308 lb) initially, which reduced to a final 30 kg (66 lb) in the 17 sec burning time. Because of this short burning time, a heat-absorbing combustion chamber of welded sheet iron sufficed.

Although some 1,300 BMW 109-548 motors were produced at the Stargard factory, development was not quite finalized, and the Schmidding 109-603 solid-diglycol fuelled rocket motor had to be used in the first test launchings. This motor produced a thrust of 150 kg (330 lb) for eight seconds only. Between April and August 1944, 225 prototype series of the X-4 were produced, and the first missile was air-launched from a Focke-Wulf Fw 190 on 11 August, 1944. Tests continued from Karlshagen using Junkers Ju 88G-1 and Ju 388 aircraft until early in February 1945. From August to December 1944, some 1,000 missile airframes were produced at Ruhrstahl's Brackwede factory, but their motors, which were delayed at BMW's Stargard works, were all destroyed by bombing. Thus, although full mass production was scheduled for January 1945, there was no longer any prospect of beginning new rocket motor production lines, and the reasonable hopes of issuing the X-4 to the Luftwaffe were not realized.

The range of attack was to have been between 1·5 km (0·93 miles) and 3·5 km (2·17 miles), with launching being made at a similar height to the target.

X-4: Span across fins 0·575 m (1 ft 10⅝ in); length including fuse nose 2·001 m (6 ft 6¾ in); body diameter 0·222 m (8¾ in).
Operational weight 60 kg (132 lb); total propellant weight 8·5 kg (18·7 lb); explosive weight 20 kg (44 lb).
Maximum permissible speed 1,140 km/h (708 mph).


# X-7 Rotkäppchen (Red Riding Hood)

During 1944 the German Army was coming under increasing pressure from enemy armour, Russian tanks proving a particular threat, since infantry were finding even their Panzerfaust weapons of limited use, primarily because of the short range at which effective hits could be made. The Heereswaffenamt (Army Ordnance Board) therefore placed urgent development orders for anti-tank missiles with several firms, including Ruhrstahl, AEG, and possibly Rheinmetall-Borsig, but only Ruhrstahl made any headway in the short time available, and their product was the X-7 Rotkäppchen.

This missile was the smallest that could be devised to do the job, and simplicity, reliability and ease of carrying were the keynotes. The shell-shaped body had two wings at its aft end, with parabolic leading and

702

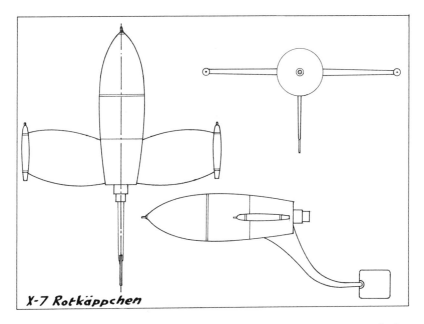

**X-7 Rotkäppchen**

trailing edges, and two small pods for the wire-link spools were attached to the wingtips. Kramer's spoiler control, used throughout the X-series, paid its biggest simplicity dividend in the X-7, because the X-4 control scheme was further simplified to use only one spoiler control. This control was attached to an arm which curved away and behind the body of the missile. The missile, which was revolved by a twist in the wings, was controlled by a joystick and similar equipment to that used for the X-4, and a gyroscope in the missile passed commands, as the spoiler control revolved through the appropriate plane.

Since only a direct hit on a tank or other armour would have any effect, a shell-type contact fuse was fitted to the nose of the warhead. For power, the WASAG 109-506 solid diglycol fuelled rocket motor was fitted in the aft part of the body. In order to give a relatively high launching thrust, followed by a longer but lower sustaining thrust, two tube-shaped charges were fitted, one inside the other. The first charge gave a thrust of 68 kg (150 lb) for 2·5 sec, after which the second charge gave a thrust of 5·5 kg (12·1 lb) for eight sec.

A few hundred X-7s were manufactured at Ruhrstahl's Brackwede factory, primarily for development purposes, but control had not been fully developed by the end of the war. Nevertheless, it appears that some of these missiles were tested by troops during the collapse on the Eastern Front in January 1945. Unconfirmed reports state that the troops were enthusiastic about the X-7, which was said to be capable of dealing even with the Stalin tanks.

In some references, mention is made of both an X-7 and X-8 missile, but

703

it is believed that these refer to the same weapon and that there was no X-8 design. The notation possibly arises out of the alleged fact that there was a proposal to adapt the X-7 as an air-to-air missile, but its performance hardly seems to have been suited to this rôle.

It is interesting to note that BMW were also requested, early in 1945, to develop an anti-tank missile, because the Army Ordnance Board was not satisfied with the progress of the other firms. The BMW team worked fast and within a few weeks had examples ready of a design similar to the X-4.

Although a solid fuelled rocket was to be used, the BMW missiles were successfully tested on Dachauer moor using the BMW 109-548 motors.

X-7: Span 0·6 m (1 ft 11⅝ in); length 0·95 m (3 ft 1⅜ in); body diameter 0·15 m (5⅞ in). Operational weight 9 kg (19·8 lb); propellant weight 6·5 kg (14·3 lb); explosive weight 2·5 kg (5·5 lb).
Maximum speed 360 km/h (224 mph); range 1·2 km (0·75 miles).

# Rheinmetall-Borsig Hecht (Pike)

Although principally associated with the production of guns, ammunition, and bombs for the German forces, Rheinmetall-Borsig AG began experimenting with solid fuelled rockets as early as 1934 and maintained an interest in an increasing variety of rocket weapons throughout the war years. This side of the work was carried out under the technical leadership of Dr Ing Hermann Vüllers and eventually expanded into the field of guided missiles.

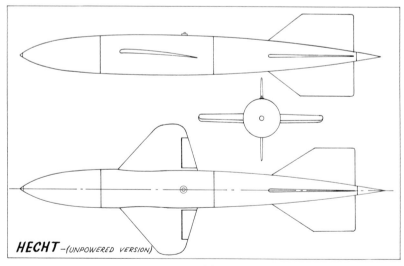

HECHT –(UNPOWERED VERSION)

Although the origins and details of Hecht are obscure, it appears to represent Rheinmetall-Borsig's first efforts in the winged missile field. The missile was for experimental work only and existed in various designs having equi-taper wings and tail units. The Hecht programme did not continue for long and was supplanted in 1941 by the Feuerlilie (Fire Lily) programme, for which there was greater interest. It is believed that aerial drops of Hecht in both unpowered and rocket-powered forms were made, the approximate data relating to the latter type.

Span 0·95 m (3 ft 1⅛ in); length 2·5 m (8 ft 2½ in); fuselage diameter 0·38 m (1 ft 3 in); total weight 140 kg (308 lb); motor thrust 60 kg (132 lb) for 25 sec; maximum speed 1,000 km/h (621 mph).

# Rheinmetall-Borsig Feuerlilie (Fire Lily)

Although described here under the heading of Rheinmetall-Borsig, the Feuerlilie missiles were only partly fostered by this company. The missile was begun as part of a high-speed research programme instituted and guided by the Forschungsführung (research control) of the RLM in

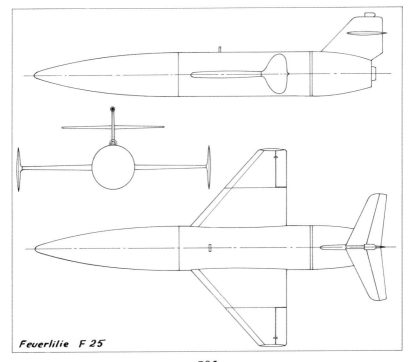

Feuerlilie F 25

order to obtain data for future guided missiles. At the same time, however, it was considered prudent to plan the missile along the lines of a flak rocket for possible future military application. Feuerlilie was produced in various sizes, principally F25 and F55 (the numbers giving the fuselage diameter in centimetres) using the basic aerodynamic shapes designed at the Luftfahrtforschungsanstalt (LFA) by Dr G. Braun and Prof A. Busemann.

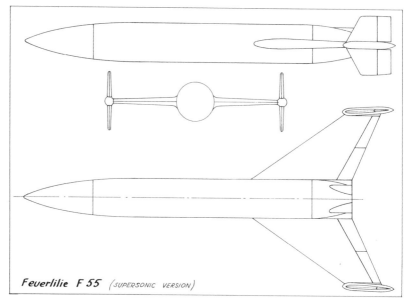

*Feuerlilie F 55* (*SUPERSONIC VERSION*)

The basic shape of Feuerlilie was a streamlined fuselage with sweptback wings mounted well aft and having small symmetrical fins at their tips. In the case of F25, there was also a single fin at the rear of the fuselage having a high-mounted tailplane with elevators working together or differentially for control.

Development was handed to Rheinmetall-Borsig early in 1942, and a very small F5 model was produced for the first tests with solid fuelled rockets. Progress was made to the F25 size which was tested both at the firm's trials ground at Leba and at the island of Greifswalder Oie, off Peenemünde. The subsonic F25 was powered with a Rheinmetall 109-505 solid diglycol fuelled rocket motor, which was in production as a glider ATO unit and gave a thrust of 500 kg (1,102 lb) for six sec. Launchings were made from an inclined ramp and also from aircraft; in the former case, the short flights were controlled by an LFA-designed autopilot, and in the latter case the longer flights were controlled by radio link.

Similar work was conducted with the larger F55 version which was designed for supersonic speeds in its last tailless versions, but it is not known if these speeds were attained. Power for the F55 was supplied by the Rheinmetall 109-515 solid diglycol fuelled rocket motor, of which

706

1,000 were produced for general experimental work. This motor gave 1,000 kg (2,205 lb) thrust for six sec. The supersonic version of the F55 was designed to use a liquid propellant motor designed by Dr Conrad of the DVK (who also designed motors for Enzian and Rheintochter). This motor used R-Stoff or Visol fuel and S-Stoff nitric acid oxidant, a self-igniting combination, to produce a thrust of 6,350 kg (13,970 lb) for seven sec. Compressed-air propellant feed and bursting-disc starting was used. The Feuerlilie programme continued until early 1945.

Feuerlilie F25: Span 1·15 m (3 ft 9¼ in); length 2·1 m (6 ft 10⅝ in); fuselage diameter 0·25 m (9⅞ in).

Total weight 120 kg (264 lb); propellant weight 17 kg (37·5 lb); payload allowance 15 kg (33 lb).

Maximum speed 840 km/h (522 mph).

Feuerlilie F55 (supersonic liquid fuelled version): Span 2·5 m (8 ft 2½ in); length 4·8 m (15 ft 9 in); fuselage diameter 0·55 m (1 ft 9⅝ in).

Total weight 470 kg (1,035 lb); total propellant weight 147 kg (324 lb); payload allowance 140 kg (308 lb).

Designed maximum speed 1,500 km/h (932 mph); ceiling 5,000 m (16,400 ft); range 7·5 km (4·6 miles).

# Rheinmetall-Borsig Rheinbote
# (Rhine Messenger)

The Rheinmetall-Borsig Rheinbote is of considerable interest as a high-speed multi-stage rocket. Built during the Second World War, it appeared as one solution to a Heereswaffenamt requirement for a rocket weapon capable of carrying about 40 kg (88 lb) of explosive over a range of 160 km (99·4 miles). Thus, it was to be a tactical Army weapon filling the gap

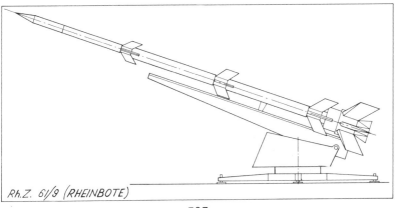

Rh.Z. 61/9 (RHEINBOTE)

707

between conventional artillery guns and the A4 rocket, and Rheinmetall-Borsig began experimenting early in 1942 with stage rockets using existing solid fuelled ATO units at first.

As initially projected, the rocket had a six-finned first stage and a four-finned second stage with 3 kg (6·62 lb) of explosive in a conical nose for sounding tests. A constant body diameter of 0·159 m (6¼ in) was used, total length was 2·7 m (8 ft 10¼ in), total weight was 110 kg (242 lb), and 34 kg (75 lb) of diglycol propellant was divided equally between the two stages. Since a velocity of only 160 km/h (100 mph) was obtained from the first stage, it was decided that a high-thrust take-off chamber with very short burning time was necessary if simple short launching ramps were to be employed. Furthermore, it was decided that spin imparted by off-set fins would increase accuracy by compensating for inaccuracies in manufacture. Adequate stage separation was obtained by simply inserting one cylindrical guide into another and allowing the exhaust from one stage to discard the burnt-out stage behind it, ignition being by time fuse.

Data from this and similar projectiles then led to the building of a three-stage rocket, which had a take-off stage of 0·19 m (7½ in) body diameter, two upper stages with 0·076 m (3 in) body diameters and a total length of 2·6 m (8 ft 6⅜ in). Total weight was 62 kg (137 lb), including 8 kg (17·65 lb), 2·8 kg (19·4 lb) and 2·8 kg (19·4 lb) of propellant for the take-off, second, and third stages respectively. A conical nose cone contained 1 kg (2·2 lb) of flash material for observation purposes, and each stage had six fins. This design, then, was the immediate predecessor of Rheinbote, which had the firm's designation Rh.Z.61/9.

Rheinbote was a four-stage ballistic rocket designed to be launched from a mobile trailer modified from the A4 transporter, known as the Meilerwagen, or from the modified mounting 41 of the 88 mm flak gun. The shortest, but greatest diameter, take-off stage was followed by stages one and two of smaller and equal diameter, while the third and final stage was of still smaller diameter and ended in a conical nose. Each stage had six fins at its base and was powered by solid diglycol propellant. The propellant in the take-off stage was arranged in bars with spaces to allow a large burning surface area; ignition was by means of an explosive charge and electrical igniter at the head of the propellants, and the exhaust discharge was from one central and six peripheral nozzles, all being spring regulated. In each of the other stages, the propellant was in the form of a tube with burning occurring on the inner and outer surfaces, the exhaust discharge being from a single plain nozzle; ignition was by means of flash powder and a clockwork fuse primed by acceleration. Guidance on the take-off ramp was given by sliding clamps on the take-off and first stages, the front clamp falling free after take-off.

Remote guidance was not used for Rheinbote, which merely achieved its aim and ballistic trajectory in the manner of an artillery shell. After launching, the take-off and first and second stages fell away at approximately 3·5 km (2·2 miles), 12 km (7·5 miles), and 25 km (15·5 miles) respectively, and so to avoid damage on the ground care had to be taken over the choice of firing site. The final stage continued with the warhead to the target, detonation being initiated by a percussion fuse. Rheinbote's maximum speed of Mach 5·55 appears to have been the highest of any German rocket, since it slightly exceeded that of the A4 rocket, but the A4 and its derivatives had greater range and altitude limits. It is not known how many Rheinbote rockets were made, but, during November 1944, the Army launched over 200 at Antwerp as part of the all-out offensive against that city. Eight A4s would have delivered the same amount of explosive, though only at eight target areas.

Rheinbote: Total length 11·4 m (37 ft 4⅞ in).
Total operational weight 1,715 kg (3,775 lb); total propellant weight 585 kg (1,287 lb); explosive weight 40 kg (88 lb).
Maximum speed 5,900 km/h (3,663 mph); maximum range was 218 km (136 miles) for which the launching elevation was 65 deg and the trajectory height was 78 km (48·5 miles); maximum flight time 4 min 20 sec.
Details of each stage are:
Take-off stage: Fin span 1·49 m (4 ft 10⅝ in); body diameter 0·535 m (1 ft 9 in); total weight 695 kg (1,530 lb); propellant weight 245 kg (540 lb); thrust 38,000 kg (83,790 lb) for one sec; maximum speed 902 km/h (560 mph).
First stage: Fin span 0·98 m (3 ft 2⅝ in); body diameter 0·268 m (10½ in); total weight 425 kg (935 lb); propellant weight 140 kg (308 lb); thrust 5,600 kg (12,350 lb) for five sec; maximum speed 1,835 km/h (1,140 mph).
Second stage: Fin span 0·8 m (2 ft 7½ in); body diameter 0·268 m (10½ in); total weight 395 kg (870 lb); propellant weight 140 kg (308 lb); thrust 5,600 kg (12,350 lb) for five sec; maximum speed 3,540 km/h (2,200 mph).
Third stage: Fin span 0·745 m (2 ft 5⅜ in); body diameter 0·19 m (7½ in); total weight including warhead 200 kg (440 lb); propellant weight 60 kg (132 lb); thrust 3,400 kg (7,495 lb) for 3·5 sec; maximum speed 5,900 km/h (3,663 mph).

# Rheinmetall-Borsig Rheintochter (Rhine Maiden)*

The experiments preceding and concerned with Rheinbote indicated the possibilities of using the multi-stage, solid fuelled rocket as a guided flak weapon in view of the high altitudes being obtained. Accordingly, Rheinmetall-Borsig received a development contract from the Heereswaffenamt (Army Ordnance Board) in November 1942, and work on the Rheintochter R-I two-stage missile began.

The R-I was of curious and interesting layout for the time. The main stage had a cylindrical body tapering fairly finely into a pointed nose where

* Wagner's *Rheintochter*, literally 'Rhine Daughter' but in usual parlance 'Rhine Maiden'.

The Rheinmetall-Borsig Rheintochter R-I ground-to-air guided missile. Although eventually cancelled, this missile was used to test many German guidance systems.

four small, rounded steering surfaces were pivoted for servo operation, while, at the aft end, were attached six large sweptback fixed fins. The exhaust from the sustainer motor was ejected through six venturii, positioned in the spaces between the six main fins, and these venturii were directed outwards, partly for stabilization and partly because the missile's warhead was situated behind the motor and fins. To the rounded base of this warhead was attached the take-off or booster section of the missile by means of a ring and explosive bolts, the fixtures being covered by a light fairing. The short cylindrical booster section had four long sweptback fins, which had inter-bracing struts, and the exhaust ejected from one central and six peripheral venturii. For both stages the motors were fuelled with solid-diglycol propellant. Launching was from an inclined ramp or converted gun mounting, as for Enzian, followed by remote joystick radio control and line-of-sight guidance.

Development of the R-I seems to have been somewhat protracted because, by the beginning of July 1944, only 34 had been fired, and total firings had only reached 45 by September 1944. Altogether, 82 examples of the R-I were launched, of which only 22 carried full guidance equipment, and the development was abandoned by December 1944, because,

710

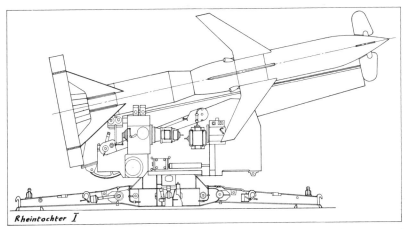

*Rheintochter I*

although the missile had a range similar to that of Enzian and Schmetterling, it only attained about half their altitude limits.

This shortcoming in altitude performance was, however, foreseen at an earlier date, and work had therefore been done on the Rheintochter R-III, which was intended as the operational version, leaving the R-I design to be used for general development work on factors such as guidance systems.

In order to obtain improved performance with the R-III, a liquid-propellant rocket motor was designed for the main stage, with much increased burning time compared with the solid fuelled motor. Apart from

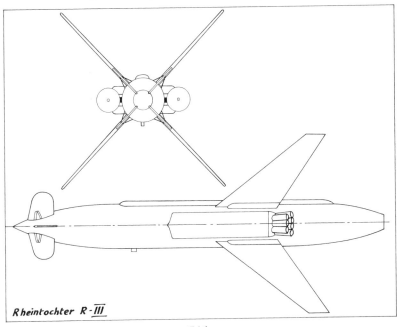

*Rheintochter R-III*

the motor change, the main stage remained much as before, with the canard layout of flying surfaces, but the rear inline tail booster section was removed and replaced by two solid-fuelled booster rockets mounted at the sides of the missile's body. The new sustainer motor was designed by Dr Conrad and was of similar layout to the motor designed for the Feuerlilie F55, though it had a much lower thrust for a longer burning time. The propellants were Visol fuel and nitric acid oxidant. The new layout was tested in the form of Rheintochter R-IIIp, which had a solid-fuelled sustainer motor, and the version with the Conrad sustainer motor was designated R-IIIf. By December 1944 six R-III missiles had been fired, and, though it is not known whether any of these had the Conrad motor, this is unlikely. In any event, time ran out for the Rheintochter programme, which in that month was cancelled in favour of more advanced or promising flak missiles. Guidance and fusing methods and proposals for Rheintochter were similar to the general plans for other flak rockets designed as blast weapons, but the R-I missile was used to test more guidance systems than other missiles.

Rheintochter R-I: Maximum fin span 2·22 m (7 ft 3⅛ in); length with booster stage 6·3 m (20 ft 8 in); length without booster stage 4 m (13 ft 1½ in); body diameter 0·54 m (1 ft 9¼ in).

Operational starting weight 1,750 kg (3,859 lb); weight at target 750 kg (1,654 lb); booster propellant weight 240 kg (529 lb); sustainer propellant weight 220 kg (485 lb); explosive weight 100–150 kg (220–330 lb); booster thrust 75,000 kg (165,375 lb) for 0·6 sec; sustainer thrust 4,000 kg (8,820 lb) for 10 sec.

All-burnt speed 1,288 km/h (800 mph); approximate speed at target 1,080 km/h (671 mph); maximum altitude 6,000 m (19,680 ft); maximum range 40 km (24·8 miles).

Rheintochter R-IIIf: Maximum fin span 2·2 m (7 ft 2⅝ in); length 5 m (16 ft 4⅞ in); body diameter approximately 0·54 m (1 ft 9¼ in).

Operational starting weight approximately 1,500 kg (3,307 lb); weight at target 685 kg (1,510 lb); booster propellant weight 172 kg (379 lb); liquid sustainer propellant weight 417 kg (918 lb); explosive weight 160 kg (353 lb); combined booster thrust 28,000 kg (61,740 lb) for 0·9 sec; sustainer thrust 2,200 kg (4,851 lb) falling to 1,800 kg (3,969 lb) over the 43 sec burning time.

All-burnt velocity below 1,075 km/h (670 mph); approximate speed at target 805 km/h (500 mph); maximum altitude 15,000 m (49,200 ft); maximum range 40 km (24·8 miles).

# APPENDICES

# The '8' Series Type Numbers

| Number | Company | Details and remarks |
|--------|---------|---------------------|
| 5 | Fieseler | Two-seat single-engined light monoplane. |
| 8 | Göppingen | Experimental unpowered one-fifth-scale model to provide data for Do 214 flying-boat project. Built by Schemp-Hirth and tested behind a motor-boat. |
| 9 | Göppingen | Experimental single-engined aircraft with a pusher propeller; provided data for the Do 335. |
| 10 | Dornier | Experimental single-seat single-engined parasol-wing monoplane; engine could be tilted for take-off; also known as the Dornier C 1. |
| 11 | Dornier | Twin-engined shoulder-wing medium bomber; served with the Luftwaffe 1934–36. |
| 11 | WNF | Four-seat twin-engined light amphibian; engines mounted above shoulder wing. |
| 12 | Dornier | Two-seat single-engined shoulder-wing amphibian for sports and touring use; engine above wing with pusher propeller. |
| 13 | Dornier | Development of the Do 11. |
| 14 | Dornier | Experimental flying-boat with shoulder-wing, stabilizing sponsons and pylon-mounted, shaft-driven, pusher propeller. |
| 15 | Dornier | RLM designation of the Dornier Militär-Wal twin-engined flying-boat. |
| 15 | WNF | Twin-engined touring monoplane. |
| 16 | WNF | Experimental light aircraft with a pusher propeller and twin tail booms; one prototype. |
| 17 | Dornier | See page 106. |
| 18 | Dornier | See page 115. |
| 19 | Dornier | Four-engined low-wing bomber with twin fins and rudders; development ordered 1935; one prototype. |
| 20 | Dornier | Projected in 1935 as aerodynamically-improved version of the Dornier Do X flying-boat. Eight-engined high-wing monoplane. |
| 22 | Dornier | See page 119. |
| 23 | Dornier | Twin-engined high-wing medium bomber with fixed undercarriage; over 100 built for the Luftwaffe. |
| 24 | Dornier | See page 121. |

| Number | Company | Details and remarks |
|--------|---------|---------------------|
| 25 | Klemm (L) | Two-seat single-engined low-wing monoplane trainer and touring aircraft. |
| 25 | Dornier | Number issued to Dornier but not used for an aircraft until 1953. |
| 26 | Klemm (L) | More powerful version of L 25. Appeared in 1929. |
| 26 | Dornier | See page 124. |
| 27 | Dornier | Number issued to Dornier but not used until 1954. |
| 29 | Dornier | Project for a medium bomber and heavy fighter in 1934 to same specification as Fw 57, Hs 124 and Ju 85/88. |
| 31 | Klemm | Four-seat single-engined touring monoplane. First built in 1931. |
| 32 | Klemm | Three-seat single-engined touring monoplane. First built in 1932. |
| 33 | Junkers (W) | See page 354. |
| 33 | Klemm | Single-seat single-engined ultra-light high-wing monoplane. Built in 1933. |
| 34 | Junkers (W) | See page 354. |
| 35 | Klemm | See page 459. |
| 36 | Klemm | Four-seat single-engined touring and competition monoplane. First built in 1934. |
| 39 | DFS | Two-seat single-engined tailless aircraft. Second version was to have a rocket motor but was abandoned in favour of DFS 40 and DFS 194. |
| 40 | DFS | Single-seat experimental rocket-powered tailless glider; replaced by DFS 194. |
| 40 | Blohm und Voss | See page 84. |
| 42 | Heinkel | Two-seat single-engined float biplane trainer. In service by 1933. |
| 43 | Focke-Wulf (A) | Three-seat single-engined high-wing cabin tourer built in 1932. Not built in numbers. |
| 44 | Focke-Wulf | See page 155. |
| 45 | Heinkel | See page 220. |
| 46 | Heinkel | See page 221. |
| 47 | Focke-Wulf | Two-seat single-engined parasol-wing, weather-reporting aircraft built in 1932. |
| 49 | Heinkel | Single-seat single-engined biplane fighter; three prototypes only. |
| 49 | Junkers | Single-engined high-altitude research aircraft; first flew in 1931. First Junkers aircraft with pressurized cabin. |
| 50 | Heinkel | See page 224. |
| 51 | Heinkel | Single-engined biplane fighter. (Went into Luftwaffe service in 1935, obsolete before Second World War). |
| 52 | Junkers | See page 357. |
| 54 | Nagler-Rolz | See page 610. |
| 54 | DFS | See page 96. |

| Number | Company | Details and remarks |
|---|---|---|
| 55 | Nagler-Rolz | See page 610. |
| 55 | Focke-Wulf | Two-seat single-engined high-wing trainer (Fw 55L). Floatplane version (Fw 55W) had a small lower wing added. |
| 56 | Focke-Wulf | See page 158. |
| 57 | Focke-Wulf | Three-seat twin-engined heavy fighter. Focke-Wulf's first all -metal aircraft. Competed with Ju 88, Hs 127 and Bf 162; only two prototypes were built. |
| 58 | Focke-Wulf | See page 160. |
| 59 | Heinkel | See page 226. |
| 60 | Heinkel | See page 229. |
| 60 | Junkers | See page 422. |
| 61 | Focke Achgelis | See page 596. |
| 61 | Heinkel | Export version of He 45. |
| 61 | Junkers (EF) | Experimental twin-engined high-altitude aircraft; two prototypes built in 1936/37. |
| 62 | Focke-Wulf | Two-seat single-engined general-purpose catapult-launched biplane. One prototype with twin floats and one prototype with central main float plus wingtip floats. |
| 63 | Heinkel | Two-seat single-engined biplane trainer, ten aircraft only. Land and floatplane variants built. |
| 64 | Heinkel | Two-seat single-engined sports monoplane. Several built for competitions from 1932. |
| 64 | Arado | Single-seat single-engined biplane fighter of 1930. Only three built. |
| 65 | Arado | Single-seat single-engined biplane fighter of 1935. |
| 66 | Arado | See page 17. |
| 67 | Arado | Single-seat experimental biplane fighter of 1933 with Rolls-Royce Kestrel engine; two prototypes. |
| 68 | Arado | See page 19. |
| 69 | Arado | Two-seat single-engined biplane trainer of 1933; only used in small numbers. |
| 70 | Heinkel | See page 232. |
| 71 | Heinkel | Single-seat single-engined sports cabin monoplane of 1933. |
| 72 | Heinkel | See page 236. |
| 74 | Heinkel | Single-seat single-engined advanced-training biplane, 1933; eight aircraft only. |
| 75 | Arado | Project. (Details unknown). |
| 76 | Arado | Single-seat single-engined advanced trainer with parasol wing similar to the Fw 56, about 10 built. |
| 77 | Arado | Four-seat twin-engined training monoplane to same specification as Fw 58; two built. |
| 79 | Arado | Two-seat single-engined sports and training monoplane of 1937. Created records and had competition successes. |

| Number | Company | Details and remarks |
|---|---|---|
| 80 | Arado | Single-seat single-engined low-wing fighter with fixed undercarriage, to same specification as Fw 159, He 112 and Bf 109, 1935; three prototypes. |
| 81 | Arado | Two-seat single-engined biplane dive-bomber, to same specification as Ha 137, He 118 and Ju 87, 1936. Three prototypes only, two with twin fins, one with single fin. |
| 84 | Junkers | Project. (Details unknown.) |
| 85 | Junkers | Twin-engined multi-purpose military monoplane of 1934, to same specification as Fw 57 and Hs 124. Ju 85 not built, supplanted by Ju 88 design. |
| 86 | Junkers | See page 370. |
| 87 | Junkers | See page 378. |
| 88 | Junkers | See page 394. |
| 89 | Junkers | Four-engined low-wing strategic bomber with twin fins and rudders. Development ordered in 1935 alongside the Do 19; two prototypes. |
| 90 | Junkers | See page 418. |
| 95 | Arado | See page 23. |
| 96 | Arado | See page 27. |
| 97 | Fieseler | Four-seat single-engined cabin monoplane tourer of 1934. |
| 98 | Fieseler | Single-seat single-engined biplane dive-bomber with fixed undercarriage and biplane tailplane; one prototype; abandoned in favour of Hs 123. |
| 99 | Fieseler | Two-seat single-engined cabin monoplane tourer of 1938; named Jungtiger. |
| 100 | Heinkel | See page 238. |
| 101 | Albatros | Two-seat single-engined parasol-wing sports and training aircraft; built in 1930. |
| 102 | Albatros | Two-seat single-engined parasol-wing sports and training aircraft; built in 1931. |
| 103 | Albatros | Experimental aircraft developed for the DVL, fitted with a variable-incidence wing. |
| 103 | Fieseler | See page 666. |
| 104 | Klemm/Siebel | See page 578. |
| 105 | Klemm | Two-seat single-engined cabin monoplane for sports and touring, 1938. Only a few built. |
| 106 | Klemm | Two-seat single-engined sports monoplane of 1939 for licence-building in USA. Only prototypes built. |
| 107 | Klemm | Two-seat single-engined cabin monoplane for advanced training and touring. Only six built, 1940. |
| 108 | BFW | See page 464. |
| 109 | BFW | See page 467. |
| 110 | BFW | See page 493. |
| 111 | Heinkel | See page 243. |
| 112 | Heinkel | See page 261. |

| Number | Company | Details and remarks |
|--------|---------|---------------------|
| 113 | Heinkel | Original designation of He 100. |
| 114 | Heinkel | See page 265. |
| 115 | Heinkel | See page 269. |
| 116 | Heinkel | See page 274. |
| 117 | Henschel | See pages 688 and 690. |
| 118 | Heinkel | Two-seat single-engined low-wing dive-bomber, to same specification as Ar 81, Ha 137 and Ju 87, 1936. Only thirteen prototypes built He 118 V4 tested by Japan as the DXHe 1. |
| 119 | Heinkel | Two-seat twin-engined low-wing fast reconnaissance aircraft or bomber. Single airscrew with shaft through glazed nose. Eight prototypes. |
| 120 | Heinkel | Large floatplane project. |
| 121 | Henschel | Single-seat single-engined advanced trainer with high wing, 1934; one prototype. |
| 122 | Henschel | Two-seat single-engined short-range reconnaissance aircraft with parasol wing and fixed undercarriage; small number produced, 1935. Developed into the Hs 126. |
| 123 | Henschel | See page 317. |
| 124 | Henschel | Three-seat twin-engined heavy fighter and bomber with twin fins and rudders, to same specification as Bf 110 and Fw 57; three prototypes built. |
| 125 | Henschel | Single-seat single-engined low-wing, advanced training and sports monoplane; two prototypes built. |
| 126 | Henschel | See page 321. |
| 127 | Henschel | Twin-engined fast bomber developed from Hs 124, to same specifications as Bf 162, Fw 57 and Ju 88; two prototypes built. |
| 128 | Henschel | See page 327. |
| 129 | Henschel | See page 330. |
| 130 | Henschel | See page 327. |
| 131 | Bücker | See page 91. |
| 132 | Henschel | See page 339. |
| 133 | Bücker | See page 92. |
| 134 | Bücker | Two-seat single-engined cabin monoplane with high-mounted folding wings; one prototype, 1936. |
| 135 | HFB | Two-seat single-engined sports biplane, 1933. |
| 136 | HFB | Experimental single-seat single-engined low-wing advanced trainer. |
| 137 | HFB | Single-seat single-engined low-wing dive-bomber with fixed undercarriage, to same specification as Ar 81, He 118 and Ju 87 in 1936; six prototypes. |
| 138 | HFB | See page 59. |
| 139 | HFB | See page 63. |
| 140 | HFB | Three-seat twin-engined multi-purpose float seaplane; three prototypes. |

| Number | Company | Details and remarks |
|--------|---------|---------------------|
| 141 | Blohm und Voss | See page 66. |
| 142 | Blohm und Voss | See page 71. |
| 143 | Blohm und Voss | See page 663. |
| 144 | Blohm und Voss | See page 73. |
| 145 | Gotha | See page 215. |
| 146 | Gotha | Twin-engined low-wing light transport and communications aircraft for three passengers. Small number built, 1935. |
| 147 | Gotha | Experimental two-seat single-engined tailless aircraft with sweptback wing with endplate fins and rudders; two prototypes, 1936. |
| 148 | Gotha | Project (Details unknown). |
| 149 | Gotha | Single-seat single-engined low-wing cabin monoplane of 1936 for advanced training; three prototypes. |
| 150 | Gotha | Two-seat twin-engined low-wing cabin tourer. |
| 151 | Klemm | Four-seat single-engined cabin tourer. |
| 152 | Focke-Wulf (Ta) | See page 207. |
| 153 | Focke-Wulf (Ta) | Single-engined fighter development of Focke-Wulf Fw 190D. |
| 154 | Focke-Wulf (Ta) | See page 211. |
| 155 | Messerschmitt | (Design taken over by Blohm und Voss.) See page 88. |
| 156 | Fieseler | See page 142. |
| 157 | Fieseler | High-performance pilotless target drone; three built. |
| 158 | Fieseler | Single-seat single-engined cabin monoplane for record breaking; twin fins and rudders, 1938. |
| 159 | Focke-Wulf | Single-seat single-engined fighter with parasol wing, to same specification as Ar 80, Bf 109 and He 112, 1935; three prototypes. |
| 160 | Junkers | See page 422. |
| 161 | BFW | See page 506. |
| 162 | BFW | See page 506. |
| 162 | Heinkel | See page 307. |
| 163 | BFW | Three-seat single-engined reconnaissance aircraft similar to Fieseler Fi 156; one prototype. |
| 163 | Messerschmitt | See page 508. |
| 164 | Messerschmitt | Twin-engined shoulder-wing communications aircraft for eight passengers. |
| 165 | Messerschmitt | Project (Details unknown). |
| 166 | Flugzeugbau Kiel | Single-seat single-engined advanced-training biplane without interplane struts; one prototype only. |
| 166 | Fieseler | Rocket-propelled target defence fighter project. |
| 167 | Fieseler | See page 147. |
| 168 | Fieseler | Project (Details unknown). |
| 170 | Heinkel | See page 232. |
| 172 | Heinkel | Improved version of He 72 trainer biplane. Two prototypes only, 1934. |

| Number | Company | Details and remarks |
|---|---|---|
| 174 | Heinkel | Project (Details unknown). |
| 176 | Heinkel | See page 276. |
| 177 | Heinkel | See page 279. |
| 178 | Heinkel | See page 290. |
| 180 | Bücker | Two-seat single-engined sports and training monoplane, 1937. |
| 181 | Bücker | See page 94. |
| 182 | Bücker | Single-seat single-engined cabin monoplane for advanced training, 1938; only a few built. |
| 183 | Focke-Wulf (Ta) | See page 626. |
| 184 | Flettner | Two-seat autogyro, 1936; one prototype only. |
| 185 | Flettner | Single-seat single-engined helicopter (using autorotation for forward flight), two contra-rotating airscrews on outriggers, 1937; one prototype only. |
| 186 | Focke-Wulf | Two-seat 'jump-start' autogyro based on the Cierva C 30. One prototype, tested 1938. |
| 186 | Junkers | Four-engined high-altitude bomber project based on the Ju 86. |
| 187 | Focke-Wulf | See page 162. |
| 187 | Junkers | Redesigned and improved version of the Ju 87. Projected in 1943 but not built. |
| 188 | Junkers | See page 424. |
| 189 | Focke-Wulf | See page 166. |
| 190 | Focke-Wulf | See page 173. |
| 191 | Focke-Wulf | See page 197. |
| 192 | Ago | Twin-engined low-wing touring and communications aircraft for up to six passengers; small numbers built, 1937. |
| 193 | Ago | Project (Details unknown). |
| 194 | DFS | Rocket-powered experimental tailless aircraft, 1939; preceded the Me 163. |
| 195 | Arado | See page 23. |
| 196 | Arado | See page 29. |
| 197 | Arado | See page 19. |
| 198 | Arado | Three-seat single-engined short-range reconnaissance monoplane designed to the same specification as the Bv 141 and Fw 189; one prototype, 1938. |
| 199 | Arado | See page 34. |
| 200 | Focke-Wulf | See page 200. |
| 201 | Siebel | Single-engined light high-wing monoplane reconnaissance aircraft with pusher propeller and low tail boom; two prototypes flown 1938. |
| 202 | Siebel | Two-seat single-engined low-wing cabin monoplane for sports and training use, 1938. |
| 204 | Siebel | See page 578. |
| 206 | Focke-Wulf | Twin-engined medium-range monoplane transport project derived from Fw 58. |

721

| Number | Company | Details and remarks |
|--------|---------|---------------------|
| 208 | Messerschmitt | Four-seat single-engined cabin monoplane with tricycle undercarriage, developed from Bf 108; two prototypes. |
| 209 | Messerschmitt | See pages 520 and 524. |
| 210 | Messerschmitt | See page 526. |
| 211 | Focke-Wulf (Ta) | Original designation of Ta 154. |
| 211 | Hütter | Two-seat twin-engined long-range development of the He 219 with a wooden wing. |
| 212 | Dornier | Experimental four-seat single-engined amphibian with pusher propeller at the tail. Sole prototype built in Switzerland, 1941. |
| 214 | Dornier | Eight-engined transatlantic flying-boat project for 40 passengers. Designed in 1941 after tests with Gö 8 model. Four pusher and four tractor airscrews. |
| 215 | Dornier | See page 126. |
| 216 | Dornier | Smaller version of projected Do 214 flying-boat for military use, with four or six engines. Not built. |
| 217 | Dornier | See page 127. |
| 218 | Dornier | Project (Details unknown). |
| 219 | Heinkel | See page 298. |
| 221 | Dornier | Project (Details unknown). |
| 222 | Blohm und Voss | See page 75. |
| 223 | Focke Achgelis | See page 598. |
| 224 | Focke Achgelis | Two-seat projected sports version of Fa 61 experimental twin-rotor helicopter. |
| 225 | Focke Achgelis | See page 603. |
| 225 | AGO | Projected fighter to compete with Me 210. |
| 226 | Blohm und Voss | Air-to-surface glider bomb; study only. Led to Bv 246 glider bomb. |
| 227 | Horten | See page 349. |
| 227 | FGP | Six-engined quarter-scale model of Bv 238 flying-boat to provide data; one example only. |
| 228 | DFS | See page 97. |
| 229 | Gotha | See page 351. |
| 230 | DFS | See page 100. |
| 231 | Arado | See page 35. |
| 232 | Arado | See page 36. |
| 233 | Arado | Twin-engined high-wing ten-passenger touring and communications amphibian. |
| 234 | Arado | See page 40. |
| 236 | Focke Achgelis | Project (Details unknown). |
| 237 | Blohm und Voss | Single-seat single-engined asymmetric layout ground-attack aircraft project; development of the Bv 141. |
| 238 | Blohm und Voss | See page 81. |
| 239 | Arado | Project (Details unknown). |
| 240 | Arado | See page 49. |
| 241 | Gotha | Twin-engined communications aircraft. |

| Number | Company | Details and remarks |
|--------|---------|---------------------|
| 242 | Gotha | See page 216. |
| 243 | Messerschmitt | Details unknown. |
| 244 | Gotha | See page 219. |
| 245 | Gotha | Project (Details unknown). |
| 246 | Blohm und Voss | See page 664. |
| 248 | Junkers | (Original designation of Me 263.) See page 547. |
| 250 | Horten | See page 344. |
| 250 | Blohm und Voss | Landplane version of the Bv 238 flying-boat. Not built. |
| 251 | Horten | See page 345. |
| 252 | Horten | See page 346. |
| 252 | Junkers | See page 429. |
| 253 | Horten | See page 348. |
| 253 | Fieseler | Two-seat twin-engined light sports aircraft; only prototypes built. |
| 254 | Focke-Wulf (Ta) | Two-seat twin-engined shoulder-wing night fighter project; improvement of the Ta 154C. |
| 256 | Fieseler | Five-seat version of the Fi 156 single-engined general-purpose STOL aircraft. Only two built. |
| 257 | Skoda-Kauba | See page 582. |
| 259 | Focke-Wulf | Project (Details unknown). |
| 261 | Messerschmitt | See page 530. |
| 262 | Messerschmitt | See page 531. |
| 263 | Messerschmitt | See page 547. |
| 264 | Messerschmitt | See page 549. |
| 265 | Messerschmitt | Single-seat twin-engined tailless fighter project with pusher propellers. |
| 265 | Flettner | See page 589. |
| 266 | Focke Achgelis | See page 598. |
| 267 | Gotha | Details unknown. |
| 268 | Junkers | Twin-jet Mistel lower component project (fighter-guided unmanned flying bomb). |
| 269 | Focke Achgelis | See page 604. |
| 270 | Heinkel | See page 232. |
| 272 | Focke-Wulf | Project (Details unknown). |
| 274 | Heinkel | See page 304. |
| 277 | Heinkel | See page 305. |
| 280 | Heinkel | See page 293. |
| 281 | Focke-Wulf (Ta) | Project (Details unknown). |
| 282 | Flettner | See page 592. |
| 283 | Focke-Wulf (Ta) | See page 633. |
| 284 | Focke Achgelis | See page 605. |
| 285 | Flettner | Helicopter project; probably based on Fl 282. |
| 286 | Junkers | Six-engined high-altitude bomber project based on Ju 86 and Ju 186. |
| 287 | Junkers | See page 431. |
| 288 | Junkers | See page 437. |
| 289 | Junkers | Project (Details unknown). |
| 290 | Junkers | See page 442. |
| 291 | Henschel | Details unknown. |

| Number | Company | Details and remarks |
|--------|---------|---------------------|
| 292 | Henschel | Details unknown. |
| 293 | Henschel | See pages 673, 679 and 681. |
| 294 | Henschel | See page 678. |
| 295 | Henschel | See page 683. |
| 296 | Henschel | See page 685. |
| 296 | Arado | Projected improvement of Ar 96 single-engined multi-purpose monoplane. |
| 297 | Henschel | See page 688. |
| 298 | Henschel | See page 692. |
| 299 | Junkers | Project (Details unknown). |
| 300 | Focke-Wulf | Four-engined 45-seat airliner project. |
| 301 | DFS | Project (Details unknown). |
| 309 | Messerschmitt | See page 553. |
| 310 | Messerschmitt | High-altitude version of twin-engined Me 210 fighter; abandoned in favour of Me 410. |
| 315 | Henschel | Missile project. |
| 317 | Dornier | See page 136. |
| 318 | Dornier | Projected version of the Do 24T-2 flying-boat with boundary layer suction wings, built by the Weser-Flugzeugbau. |
| 319 | Heinkel | Twin-engined night fighter project based on He 219 but with single fin and rudder; abandoned in favour of He 419. |
| 320 | Messerschmitt | Project (Details unknown). |
| 321 | Messerschmitt | See page 555. |
| 322 | Junkers | See page 446. |
| 323 | Messerschmitt | See page 557. |
| 325 | Focke Achgelis | Project (Details unknown). |
| 328 | Messerschmitt | See page 561. |
| 329 | Messerschmitt | Tailless fighter-bomber project based on the Me 265. |
| 330 | Focke Achgelis | See page 606. |
| 331 | DFS | See page 104. |
| 332 | DFS | See page 105. |
| 333 | Fieseler | See page 154. |
| 334 | Arado | Project (Details unknown). |
| 335 | Dornier | See page 137. |
| 336 | Focke Achgelis | Proposed powered version of the Fa 330 gyro kite. Built in modified form in France after the war. |
| 337 | Junkers | Project (Details unknown). |
| 339 | Flettner | Single-engined twin-rotor helicopter project for about 20 passengers. |
| 340 | Arado | Twin-engined twin-boom medium bomber project. |
| 341 | Berlin | Twin-engined low-wing research monoplane with prone pilot; only one built. |
| 342 | WNF/Doblhoff | See page 587. |
| 343 | Heinkel | Four-engined jet-propelled general-purpose medium bomber project. |

| Number | Company | Details and remarks |
|--------|---------|---------------------|
| 344 | Ruhrstahl/Kramer | (Also known as X-4.) See page 700. |
| 345 | Gotha | Shoulder-wing cargo glider. One prototype built. |
| 346 | DFS | See page 636. |
| 349 | Bachem | See page 55. |
| 352 | Junkers | See page 448. |
| 356 | Fieseler | Project based on the Fi 156. |
| 362 | Messerschmitt | Project for a three-engined jet airliner. |
| 368 | Messerschmitt | Project (Details unknown). |
| 388 | Junkers | See page 450. |
| 390 | Junkers | See page 455. |
| 391 | Focke-Wulf | Project based on the Fw 191 bomber. |
| 396 | Arado | See page 54. |
| 400 | Focke-Wulf (Ta) | Six-engined shoulder-wing heavy bomber project with twin fins and rudders. |
| 409 | Messerschmitt | Single-engined fighter project based on Bf 109/Me 209/Me 309 series. |
| 410 | Messerschmitt | See page 566. |
| 419 | Heinkel | Twin-engined night fighter developed from the He 219 with enlarged wing; only seven built. |
| 423 | Messerschmitt/ Zeppelin/ Sud-Ouest | Projected development of the Me 323 transport. |
| 430 | Gotha (Ka) | Transport glider with shoulder-wing, tricycle undercarriage, tail boom and single fin and rudder, developed from the Go 242B glider; at least one prototype built. |
| 432 | Arado | Development of the Ar 232B-0 four-engined transport to make extensive use of wood and steel construction; prototype not completed. |
| 435 | Dornier | Development of the Do 335 fighter. |
| 440 | Arado | Twin-engined multi-purpose aircraft based on the Ar 240; four aircraft only. |
| 446 | DFS | Project (Details unknown). |
| 488 | Junkers | See page 457. |
| 491 | Focke-Wulf | Project based on the Fw 191 and Fw 391 bombers. |
| 510 | Messerschmitt | Projected development of the Me 410 twin-engined multi-purpose aircraft. |
| 523 | Zeppelin/ Sud-Ouest | Projected development of the Me 323 and ZMe 423 transports. |
| 532 | Arado | Projected development of Ar 432. |
| 535 | Dornier | Development of Do 335 with rear piston engine replaced by a turbojet. |
| 609 | Messerschmitt | Project for coupling two Me 309 fighters together (side-by-side) to produce a twin-engined long-range fighter-bomber. |
| 632 | Arado | Projected development of the Ar 432 four-engined transport aircraft. |
| 635 | Dornier | Project for coupling two Do 335 fighters together (side-by-side) to produce a four-engined long-range reconnaissance aircraft. |

*Company abbreviations used in Appendix 1.*

BFW   Bayerische Flugzeugwerke AG
DFS   Deutsches Forschungsinstitut für Segelflug
FGP   Flugtechnische Fertigungsgemeinschaft Prague
HFB   Hamburger Flugzeugbau GmbH (Blohm und Voss)
WNF   Wiener-Neustädter Flugzeugwerke

# List of German Aircraft Projects

To supplement the section on fixed-wing aircraft projects (which was necessarily condensed) this appendix lists known projects together with brief details. In general, projects have been omitted where designations are unknown but, in any case, it is doubtful if a definitive list can ever be compiled. It is therefore impossible to deduce from this list that a certain company worked on the greatest number of projects. Most project designations were simply prefixed P for Projekt but, within the Arado company, the prefix E for Entwurf (project) was used while, within the Junkers company, the prefix EF for Entwicklungsflugzeug (development aircraft) was used.

Many of the aircraft listed were based upon engines which were also in project form at the time. In the following list, engine designations have been abbreviated. Turbojets and rockets have their power given in kg (static thrust) and propeller-turbines have their power given in ehp, all other engines being of the piston type.

| *Name* | *Brief details* | *Engine* |
|---|---|---|
| | **Arado** | |
| E.240 | Original designation of Ar 240. | Two 1,475 hp DB 605 |
| E.340 | Original designation of Ar 340. | Two 2,500 hp Jumo 222 |
| E.370 | Original designation of Ar 234. | Two 900 kg Junkers 004 |
| E.375 | Fast bomber. | Two 2,780 kg Junkers 012 |
| E.377 | Mistel lower component project. | Two 800 kg BMW 003 |
| E.380 | Floatplane development of Ar 196 with folding wings. | One 1,600 hp BMW 801A |
| E.381 | Rocket-powered midget fighter. | One 1,700 kg HWK 509 |
| E.385 | Fast bomber. | Two 3,400 kg BMW 018 |
| E.395 | Fast bomber and reconnaissance aircraft. | Four 1,300 kg HeS 011 |
| E.430 | Passenger flying-boat similar to Ar 233. | Two 1,000 hp BMW 323R |
| E.440 | Powered glider. | Two 1,600 hp BMW 801L |
| E.500 | Bomber project with twin booms. | Two piston engines |
| E.561 | Heavy fighter. | One piston engine |
| E.580 | Lightweight fighter designed to same specification as He 162. | One 800 kg BMW 003 |
| E.581 | Delta-wing jet fighter. | One 1,300 kg HeS 011 |
| E.651 | Heavy fighter. | One piston engine |
| Ar I | Night fighter with delta wing. | Two 1,300 kg HeS 011 |
| Ar II | Night fighter with swept wing. | Two 1,300 kg HeS 011 |

| Name | Brief details | Engine |
|---|---|---|
| | **Blohm und Voss** | |
| P.1 | Fighter. | One 550 hp BMW XV |
| P.4 | Single-seat trainer, developed into Ha 136. | One 160 hp Sh¹14A |
| P.5 | General-purpose aircraft. | One 750 hp BMW VI |
| P.6 | Dive-bomber. | One 550 hp BMW XV |
| P.6a | Dive-bomber, developed into Ha 137A. | One 650 hp BMW Hornet |
| P.6b | Dive-bomber, developed into Ha 137B. | One 525 hp Rolls-Royce Kestrel |
| P.7 | Biplane dive-bomber. | One Wright Cyclone |
| P.8 | Flying-boat. | Two 550 hp BMW XV |
| P.9 | Twin-boom flying-boat. | Two piston engines |
| P.10 | General-purpose aircraft. | One piston engine |
| P.11 | Carrier-based dive-bomber, development of Ha 137. | One 725 hp BMW 132A |
| P.12 | Flying-boat. | Three 600 hp Jumo 205C |
| P.13 | Flying-boat. | Four 600 hp Jumo 205C |
| P.14 | Reconnaissance flying-boat. | Four 600 hp Jumo 205 |
| P.15 | Floatplane, developed into Ha 139. | Four 600 hp Jumo 205 |
| P.16 | Floatplane. | Four 600 hp Jumo 205 |
| P.17 | Floatplane. | Four 600 hp Jumo 205 |
| P.18 | Asymmetric fighter. | One 540 hp Jumo 210 |
| P.19 | Reconnaissance aircraft, developed into Ha 140. | Two 540 hp Jumo 210 |
| P.20 | Bomber/reconnaissance version of Ha 139. | Four 600 hp Jumo 205C |
| P.21 | General-purpose aircraft. | One 540 hp Jumo 210 |
| P.22 | Fighter. | One 540 hp Jumo 210 |
| P.23 | Development of P.22 with increased span. | One 540 hp Jumo 210 |
| P.24 | Fighter-trainer for Japan. | One 400 hp piston engine |
| P.25 | Dive-bomber. | One 540 hp Jumo 210 |
| P.27 | Dive-bomber. | One BMW-Bramo 333 |
| P.28 | Rotating-wing twin-boom aircraft. | One 600 hp BMW 112 |
| P.29 | Passenger transport. | Four BMW 132, Jumo 205, Jumo 206 or DB 600 |
| P.33 | Long-range bomber. | Two 700 hp Jumo 206 |
| P.37 | Development of Ha 139. | Four 600 hp Jumo 205C |
| P.38 | Development of Ha 139. | Four 880 hp Jumo 208 |
| P.39 | Bomber. | Four 600 hp Jumo 205C |
| P.40 | Asymmetric ground attack aircraft. | One 910 hp DB 600 |
| P.41 | Improved version of Ha 137. | One 540 hp Jumo 210 |
| P.42 | Twin-boom flying-boat. | Six 700 hp Jumo 206 |
| P.43 | Flying-boat. | Six 700 hp Jumo 206 |
| P.44 | Asymmetric reconnaissance aircraft. | One Jumo 210, Bramo 329 or DB 600 |
| P.45 | Passenger transport with rocket-assisted take-off. | Six 700 hp Jumo 206 |
| P.46 | Development of Ha 142. | Four Wright Cyclone |

| Name | Brief details | Engine |
|------|---------------|--------|
| P.47 | Development of P.45. | Four Bramo 329 |
| P.48 | Bomber version of Ha 142 for Japan. | Four 725 hp BMW 132 |
| P.49 | Passenger floatplane. | Four 725 hp BMW 132 |
| P.50 | Freight floatplane. | Six 600 hp Jumo 205 |
| P.51 | Freight floatplane. | Four 725 hp BMW 132 |
| P.52 | Passenger floatplane. | Four 725 hp BMW 132 |
| P.53 | Passenger floatplane. | Four 900 hp Bramo 323 |
| P.54 | Passenger flying-boat developed into Bv 222. | Six 725 hp BMW 132 |
| P.55 | Improved version of Ha 140. | Two 725 hp BMW 132 |
| P.56 | Seaplane dive-bomber. | Two 1,100 hp DB 601 |
| P.57 | Flying-boat. | Two 800 hp BMW 132H |
| P.58 | Naval dive-bomber. | Two 1,100 hp DB 601 |
| P.59 | Torpedo- or dive-bomber. | Two 1,100 hp DB 601 |
| P.60 | Flying-boat. | Four piston engines |
| P.61 | Improved version of Ha 138. | Four piston engines |
| P.62 | Asymmetric Naval dive-bomber. | One 2,700 hp DB 606 |
| P.63 | Fast bomber. | One Jumo 212B |
| P.64 | Long-range aircraft. | Three 700 hp Jumo 206 |
| P.65 | Attack version of Ha 141. | One piston engine |
| P.66 | Naval dive-bomber. | Two 1,200 hp Jumo 211D |
| P.67 | Large mine-laying aircraft. | Four 1,550 hp BMW 139 |
| P.68 | Mine-laying version of Bv 222. | Four 1,550 hp BMW 139 |
| P.69 | Target drone. | One 240 hp HM 508 |
| P.70 | Fast bomber. | Two Jumo 211 or DB 601 |
| P.71 | Bomber and heavy fighter. | Two 1,200 hp Jumo 211D |
| P.72 | Attack version of Ha 141. | One 725 hp BMW 132A |
| P.73 | Bomber with pusher propellers. | Four 1,200 hp Jumo 211 |
| P.74 | Multi-purpose version of Ha 141. | One 1,200 hp Jumo 211 |
| P.75 | Multi-purpose version of Ha 141. | One 1,550 hp BMW 139 |
| P.76 | Long-range reconnaissance version of Bv 222. | Six 1,600 hp BMW 801 |
| P.77 | Similar to P.76. | Six 1,500 hp Jumo 208 |
| P.78 | Long-range floatplane. | Six 1,500 hp Jumo 208 |
| P.79 | Long-range floatplane. | Four 3,000 hp Jumo 218 |
| P.80 | Trans-ocean floatplane. | Four 3,000 hp Jumo 218 |
| P.81 | Long-range aircraft. | Four 3,000 hp Jumo 218 |
| P.83 | Transatlantic aircraft. | Four 3,000 hp Jumo 218 |
| P.84 | Long-range aircraft. | Four 3,000 hp Jumo 218 |
| P.85 | Transatlantic aircraft. | Four 3,000 hp Jumo 218 |
| P.86 | Transatlantic aircraft. | Four 3,000 hp Jumo 218 |
| P.88 | Long-range heavy fighter. | Two 1,580 hp BMW 801 |
| P.89 | Long-range heavy fighter. | Two 2,700 hp DB 606 |
| P.90 | Long-range heavy fighter. | Three 1,580 hp BMW 801 |
| P.92 | Passenger aircraft. | Three 800 hp Jumo 207 |
| P.94 | Improved Bv 138 flying-boat. | Three 950 hp Jumo 207 |
| P.95 | Development of Bv 222. | Six 1,000 hp Bramo 323 |
| P.96 | Development of Bv 222. | Six 1,500 hp Jumo 208 |
| P.97 | Development of Bv 222. | Six 1,600 hp BMW 801 |

| Name | Brief details | Engine |
|------|---------------|--------|
| P.98 | Development of Bv 222. | Four 1,600 hp BMW 801 |
| P.99 | Development of Bv 222. | Six BMW 800 |
| P.100 | Target drone. | none |
| P.101 | Target drone. | none |
| P.103 | Asymmetric airliner. | Three 1,580 hp BMW 801 |
| P.104 | Airliner with tail-mounted engine. | Three 700 hp Jumo 206 |
| P.105 | Development of Bv 222. | Four 2,500 hp Jumo 222 |
| P.106 | Development of Bv 222. | Four 2,500 hp Jumo 222 |
| P.107 | Development of Bv 222. | Four 2,500 hp Jumo 222 |
| P.108 | Development of Bv 138. | Three 1,500 hp Jumo 208. |
| P.109 | Development of Bv 138. | Two 1,500 hp Jumo 208 and one 600 hp Jumo 205 |
| P.110 | Development of Bv 138. | Three 1,500 hp Jumo 208 |
| P.111 | Asymmetric version of Bv 138. | Three 1,500 hp Jumo 208 |
| P.112 | Development of P.111. | Three 1,500 hp Jumo 208 |
| P.113 | Asymmetric seaplane. | Three 1,500 hp Jumo 208 |
| P.114 | Heavy fighter version of Bv 141. | One 1,600 hp BMW 801 |
| P.116 | Development of Bv 222. | Six 1,600 hp BMW 801 |
| P.117 | Development of Bv 222. | Four 1,600 hp BMW 801 |
| P.118 | Development of Bv 222. | Six BMW 800 |
| P.119 | Development of Bv 222. | Four 2,500 hp Jumo 222 |
| P.122 | Maritime patrol floatplane. | Four 800 hp Jumo 207 |
| P.123 | Double-hull patrol flying-boat. | Four 800 hp Jumo 207 |
| P.124 | Maritime patrol flying-boat. | Four 800 hp Jumo 207 |
| P.125 | Maritime patrol floatplane. | Four 800 hp Jumo 207 |
| P.127 | Fighter. | One 1,750 hp DB 603 |
| P.128 | Asymmetric fighter. | not known |
| P.129 | Fighter. | not known |
| P.131 | Airliner with tail-mounted engine. | Three 800 hp Jumo 207 |
| P.134 | Fast bomber with pusher propeller. | One 3,800 hp DB 613 |
| P.135 | Asymmetric fast bomber. | One 3,800 hp DB 613 |
| P.138 | Long-range reconnaissance flying-boat. | Two 2,500 hp Jumo 223 |
| P.139 | Flying-boat. | not known |
| P.140 | Passenger aircraft. | Two 1,700 hp BMW 801D |
| P.141 | Asymmetric passenger aircraft. | Three 1,000 hp Bramo 323 |
| P.142 | Passenger aircraft with rotating wing. | Two 1,700 hp BMW 810D |
| P.143 | Similar to P.142. | not known |
| P.144 | Maritime patrol aircraft. | Four 2,500 hp Jumo 223 |
| P.145 | Maritime patrol floatplane. | Four 2,500 hp Jumo 223 |
| P.146 | Development of P.144 for DLH. | Four 2,500 hp Jumo 223 |
| P.147 | Development of P.142 as a transport. | Two 1,700 hp BMW 801D |
| P.148 | Flying-boat. | not known |
| P.149 | Flying-boat. | not known |
| P.150 | Transatlantic flying-boat. | Four 2,500 hp Jumo 223 |
| P.155 | Asymmetric dive-bomber. | One 2,500 hp Jumo 222 or 1,700 hp BMW 801 |
| P.160 | Transatlantic flying-boat. | Six 3,900 hp BMW 803 |

| Name | Brief details | Engine |
|------|---------------|--------|
| P.161 | Landplane version of Bv 238. | Six 1,700 hp BMW 801D |
| P.162 | Bomber. | One 3,800 hp DB 613 |
| P.163 | Heavy fighter-bomber. | One 3,800 hp DB 613 |
| P.164 | Bomber. | One 3,800 hp DB 613 |
| P.165 | Asymmetric bomber. | One 2,500 hp Jumo 222 |
| P.166 | Fast bomber. | Two 2,500 hp Jumo 222 |
| P.167 | Twin Bv 250 landplane. | Twelve 1,750 hp DB 603 |
| P.170 | High-speed bomber. | Three 1,700 hp BMW 801D |
| P.171 | Fast bomber. | Two 1,700 hp BMW 801D |
| P.172 | Dive-bomber. | One 1,700 hp BMW 801D |
| P.173 | Long-range bomber. | Six 1,700 hp BMW 801D |
| P.174 | Glider bomb. | none |
| P.175 | Parasite or hook-on fighter. | One turbojet. |
| P.176 | Armoured version of asymmetric Bv 237. | One 1,700 hp BMW 801D |
| P.177 | Asymmetric jet fighter-bomber. | not known |
| P.178 | Asymmetric jet fighter-bomber. | not known |
| P.179 | Fighter-bomber. | One 1,700 hp BMW 801D |
| P.180 | Fighter-bomber with rotating wing. | One 1,700 hp BMW 801D |
| P.181 | Fighter-bomber. | One 1,700 hp BMW 801D |
| P.182 | Fighter-bomber. | not known |
| P.183 | Long-range patrol aircraft. | Six 1,970 hp BMW 801E |
| P.184 | Long-range patrol aircraft. | Four 1,970 hp BMW 801E |
| P.185 | Ground attack aircraft. | not known |
| P.186 | Glider-fighter. | none |
| P.187 | Landplane version of Bv 222. | Six 1,800 hp BMW 801TJ |
| P.188 | Jet bomber with compound swept wing. | Four 1,000 kg Junkers 004C |
| P.190 | Jet fighter. | One 890 kg Junkers 004 |
| P.191 | Flak suppression aircraft. | Eight 1,700 hp BMW 801D |
| P.192 | Ground attack aircraft. | One 1,900 hp DB 603G |
| P.192 | Ground attack aircraft. | One 1,780 hp Jumo 213A |
| P.193 | Ground attack aircraft with pusher propeller. | One 1,780 hp Jumo 213A |
| P.194 | Asymmetric ground attack aircraft with turbojet boost. | One 1,700 hp BMW 801D and one 800 kg BMW 003 |
| P.195 | Turbo-supercharged high-altitude fighter. | Two 2,060 hp Jumo 213F |
| P.196 | Jet twin boom ground attack aircraft. | Two 800 kg BMW 003 |
| P.197 | Jet fighter. | Two 800 kg BMW 003 or two 890 kg Junkers 004 |
| P.198 | High-altitude jet fighter. | One 3,400 kg BMW 018 |
| P.199 | High-altitude jet fighter. | One 890 kg Junkers 004 |
| P.200 | Transatlantic passenger flying-boat. | Eight 3,900 hp BMW 803 |
| P.201 | High-altitude rocket-powered interceptor. | One HWK rocket unit |
| P.202 | Jet fighter with swing wing. | Two 800 kg BMW 003 |
| P.203 | Night fighter with turbojet boost. | Two 1,700 hp BMW 801D and two turbojets |

731

| Name | Brief details | Engine |
|------|---------------|--------|
| P.204 | Ground attack aircraft with turbojet boost. | One 1,700 hp BMW 801D and one turbojet |
| P.205 | Development of Bv 155 fighter. | One 1,900 hp DB 603G |
| P.206 | Long-range bomber. | Two 4,000 hp As 413 and two 1,780 hp Jumo 213 |
| P.207 | Fighter with pusher propeller. | One 2,500 hp Jumo 222, one 4,000 hp As 413 or, one 1,750 hp DB 603 |
| P.208.01 and 02 | Tailless fighter with pusher propeller. | One 2,500 hp Jumo 222F or one 4,000 hp As 413 |
| P.208.03 | Tailless fighter with pusher propeller. | One 1,980 hp DB 603L |
| P.209 | Jet tailless fighter with sweptforward wing. | One 1,300 kg HeS 011 |
| P.210 | Jet fighter. | One 1,300 kg HeS 011 |
| P.211 | Jet fighter (Volksjäger). | One 800 kg BMW 003 |
| P.212 | Tailless jet fighter. | One 1,300 kg HeS 011 |
| P.213 | Pulse-jet powered lightweight fighter. | One 300 kg As 014 |
| P.214 | Piloted tailless flying bomb (pilot to bale out after aiming). | not known |
| P.215.02 | Tailless jet night-fighter. | Two 1,300 kg HeS 011 |

**BMW**

| | | |
|---|---|---|
| Schnellbomber I | Heavy bomber with compound swept wings, turbojet and propeller-turbines. | Two 3,400 kg BMW 018 and two 6,570 ehp BMW 028 |
| Schnellbomber II | Propeller-turbine bomber with sweptforward wings. | Two 6,570 ehp BMW 028 |
| Strahlbomber I | Jet bomber. | Six 800 kg BMW 003 |
| Strahlbomber II | Tailless jet bomber. | Two 3,400 kg BMW 018 |

**Daimler-Benz**

| | | |
|---|---|---|
| P.A. | Combination or composite aircraft. Upper component: propeller-turbine powered carrier aircraft. | Four or six 3,300 ehp HeS 021 |
| | Lower component: jet bomber with V-tail. | Two 3,400 kg BMW 018 |
| P.B | Carrier aircraft (upper component) with four tractor and two pusher airscrews. To carry one Project C bomber or five Project D flying bombs. | Six 1,900 hp DB 603G |
| P.C | Jet bomber. | One 1,275 kg DB 007 |
| P.D | Ramjet-powered flying bomb. | One ramjet. |

Daimler-Benz also proposed several turbojet and propeller-turbine powered fast bombers, reconnaissance and fighter aircraft, but no project designations have been recorded.

732

| Name | Brief details | Engine |
|------|---------------|--------|

**Dornier**

| Name | Brief details | Engine |
|------|---------------|--------|
| P.247/6 | Fighter-bomber with pusher airscrew. | One 2,000 hp Jumo 213T |
| P.252 | Three-seat night and bad-weather fighter with contra-rotating pusher propellers. | Two 1,750 hp Jumo 213J |
| P.256 | Jet heavy fighter developed from Do 335. | Two 1,300 kg HeS 011 |
| P.—? | Jet fighter with canard layout. | Three 1,300 kg HeS 011 |

**Focke-Wulf**

| Name | Brief details | Engine |
|------|---------------|--------|
| P.82114 | Dive-bomber with parasol wing. | One 950 hp DB 600 |
| P.222.001 | High-performance fighter. | One 2,500 hp Jumo 222 |
| P.222.004 | Three-seat day and night fighter with piston engine and turbojets. | One 2,500 hp Jumo 222 and two 800 kg BMW 003 |
| P.222.010 | All-weather fighter similar to P.222.004. | One 2,500 hp Jumo 222 and two 800 kg BMW 003 |
| P.222.018 | High-performance fighter. | One 2,500 hp Jumo 222 |
| P.0310.025.1006 | Bad-weather or high-altitude fighter. | One 4,000 hp As 413 |
| P.0310.224.20 | Long-range bombing and patrol aircraft. | Four 1,970 hp BMW 801E |
| P.0310.224.30 | Long-range bomber. | Six 1,970 hp BMW 801E |
| P.0310.225 | Long-range bomber with twin tail booms. | Four 1,700 hp BMW 801D |
| P.0310.237.2 | High-altitude fighter. | One 1,750 hp DB 603 |
| P.0310.251.13 | Night and bad-weather fighter with pusher propeller and turbojets. | One 2,500 hp Jumo 222 and two 800 kg BMW 003 |
| P.413.001 | High-altitude fighter. | One 4,000 hp As 413 |
| P.011.001 | Jet fighter with twin tail booms and rocket boosting. | One 1,300 kg HeS 011 and one 1,700 kg HWK 509 |
| P.011.018 | Jet fighter. | One 1,300 kg HeS 011 |
| P.011.025 | Jet fighter. | Two 1,300 kg HeS 011 |
| P.011.045 | Two-seat jet night fighter. | Two 1,300 kg HeS 011 |
| P.021.009 | Propeller-turbine powered fighter bomber. | One 3,300 ehp HeS 021 |
| P.? | Rocket-powered fighter. | One 1,700 kg HWK 509 |

1000 × 1000 × 1000 Bomber Projects

| | | |
|------|---------------|--------|
| Version A | Jet bomber with sweptback wing. | Two 1,300 kg HeS 011 |
| Version B | Jet bomber with delta wing. | Two 1,300 kg HeS 011 |
| Version C | Jet bomber with sweptback wing. | Two 1,300 kg HeS 011 |

As will be realized, there are a large number of undiscovered Focke-Wulf projects.

| Name | Brief details | Engine |
|---|---|---|
| | **Gotha** | |
| P.3 | Heavy fighter to same specification as the Ju 88. | Two 950 hp DB 600 |
| P.8 | Fighter. | Two 240 hp As 10C |
| P.9 | Sports aircraft. | One 80 hp HM 60R |
| P.10 | Touring aircraft. | Two 240 hp As 10C |
| P.11 | Basic trainer. | One 100 hp HM 504 |
| P.12 | Touring aircraft. | Two 100 hp HM 504 |
| P.14 | Fighter (P.14.012 was a float-plane). | Two 465 hp As 410 |
| P.16 | Light fighter. | One 465 hp As 410 |
| P.17 | Training aircraft. | One 50 hp Zündapp 092 |
| P.20 | Fighter. | Two 240 hp As 10C |
| P.21 | Training aircraft. | One 100 hp HM 504 |
| P.35 | Twin-boom transport. | Two 880 hp BMW 132D |
| P.40B | Asymmetric transport. | One 1,600 hp BMW 801 |
| P.45 | Transport. | One 1,100 hp Jumo 211 |
| P.46 | Twin-boom transport. | One 1,100 hp Jumo 211 |
| P.47 | Cargo glider. | none |
| P.50 | Canard cargo glider. | none |
| P.52 | Jet fighter. | Two 890 kg Junkers 004 |
| P.53 | Jet fighter. | Two 890 kg Junkers 004 |
| P.56 | Mistel type glider auxiliary fuel tank. | none |
| P.57 | Mistel type glider bomb. | none |
| P.58 | Cargo glider. | none |
| P.60C | Tailless jet night fighter. | Two 800 kg BMW 003 or two 1,300 kg HeS 011 |
| | **Heinkel** | |
| P.1041 | Original designation of He 177. | Two 2,650 hp DB 606 |
| P.1054 | Transport. | Two piston engines |
| P.1060 | Original designation of He 219. | Two 1,750 hp DB 603 |
| P.1062 | Fighter. | One 1,750 hp DB 603 |
| P.1063 | Bomber. | Two turbojets |
| P.1064 | Long-range bomber. | Six piston engines |
| P.1065 | General-purpose aircraft. | Two piston engines |
| P.1066 | General-purpose aircraft. | Two piston engines |
| P.1068 | Predecessor of He 343 jet bomber. | Two or four turbojets |
| P.1069 | Fighter. | One turbojet |
| P.1070 | Flying wing. | Two or four turbojets |
| P.1071 | Asymmetric fighter. | Two piston engines |
| P.1072 | Bomber. | Four piston engines |
| P.1073 | He 162 predecessor. | One 800 kg BMW 003 |
| P.1074 | Fighter. | Two piston engines |
| P.1075 | Coupled Do 335, developed into Do 635. | Four 1,750 hp DB 603 |
| P.1076 | Fighter with contra-rotating airscrews and sweptforward wing. | One 1,750 hp DB 603 |
| P.1077 | 'Julia'. Rocket-propelled fighter. | One 1,700 kg HWK 509 |

| Name | Brief details | Engine |
|---|---|---|
| P.1078 | Tailless jet fighter. | One 1,300 kg HeS 011 |
| P.1079 | Jet-propelled night and heavy fighter. | Two 1,300 kg HeS 011 |
| P.1080 | Tailless fighter. | Two ramjets |

**Henschel**

| Name | Brief details | Engine |
|---|---|---|
| P.54 | Airliner. | Two 1,700 hp BMW 801 |
| P.72 | Airliner. | Two 1,700 hp BMW 801 |
| P.75 | Fighter. | One 2,200 hp DB 610 |
| P.76 | Ground attack aircraft. | Two 700 hp Gnome/Rhône 14M |
| P.80 | Original designation of Hs 130E. | Two 1,750 hp DB 603 |
| P.87 | Canard fast bomber. | One 2,200 hp DB 610 |
| P.122 | Tailless jet bomber. | Two 3,400 kg BMW 018 |
| P.135 | Tailless jet fighter. | One 1,300 kg HeS 011 |
| P.? | Twin-boom transport. | Two piston engines |

**Horten**

| Name | Brief details | Engine |
|---|---|---|
| Ho XIIIA | Experimental flying-wing glider to precede Ho XIIIB. | none |
| Ho XIIIB | Supersonic flying-wing jet fighter with rocket boost. | One 800 kg BMW 003 and one rocket engine |
| Ho XVIIIB | Flying-wing jet bomber. | Six 1,050 kg Junkers 004H |

**Junkers**

| Name | Brief details | Engine |
|---|---|---|
| EF 008 | Jet bomber. | Four turbojets |
| EF 009 | Jet fighter with engines around the nose. | Ten small turbojets |
| EF 010 | High-speed jet aircraft designed for record breaking. | Two turbojets |
| EF 011 | Rocket-propelled fighter. | Two HWK rockets |
| EF 012 | Jet bomber. | Four turbojets |
| EF 015 | Jet bomber. | Four turbojets |
| EF 017 | Jet fighter. | Two turbojets |
| EF 018 | Jet fighter. | Four turbojets |
| EF 019 | Jet fighter. | Two turbojets |
| EF 61 | High-altitude research aircraft. | Two 950 hp DB 600A |
| EF 73 | Medium bomber developed into Ju 288. | Two 2,500 hp Jumo 222 |
| EF 77 | Airliner project, developed into Ju 252. | Three 1,000 hp BMW 132 |
| EF 101 | Long-range mother aircraft carrying a high-altitude reconnaissance aircraft. | Four 3,800 hp DB 613 (mother aircraft), one piston engine (parasite aircraft) |
| EF 125 | Jet bomber with sweptforward wing, forerunner of Ju 287. | Two 2,780 kg Junkers 012 or two 3,400 kg BMW 018 |
| EF 126 | 'Elli'. Lightweight pulse-jet propelled fighter. | One 500 kg As 044 |
| EF 127 | Rocket-propelled interceptor. | One 1,700 kg HWK 509 |
| EF 128 | Tailless jet fighter. | One 1,300 kg HeS 011 |
| EF 130 | Flying wing jet bomber. | Four 800 kg BMW 003 |

| Name | Brief details | Engine |
|------|---------------|--------|

**Lippisch**

| Name | Brief details | Engine |
|------|---------------|--------|
| DM 2 | Subsonic delta wing jet research aircraft. | One turbojet |
| DM 3 | Supersonic delta-wing rocket-propelled research aircraft. | Two rocket engines |
| DM 4 | Supersonic delta-wing rocket-propelled research aircraft. | Two rocket engines |
| P.01.114 | Experimental tailless rocket-propelled aircraft (similar to Me 163). | One 3,000 kg HWK rocket |
| P.11 | Jet-propelled version (with rocket boosting) of Me 265 tailless fast bomber project. | Two 890 kg Junkers 004 and two rocket engines |
| P.13a | Ramjet-propelled delta-wing fighter. | One ramjet and one rocket engine |
| P.20 | Development of Me 163 fighter with rocket engine replaced by a turbojet. | One 1,000 kg Junkers 004C |

**Messerschmitt**

| Name | Brief details | Engine |
|------|---------------|--------|
| P.1059 | Forerunner of Me 209 V1 record-breaking fighter. | One piston engine |
| P.1064 | Forerunner of Me 261. | Two piston engines |
| P.1065 | Forerunner of Me 262. | Two turbojets |
| P.1079 | Single-seat aircraft to study various turbojet installations. | One or two turbojets |
| P.1085 | Medium-range heavy bomber. | Four piston engines |
| P.1091 | High-altitude fighter. | One 1,750 hp DB 603 |
| P.1092 | Jet fighter. | One 1,000 kg Junkers 004C |
| P.1099 | All-weather jet fighter with a 50 mm cannon. | Two 1,000 kg Junkers 004C |
| P.1100 | Two-seat jet bomber. | Two 1,000 kg Junkers 004C |
| P.1101 | Jet fighter. | One 1,300 kg HeS 011 |
| P.1102 | Unarmed jet bomber. | Three 800 kg BMW 003 |
| P.1104 | Rocket-propelled fighter. | One 1,700 kg HWK 509 |
| P.1106 | Jet fighter with butterfly tail. | One 1,300 kg HeS 011 |
| P.1107 | Jet bomber with butterfly tail. | Four 3,400 kg BMW 018 |
| P.1108 | Jet bomber with butterfly tail. | Four 1,300 kg HeS 011 |
| P.1110 | Jet fighter with sweptback wing. | One 1,300 kg HeS 011 |
| P.1111 | Tailless semi-delta-wing jet fighter. | One 1,300 kg HeS 011 |
| P.1112 | Tailless jet fighter. | One 1,300 kg HeS 011 |
| P.1113 | Tailless jet fighter. | One turbojet |
| P.1116 | Jet fighter similar to P.1106. | One 1,300 kg HeS 011 |

**Skoda-Kauba**

| Name | Brief details | Engine |
|------|---------------|--------|
| P.14 | Ramjet-propelled fighter. | One ramjet engine |

**Zeppelin**

| Name | Brief details | Engine |
|------|---------------|--------|
| Rammer | Ramming fighter with prone pilot. | One 1,000 kg Schmidding 533 rocket |

# INDEX OF AIRCRAFT AND MISSILES

# Index of Aircraft and Missiles

This index lists all the German aircraft, missiles and projects mentioned in the introduction, the main text and Appendix 2 of the book. Where a major reference is made to a type, the page number concerned appears first and is emphasized by the use of italics. Appendix 1, which details the German '8' series type numbers and can be found on pages 713–724, provides additional references in a numerical sequence.

740